THE REAGAN PRESIDENCY AND THE GOVERNING OF AMERICA

*A Conference Sponsored by
the Changing Domestic Priorities Project
of The Urban Institute*

THE REAGAN PRESIDENCY AND THE GOVERNING OF AMERICA

Edited by
Lester M. Salamon and Michael S. Lund

INDIANA
PURDUE
LIBRARY
FORT WAYNE

The Changing Domestic Priorities Series

John L. Palmer and Isabel V. Sawhill, Editors

JK
271
.R332
1984

 THE URBAN INSTITUTE PRESS · WASHINGTON, D.C.

Copyright © 1984
THE URBAN INSTITUTE
2100 M Street, N.W.
Washington, D.C. 20037

INDIANA
PURDUE
LIBRARY
FORT WAYNE

Library of Congress Cataloging in Publication Data
Main entry under title:

The Reagan presidency and the governing of America.

  (The Changing domestic priorities series)
  Includes bibliographies.
  1. United States—Politics and government—1981–
Addresses, essays, lectures. I. Salamon, Lester M.
II. Lund, Michael S., 1941–   . III. Series.
JK271.R332 1985   973.927   84-27065
ISBN 0-87766-370-X (cloth)
ISBN 0-87766-347-5 (pbk.)

Printed in the United States of America

9 8 7 6 5 4 3 2

2/11/86 jl

BOARD OF TRUSTEES
Carla A. Hills
Chairman
Katharine Graham
Vice Chairman
William Gorham
President
Warren E. Buffett
John J. Byrne
Joseph A. Califano, Jr.
William T. Coleman, Jr.
John M. Deutch
Anthony Downs
Joel L. Fleishman
Philip M. Hawley
Aileen C. Hernandez
Ray L. Hunt
Robert S. McNamara
David O. Maxwell
Lois D. Rice
Elliot L. Richardson
George H. Weyerhaeuser
Mortimer B. Zuckerman

LIFE TRUSTEES
John H. Filer
Eugene G. Fubini
Vernon E. Jordan, Jr.
Edward H. Levi
Bayless A. Manning
Stanley Marcus
Arjay Miller
J. Irwin Miller
Franklin D. Murphy
Herbert E. Scarf
Charles L. Schultze
William W. Scranton
Cyrus R. Vance
James Vorenberg

 THE URBAN INSTITUTE is a nonprofit policy research and educational organization established in Washington, D.C., in 1968. Its staff investigates the social and economic problems confronting the nation and government policies and programs designed to alleviate such problems. The Institute disseminates significant findings of its research through the publications program of its Press. The Institute has two goals for work in each of its research areas: to help shape thinking about societal problems and efforts to solve them, and to improve government decisions and performance by providing better information and analytic tools.

Through work that ranges from broad conceptual studies to administrative and technical assistance, Institute researchers contribute to the stock of knowledge available to public officials and to private individuals and groups concerned with formulating and implementing more efficient and effective government policy.

Conclusions or opinions expressed in Institute publications are those of the authors and do not necessarily reflect the views of other staff members, officers or trustees of the Institute, advisory groups, or any organizations which provide financial support to the Institute.

THE CHANGING DOMESTIC PRIORITIES SERIES

Listed below are the titles available, or soon to be available, in the Changing Domestic Priorities Series

Books

THE REAGAN EXPERIMENT
An Examination of Economic and Social Policies under the Reagan Administration (1982), John L. Palmer and Isabel V. Sawhill, editors

HOUSING ASSISTANCE FOR OLDER AMERICANS
The Reagan Prescription (1982), James P. Zais, Raymond J. Struyk, and Thomas Thibodeau

MEDICAID IN THE REAGAN ERA
Federal Policy and State Choices (1982), Randall R. Bovbjerg and John Holahan

WAGE INFLATION
Prospects for Deceleration (1983), Wayne Vroman

OLDER AMERICANS IN THE REAGAN ERA
Impacts of Federal Policy Changes (1983), James R. Storey

FEDERAL HOUSING POLICY AT PRESIDENT REAGAN'S MIDTERM
(1983), Raymond J. Struyk, Neil Mayer, and John A. Tuccillo

STATE AND LOCAL FISCAL RELATIONS IN THE EARLY 1980s
(1983), Steven D. Gold

THE DEFICIT DILEMMA
Budget Policy in the Reagan Era (1983), Gregory B. Mills and John L. Palmer

HOUSING FINANCE
A Changing System in the Reagan Era (1983), John A. Tuccillo with John L. Goodman, Jr.

PUBLIC OPINION DURING THE REAGAN ADMINISTRATION
National Issues, Private Concerns (1983), John L. Goodman, Jr.

RELIEF OR REFORM?
Reagan's Regulatory Dilemma (1984), George C. Eads and Michael Fix

THE REAGAN RECORD
An Assessment of America's Changing Domestic Priorities (1984), John L. Palmer and Isabel V. Sawhill, editors (Ballinger Publishing Co.)

Conference Volumes

THE SOCIAL CONTRACT REVISITED
  Aims and Outcomes of President Reagan's Social Welfare Policy (1984), edited
  by D. Lee Bawden

NATURAL RESOURCES AND THE ENVIRONMENT
  The Reagan Approach (1984), edited by Paul R. Portney

FEDERAL BUDGET POLICY IN THE 1980s (1984), edited by
  Gregory B. Mills and John L. Palmer

THE REAGAN REGULATORY STRATEGY
  An Assessment (1984), edited by George C. Eads and Michael Fix

THE LEGACY OF REAGANOMICS
  Prospects for Long-term Growth (1984), edited by Charles R. Hulten and Isabel
  V. Sawhill

THE REAGAN PRESIDENCY AND THE GOVERNING OF AMERICA
  (1984), edited by Lester M. Salamon and Michael S. Lund

Advisory Board of the
Changing Domestic Priorities Project

Martin Anderson, Hoover Institution

John Brademas, President, New York University

Hale Champion, Executive Dean, John F. Kennedy School of
Government, Harvard University

Nathan Glazer, Professor of Education and Sociology,
Harvard University

Aileen C. Hernandez, Partner, Aileen C. Hernandez Associates

Carla A. Hills, Partner, Latham, Watkins & Hills (Chairman)

Juanita M. Kreps, Economist and former Secretary of Commerce

Thomas G. Moore, Hoover Institution

Richard F. Muth, Professor of Economics, Stanford University

Eleanor Holmes Norton, Professor of Law, Georgetown University

Paul H. O'Neill, Senior Vice President—Planning and Finance,
International Paper Company

Peter G. Peterson, Chairman, Peterson, Jacobs and Company

Henry B. Schacht, Chairman, Cummins Engine Co., Inc.

Robert M. Solow, Professor of Economics, Massachusetts Institute of
Technology

Herbert Stein, Professor of Economics, University of Virginia; Senior
Fellow, American Enterprise Institute

Arnold Weber, President, University of Colorado

Daniel Yankelovich, Chairman, Yankelovich, Skelly and
White, Inc.

CONTENTS

Foreword   xiii

Acknowledgments   xv

GOVERNANCE IN THE REAGAN ERA: AN OVERVIEW /
Lester M. Salamon, Michael S. Lund   1

PART ONE
THE PHILOSOPHY OF GOVERNMENT

RONALD REAGAN—REVOLUTIONARY? / *Theodore J. Lowi*   29

THE THEORY OF GOVERNANCE OF THE REAGAN
ADMINISTRATION / *James W. Ceaser*   57

PART TWO
POLICY FORMULATION

THE BUDGET AS AN INSTRUMENT OF PRESIDENTIAL
POLICY / *Allen Schick*   91

Comments / *James M. Verdier*   126
Comments / *Robert D. Reischauer*   131

EXECUTIVE OFFICE POLICY APPARATUS: ENFORCING THE
REAGAN AGENDA / *Chester A. Newland*   135

Comments / *Ben W. Heineman, Jr.*   169
Comments / *Stephen J. Wayne*   176

PRIVATE-SECTOR INITIATIVES IN THE REAGAN ERA: NEW
ACTORS REWORK AN OLD THEME / *Renée A. Berger*   181

Comments / *Denis P. Doyle*   212
Comments / *John B. Olsen*   216

PART THREE
POLITICAL SUPPORT

THE REAGAN PHENOMENON AND PUBLIC ATTITUDES
TOWARD GOVERNMENT / *Everett Carll Ladd*   221

Comments / *Daniel Yankelovich*   250
Comments / *David E. Price*   253

A NEW PRESIDENT, A DIFFERENT CONGRESS, A
MATURING AGENDA / *Charles O. Jones*   261

Comments / *Norman J. Ornstein*   288
Comments / *James L. Sundquist*   292

INTEREST GROUPS AND THE REAGAN PRESIDENCY /
Harold Wolman, Fred Teitelbaum   297

Comments / *Michael J. Malbin*   330
Comments / *Milton D. Morris*   334

PART FOUR
POLICY IMPLEMENTATION

THE REAGAN ADMINISTRATION AND THE RENITENT
BUREAUCRACY / *Laurence E. Lynn, Jr.*   339

Comments / *Hugh Heclo*   371
Comments / *Richard P. Nathan*   375

THE PERMANENT GOVERNMENT IN AN ERA OF
RETRENCHMENT AND REDIRECTION / *Edie N. Goldenberg*   381

Comments / *Frederick C. Mosher*   405
Comments / *Alan K. Campbell*   410

NEW FEDERALISM, OLD REALITIES: THE REAGAN
ADMINISTRATION AND INTERGOVERNMENTAL
REFORM / *David R. Beam* 415

Comments / *Hale Champion* 443
Comments / *Marian Lief Palley* 448

PRIVATE-SECTOR INITIATIVES OR PUBLIC-PRIVATE
PARTNERSHIPS? / *Marc Bendick, Jr., Phyllis M. Levinson* 455

Comments / *Denis P. Doyle* 480
Comments / *Edwin B. Knauft* 486

About the Authors 491

Participants in the Conference 499

FOREWORD

In late 1981, The Urban Institute initiated a project—Changing Domestic Priorities—to examine the course and consequences of shifts in domestic policy occurring under the Reagan administration. This volume, a product of this project, is one of six collections of analyses by leading scholars on subjects of considerable national interest in the 1980s. The other five volumes are focused upon social welfare, economic growth, budget policy, natural resources and the environment, and regulatory policy.

The subject of the present volume is the effect of the Reagan administration on America's politics and its governing institutions and processes. Such a focus is essential to a project that examines the nation's changing domestic priorities. Much of the impact that the Reagan administration has wanted to have on national priorities lies precisely in the area of changing the existing conception of government. More than any recent president, Ronald Reagan has challenged prevailing notions concerning the scope and structure of government. The specific changes the administration has proposed for the various domestic program areas of the federal government are thus linked to more fundamental notions concerning where and how government ought to operate. It is crucial that a systematic assessment be made of how the administration has sought to change the government and wider political system and how successful it has been.

A second reason for the focus on this subject relates to the subjects of the other five volumes in the series. In order to explain fully the extent to which the administration's desired program changes have been accomplished, it is important to examine how the administration's philosophy and actions have interacted with preexisting ideologies, policy processes, and governing institutions—Congress, the political parties, interest groups, and so on.

The thirteen chapters in this book came out of an Urban Institute conference on "Governance in the Reagan Era" convened by the editors in December 1983 and attended by over forty expert observers of American government and politics. The chapters are based on papers commissioned for this conference from a respected group of analysts who were asked to describe and evaluate the effects of the Reagan presidency within their respective areas of expertise—such as political philosophy, public opinion, Congress, the Executive Office of the President, the civil service—and to put that impact in perspective in terms of recent trends. Additional experts were asked to provide written commentaries on the papers. Both the papers and the commentaries were then revised during the spring and early summer of 1984. While a few important aspects of the Reagan impact are not covered, such as on the courts, the book provides broad and varied insights by some of the most astute students of American government into the operation of the Reagan presidency and into its larger significance for American political life.

The volume begins with an overview chapter by the editors that first reviews what the separate chapters say about how the Reagan administration managed to deal with three major problems that beset the American political system in the 1970s—the crisis of ideas, the crisis of political support, and the crisis of public management—and then steps back from the individual spheres of political action covered in the separate chapters to draw overall conclusions about the impact of the Reagan administration's first term on governance in America.

The chapters in Part One deal with the distinctive philosophy of government that has influenced the Reagan administration's substantive program and its methods of governing the nation—an essential part of the assessment of an administration for which ideology has played such an important role. The papers in Part Two focus on the mechanisms for translating ideas into concrete form, including the Reagan administration's use of the budget formulation process, the staffing and institutional apparatus of the Executive Office of the President, and the special presidential task force. In Part Three attention turns to three forces that are essential for mobilizing political support behind a president's objectives—American public opinion toward government and public policy, presidential relations with Congress, and national interest groups. The final part of this volume focuses on how the Reagan administration has interacted with institutions and processes that are involved in the implementation of public policy. The topics examined include the ability of presidentially appointed federal agency directors to transform an agency's operations, the federal civil service, relationships between the federal government and the states, and public sector-private sector relationships.

John L. Palmer
Isabel V. Sawhill
Editors
Changing Domestic Priorities Series

ACKNOWLEDGMENTS

This book required the individual and cooperative efforts of a number of persons. We are especially grateful to the authors of the individual chapters and the commentaries. We also wish to thank all the participants in the conference "Governance in the Reagan Era" for their insights, which made the conference discussions extremely fruitful and stimulating.

Theresa Walker and Marie D. Baker are to be thanked for their efficient work in moving the many pieces of the book from first draft form through to final copy, and the editing skills of Molly Ruzicka were invaluable.

Finally, the editors are grateful to Harriet Page for her assistance in arranging the conference and to Marla Taylor for her able work, under great pressure at times, in managing the preparation of several parts of the book.

The support of these efforts by the Ford Foundation and the John D. and Catherine T. MacArthur Foundation is also gratefully acknowledged.

GOVERNANCE IN THE REAGAN ERA: AN OVERVIEW

Lester M. Salamon and Michael S. Lund

In the decade prior to Ronald Reagan's election as president in 1980, confidence in the effectiveness of American government reached a low ebb. Vietnam and Watergate led many citizens to distrust public officials. Large numbers of voters expressed discontent with government's rising costs by supporting referenda to cut state and local taxes. Doubts about government also increased among social scientists, with some claiming that the Great Society programs of the 1960s had accomplished very little and had created new problems.

Not only did the substance of government policy become a subject of concern; so did the political process itself. In particular, the political system seemed to be suffering from three interrelated crises: first, "a crisis of ideas" reflecting discontent with the theory of positive government that had dominated the political agenda for more than a generation; second, a "crisis of political support" growing out of an erosion in the broad public backing needed for government initiatives, the proliferation of new issue and interest groups, and the weakening of such integrating institutions as political parties; and third, a "crisis in public management" resulting from the greatly enlarged scope of public activity and the cumbersomeness of many of the mechanisms through which government was seeking to carry out its responsibilities. These problems were perceived to be so deep-seated, in fact, that proposals surfaced among serious observers of American government for fundamental structural reform in the political system, such as placing members of Congress in the president's cabinet as in the British model, lengthening the president's term to six years, and passing a balanced budget amendment to the U.S. Constitution. As the decade closed, a panel of prominent leaders convened by the National Academy of Public Administration warned that recent political and governmental trends were "threatening America's capacity for self-government."[1]

To those dismayed at the state of the political system, the first nine months of the Reagan administration gave cause to sit up and take notice. Whether or not one agreed with the administration's policies, it was hard not to be impressed by the administration's apparent impact on American politics and government. An authentic conservative had won a clear victory in the November 1980 presidential election. Soon after his administration took the reins of power the following January, major portions of its bold program were moving through Congress. The nation was being led in a direction distinctly different from that of the past, and public support for the change seemed strong. Even more remarkably, evidence from opinion polls suggested that the public's respect for government in general, not just for Reagan, was on the rise. As the effects of the administration's program unfolded in subsequent years, some began to feel that the American political system was working again. By early 1984, a prominent political writer was ready to conclude that "Ronald Reagan had made a mockery of the conventional wisdom that the country was ungovernable."[2] And the president's 1984 landslide election suggested quite strongly that a substantial portion of the public shared that view.

Other observers cautioned, however, that Reagan's successes have been greatly exaggerated. Most of the first-term successes, they noted, occurred in the early months of the administration and are therefore typical of the traditional "honeymoon" period every administration enjoys. After this the administration faced notable setbacks, such as with regard to its federalism proposals and the increasing difficulty it has had in getting its annual budget recommendations through Congress. A huge budget deficit, which eluded political resolution, belied the confident predictions of Reaganomics and cast a shadow over the economic recovery. Serious questions were also being

---

1. National Academy of Public Administration, *A Presidency for the 1980s* (Washington, D.C.: National Academy of Public Administration (1980), p. 1. For examples of recent proposals to re-structure American government and politics, see Kevin Phillips, "An American Parliament," *Harper's* (November 1980), pp. 14–21; Lloyd N. Cutler, "To Form a Government," *Foreign Affairs*, vol. 59 (Fall 1980), pp. 126–143; Lloyd N. Cutler, "Getting Rid of Incoherent Government," *Washington Post*, March 27, 1983, p. B1–B4; Charles M. Hardin, *Presidential Power and Accountability: Toward a New Constitution* (Chicago: University of Chicago Press, 1974); and James MacGregor Burns, *The Power to Lead: The Crisis of the Modern American Presidency* (New York: Simon and Schuster, 1984).

2. Richard Reeves, "The Ideological Election," *New York Times Magazine*, February 19, 1984, p. 29. For evidence of increased public confidence in government between 1980 and 1982 see Arthur Miller, "Is Confidence Rebounding?" *Public Opinion* (June/July 1983).

raised about Ronald Reagan's apparent inability to grasp, or take an interest in, much of the substance and detail of the vast government under him. To skeptics, the Reagan performance seemed more mixed, not so atypical of American presidencies generally, and therefore further evidence of fundamental problems in the political system.

These contrasting assessments of the political impact of the first four years of the Reagan presidency pose the chief issues examined in this volume. Its subject is the Reagan effect on American governance. By governance, we mean the concepts, processes, and institutions through which public policies are formulated, enacted, and carried out. Behind all the drama—the claims of Reagan supporters, the polemics of opponents, the stereotypes of the media—what in American politics and government has really changed under Reagan and what has stayed the same? What has been the impact of this administration on the capacity of the political system to function effectively—to reach decisions, to carry them out, and to maintain public trust? How has this administration dealt with the obstacles that seemed to frustrate effective governance in the 1970s? And what is its longer-term impact likely to be on the operation of the presidency, the executive agencies, Congress, and the broader political system?

These questions are as compelling for the general citizen as they are significant for the student of modern American government and politics. But relatively little effort has been made to answer them systematically. Most analyses of the "Reagan Revolution" have been confined to the substance of the administration's policies—social, economic, military, and foreign—and the effects of these policies on American society and the world. Little sustained interest has been focused on the impacts of the Reagan experience on the workings of government itself or on the nation's political behavior, thinking, and institutions.[3]

Yet these impacts are just as essential to assess. In the first place, substantive policies are heavily shaped by such political phenomena—by the assertion and reconciliation of clashing values, by the mobilization of

---

3. Some aspects of the Reagan impact on governance during the administration's first two years are covered in Fred I. Greenstein, ed., *The Reagan Presidency: An Early Assessment* (Baltimore: Johns Hopkins University Press, 1983); Norman J. Ornstein, ed., *President and Congress: Assessing Reagan's First Year* (Washington, D.C.: American Enterprise Institute for Public Policy Research, 1982). For analyses of the substantive program of the Reagan administration and its effects, see John L. Palmer and Isabel V. Sawhill, eds., *The Reagan Experiment: An Examination of Economic and Social Policies Under the Reagan Administration* (Washington, D.C.: The Urban Institute Press, 1982), and John L. Palmer and Isabel V. Sawhill, eds., *The Reagan Record: An Assessment of America's Changing Domestic Priorities* (Cambridge, Massachusetts: Ballinger Publishing Company,1984).

political support, and by the exercise of governmental authority. To make sense of an administration's policies, therefore, it is important to understand how its political philosophy and its governing methods interact with existing political processes and organizations to influence its actions and achievements.

In the second place, however, governing philosophies, institutions, and processes are important in their own right, as ends in themselves. They are the mechanisms through which conflicting values and interests are resolved and central values protected. It is therefore necessary to evaluate a presidency not only in terms of its success in advancing its favored programs or policies but also in terms of its impact on the nation's political heritage and governing institutions.

Finally, these issues are especially important in the case of the Reagan administration because it has made questions of governance—such as the roles and responsibilities of public and private institutions and of different levels of government—a central part of its program. For this administration, governance issues and substantive program issues have overlapped to an unusual degree.

The Reagan victory in the 1984 presidential election makes the question of this administration's impact on American governance all the more significant. It means that the Reagan administration's opportunity to affect the operation of the political system will be more extensive, and by suggesting public approval of the Reagan approach to governing, it makes this approach a standard against which future administrations will be judged.

This book seeks to formulate a "political impact statement" on the Reagan presidency, at least as of 1984. In the following twelve chapters, expert analysts of American government, politics, or policy examine the effects that the Reagan administration has had on ideas, procedures, and organizations that play major roles in the functioning of the American political system. Each of the chapters, as well as the commentaries that follow, seeks to assess not only how the Reagan administration performed during its first term but also what its longer-term impact is likely to be on the underlying forces at work.

The remainder of this overview highlights the major findings of these chapters and puts them into the context of the three fundamental problems of governance identified earlier. We then step back from the individual chapters and, drawing on the papers, a conference discussion of them, and other sources, identify what for us are the essential conclusions about the impact of the Reagan administration on governance in America as of late 1984.

The Reagan Presidency and the Dilemmas of Governance

The Crisis of Political Ideas

Ronald Reagan came to office at a time of extraordinary ideological ferment in the United States. During the thirty years following the New Deal of the 1930s, an implicit political consensus gradually took shape at the national level in support of an activist federal government responsible for stabilizing the economy and available to assist those in need. Though never unchallenged, it appeared by the mid-1960s that liberalism had truly arrived as the dominant ideology of the nation. Indeed, even the two Republican administrations that succeeded the Great Society era of Lyndon Baines Johnson operated within its basic world view, tidying up and consolidating the gains liberalism had attained in some areas, and even advancing them in others.

But appearances were deceiving. As one close observer noted, many of the Great Society measures passed without "the necessary majority" of popular support.[4] In subsequent years, as the scope of the federal enterprise expanded and the economy appeared to falter, serious questions began to surface about the effectiveness of many of the Great Society and related programs, and about their broader effect on the nation's social and economic life. These doubts intensified in the early 1970s as the federal government found itself thrust into the middle of a host of touchy social disputes and as it acquired new responsibilities—protecting consumers, the environment, and workers—that many perceived as threatening economic growth. Within a decade of its apparent political triumph, therefore, liberalism found itself on the defensive before a vigorous new conservative assault emboldened by right-wing social and moral doctrines. Even many long-time advocates of activist government began to question main-line liberalism's assumptions about the benefits of government involvement.

Though capitalizing on the growing political hostility to liberalism, Richard M. Nixon did not seek to chart an alternative course for the nation. Nor did Jimmy Carter manage to restore faith in the liberal creed or formulate a variant that could command public respect. Consequently, by the 1980 presidential election, the stage was set for a new ideological direction. What is more, by virtue of his lengthy apprenticeship as spokesman for the resurgent

---

4. Robert C. Wood, *The Necessary Majority: Middle America and the Urban Crisis* (New York and London: Cambridge University Press, 1972).

conservative cause, Ronald Reagan was an ideal candidate to attempt such a redirection. The result was one of the most uncharacteristically ideological campaigns, and one of the most self-consciously ideological presidencies, in modern American history.

But what set of ideas does Reagan stand for? What is the ideology that animated his campaign, and how effective has his administration been in developing mechanisms to translate that ideology into concrete action?

One important strand of the Reagan ideology is traditional laissez-faire conservative hostility to government involvement in social and economic life. Government domestic programs are perceived as wasteful at best and destructive of personal liberty and individual initiative at worst. Hence, Reagan has assaulted liberal social welfare programs, government job programs, and consumer and environmental regulations. Coupled with this philosophical hostility to the substance of many government programs, as James Ceaser's paper in this volume points out, is a distinct theory of governance that attributes the perceived poor performance of the federal government and the presidency to the excessive crush of issues they were being asked to handle. The Reagan approach sought to unclog the federal government's policy channels and administrative apparatus by challenging the assumption that the federal government must devise a program to deal with every social or economic circumstance some group considers to be a national problem. Instead, the Reagan philosophy of governance calls for a greater degree of selectivity in the assumption of federal responsibilities and a far higher degree of reliance on state and local governments and the private sector to resolve problems than was true in the recent past.

But laissez-faire hostility to government hardly exhausts the Reagan version of modern conservatism. To the contrary, the Reagan ideology is a mixture of conservative economic doctrines and populist moral and social tenets. The result, as Theodore J. Lowi argues in his chapter, is hardly blanket opposition to the extension of government authority. Rather, Ronald Reagan's political philosophy endorses the extension of governmental authority in a variety of spheres. The key distinction between Reaganism and liberalism, in other words, is not that one opposes the exercise of government authority and the other supports it. Rather, the key distinction has to do with the arenas where each considers government authority to be appropriate.

Under liberalism, government action is considered appropriate where it is needed to control conduct that, in Lowi's phrase, is "deemed to have harmful consequences." It is not, in other words, the inherent nature of the conduct, but the nature of the consequences that flow from it, that provides the rationale for government involvement. By contrast, under the new conservatism manifested in the Reagan administration, government action is considered appropriate to influence behavior "deemed good or evil in itself." Thus the Reagan philosophy condones government involvement in matters concerning abortions, the dispensation of birth control information, the work and sexual behavior of welfare recipients, prayer in the public schools, and a variety of other similar topics that liberals would prefer to leave to individual choice.

The Reagan proposals to shift more of the responsibility for governing from the federal level to the state and local levels are fully consistent with this ideology, both because the protection of "public morals" has traditionally been a state and local responsibility and because the business, small-town, and traditional religious political values that underlie the Reagan political philosophy are much more dominant at this level. Devolution is thus viewed not simply as an administrative strategy sought for reasons of efficiency, but as a political strategy pursued to provide advantages for a specific set of interests and perspectives.

As with any administration, however, the task of the Reagan presidency was not only to articulate a vision about where it wanted to lead the nation, but also to translate that vision into concrete, actionable terms. An assessment of the administration's impact in the realm of ideas must therefore go beyond scrutiny of its philosophical content and examine the extent to which it developed procedures and mechanisms to turn its philosophical tenets into specific programs of action.

The Reagan administration approached this policy-development task with considerable forethought and energy. Despite its emphasis on the need for devolution and decentralization, however, it did this by centralizing policy development in the Executive Office of the President even more than had previous administrations. To accomplish this end, the administration revised the budget process and established a network of White House committees and staff. In addition, the administration made use of the time-honored device of appointing a presidential commission on particular issues where it was necessary to "pre-cook" political consensus or mobilize potential allies.

The budget was by far the principal vehicle the Reagan administration used to translate its philosophical tenets into programmatic form. More than most recent presidents, Ronald Reagan has sought to use the federal budget to enforce his policy preferences on the federal establishment, interest groups, and Congress. The fact that a primary goal of the administration was to cut back on federal involvement in a number of domestic policy fields made the budget a natural candidate for this role. But it was still necessary for the administration to make major alterations in the budget process, which traditionally relied heavily on agency initiative and decentralized treatment in Congress. In particular, as reflected in Allen Schick's chapter, the Reagan administration adopted a highly centralized, top-down approach to federal budgeting, which left little room for agency input.[5] It then took advantage of the reconciliation provisions of the 1974 Congressional Budget Act to centralize control in Congress as well, concentrating the action in the Budget Committees and reducing the early budget battle to a few, well-publicized votes. The administration did this by changing the timing of the process, moving to the very beginning the binding "reconciliation" measure that was supposed to come at the tail end of the process to clear up remaining inconsistencies, and using that binding measure to short-circuit the rest of the procedures.

In the first year of the administration, this strategy was highly successful. The Omnibus Budget and Reconciliation Act that passed Congress in the summer of 1981 incorporated a significant portion of the administration's budget and policy objectives. As Schick shows, however, the administration's budget record in the remainder of its term was far more mixed. Although it cut back on government revenues and boosted defense spending, the administration did not make significant further progress in achieving the domestic spending cuts it sought. Nor did it manage to limit the growth of "uncontrollable" entitlement spending. As a result, the administration found itself in a tighter and tighter budgetary box.

One reason for this disappointing record, Schick asserts, is that the administration was so preoccupied with short-run successes that it overlooked opportunities to strengthen the institutional devices that are needed to exert control over the budget in the long run. In fact, the administration's initial use of the nascent congressional budget process struck many in Congress as so heavy-handed that it put a severe strain on the entire process. This was so not only because the administration altered the formal timetable, but also because it crammed a considerable amount of authorizing legislation into the reconciliation bill to the dismay of the authorizing committees, and then moved the package through so quickly that many members hardly knew what they were voting for.

Beyond this, the administration was highly inconsistent in its support for the congressional budget process. Having overused the Budget Committees and budget procedures in its first year, the administration then turned its back on them in 1982, when the Budget Committees and moderates in Congress

---

5. See also Hugh Heclo, "Executive Budget Making," in Gregory B. Mills and John L. Palmer, eds., *Federal Budget Policy in the 1980s* (Washington, D.C., The Urban Institute Press, 1984) pp. 255–291; and Frederick C. Mosher and Max O. Stephenson, Jr., "The Office of Management and Budget in a Changing Scene," *Public Budgeting and Finance*, vol. 2, no. 4 (Winter 1982), pp. 23–41.

resisted the administration's rosy economic assumptions and sought a budget compromise more in line with the developing economic realities. A similar pattern emerged in 1983, and both years the administration's proposals went nowhere.

Nor did the administration make much progress in institutionalizing its top-down budget process within the Executive Office of the President. As a consequence, intense, personal lobbying was regularly required on the part of the budget director to achieve marginal reductions in spending levels, while the vast bulk of the budget went unaffected. Far from signifying presidential strength, therefore, the "budgetization" of the national policy debate and the growing preoccupation with an expanding federal debt that occurred during the early 1980s is instead, in Schick's view, a sign of presidential weakness despite the success Reagan has had in shifting fiscal expectations.

Although the budget was the primary vehicle for giving concrete form to the Reagan political philosophy, the Reagan administration also followed the tradition of its liberal predecessors in developing a large and complex White House institutional structure to formulate and promote its policy ideas. At the heart of this structure were three key White House aides—James A. Baker, III, Edwin Meese, III, and Michael Deaver. These three individuals functioned as a kind of "subcommittee of the presidency," hammering out administration positions and communicating them to the media, Congress, and other parts of the administration. Beyond this troika, however, the administration created a more elaborate policy apparatus consisting of an Office of Planning and Evaluation, a domestic policy staff, and a network of Cabinet Councils.

As Chester A. Newland shows in his chapter, these units have performed a somewhat different function during the Reagan years than did their counterparts under previous presidents. In particular, they have served more as communicators and enforcers of centrally determined policy positions than as mechanisms for active deliberation over priorities. This reflects the administration's philosophical hostility to an activist federal government and the fact the Reagan's policy positions were largely shaped in advance by the task forces that operated during the pre-inauguration transition period. What was needed in the White House, therefore, was not a policy development apparatus but a mechanism to gather political intelligence in order to gauge public and media response to the president's actions, and a means to avoid having the administration's appointees "go native" once exposed to the professionals in the agencies they were charged with overseeing.

In at least one major area—the promotion of "private-sector initiatives"—the administration's ideology required setting up new programmatic initiatives to translate its ideas into concrete form. To help it perform this function, it turned to another common vehicle for presidential policy development: the presidential task force or commission. Thus was born the President's Task Force on Private Sector Initiatives, a group of prominent corporate, foundation, and philanthropic leaders given the job of devising ways to stimulate private-sector activity to respond more effectively to local needs and help compensate for cuts in government programs.

As recounted by Renée Berger in her chapter, this effort had great difficulty getting off the ground. Saddled with a nebulous structure and role, lacking in resources, uncertain over its goals, and placed in the uncomfortable position of appearing to be a cover for the administration's proposed budget cuts, the Task Force never rose much above a public-relations effort. The Task Force leadership eschewed information gathering or in-depth analysis of existing public-private partnerships, even that of think tanks sympathetic to the administration's position. Although usefully raising consciousness about the need for private-sector involvement in social problem solving, the Task Force made little measurable headway in developing a serious program of private-sector action or public-private cooperation. In the process, it suggested that, where the Reagan administration sought new initiatives as opposed to budget cuts, it had as much difficulty translating its philosophical beliefs into concrete form as did many of its predecessors.

The Crisis of Political Support

If Ronald Reagan came to power at a time of considerable ideological discontent, he also took office at a time of political disarray and stalemate arising from a widespread public loss of confidence in government, the proliferation of organized interests and social movements, and the weakening of a number of crucial integrating institutions, such as political parties. Under the circumstances, it became increasingly difficult to assemble the majorities needed to deal with major national problems.

How well has the Reagan administration coped with these problems? To what extent has it managed to put together a durable governing coalition—in the country as a whole and in Congress? Did the 1980 election signify a major realignment of political attitudes and party loyalties? Was this confirmed or altered in the midterm elections of 1982? Has Reagan succeeded in breaking the hold of powerful interest groups over the policy channels in Congress?

Viewed from afar, the Reagan administration's record for mustering political support for its policies appears impressive indeed, particularly against the backdrop of recent presidencies. On closer scrutiny, however, this record seems much more uneven.

Although Reagan won a stunning electoral victory in 1980, for example, the election hardly represented an endorsement of the conservative program Reagan articulated in the campaign. Aside from the dislike for the presidency of Jimmy Carter, the most that can be read from the 1980 election returns is a voter preference for something new to replace the policies of the recent past. In no sense were the voters expressing a preference for the conservative economic policies or fundamental opposition to the concept of positive government. To the contrary, as Everett Carll Ladd documents in his chapter, voters in the 1980 election were highly ambivalent toward government: They were opposed to its rising costs but generally supportive of its benefits. In the 1980 campaign Ronald Reagan did not win over large numbers of adherents to his conservative world view or the Republican Party. The proportion of voters who espoused conservative and liberal positions remained about the same in 1980 as in earlier periods, as did the proportion identifying themselves as Democrat and Republican. Nor was any basic change in political alignment apparent in the 1982 midterm election. Voters liked Reagan and seemed willing to give his program a chance, even while disagreeing with key parts of his agenda and resisting identification with his overall ideology. In Ladd's view, therefore, there is little in Reagan's election that suggests a basic electoral realignment or the emergence of a strong two-party system dominated by highly committed partisans taking clearly opposing stands on fundamental issues. Rather, despite the evidence that David Price presents in his commentary on Ladd's paper that both the Republicans and Democrats are improving their parties' organizational capacities to win voter support for their candidates, personal rather than ideological or partisan attachments seem to dominate the political scene, as the number of independents continues to grow and the number of strong party identifiers continues to decline.

Although the polls hardly support an interpretation of the 1980 election as a turning point in public attitudes and party affiliation, the margin of victory was sufficient to give a different impression to those in the media and in Congress who had to deal with the election results politically before the polling results were in. This was particularly true because the president's party took control of the Senate for the first time in decades. The upshot, as Charles O. Jones points out in his chapter, was an unusual degree of congressional acquiescence in the new administration's early proposals. By putting a bold program of domestic budget cuts, defense increases, and tax reductions before Congress soon after Reagan's election and in the wake of the assassination scare, and by pushing for this program vigorously, the administration was able to score an impressive string of early legislative victories and to establish a reputation for itself as a "winner."

Impressive though these early victories were, however, they were not followed by comparable achievements in subsequent years. To the contrary, after the initial budget and tax triumphs, the Reagan administration and Congress settled into a "cold war" standoff across a broad front. Determined to enact its program intact, the administration refused to bend enough to help Republican moderates forge a governing coalition with their Democratic counterparts on the budget. The result was a deadlock over the key elements of the remaining Reagan agenda, albeit a deadlock that left the earlier achievements largely in place.

Beyond its effect on voters and Congress, the Reagan administration also influenced the prospects for generating political support and overcoming political fragmentation by virtue of its dealings with political interest groups. The Reagan program of domestic spending cuts, devolution of programmatic authority to the states, and revision of federal consumer and environmental regulation constituted a frontal assault on a broad assortment of influential groups—groups that, according to conventional wisdom, dominated the policy process because of the links they enjoyed with powerful allies in Congress and in the federal establishment. How is it, then, that the administration made significant progress? And what does this tell us about the seemingly invincible power of interest groups and the consequences of fragmentation of political influence?

Part of the answer to these questions can be found in the tactics the administration employed and the nature of the interest groups it targeted for assault. As Harold Wolman and Fred Teitelbaum report in their chapter, the Reagan administration caught many groups by surprise. What is more, by focusing heavily on the Congressional Budget Committees rather than on the Appropriations Committees for its initial budgetary thrust, the administration engaged the groups on terrain with which they were largely unfamiliar. Finally, while adversely affecting liberal and social welfare groups, which tend to be relatively weak, the administration worked in concert with many business groups. It was not, therefore, a challenge to interest-group power per se that the administration launched, but a challenge to a particular set of interests. Indeed Wolman and Teitelbaum present evidence that suggests that the administration's decentralization efforts, if sustained over the long run, would likely shift power further away from the poor, at least in low-income states and states with high minority and poverty populations.

While achieving some notable victories in the face of strenuous interest-group opposition, however, the Reagan administration has by no means broken the hold even of liberal, labor, and consumer interest groups on the national policy process. To the contrary, in many fields—such as environmental protection—the administration's blitzkrieg tactics and outspoken appointees helped groups to mobilize new adherents and to reactivate existing ones. In addition, many groups began to alter their operations in the face of the new realities—for example, by focusing more of their lobbying efforts on the state government level and by turning more heavily to grass-roots organizing. In fact, the administration's frontal attack on the liberal-labor-consumer wing of the interest-group state may ultimately prove to be self-defeating, stimulating a resurgence of group strength. Certainly the difficulties the administration encountered in trying to move beyond its initial 1981 budget conquests lends credence to this view.

The Crisis of Public Management

Underlying the ferment over political ideas and the difficulties in mustering the necessary majority support for government action during the 1970s was a serious decline in confidence in the manageability of the governmental enterprise, particularly at the federal level and in federal-state relations. Whether accurate or not, the view was widespread by the mid-1970s that the federal government was poorly run, that its policies were not being implemented well, and that it was mired in bureaucratic procedures and intruding too heavily into the operations of too many types of institutions.

The Reagan administration was sympathetic to this widespread complaint. Consistent with its philosophical hostility to many of the social programs and regulatory initiatives of the recent past, however, it set out to solve the problem not so much through reorganization or management reform at the federal level as by reducing the range of activities in which the federal government was involved, and by reducing the amount of "management" the federal government engaged in even for those functions it retained. In other words, the administration proposed to cure the problems of federal management by eliminating—or seriously curtailing—major segments of the federal operation. Still it was necessary to secure control over the federal establishment and to devise ways to shift responsibilities to other levels of government and the private sector.

One mechanism the Reagan administration used to accomplish at least the first of these purposes, as noted earlier, was the network of Cabinet Councils supervised by presidential aide Edwin Meese. In addition, the administration devoted an extraordinary amount of effort to locating subcabinet officials who shared the administration's basic ideology. Reflecting this, as Edie Goldenberg shows in her chapter, the Reagan administration has filled a larger proportion of the executive positions in the government with noncareer political appointees than was the case in any prior administration.

Ultimately, however, the administration's success in gaining effective control of the executive agencies and implementing its policy priorities depended heavily on the skill of the individuals put in charge of the various agencies. This is clearly apparent in Laurence E. Lynn, Jr.'s chapter analyzing the experiences of five Reagan appointees in changing the core activities of the agencies they were named to head. Aside from the nature of the opportunity each faced and the personality and management experience each brought to the job, the chief factor explaining the success or failure of these appointees appears to have been the extent to which they developed a clear management strategy that took into account the realities of agency operations and the interests and incentives of agency personnel. Where skills and sensitivities lined up well with agency dynamics, and where a careful management plan was developed, Lynn finds, far more change could be effected in basic agency operations than conventional wisdom might have predicted. The record of these appointees was therefore mixed, with some achieving changes in their agencies' operations and others falling significantly short.

In addition to naming highly committed Reagan partisans to positions of authority within executive departments and agencies and relying on them to implement the president's goals, the Reagan administration also affected the operation of the federal establishment through its personnel policies. Throughout the campaign and into the first years of his administration, Reagan made the federal civil service the whipping boy of his rhetoric. The overall image that emerged was that of a bloated and misdirected behemoth staffed by incompetent zealots, hardly an image likely to encourage bureaucratic self-esteem. On a more concrete level as well, as Edie N. Goldenberg contends in her chapter, the administration has made life tough for the federal work force. To be sure, increases occurred in the salaries of top executives and some progress was made in recruiting women and minorities. But the administration also instituted sizable reductions-in-force, took advantage of the provisions of the 1978 Civil Service Reform Act to shift around numerous top-level personnel, and reduced training and professional development programs. In addition, many civil service professionals were cut out of effective participation in key policy deliberations by virtue of the top-down budgeting procedures and centralized policy development practices. The overall effect of these actions, in Goldenberg's view, was to subject the permanent officials in the federal government to much tighter political control by the administration, and to de-emphasize the independent, professional roles that civil servants can play.

In its effort to reduce the amount of management required at the federal level, the Reagan administration also proposed major changes in the role of the federal government relative to states and local governments. In the first place, the administration proposed to transform a number of federal, categorical grant programs into block grants to the states, with only minimal federal control over the use of the funds. Beyond this, however, the administration came forward with a plan to swap certain functions between the federal government and the states, with the federal government taking over Medicaid, and state government, aided by a temporary federal trust fund, taking most of the rest, including Aid to Families with Dependent Children and food stamps. As David R. Beam makes clear in his chapter, this latter proposal harked back to an earlier, pre-New Deal theory of intergovernmental relations that viewed the federal government and state governments as operating in wholly different and separable fields, rather than as cooperating with each other across a broad front as is commonly the case in most domestic program areas.

Although a number of the administration's block-grant proposals passed in the initial Omnibus Budget and Reconciliation Act of 1981, most did so in significantly watered-down form, with the largest programs deleted and with some of the federal requirements retained. Beyond this, the administration got nowhere with its more ambitious scheme for shifting domestic program responsibilities to the states in return for federal takeover of Medicaid costs and sharing of windfall profits and selected excise tax receipts. The reasons for this, Beam suggests, were partly tactical—the administration's selection of a set of proposals that were alien to most of the groups interested in intergovernmental reform, its failure to present them effectively or argue for them convincingly, and the accident of timing that states were asked to take on new functions at a time when federal support was declining and recession was eating away at their revenues. But more basic factors were also at work—the public's continued expectation of active federal involvement in serving public needs and the difficulties of generating serious public interest in the arcane topic of intergovernmental reform. The result has been to limit significantly the administration's headway on this aspect of its governance agenda, though some progress was made in revising the expectation of continued growth in federal aid to states and in easing at least some of the restrictions of the grant system.[6]

Similar roadblocks were also encountered in moving ahead with another facet of the administration's effort to ease the burden on federal management: namely, its efforts to increase reliance on private-sector institutions to replace federal program activity. As noted earlier, the administration's effort to utilize

6. For further information of these points, see George E. Peterson, "Federalism and the States: An Experiment in Decentralization," in Palmer and Sawhill, eds., *The Reagan Record*, p. 257ff.

a private-sector task force to develop a program in this area fell far short of the claims made for it. The reason for this was not simply the character and operation of this task force. Even more important were the incentives and resources of the major private-sector institutions the administration turned to for help—corporations, foundations, and other sources of private charitable support and voluntary action. As Marc Bendick, Jr. and Phyllis M. Levinson note in their chapter, these institutions do not have the capability or the incentive to replace federal resources, but they do have special advantages that, in cooperation with government, could be used to improve the delivery of services. By stressing "private-sector initiatives" instead of "public-private partnerships," however, the administration may have lost important opportunities to make use of these advantages and build private-sector institutions more effectively into the operation of public programs.

A Summing Up: The Reagan Impact on Governance

What the discussion above makes clear is that in each of the major fields of political life—from the realm of political ideas to that of policy implementation—the Reagan administration's impact during its first term was decidedly mixed—more extensive than many would have predicted but far more limited than some popular accounts suggest. What overall conclusions can we draw, then, about the impact of the Reagan administration on the American polity? How well did it overcome the obstacles to effective governance that seemed to dominate the political scene when it entered office? Did the experience of this administration refute the theories prominent in the 1970s that the American presidency was unworkable and the American political system in deep trouble, requiring structural reform? What enduring legacy, if any, is this administration likely to leave for the American polity and for its own second term?

In this section we step back from the individual institutions and processes and, drawing on the conference chapters and commentaries, a conference discussion of them, and other research[7] reach some bottom-line judgments about how the Reagan administration fared in the area of governance in its first term. In particular, three observations about the implications of the Reagan presidency for governance in America seem appropriate, relating to its role in defining the terms of the national policy debate, its success in

---

7. See particularly Lester M. Salamon and Alan J. Abramson, "Governance: The Politics of Retrenchment," in Palmer and Sawhill, eds., *The Reagan Record*, pp. 31–68.

forging a solid governing majority, and its impact on governmental institutions.

Agenda Setting and Public Confidence

In the first place, the Reagan administration appears to have succeeded significantly in shifting the terms of the national policy debate and in restoring, in the process, a considerable measure of public confidence in the presidency and in the workability of the political system. More than many of his predecessors, Ronald Reagan articulated a coherent new direction for national policy, sought public support for that new direction, and then got a substantial portion of it enacted and put into place.

In neither its general philosophy nor its theory of governance was the Reagan administration wholly consistent. As noted earlier, Reagan's world view combined traditional laissez-faire precepts with a more statist social philosophy that condoned the use of governmental authority to enforce discipline and control "immoral" social behavior. Furthermore, the administration's eagerness to reduce policy congestion at the center of the political system did not prevent it from centralizing control over executive branch policy development and political negotiation in the crucial areas of budgeting, program restructuring, and regulatory reform far more extensively than did previous administrations.

Despite these apparent contradictions, the Reagan administration did articulate a policy course for the nation that was reasonably clear, markedly different from what had gone before, and responsive to at least one facet of the popular mood. More than that, the administration put a significant portion of this new direction into operation. It did this most forcefully through passage of two landmark pieces of legislation: first, the 1981 Omnibus Budget and Reconciliation Act, which greatly expanded military spending, made significant cuts in a variety of domestic programs, and merged a number of categorical grant programs into block grants; and second, the Economic Recovery Tax Act of 1981, which reduced tax rates for both individuals and corporations and put a lid on further revenue growth by "indexing" tax rates beginning in 1975 so that rates decline when inflation increases.

Though the administration did not get everything it requested, these two pieces of legislation fundamentally changed the context of the national policy debate, and in the direction Reagan wanted. By reducing government revenue and clamping down on its future growth, the tax act in particular virtually guaranteed that new program initiatives would face extremely unfavorable odds and that key constituencies would have to battle mightily just to maintain existing benefits in the face of growing federal deficits. Moreover, through a series of administrative moves by its appointees, the administration limited the zealousness of enforcement in the social regulatory area and created a "hunker-down" atmosphere that placed the burden of proof back with the advocates of regulatory protection. The result has been a severe ratcheting down of expectations that has had ramifications throughout the political system.

Several factors seem to account for the Reagan administration's success in altering the terms of the national policy debate in this fashion. One was the apparent clarity and straightforwardness of the administration's basic philosophy, with its simple appeal to cut domestic spending, increase defense spending, and limit federal regulation. Equally important was the 1980 election, which, though hardly yielding a voter endorsement of the Reagan philosophy, nevertheless created a presumption that the electorate was eager for a change. A third factor was the speed with which the administration moved and the skill with which it took advantage of the reconciliation provisions of the Congressional Budget Act. The Reagan administration did not spend months analyzing possible alternative courses of action or endlessly reviewing the details of what it was proposing with myriad interest groups and congressional advocates. Rather, it assembled its proposals quickly on the basis of best estimates and hunches and moved boldly to gain acceptance for them in the warm afterglow of the election, thus catching its opponents thoroughly off guard.

Finally, the administration's success in changing the terms of the national policy debate resulted in no small part from the extraordinary political and communications skills of Ronald Reagan. By personalizing and humanizing the presidential office, Reagan managed to take the edge off what would otherwise have been perceived as insensitive policy directions. He did this by effortlessly projecting a basically ingenuous personality, by using anecdotes and homiletic appeals to widely felt values, and by conveying an unpretentious, friendly manner that avoided impersonal statistical argument, complex reasoning, and expressions of intense emotion such as bitterness or sarcasm. Reagan's operational style reinforced this image, leaving to White House aides and cabinet members much of the nitty-gritty detail of program content and political deal-cutting, while reserving for the president the high ground of general philosophy and public mobilization.

As a result of this style, the public dissociates its evaluation of the Reagan administration and its policies as a whole from its estimation of Reagan himself. Drawn to his attractive personality, large numbers of Americans have been willing to forgive Reagan or not hold him accountable for major failures of his administration. The political payoff for Reagan is that the positive feeling he instills toward himself helps to carry support for his policies, even though the policies per se are not being endorsed. Coupled with the strong performance of the economy, this contributed importantly to Reagan's overwhelming victory in the 1984 election.

Stalemate and Lost Opportunities

While making significant progress in shifting the terms of the national policy debate, however, the Reagan administration has hardly escaped the prevailing realities of American political life or altered them in any fundamental way. To the contrary, the early successes of the Reagan administration were not unlike the "honeymoon" periods of other administrations that have entered office with a modicum of electoral momentum. Despite the drama of its early successes, the Reagan administration ultimately failed to gain control of the federal budget as it had intended. Rather, it encountered a serious stalemate in Congress as it attempted to move forward from the budgetary beachhead it established in 1981. Similarly, it made little headway in translating its regulatory initiatives into legislative form, with the result that many of the regulatory changes it pursued through administrative means were reversed in the courts.[8] In addition, the efforts to devolve authority to state and local governments and to the private sector ended up far short of their marks.

In large part, these failures resulted from the resurgence of political forces that had been thrown off balance by the early Reagan initiatives, and from the results of the 1982 Congressional elections, which undercut Reagan's "working majority" in Congress. In part, however, they also reflected blind spots in the administration's outlook and approach that led to significant missed opportunities. This was certainly the case in the regulatory arena, where outspoken appointees effectively pulled the rug out from under the broad coalition that had formed in support of moderate regulatory reform, dooming many of the administration's regulatory objectives.[9] Similarly, opportunities for making further headway on intergovernmental reform and on private-sector initiatives were undermined by policy actions that took too little account of prevailing patterns of cooperation between the federal government and both state and local and private-sector institutions.

Behind these individual cases, moreover, was a broader failure of this administration to take full advantage of the political resources it might have

---

8. This point is developed more fully in Salamon and Abramson "Governance: The Politics of Retrenchment," Palmer and Sawhill, eds., *The Reagan Record*, and in ," George C. Eads and Michael Fix, *Relief or Reform? Reagan's Regulatory Dilemma* (Washington, D.C.: The Urban Institute Press, 1984).

9. *Ibid.*

tapped had it pursued a less ideological approach. The administration was far less vigorous than it might have been in forging a reliable coalition with moderates of both parties in Congress on the budget. On numerous occasions, the administration left potential moderate leaders in Congress "twisting in the wind" on budget compromises that the administration sorely needed. Similarly in the administration's dealings with state and local government officials, with leaders in the philanthropic community targeted for involvement in the private-sector initiatives, and with the federal civil service itself, it pursued a take-it-or-leave-it approach that denied it potentially important insights and support. By stressing private-sector initiatives instead of public-private partnerships, for example, the administration made corporate and philanthropic leaders suspicious that they were being set up as scapegoats for the administration's budget cuts, when in fact these leaders were more than willing to take a larger part in social problem solving in cooperation with government.[10] Likewise, many Reagan appointees spurned help from the career civil service. Instead of meeting such potential allies halfway, the administration too often seemed more eager to make a point than to make things work.

Institutional Costs

This brings us to the final point, which has to do with the administration's longer-term impact on the effectiveness of America's basic political institutions and processes. What is at issue here is not how successful the administration was in getting its own program adopted, but what impact it has had on the functioning of our overall system of democratic government. Of special concern is how this administration has affected the balance that is supposed to exist in American political life between the dispersion of political power in order to guarantee meaningful access to political decision making and the need for sufficient coherence and integration to permit joint action on pressing societal problems. A tension has long existed between these forces of fragmentation and integration in the American political system, but it has intensified in recent decades as a consequence of the decline of public confidence in government, the proliferation of issue and interest groups, the growing dispersion of power in Congress, and the progressive weakening of some potentially integrating institutions such as political parties.

This situation has special implications for the presidency because of the distinctive role the presidency plays in maintaining a balance between these

10. Lester M. Salamon, "Nonprofit Organizations: The Lost Opportunity," in John L. Palmer and Isabel V. Sawhill, eds., *The Reagan Record*.

two sets of forces. As the only nationally elected political leader, the president is in a better position than most political figures to articulate the national interest and bring to bear a society-wide perspective in policy disputes. The problem is that over the long run the presidency cannot perform this integrating function by itself. For one thing, power is too dispersed for that. For another, the range of issues requiring a system-wide perspective is too great even for the presidency to handle by itself without being spread too thin. In addition, the public is too fickle to grant a president enough influence over the long run to withstand the powerful centrifugal forces in this system on his own, and even if a president were granted such influence, it would not likely carry over to a successor. Finally, a presidency imbued with enough power to overwhelm potential opponents regularly without other help would raise dangers of a different sort—that other channels of political expression were being closed and other legitimate interpretations of the public good ignored.

Fortunately, however, the presidency is not alone in performing a potentially integrating function in the political system. Several other institutions share with the presidency a national perspective and a potentially integrating role. These include the professional institutions and processes of the Executive Office of the President and of the executive branch more generally, the leadership in Congress, and the political parties. Over time, the best hope for a proper balance between the centrifugal and centripetal elements in the political system, and thus for the long-term health of our basic political order, is to strengthen all of these integrating institutions and to encourage meaningful collaboration among them.

Although the viability of these other institutions rests on a number of factors, the presidency itself plays an important role. The dilemma for each president, however, is that working with and through these other integrating institutions has costs as well as advantages since these other institutions inevitably have somewhat different perspectives and bases of power. In the short run presidents can often do better on their own, taking advantage of their own popularity—however fleeting—and of the fragmentation of political power to muster their own majorities, even if this undercuts the influence of other integrating institutions. Presidents frequently find themselves forced to choose between the short-run goal of pursuing their own programs without compromise, though at some cost to the viability of these other institutions, and the longer-run goal of working through—and thus strengthening—the other integrating institutions, but at the cost of some compromise of presidential goals.

In general, the Reagan administration has tended to take the former of these two courses. Eager to move quickly to take advantage of its substantial electoral victory, the administration early adopted a style of operation that resembled a military campaign. A handful of key White House aides exerted effective control over policy development and political mobilization, and loyal lieutenants carried the orders to the troops. By developing a coherent program at the center, by establishing clear priorities for presidential involvement, by making ample use of the persuasive powers of the president to focus attention on this central program and espouse its basic values, by avoiding the use of presidential resources for "fringe" issues, and by cutting deals directly with individual legislators, the administration managed to achieve a significant political breakthrough that exceeded prevailing expectations. In the process, it defined a style of presidential policy management and agenda-setting that is likely to serve as a standard and guide for other occupants of the office.

While this style of operation enabled the administration to achieve an important victory, however, it did little to strengthen, and in significant respects it weakened, some of the other institutions that presidents and the nation have historically needed to help promote a system-wide perspective. Nor has the administration acted in the period since its initial 1981 victories to buttress these institutions or even to institutionalize its own stylistic innovations. This is apparent in the administration's treatment of the institutions and processes both of the executive branch and of the wider political system.

Executive Institutions.   With regard to the institution of the presidency itself, the Reagan administration has succeeded in magnifying the role that the presidency plays on the center stage of American political life and in keeping the spotlight of national politics beamed steadily on the Oval Office. In so doing, Reagan eschewed past conservative notions of a relatively passive presidency that limits its authority in deference to the prerogatives of Congress or other institutions, and he extended instead the tradition of the activist presidency amplified by Franklin Delano Roosevelt and subscribed to by all subsequent presidents with the exception of Dwight D. Eisenhower. As Lester M. Salamon and Alan Abramson put it recently, Reagan "adopted the approach of Wilson and Roosevelt in order to pursue the objectives of Coolidge and Harding."[11]

Much of this centralization in Reagan's case was motivated by distrust of the existing centers of policy and political advice both within and outside the executive branch. However, as a result, professional staff even within the Executive Office of the President, such as those in the Office of Management and Budget (OMB), were not effectively involved in a number of major policy decisions. OMB staff had only minimal substantive input into the initial budget decisions that shaped the administration's priorities for the next four years,

---

11. Salamon and Abramson, "Governance: The Politics of Retrenchment," Palmer and Sawhill, eds., *The Reagan Record*, p. 41.

and the top-down budgeting procedures the administration adopted left agency staff out of the loop as well. Although OMB has recovered part of its professional role, the top-down procedures that work in practice have never been institutionalized, so that the formal budget process run by OMB and the agencies, and the informal budget process run by the president's staff, operate on different tracks. While such an arrangement is tolerable in the short run, over time it takes a toll on established routines, of which the budget process has long been one of the most effective.

Similarly, the Reagan administration has tended to downplay the idea that the nonappointed portion of the executive branch has a legitimate role to play in national policy formulation. In the process, it has done little to strengthen, and on balance has probably undercut, the concept of a professional Senior Executive Service created by the Civil Service Reform Act of 1978. Pressure has been placed on the bureaucracy to cut costs, but far less has been done to improve program effectiveness. In fact, some of the basic information resources needed to gauge program effects have been sharply cut back.

The Reagan administration's record in the area of executive branch institutional development is not, to be sure, entirely negative. For example, it has created an elaborate new system for tracking budgetary decision making in Congress so that the administration can participate in the process more effectively. It has also extended the procedures for Executive Office scrutiny of regulations begun under Presidents Gerald R. Ford and Jimmy Carter, and it has taken steps to strengthen financial controls in the executive branch. It has also furthered the review of federal credit activities and accelerated the move to establish a regular credit budget. In addition, its "Cabinet Councils" have improved internal executive branch communication. Beyond this, the administration has given greater salience to the potential role that both private-sector institutions and state and local governments can play in dealing with public problems.

Overall, however, the Reagan administration has weakened more than strengthened the more permanent institutions of presidential management, has undermined the morale of the civil service, has taken a narrow auditing approach to improving management in the executive branch, has done little to encourage competent professionals to serve in the federal government, and has overlooked opportunities to strengthen existing partnership arrangements between the federal government and other institutions at the state and local level and in the private sector.

Representative Institutions. A similar observation applies to the administration's handling of Congress and other representative institutions. The retrenchment program that the Reagan administration proposed to Congress in 1981 fundamentally challenged the prevailing pattern of constituency politics on Capitol Hill. To deal with this, the administration initially used one of the most important integrating devices Congress had devised for itself in recent years—the Congressional Budget Act of 1974. However, the omnibus reconciliation measure that the administration got Congress to accept in the summer of 1981 represented such a heavy-handed use of the budget procedures that its real effect may have been to weaken the congressional budget process rather than strengthen it. In addition, by relying, at least in the House of Representatives, not on the existing party leadership but primarily on an ad hoc group of young mavericks, the "Boll Weevils," to conduct its budget negotiations, the administration alienated both Republican and Democratic leaders.

Coupled with the 1982 election results, this mode of operation led to a stalemate between Congress and the administration that is still unresolved, that has put the federal government into continual fiscal turmoil, and that leaves deficits growing at alarming rates. More important, the role of the congressional leadership and of the congressional budget process was thrown into limbo. Again the administration sought short-term victories at the cost of longer-term improvement in the functioning of key integrating institutions and centers of power.

The situation with regard to parties and interest groups is more a blend of good and bad. On the positive side, the administration's highly partisan style has increased party voting in Congress, at least since the Boll Weevil defection in 1981. The Republican Party has developed sophisticated machinery for mobilizing funds and voters, stimulating parallel—if less well-developed—efforts on the part of Democrats. Finally, the administration made important headway in breaking the hammer-lock that liberal, labor, environmental, educational, and social welfare groups were reputed to hold on national policy channels, and it thereby created possibilities for pursuing new approaches to solving national problems.

These developments have hardly affected the functioning of parties or interest groups in a fundamental way, however. To the contrary, the Reagan administration has done little to buttress the Republican party leadership in Congress. By giving vent to the more conservative elements in the Republican Party, moreover, the administration has strained the loyalties of Republican moderates. While weakening the hold of essentially "liberal" interest groups, the administration has strengthened the grip of more business- and conservative-oriented groups. Indeed, through its defense buildup it may have replaced the "social pork barrel" about which Budget Director David Stockman had expressed such concern in the 1970s with a "military pork barrel" even more extensive in scope.[12] What is more, the administration's actions in several areas created backlashes that inadvertently shored up some of the social welfare and environmental groups the administration was assaulting.

Conclusion

The Reagan administration has demonstrated that with careful attention and a solid strategy, a popular president can make major inroads in defining the national agenda and shaping the content of at least a few key elements of national policy. In the process, it has shown that the political system can respond when an effective politician occupies the White House and makes sensible use of the resources available. At the same time, the administration has made little attempt to institutionalize its approach, and, in some cases, has actually weakened institutions, processes, and centers of influence that are important to the long-run health of the political system and to the capacity of the presidency to perform its integrating function in American politics. While this has not seriously affected the administration during the first term, it promises to be far more important during the second, especially in view of the perpetuation of split party control of Congress, which puts a premium on the other integrating institutions and coalition-building skills that this administration tended to neglect in its first term. With a number of politically difficult policy dilemmas—such as the sky-rocketing budget deficit and rapidly escalating Medicare costs—looming on the nation's political agenda, it seems clear that continued inattention to these processes and institutions for achieving consensus and building long-run governmental capacity would be costly indeed. In the meantime, set against the record of prior, "failed" presidencies, the Reagan administration's first term accomplishments, though partial, deservedly attract praise.

---

12. David A. Stockman, "The Social Porkbarrel," *The Public Interest* (Spring 1975), pp. 3–30.

PART ONE

THE PHILOSOPHY OF GOVERNMENT

RONALD REAGAN—REVOLUTIONARY?

Theodore J. Lowi

If Ronald Reagan leaves no other legacy, he should be long remembered for forcing a reexamination of some basic premises of American government. For most of the twentieth century, indeed the past two centuries, the American public philosophy has been a variant of liberalism. Louis Hartz called it the "liberal tradition."[1] It may be also called the liberal consensus, a consensus so widely shared that it has effortlessly suppressed all alternatives. Ronald Reagan's conservatism has dared to dissent, and his dissent has sent armies of intellectuals back to their dictionaries and treatises, not so much to examine conservatism as to refamiliarize themselves with liberalism. Confusion is not confined to academia. It is widespread, and is preventing adequate evaluation of the changes that are taking place and of Ronald Reagan's contribution to them.

In 1961 Daniel Bell could write *The End of Ideology*, and President John F. Kennedy could endorse it in his 1962 Yale Commencement address.[2] Twenty years later, Ronald Reagan's policies would question whether the obituary was not a bit premature. Liberalism had not put an end to ideology; it had simply obliterated the alternatives and obfuscated its own ideological and philosophical base. Significant debate between opposing public philosophies disappeared during this century, leaving a dialogue between variants of liberalism. Since Americans have always thought of themselves as a pragmatic people unburdened by ideology, there has been no apparent discomfort in the fact that political debate has seemed to run the gamut from A to B.

---

1. Louis Hartz, *The Liberal Tradition in America* (New York: Harcourt Brace & World, 1955).
2. Daniel Bell, *The End of Ideology* (New York: Collier Books, 1961).

One variant of liberalism was laissez-faire liberalism, which prevailed toward the end of the nineteenth century and was known sometimes as market liberalism or free enterprise. Nowadays it is known as libertarianism. Oddly, it also came to be identified with conservatism, but this was mainly for lack of any important, real conservatism until the 1970s. The more recent variant of liberalism, a pro-state liberalism, pushed the nineteenth-century variety into a conservative box simply because it was older. Pro-state liberalism shares most of the social ethic of the older market liberalism, except for the confidence that free enterprise is the best guarantor of individual freedom and prosperity.

Although this newer type of liberalism is often identified as New Deal liberalism, it actually became the dominant variety before the New Deal. But the New Deal gave it an electoral base that lasted into the 1970s. The longer pro-state liberalism remained as the public philosophy, however, the weaker its intellectual powers became, until its contradictory and self-defeating qualities began to outweigh its virtues. In its deterioration, pro-state liberalism became "interest-group liberalism," whereby its broad vision of using government to expand freedom was replaced by its embrace of a process in which corporate groups (of business, labor, agriculture, and other organized interests) were provided with direct and legitimate involvement in policymaking and in which group support became the primary basis of policy justification. Interest-group liberalism sees as both necessary and good that the policy agenda and the public interest be identified in terms of the organized interests in society.[3]

The decadence of pro-state interest-group liberalism led to its collapse in the 1970s, the reasons for which are explored in detail later in this paper. What is important to note here is that the national breakdown of the liberal consensus in the 1970s made way for two minority administrations. The first of these was that of President Jimmy Carter, whose rise to power is one of the most remarkable political stories of this generation. Starting with nothing but a base in Georgia and a reputation as a "New South" politician, Carter succeeded by cleverly positioning himself among the several Democratic presidential candidates who so fragmented the primary electorate. All Carter had to do to build a bandwagon was to exceed expectations as these were defined for each candidate by the media experts. His four years in office combined lame populism with a hint of antinational government libertarianism and the appearance of instinctive honesty in contrast to the moral obtuseness

---

3. Theodore J. Lowi, *The End of Liberalism* (New York: W.W. Norton & Co., 2nd ed., 1979).

of Watergate. The Carter administration was a mere holding operation that held almost nothing.

The second minority administration is that of Ronald Reagan, which is more accurately a minority of a minority. Although the conservatives were always the distinct minority wing of the Republican party, Reagan was able to capture the 1980 presidential nomination mainly because of the fragmentation of moderate and liberal Republicans. With the nomination in hand, Reagan rallied the entire GOP around his appeal for a radical response, not to Carter but to the "Roosevelt Revolution"[4] itself. Reagan's presidency thus represents the first real conservative confrontation of liberalism nationally since the rise of big government. Richard M. Nixon, a self-proclaimed conservative, proved to be a liberal president who simply operated with a coalition of interest groups different from that of the Democrats. Dwight D. Eisenhower, who likewise professed to be a conservative, was a consistent libertarian liberal. Herbert Hoover was also a nineteenth-century libertarian liberal, albeit a complex one in that he favored voluntary collectivism as an alternative both to rampant individualism and to state collectivism. Calvin Coolidge came to the White House with a reputation as a severe Yankee conservative, a reputation that was well deserved on the basis of his tenure as governor of Massachusetts, during which he cracked down on organized labor and attested to all the eternal verities being threatened by unions and by anarchists and other subversives. But as president, Coolidge was a consistent libertarian liberal who lived faithfully by his one memorable maxim, "The business of America is business."

President Reagan's publicly expressed admiration for President Coolidge encourages a comparison of the two leaders' approaches. Although Coolidge abandoned his conservatism when he moved from governor to vice-president and then to president, Reagan held steadfastly to his. And although as president, Coolidge vigorously attempted to maintain the status quo, President Reagan has worked hard to make things happen. The main difference between the two presidents' political thought is that Reagan has worked hard to establish in or through the national government a program that resembles Coolidge's (and Reagan's own) program for *state* government. As president, Reagan is neither a libertarian nor a New Deal liberal. That is precisely what makes his tenure a true ideological departure and not just another administration with a different interest-group base.

To elaborate further, what is the Reagan difference? What distinguishes Reagan's conservatism from liberalism and from the philosophy of those who

---

4. Ernest K. Lindley, *The Roosevelt Revolution: First Phase* (New York: Viking Press, 1933).

mistakenly call themselves conservatives? Will the Reagan Revolution leave a legacy comparable to that of the Roosevelt Revolution? These are the questions that this paper seeks to answer. I begin with an examination of the liberal tradition from which Reagan is a departure, an exercise that will permit an appreciation of Reagan conservatism and of its prospects.

American Liberalism and Its Alternatives

Liberalism in the United States has assumed many forms and faces. Notable examples can be found in the writings of Presidents James Madison, Thomas Jefferson, and Andrew Jackson. Abraham Lincoln's approach to the Union is another example. Laissez-faire or market liberalism is still another example, a once-dominant philosophy that continues to enjoy a considerable following. Progressivism was one reaction to laissez-faire liberalism, but is itself a variant of liberalism. The liberal tradition is found not only in politics and government but in virtually all social institutions—for instance, there is liberal education, religious liberalism, liberal marriage, and liberal penology.

Liberalism is grounded in individualism and is necessarily tentative about moral absolutes. According to the tenets of liberalism, although each individual ought to have a moral code, there are so many definitions of goodness and virtue that no one code can be set too far above another. A recent statement by a critic of liberalism defined the concept with uncommon clarity and efficiency:

> [Liberalism] is an ethic that asserts the priority of the right over the good. . . . Its core thesis can be stated as follows: Society, being composed of a plurality of persons, each with his own aims, interests, and conceptions of the good, is best arranged when it is governed by principles that do not *themselves* presuppose any particular conception of the good. What justifies these regulative principles above all is not that they maximize the social welfare or otherwise promote the good, but rather that they conform to the concept of *right*, a moral category given prior to the good and independent of it.[5]

Liberals have subscribed to justice over virtue because justice is inevitably concerned with the fair treatment of each individual. But since there is no absolute and substantive definition of justice, liberals are forced to embrace procedures over ends, means over morality. Morality has its place, says the liberal, but only in private life. In the public sphere, liberalism takes a moral position against morality (the most concrete manifestation of this being the separation of church and state). In public life, all morality becomes

---

5. Michael Sandel, *Liberalism and the Limits of Justice* (New York: Cambridge University Press, 1982), p. 1. Emphasis in original.

interests, and all interests are equal—except interest in the rules and procedures that enable private moralities to coexist.

Since government is at bottom moral force, liberalism would seem to be a flimsy public philosophy from which justifications for the use of government power must be drawn. Government is essentially a collective phenomenon, whereas liberalism exists for the individual. Government is built on coercion, though legitimate coercion, whereas liberalism is antagonistic to any such limit on liberty. Government is involuntary, whereas liberalism is literally built on free choice. Liberalism in all its forms has appeared to be antistatist. But appearances are deceiving. Liberalism has turned out to provide a solid basis for government, a particular kind of government, in that liberalism asserts a justification, indeed an obligation, to use government authority over *conduct deemed to have harmful consequences.* According to the precepts of liberalism, no absolute judgments about the goodness of conduct are necessary. Neither must conduct or the controls over conduct be related to some larger end. Consequences are empirical and demonstrable and refer to effects of pleasure and pain, loss and gain, dependence or independence. Any theory or argument alleging damaging results that is supported by plausible evidence and that flows from identified conduct will be taken seriously as a potential public policy. This helps explain the strong kinship between liberalism and science. The liberal state could hardly exist without science. This is not just a matter of liberalism's commitment to individual rationality. The relationship is much more specific, wherein every proposal for the expansion of government requires a plausible empirical case—in essence a "Brandeis brief"[6]—and the most plausible empirical case is one that can claim to be scientific.

The distinctive quality of liberalism is best appreciated in relation to its alternatives. Take, first, the Right, conservatism. As opposed to liberalism, conservatism is more confident that moral absolutes can be known and, once known, that they ought to be imposed by law. Nothing is more irksome to genuine conservatives than the moral uncertainty of liberals. In stark contrast to liberalism, conservatism can justify the extension of government authority over all conduct deemed good or evil *in itself.* Conservatives are not averse to considering consequences. However, consequences for conservatives are of a higher order, indeed a higher moral order. Relevant consequences of conduct pertain to how they relate to virtue, to the good of the community, to the corruption or elevation of the moral fiber of the individual, and so forth.

---

6. In 1908 Louis Brandeis made successfully, for the first time, an argument before the Supreme Court based on social facts and statistics demonstrating the harmful consequences of certain kinds of employment.

There is today a widespread misconception that conservatism and libertarianism are either related or that they are one and the same. As suggested earlier, libertarianism is a modern name for the form of liberalism predominant in the late nineteenth century. The current misconception is based upon the coincidence of libertarian and conservative attitudes toward national policies in the 1970s and 1980s. Both systems have been opposed to numerous national government programs, but for very different reasons. Libertarians are truly antistatist. Conservatives, on the other hand, are pro-statist, so long as the state operates according to conservative principles.

In contrast to the Right, the Left, in particular the socialist Left, is generally more optimistic about the capacity of individuals to shape their own lives, but it shares with conservatism the confidence that absolute values can be discovered and, once discovered, that they should be imposed by government. The Left sees in both liberal governments and conservative governments a conspiracy of wealth and privilege. In terms of moral codes, the Left is just as committed as the Right to the imposition of moral principles through law; however, the two differ as to which moral principles should be imposed. A genuine leftist would tend to view capitalism as an immoral social order and would be inclined to define injustice according to distributions of wealth.

Raymond Williams puts the three outlooks (Left, Right, and liberalism) in proper relation to each other. His treatment is especially useful because he is writing from the perspectives of England, where he is a professor at Cambridge University, and of the European Left, to which he pays intellectual loyalty:

> Liberal as a term of discourse has been under regular and heavy attack from conservative positions, where the senses of lack of restraint and lack of discipline have been brought to bear, and also the sense of a (weak and sentimental) generosity . . . and of a lack of rigour. . . . But *liberal* as a pejorative term has also been widely used by socialists and especially Marxists. This use shares the conservative sense of lack of rigour and of weak and sentimental beliefs. . . . [Liberals] reply to socialists that they are concerned with political freedom and socialists are not. But this masks the most serious sense of the socialist use, which is the historically accurate observation that *liberalism* is a doctrine based on *individualist* theories of man and society and is thus in fundamental conflict not only with *socialist* but with most strictly social theories.[7]

Not every conservative precisely fits the definition of conservatism, nor does every leftist or liberal conform exactly to the respective definitions of their ideologies as I have developed them here. This fact emphasizes the important point that each of these ideologies is a distinct dimension of political

---

7. Raymond Williams, *Keywords—A Vocabulary of Culture and Society* (New York: Oxford University Press, 1976), p. 150. Emphasis in original.

thought. The Left, for example, cannot be defined by adding a "not" to each of the tenets of the Right. And liberalism is not a midpoint or compromise between extremes of Right and Left. Each ideology has its own tradition, and each derives from a classic literature in political philosophy. And, since each is a separate body of principles, each is a separate continuum upon which an individual can be placed at a moderate or extreme (or purist) position. It is probably one of the distinctive marks of liberalism that the idea of an extreme liberal sounds like an internal inconsistency. Nevertheless, there are moderate and extreme liberals just as there are moderate and extreme conservatives. The manner in which extreme liberalism contributed to its own downfall in the 1970s is discussed later in this paper. But the point here is that liberalism (including libertarianism) is an intellectual world apart both from conservatism and from the Left. However, no further discussion of the Left is necessary here because the Left has never found a comfortable place in American politics. This is attributable less to suppression than to a federal system that well accommodates local conservatism and national liberalism.

The federal system is extremely significant because the U.S. Constitution did not just create two layers of government; it provided also for a specification of functions between the two. The Constitution made state governments responsible for the laws pertaining to the moral order of society and assigned to the national government a list of rather practical, albeit important, tasks. In constitutional theory this list of tasks is called the "expressed powers." All other powers were "reserved" to the states or to the people who, in their wisdom, could delegate them to the state governments. These reserved powers are also called the police powers, which can be defined as responsibility for the health, safety, and morals of the community. States are not excluded from liberal legislation, but virtually all the legislation that would qualify as conservative and that would be approved by conservatives is state legislation. Examples include family laws, morality laws, most of the property laws, and virtually all the basic human obligations that are comprehended under the criminal law. The essence of James Madison's view of the Constitution was that federalism could tolerate a "moral majority" in any one state but would render extremely difficult the prospect of that majority becoming a national majority.

When the national government began to grow in the twentieth century, it expanded along liberal lines, justifying each extension of its authority in terms of particular problems and consequences. Prohibition of alcohol was one of the few truly conservative programs ever undertaken by the national government, and this was literally imposed upon the federal government through a constitutional amendment. Recent national issues that involve morality and that have mobilized genuine conservatives, such as abortion and school prayer, are not issues of national policy but are efforts to reverse Supreme Court decisions that put limits on the powers of state governments to enter into these fields. A fairly clear distinction has therefore been maintained between state-level conservatism and national-level liberalism that gives concrete reality to the distinction between conservatism and liberalism being pursued here.

The growth of liberalism in government helps to explain why it is easier to find prominent national exponents of liberalism than of conservatism. Liberals have found their natural habitat in national government and national policies. Presidents have tended to be liberal, as have journalists and political scientists. Although there is no shortage of conservatives, the fact that, traditionally, they have been involved in state governments has distanced them from national awareness and recognition. Those who ascend to positions of power in national government have also tended toward liberalism. Note, for example, that historian Richard Hofstadter felt it necessary in his classic work *The American Political Tradition* to treat Theodore Roosevelt as "the Conservative as Progressive," and Woodrow Wilson as "the Conservative as Liberal."[8] American conservatism, almost by its nature, is parochial; and I use that word advisedly. The dictionary defines *parochial* as referring to matters of the parish, with an additional and more recent meaning being narrowly local in orientation. American conservatism is reflected in both definitions: The responsibility of the parish is uppermost, and conservatism finds its true expression where matters such as religion and morality are seated in real localities with real families and institutions, real histories, and real traditions. *Parochial* has come to have negative connotations and is pitted against haloed terms such as *cosmopolitan*, *sophisticated*, and *relativistic*. Yet the latter are necessary characteristics if one is to deal in the nation, in the world, and in conflicting values that are likely to call forth toleration if not relativism.

The Conservatism of Ronald Reagan

The discussion so far points directly toward the conservatism of Ronald Reagan and to the virtual uniqueness of his passage from state government to national government as an untransformed conservative. A brief review of Reagan's agenda as president will demonstrate not only that he is a consistent

---

8. Richard Hofstadter, *The American Political Tradition* (New York: Vintage Books, 1954), pp. 206 and 238.

conservative but that he is also more programmatic than any recent president, including Franklin Delano Roosevelt. After all, no one knew Roosevelt's specific positions and plans until after he became president in 1933. If there was a referendum on the Roosevelt program, that was in 1936, not in the campaign of 1932. In contrast, Ronald Reagan's program was clear for all to see before the 1980 election. Illustrations of Reagan's conservatism are grouped here for convenience into four general categories, which are neither logically exclusive nor exhaustive.

Deregulation and Decentralization

The Reagan commitment to deregulating the national government and to decentralizing to state and local governments is obviously sincere. But such policies are in no way tantamount to Reagan's oft-repeated aim of "getting the government off our backs." Reagan is a conservative, not a libertarian; his commitment has been toward a shift of authority rather than a release of it. In fact, if one listens carefully enough through the household noise, one can hear in Reagan's conservatism a greater willingness than that of the liberals to acknowledge the inevitability of the exercise of authority. Liberals have been so eager to mask the controls in government programs that they have converted themselves into interest-group liberals replete with such devices as community action, cooperative federalism, and involvement in agency decision making.

President Reagan has pursued deregulation on several fronts. He has tried to weaken the guidelines that restricted the discretion of state and local officials in implementing federally aided programs, so as to leave them freer to combine, to cut, or to discontinue certain activities even where these embodied explicit national goals. Reagan has also used the Office of Management and Budget (OMB) to extend the Carter principle of cost-benefit analysis as applied to the issuance of new regulatory rules. This requirement, essentially of a "regulatory impact statement," both delays and weakens the issuance and implementation of regulatory rules. (The average time it takes for the Environmental Protection Agency [EPA] to issue a new rule is now over thirty months.) President Reagan has also used OMB and the White House to encourage, wherever and however possible, administrators of regulatory agencies to implement their statutory responsibilities much less vigorously than in the past. Many critics, especially in the antitrust and civil rights fields, would argue that the president has gone so far in this direction as to violate the spirit if not the letter of existing regulatory statutes.

None of these efforts is devastatingly new or bold. Deregulation had become a popular policy under the Carter administration, and a good case can be made that Carter advanced the cause of deregulation farther and more dramatically than did Reagan. Note in this regard that President Reagan avoided confronting Congress with any important requests for deregulatory legislation that would result in the termination of an agency. President Reagan has restricted his efforts to pursuing results that could be accomplished either through executive action or inaction. And, although it is true that he has refrained from requests for any new major regulatory statutes, it should be observed that new regulatory programs come in spurts and that the most recent binge of regulatory programs occurred during the 1970s. Therefore, sobriety in this field had already returned to Congress *by the time Reagan took office.*

It should be remarked here that Reagan stuck to his administrative guns and was rather shy in confronting Congress with new requests to deregulate. But a more important point is that what Reagan was ultimately trying to accomplish was considerably more important to him than merely relieving major corporations of some of their regulatory burdens. Reagan's goal as a conservative was to try to shift and extend government authority toward realms where government concerned itself with the morality of conduct. It is important in this connection that Reagan favored the "Right to Life" amendment to the Constitution. It is equally significant that he favored an extension of the Hyde amendment that eliminated abortion cases from eligibility for Medicaid. It is also noteworthy, as well as a measure of Reagan's consistency as a conservative, that his administration sought to extend Section 504 of the Rehabilitation Act, so as to protect the rights of infants born with serious disabilities. He did this over the intense opposition of the medical community, which did not want to be regulated in regard to decisions about the civil rights of infants who could be kept alive only by extremely expensive artificial means. Further proof of Reagan's consistency lies in his firm support of the school prayer amendment. Another example along these lines is Reagan's gleeful embrace of the moral and disciplinary aspects of the report of the Commission on Excellence in Education.[9] It is impossible to believe that President Reagan was unaware of the regulatory implications of his approach to solving the crisis of mediocrity in American elementary and secondary schools.

A review of these positions and of the regulatory programs implicit in them confirms fairly strongly that Reagan wants to extend rather than restrict the reach of government. He simply wants other than a liberal government. The abortion (Right to Life) amendment would restore to the states the power to make criminal or to regulate in a variety of ways the conduct of women

---

9. U.S. National Commission on Excellence in Education, *A Nation at Risk: The Imperative for Education Reform* (Washington, D.C., 1983).

toward their own bodies. One need not confront the merits of the case to appreciate that the range, scope, and sanctions of government would be expanded tremendously if the abortion amendment were passed and rigorously implemented. Every pregnant woman would be a potential target for a case of manslaughter. A moral meaning could be put upon every tennis game or aerobics class joined by a pregnant woman. Was her miscarriage a case of negligence? Indeed, was it a premeditated act? What are the liabilities of her doctors and nurses and of the hospital? The coverage of a large existing regulatory program, such as that of the Occupational Safety and Health Administration (OSHA), is modest in comparison to the coverage of the regulatory programs that are likely to flow from an amendment to the Constitution that returns this kind of power to the state governments. The Hyde amendment, one of the few national conservative policies, contributes the same moral meaning to the issue. And identical implications stem from the proposed constitutional amendment enabling the states to regulate the exercise of religious beliefs in the schools. Finally, although thousands of people may sympathize with Reagan's appeal for discipline as an approach to the solution of problems in secondary schools, such an approach is not the mark of a libertarian but of a conservative. A Reagan republic would be a nation founded upon small-town, perhaps California-small-town, Christian values. Richard Nixon probably espoused the same values, but since he was basically a liberal in his national public life, he was not trying to construct a republic along those lines, but only to divert the liberal system he inherited toward his coalition of groups rather than toward those of the Democratic party.

Decentralization, or devolution, of programs and services from the national to the state and local governments can best be understood in the same context as deregulation. President Reagan was historically incorrect in suggesting that we "turn back" these powers to the states, since most of the regulations and services adopted by the national government in the twentieth century have been in fact additions to and not usurpations of the powers of state governments. Nevertheless, Reagan has sought a much more extreme version of decentralization than did any of his recent predecessors, despite the emphasis put upon decentralization by Carter, Nixon, and, for that matter, Lyndon Baines Johnson. For each of these former presidents, decentralization to the states was seen as a means of improving the administration of and the public's access to programs that were to remain the same size or grow. Democrats were highly suspicious that President Nixon had a hidden agenda of budget reduction behind his sharing, his block grants (special-revenue sharing), and his localized Family Assistance Plan. But such an intention seems more in the minds of the observers than it was inherent in Nixon's proposals. Whatever the case with Nixon, it was certainly true that Johnson and Carter intended decentralization to expand and/or to democratize national and nationally funded programs. Not so, however, with President Reagan, who has explicitly and unabashedly coupled decentralization with a strong commitment to cuts and to downright elimination of national programs. Although it is true that "no large-scale devolution of federal fiscal or regulatory functions has been accomplished" during the Reagan administration,[10] the mark of any president is what he sought rather than what he got.

President Reagan sought devolution to the states for one reason. In his own words:

It's far easier for people to come to Washington to get their social programs. It would be a hell of a lot tougher if we diffuse them and send them out to the states. All their friends and connections are in Washington.[11]

Another factor associated with decentralization is the stronger average conservatism of state and, especially, of local governments as compared to the national government. Even in states with a more liberal reputation than most, such as New York, there is a more powerful element of conservatism. For example, implementation of welfare programs in the states is closely tied to law enforcement and to private charity, which traditionally make a greater distinction between the deserving and the undeserving poor than do national decision makers and welfare administrators. Added to this viewpoint are the severe limitations on state and local tax resources. Moreover, to ensure that state and local governments would be more restrictive, President Reagan opposed all versions of revenue sharing. His offer of a $28 billion national trust fund to help the states finance some of the decentralized programs was to be a temporary fund phased out over a four-year period.

President Reagan obviously recognized that successful devolution meant, among other things, that there would be extensive disparities of services among the states. However, he chose to assume that this would be the result of bad management rather than of disparities in resources. His solution to the problem of inequality of wealth among the states was as follows:

If a state is badly managed, the people will either do one of two things: They will either use their power at the polls to redress that, or they will go somewhere else.[12]

Another Reagan proposal that strongly confirms the conservative motivations behind devolution was his strong support of proposals to eliminate the legal services program. Though small, this program had been a major instrument of liberal interest groups to advance the interests of the poor through

---

10. See paper by Beam in this volume.
11. Quoted in paper by Beam in this volume.
12. Quoted in paper by Beam in this volume.

legal action, lobbying, and consciousness raising. Such groups had been particularly effective at expanding participation in Aid to Families with Dependent Children (AFDC)/Medicaid by making low-income people aware of their eligibility and by bringing class-action suits and other legal actions to assure that the eligibility was expanded and maintained. These latter points lead directly to the next category of policies, the welfare state.

The Attack on the Welfare State

Essential to a comprehension of Reagan's conservatism is his fundamental opposition to the welfare state. Although Reagan is too realistic to mount a full-scale attack on national welfare, his concept of the good society is nevertheless one whose "safety net" is voluntary local charity, not compulsory national welfare.

To the liberal, most people become dependent through imperfections in the economy or through natural catastrophies, not through any particular fault of their own. Since, according to liberalism, dependency is a national objective and a national phenomenon, the response ought to be national, regular, and obligatory. Thus, for the liberal, the concept of the welfare state is an appropriate one.

President Reagan's response to the welfare state has been consistent, if not systematic. One of the more indicative aspects of Reagan's conservatism toward welfare is the decentralization itself. This of course includes his effort to reduce and to eliminate, wherever possible, urban policies, housing policies, the Comprehensive Employment and Training Act (CETA), and other rehabilitation policies. But decentralization aims at bigger game—the welfare state itself. Decentralization has involved a serious proposal for a "turnback" of as much welfare as possible to the states, even to local agencies where possible. No secret has been made of the president's desire to reduce drastically the cost of welfare, or of the intention of the White House to use decentralization, among other things, as a means toward that end. Reduction is to be severe, limited only by the vague but solemn promise to maintain a "safety net." In 1982 President Reagan proposed a deal wherein the national government would assume all the costs of Medicaid ($30 billion in 1982, with continued growth projected) if the states would accept responsibility for AFDC and Food Stamps. If this proposal had been accepted by Congress and the states, it would have meant an immediate cutback in the latter programs, precisely because they have been financed until now as a joint national-state venture. But beyond this, the arrangement would have been a handy and effective way to shrink Medicaid, because Medicaid eligibility has been pegged to AFDC, which is the most unpopular of the welfare programs and has the least effective constituency. Without the national welfare administrators and national professional welfare groups to lobby in Congress and to defend Medicaid and AFDC, both would decline perceptibly. Reference can be made again to Reagan's observation that it is "a hell of a lot tougher" to defend social programs if they are diffused among the states.

Of equal weight from an ideological standpoint is the moral cast put on welfare issues by Reagan officials, particularly by their effort to establish a distinction between the deserving and the undeserving poor. This distinction is truly a "turnback," or rather a throwback, to nineteenth-century charity, in which local elites differentiated between the deserving and undeserving poor according to their own discretion. This general distinction is reinforced by continual stress on eligibility, on the elimination of chiselers, on the problem of illegitimacy, on the alleged contribution of welfare to the moral decline of individuals and families, and on the alleged contribution of welfare to the immoral preference of a supposed large number of dependent people for a free meal rather than a job. The Reagan administration has tried to establish public assistance as being synonymous with the undeserving poor. Liberal welfare supporters recognize that chiseling can be a problem and that welfare can discourage work. Nevertheless, the liberal approach to welfare seeks to achieve justice as well as fairness through general rules, implying rights without stigma. To a liberal, welfare chiseling is no greater a problem for a welfare system than stealing by clerks is a problem for a large department store. In contrast, the conservative approach to welfare, being derived from the traditional concept of charity, operates case by case, making judgments as to the truly needy and the truly meritorious. This was the reasoning behind the impolitic remarks of White House Counselor/Attorney General Designate Edwin Meese, III, in late 1983, when he observed that there was no authoritative evidence of real hunger, that some people with money are going to soup kitchens and that "those who are truly in need have been taken care of."[13] He was probably surprised at the widespread negative response, because he was trying to make a rather traditional conservative distinction. The public reaction suggests that there is a limit to the success the Reagan administration can achieve by infusing welfare with morality.

In line with the distinction made between the deserving and the undeserving poor is the special attention given by President Reagan to the desirability and capacity of the private sector to pick up the slack of reduced public welfare support. The actual pattern of private welfare makes it virtually a code word for a conservative, moral approach to welfare. In the first place,

---

13. New York Times, "What Meese Said to Reporters," Dec. 15, 1983, p. B-13.

corporate contributions to charity seem to be unresponsive to the very wide cuts in corporate income taxes. Needless to say, corporate giving has not increased in proportion to the tax relief. Second, at least half of all charitable contributions go to churches and church-related organizations. Therefore, however generous churches might be, this source of welfare certainly has a moral dimension attached to it. Third, most local charitable groups, church related and nonchurch related, are in the business of providing quality-of-life services rather than essential safety-net services. It is unlikely that Kiwanis Clubs will give up kiddie baseball for services to the "truly needy."[14]

Even though Reagan has failed to get very much welfare reform from Congress, his proposals coupled with his lectures have to a certain extent put the welfare state on the defensive. Liberals were cooperative with the Reagan administration up to a point, because they welcomed his willingness to confront the costs of welfare. But there is probably no issue on which liberals and conservatives are farther apart than that of whether welfare should have a moral dimension attached to it.

Tax Cuts

"Getting the government off our backs" would have sounded superficial had it not included tax relief. But there are different kinds of relief, and President Reagan's was severely and unashamedly regressive. In effect, he sought to revise and restructure the economy by favoring the wealthy investor over the healthy consumer. This is theoretically defensible, especially in the context of ideological conservatism.

In the area of tax reform, Reagan got virtually all that he sought—most of the policies of which were embodied in the Economic Recovery Tax Act of 1981. The main feature of this extremely important tax legislation was a slightly scaled-down version of the Kemp-Roth bill, which called for an across-the-board reduction of one-third in the total income tax burden. Spread roughly over three years, Reagan's moderately compromised version provided for a 5 percent reduction the first year and 10 percent reductions in each of the two succeeding years. Second, the top marginal rate for all earnings was reduced from 70 percent to 50 percent, and the maximum taxation on capital gains was reduced from 28 percent to 20 percent.

Since this was an across-the-board tax cut, all income groups would receive the same percentage reduction. This means that after-tax incomes rise

---

14. See paper by Bendick in this volume on the consequences of government reliance on charitable giving to supplement public welfare.

by significantly greater percentages as one moves up from bracket to bracket. This is not something President Reagan tried to hide. But the full regressiveness of his approach was either hidden or was left unstressed, particularly because no mention was made of the Social Security tax burden that had been increased during the 1970s, when the rate of taxation was hiked to 6.7 percent and the wage base subject to Social Security taxation was allowed to move up to $37,800 (still rising in 1984). This meant that the Reagan tax cut was not only directly favorable to the higher-income brackets but was all but meaningless to people whose incomes were below the Social Security wage base. These individuals would continue to pay Social Security tax on all of their income, whereas a person earning double the ceiling had only half the Social Security tax liability. House Speaker Thomas P. O'Neill, Jr., and other critics were exaggerating only moderately when they accused President Reagan of writing a tax bill for the rich. It was more truly a tax bill for the investor, based on the assumption that a dependable increase in retained earnings would produce a surplus that would result in significant increases in investment. There was of course no guarantee that the surplus would be invested in things that would increase productivity. Economist Robert B. Reich, among others, has suggested that it is more likely that the surplus will go into what he calls "paper entrepreneurialism," with mergers and other expansions that do not represent increased real growth or increased productivity.[15]

Whatever the actual outcomes, the tax cut was clearly motivated by the assumption that America's prosperity comes from the top, from the wealthy elite who are perceived to do more for society from their retained earnings than consumers would from marginal increases in capacity to consume.

Another important feature of the Reagan tax reform was the indexing of the tax structure, whereby the tax brackets, the standard deduction, and the personal exemption will, by 1985, be adjusted automatically according to the Consumer Price Index. These provisions are aimed at eliminating "bracket creep," a situation in which inflation pushes people into higher and higher tax brackets, subjecting them to disproportionately higher tax liabilities. Although no simple case can be made that indexing is in itself conservative, it does seem to reinforce the rest of the Reagan tax approach, relieving those persons whose incomes are most likely to keep abreast of or exceed the rate of inflation. Indexing is not particularly relevant, if relevant at all, to those whose incomes are likely to decline relative to the inflation rate.

15. Robert B. Reich, *The Next American Frontier* (New York: Times Books, 1983), especially chapter 13.

Finally, by expanding eligibility for individual retirement accounts (IRAs) to workers already covered under private pension plans and by permitting deductions for contributions to an IRA of up to $2,000 per year, the Reagan tax law put an extra premium and an extra stamp of approval on saving. This is relevant only to those persons who earn enough money to be able to save. Whatever law President Reagan has for people who prefer work to welfare, his fiscal policies were certainly not aimed at rewarding them.

Foreign Policy and Military Policy

Although all administrations in the twentieth century, Democratic and Republican, have been relatively conservative on foreign policy, President Reagan's tenure has contributed an unusually forceful element of moral fervor. The historian and diplomat George Kennan has criticized the American approach to foreign policy as legalistic and moralistic. Many others have recognized the inclination of American leaders to distrust and to avoid diplomacy ("open covenants, openly arrived at"). Some call it Victorian. But at bottom it is conservative, and Ronald Reagan is the conservative's conservative. Although Cold War and bipolarity theories were developed during Democratic administrations and were enriched during the Eisenhower administration, Reagan restored them and brought them to new intensities of morality with his treatment of the Soviet Union as "an evil empire." His view is fiercely antidétente, adamantly opposing serious arms control negotiation until the United States possesses clear military superiority (whatever that is). He has given the military virtually carte blanche in weapons procurement and in research and development (R&D), and the military presence he favored throughout the world went much farther than what much of the military itself wanted. Again, although every American president has had a tendency not only to escalate the meaning of a foreign policy conflict but to see America's vital interest at stake and to withdraw critical issues away from diplomats, few presidents during peacetime have gone as far as President Reagan. Even the distinguished *Wall Street Journal* editorial writer Vermont Royster noted in his first 1984 op-ed column the startling range of foreign entanglements during the Reagan administration: in Lebanon with Marines, aircraft carriers, battleships, and destroyers; in Grenada with attack forces and then a lingering military presence; in El Salvador with a large but indeterminate commitment of advisers, supplies, and semicovert support; in Honduras with troops on chronic maneuvers both to maintain a military presence in Central America and to provide support and cover for insurgent activities in Nicaragua; in and near Nicaragua with a variety of covert and overt military involvements; in the Caribbean at large with a sizable naval presence; in the Mediterranean with naval and air force presence, focusing not only on Lebanon but on Libya and the Organization of Petroleum Exporting countries (OPEC); and in general an assertion of our "vital interests" as well as the total involvement of our "credibility" in each of the countries so identified.[16]

The conservatism of these actions is underscored by their association with the unprecedented buildup in the Pentagon budget, along with the unparalleled reduction in the rate of increase in domestic expenditures. And then there is the budget deficit, also a first in its size and its rate of growth. A budget deficit is in itself neither liberal nor conservative. Liberals defend deficits when deficits are associated with economic growth. Conservatives can also defend deficits when these arise out of proper uses of authority— military in particular. Bear in mind, also, that so long as there is a large budget, liberal or conservative, no prospect exists for getting the government off our backs.

Why the Reagan Revolution Will Fail

As a programmatic president, Reagan promises to rate second only to FDR. But that evaluation is based on what he has sought. It is quite another matter to evaluate whether he will leave an important legacy. What Reagan strived for defines his conservatism. What he got, and will get, defines conservatism's success and the probability of its endurance. Reagan's success does not require that he repeal the New Deal. In fact, conservatives would maintain or restore some New Deal legacies, not the least of which are presidential power and administrative discretion. Since conservatism is not libertarianism, conservatives are not interested in weak and small government but in strong government by good people, people of honor and of good judgment, and people who are committed to patriotic American values. Rule of law and due process are much less important when good people who can make right decisions are holding high office.

Most of all, since inevitably the business of the Reagan Revolution will be incomplete, Reagan and all conservatives probably want to create for themselves an equivalent of the Roosevelt Coalition that would last two or more decades beyond Reagan, so that the Reagan agenda and the terms of discourse would continue as though he were still president. There are at least three reasons, however, why President Reagan will fail and conservatism will

---

16. Vermont Royster, "Thinking Things Over—Wherever is a Big Place," *Wall Street Journal*, Jan. 11, 1984, p. 28.

leave no legacy greater than the marginal contributions any ordinary administration leaves. Few presidents in history have had greater personal skills
and have enjoyed the affections of more Americans than Ronald Reagan. But
personal skills and an attractive personality cannot be willed to others. The
evaluation here is of an ideology seeking to become the public philosophy.
Following is a delineation of the three reasons why conservatism will not
prevail.

1. The Flawed Presidency

First of all, President Reagan will fail for the same reasons all five of
his recent predecessors failed. The presidency has become an impossible job,
not because Roosevelt's successors were men of so much smaller stature, but
because the presidency has become too big, even for the likes of FDR.

The decline of the political parties has left the president with no standing
organization, nobody to share responsibility for outcomes, in a government
of which so much more is expected now than in the 1930s. The president
must personally mobilize the masses, and this requires the use of tremendously
exalted rhetoric, leading to great expectations that are doomed to disappointment. Even modest successes look like failures.

As a consequence, public opinion polls show a dramatic decline in
approval ratings for each president since Kennedy. In response to the general
question "Do you approve of the way the president is doing his job?" the
rating for each president starts off in the upper 60 percent range, well above
the vote he received in his electoral victory. But once the honeymoon is over
and as the months pass, that approval rating drops well below 50 percent.
The only factor guaranteed to elevate the approval ratings is an important
foreign policy event, and this upward tendency is a mere "blip" in an otherwise downward tendency.

This means that presidents exhaust their popular support as they use it.
They are left with little time to achieve their legislative goals, much less to
create and institutionalize political arrangements that will last into a second
term and beyond.

President Reagan has not managed to escape this tendency, although for
a time he enjoyed an unusual maintenance in approval ratings beginning in
the last quarter of 1983. A closer look will show that his increased approval
ratings can be attributed to a series of important foreign policy events, starting
with the Soviet Union's shooting down of the Korean Airlines passenger plane
on September 1. During December 1983, as dramatic events subsided and
foreign affairs returned to their usual morass, the Reagan approval rating
began to drop once again. It held up well enough to encourage him to run

for reelection; but even if it continues to hold up through November, the negative ratings he receives for his performance on specific issues (such as unemployment, interest rates, trade, defense, and foreign policy) suggest that he will not be able to escape the high expectations and harsh judgments of the American people as to "what the president has done for us lately."

2. The Mythical Reagan Majority

A second reason why President Reagan will fail is that his popular base is broad but very thin. That is to say, his electoral victory in 1980 was not the victory of a conservative majority, and there is little sign that he can provide for himself a voter realignment comparable to the 1932 realignment that sustained the New Deal into the 1960s.

A brief look behind the 90 percent electoral vote and the 51 percent popular vote reveals the weakness of the Reagan victory. For example, Reagan in 1980 did significantly better than President Ford in 1976 in only ten states, and Ford actually carried five of those states. In the seven most urbanized states, Reagan either did less well or barely improved on Ford's performance. Turning from the vote to the surveys, Reagan does not perform much better. Every review of the opinion studies or of the exit polls shows that a large, if indeterminate, proportion of Reagan's support came from people who went to the polls to vote *against* President Carter. A recent, exhaustive review of the survey data by political scientist Stanley Kelley reveals that still another substantial portion of the Reagan vote was provided by people who preferred Reagan but only on a few issues. That is to say, they were weak supporters of Reagan. Based on the anti-Carter voting and the weak Reagan voting, Kelley, among others, has been led to conclude that the Reagan majority was a weak majority, showing no signs of a conservative constituency with strong and broadly shared conservative values.[17]

Pursuing further the inevitable Roosevelt comparison, 1984 could be the true Reagan referendum, consolidating the 1980 victory with his personal popularity into a lasting Reagan majority. But the comparison deteriorates quickly. In the third and fourth years of the Roosevelt era, Roosevelt was still in control, adding successes to his legislative program and overwhelming his congressional and electoral opposition. President Reagan, by contrast, had only one good year of legislative triumphs, although they were genuine and dramatic ones. Since that time he has been fighting political trench

---

17. Stanley Kelley, *Interpreting Elections* (Princeton: Princeton University Press, 1983), chapter 9. See also paper by Ladd in this volume on the Reagan mandate and public attitudes toward government.

warfare, without a solid victory, without a solid Republican party, and no longer filling his opponents with fear. What was just beginning to materialize for Roosevelt in years three and four began to vanish for Reagan in year two. If Reagan should win again in 1984, in all likelihood he will do so with another weak majority and will face the prospect of four years of trench warfare. This is not the stuff of realignment or revolution.

3. The Historic Resiliency of Liberalism

President Reagan will fail because liberalism is too well entrenched in the national system of government. This system includes the welfare state; the regulation of capitalism; the ironing out of the most egregious disparities among states and regions; and the handling of the most flagrant departures from racial and economic equity. Most of all, the system comprises a fear of any one set of parochial values having any long or significant national influence. Ronald Reagan is a conservative president in a liberal institution. Far from being able to change the model, he can barely put on the brakes, much less turn the steering wheel. Recent studies have shown that the rebelliousness of the American people against big government in the 1970s was markedly more superficial than appeared at the time. During those years, thousands of people complained about the costs and burdens of regulation, the wastes of services, and bureaucratic red tape and inefficiency. There were tax revolts throughout the country and bond-issue referenda by the hundreds were rejected. But careful analysis of the opinion data shows that citizens opposed the costs of government without rejecting the programs or governments themselves. A substantial percentage of Americans felt that if taxes and program budgets were cut, the programs could be sustained by greater efficiencies.[18] Moreover, it would appear that the national government is accepted precisely because it has become all the things states are not and cannot be—national and international versus parochial; competitive with capitalism versus cooperative with it; concerned with consequences rather than with moralities.

One question remains and is dealt with in the section following: If liberalism is so well ensconced, why did it collapse in the 1970s, rejected by both political parties? The response to this question, however inadequate, could shed light not only on the nature and strength of the Reagan Revolution but also on the future of American government.

---

18. S.M. Lipset and William Schneider, *The Confidence Gap* (New York: The Free Press, 1983). See also paper by Ladd in this volume.

Life after Reagan

Why Liberalism Collapsed

There are two levels of explanation for the political demise of liberalism in the 1970s. The first level is simple, straightforward, and conventional: Liberal administrations and liberal majorities in Congress persisted in expanding existing programs and creating new programs despite consistent voter rejection of each administration and despite persistent survey results showing disaffection with national government. Both parties were expansionist, and both suffered voter disaffection. Disaffection went so far that a complete outsider, Jimmy Carter, could be nominated and elected president by running against the very government over which he sought to preside.

But persistence despite disapproval is an explanation that begs the question. Why *did* liberals persist despite disapproval? Were they ignorant of or apathetic to public sentiment? Were they insensitive to costs and oblivious to benefits? Were they simply victims of habit or of their own supporting interest groups? The answer may be yes to each of these questions, but the second level of explanation must probe more deeply to an examination of the hypothesis that something inherent in liberalism led to its collapse.

Exploration of this hypothesis requires a return to the definition of liberal government given earlier: Liberal government displays concern not for the morality but only for the material, measurable consequences of conduct. This is obviously a reasonable attitude, one that does not seem to possess the seeds of its own downfall. But note further that under *some* conditions, any and all conduct can produce harmful consequences. For example, there is nothing morally wrong with raising pigs in your own backyard. However, if a medical theory plausibly demonstrates that pigs are associated with a disease, a liberal majority in the legislature will feel some degree of obligation to forbid or stringently regulate the raising of pigs in urban areas.

Mark well the importance of theory to the liberal philosophy of government. All liberal policies are based on some theory about causes and consequences. Some theories are confirmed beyond reasonable doubt, with solid evidence and experience. Examples of conduct that surely produces harmful consequences would include driving while intoxicated, associating with others while carrying certain diseases, or selling products on the basis of false advertising. Some theories about causes and consequences are moderately well documented, such as the relationship between certain food additives and cancer or between the use of fossil fuels and acid rain. But some theories remain very poorly confirmed, or at least the documentation is flimsy. Sometimes the theory involves a very general cause for a very specific effect, such as the relationship between unemployment and crime or between smog and respiratory disease. At other times, the theory is poorly supported because, although the connection between cause and effect may be understood, there is no agreement as to the threshold of vulnerability, or the requirement of intervening variables, or the amount of time required for the effect to be experienced. Is the demonstration sufficient if enhanced cancer levels show up twenty years after exposure to one part per billion of benzene in the air? Is the demonstration sufficient if the data came from experiments on rats, without direct knowledge of the applicability to human beings or of the appropriateness of the amounts involved, such as occurred with the saccharin experiments?

The point here is this: Since any conduct *can* produce injury, then *all* conduct becomes government responsibility and comes under government surveillance. Not all conduct will be in immediate jeopardy of some kind of control, but all conduct comes within the purview of liberal government. The liberal approach to government has made government a magnet and has rendered representatives powerless to say no or to establish priorities among theories and needs. If a theory points to consequences, there is an obligation to act upon it. In fact, during the last two or three decades, the legislative process has not even required that legislators be knowledgeable about what to do or how to do it. It simply accepts the theory ("whereas . . .") and indicates that there is an injury and a likely cause ("here's the problem . . ."); then it delegates to an administrative agency the responsibility for doing something about it ("go deal with it . . .").

Consequently, liberal government is almost impossible to limit. Liberalism tends to universalize the scope and responsibility of government, and science then makes the liberal argument almost unassailable. This, then, is a general explanation that helps to define why liberal governments tend to grow, despite costs and despite ignorance of how to achieve the goal specified by the theory. It also helps to explain why liberal legislation has grown broader and broader in scope, has become more and more abstract in definition, and is more and more universal in its applicability. Since science always tends to define the total system of which any given phenomenon is a part, so liberalism attempts to define any given effect as a part of some hypothetical total universe. The chain of causation can be infinite. Out of this emerges the concept of social cost. In other words, we must act now to regulate or to improve upon a given state of affairs, because it will cost a great deal more in retribution or in rehabilitation if we wait until later to act. To return to the original question, this is why the last decade prior to the political collapse of liberalism was one of almost exponential expansion in regulatory, welfare, and service programs. Even liberals themselves were expressing fears of runaway costs and national insolvency in the face of their own legislative and administrative actions.

Waiting for the Third Republic

Nevertheless, conservatism is not the answer to the chronic crisis of public philosophy in the national government. Liberalism in the 1970s was at an intellectual dead end, but conservatism turned out not to be the answer. National, multinational, and international economic problems, after all, cannot be confronted with parochial perspectives. Hundreds of sectional, racial, ethnic, and other minorities cannot be managed from the perspective of one minority that is no larger, no broader in perspective, and no more righteous than the others. The United States as a nation does not have a unified white Christian majority, let alone a small-town southern California variant of it. And neither this minority nor any other minority, so far as anyone knows, has a special connection to the source of all that is true and virtuous.

Conservatism is, therefore, an interlude. Ironically, it may not even be successful enough or last long enough to permit liberalism to regenerate. In politics there is no substitute for defeat. A party defeated is much more open to new ideas, new social forces, new leadership, new patterns of interest, new procedures, and new perspectives. In 1984 at least, the leading Democratic alternatives to President Reagan looked like the same Democrats who gave us the collapse of liberalism in the 1970s. Despite talk about new ideas inside the Democratic party, these are difficult, if not impossible, to find. If the Democrats win in 1984, they are likely to validate the interest-group liberalism of the epoch I have called the Second Republic.[19] A Reagan re-election will probably suppress Republican liberalism for still another decade. In neither party, therefore, is there much evidence of a fundamental revision of liberalism that is aware of its own limitations and yet committed to ideas that are a more effective answer to the extraordinarily appropriate criticisms that the Reagan administration and others have thrown at them.

This continuing derangement and disorientation of liberalism provides, in a perverse way, insight into the near future. Two scenarios can be prepared from the present morass—one of relatively high probability, the other of much lower probability. And, as usual, there is an inverse relationship between probability and desirability.

The high-probability scenario is one of stalemate and drift, in which Reagan conservatism has been discredited, leaving two disoriented political

19. Theodore J. Lowi, *The End of Liberalism* (New York: W.W. Norton & Co., 1979).

parties, relatively equally matched at the national level, competing intensely for the dead center—whatever and wherever that is. This scenario anticipates a standoff not between two vying public philosophies backed by political parties but between two diffuse partisanships, each of whose leaders sees himself as close enough to the presidency to reject any substantial innovations. Competition is an important and positive factor in virtually all American economic or political theories. And history will probably confirm that competition has generally been a positive force. Nevertheless, American history will also demonstrate that if an extremely small number of large firms in an oligopolistic market are very closely balanced in size and resources, each of the firms becomes quite "conservative," in the sense that each would resist any but marginal departures from whatever strategies are currently paying off. The same is true of two very evenly matched political parties. If each party is already close to victory, the leadership would be loath to consider anything but marginal changes of strategy—such as minor adjustment, fine tuning, and so forth. Why consider large departures and innovations if we are already close to victory doing what we have been doing up to now? Substantial departures would violate one of Murphy's laws: "If it ain't broke don't fix it."

Forty years have passed since the last Roosevelt election, and Republicans and Democrats have held the presidency twenty years each. This is true despite the fact that there are substantially more enrolled and self-identified Democrats than Republicans; but this means only that the Republicans are generally forced to stick as close to the Democrats as possible in order to encourage ticket-splitting. This also clarifies just how unusual Ronald Reagan is. He is the leader of the minority wing of the minority party. Once he has personally gone from the scene, there is likely to be little incentive on the part of other Republican leaders to depart from their resemblance to the Democrats, considering the payoff of that strategy over most of the past forty years. There is little chance that any Republican successor to Ronald Reagan would keep the faith. Their efforts will fit well the George Wallace model, that "There ain't a dime's worth of difference between the two parties."

There are fates far worse than stalemate and drift, however. After the period of great domestic expansion in the early 1970s and the period of dynamic decentralization coupled with military concentration in the early 1980s, many would surely welcome a period of stalemate. Call it consolidation to put it in a favorable light. But consolidation by choice is one thing. Stalemate as a result of institutional weakness and leadership failure is another. In the difference is a great danger; in a period of stalemate, frustration can lead to mass mobilization around a charismatic leader or dynamic social movement. The potential for inflation, stagflation, high unemployment, environmental disaster, and international military crisis continues to be high enough to require more institutional and leadership capacity than the present two parties can provide. These parties have created a national government that relies heavily on a presidency that has the capacity to govern and on presidents who have the capacity to mobilize the American people.

Brief further reflection upon the pattern of presidential approval referred to earlier provides some sense of the risks in a governmental structure with a plebiscitary presidency if the government is bogged down for too long in organized stalemate. If a president's only dependable means of mobilizing the public in order to maintain control of Congress and the Washington, D.C., community is an international incident, then each president will have to keep a score of international contingency plans in his tool kit of leadership. We can see rather clearly from the international events of 1983 that so buoyed President Reagan's approval ratings that, although international events are relatively easy to turn on, they are not so easy to turn off. We can no longer afford, if we ever could, a domestic system that depends upon international events to goad the country out of domestic doldrums. Thus, great advantages are matched by great disadvantages in this scenario.

The second, low-probability scenario is the restructuring of party politics to permit the regeneration of a new liberalism appropriate to the substantial and substantive innovations the national government will require to survive into the twenty-first century. This sort of change could take place within the present two-party system, but only if one of the parties is defeated badly enough to provide incentive for absorption of new ideas and commitment to fundamental rather than marginal strategies. The record of the past forty years does not, however, give any indication of that possibility. Both parties have remarkable staying power. Democrats seem to have a lock on slightly more than 50 percent of all legislative seats; and Republicans seem equally unassailable in their near-majority status, remaining sufficiently satisfied so long as enough Democrats will help Republicans elect the president often enough to keep the bureaucracy honest. Another problem with a new public philosophy or with substantial innovations of any sort through the two parties is their very lack of structure. *There is virtually nothing left of the parties to realign.* Except for continuing Democratic/Republican partisanship, there is no continuity to break. The two-party system is a fluid arrangement that ebbs and flows easily, usually as a negative reaction to any presidential incumbent. The two parties prove too adaptable at the margins to require adaptation at the core.

All in all, therefore, the two-party system is not only institutionally unsuitable for generating the new national public philosophy, but it is more generally unsuitable to provide the kind of organized partisanship that large, modern, Western-style governments require. This problem is not limited to the United States. The two-party system has proven unable to adapt anywhere to large, modern, programmatic governments. None of the large liberal states of the world have two-party systems. Two-party politics is a shambles in Great Britain and never took hold in France, despite strongly favored conditions in the Fifth Republic. Japan has a modified one-party system. Germany may be the most interesting case from the standpoint of the United States, because a quite small third party significantly shapes the structure of the two major parties there.

All this is to say that a third party, even a small third party, could easily change the political map of the United States. The third party would relieve the two major parties of having to be all things to all people. This would enable the two major parties to define more clearly the minorities they actually represent, thus enabling them to stabilize themselves sufficiently to develop an institutional structure.

Of equal importance is the impact a permanent third party would have on the presidency. Since the Constitution would not change, the president would continue to be elected by the present system of a popular vote followed by an electoral vote. However, a third party would so increase the probability of a stalemate in the electoral college that rational strategy would require all presidential candidates to look to the House of Representatives as the place where the final decision would have to be made from time to time. Even if election in the House happened only infrequently, its enhanced probability would nevertheless redefine the constituency of the president, from what it has become—a mass plebiscitary base—to a much more parliamentary constituency. The president would have to be much more concerned with building and maintaining a coalitional base in the legislature, and the legislature would have to act much more regularly as a mediating influence between the president and the masses. The presence of a third party and the drawing of the presidency more into the legislature would bring the national government of the United States into close resemblance with the French government under the Fifth Republic. The president of France is popularly elected, with a runoff two weeks later in case no candidate wins an absolute majority in the first election. Presidents are elected to seven-year, repeatable terms; but more interestingly, the Fifth Republic constitution calls for a premier, who is appointed by the president along with the other members of the government. Although the Fifth Republic constitution creates an extremely strong president, who is in some respects even stronger than the American president, it also provides for a much closer working relationship between president and parliament—proving definitively that a strong president is not incompatible with close parliamentary responsibility and accountability. Since the French fashioned their

1958 constitutional structure after ours, and since they gained a tremendous amount of stability and effectiveness as a consequence, the United States would do well to gather inspiration from the French model. We badly need the benefits of an independent executive coupled with those of parliamentary democracy. This was anticipated by the framers of the original U.S. Constitution when they provided for final selection of the president by the House of Representatives and a variety of "checks and balances," precisely on the assumption that there would be a continuity rather than alienation between the two branches of government.

A third party and a somewhat more parliamentary system could be the mark of a new, or what I would call Third, Republic. Such an important change in structure would either reflect or cause a change in public philosophy. Every regime develops politics consonant with itself, and a distinctive public philosophy is a major aspect of that politics. Such a change of structure may be the only way for the United States to refashion its liberalism and meet its future head on; but that is the very reason why this scenario has a low probability of occurring.

If Ronald Reagan leaves any legacy at all, it may well be in the lesson that we have nothing to fear from substantial innovation, including substantial institutional reform. Generally, institutional reform is not only frightening but also exceptionally difficult to dramatize politically, as compared to the championing of exciting policy proposals involving billions of dollars for new services, industrial vitalization, or fancy military hardware. That is why the economist has replaced the lawyer and the philosopher as the source of important ideas in American politics. President Reagan is the exception because he has the character of the innovator in a two-party system that has produced few innovations. Reagan combines boldness with political naiveté, a simple belief system, and a willingness to lose big. In a stable and established politics, the preferred leadership traits are opposite to those of prudence, sophistication, a complex analytic mind, and a cost-benefit approach to policies. It is no coincidence that the most important innovator among all recent presidential candidates was from the minority wing of the minority party. By a quirk of fate, Ronald Reagan was elected; but his administration illustrates mainly that innovation in our system is growing more infrequent and difficult. Even if his conservative morality does not prevail, there is a moral to his story that should not be allowed to die. During the same forty years in which Democrats and Republicans have been relatively evenly matched, Americans have been advising hundreds of countries and thousands of political leaders throughout the world about how to reform their institutions. The lesson of Ronald Reagan is that the time may have come for us to begin taking our own advice.

THE THEORY OF GOVERNANCE OF THE REAGAN ADMINISTRATION

James W. Ceaser

In his 1981 inaugural address, Ronald Reagan promised the nation a "new beginning." Claims to newness of one sort or another are, of course, typical of inaugural rhetoric. What was untypical was that six months later many political analysts were proclaiming that President Reagan had in fact delivered on his promise. Although the scope of the change, as indicated by the journalistic expression "Reagan Revolution," was frequently exaggerated, and although some important continuities existed between the policies of President Reagan and President Jimmy Carter, the transformation in American politics that took place in 1981 was probably greater than any that has occurred since the inauguration of Franklin Delano Roosevelt in 1933.

The Reagan administration's "new beginning" represented an effort to change not only what government should do but also how the instrument of government should be used. In the 1980s few observers in Washington, D.C., could help but notice that after the administration's first dramatic months of budget cuts and tax reductions, the pace of politics slowed remarkably by comparison with the previous four years. In place of a crowded agenda and a near universal expectation that government would be constantly adopting new policies, observers found themselves awaiting the results of a few major initiatives. Was there, apart even from the content of Reagan's program, a new theory of how to run the government?

This paper addresses this question by examining the nature of the Reagan administration's *theory of governance*. By a theory of governance, I mean a set of ideas relating to how to make the national government function properly—that is, how to make it function in accordance with a chosen constitutional form and, within that form, with efficacy. A theory of governance deals with issues such as the proper source of authority for national institutions, a recommended scheme for apportioning power among and within the institutions, the kind of agenda that the government can manage, and general strategic notions about how to make the government work in practice. In most discussions of governance in the United States, not all of these questions are opened to debate on first principles, since nearly everyone accepts as a given the broad framework of government established in the Constitution. Yet because the Constitution does not answer all of these questions and is subject to interpretation on many points, there is still much room for theorizing and controversy.

Theories of governance do not comprise the whole, or even the main, of the ideas that shape national political programs. In thinking, for example, of today's two major labels—liberalism and conservatism—one is likely to first think of certain content goals, such as equality or economic liberty, and only thereafter of ideas about how the national government should function. A theory of governance therefore makes up only one segment of a (possible) larger "public philosophy" that offers guidance on three other fundamental issues: (1) the ends of society (meaning, generally, an interpretation of the consensual values of liberty, equality, democracy, and progress); (2) the role of government, and of the different levels of government, in society; and (3) the role that the United States should play in the world.

The elements that comprise a public philosophy are linked in a complex relationship that has never been studied systematically. Most discussions of the role of ideas in American politics, however, assume (though they employ differing terminology) that among the elements of any public philosophy, a theory of governance is more caused than causal.[1] Thus, in accounts of the development of liberalism, it is usually said that liberals in the 1930s embraced certain ideas about the ends of society (mainly, a new interpretation of liberty as the freedom *from* want); that this belief led to new assumptions about the proper role of government in society (mainly, the insistence on a much more active role for government, especially for the federal government); and that these two ideas in turn dictated the development of a new theory of governance (mainly, the call for the powerful, modern presidency and the modern administrative apparatus). Somewhat later, in the 1940s and 1950s, liberals embraced the idea of the United States as the protector of freedom in the world, adding further weight to the call for a more active government and a stronger presidency.

---

1. Establishing the relative weight of the four elements that comprise a public philosophy is a matter for empirical investigation. It is likely that the importance of these elements varies from one public philosophy to another.

The complex relationship among the elements of public philosophy means that treating a "theory of governance" in isolation risks abstracting from reality and assigning more importance to governance as a causal factor than it deserves. This bias may not be without a certain value, however, for a theory of governance may be a much more important element in a public philosophy than is commonly acknowledged. Because of the complicated system of government that exists in the United States, American political thinkers have traditionally given a great deal of attention to the problem of how to run the government and not just to the content goals it should serve. In the case of modern conservatism, I will attempt to show the very considerable degree to which the Reagan program has been a response to a perceived crisis in governance that has required a rethinking of the previously dominant theory of governance.

Ideas in American Political Development

Discussing a theory of governance assumes that ideas have an important effect on political development, an assumption seemingly so commonsensical that only academic political science could have rendered it suspect. In fact, for many years, political scientists who analyzed American politics gave little weight to the role of ideas in accounting for policy changes or institutional developments. This neglect of ideas resulted from a number of causes: the absence of ideological conflict in the 1950s and early 1960s, when modern political science achieved prominence in many American universities; the effort to transform political science into a hard science and therefore to banish soft variables like ideas; and the confused notion that studying ideas automatically places one in the fuzzy netherland of normative theory.

The situation has changed dramatically in the last several years, and leading scholars of institutions and policy now typically refer to the significance of ideas, not to ventilate their own preferences but to explain how and why things happen.[2] This change is attributable to a fact no more complicated than that political scientists found they could not understand the empirical world without taking into account the role of ideas.

Perhaps the most sweeping contemporary claim for the influence of ideas in American politics is found in the work of one of America's foremost political scientists, Samuel Beer, who claims that policies and institutional

---

2. See James Q. Wilson, "American Politics Then and Now," *Commentary* (February 1979), pp. 39–46.

developments radiate from a dominant "public philosophy," which he defines as an "outlook on public affairs which is accepted within a nation by a wide coalition and which serves to give definition to problems and direction to governmental policies."[3] So comprehensive a statement obviously invites challenges about the relative weight of ideas compared to other factors that may account for political change, such as economic and technological developments, political events, and institutional relations. Even those disposed to accept the importance of ideas may question whether they flow, as Beer suggests, from a single unified whole or whether they develop in a more piecemeal, ad hoc fashion.

Whatever the validity of such objections, it is clear that they cannot be discussed until the concept of a public philosophy itself has been elaborated more precisely. This requires that one specify the kinds of ideas that comprise American public philosophies, how a public philosophy develops, and how one public philosophy replaces another.

Following is a brief review of the assumptions on which this paper is based:

1. The ideas that make up American public philosophies derive chiefly from certain fundamental building blocks within the tradition of American political thought that can be traced to the dialogue between the Federalists and the anti-Federalists. To the extent that new ideas are imported from the outside, they are generally presented and interpreted through the lenses of these American ideas.[4]

2. These ideas do not develop in a fixed and predictable pattern based on any dialectic contained in the ideas themselves. I cannot, for example, agree with the diagnosis of political scientist Samuel Huntington, who traces the development of ideas to the unfolding of a single tension within the revolutionary principle.[5] On the other hand, it is not the case that the process of development is so open-ended that no statements can be made about the possible progression of ideas in advance of the moment that they are devised. Rather, the process of development is constrained by the building blocks just

---

3. Samuel Beer, "In Search of a New Public Philosophy," in Anthony King, ed., *The New American Political System* (Washington, D.C.: American Enterprise Institute, 1979), p. 5.

4. For the development of these ideas see Herbert Storing, *What the Antifederalists Were For* (Chicago: University of Chicago Press, 1981); William Schambra, "The Roots of the American Public Philosophy," *The Public Interest*, vol. 67 (Spring 1982), pp. 36–48; and the recent doctoral dissertations at the University of Virginia by David Nichols and William Connelly, Jr.

5. Samuel Huntington, *American Politics: The Promise of Disharmony* (Cambridge, Mass.: Harvard University Press, 1981).

mentioned, which are combined and recombined in different ways, although not in any fixed inevitable patterns.

3. A change of public philosophies, insofar as such changes can be explained by reference to ideas and not other factors, becomes more likely to the extent that the existing public philosophy enters—and is perceived to enter—a crisis in which the major tenets of the philosophy no longer seem to conform to developments in the real world or in which components of the philosophy begin to operate at cross-purposes with one another.

One important implication of these assumptions for this analysis is that the ideas that comprise any American public philosophy (and therefore its theory of governance) do not emerge full-blown as packaged ideologies, as one sometimes finds with party programs in European democracies. Rather, American public philosophies are often forged pragmatically by a process of reaction against the elements of the existing public philosophy and the construction, often tentatively, of a "positive" alternative. American public philosophies define themselves as much by what they are against as by what they are for. Thus, to understand Reagan's theory of governance, one cannot analyze it in isolation but must view it initially in the light of what preceded it. The widely discussed "crisis" of liberalism in the 1970s involved tensions not just about the fundamental ends of society or the obligations of government or America's role in the world, but also about how to operate the government. Reagan's theory of governance was adapted in part to resolve some of these problems.

Changing Elements in Governance: From Carter to Reagan

President Reagan's "new beginning" was intended to break not just with the policies of the Carter administration, but with those of an entire era said to be dominated by the public philosophy of liberalism. As Reagan told a group of reporters in 1982, "We have started government on a different course, different from anything we've done in the last half century since Roosevelt began the New Deal."[6] Although the philosophy of liberalism was

6. Public Papers of the Presidents, Ronald Reagan 1982 I, p. 54; January 20, 1982, interview with reporters from the *Los Angeles Times*. President Reagan has made clear in speeches and interviews that the era of liberalism should be dated from the New Deal and that his attempt has been to reverse the trend of steady growth in domestic government spending that began at that time. However, Reagan in some instances distinguishes between two phases of liberalism—the New Deal and the Great Society—and argues that his main disagreements lie with the second and not the first. See Ronald Reagan, Speech of March 13, 1984.

not always as evident in the Carter presidency as in earlier Democratic administrations, comparing the Carter and the Reagan administrations on three fundamental points relating to the question of governance should provide a clear contrast between the old and the new.

The first point relates to the nature of the policy agenda of the two administrations. The transformation can be characterized as a change from an attempt at complex policy agenda under President Carter's tenure. The Carter administration's approach to the agenda, particularly in its early years, consisted in proposing a large number of policy initiatives, "in the first six months the greatest outpouring of new proposals . . . to Congress by any first term president since Franklin Delano Roosevelt in 1933."[7] Nearly all of these were said to be important and deserving of immediate action.

Imbued with a "technocratic" perspective toward problem solving, Carter seemed to view the task of governing in terms of the management of complex and interrelated policies. Some saw in this engineering approach, and particularly in the stress on sound management and budgeting reforms, a conservatism reminiscent of President Herbert Hoover. Yet the administration's program as a whole revealed that this technocratic approach was designed not to limit but to manage the complexities of the advanced stages of liberalism. In its understanding of the capacities of government, the administration believed that our system could be operated as a sophisticated machine capable of responding quickly and rationally to numerous and complex problems without being unduly compromised by "political" considerations.[8]

This view of governance, while never completely abandoned, ran counter to certain inhospitable realities of the American political system. The administration's complex and ambitious program seemed to confuse the public and ultimately to paralyze the operation of government. Evidently not as sophisticated as the president hoped, the governmental machine ceased to function effectively, its "circuits" overloaded. The consensus of observers was that the administration had failed to establish clear and simple priorities, a judgment ultimately confirmed by Hamilton Jordan, White House chief of staff: "My most basic regret is that in doing so many things, we never clearly fixed in the public mind a sense of our priorities."[9]

7. Austin Ranney, "The Carter Administration," in Austin Ranney, ed., *The American Elections of 1980* (Washington, D.C.: American Enterprise Institute, 1981), p. 18.

8. See James Fallows, "The Passionless Presidency," *Atlantic Monthly*, vol. 243, no. 5 (May 1979), pp. 33–46; "A Talk with Brzezinski," *Encounter*, vol. 56, no. 5 (May 1981); Herbert Storing, "American Statesmanship: Old and New," in Robert Goldwin, ed., *Bureaucrats, Policy Analysts, Statesmen* (Washington, D.C.: American Enterprise Institute, 1980).

9. "Jordan Takes Stock as He Packs Up His Memories," *New York Times*, December 4, 1980, p. 22.

Under Reagan, by contrast, a concerted effort was made from the outset to fix a few key items as priorities and to keep all other matters off the policy agenda. Until an item was addressed, nothing new was added, even when some administration officials deemed an initiative worthy of the agenda.[10] Thus during the first year, for example, the administration pursued only a few objectives—domestic spending cuts, an increase in military spending, and a reduction in marginal tax rates. As Hugh Heclo, one political scientist, observed:

> By drastically narrowing his priorities to a few economic road signs, the President appeared to rise above the prevailing policy congestion. In place of ambiguity and trade-offs appeared simplicity and decisions. . . . By drastically limiting White House priorities, the president seems to rise above the confusion and squabbling of a congested policy environment.[11]

As a consequence of this approach, there was seldom any doubt in 1981, either among elites in Washington or within the public at large, about what the administration wanted. As time went on, the agenda on occasion became less focused, particularly when mid-course corrections were made after the 1982 congressional elections. Never, however, was the agenda very large or complex. Simplicity remained the hallmark throughout.

The Reagan administration's approach reflected a very different conception of governance. It viewed governing much less in technical terms and more in political terms. The problem in governing was not just to find the right program, but a program that could be put into effect in our political system. The constitutional system, particularly the separation of powers, imposed certain constraints on how to achieve any political objective and on how many objectives could be achieved at once. To govern meant accepting—indeed embracing—these constraints. This did not mean that *what* was sought could not be bold—indeed, the changes that the administration obtained in 1981 were, by the standards of American policymaking, very significant. Yet the means by which these objectives were pursued reflected the administration's perception of operating in a political environment that required the development of a political strategy based on mobilizing the public and congressional supporters by means of appeals to a few clear-cut ends. Nuances were often ignored. Even if its "ideal" policy agenda had been more complex,

---

10. Consider, for example, how the White House rebuffed efforts by Secretary of State Alexander Haig in 1981 to make the issue of communism in Central America more prominent. The president's closest aides did not want to "divert attention from the economic program that was his [Reagan's] overriding priority" [I.M Destler, "The Evolution of Reagan Foreign Policy," in Fred I. Greenstein, ed., *The Reagan Presidency: An Early Assessment* (Baltimore: John Hopkins University Press, 1983), p. 137].

11. Hugh Heclo, "One Executive Branch or Many," in Anthony King, ed., *Both Ends of the Avenue* (Washington, D.C.: American Enterprise Institute, 1983). p. 47.

the administration's assumption was that the political system could not enact it. If a corresponding mechanical analogy can be devised to compare with the Carter administration's image of the political system as a sophisticated machine, one might liken the Reagan conception to that of an old but reliable steamer: You set it in motion, fix its destination, nurse it along, but avoid complex maneuvers.

The second major difference between Reagan and Carter relates to their understandings of the source of legitimate authority for the presidency and, in some measure, for the government as a whole. Here the contrast, which is one more of degree than of kind, can be characterized as a shift from an avowedly populist conception of authority and leadership under President Carter to a slightly more representative conception under President Reagan.

Virtually every writer analyzing Carter's campaign and presidency has stressed the populist nature of his conception of leadership. Yet few have defined precisely what populism in this context means. One of the reasons is that all American leadership today tends to be highly popular, if not populist, which makes it difficult to draw clear distinctions. Populism as a concept rests on an intuitive grasp of degree—of how far leaders go in resting their legitimacy on a direct relationship to the people. Populism can best be understood in contrast to republicanism, a term that suggests leaders who emphasize the forms and powers of their offices as the basis of their authority. Although elective offices must be ultimately dependent on the will of the people, and subject to pressures of public opinion, the republican view emphasizes that these offices are constituted to retain a realm of independent discretion. Populism, on the other hand, suggests that the sole legitimate source of authority lies with the people's wishes, usually as interpreted by the leader. Hierarchic authority, including the normal prerogatives of governmental institutions, are called into question and regarded suspiciously as a possible cover for machinations against the people. The populist leader may make a special point of demonstrating his "oneness" with the people against these institutions and of stressing his unwillingness to "play the game" of dealing with them.

If President Carter regarded the business of governing as complex management, he nonetheless assumed that the source of legitimacy for government derived from some kind of "direct relationship" between the leader and the people. This direct relationship was based less on any congruence between the leader and the people with regard to specific policies or even specific political principles than on a special community of trust. Thus President Carter called for "a government as good as our people," "a government as filled with love as our people."[12] As Vivien Hart, a political scientist, has written:

---

12. Cited in Beer, "In Search of a New Public Philosophy," p. 43.

Carter stood precisely with the distrustful Populists of the 1890s in his constant campaign assertion of the necessity of bringing government closer to the people, and of the people's capacity to rise to the responsibility. . . . [He] combined to great rhetorical effect the Populist language of aspiring to involve all the people more closely and continuously in government with denunciations and proposals in the name of the managerial criterion of efficiency.[13]

Although Carter relied more on such themes during the campaign than after he took office, he never abandoned his populist style and—very revealingly— he returned to it at some of his moments of tribulation, such as the period of the "malaise" crisis in July and August 1979, in an effort to reinvigorate his legitimacy.

In seeking the understanding of the source of legitimacy for governing institutions under the Reagan administration, one encounters a certain ambiguity among present-day conservatives. The traditional conservative position has been to protect the prerogatives of established institutions against the pressures of populist sentiments. Yet the conservatism of the past decade has added another strain, the New Right, which has clearly been more populist in orientation, identifying wisdom with the popular will, showing little respect for established representative institutions, and building a community of interest on the basis of mistrust for authority.

While Ronald Reagan has long had close ties to the New Right and has clearly been the choice of most of its adherents since 1976, as president, Reagan has by and large avoided populist statements about presidential leadership or the foundations of governmental authority. He has, to be sure, continued to attack the development of "big government" in the name of the people, although his attack has been more a condemnation of the *use* of government than of the source of legitimacy of its institutions; and he has successfully employed speeches on many occasions to mobilize public opinion on behalf of his programs, although such use of the rhetorical dimensions of the office has long been considered a normal and legitimate element of modern presidential leadership. In attempting to discover whether there has been a change under the Reagan administration from a populist to a more republican view of institutional authority, it is important to consider what is *not* being said and done as much as what is said and done. Among those who comment on the presidency, almost all references to populism as a source of leadership have ceased, largely because they seem to have no relevance in describing the Reagan presidency. Reagan makes no claims of having a special relationship with the American people and seldom belabors or agonizes over the nature of his own or his institution's legitimacy. As Meg Greenfield, a col-

---

13. Vivien Hart, *Distrust and Democracy* (London: Cambridge University Press, 1978), p. 190–196.

umnist for *Newsweek*, has written: "[Reagan] is the first president in years who has, at least so far, failed to cultivate the image of crisis and ordeal and almost unbearable testing."[14]

Some traditional conservatives have faulted President Reagan for not engaging in a direct campaign against populist themes in American politics.[15] Yet Reagan has made some changes in style. In his dealings with other power centers, in particular with Congress, Reagan made it clear from the beginning that while he would press vigorously for his policies, he would not question the essential legitimacy of official institutions and would work with, rather than against, the Washington, D.C., establishment.[16] This has not meant, however, complying with the desire of some in Congress for a weak presidency. On the contrary, basing his case on constitutional powers, Reagan has pressed his conception of a strong presidency and sought to prevent congressional intrusions on presidential discretion, particularly in foreign affairs.[17]

The third and final point of comparison between the Carter and Reagan administrations relates to views on the part of both governing officials and the public at large about the workability of the American presidency and of the American political system. The transformation here can be characterized as a change from a perception of crisis and ungovernability under the Carter administration to a perception of relative confidence that the system works in its usual—that is, minimally efficient—way under the Reagan administration.

Widespread sentiment began to develop after Carter's first year in office that the structural design of the government was inadequate to meet the tasks of governing. The system, it was said, was too fragmented and its policy-making machinery too dispersed to deal with the problems of complex management in a modern regime. In particular, many came to consider the American presidency, the fulcrum of the system, as an institution in serious trouble.

---

14. Meg Greenfield, "How Does Reagan Decide?" *Newsweek*, February 20, 1984, p. 80.

15. Harvey C. Mansfield, Jr., "The American Election: Towards Constitutional Democracy?" *Government and Opposition*, vol. 16, no. 1 (Winter 1981), pp. 1–18.

16. See "Reagan Courts Legislators in Visit to Hill," *Congressional Quarterly*, vol. 38, no. 47 (November 22, 1980), p. 3389. As Charles O. Jones has pointed out, Reagan's style has been that of a constant communicator with Congress, in contrast to an independent (and sometimes suspicious) style characteristic of Presidents Nixon and Carter. See Charles O. Jones, "Presidential Negotiations With Congress," in Anthony King, ed., *Both Ends of the Avenue* (Washington, D.C.: American Enterprise Institute, 1983), pp. 96–130; also paper by Jones in this volume.

17. The president reluctantly had to concede the force of the War Powers Resolution when introducing troops into Lebanon. But throughout his term he has called for greater discretion for the presidency in foreign affairs. See "Reagan Goes on the Attack," *Newsweek*, April 16, 1984, pp. 24–25.

Scholars issued analysis after analysis describing the "crisis" of the presidency, and President Carter himself, during the summer of 1979, seemed to adopt this view. Many observers began to speak of the need for dramatic institutional changes in the presidency and the political system.

During Reagan's first year, by contrast, there was a remarkable shift in perceptions about the capacity of the system to act, even if many did not agree with how it was acting. Virtually all talk about a crisis of ungovernability and the demise of presidential leadership ceased. As Fred I. Greenstein remarked:

> Reagan and company reversed the notion that presidents were becoming increasingly powerless. By the summer of 1981, in a striking display of political skill that took advantage of such circumstances as a Republican-controlled Senate and a Democratic party in disarray, Reagan forces had achieved dramatic results on Capitol Hill above and beyond the administratively induced changes introduced by presidential appointees.[18]

This reversal took place, it should be observed, *without* aid of any change in the basic institutional structure of government, except perhaps for Reagan's use in one instance of the reconciliation process under the Budget and Impoundment Act of 1974. Reagan was able to assemble the requisite power by relying on sources of authority that have been available on certain occasions to presidents in the past: a large electoral victory, a substantial increase of fellow party members in Congress, and a party united on certain principles.

Did this mean, therefore, that the case that political analysis had built about the growing fragmentation of our institutional processes was incorrect? Not necessarily. Any careful argument about the status of institutions must be based on long-term assessments, and it is possible that Reagan's success was owed in large part to powerful short-term factors that temporarily masked and overrode certain long-term tendencies. In fact, by 1984 many observers again were complaining, if not exactly about fragmentation, about an institutional incapacity of government to resolve the deficit problem, and some, including President Reagan, were recommending institutional changes (e.g., an item veto or a budget-balancing amendment) to help resolve the problem. On balance, however, it seems clear that: (1) the administration's performance overall and especially in the first two years disproved at least the most extreme claims about the ungovernability of the American political system, and (2) within both the government and the nation there has been a decided move away from the attitude that the presidency and our political system are in crisis.

---

18. Fred I. Greenstein, "The Need for an Early Appraisal of the Reagan Presidency," in Fred I. Greenstein, ed., *The Reagan Presidency: An Early Assessment* (Baltimore: Johns Hopkins University Press, 1983), p. 6.

Elements of the Liberal Theory of Governance

While many would hold that the changes just cited have no connection with one another, let us consider whether they can be tied together in a systematic way. First, it may be that the properties of each administration reflect more than just tactics or haphazard effects, but also the intentions (or consequences) of two different theories of governance, described here as liberal and conservative. Second, it may be that these three changes are linked together in a partial cause-effect relationship in which, at least in the view of conservatives, the crisis in governance of the late 1970s has abated, in part because the agenda of government has been limited and (perhaps) because the asserted foundation of legitimacy has been made less populist.

Clearly there are objections that can be raised to any attempt to explain developments at such a theoretical level. There is no need, of course, to deny that other factors, including the personalities of the two presidents and their short-term tactics, have played a major role. A more obvious difficulty lies in identifying the Carter presidency with a liberal theory of governance, in particular on the matter of setting priorities and working the system effectively. In contrast to President Carter, certain liberal presidents set clear priorities and were remarkably successful in leading Congress and the nation. Indeed, in this regard, President Reagan apparently has taken President Franklin Delano Roosevelt as his model for governance. What I will argue, however, is not that the Carter administration was like that of other liberal presidents, but rather that its ideas about governing were, in the main, a logical outgrowth or consequence of the liberal theory of governance in its later stages; and that important elements of Reagan's approach were adapted in response to the liberal theory and not just to the peculiarities of President Carter's administration.

The Agenda and the Concept of Policymaking

The large number of items on the agenda during the Carter administration was a logical, if not inevitable, outcome of the liberal public philosophy. Since its inception, the core of the liberal idea has been to expand the purview of government—and in particular the federal government—into new domains of society in order to prohibit, modify, stimulate, or create certain activities and forms of behavior. The objective of this expansion has been a fluid and evolving notion of social justice. The expansion of government has been encouraged by modern social science, which, particularly in the early years of liberalism, tended to support the view that increased knowledge of social processes could be readily employed to help devise policies of intervention by public authority that could achieve many of the liberals' goals for social justice.

As a consequence of the liberal idea, sanctioned by social science, many have come to accept a theory of governance under which it is assumed that for every major block of social activity, there should be a corresponding public policy. Thus, we have an economic policy, a housing policy, an energy policy, and so forth. Under the Carter administration, efforts were made to develop an urban policy, a family policy, and a neighborhood policy; and among neoliberals today, the key buzz words heard are "incomes policy" and "industrial policy."

The continual use of the word *policy* in political discussion today reflects an important development. To speak of a policy for any given area of activity already implies that that area is a matter for legitimate superintendence by government. Of course, policy analysts who discuss and advocate policies do not always call for extensive public intervention or regulation, and in recent years they have tended to be somewhat more cautious in doing so. Nonetheless, whether or not a policy eventuates in a program for large-scale intervention, the very idea of developing a policy for a particular area calls into question the juridical significance of a public versus a private sphere; similarly, the very idea of developing a *federal* policy calls into question the juridical significance of a federal versus a state or local sphere. Once an area of social activity is demarcated for the formulation of a policy, the legal injunction fades from view: the criteria employed for deciding on intervention or abstention tend to be based not on juridical considerations, but on "policy" considerations, that is, what produces a plan to solve the problem at hand.

The liberal agenda, of course, has changed from one era to another, but almost every activity for which a policy has once been implemented tends to remain within the scope of government and thus to become a possible item on the current agenda, albeit often in only a small way. Liberalism in its modern sense, meaning an active federal government, only began to be accepted as part of the national public philosophy in the New Deal era, when the term *liberalism* was first appropriated by Franklin Delano Roosevelt and made a part of the common political vocabulary. The immediate crisis—the depression—brought forth as a response an explicit economic policy and began a transformation in thinking, by now complete, under which the federal government, and in particular the president, is deemed responsible for ensuring a healthy economy. As Samuel Beer has written: "Before Roosevelt the issue of national action to sustain and direct the economy did not arise . . . the question of 'government management of the economy' . . . was simply not on the agenda.[19] If the government before the 1930s could be held responsible for the sin of committing an error that allegedly made the economy falter, it would now be held responsible for the sin of failing to take the necessary steps to make the economy work well. Indeed, under the *then*-prevailing assumptions of social science (Keynesian economics), a sin of commission was hardly worse than a sin of omission, for it was supposed that the tools now existed to ensure prosperity.

During the Johnson administration a new phase in liberalism was launched as a large number of policy areas were suddenly added to the agenda of national politics. The expansive attitude toward policymaking that lay behind the Great Society is explained by Harry McPherson, one of Johnson's top advisers:

> But a new philosophy of government had emerged since New Deal days. In essence it held that our problems were more of the spirit than of the flesh. People were suffering from a sense of alienation from one another, of anomie, of powerlessness. This affected the well-to-do as much as it did the poor. Middle-class women, bored and friendless in the suburban afternoons; fathers, working at "meaningless" jobs, or slumped before the television set; sons and daughters desperate for "relevance"—all were in need of community, beauty, and purpose, all were guilty because so many others were deprived while they, rich beyond their ancestors' dreams, were depressed. What would change all this was a creative public effort: for the middle class, new parks, conservation, the removal of billboards and junk, adult education, consumer protection, better television, aid to the arts; for the poor, jobs, training, Head Start, decent housing, medical care, civil rights; for both, and for bridging the gap between them, VISTA, the Teacher Corps, the community action agencies, mass transportation, model cities.[20]

Although it would be an exaggeration to say that all of these ventures had the backing of experienced policy analysts—indeed today many policy analysts look back with horror at the amateurism of those who claimed the scientific mantle—it is undeniable that social scientists helped supply the ideas that underlay many of the Great Society programs. It was, in fact, the heyday for social science, as the "new professionals" within the government who had been trained in the social sciences stepped in to help devise the new programs, borrowing freely from current theories floating around academia.[21] The era of the policymaking state had arrived.

---

19. Beer, "In Search of a New Public Philosophy," p. 7.

20. Harry McPherson, *A Political Education* (Boston: Atlantic Monthly Press, 1972), pp. 301–302.

21. Beer, "In Search of a New Public Philosophy," p. 18. Beer writes here, "In perhaps the greatest novelty of all, the social sciences of psychology, economics, sociology, and even political science seemed to achieve in their 'behavioral revolution' the capacity for specific social control necessary to make them the foundation of government action."

When President Carter took office in 1977, much had changed since the Johnson years. Economic growth had slowed, making it difficult to hide the cost of new initiatives by financing them "freely" from an expanding economic pie. The claims on government, in large part resulting from the programs already in place, had increased enormously, putting more pressure on the agenda and exhausting additional revenues. Finally, policy science—or what is now commonly accepted as such—had become much more cautious and hardheaded, owing in part to the perception that many of the Great Society programs had failed and in part to the growing reliance on microeconomic theory as the methodological core of the new policy analysis. Indeed, in a revealing development, Henry Aaron of the Brookings Institution launched what was perhaps the first attack by a liberal on social science in a half century. Admitting that social science had in the past been allied to liberal causes, Aaron argued that this had resulted from a prescientific commitment of social scientists, which formed the general context into which they fitted their research. Shorn of such a commitment and left to its own devices, social research, said Aaron, has a "conservative effect" because, with all its conflicting theories and evidence, it tends to "corrode any simple faiths around which political coalitions are built" and because it is harder and more expensive to establish definitely that a program will work than to raise possible objections to it.[22] To sustain liberalism, in Aaron's view, one needed a bit more commitment and a bit less science.

The perception of growing constraints in the economic and political environment led the Carter administration to respond with more caution than was typical, certainly, of the Johnson years. From the viewpoint of many liberals who claimed to be keeping the faith (and who ended up supporting Senator Edward Kennedy for president in 1980), President Carter was seen as at best halfhearted in his commitment to liberalism. From a different perspective, however, the dispute here involved nothing more than that of whether to regard the glass as half empty or half full. Granting Carter's caution in relation to some of his more liberal critics, it nonetheless remains that the new programs proposed in the first two years of his term were fairly ambitious in scope and reflected, as in his employment and urban programs, a liberal policymaking approach. The urban program was perhaps the most typical in this respect, described by Anthony Downs in the Brookings Institution's *National Priorities* series as "promising to do just about everything good conceivable for just about everybody in all

22. Henry Aaron, *Politics and Professors* (Washington, D.C.: The Brookings Institution, 1978), pp. 158–159.

urban areas."[23] Even when President Carter decided in his last two years on a program of restraint in domestic spending, it did not prevent the administration from continuing to view the activity of governing in terms of developing new policies. As the administration was leaving office, it was proposing a new neighborhood policy and investigating a complicated new incomes policy.

Whatever the differences of objectives and style among the liberal presidents, there has nevertheless been a common underlying theme in their theory of governance. Governing consists of examining new issues or problems and devising a governmental response to manage the problem. Governing is creative policymaking, and we live in a policymaking state. After years of adding more and more policy responsibilities to government, it is not surprising that one ends up with an increasing set of demands and therefore a very full agenda. Nor is it surprising that a responsible leader would, under such circumstances, view the task of governing as that of complex management. Unless one loses faith in the entire liberal project, the operative view is that the government is—or ought to be—an instrument for handling the complexities that derive from a policymaking state.

The policymaking idea of governance has had a substantial impact on the governmental process. It has resulted in the development of a new quasi-institutional network that has been grafted onto the traditional decisionmaking process. This new network, however, is fraught with a profound contradiction—a contradiction between its rational policymaking component and its interest group politics component.

On the one hand, Washington has come to be populated with numerous centers for policy analysis, both inside and outside of the government. These centers are in the business of blocking out various areas of social activity for study and for the recommendation of one kind of national policy or another. The effort is to formulate policy on the basis of a rational understanding of the issues. Knowledge is the handmaiden of power, and the characteristic method of conducting politics is by "issue-networking" rather than by raw bargaining or political threats. Positions are promoted by means of conferences and the publication of policy papers, not by means of quiet trips to local golf clubs. Although this method of conducting business does not conform with the hard-headed picture, so beloved among journalists, of how real power is exercised in Washington, it nonetheless is the case that the policy-analysis

---

23. Anthony Downs, "Urban Policy," in Joseph Pechman, ed., *Setting National Priorities: The 1979 Budget* (Washington, D.C.: The Brookings Institution, 1978).

community has been the chief source for new governmental initiatives in recent years.[24]

On the other hand, once an area of social activity has been marked for federal policy purview, and particularly after a policy has been formulated and a program put into place, various interest groups flock to the nation's capital to promote and protect their particular interests. Some of these are traditional interest groups that have had a long history of activity in politics at other levels of government and that decided to establish or augment a presence in Washington, D.C. Other groups have more or less been created in response to policies and programs. Whatever the case, however, interest-group activity has grown immensely in Washington, D.C., especially since the period of the Great Society, paralleling the growth of the policy-analytic community.

It cannot be said, of course, that these two networks live in constant tension with one another. Groups likely to profit from a proposed policy become the temporary allies of the policy analysts who devise the programs, and policy analysts often find the information that interest groups supply to be helpful to their policy studies. Thus there has been considerable cross-fertilization of styles of doing business. Lobbyists in particular have had to learn how to "interface" with policy analysts and can now often be found roaming the Dupont Circle area with some kind of analytic study tucked under their raincoats.

Yet as a general rule, the interest-group network tends to reduce the discretion of policy analysts and to make it more difficult for the government to accommodate the "advances" in knowledge that emerge from the study of the social problems. The interest groups, after all, have their interests to protect and are unlikely to applaud new analyses, whatever their technical merit, that suggest the need for changes unfavorable to their group. The decision-making process, which from the policy analysts' viewpoint should be rational, suddenly becomes constrained and confined by group concerns, and the policy analysts may feel the temptation to turn their backs in disgust at this intrusion of politics into the political process. It was precisely this contradiction between rational policy analysis and "politics" that troubled and dismayed so many in the Carter administration and led Carter to attack special interests in his "crisis of confidence" speeches.

The Liberal Theory of Legitimacy: Populism and Reform

If the notion of complex management can be considered a logical—and even an inevitable—outgrowth of liberalism, can the same be said of pop-

---

24. Samuel Beer, "Federalism, Nationalism, and Democracy," *APSR*, vol. 72 (March 1978), pp. 9–21.

ulism? Here, the answer must be more ambiguous. From the moment of its establishment, proponents of the liberal idea never ceased stressing that it was designed to serve the interests of the "common man." The original emphasis in liberalism, however, was on the *programs* that would benefit the common man, not on empowering the common man to govern directly. For the most part, liberalism respected hierarchy and concentration of authority, particularly in those institutions deemed necessary for putting into place the liberal program, such as the Democratic party and the presidency.[25]

Yet by the 1970s liberalism had become wedded to a general theory or impulse known as "reform," and there is no question that populism is a direct and logical outgrowth of that theory. President Carter's style no doubt had its unique or idiosyncratic characteristics, but his populist themes were already implicit in the reform theory of governance. Populism, as many now believe, may have been detrimental to the substantive goals of liberalism, but its emergence was not a mere aberration from the course of development of liberalism in its recent stages.

The main elements of this reform are now widely known: a commitment both to "opening" the political process to democratic procedures and to undermining centers of hierarchic authority; with respect to the political parties—where the doctrine was launched and had its greatest impact—a call to end prerogatives and privileges for party organizations and to open the nominating process to the direct control of the citizenry; in Congress, an attack on the hierarchies of the committee system, on many of the norms that supported concentration of power, and on rules of secrecy in certain committee deliberations; in executive-legislative relations, a joining in on the attack against the "imperial presidency"—a common cry, too, of advocates of "congressional government"; and finally, the proposal of a series of laws and amendments to democratize the political process, including plans for national party primaries, a direct election of the president, and a national referendum and recall. All of these elements were supported by a powerful rhetoric that celebrated the wisdom of the people and that said little if anything in defense of republican themes. It was but a small and logical step from this general theory of governance to populist leadership.

---

25. Beer, "In Search of a New Public Philosophy," p. 27. Beer also writes here that the New Deal politics required "some degree of organization. . . . But in the eyes of many champions of participatory democracy such a politics represented precisely those impersonal bureaucratic, centralistic tendencies that were dehumanizing American society."

Whatever the exact reason for the marriage of reform and liberalism, the union created new tensions in the liberal theory of governance.[26] First, there was the obvious tension between the attack on the presidency and the celebration of congressional government on the one hand and the call for government by complex management and rationality on the other. The latter objective clearly demands more, not less, hierarchic authority and thus a stronger presidency, a view that President Carter came to share.[27] On this point, the original liberal theory of governance was clear and consistent. Seeking to extend the role of government and to create a vast new administrative apparatus, liberals were originally the partisans of a much stronger executive, and some even went so far as to propose a fundamental change in the constitutional system that would abolish the separation of powers and endow the executive with the power necessary to create and manage the new policymaking state.

A second tension created by the union of reform and liberalism resulted from the call for more democracy, openness, and access on the one hand and the insistence on rational policy analysis on the other. Although the intention of the reform movement in "opening" the system was apparently to promote public dialogue on the common good or the general will, one of its effects has been to give much greater access to the claims of various interest groups. The new structure of Congress, with its myriad subcommittees, allows groups multiple points of access, while the open procedures, such as public conference committee meetings, remove shields that members formerly could employ to protect themselves from group pressures. In the presidential nomination process, the loss of power by the party organizations has enabled another layer of organized entities—the interest groups—to exercise a growing influence.

All this has meant that the political system—which already, because of the separation of powers, was open to the penetration of interest groups—has become even more vulnerable to the pressures of particular interests. Such

---

26. Exactly why this doctrine of reform was adopted and promoted by the main exponents of liberalism is an interesting subject for speculation. Some have claimed that it represents a natural working out of the "popular" ideas underlying the original liberal program; others have attributed it to the emergence of a new strain of "romantic," antihierarchic Rousseauism emanating from the New Left; and others still have attributed it to a loss of purpose among liberals on the objectives of their policy, which many then sought to hide by recourse to a new common front on procedures.

27. A great part of Carter's farewell address (January 14, 1981) was dedicated to a defense of the presidency. After discussing the problems related to "single-issue groups," President Carter argued: "Because of the fragmented pressures of these special interests, it's very important that the office of the President be a strong one and its constitutional authority be preserved." *Public Papers of the Presidents, 1981*, "Farewell Address to the Nation," pp. 2889–2893.

a system is scarcely compatible with the demands of rational policymaking and complex management.

The Crisis in the Liberal Theory of Governance

By the end of the 1970s, many commentators on American politics had begun to speak of a crisis in liberal political thought. By crisis they were referring to the various contradictions among liberal policy goals—the battles between old and new liberals on issues such as America's role in the world and affirmative action—and to the failures of liberal programs to realize their objectives. Clearly, also, liberalism was suffering from severe internal stresses in its theory of governance. As President Carter himself conceded: "What you see in Washington and elsewhere in the country is a system of government that seems incapable of action. . . . Often you see paralysis and drift. . . . We have lost confidence in our government. . . ."[28]

The major elements of that crisis have been expressed in terms of the contradictions analyzed here between the goals of rational policymaking and government by complex management on the one hand and the emergence, as a consequence of liberal theory or practice, of institutional arrangements that thwarted the accomplishment of these goals on the other hand. Chief among these contradictions have been: (1) the development of a large interest-group network in Washington, (2) a (temporary) attack on the powers and prerogatives of the president, and (3) an opening of the system to greater influence of interest groups, by the dispersion of power in Congress and by the loss of party control over the nomination of candidates.

The fundamental problem underlying these contradictions may be defined in terms of a basic question: Even if, in principle, there are good policies in many different areas of social activity that would improve society, can they be enacted and maintained, beyond a certain number or beyond a certain degree of complexity, by a democratic political system, especially one characterized by a system of separation of powers and multiple points of access? Or, on the contrary, are the demands and strains on government inherent in a fully developed policymaking state simply more than the system can handle? Can our political system support the project of the policymaking state, or is the result of trying to make it do so likely to be the breakdown in the capacity of democratic government to function effectively and the advent of one form or another of "corruption"?

---

28. Jimmy Carter, Speech of July 15, 1979, *Public Papers of The Presidents 1979*, "Energy and National Goals," pp. 1235–1241.

This problem confronted modern liberals rather suddenly. Their view all along had been that governing consisted of finding good policies, but few considered the problems inherent in managing so many good policies at once. The implicit assumption always seemed to be that the government should be able to adjust to the demands of the policymaking state and that the outer limits of government responsibility should be fixed by judgments of the efficacy of policies and not by any "costs" imposed by maintaining the government itself. When the government ceased to function well under the Carter administration, the response was therefore not to adjust the policy agenda to what the government could accomplish but to alter the structure of the government or to change the political environment so that government could perform its role. The liberal reaction to the difficulties encountered in the late 1970s seemed to follow the usual last resort of the do-it-yourselfer: If it doesn't fit, force it.

The effort to "force it" assumed some unique forms. First, President Carter sought to reduce the stranglehold of interest groups, not through structural or institutional changes that would alter the incentives under which they operated, but by a change in the basic political culture—a kind of moral regeneration that would limit and discipline the special interests. This was the most important theme of Carter's "moral crisis" speech, which outlined the problem of a "Congress twisted and pulled in every direction by hundreds of well-financed interest groups. . . ."[29]

Second, Carter sought to rejuvenate the office of the presidency, after coming to the conclusion that it lacked the force and energy to move the nation. In some measure, this step was directed against the doctrine of constraints that the reform movement had placed on the presidency. The president accordingly sought to revitalize the office of the chief executive by connecting it more closely to the people.

Third, there was an effort to overhaul the entire constitutional structure. By the last year of Carter's term, some analysts within the White House concluded that the problem was structural (not moral) and that it went much deeper than merely the president redefining his relationship with the American people. Since our government as constituted could not handle the task of complex management, it was necessary to change the structure of government so that it could. According to Lloyd Cutler, President Carter's chief counsel:

> The separation of powers between the legislative and the executive today, whatever its merits in 1793, has become a structure that almost guarantees stalemate today. . . . During the second half of this century our government has adopted a wide variety of national goals. Many of

---

29. Ibid.

these goals—checking inflation, spurring economic growth, reducing unemployment, protecting our national security, assuring equal opportunity, increasing social security, cleaning
up the environment, improving energy efficiency—conflict with one another. For balancing
choices like these . . . it is almost impossible to achieve a broad consensus. . . . we need to
find a way of coming closer to the parliamentary concept of forming a government, under
which the elected majority is able to carry out an overall program. . . .[30]

In a sense, then, liberal thought in the late 1970s had come full circle,
echoing the views of many liberal thinkers of the last generation who had
called for "party government" on the British model. According to the modern
liberal theorists like Cutler, the complex policymaking state requires a system
of hierarchic management, which the American Constitution does not permit.
(Strangely, however, these critics have been silent on the question of whether
the liberal idea of reform and populism has not itself made the problem of
fragmentation much worse.) What these modern liberals are arguing is nothing
less than that the goals of liberalism cannot be obtained within our system.
Here was a clear acknowledgment by liberals of the existence of a crisis in
the liberal theory of governance.

The Conservative Response

Modern conservatism cannot now be said to be the nation's public philosophy, for it has yet to win a sufficient number of electoral endorsements
to prove its dominance. Public opinion surveys from the middle of the 1970s
documented a growing skepticism about the major tenets of liberalism, but
at the same time they showed no mass conversion to conservative principles.
Most analysts of the 1980 election interpreted the vote as mainly a rejection
of Jimmy Carter and a tentative endorsement of Ronald Reagan's right to
experiment with some of his ideas. At most, therefore, modern conservatism
can be counted a strong candidate for becoming a new public philosophy,
one whose fate is tied to the public's judgment of the Reagan administration
in the 1984 election and beyond.

It is questionable, moreover, whether modern conservatism as yet em-
braces a full-blown theory of governance. American public philosophies, as
noted earlier, do not generally emerge as complete systems but develop di-
alectically from criticism of the previously dominant public philosophy and
from confrontation with the experience of governing. The modern conservative alternative—if one assumes that the Reagan administration embodies

30. Lloyd Cutler, "To Form a Government," *Foreign Affairs*, vol. 58, no. 1 (Fall 1980), pp. 126–143.

a view distinct from its Republican predecessors—has had comparatively little time in which to test and hone its ideas. The most one can expect to examine at this point, therefore, are the main lines of probable development.

The Central Issue: Simplification of Governance

Theories of governance emerge from actions no less than words. As noted earlier, the Reagan administration has already moved without fanfare to place governmental authority on a less populist foundation and to assert, if not yet to win, some of the prerogatives for the presidential office that were lost in the aftermath of Watergate. Clearly, however, the key element of the nascent conservative theory of government has centered on a point where actions and words have often converged: on consolidating the political agenda and, implicitly at least, on attacking the basic idea of the policymaking state.

The change sought by the Reagan administration can be described as follows: Whereas liberals have sought to make our political system fit their notion of the policymaking state, conservatives seek to tailor an agenda that can fit the capacities of our political system. The Reagan administration has proceeded to simplify the agenda—to focus on a few major issues and to adopt nonpolicies or antipolicies—in part because of the White House's assessment of what our political system can handle. What the liberal theory of complex management has failed to take into account, in the conservative view, are the "costs" for the political system itself of attempting to manage too much.

The movement to simplify is evident in President Reagan's political rhetoric, which is characterized by its adherence to a limited number of clear and direct principles. Many of the president's critics never tire of accusing him of being simplistic; oddly, however, they recognize his success as a "Great Communicator" and acknowledge that this success rests in no small part on his capacity to make clear a few central ideas. Modern conservatives may well operate on the assumption that there are limits to the degree of complexity and dissonance that can be effectively communicated to democratic publics without confusing them and making them feel helpless. This view of rhetoric reflects a theory of governance that holds that what a democratic government should do and how it should do it must take into account constraints related to how public opinion can be shaped and educated.

Along with the effort to simplify the nature of public appeals, modern conservatives also hold that the *tasks* of government must be simplified. For government to "work," especially in a separation-of-powers system, it can only handle so many demands and tasks before it loses the capacity to respond effectively. In the view of David Stockman, Reagan's director of the Office of Management and Budget, the nation has long since lost this capacity: "The government is overloaded at the national level . . . we simply can't make wise decisions on the thousands of issues that come before us."[31] The president elaborated further on this point, linking it to his view of the original intentions of the policy capacities of the federal government:

> [The Founding Fathers] knew well that if too much power and authority were vested in the central government, even if intended for a noble purpose, not only would liberty be threatened but it just wouldn't work. . . . I think during the last decade and before, we've gotten a taste of just what [they were] warning us about. So much power had centralized in Washington that frustration and stagnation ruled the day.[32]

To help reduce the load on the federal government, conservatives take seriously the idea of juridical divisions between the public and private spheres and between the federal and the state and local spheres. As President Reagan stated in his inaugural address, "It will be my intention to curb the size and influence of the federal establishment and to demand recognition of the distinction between powers granted to the federal government and those reserved to the states or to the people."[33] These juridical divisions, even if not as absolute as much of the conservative rhetoric might suggest, can serve—especially if they are regarded as nearly absolute—to protect the federal government from excessive demands and to limit the size and scope of its responsibilities.

Of course, conservatives believe that limiting the role of the federal government is important, irrespective of the consequences for governance in the narrow sense, because of their interest in promoting key conservative values such as economic liberty and self-reliance. Most commentators, in fact, assume that conservatives derive their view of the limited role of government almost entirely from considering these ends and not from an independent analysis of the issues of governance. Yet this view, it seems, seriously underestimates the significance that conservatives now attach to the issue of governance as an important question in its own right. The crisis of government as identified by conservatives involves not just what government should do but what it can do.

The Attack on the Policymaking State

To solve the crisis of governance, conservatives hold that it is necessary to change expectations about the capacities and limits of government. This

---

31. Quoted in paper by Wolman and Teitelbaum in this volume.
32. "Prayer in School," Radio Address to the Nation, February 25, 1984, *Weekly Compilation of Presidential Documents*, vol. 20, no. 9 (March 5, 1984).
33. "Inaugural Address of President Ronald Reagan." *Weekly Compilation of Presidential Documents*, vol. 17, no. 4 (January 26, 1981).

has translated into conservative resistance to the "policymaking mentality" that has given rise to the modern policymaking state. In its place, conservatives seek to promote (or protect) a mentality based on juridical distinctions and a "political" or prudential logic. At issue in this debate is a basic difference between the liberal and the conservative theories of governance.

A guiding tenet of American liberalism is its objective of "rationalizing" both society and the process of governing—that is, including more areas of societal activity for explicit scrutiny, with the goal of developing a general policy to improve society. Contemporary liberals have attempted to change the character of political discourse by arguing that even where there is no explicitly legislated general federal policy for a given area of societal activity, a policy of sorts may be said to exist because (a) certain government actions taken on an ad hoc basis may already exercise an influence on the activity in question, and (b) a "decision" has in effect been made, whether consciously or not, *not* to take action, which "decision" can be said to have a profound impact when compared to the situation that would have resulted had certain actions been taken. In this view, once it is established that government has a policy, the only relevant question is whether the current policy is as rational as any conceivable alternative. Since not taking any action is said to be as much of a "policy" as acting, it has no greater claim to legitimacy; or, to reverse the proposition, an interventionist plan has, a priori, no less claim to legitimacy than a non-interventionist plan. All policy options enjoy a right of equal opportunity, if not in the eyes of Nature's God, then at any rate in the calculations of cost-benefit analysis.

Conservatives, however, tend to resist this mode of thinking and to avoid using the policymaking vocabulary. To admit that either a series of ad hoc measures or the nonexistence of action constitutes a "policy" has the political effect of putting large-scale and systematic intervention on the same footing, thereby undermining the presumption in favor of a limited government (if indeed that presumption still exists). The consequence of opening up all matters to "rational" policy analysis, where rationality is, in reality, often much weaker than the claims made on its behalf and where it is often used as a cover for various political appeals, is to make it more likely that more areas of social activity will be put on the agenda and that public authority will be significantly expanded. For the conservative, the logic (and language) of policymaking should be subservient to a prior political logic (and language) that protects certain political objectives. According to this way of thinking, there may be considerable wisdom in refusing to view all governmental decisions as elements of policymaking. Pressed repeatedly by a reporter to spell out his planned "new policies" and "new initiatives," President Reagan replied: "If there are new programs that'll be beneficial, why yes. . . . But right now I think a great deal of our problem is that government has attempted to do a great many things that aren't government's proper role."[34]

Of course, the conservative's resistance to a policymaking approach is not automatic or absolute. Many in the Reagan administration and in conservative think tanks make extensive use of policy science—in particular of analysis that derives from microeconomics. This is not unexpected: By and large the conclusions derived from microeconomic analyses have supported approaches that are much less interventionist than many current policies, and conservatives have therefore relied on them extensively to lay the foundation for new conservative alternatives (antipolicies) that seek to undo some of the interventionism of recent times. Yet, while policy science can be helpful to conservatives in combating schemes for intervention, one might say that the more vague policymaking mind-set described in the preceding paragraphs is not. It is this mind-set and its attendant impact on the terms of political discourse that is one of the greatest threats to conservative values today.[35]

The Political Strategy of the Conservative Response

In addition to this effort to change perceptions about the process of governing, conservatives have sought programmatic and institutional changes that would reduce the incentives of participants to make demands on the federal government. The main components of this strategy have been: (1) a shift of public-regulated responsibilities back to the private sphere, (2) a shift of responsibilities from the federal government to the states and localities, (3) a change in the expectations of the "new dimension" of modern government—that is, the policy analytic/interest-group network, and (4) a change in the "fiscal constitution" or underlying doctrine of public finance. The first of these components involves the obvious attempt to reduce the overall load on government by removing demands and pressures from the agenda of federal politics. Deregulation and resisting the demand for a federal "industrial policy" have been part of the Reagan program. As these matters are discussed elsewhere in this volume, this paper will concentrate more attention on the other three.

Federal-State Relations.   Talk of a fundamental redistribution of responsibilities between levels of government has been one of the most prominent themes of the Reagan administration. The administration has sought to

---

34. *Weekly Compilation of Presidential Documents*, vol. 20, no. 12 (March 21, 1984).
35. See Steven Rhoads, *The Economist's View of the World* (London: Cambridge University Press, forthcoming).

accomplish this redistribution by means of a change in the nature of the grant program, under which more grant money would be given in the form of block grants rather than categoric grants; a cessation of most new federal initiatives, which, by leaving the states as the only important source of new initiatives, would have the second-order effect of increasing the states' range of responsibilities; and by an historic sorting-out process—the "new federalism"— under which there would be a kind of "constitutional" settlement (without a formal constitutional amendment) in regard to the functions that the federal and the state governments would assume.

Of these three strategies, the last would clearly be the most direct way to ensure an institutional change that would endure beyond the current administration. The president, however, had no success with his new federalism plan in 1982, and the idea of a direct frontal assault on the question of federalism was dropped. The first two strategies are less certain to produce major changes, since they are not supported by any explicit recognition of new roles for the two levels of government; nevertheless, if adhered to consistently, they could over a period of years alter fundamental patterns of behavior and accomplish silently as much or even more than a "constitutional" settlement. In pursuing these two strategies, the administration has been quite successful. A greater reliance on block grants has reduced federal discretion in intergovenmental relations; and, more importantly, the paucity of new federal programs and the public assertions that new initiatives must come from the states have had a significant impact. Several new policy areas, which almost certainly would have resulted in new programs by the federal government under an administration holding a liberal theory of governance, have become domains for action by the states, educational policy being perhaps the most prominent example.

The New Dimension. The Reagan administration has sought to lessen the influence of the policymaking and interest-group network in Washington, D.C. While it has employed (like the Carter administration) a rhetoric of moral invective against interest groups, it has also adopted a strategy for changing the expectations of these groups by reducing their *incentive* to operate in Washington: If there is nothing to gain from the federal government, there is less reason to exhaust resources by lobbying in the nation's capital. In respect to incentives, if not yet to long-term expectations, the Reagan administration has already had a significant impact. There has apparently been a reduction in the size of the interest-group network in the nation's capital and a transfer of focus on their part to lower levels of government. The only question at this point is whether these changes represent a new pattern of behavior or merely a temporary tactical shift that would be quickly reversed by a change in the party holding the presidency.

The Fiscal Constitution.   The fiscal constitution refers to the dominant view, as reflected in the practices of government, of the doctrine of public finance. A position respecting the fiscal constitution may be an integral part of, or an important influence on, a theory of governance.

Supply-side economics is the controversial economic theory that has influenced the Reagan administration's practice of public finance (at least in the short term). It is not known, and may never be known, to what extent the president and his advisers subscribe to every tenet of this theory, as it has been judged within the administration as a doctrine of *political* economy and not just as an economic doctrine. A modern doctrine of political economy is political in at least three senses: (1) in its potential to win votes (an electoral concern), (2) in its potential to be comprehensible and ''sellable'' to the public (no economic doctrine can be sustained in a democratic system unless it wins a popular constituency), and (3) in its effects on helping to carry out key political objectives espoused independently of economic consideration—for example, reducing (or expanding) the scope of government, or decentralizing (or centralizing), political power.

The last consideration is extremely important, since in modern politics the responsibility of government for economic well-being has emerged as one of the dominant concerns in the political system. Under this view, political values, rather than taking precedence over economic assumptions, are often ''hidden'' behind them. Thus, instead of arguing that there are certain political objectives to accomplish whose economic consequences are not clear, politicians today tend to argue that they have an economic doctrine that can bring prosperity, and that incidentally it brings along with it the necessity of enacting certain political changes as well. Politics, at least ostensibly, has been mortgaged to economics.

It is a mistake, accordingly, to believe that political leaders judge a doctrine of economic theory solely on the grounds of their judgment of its economic performance. They also consider—and, up to a certain point, quite legitimately—the political ramifications of adopting a particular economic theory. (Indeed, to the extent that political leaders become more skeptical of the claims of the effects of various economic theories, the political consequences of alternative economic theories may loom more important in their calculation.) Generally, however, one may assume that politicians' deliberations on doctrines of political economy are not either/ or propositions in which the economics is thought to be completely sacrificed to the politics or the politics to the economics. The two probably tend more or less to be believed together. Thus, the Keynesian doctrine of political economy served for many years as an ideal theory of public finance for liberals.[36] As an economic doctrine, it offered a set of nostrums for how to make the economy function well—in other words, how to make it grow with high employment and without high inflation. As a political doctrine it provided a marketable popular theory that promised to bring prosperity and legitimated the growth of the public sector. Liberals could thus argue that the same programs that assured the health of the economy also permitted an expansion of the policymaking domain of the government and provided for greater social justice. Supply-side economics offered the same prospect, in reverse, for some conservatives.

As an economic doctrine, supply-side theory holds that the key to producing economic growth is to increase incentives to produce. This can be done only by cutting the amount of nonproductive expenditures—in other words, the size of government expenditures—and by reducing the marginal tax rates. The novel element of this theory was its assertion that a decrease in marginal tax rates was more important in the short run than balancing the budget, because any effort to balance the budget at current (or a higher) level of government expenditures would leave a weak economy without any prospect for sustained growth (and, hence, without any real prospect of balancing the budget). According to this logic, the order of business was to cut government expenditures and marginal tax rates, even if in the end the budget were not brought into balance. The most optimistic corollary—the ''voodoo'' element—was that the growth engendered by these changes would eventually generate more tax revenues and permit the budget to be balanced.

For some conservatives, the most troubling element of this theory was not its optimism but its radical assertion about the capacity of economics as a science to predict and control social behavior. The claims of supply-side economics are no less vaunted than were those of the liberal Keynesian economic doctrine. If Keynesian economics asserted that there was a science of economics that could made the economy work by means of governmental manipulation, supply-side economics was no less confident in arguing that there was a science of economics that could make the economy function perfectly by reliance on the market. The risk, of course, is that the whole of the conservative public philosophy and theory of government is wagered on the performance of the economy—a wager the Reagan administration clearly lost in 1982 but appeared to be winning in 1984. While there are no doubt

---

36. I am using *Keynesian* here to refer not necessarily to what Keynes himself said, but to the way he was interpreted by a group of American economists who appropriated his name. For a discussion of this distinction, see Herbert Stein's *Presidential Economics* (New York: Simon & Schuster, 1984), pp. 45–50.

better and worse doctrines of political economy, some conservatives have objected to the idea of linking their political principles to the fate of the short-term performance of the economy. Whether, in modern politics, it is possible to dissociate the two is a question no one has answered.[37]

As a political doctrine, in addition to the political appeal it may have had in 1980, supply-side economics was remarkably efficient in helping the administration to attain its political objectives of reducing the rate of built-in growth in domestic federal spending and taxes. In 1981 the supply-side argument that the only way to stimulate economic recovery was to cut domestic spending and reduce taxes was a direct political aid. After 1981, the theory worked in an indirect and perhaps unforeseen way by leaving the nation a budget deficit so large that it was difficult to contemplate any new, massive federal expenditures. Supply-side economics thus enforced a kind of budgetary discipline (on domestic, nonmilitary spending) and helped to turn the focus of political activity back to the states. As President Reagan said in one news conference: "Very few of you have realized that for the last three years, unlike the last fifty, there haven't been arguments going on in Washington about whether or not and what to spend additonal money on. The arguments have been on where do we cut."[38]

Yet, if functional as a short-term strategy, the idea of maintaining budgetary discipline by running large deficits may not prove viable over the long run. Apart from the increased costs of carrying a deficit and the (possible) adverse effects on the economy, there is the psychological problem of becoming inured to large deficits. What is an unacceptably large deficit this year may be perfectly acceptable by next year.

Conclusion

In its attempt to implement a new theory of governance, the Reagan administration thus far has enjoyed only a partial success. Certain steps within the discretion of the president have been taken, such as waging a battle to protect presidential prerogatives in the conduct of foreign affairs and minimizing the populist basis of presidential authority. Yet the most ambitious plans to change the institutions of government, such as the plan for new federalism and the budget balancing amendment, have not been achieved.

---

37. Harvey C. Mansfield, Jr., "The American Congressional Election: Reagan's Recalcitrant Economy," *Government and Opposition*, vol. 18, no. 2 (Spring 1983), pp. 144–156.

38. *Weekly Compilation of Presidential Documents*, vol. 20, no. 12 (March 12, 1984), p. 400.

This result has led some to argue that after one term the Reagan administration has failed to "institutionalize" its "conservative revolution." As Hugh Heclo and Rudolph Penner argued in 1982, "Very little of the Reagan agenda has, as yet, been institutionalized in government. . . . There has not been landmark legislation or other actions that could be expected to bring long-term changes in the way government works in Washington."[39]

Yet this claim may exaggerate the extent to which the *direct* manipulation of institutional factors is responsible for creating the most enduring transformations of the American political system. Many changes result from new patterns of behavior that evolve in response to different ideas and different programs. It is only after a certain time, when these patterns become more or less permanently fixed, that they are then judged with the aid of hindsight to have been major institutional changes. This was the case, for example, with many of the changes in federal-state relations that occurred in the New Deal era. It would be a mistake, therefore, to underestimate the possible cumulative impact of the patterns of behavior that have begun to emerge since 1981, although most of these will require at least one more conservative administration before becoming permanent fixtures of a new institutional environment.

39. Hugh Heclo and Rudolph Penner, *National Journal*, January 23, 1982.

PART TWO

POLICY FORMULATION

THE BUDGET AS AN INSTRUMENT OF PRESIDENTIAL POLICY

Allen Schick

President Ronald Reagan and his budget director, David Stockman, have dominated federal budgeting during the early 1980s. This paper considers whether these national leaders have significantly altered budgetary practice and whether the changes they have instituted are likely to endure—in other words, a decade or more from now, will we look back at the Reagan era solely in terms of personalities whose imprint was deep but transitory, or will we find that the conduct of budgeting was changed in ways that affected succeeding administrations?

In its early years the Reagan administration concentrated on the substance of budget policy to the virtual neglect of the machinery of government. The administration's frenetic, improvisational budgeting style, with its numerous appeals for public support and seemingly endless rounds of brinksmanship and negotiation, suggests that although federal programs and priorities have been significantly altered, the budgetary process that Ronald Reagan bequeaths to his successors may be the same one he inherited in 1981. Thus far in the 1980s there has been no "big-bang" budget innovation comparable to planning-programming-budgeting (PPB) in the 1960s or to zero-base budgeting (ZBB) in the 1970s. Rather than building new institutions, the Reagan administration appears bent on attenuating old ones, for its top-down, centralized mode of budgeting impairs the role both of departments in preparing requests and of the Office of Management and Budget (OMB) in reviewing them.[1]

---

1. For a discussion of how top-down budgeting has impaired budgetary patterns, see Hugh Heclo, "Executive Budget Making," in Gregory B. Mills and John L. Palmer, *Federal Budget Policy in the 1980s* (Washington, D.C.: The Urban Institute Press, 1984), pp. 255–291.

Yet this behavior may itself be an effort to alter or at least to dislodge budgetary practice. Significantly, the administration's tactics have been similar to adaptations under way in a number of other industrialized democracies that, like the United States, are beset by a mismatch between the established routines of budgeting and the demands placed on the budgetary process by contemporary economic and political conditions.[2] None of these countries (with the exception of Canada) has devised a new budgetary system; all have sought ad hoc means of coping with the incapacity of their conventional processes. The breakdown of established institutions may be a prerequisite for far-reaching innovation, or it may portend the incapacity of contemporary democracies to cope with the budgetary demands placed upon them.[3]

When Ronald Reagan and David Stockman took command of the budgetary process in 1981, its effectiveness as an instrument of presidential policy was doubtful. In March 1981 I wrote that

> the shocks administered to the federal budget by Ronald Reagan shortly after he took office in January 1981 were more than an attempt to reorder government priorities by spending more on defense and less on social programs. The President wanted to reestablish White House control over the budget; he wanted it to be a statement of his policies rather than a testament to presidential impotence.[4]

The Reagan administration has weakened budgetary institutions because these get in the way of presidential objectives—objectives not just of conservative presidents but of all chief executives who would redirect national budgetary policies. If this administration leaves a meager institutional legacy, it will be because in these times it has proven more convenient to tear down and improvise than to make durable structural changes.

The Reagan administration is one episode in the long flow of budgetary history. To understand this episode, one must begin with the problems that faced budgeting before the electoral tide of 1980 swept a conservative president into office. What the Reagan administration has done in the budgeting field is largely a response to the conditions it found when it first tackled the federal budget. Liberal presidents might not have reacted in the same way,

---

2. Countries that have made piecemeal but significant changes in their budget practices include Australia, Denmark, the Netherlands, and the United Kingdom.

3. This statement is based on my study, currently underway, "The Capacity to Budget," which has been undertaken by the Organization for Economic Cooperation and Development (OECD) to compare the effects of recent economic and political pressures on the budgetary practices of industrialized democracies. Useful insights on contemporary budget developments are presented in Daniel Tarschys, "The Scissors Crisis in Public Finance," *Policy Sciences*, vol. 15 (1982), pp. 205–224.

4. Allen Schick, "The Problem of Presidential Budgeting," in Hugh Heclo and Lester M. Salamon, eds., *The Illusion of Presidential Government* (Boulder, Colo.: Westview Press, 1981), p. 85.

but they would have faced many of the same problems. So also will future presidents, unless the capacity of budgeting is restored or unless other processes are devised to take its place.

Ronald Reagan's Budget Problem

Despite several waves of innovation, the formalities of federal budgeting have remained remarkably unchanged since the process was designed more than sixty years ago. Stripped to its basic routines, the process revolves around the formulation of requests by government agencies, review by OMB (the Bureau of the Budget from 1921 to 1970), submission of the president's recommendations to Congress, and appropriation of funds to agencies by Congress. These four stages link to form a self-contained, insular process whose purpose is to provide the financial resources spent by the government.

During most of the first half-century of executive budgeting, the federal government made budgets by talking to itself. Budgetary discussions and the flow of data and proposals were closed to outsiders: Agency requests were sealed and leaks were rare; Budget Bureau hearings and the budget director's review (at which most budget decisions were finalized) were conducted behind closed doors—the president's budget really was news because few details were known before its official release; and the Appropriations Committees met and marked up their bills in executive session. The results of the private discussions were revealed to outsiders in budget documents and appropriations bills, but outsiders did not formally participate in the process. An Appropriations Committee member once explained why the committee heard so few outside witnesses: "Budget and appropriations are operations in support of the government. It's between the legislators and the administrators, and the public isn't involved—well, they're involved indirectly but not directly."[5]

Undoubtedly, the insular budgetary process was permeated by outside influences such as economic conditions and political demands, but these influences usually were brought to bear indirectly, through requests by administrative agencies and legislative actions by members of Congress. Consequently, the correspondence between budget decisions and outside preferences was uncertain, though it was often assumed.[6]

---

5. Quoted in Richard F. Fenno, *The Power of the Purse: Appropriations Politics in Congress* (Boston: Little, Brown & Co., 1966), p. 343.

6. This is one of the assumptions underlying Aaron Wildavsky's *The Politics of the Budgetary Process*, 4th ed. (Boston: Little, Brown & Co., 1984), but Wildavsky's failure to examine budgetary outcomes leaves one without a basis for examining whether budget decisions do correspond to political preferences.

Budgeting was organized around a series of routines that stabilized the roles and relationships of participants, ensured that required tasks were completed on schedule, and legitimized the outcomes. Some routines (such as the annual budget timetable and the instructions for submission of estimates) were formal; others (such as incremental norms, which narrowed budgetary attention to proposed spending increases) were informal. Despite the insularity of the process, there generally were few surprises when the budget was released and appropriations reported. The routines made the process and outcomes flowing from it predictable.

The closure and routinization of budgeting conformed to the structure and role of the federal government from the 1920s through the early post–World War II period. Most of the budget was spent by agencies on their own operations; it made sense, therefore, for the process to be closed. In general through this period, fiscal policy was static or limited, and decisions made early in the process concerning total revenues and expenditures were usually adhered to in later budgetary stages.[7]

The president's role in budgeting was defined by routines that enabled him to advance salient objectives without investing inordinate time in the process. The president made tentative decisions early on and then withdrew until the Budget Bureau reviewed agency requests, after which he attended to a small number of appeals. By concentrating on incremental issues, the president avoided searing budget battles and still got his way on most of the things that mattered to him.

The Budget Bureau, as master of the information flow, had no serious challenger for control of the budget process. Most of the bureau's decisions were accepted (if only grudgingly) by agencies, and even the Appropriations Committees, which resented the bureau's influence, did not really question its lead.[8] Indeed, most spending decisions made by these committees were

---

7. This finding emerges from a study of presidential budgeting by David C. Mowery, Mark S. Kamlet, and John P. Crecine, "Presidential Management of Budgetary and Fiscal Policymaking," *Political Science Quarterly*, vol. 95, (1980), pp. 395–425. The authors found that during the Eisenhower era, budget decisions conformed to relatively fixed targets set early in the process, but that in later administrations the targets were regarded as provisional numbers that were expected to change in the course of the process.

8. Richard F. Fenno sums up the House Appropriations Committee's view of the president's Budget Bureau as follows: "The Committee's view is that the Bureau does not, cannot, and should not function as an adequate guardian of the Treasury. A sizable minority of the Committee members interviewed expressed outright antagonism toward the Bureau. . . . The critics expound the theme that the Bureau is 'arrogating unto itself' the constitutionally grounded task of the Committee. . . .

"Whatever the attitude—and this is the crucial point—all members agree that the estimate prepared by the Budget Bureau is the place to begin and not a figure that should be accepted as authoritative" (Fenno, *The Power of the Purse*, p. 101).

incremental adjustments to the president's budget. Although the Appropriations Committees claimed to be watchdogs of the Treasury Department, they effectively protected presidential interests in Congress.

With presidential/Budget Bureau power virtually undisputed, it was possible to decentralize budgeting without jeopardizing presidential interests. Budget preparation was mostly bottom-up, with agencies preparing their requests with little policy guidance from the White House. The agencies—not the Budget Bureau—defended the president's budget in Congress; yet they rarely breached the rules that barred them from actively soliciting higher appropriations than the president had recommended. The appropriations process was fragmented—with more than a dozen separate spending bills each year and an equal number of quasi-autonomous appropriations subcommittees in each chamber—yet the totality of the actions resulting from these various processes usually did not significantly conflict with the president's budget preferences.

In sum the president exercised control with a light touch, intervening at key points but permitting executive agencies and congressional committees to conduct their business without heavy White House involvement.

Displacement of Presidential Budgeting

The president is still the nation's chief budget maker, but his influence is not as pervasive as it once was, and to be felt it must be exercised much more forcefully than was previously true. No single event or change has been the turning point in weakening the president's hold on the budget; rather, the displacement must be explained as the cumulative effect of a large number of small changes in budgeting.

This evolution has been most pronounced in the changing composition of the federal budget. As already mentioned, as late as the early postwar period, most of the budget was spent by agencies on their own operations. Today, over three-quarters of the funds appropriated to agencies are passed through to outsiders who actually spend the funds provided by the government. Each year, more than $100 billion is transferred to state and local governments, more than $100 billion to bondholders, more than $400 million to beneficiaries of federal entitlements, and tens of billions of dollars to contractors and other countries.

In the face of this radical transformation, the routines of budgeting have continued relatively intact from year to year. It is still government talking to itself, as if it alone had a stake in the outcomes. But how are the interests of outsiders—who do not directly receive appropriations but who actually spend most of the money—conveyed to executive and congressional budget makers? How do agencies proceeding in bottom-up fashion articulate claims in behalf of the real spenders? How does Congress satisfy these claims by making appropriations to agencies that are not the real spenders?

As the composition of the budget changed, resources were allocated increasingly through legislative rather than budgetary decisions. Legislation shaped the great entitlements programs that now consume half of the budget, as well as the hundreds of grant programs that tripled the state-local share of federal outlays from 5 percent in 1950 to 15 percent in 1975. Budgeting by legislation is a political process in which interested parties (whether inside or outside government) try to influence the outcomes. The process is conducted in the continuing relations between agencies and their clients, in the use of media to shape public opinion, in the lobbying of congressional committees and members, and by any other means that has the potential to improve an interest group's budget status.

A politicized budget process cannot abide the closure that attended the routine administrative process nor can it permit budgeting to be confined to a small band of participants. Hence, as an expanding percentage of the budget has been spent by outsiders, the process has been increasingly opened to their influence. Leaks of agency requests to OMB have become common, as have news stories on OMB "marks" and "passbacks" to agencies.[9] On occasion, the letters of appeal spent by agencies to the president have made their way to news outlets and congressional offices before the White House has issued its final decisions. The result is that most of the key budget decisions are known before the budget is released. The opening up of the budget process has also affected congressional behavior, in that most appropriations hearings and markups are now open.

In addition, there has been a considerable increase in the number and variety of budgetary participants. On the executive side, White House aides have major roles in bringing the interests of affected groups to the president's attention. They often participate in internal OMB budget reviews and in the president's consideration of agency appeals. In Congress, the Budget Committees have been added to the roster of participants, and most authorizing committees have become more informed and active on budget matters than they were a decade ago. They have also become more influential as an increasing portion of the budget is decided in "backdoor legislation" that

---

9. Terminology often is indicative of changes in behavior. *Ceilings*, which convey a sense of finality, became *marks*, which suggest tentativeness. The term currently in use—*passbacks*—suggests the greater strength of agencies in contesting OMB budget recommendations.

bypasses the appropriations process. With the establishment of the Congressional Budget Office (CBO) and the enlargement of legislative staffs, a legion of committee and member aides now are involved in budgeting on Capitol Hill.

If more openness and participation were the only by-products of the changed composition of the federal budget, the president's budget capacity would not be measurably diminished. But these changes have rippled through the budget process to weaken the president's ability to get his way. When the president and his aides review budget requests, they must reckon with the possibility that agencies and interest groups will use leaks, congressional allies, and sympathetic media to publicly challenge the budget that is still in the making. The problem is not simply that the White House must be sensitive to how others will react to the budget, but that the president cannot easily manage budget perceptions and expectations by controlling the flow of information. In the past, one of the great sources of presidential strength was the secrecy that shrouded the budget and veiled its questionable assumptions, conflicts, and compromises from the public view, so that when the budget finally emerged, it was almost as if Zeus had given of his wisdom and beneficence to the populace.

The open bickering that now typically precedes release of the budget taints the way it is subsequently received. Almost immediately after it is officially unveiled, the budget is likely to be challenged (and in some years discredited) by the instant analyses that flow from interest groups, research organizations, and congressional staffs and that subject its economic assumptions, spending priorities, and policy recommendations to in-depth examination. No longer in command of the sources of budgetary data and wisdom, the president finds that Congress treats his budget as just one of a number of options that might be considered.

As the budget process has become more transparent and the circle of participants wider, the White House has perceived a need for more "eyes and ears" to deal with affected parties. As a consequence, the executive office has been staffed with aides who keep in touch with recipients of federal dollars (such as state and local governments) and advise the president on specialized issues such as agriculture and energy. These staffs attend OMB reviews, negotiate with agencies and interest groups on budget matters, and provide the president with an array of budget options. The president now hears more varied views than he did when OMB held full sway over the budget process, and he has a greater opportunity to weigh budget issues in terms of the effects on, and possible reactions of, outsiders who have a stake in the outcome. But there also is more conflict within the president's orbit as the various participants compete for presidential attention and support. In the process, the president's budget competence may be eroded by perceptions that his office is torn by contention and indecision.

The extent to which the president is incapacitated by the transformation of budgeting depends in large measure on economic conditions. When the economy is buoyant, as it was in the early postwar era, the president can influence the budget by controlling the allocation of incremental resources. Even if mandatory entitlements and pressure from interest groups bar him from making major changes in the "base," he can put his mark on the budget by increasing the resources for the programs he cares about. Inasmuch as incremental resources for program expansion are not taken from current programs, the president can confidently expect much of his legislative program to be approved by Congress. This incremental behavior can persist despite the ups and downs of the business cycle, provided that the downturns are brief and the recoveries vigorous. During recessions, the government can take a countercyclical stance and, by allowing automatic stabilizers and discretionary expenditures to prop up the economy, continue to behave as if increments were still available to it. If the downturns are protracted, however, and/or the recoveries weak, high unemployment will drain the public sector of incremental resources. If stagnation is accompanied by high inflation (as it was in the 1970s), indexed entitlements might compel the government to spend resources not provided by economic growth. Without incremental resources available for program growth, the president's budget role might be limited to estimating the future cost of past decisions.

The foregoing paragraph assumes that the president wants to expand federal programs. In fact, this has been the posture of most presidents from Franklin Delano Roosevelt to Jimmy Carter. An incrementalist president can significantly alter budget priorities without curtailing (in nominal terms) the resources provided to any sector of the budget. He can accomplish this objective by having the various parts of the budget grow at different rates. If, however, the president wants to cut back on government, he must do something about the rising costs of past decisions. No matter how vigorously he prunes agency requests, this budgetary objective will be thwarted if entitlements and other mandatory expenses are permitted to continue their upward trend.

Prior to the Reagan administration, no president since the New Deal had sought a substantial curtailment in the size of government. Reagan's budget problem, therefore, was partly rooted in substantive policy, but the problem would have confronted any president faced with a sluggish economy and expansive entitlements.

Incapacity of the Budget Process

In the chaotic aftermath of his landslide election, Reagan hardly attended to the budgeting machinery. He had more pressing matters to deal with—a looming economic crisis and a determination to cut tax rates and to increase defense spending while shrinking the overall size of government. A sense of urgency and opportunity pervaded the new administration that saw Republican capture of the Senate and the prospect of a renascent conservative coalition in the House of Representatives as a once-in-a-political-generation opportunity to revamp the nation's economic policy and its budget priorities. But if structural changes in the budgeting process had to be relegated to the sidelines, Reagan and Stockman were certainly aware that problems resulting from these processes had also plagued previous administrations. These problems included:

1. *Uncontrollable and unbudgeted expenditures.* When the Reagan administration took office, more than three-quarters of total federal outlays were "uncontrollable under existing law,"[10] compared to less than 60 percent of total outlays a dozen years earlier when comparable statistics were first compiled. The level of mandated expenditures—principally social insurance and income transfer programs—cannot be determined by budgetary actions alone. If the government underestimates the amounts required for mandatory programs or if appropriations are insufficient to cover required costs, additional funds have to be provided, regardless of the condition of the economy or of other claims on the budget. The only way to curtail these expenditures is to the change the laws that require them, but this entails legislative approval, which, in ordinary times, is hard to obtain.

   Mandatory expenditures not only consumed the bulk of the budget, they also accounted for most of the year-to-year rise in public expenditures. Even before he prepared the budget, the president discovered that virtually all of his spending discretion was crowded out by uncontrollable spending. Moreover, because many of these expenditures were linked to the performance of the economy, they forced frequent, and sometimes unwanted, shifts in budget policy. Indeed, in the Carter years, changes *within* budgets were more sig-

---

10. The term "uncontrollable under existing law" has been devised by the U.S. Office of Management and Budget to cover various fixed costs and obligations. Each year, the U.S. Budget reports on the expenditures deemed to be uncontrollable under existing law.

nificant than changes *between* budgets, as evidenced by revenues and expenditures that deviated substantially from anticipated levels.

Uncontrollables stood in the way of a number of Reagan objectives; they threatened the shift from domestic to defense spending, because most uncontrollable spending went for nondefense programs. In 1980 (the last complete fiscal year prior to the Reagan administration) approximately two-thirds of the defense budget was deemed to be controllable, while more than 80 percent of nondefense spending was classified as uncontrollable. Uncontrollables also accounted for much of the upward, unbudgeted creep in the relative size of the federal government.

2. *Unstable budgets.* In the years leading up to the Reagan administration, budgeting became an unstable process, with numerous mid-course jolts during each fiscal year. Fresh economic news or shifts in political sentiment swayed the president from his intended budget course before Congress had an opportunity to act on his original proposals. The result was that budgeting became a virtually continuous, rather than a cyclical, process. Continuous budgeting had a number of adverse side effects: heightened political conflict, expedient and unreliable economic forecasts and assumptions, and a shortened time horizon. Continuous budgeting also destroyed budget routines and made it easier for Congress (and interest groups) to discredit or compel revisions in the president's budget after its submission. Instead of regarding the budget as the starting point for its subsequent actions, Congress saw the budget simply as one stage in the year-round process of negotiating with the White House. In this process, rather than merely making (formerly marginal) changes in the budget, Congress could demand that the president revise his own revenue and spending plans. This is exactly what happened to Jimmy Carter less than a year before Reagan was sworn into office.

3. *Ineffective fiscal policy.* During its prime in the postwar era, the budget came to be seen as a reliable instrument of economic stabilization. Governments were confident that they could ensure continued growth (despite some recessions) while maintaining high employment and low inflation. Moreover, it was possible for these objectives to be accomplished without large deficits and without enlarging the relative size of the federal sector. However, in the 1970s, two oil shocks, stagnation, and high interest rates robbed the government of confidence in the budget as an instrument of fiscal policy. Where once the budget was thought to stabilize the economy, now the

economy destabilized the budget. Rather than the budget restoring the economy to vigor, now budget health could not be achieved unless the economy first recovered. This budgetary conundrum led to the stop-go policies described earlier, as administrations lurched from one course to another in search of something that would work.

4. *Fragmentation and independence of congressional budgeting.* The establishment of the congressional budget process in 1974 was a mixed blessing for the White House. It brought some consolidation to legislative consideration of financial matters, but not necessarily on presidential terms. The new Budget Committees quickly became the marshaling point for congressional opposition to President Gerald R. Ford's tax and expenditure policies. By the time Jimmy Carter became president in 1977, the committees were sufficiently entrenched to strongly shape the economic and budget proposals he submitted to Congress. The new Congressional Budget Office was building a reputation as a skilled puncturer of presidential economic assumptions and a bold second-guesser of the president's policies. The congressional budget process was hailed by leading congressional members as a declaration of independence from presidential budgetary influence, and with Democratic cohesion in the House and bipartisanship in the Senate, it was working out that way.

But presidents were not troubled by the budget process alone. They also had to deal with tax matters in the custody of the Ways and Means and Finance Committees; the Appropriations Committees, which were behaving as spending advocates rather than as budget cutters; and the authorizing committees, which had muscled themselves piecemeal into positions of budgetary influence. The many participants provided multiple channels for those seeking to undermine the president's budget policies. The president had to keep watch over all the areas in which Congress made money decisions, and he could never be certain that success at one stage would bring victory at the next.

Ronald Reagan's budget prospects in Congress were markedly enhanced by the 1980 elections. Nevertheless, a wily and recalcitrant Congress still had the means to thwart Reagan's budget objectives. It could vote with him (on budget resolutions) for lower spending and smaller deficits, then ''nickle and dime'' the policy to death by adding small amounts to a large number of programs; it could kill proposed savings in entitlements simply by failing to act on them; it could vote less for defense than the president wanted but more for domestic programs; it could attach spending items to veto-proof legislation; and so on. Reagan and his budget aides indeed sensed that if the Congress that convened in January 1981 were to behave as usual, his budget objectives would be undermined.

5. *An irrelevant executive budget process.* If Reagan was confronted by a potentially contentious congressional budget process, he was furthermore armed with an executive process ill suited for the problems at hand. Bottom-up budgeting was ineffective because it relied on agencies to generate requests and to monitor congressional compliance with his budget. Agencies could be expected to submit incremental requests and to drag their feet when called upon to propose retrenchments. Moreover, the process was still organized as if most spending decisions were made by discretionary appropriations. Reagan could have prevailed on every discretionary issue and still lost the battle of the budget. He needed a budget process that was centered around the White House and its concerns, not around the particular interests of federal agencies.

From Dunkirk to Blitzkrieg to Stalemate

Shortly after the 1980 election Stockman moved boldly to make budget policy the cornerstone of the new administration's economic and political policy. In his "Dunkirk memorandum" prepared for the president (and cosigned by Congressman Jack F. Kemp), Stockman argued for sizable spending cutbacks to curtail the deficit and avert an economic crisis.[11] The memorandum, and Stockman's appointment as OMB director, gave him license to attack the structure of domestic programs that had been erected over the previous half century. Within a month after inauguration, Ronald Reagan unveiled a Program for Economic Recovery that called for $45 billion less spending in fiscal year (FY) 1981 than Jimmy Carter had requested in his farewell budget for the same fiscal year.[12] The president also proposed $200 billion in reductions spread over the next three fiscal years, and he projected a drop in the budget's share of the gross national product (GNP) from an estimated 21 percent in FY 1981 to 19.3 percent in FY 1984. The Reagan

---

11. The memo bore the signatures of David Stockman and Congressman Jack Kemp of New York. Excerpts appeared in the *New York Times*, December 14, 1980.

12. See Ronald Reagan, *A Program for Economic Recovery* (February 18, 1981), containing the president's address to Congress on his budget and economic program, along with a discussion of major policy proposals.

program envisioned a growth in defense from one-quarter to one-third of total expenditures and a corresponding drop in domestic discretionary spending other than "social safety net" expenditures from 29 percent to 18 percent of the total. Along with spending reductions, the president asked for a three-year tax reduction that would slash almost $150 billion from annual revenues by FY 1984 but would still produce a balanced budget in that fiscal year.

Although both the tax and spending reductions were to be spread over a number of years, presidential success hinged on having them all enacted at the start of the new administration. On the revenue side, this entailed three annual 10 percent tax cuts to be adopted in one law; on the expenditure side, the Reagan team skillfully exploited the congressional reconciliation process to have the program reductions combined in an omnibus bill. The reconciliation procedure (first used successfully in 1980) provided for Congress to instruct committees (in a budget resolution) to report legislation changing the levels of revenues or expenditures for programs in their jurisdiction, and for the recommended changes to be considered in an omnibus reconciliation bill. This device made it possible for the administration to compel recalcitrant committees (especially those in the Democratic-controlled House) to report legislation that they might have otherwise been able to pigeonhole. As used in 1981 the reconciliation instructions required the affected committees to report spending reductions for each of the next three fiscal years, thereby enabling Reagan to achieve multiyear cutbacks in one measure.[13]

Further assistance was provided by the Republican capture of the Senate, as well as by remarkable Republican cohesion on key budget votes in both chambers.[14] The new Senate Republican leadership quickly mobilized to put the president's program on a fast track, adopting a budget resolution/reconciliation package more than a month before the date prescribed by the Congressional Budget Act. Although this resolution was not acted upon by the House (the Senate later passed another budget resolution that also accommodated the president's demands), it did set the stage for the budgetary blitzkrieg that led to the enactment of most of the tax and spending cuts in the summer of 1981. The House succumbed to intense White House pressure—Reagan made several appeals for public support on prime-time television and held dozens of one-on-one meetings with moderate Republicans and marginal Democrats—and narrowly adopted the budget resolution and reconciliation bill

13. For a discussion of the reconciliation process, see Allen Schick, *Reconciliation and the Congressional Budget Process* (Washington, D.C.: American Enterprise Institute, 1981).

14. Reagan's budget strategy is analyzed in Allen Schick, "How the Budget Was Won and Lost," in Norman J. Ornstein, ed., *President and Congress: Assessing Reagan's First Year* (Washington, D.C.: American Enterprise Institute, 1982), pp. 14–43.

favored by the president. The tax cuts, which were scaled back to 25 percent (rather than 30 percent) over three years, were enacted into law after a bidding war between House Democrats and the White House that led to the addition of generous business depreciation allowances to the bill.

Although the spending reductions cut a broad swath through the domestic budget—cuts in more than two hundred accounts totaled more than $100 billion—the administration got significantly less than it asked for or that Congress believed it was giving. "There was less there than met the eye," Stockman confided in his famous interviews published in the *Atlantic Monthly*.[15] Both the Democrats and Republicans had reason to exaggerate the size of the reduction, the latter in order to claim more savings and the former in order to save more programs.

Regardless of how the savings were computed, it quickly became evident that they would not suffice to cover a growing budget deficit. Barely a month after he signed the tax and reconciliation bills into law, Reagan returned to Congress with new demands for cutbacks and for revenue enhancements to restore some of the lost revenues. Congress, however, refused to comply. Rather than using expedited procedures to cut through legislative recalcitrance, Congress followed the regular order and considered the president's request in a series of appropriations bills. This tactic enabled opponents to effectively organize against the new cutbacks. Congress also made skillful use of continuing resolutions (which provide interim funding to agencies that have not yet received their regular appropriations for the new fiscal year) to force the president to accept higher domestic spending than he preferred. In November 1981 President Reagan closed down much of the federal government by vetoing a continuing resolution that did not include $8.5 billion in additional spending cuts that he had sought, but within days he signed another continuing resolution that also failed to enact the desired cutbacks.

In 1982 the president and Congress fought to a budgetary stalemate, with neither side strong enough to consistently prevail over the other. The year began with submission of a budget that projected a $90 billion deficit but that was estimated by the CBO to carry a $120 billion shortfall. The year ended with unemployment soaring to 10.8 percent and the deficit reaching toward $200 billion. In between, there were numerous budgetary confrontations between the president and Congress, frequent threats to veto "budget-busting" appropriations, brinksmanship over tax legislation, and the enactment of spending bills above the president's request but below the level wanted by congressional Democrats.

---

15. Quoted in William Greider, "The Education of David Stockman," *Atlantic Monthly*, December 1981.

The worsening economic and budget conditions led to a summit conference between presidential aides and congressional leaders (the "gang of 17"), which broke up in disagreement over tax and budget policy. Congress passed and the president vetoed two supplemental appropriations that contained billions more for domestic programs than the president was prepared to accept. Congress retreated and approved a trimmed-down bill that the president signed in July 1982. Two months later, however, Congress passed another supplemental appropriations bill with $1 billion more for domestic programs and $2 billion less for defense than Reagan had budgeted. This time Congress prevailed and it overrode the White House veto.

Despite initial resistance, the president accepted tax legislation that was expected to bring almost $100 billion additional revenues to the Treasury over a three-year period. But in the give-and-take, the president won adoption of assorted cutbacks that totaled $30 billion over the same period. The year's budget battles ended with the president signing a continuing resolution that added billions above his budget for education, health programs, and employment but that sliced $17 billion from the amount budgeted for the defense buildup.

Presidential-congressional budget conflict resumed in 1983, and once again stalemate ensued. The president's bargaining position was weakened by the midterm election, which added twenty-six Democratic seats in the House and broke the Republican-conservative Democratic stranglehold. The budget (for FY 1984) projected a $189 billion deficit and continuing economic adversity. Congress exhibited a great deal of independence in cutting the defense increase in half, but it was unable to win White House support for a tax increase to narrow the deficit. Significantly, however, the appropriations bills moved through Congress much more expeditiously than they had in previous years, and ten of the thirteen regular bills were enacted into law. Presidential threats to veto appropriations that exceeded the budget were not implemented. The president even signed fiscal 1984 appropriations for the Departments of Labor and Health and Human Services that totaled $8.6 billion above his request.

It is difficult to calculate whether Congress or the president came away from the give-and-take with the better part of the bargain. The White House prevailed on tax policy, because once the multiyear tax cut was enacted, the president could afford to be intransigent. His willingness to accept some tax increases in 1982 enhanced his opposition to a repeat performance in 1983. Congress came out slightly ahead on regular appropriations bills, but at the price of rather modest supplementals. Existing programs were generally protected against another round of retrenchment, but the Democrats were compelled to abandon most of their contemplated expansions.

The Tactics of Budget Control

The budget story chronicled in the previous section shows that the president has combined steadfastness in budget policy with flexibility in budget tactics. As his first term draws to a close, Ronald Reagan speaks as firmly about the virtues of smaller government and lower taxes as he did in the 1980 campaign. The wavering and ambivalence that characterized previous administrations has been replaced by a determination to stay the course. The president remains convinced that the best expenditure policy is a tax cut, and he has therefore opposed strong congressional demands for a bipartisan accommodation to narrow the deficit through tax increases, moderation of the defense buildup, and some additional domestic cutbacks. By keeping a lid on tax increases, the president believes that he will force Congress to accept lower domestic spending.

But each year's budget has followed a somewhat different route. Through budgetary blitzkrieg, the president imposed most of his demands on Congress in 1981. In 1982 presidential aides and a congressional "gang of 17" tried but failed to reach agreement on a budget resolution, after which the president reluctantly accepted a small tax increase engineered by Senate Republicans. In 1983 the president and Congress battled to a budgetary stalemate as the White House succeeded in protecting its multiyear tax cut, congressional Democrats restored some of the additional domestic cuts proposed by the president, and the defense increase was cut to about half the requested amount. The president launched the 1984 budget cycle with a call for a bipartisan executive-legislative commission to tackle the awesome deficit, but this proposal was quickly forgotten in the hustle of election-year politics.

I would argue that the failure of the White House to make significant structural changes in the budgetary process has been due in part to its emphasis on budgetary tactics. A government bent on curtailing expenditure must be extremely sensitive to the potential reaction of those who would be adversely affected. It cannot merely propose cutbacks and then let the budget process run its course, as might be appropriate if it were seeking incremental growth. It has to devise tactics that improve its probability of success. In this environment, tactical aspects of budgeting—such as how the cutbacks are presented to the public and to Congress, and the position of OMB vis-à-vis spending agencies—have become quite important. These strategies uproot budget routines because they vary from one budget cycle or political season to another, the only common element being an opportunistic assessment of what is most appropriate for the objectives of the moment. The budget process is plotted as if it were a military campaign. Should the White House and OMB ask for unrealistic cuts in the hope that this ploy will improve their

changes of winning some reductions? Should they act without advance warning in the hope that the shock treatment will overwhelm the opposition before
it can be effectively mobilized? Or should they try to build political support
for retrenchment by consulting with affected groups or by openly airing the
fiscal problems that compel them to make cutbacks?

OMB's tactical orientation explains the unusual manner in which it has
launched some budget cycles under Stockman. Rather than following the
customary practice of looking ahead to the economic and financial prospects
for the next year, OMB has sometimes looked back at the results of the cycles
of the previous one or two years, to determine which tactics were successful
and which were not. This retrospection makes sense if the quality of the
budget process is measured in terms of the degree to which the president's
proposals have been implemented; however, it is not sensible if the quality of
budgeting is evaluated in terms of the programmatic choices flowing from it.

Tactical behavior can disrupt budget routines because it encourages participants to seek ways of gaining an advantage with respect to others, rather
than attempting to reach budgetary agreement. The budget cycle can become
irregular when big, controversial packages have to be assembled, debated,
and implemented. Moreover, tactical thinking leads participants to explicitly
alter or disregard routines so as to improve their bargaining position. In late
1983, after OMB had started to review its requests for FY 1985, agencies
were instructed to submit new, lower requests. While they were preparing
revised requests, OMB continued to prepare final budget recommendations
for the president based on its review of the original estimates. This tactic
strengthened OMB's budget-cutting position, but at the expense of an orderly
budget process.

Packaging the Budget

A major tactical consideration revolves around the issue of whether the
cutbacks should be grouped into a single package or split into a number of
separate votes. One advantage of a package—such as the reconciliation bill—
is that it enables the government to argue that the burden of restraint is widely
(and fairly) distributed. Another is that it enables the president to insist that all
the cutbacks be acted on as a unit, thereby weakening opposition to individual
reductions and making it easier for legislators to support the whole package.

After its initial success in the spring and summer of 1981, the Reagan
administration was forced into piecemeal negotiations with various authorizing
committees and appropriations subcommittees over their parts of the budget.
There is a definite link between the concentration of budgetary power in 1981
and its dispersion in subsequent years. The unprecedented packaging of so

much substantive legislation and spending matters in a single measure ignited widespread fears on Capitol Hill that the Budget Committees, armed with the power to force other committees to report legislation, would bypass the regular committee process and dominate Congress. The 1981 experience poisoned the well for reconciliation and led to a much more limited use of this process in the 1982–1984 period.[16]

Without full use of reconciliation, the administration has been forced to negotiate on a piece-by-piece basis with committees over programs in their jurisdiction. These negotiations are not over packages to curtail total expenditure of the deficit but over particular items of expenditure. Moreover, these fragmented negotiations are not usually with congressional leaders or Budget Committee members but with spending advocates who are determined to get as much as they can for programs they care about. The White House has found that these advocates are everywhere on Capitol Hill, in both political parties, in both chambers, and in both authorizing and appropriating posts. From this perspective, Stockman's endless budget negotiations and the overuse of the threat of a presidential veto can be seen as evidence of presidential weakness, despite the outward appearance of strength.

In this piecemeal relationship, the best the White House can hope for are partial victories. Under threat of a veto, committees have somewhat moderated their demands, but they have forced the president to accept more spending for social programs and less for defense than he wanted. Reagan has skillfully alternated praise of Congress's bipartisan cooperation with attacks on its budget-busting proclivities, but he has been reluctant to veto spending legislation that diverges significantly from his budget policy. His cause was injured by the 1982 recession and by congressional weariness over protracted budget battles. High unemployment stimulated legislative pressure for jobs bills, for aid to the poor, and for assistance to hard-pressed communities. It also gave rise to feelings that the president's program is unbalanced and unfair and that domestic programs should not be so sharply reduced when defense spending is booming.

Working the Hill

The short-term tactical considerations that have driven White House–congressional budget relations have resulted in little value being placed on

---

16. The 1981 reconciliation process was applied to discretionary authorizations, as well as to revenue legislation and entitlements. That extensive use generated a great deal of opposition from the authorizing and Appropriations Committees. Therefore, since then, reconciliation has not been applied to discretionary authorizations.

the development of structures to promote trust between the two branches and to facilitate timely and responsible budget action. The main losers have been the Budget Committees, whereas the big winners have been the Appropriations Committees. After exploiting the budget process to obtain the Omnibus Reconciliation Act of 1981, the White House downgraded the value of the Budget Committees when they produced resolutions at variance with its budget objectives. In 1983 the budget process in Congress nearly collapsed when the White House successfully pressured Senator Pete Domenici to delay markup of the budget resolution and when Secretary of Defense Caspar W. Weinberger (and other executive officials) let it be known that they preferred no resolution to one that did not fully subscribe to their budget objectives. This short-term emphasis on tactics has given the administration a few budget victories but no durable means of support from those in Congress who share the president's guardianship values. It has, moreover, undermined the potential for comprehensive negotiations on the budget and has made it more difficult for Congress to approve significant program retrenchments. It also has forced the White House into one-bill-at-a-time negotiations in which it faces program advocates rather than budget guardians.

The locus and outcome of these negotiations depend on the issue under dispute. In the case of mandatory entitlements, OMB must deal with authorizing committees, which can block changes sought by the White House. Lacking action-forcing, comprehensive reconciliation, presidential aides negotiate from a position of weakness. In 1983, for example, the agriculture committees successfully pressured the president to sign a bill strongly opposed by his budget director, using the argument that the president's budget policy would be more adversely affected by a veto. The White House has a stronger role when new authorizations are advanced, because it can use the threat of a veto to thwart legislative initiatives.

The appropriations process has also been affected by the Reagan style of executive-legislative relations. The status of the Appropriations Committees has been enhanced by the decline of the Budget Committees, and the role of the former has varied with the behavior of the latter. In 1982 the Appropriations Committees maneuvered to obtain passage of a continuing resolution fattened by numerous items that the president might have warded off had they been presented to him through regular channels. But in 1983 most of the regular appropriation bills were enacted by the close of the session (though not by the start of the fiscal year), and the continuing resolution was a relatively lean measure. Rather than being used as a vehicle for "Christmas-tree" spending schemes as had been common in recent years, the continuing resolution was generally limited to interim funding for agencies that lacked regular appropriations. Many of the spending initiatives that might have drawn presidential wrath were shunted aside to supplemental measures.

It is too early to ascertain whether this recent behavioral change will last, but it may depend on the role of the Budget Committees. At the apogee of the budget process in 1981, the budget resolutions and the reconciliation bill determined subsequent appropriation decisions. Because budget cutting affected discretionary programs that are the stock-in-trade of the appropriations process, the Appropriations Committees were bereft of a useful role in the legislative process. They could not cut programs, because that task had already been accomplished. In quest of a niche of their own, the Appropriations Committees acted as program advocates, a role they had been moving toward in the previous decade.[17] These committees led the battle against the second round of budget cuts demanded by President Reagan in September 1981. In 1982 they willingly provided more funds than the president wanted, though they kept within the limits set in the budget resolution. When the budget process was threatened with paralysis in 1983 and 1984, the House Appropriations Committee came forward with its bills without waiting for adoption of the budget resolution. Seeing an opportunity to demonstrate that it could responsibly handle the budget without the overlay and frictions of the budget process, the committee reclaimed its role as guardian of the purse by playing the incremental role in which it had long excelled. It doled out increases to existing programs, was stingy in its treatment of new programs, and made sure that the appropriations process operated smoothly by moving the regular bills through Congress and freeing the continuing resolution of most extraneous matters.

The Reagan Budget Legacy

Although it has approached the annual budget battles in tactical terms and has made little effort to restructure the budget process, the Reagan administration has contributed to the evolution of budgeting in a manner consistent with patterns that began to emerge before Reagan's inauguration. This section looks at four of these developments: centralized budgeting, a more active presidential role in the legislative process, multiyear budgeting, and a more comprehensive resource allocation process. These developments are logically linked to the changing composition of the budget, a factor identified

---

17. For a discussion of this role shift, see Allen Schick, *Congress and Money: Budgeting, Spending, and Taxing* (Washington, D.C.: The Urban Institute, 1980), chapters 10 and 11.

early in this paper as a prime source of presidential incapacity. Each development in its own way is an effort to adapt federal budgeting to the fact that resources can no longer be controlled through conventional budget routines alone. Although these adaptations are associated with the Reagan administration, it is important to note that the initiative and support for some of them have stemmed from the legislative branch (and particularly from the Budget Committees) and that these developments respond as much to congressional budget problems as to presidential ones.

Two other budget developments are also examined in this section, but they were inspired by different considerations. One is the administration's fiscal policy; the other is its emphasis on financial control.

The Budget as an Instrument of Economic Policy

In the Carter years, fiscal policy was virtually paralyzed by mandated expenditures, by a wide discrepancy between assumed and actual economic conditions, by loss of confidence in Keynesian prescriptions, and by the confluence of inflation and unemployment. Budget decisions made to ameliorate one of these economic ills would exacerbate the other, forcing politicians to change course before their policies had a chance to work. The results were inconstancy in fiscal policy and budget outcomes that varied sharply from those sought by the president.

Reagan's "supply-side" approach was an effort to break out of this policy morass and to thereby restore the budget's usefulness for economic policy. According to this approach, tax cuts and curtailment in the relative size of the federal sector would make fiscal policy once again effective. Spending on particular programs would be forced downward by shrinkage of the resource base of government. Smaller government would revitalize the economy by encouraging work, savings, and investment. And both inflation and joblessness would drop.

Neither the economy nor the budget has behaved as contemplated. The tax cuts have not significantly spurred saving nor have they fed back to the Treasury the sums taken away by the 1981 legislation. With booming defense spending and only partial realization of the proposed domestic cutbacks, the prospect of a balanced budget has given way to huge and seemingly intractable deficits. Inflation has been lowered, but at the price of high unemployment. Economic recovery has been vigorous; however, the path taken to achieve it has been costly.

Economists will continue to argue over supply-side theory, but the political verdict already is in. The theory has failed, and as a consequence the nation still lacks a viable fiscal policy. The $200 billion deficits projected through the 1980s are one measure of failure. Deficits of this magnitude may prove to be economically manageable, but politically they convey the powerful message that the policy has failed. Even those who believe that big deficits do not contribute to inflation or to high interest rates cannot argue that the current ones are the result of deliberate policy choices. The deficit, rather, is the residual of all the budgetary actions and inactions of the executive and legislative branches; it was not chosen on the basis of a fiscal rule.

A second sign of policy failure is high unemployment, which may afflict the economy for many years. One of the principal political attractions of Keynesian and supply-side economics was the expectation that both inflation and unemployment would be mitigated. Budget policy would benefit much of the population without imposing significant costs on any sector. The Reagan administration may be right in making inflation its first target, but high joblessness is likely to lead to pressure for a reversal in economic policy.

A third problem is the continued growth in spending. The federal sector has not receded relative to the overall economy; indeed, its relative size is significantly larger than when Reagan entered office. The parts continue to drive the totals, as high defense spending, interest on the growing debt, mandated increases in entitlements, and discretionary appropriations exert upward pressure on the budget. This pressure suggests that the president has not succeeded in moderating the budgetary expectations of the recipients of federal dollars. The multiyear cutbacks enacted in 1981 forced many claimants to shift their immediate objective from program enlargement to damage limitation, but one or two seasons of budgetary disappointment have not uprooted long-entrenched expectations. Congress and interest groups still are poised to push domestic spending well above Reagan's budgeted levels. Several FY 1984 and 1985 appropriations were significantly above budget.

The Reagan fiscal strategy might have worked if the federal government still consisted principally of agencies spending money on their own operations. By trimming agency requests, the president might have been able to keep them in line with his budget policy. But most of the domestic budget is sucked up by a small number of transfer programs whose beneficiaries are mobilized to protect their interests. The president has won some battles against weak interests (welfare recipients, for example) but he has not taken many benefits away from strong ones.

The Reagan policy plays to the well-known preference of the American people for smaller government and lower taxes, but it has not come to grips with the fact that the American people also want maintenance of services and benefits.[18] The contradictions in the Reagan budget plan are the contradictions of public opinion. Unless the latter are resolved, the former cannot be either.

Centralized Budgeting

In a volume in the Urban Institute's Changing Domestic Priorities series, Hugh Heclo analyzes the shortcomings of top-down budgeting as it has been practiced by David Stockman, claiming that it has been destructive of budget routines and has debilitated OMB's institutional capacity. Top-down budgeting, he claims, has led also to insatiable demands for data, while cutting off the flow of analysis and evaluation needed to enrich budgetary data.[19] Yet two considerations compelled the administration to centralize budgeting: the first was its drive to curtail expenditure; the second was the changed composition of the federal budget discussed earlier in this paper.

Bottom-up budgeting relies on agencies to submit claims for resources, with little central guidance. OMB then trims the requests to fit the president's budget. This arrangement is oriented to incremental growth in expenditure, for once demands have been presented to OMB, they strongly influence the outcome. If the White House seeks retrenchment, however, OMB cannot merely react to spending demands; it must close off pressure for more money before it is too late. Centralized budgeting has enabled Reagan and Stockman to put their stamp on the budgets submitted to Congress. Unlike incremental budgets, these have been made by the White house and OMB, not by the spending agencies.

If top-down budgeting were merely a response to the perceived need for retrenchment, it would endure only so long as budget parsimony. But if it derives from the need for a new decision-making structure for budgeting, then it might persist even if the domestic spending constraints imposed by the Reagan administration were relaxed. Yet, the durability of top-down budgeting is hampered by the lack of a structure to implement it. The ongoing routines of bottom-up budgeting are organized around the preparation of agency requests, but centralized budgeting has been based on the work style of OMB Director Stockman. Top-down budgeting has been imposed improvisationally on the existing budget structure, with the result that existing routines have become less useful and no new ones have taken their place.

---

18. These contradictions are analyzed in Royce Crocker, "Federal Government Spending and Public Opinion," *Public Budgeting and Finance*, vol. 1, no. 3 (Autumn 1981), pp. 25–35. See also paper by Ladd in this volume.

19. See Heclo, "Executive Budget Making," in *Federal Budget Policy*, pp. 255–291.

The prospects for entrenchment of centralized budgeting are furthermore called into question by the failure to devolve financial management powers to agencies. Agencies have not only been called upon to make do with less money, but they also have less say over the dollars they get. A flow of OMB directives have narrowed agency discretion. This administration does not trust federal managers to do the right thing; therefore, it is unwilling to entrust them with greater responsibility for the details of expenditure. The problem for OMB and the president, however, is that the federal budget is too big and sprawling for them to exercise effective control by managing the details. If they worry about the number of personnel, travel and printing costs, the use of consultants, and so forth, they may neglect the major factors that propel federal expenditures.

Executive-Legislative Relations

During the Reagan-Stockman era, OMB has been mobilized to serve the director's continuing need for up-to-date data on congressional activity. OMB's Central Budget Management System (CBMS) provides Stockman with current data on the status of budget-related legislation and on the estimated impact of pending measures on the president's budget. With this scorekeeping capability, Stockman continually cajoles committees and members to produce legislation more in line with the president's budget than they might if left to their own designs. With calculator and data in hand, Stockman appears to be ubiquitous on Capitol Hill, rushing from one meeting to another and pressuring Congress to budget according to his numbers. His pace is frenetic because Congress is a spasmodic and disorganized institution, with many things happening simultaneously.

To serve their director's insatiable need to know what is happening in Congress, OMB staff regularly attend hearings and markups and report back to him on the progress of budget-related legislation and on issues that might pose problems for the president's spending or revenue policies. Staff have been deployed, Hugh Heclo has suggested, in much the same manner as are legislative aides in Congress.[20] The perspective is short-term, and the daily schedule is driven by the opportunities or crises of the moment.

This congressional orientation is a far cry from the old Budget Bureau, which withdrew from the scene once the president's budget was submitted to Congress. Under that system, the budget director and other administration spokespersons participated in overview hearings conducted by the Appropri-

20. Ibid.

ations Committees or the Joint Economic Committee, but responsibility for defending the particulars of the budget fell to the spending agencies. The president and the Budget Bureau could limit their involvement in congressional business because they were confident that most appropriations would be close to the recommended levels.

The old style is unsuited for contemporary budget conditions, however, and no bemoaning the loss of institutional competence will bring it back. Indeed, the Stockman behavior is a continuation of trends that began in the 1960s and accelerated after passage of the 1974 Congressional Budget Act. There has been increased exposure of the president's budget organization to congressional activity. Prior to the 1960s the budget director rarely appeared on Capitol Hill; since then, he has testified with increasing frequency at congressional hearings; and in the 1970s, he was made subject to Senate confirmation. The entire budget organization also has become more sensitive to congressional activity because of the transformation of the budget discussed earlier. The emplacement of politically appointed associate directors (PADs) in OMB's chain of command gives it greater capacity to deal with the growing number of committees and members active in the budget field.

One factor that has not changed is the responsibility of agencies to justify their budgets before appropriations subcommittees. Nevertheless, this elaborate ritual has become increasingly irrelevant to budget outcomes. Most funds are spent by recipients who lack a formal role in the appropriations process, while the "salaries and expenses" accounts on which the appropriations subcommittees concentrate are a declining portion of total expenditure. Cross-agency issues such as intergovernmental finances and assistance to target groups have been neglected in the appropriations process, which is still organized to review agency budgets rather than federal programs.

The new budget process has a centralizing potential because it provides for Congress to adopt budget resolutions spanning all federal revenues and expenditures. The process offers the president a more cohesive means of monitoring and influencing congressional activity than was possible before the Budget Committees were created. But this potential was not realized during the first years of the process. During Ford's presidency, policy disputes between the Republican White House and the Democratic Congress interfered with their common interest. When Carter was elected, extensive negotiations between the president-elect and congressional leaders led to an economic stimulus package of tax cuts and spending increases. OMB did not play a role in these negotiations, but Budget Committee leaders did.

Formal negotiations between OMB (and other presidential officials) and congressional leaders occurred in March 1980, two months after President Carter submitted his fiscal 1981 budget to Congress. Reaction to the budget was adverse, as interest rates and inflation continued their upward spiral. The resulting lengthy negotiations led to submission of a revised budget with lower spending and a projected surplus.

This virtually unprecedented summit conference broke new ground in presidential-congressional relations and established a basis for negotiation between the legislative and executive branches that has continued with Reagan. But there are two important differences between the 1980 precedent and subsequent relationships: First, in 1980, the two sides bargained from a sense of parity and shared interests, while in the Reagan years they have been brought together to iron out important differences between the two branches; second, in 1980 and in the first year of the Reagan administration, congressional leaders spoke for the legislative branch, but since then a fragmented Congress has engaged in numerous piecemeal negotiations with OMB and White House officials.

The spirit of consensus that animated the 1980 negotiations was chilled by Reagan's electoral triumph. Armed with a mandate and spurred by a sense of crisis, the President and OMB eschewed time-consuming negotiations. The terms of budgetary compliance were dictated to the newly Republican Senate by the Reagan White House, and the necessary votes in the House were secured by pressure applied to bollweevils and to other marginal Democrats. Rather than bargaining with Congress, the president bypassed it in television appeals for mass support. However, once the advantages of the president's honeymoon and the perceived crisis were dissipated, the president and OMB had to come to the bargaining table and deal on a more equal footing with congressional leaders. The fact that the terms and conditions of bargaining have differed from year to year strongly suggests that the president's role in congressional budgeting has not stabilized.

Multiyear Budgeting

In the past, budgeting for the expenditures of government agencies was effectively conducted in a one-year framework. The president would recommend and Congress would appropriate an amount to be spent by agencies in the next fiscal year. This process was well-suited for marginal adjustments that keyed spending levels to changes in political and economic conditions.

But when the bulk of expenditure goes to outsiders, as is now the case, the lead time for budget control lengthens. State and local governments require some advance notice if there is to be a substantial change in the level or purpose of federal assistance; recipients of transfers need time to adjust to losses in take-home pay; and payments to contractors depend more on past commitments than on current budget decisions. Because of these lead times, if the president were to propose, and Congress to approve, significant budget reductions, the impact on the next year's spending would be relatively small. However, these cutbacks can make a big dent in spending for the years further in the future. To budget for these cutbacks requires multiyear decisions stretching beyond the scope of the annual budget.

The House and Senate Budget Committees began to move to multiyear budgeting during the Carter administration. A major advance occurred in 1981 with the issuance of three-year reconciliation instructions to congressional committees and the enactment of more than $100 billion in cutbacks spread over the 1982–1984 period. Packaging was used to overcome the limits of an annual budget. By phasing in the reductions over a three-year period, Congress made them a bit more acceptable to affected groups and also ameliorated the disruptions that might have occurred if they had been put into effect without delay. But judging from the Reagan administration's experience, multiyear packages tend to lose popularity as the government continues in office and as opposition to them grows. The perceptions or conditions that initially prompted the multiyear reductions often change or prove to be incorrect, making it necessary to reopen issues that were settled one or two years earlier. In 1983, for example, President Reagan had to fight efforts to restore some cutbacks approved during his first year in office.

The quality of multiyear budgets depends on the reliability of their economic assumptions. There has been a tendency under both Republican and Democratic regimes to base the budget on optimistic assumptions about future economic growth, inflation, unemployment, and interest rates. The first Reagan budget presented in 1981 showed a rosy forecast about the deficitless future that would ensue from vigorous economic recovery—a future of low inflation and low unemployment levels. The problem with erroneous forecasts is that current budget policy often is based on them. Thus, multiyear budgeting, rather than strengthening financial control, can lead to escapist decisions.

The Reagan administration has had a checkered record in economic and budgetary forecasting. After optimistic projections in both 1981 and 1982, it issued a dire forecast in 1983, only to shift back to a more buoyant outlook in the preelection budget presented in 1984. Although the Reagan presidency has made greater use of multiyear techniques than its predecessors, it has not used them to come to grips with the deficits forecast for future years.

Comprehensive Budgeting

The conventional budget process described in the first part of this paper usually had a simple financing arrangement—Congress would appropriate funds for the expenses of government agencies. As more of the budget came to be composed of transfers to outsiders, however, the government devised a wider array of means to provide assistance. In addition to direct appropriations, assistance was provided by lending funds to eligible beneficiaries; by guaranteeing loans to them; by granting deductions, credits, and other reductions in tax liability; and by other forms of subsidy. Because such subsidies were nontraditional financing mechanisms and did not entail direct appropriations, they were typically excluded from the federal budget. It is often argued that loans, tax expenditures, and other "off-budget" assistance were developed to evade budget control. However, a more balanced view holds that these devices also grew because of the enlarged role of the federal budget in providing assistance to firms and households.

One of the major developments of recent years, under prodding from Congress, has been the use of a credit budget for setting forth total direct and guaranteed loans and allocating these totals among the various budget functions. The credit budget parallels the regular budget. The president recommends limits on direct and/or guaranteed loans for each account having these transactions. Congress authorizes credit programs in the same manner that authorizing legislation establishes direct expenditure programs. A credit budget is included in each budget resolution. The final step in credit budgeting is the enactment of limits on annual loan activity in appropriations bills.

Tax expenditure budgeting has also emerged, although much of this predated the Reagan administration. Tax expenditures—the revenues lost through deductions, exclusions, and other special provisions—are reported in the federal budget, but they are not directly controlled through the budget process.

Financial Control

Multiyear control and more comprehensive budgeting emanated from the congressional budget process and were applied by OMB to the executive budget process. OMB has also followed Congress's lead in strengthening financial management in federal agencies. Congress has passed laws (in some cases over executive branch opposition) bolstering the role and independence of inspectors general; it has established standards of "internal control"; and it has legislated concerning debt management. The Federal Managers' Financial Integrity Act of 1982 (PL 97-255) requires federal agencies to maintain systems of accounting and administrative control in accordance with standards prescribed by the controller general. Pursuant to this law, OMB issued circular A-123 (August 16, 1983), governing the internal control systems of federal agencies. OMB also has issued instructions for the control of travel costs, consulting services, procurement, and paperwork. In 1982 OMB launched Reform '88, a drive to improve debt collection, audit recoveries, cash management, personnel usage, information systems, and other aspects of financial management.

This emphasis on economy and efficiency is a throwback to two earlier periods of budgeting: the 1920s when the executive budget process was installed and the first order of business was to impose centralized control on government agencies accustomed to a great deal of financial independence; and the 1950s when Congress passed a number of laws dealing with financial management. Like the two earlier periods, the Reagan era has sought retrenchment in expenditures, and, with the exception of defense, there have been few program expansions.

Toward More Effective Presidential Budgeting

The attention given to the budget during the first Reagan years might lead one to conclude that it is once again an effective instrument of presidential policy. Legislative issues have been defined, priced, and decided in budgetary terms. In defense programs, the debate has revolved around the amount of real growth; in domestic programs, the key issue has been the size and incidence of cutbacks. Presidential-congressional relations have been dominated by bargaining over spending and tax bills, and the legislative agenda has been congested with budgetary business. The president has repeatedly used prime-time television to take his budget case to the people, and the Reagan budget policy looms large in the 1984 election campaign.

The public display, however, masks the manner in which Reagan has distanced himself from everyday budget matters. This president probably spends less time on budget preparation than did any of his recent predecessors. He has consigned most agency appeals to a budget review board that acts in his name but that blocks cabinet members from the Oval Office. Whatever his personal reasons for adopting this role, Reagan has sensibly avoided entanglement in the details and pressures of budgeting, thus allowing him to keep a focus on basic objectives: lower taxes, more for defense, and less for domestic programs. Once in a while, presidential distance has generated public controversy or confusion, as it did in 1982 when Stockman and Weinberger squabbled over the defense budget, and in 1983 when agencies exploited conflicting White House signals and initially submitted requests well above the levels Reagan wanted.

Rather than indicating that the budget has become an effective instrument of presidential power, the ''budgetization'' of national policy may attest to the continued weakness of the budgetary process. If Reagan really had won in 1981 when Congress enacted much of his spending and tax program, the budget would have receded in importance. Sustained attention to the budget has been due to (1) the failure of the economy to perform according to presidential expectations; and (2) protracted conflict between the White House and Congress over budget policy.

If the diagnosis of budget problems presented here is accurate, then it should be apparent that the Reagan initiatives have not significantly changed the situation. Most adjustments have been tactical rather than structural, and most have been concerned with substantive policy rather than with budgetary procedure. The agenda of budget problems remains crowded.

In terms of whether any of these initiatives will endure, I think it doubtful that any major change in practice will carry over from the first Reagan administration to the next president's term. Reagan has retaught us the importance of combining mass appeals to the public with one-on-one visits with members of Congress, but he has not taught us how a president lacking his gifts in political communication can be as successful as he has been. Nor has he given us reason to believe that the next president will have an easier time managing an open budget process that remains as vulnerable as it was in 1980 to political pressure and economic flux, that is driven by mandatory programs that account for most of the year-to-year expenditure growth, and that is decided in legislative bodies that fragment budgetary power among three overlapping sets of processes—authorizing legislation, appropriation measures, and budget resolutions.

The situation described in the beginning of this paper applies as much to the 1984 presidency as it did to the pre-Reagan White House. The economy still destabilizes the budget, mandatory costs still drive up expenditures, the president's budget still is beset by leaks and challenges before it reaches Capitol Hill, and (with the remarkable exception of 1981) the president still has great difficulty in getting his major recommendations through Congress.

The administration, it would seem, blames Congress for the budget's difficulties. In 1982 the president castigated Congress's "Mickey Mouse" budget process, and in 1984 Reagan resurrected the idea of an item veto as a means of diminishing congressional profligacy. When viewed more objectively, however, budgetary inadequacy can be seen to exist in both of the political branches of government. If Congress were more accommodating to the president, his budget problems still would not vanish. Moreover, Congress has contributed more than its fair share to budget improvement. Reconciliation, multiyear controls, baselines, scorekeeping, credit budgeting, and the demand for improved financial management have been initiated or strongly pushed by Congress in recent years.

It would not be difficult to identify a large number of budget practices in need of improvement. For instance, economic assumptions and budget forecasts have often been wide of the mark; budgetary decisions have frequently been made without benefit of evaluative findings; significant transactions are excluded from the budget; Congress habitually fails to complete its budget work in a timely manner; OMB usually inaccurately estimates the outlays of federal agencies. But rather than compose a lengthy "improvements" list, it is more appropriate here to identify shortcomings in budgetary practice that detract from a well-functioning presidency. In the paragraphs following, three areas are singled out for brief consideration: the role of the president's budget office; relations of the executive branch with Congress; and control of expenditures.

The Role of OMB

The Office of Management and Budget has had a protracted role crisis since it was created in 1970. The conversion of the old Budget Bureau into a new OMB had two explicit aims: to separate policymaking from the routines of budgeting and to bolster OMB's management capabilities. Neither objective has been realized and both have generated considerable instability and uncertainty in the organization. The separation of policy from budgeting was to be accomplished externally through establishment of a presidential Domestic Policy Staff and internally through the inclusion of political appointees in OMB's chain of command. The internal change has been more successful (and also more controversial) than the external one, but neither change has satisfactorily come to grips with the problems of, first, how to ensure high-quality performance in an institutional staff that no longer has direct access to White House policymakers and, second, how to link the routines of budgeting to the nonroutines of policymaking. Stockman's dazzling success should not obscure the fact that the organization he heads is unsure of its role or of the proper demarcation between the policy and budget spheres.

OMB's search for a niche in management has caused it to embrace and quickly abandon a succession of management innovations: the joint OMB–agency management teams set up in 1972 to review agency management plans were discontinued in 1973; the management-by-objectives process that was launched with so much fanfare in 1973 fell into disuse a few years later; the 1976 issuance of circular A-113, with its long checklist of administrative management procedures, was rescinded in 1977; the management-oriented zero-base budgeting system that arrived with Jimmy Carter in 1977 lapsed into oblivion before the next administration took office; and the latest management model, Reform ' 88, has had no more success than its predecessors in penetrating the routines of budgeting.

While policymaking and management can be regarded as poles of a government process, both suffer from the transformation of budgeting discussed previously. Whereas OMB is still largely oriented (and organized) along departmental lines, policymaking spills across agencies. Policymaking, furthermore, cannot abide the regularities and constraints of budgeting; it must not only be imbued by the personalities and styles of its makers, but it must adapt to the opportunities or problems of the moment. As budgeting becomes more the means of making presidential policy, it must break out of the routines into which its process is confined. If Stockman destabilized OMB, he did it to enhance OMB's capacity to serve the needs and interest of the president. If the next budget director restores some order to OMB, it might be because the budget process's role in driving policy will have been curtailed.

The management role suffers from the fact that budgeting is not really a managerial process any longer, at least not in the sense that management is thought of and practiced in the private sector. The Grace Commission in 1983, like the Ash Council more than a dozen years earlier, recommended that budgeting be subordinated to a wide array of management functions. This will not happen in the federal government. For those who want to give higher priority to public management, the only solution may be to establish a separate management agency, leaving OMB to the routines of budgeting and the spasms of policy. However, if management cannot successfully coexist with budgeting, one cannot be confident that it will flourish alone.

Relations with Congress

Budgetary power has been shared by presidents and Congress throughout American history, by virtue of the fact that while Congress authorizes expenditures, the executive branch makes them. The budgetary relationship between the legislative and executive branches of government has been greatly affected by two seemingly disparate but, in my view, closely linked developments: the transformation of budgeting from a closed process for financing government agencies into an open process for providing benefits to Americans; and the transformation of Congress from a relatively closed and disciplined institution into a more open and fragmented body. The two developments have fed on one another: Congress could not remain as structured and closed when the government was reshaping itself into a distributor of benefits to the public at large; and a more open Congress is more likely to increase the flow of benefits to outsiders. Together, these developments have made federal budgeting more difficult and problematic for the chief executive.

A contemporary president faces a Congress equipped with three parallel processes, as mentioned earlier, for making spending decisions: authorizing legislation, appropriations measures, and budget resolutions. This multiplicity of processes overloads the legislative calendar, it severely burdens executive officials who must bargain with many more committees and legislators than before, it invites delay and confusion, and it opens the door to conflicting decisions and expectations from the legislative branch. In today's Congress a success in one of the budget processes does not ensure success in the other processes (as Ronald Reagan has discovered), while a defeat in one stage still permits combatants to reopen the issues at a later date.

As previously discussed, Reagan has played the processes off against one another, allying himself with the budget-reconciliation process in 1981 and with the appropriations process in 1983. The president has a potentially active role in shaping the distribution of budgetary power in Congress. If he encourages Congress to deal with the budget as a package, he thereby bolsters the Budget Committees; if he insists that the budget be acted upon piecemeal, he strengthens the role of the Appropriations Committees. While the posture of the president may vary from year to year, I would argue that it is in the long-term interest of the White House to improve the budget capacity of Congress. The reason for this is that both branches are exposed to intense pressure from outside beneficiaries; only if they make common cause can they withstand those pressures. They can unite in an extragovernmental organ such as the 1982 Greenspan Commission, which put together the Social Security package enacted by Congress; or in an informal group such as the White House–congressional team that recast Jimmy Carter's 1980 budget or the "gang of 17" that failed to reach agreement in 1982. I would not be surprised if presidential-legislative budget negotiations were to become commonplace, though it is highly unlikely that they will become institutionalized in the near future.

The president can make it easier for Congress to retrench expenditures and recast priorities. To do so requires that the chief executive join with Congress in taking unpopular budget actions, whether they be to cut benefits or to raise taxes. That Ronald Reagan remained on the sidelines in 1983 while congressional leaders looked to the White House for support in deficit-reduction efforts attests to the opportunistic posture he has taken toward Congress. He has obtained political victories from Congress, but he has thereby improverished the capacity of both branches to manage the budget.

Expenditure Control

The methods of expenditure control (whether for retrenchment or expansion) suitable for financing agencies are largely ineffective in controlling the distribution of benefits to outsiders. Agency spending usually is decided at the margins through incremental (or, less frequently, decremental) budget recommendations and appropriations. Resource flows to outsiders are determined by legislative requirements and economic conditions that may conflict with the president's immediate budget interests.

Devices such as the item veto would do little to improve expenditure control, though they might enhance presidential power at the expense of Congress. A president armed with an item veto might be able to bludgeon Congress into accepting his priorities on discretionary programs, but an item veto would not make a dent in mandatory expenditure.

Presidential expenditure control is not well served by the routines of bottom-up budgeting in which agencies labor for months to prepare detailed estimates and justifications that are screened by presidential aides and (usually) reduced somewhat before being forwarded to Congress. The fact that presidential-legislative negotiators can rewrite the executive budget in days suggests that the millions of work hours dedicated to preparing the annual budget are mostly irrelevant to centralized budget making.

The manner in which these negotiations have proceeded offers a clue to how a presidentially oriented budget process might be structured. Rather than working with detailed estimates, the negotiators would concentrate on a small number of categories that (with the notable exception of defense) cut across departmental lines. The main categories are defense, discretionary domestic programs, and one or more categories of entitlement programs. The small number of categories means that the central budget makers have to make only a modest number of decisions. Having decided how much to take from or give to each of the categories, the detailed budget work can then proceed according to presidential (or congressional) plan.

Many things are potentially wrong with this top-down approach. It destroys the routines of budgeting, requires that the principal decisions be made without knowledge of how they would affect particular programs, and breaks the chain of relationships that link federal agencies to the White House. But these problems could be overcome if presidentially oriented budgeting were institutionalized and did not rely so heavily on the ad hoc methods that have been used in recent years. A properly organized presidential process would include means of informing central budget makers of the main choices at hand and of the implications of each, including the effects on and interests of government agencies.

Conclusion

A presidentially oriented budget system will not be easy to design and install. The approach requires much more than a recasting of the processes of budgeting; it must also be built on a fresh consideration of the concept of governance in the late-twentieth century.

This paper has treated budgeting as if it were a self-contained process, independent of the overall governmental environment in which it operates. Such is not the case, however. The problems of budgeting depicted here are the problems of governance. Consider the implications for the conduct of government of the fact that three-quarters of the federal budget is transferred to outsiders. This country has functioned for almost two hundred years with the notion that as chief executive the president presides over an executive establishment that constitutes the U.S. government. But the president is not chief executive of the fifty states and thousands of local governments that obtain $100 billion in federal grants, or of the 36 million Americans who receive Social Security checks each month, or of the State of Israel, which spends more federal dollars than does the U.S. State Department on its own operations, or of the armies of defense contractors whose budget take exceeds that of the U.S. Army.

Until we comprehend what is involved in governing a government of political networks rather than a government of administrative compartments, we will not know how to manage a presidential budget system. When the problems of governance are resolved, then—and only then—will those of budgeting also be solved.

James M. Verdier

Modest Changes Would Help

Allen Schick's paper identifies two central problems of federal budgeting: the president has lost control of the executive budget process and Congress has at least one budget process too many. As Schick's paper suggests, these two problems may have a common solution. To see why this is so, it is useful to step back and ask: First, what purposes should the executive and congressional budget processes serve for the president and Congress? And, second, what major problems must those processes deal with over the next decade?

Purposes of the Executive Budget Process

The executive budget process should serve the president primarily by helping him pursue a few of the high-priority goals of his presidency. The present process, as Schick's paper demonstrates, is not well suited to this purpose, since it dissipates the president's efforts in the tasks of clerkship. Much of what the president does in the executive budget process aids the purposes of others—executive agencies, Congress, the media, interest groups, and program beneficiaries. The budget process provides them with a way to get and keep their concerns on the national agenda.

The executive budget process is designed principally to deal with the "small change" of budgeting—the 25 percent of the budget accounted for by everything other than defense, Social Security, Medicare and Medicaid, and interest on the debt. There is not much a president can or should do about these thousands of small programs—everything from vocational education to rural electrification—but the current budget process makes each of them a potential presidential issue.

President Reagan managed to rise above the limitations of the executive budget process in his first six months in office by acting as if it did not exist. He was assisted in no small measure by the temporary dominance of David Stockman over the rest of the executive branch, the unprecedented unity among congressional Republicans, and the public's inclination to give the new president's program a chance. But this could not last. With no institutional roots, the president's initial success in limiting the agenda proved highly vulnerable both to changes in economic conditions and to the usual erosions that occur when presidential honeymoons are over.

The president needs a budget process that can clear away the underbrush and enable him to focus consistently on the big budget issues that are of presidential dimensions. For the next decade the list is short: defense, pensions, health, and revenues. OMB as it currently operates is not in a good position to deal with those issues. The main expertise in each area is in the agencies directly involved: the Department of Defense, the Department of Health and Human Services, and the Treasury Department. Each area is highly volatile politically and highly visible. Strong congressional committees devoted to these issues must be dealt with directly and continuously. This is not a process that can be left to technicians; it requires political skills of the highest order.

Inevitably a president and his closest aides must work directly with the agencies involved and with Congress on these big budget issues. OMB can certainly assist the president, warning him of possible agency biases and making sure he is aware of institutional and issue histories in the agencies and Congress. But OMB cannot carry the big load over the long term; its expertise on the big issues is too thin and its ties to Congress too underdeveloped.

OMB in its present form is better geared to a different task: keeping as many smaller budget issues as possible off the president's agenda. To a large extent this is what OMB already does. Thousands of issues that a president ought not to have to deal with are stopped short of the White House by OMB. A president who seriously wanted to use the budget process for his own purposes, however, would try to make the screening process tighter than it now is. This might involve some seemingly arbitrary rules—for example: no issue of less than X billion dollars will come to the president. Screening rules could also entail more fundamental institutional changes. For instance, a president might decide that within an overall spending ceiling (based on agencies, budget functions, or broader categories), agencies themselves would be left to work out the actual allocation of spending with the relevant committees in Congress and with OMB. As Schick points out, most of the important spending decisions are now determined by legislative formulas anyway, so leaving the president out of the loop would not be a major change in practice. The president would retain the option to intervene on issues he considered important, but that would be his choice, not one forced on him by others.

The foregoing description of OMB's role may largely conform to the way the process now operates under President Reagan, but it contrasts sharply with at least the public perception of how it operated under Presidents Carter, Ford, and Johnson, who immersed themselves in budgetary detail and welcomed responsibility for a host of small decisions. As Reagan has demonstrated, a president has much to gain by explicitly distancing himself from these diversions.

As an extension of this decentralization of decision making on smaller issues, responsibility for program management could be left more to the agencies than it now is, with OMB bowing out of its current managerial role. With the agencies operating within an overall presidential ceiling, the president's major interests could be protected without intrusive micromanagement from a central agency.

For this ordering of budgetary responsibilities in the executive branch to work, however, the president must have institutional allies in Congress. If not, those who are stopped short of the president in the executive branch will make an end run through Congress and force their way onto the president's agenda whether he likes it or not. The president needs congressional allies who have an interest in keeping small issues off the big agenda. Those allies are already there, in the form of the Budget Committees in the House and the Senate. But for institutional ties to develop, a president must work with those committees consistently, year after year. The alliance cannot be one of convenience, cast aside whenever it does not serve the short-term needs of one of the parties.

The modifications in the executive budget process that I have suggested could also serve the interests of Congress, including the authorization and Appropriations Committees as well as the Budget Committees. The reason for this is that much of the conflict and frustration that have attended the budget process in Congress emanate from the same forces that are at work in the executive branch—too many programs, players, and layers, resulting in decision overload at the top. Common problems beget a common solution—decentralized decision making for the small issues and centralized decision making for the big ones. A closer look at the purposes of the congressional budget process and the issues it must deal with over the next decade will illustrate how this might evolve.

Purposes of the Congressional Budget Process

The main purpose of the congressional budget process, in my view, is to make congressional budget decisions more visible and understandable, so that both Congress as a whole and individual members can be held more accountable. The current budget process does not serve that purpose as well as it might, because it is still much too complicated and difficult for outsiders to fathom. It is evolving in promising ways, however. Movement toward a common baseline and toward common economic assumptions has helped make the process more manageable and comprehensible, while the increasingly common practice of dividing budget resolutions into a few "big-picture" categories—defense, entitlements (means-tested and other), and nondefense discretionary—has helped to clarify the major choices members must make.

The congressional budget process has suffered since its inception from the strains of competition between the Budget Committees and other budget participants. The Appropriations, tax, and authorization committees all have found themselves regularly at odds with the Budget Committees, because they occupy large parts of the same turf. The Budget Committees have value for the other committees as flak catchers—if you have to raise taxes or cut spending, it is better to have someone else to blame for it—but that has not been enough to lessen the strains significantly.

As Schick's paper contends, Congress has at least one budget process too many. Ideally, there should not be separate authorization, Appropriation, and Budget Committees. It is not likely that any of these committees will wither away in the near future, however. What is possible is a reordering of responsibilities among them in a way that will simplify decision making and require fewer decisions by Congress as whole.

The congressional budget process, like the president's, has dissipated itself to some extent in the minutiae of budgeting. When more than 75 percent of projected federal spending in 1989 is accounted for by just four areas of the budget—defense, Social Security, Medicare and Medicaid, and net interest—and when nearly 90 percent of the projected spending growth between 1984 and 1989 is accounted for by those same four areas, the Budget Committees really do not need to concern themselves with much else on the spending side of the budget.

If the Budget Committees were to focus primarily on these big issues, their day-to-day dealings with the other committees would be much less debilitating, and the budget process itself would consume much smaller amounts of congressional time. The Budget Committees could do this by setting overall spending ceilings and revenue floors for a few large budget categories and then leave it to the committees with direct jurisdiction to work out the details themselves. The Budget Committees already follow this model in the revenue and defense spending areas. This gives the tax and military committees the backing they need to enable them to make the hard choices that deficit control requires, without the intrusiveness and poaching on prerogatives that can occur if budget controls become too precise and direct.

The same approach could be followed in other areas. The tax committees could be given an overall target for Social Security and Medicare, while the Appropriations Committees could be given an overall target for all the programs over which they have jurisdiction, perhaps broken down between defense and domestic. Some steps toward this approach with respect to appropriations were taken in the Senate in 1984. The more detailed breakdown of the budget resolution into twenty functional categories, and the elaborate allocation of spending targets to committees (crosswalking), could be downplayed or eliminated.

Changes of this kind in the congressional budget process, along with the parallel changes in the executive budget process suggested earlier in these comments, would enable Congress, the president, and the public to concentrate on the central issues of budgeting over the next decade. Cutting spending on defense, pensions, and health and increasing taxes will still be extremely difficult. No changes in the process can make those hard choices disappear. But focusing presidential and congressional attention on the big budget issues in a way that makes it easier for the public to understand what is at stake strikes me as an essential task of governance in the 1980s and one that relatively modest changes in presidential and congressional budget processes can help to achieve.

More Credit Is Due

Federal budget policy has dominated the news during the Reagan administration's first three and a half years. Taxes have been cut, domestic programs have been curtailed, defense spending has increased, and deficits have soared. The president controlled Congress's budget process one year, confronted it another, and ignored it a third. Allen Schick's paper examines this record of accomplishment and turmoil to determine whether it has brought about any significant changes in budget practices, changes that could overcome the fundamental inadequacies that characterized the budget process when Ronald Reagan took office. The paper concludes that the administration, to date, has left a meager institutional legacy, has made no durable structural changes and that, therefore, its short-run achievements are likely to be eroded by the actions of succeeding administrations.

On Budgetary Shortcomings

This judgment is both too harsh and premature. Certainly, the administration has done little to deal with the five fundamental shortcomings of the budget process identified by Schick—namely, the growth of uncontrollable and unbudgeted expenditures, the instability of the budget, the ineffectiveness of fiscal policy, the fragmentation and independence of congressional budgeting, and the irrelevance of the executive budget process. However, Schick has presented a challenge that no administration could meet even halfway. The first of these problems has its roots in the indexed entitlement programs that the nation wants to provide its citizens; the resultant budget problem is an unfortunate but unavoidable by-product of living in a civilized society that wants to guarantee the real value of the "social safety net." The second and third problems, the unstable budget and ineffective fiscal policy, are attributable largely to the recent wild gyrations of the national and world economies, over which any president has but limited influence. The fourth problem, the institutional weaknesses of Congress, cannot easily be addressed or affected by the president, especially when Congress is not in a mood for reform. Only the continued irrelevance of the executive budget process can be blamed on Ronald Reagan.

But here Schick's pronouncement of failure is premature. As the paper accurately points out, significant changes have begun to occur. Budget decision making has become more centralized both in OMB and the White House. Top-down budgeting has replaced bottom-up budgeting. This has led to the destruction and emasculation of old institutions and capabilities, including a major reduction in the role of cabinet secretaries and of their departmental budget offices. If one believes that these parts of the executive branch consorted with interest groups and congressional committees to incrementally expand the scope of federal policy and to increase federal spending, this institutional emasculation is a significant accomplishment. The task of dismantling the old order is no small undertaking; simultaneously building a new institutional order may not be possible.

Whether these changes persist or are reversed will depend on the decisions of future presidents and the capabilities of their OMB directors. In several respects the climate is good for the continuation of these developments. Inadvertently, to be sure, the president has created an austere budget outlook that will dominate the remainder of the decade. Faced as the nation is with huge structural deficits, spending retrenchment and tax increases will be required year after year. Such an atmosphere will make it difficult to revert to incremental, bottom-up budgeting or to decentralized budget decision making. Already the budgetary expectations of interest groups, politicians, congressional committees, program administrators, and state and local governments have been lowered considerably. Program preservation, rather than expansion, has become the mark of success.

New Institutional Structures

The new institutional structures of an altered budget process may evolve in this environment. OMB has recently developed new capabilities that allow it to track and promote the president's overall budget objectives in the increasingly assertive and fragmented Congress. This new role of a centralized executive budget process has compromised and eroded some of OMB's old strengths and capacities. This is unfortunate, but it may be the necessary price of change.

If the deficit pressure continues, the ad hoc procedures of the past few years could well develop into new routines. A major step in this direction would be the formalization of the White House–congressional budget ne-gotiations that have characterized four of the past five budget cycles. These negotiations have concerned the big budget issues: How large should the tax increase be? How fast should real defense spending increase? What level of austerity should be imposed on discretionary domestic spending? Should re-ductions be made in cost of living adjustments (COLAs) or changes made in basic entitlement legislation? Negotiations between the White House and Congress are an effective way for a centralized executive decision-making process to interact with fragmented congressional budget power. The big issues of these negotiations are, and rightfully so, the focus of presidential involvement and bipartisan collaboration with leaders of Congress. The de-cisions concerning the allocation of available resources across programs, weapon systems, and budget accounts can be left to the old mechanisms.

The procedure of packaging the major budget decisions in a reconciliation bill, a budget resolution, or an omnibus budget bill may also become routinized in the remainder of the decade. Already, the reconciliation tool has been tried and proven to be a capable, although far from perfect, mechanism for im-plementing the large-scale decisions reached by the White House and Con-gress. Packaging reduces the number of painful decisions that Congress must make, it allows the president and Congress to share the political cost of cutting programs and raising taxes, and it reduces such costs by directing attention to the general benefit of deficit reduction rather than to the pain of specific program cuts or tax hikes. By the end of the decade a formalized two-stage budget decision-making process could emerge—the large issues being decided by new institutions and routines and the smaller ones being left to the old system.

Since such new institutions and routines are not yet in place, Schick's conclusion that Reagan's budget legacy is very much in doubt is certainly correct. But the president cannot be faulted for failing to try to change the institutional environment. He made two serious attempts to fundamentally alter the budget process. The first attempt was his support of a constitutional amendment to limit spending growth and to balance the budget. This was approved by over two-thirds of the Senate but fell forty-six votes shy of two-thirds of the House in October 1982. The second attempt was the request contained in Reagan's fiscal year 1985 budget message for a constitutional amendment granting the president power to veto individual items in appro-priations bills. This proposal was defeated by the Senate in the spring of 1984. Although one may debate the desirability of these two efforts, approval of either would have forced institutional changes far more profound than any that have occurred during recent administrations. No recent president except Richard Nixon has had a lasting impact on the federal budget process; ironically, Nixon's impact was the backlash from his impoundment policies, which generated support for the Congressional Budget Act of 1974. Some of the much-heralded budget initiatives of recent presidents—planning, programming, budgeting (PPB) and zero-base budgeting (ZZB)—have come and gone, leaving the budget landscape largely unchanged.

If President Reagan had pursued as his primary objective the long-run fundamental reform of the institutions of budgeting rather than the short-run tactical objectives of lower taxes, domestic spending cuts, and a defense buildup, he would probably have failed to achieve either. Procedural and institutional reform are not topics that compel action, generate enthusiasm, or grab the attention of the media and the public. Americans do not want to believe their president is constrained by ineffectual institutions and procedures. If the president had argued that the mandate of the 1980 election required procedural or institutional changes before tax and spending changes could get under way, the public would have called this a cop-out. Yet such changes may well happen unintentionally rather than by design. By unleashing a set of forces that will control the course of budgeting for the next few years, the new institutions that the president did not propose directly could evolve over the balance of the decade.

The first four years of the Reagan administration have not markedly changed the degree to which the economy destablizes the budget, the extent to which mandatory costs push up overall spending, the ability of fiscal policy to stabilize the economy, or the capacity of Congress and the executive branch to operate smoothly and effectively on budget matters. However, Reagan's budget policy has started us toward a budget process that is more centralized and more focused on big issues and hence better able to operate in a world characterized by rapidly changing economic circumstances, mandated spending, and fragmented congressional budgetary powers.

EXECUTIVE OFFICE POLICY APPARATUS: ENFORCING THE REAGAN AGENDA

Chester A. Newland

This paper examines the domestic policy apparatus of the Executive Office of the President (EOP)—what was inherited by the Reagan administration and what has been done with it. Developments of EOP policy machinery prior to Reagan are traced first to highlight long-term issues of presidential policy structure that have persisted in the Reagan era. Transitional activities are then discussed as being central to initial efforts to implement Reagan's 1980 campaign pledges. The chief focus of this paper, however, is on how the Reagan White House has structured and used principal EOP units. Primary attention is devoted to the top presidential advisers in the White House Office, to the newly created Office of Planning and Evaluation (OPE), and to the Office of Policy Development (OPD) and its Cabinet Councils. The attention given in this paper to the Office of Management and Budget (OMB) is limited to its nonbudgeting policy roles. In its budgeting function, OMB has been so crucial to policy development in this administration that it is examined separately in the paper by Schick in this book. The Council of Economic Advisers (CEA) and other EOP units are touched on here only in relation to other matters.

In contrast with developments under Reagan's recent predecessors, this administration has used the EOP policy apparatus to enforce a fixed agenda. In addition, Reagan's staffing of the EOP and of key agency positions with partisan and personal ideological loyalists and the insulation of policy processes from career service perspectives and from professional expertise has been greater than ever before.

Reagan's firm purpose has been to advance the cause of limited government and self-governance, with enhanced defense expenditures and support of relatively unrestrained private enterprise.[1] While for many those goals are matters of philosophy, subject to pragmatic implementation, they have been pursued in significant measure by the Reagan administration as an unswerving ideology. The president has sought to lead a counterrevolution to the social and political trends of the past fifty years.

Some Reagan policies in support of that ambitious goal have suffered ruin: the balanced budget commitment, state-centered federalism, and some regulatory reform objectives (as in the Environmental Protection Agency [EPA] debacle). Other major policies have emerged painfully through congressionally dominated compromises only after dramatic administration failures that were conceived not by chance but from a decisive vision from the Right. Examples are the administration's aborted 1981–1982 Social Security proposals, followed by 1983 reform; and the drastic 1981 tax cuts, modified by nearly $100 billion of corrections in 1982. Successes have occurred also: a sharp drop in inflation and 1984 long-term economic growth indicators of 4 percent, though initially preceded by the highest unemployment since the Great Depression; an overall reduction of domestic spending from 14.3 percent of the gross national product (GNP) in 1981 to a 13 percent range in 1984, offset by increased debt-service costs; and enhanced defense spending, up from a trough of 5.6 percent of GNP in 1973 toward an objective of 8.1 percent by 1988, accompanied by an overall increase of the budget as a percentage of GNP from 22.5 percent in 1980 to 24.5 percent at the outset of 1984.

Reagan succeeded most vividly in his first three and one-half years in office, in contrast with his recent predecessors, in maintaining positive identification with his agenda and personal detachment from the policy failures associated with it. EOP policy machinery under the direction of White House Counselor Edwin Meese, III, was used primarily to sustain both that agenda and the president's associated popular image with it. Meanwhile, compromises essential to workable government after the first year resulted largely from congressional initiatives in politically oriented exchanges with the "James Baker" side of the White House and with OMB's director David Stockman. By Reagan's fourth year, over half of the units of the Office of Policy Development were barely functioning, and what remained continued to be oriented to low-visibility agenda enforcement and internal management. As

---

1. On the Reagan agenda, in addition to other sources cited in these notes, see John L. Palmer and Isabel V. Sawhill, *The Reagan Experiment* (Washington, D.C.: The Urban Institute, 1982); Lou Cannon, *Reagan* (New York: G. P. Putnam's Sons, 1982); Chester A. Newland, "The Reagan Presidency: Limited Government and Political Administration," *Public Administration Review*, vol. 43, no. 1 (January/February 1983), pp. 1-21.

the 1984 election approached, efforts turned more to the cabinet as a potential arena for positive projection of Reagan's ideology.

Reagan's use of the EOP policy apparatus brings three long-standing issues of the presidency into focus. First is how to obtain a workable balance of policy involvement between Congress, the agencies, and the EOP. Second is how to achieve an optimum mix in the executive branch of institutionalized professional expertise and transient personal loyalists and partisan politicians. Third is how to strike a balance of centralization and dispersion of EOP policy responsibilities without fragmentation of authority and direction. Behind all three of these issues is a fundamental challenge for a successful presidency: how to achieve a reasonable measure of strategic, deliberate presidential policy leadership in an environment of political and other forces that favors quick, reactive behaviors.

The Inherited Policy Apparatus

All of these long-term issues played a part in the creation of the Bureau of the Budget (BOB) in 1921, and they were crucial in its transfer in 1939 to the newly created EOP. The issues were defined differently then, however, as propositions of positivist political science and orthodox public administration. From the Reform Era through the early years of the EOP, this orthodoxy prevailed: Congress set policy, with extensive interaction with agencies and with increasingly strong presidential leadership; institutionalized professional expertise in the agencies and in the EOP, particularly in the BOB, guided presidential policy involvement; and the EOP remained small and streamlined, with key political leadership in the cabinet to implement programs subject to general congressional policy determination and oversight. By the time of Presidents Harry Truman and Dwight D. Eisenhower, the BOB was firmly institutionalized as a nonpartisan, professionally staffed agency. According to "principles of good government," it prepared the president's annual budget, cleared the legislative program, acquired administrative information, performed administrative management assignments, and proposed executive reorganizations.

Forerunners of the extended presidential policy apparatus of later years emerged in the 1940s.[2] Under Truman, the cabinet was initially used almost

---

2. For a more detailed analysis of historical development of the EOP policy apparatus, see Lester M. Salamon, "The Presidency and Domestic Policy Formulation," in Hugh Heclo and Lester M. Salamon, *The Illusion of Presidential Government* (Denver: Westview Press, 1981), pp. 177-201. See also: Margaret Jane Wyzomirski, "The De-Institutionalization of Presidential Staff Agencies," *Public Administration Review*, vol. 42, no. 5 (September/October 1982), pp. 448-458.

as a board of directors. Later, however, when the nation was immersed in the Korean Conflict, the National Security Council (NSC) became Truman's principal meeting forum. Eisenhower again stressed reliance on the cabinet as an advisory body, and in 1954 he established a two-person cabinet secretariat. Use was made also of several subject-oriented interagency councils and committees that operated independently of one another. But despite those cabinet-oriented innovations, the BOB's policy role survived with orthodox integrity.

Emergence of Distinct Policy Responsibility in EOP

The Golden Era of orthodoxy in action began to decline in the administrations of John F. Kennedy and Lyndon Baines Johnson. Two crucial changes in presidential staff apparatus occurred in the dozen years following the early 1960s. Policy staff functions were increasingly separated out of the BOB, and partisan politicization increased.

Kennedy reacted against the institutional apparatus of the Eisenhower years, eliminating the cabinet secretariat, reducing cabinet meetings to a bare minimum, and trimming national security affairs machinery. He appointed political task forces prior to and after his election to develop policy topics or fields. By late December 1960 Kennedy had eleven such groups in foreign affairs and eight in domestic policy.[3] Although his BOB directors, David Bell and Kermit Gordon, both professional economists, did not disturb the bureau's character with respect to budget or other routines, policy influence began to slip away.

Under President Johnson the slip became a landslide. Johnson used more policy task forces than Kennedy, and with a change learned from Franklin Delano Roosevelt: Johnson's task forces functioned mostly off-the-record. Some of Johnson's reports, like that of Ben Heineman, Sr.'s, Task Force on Government Organization, did not become public during Johnson's presidency. Others did, with the president giving them broad credit for securing passage of 207 pieces of legislation—in Johnson's words, "landmark achievements of my Presidency."[4]

Johnson assigned Joseph Califano and Larry Levinson the nearly impossible task of coordinating development of Great Society policy. Subsequently, the BOB's role diminished, not only through loss of policy coordination

---

3. Arthur M. Schlesinger, Jr., *A Thousand Days* (Boston: Houghton Mifflin Co., 1965), p. 160.
4. Lyndon Baines Johnson, *The Vantage Point* (New York: Holt, Rinehart & Winston, 1971), p. 328.

authority but also because Califano and others detailed personnel ad hoc and used them in policy roles without respect to traditional BOB institutional integrity or professional restraint.

In his memoirs, President Johnson stated his view on the institutionalized presidential policy apparatus in terms that are relevant to later developments:

> Previously, the standard method of developing legislative programs had consisted of adopting proposals suggested by the departments and agencies of the government. The Bureau of the Budget and to a lesser degree the White House staff would analyze the suggested measures and submit them to the President. From this process derived the programs that an administration presented to the Congress. I had watched this process for years, and I was convinced that it did not encourage enough fresh or creative ideas. The bureaucracy of the government is too preoccupied with day-to-day operations, and there is a strong bureaucratic inertia dedicated to preserving the status quo. As a result, only the most powerful ideas can survive. Moreover, the cumbersome organization of government is simply not equipped to solve complex problems that cut across departmental jurisdictions.[5]

Although Johnson eschewed the bureaucracy for development of policies, he trusted the governmental apparatus and career personnel to implement them. He devoted virtually no attention to administrative requirements or to the problems entailed in governmental expansion as a result of Great Society programs. He viewed institutionalized machinery as too conservative and too incremental for rapid governmental change, but he was confident of the bureaucracy's willingness to expand programs once the policies were set in place.

Splitting Off Policy from BOB—the Domestic Council

Two 1966 studies, one by the BOB and the other by the Heineman Commission, recommended creation of a specialized policy staff within the Bureau of the Budget. In part, the BOB study was a futile defensive measure against the evident deterioration of the institution under Johnson. Both studies recommended that a presidential policy staff should function on the basis of institutionalized expertise and professionalism. Johnson took no action on those recommendations and change was deferred to the Nixon administration.

Initially, Richard M. Nixon used several cabinet-level bodies—a Council for Urban Affairs, a Council for Rural Affairs, an Environmental Quality Council, a Council on International Economic Policy, and a Cabinet Committee for Economic Policy. That policy management approach was soon discontinued, however, as being too fragmented and time consuming. Statutory reorganization of the BOB and creation of a new policy apparatus was

---

5. Ibid., p. 327.

proposed, following recommendations by the Ash Council. A Domestic Council was created by law as a cabinet-centered decision-making body to be staffed by both career experts and noncareer personnel. In fact, the new apparatus quickly developed under John Ehrlichman (President Nixon's Domestic Council director) into an EOP staff-dominated agency composed entirely of partisan political appointees. Ehrlichman staffers employed interagency task forces, but these became vehicles for isolating cabinet officers from the president and from channels of direct EOP control of subordinate agency levels. Nixon's OMB also became deeply layered with partisan officials, and numerous other EOP political offices flourished, often in competition. A curious mixture of extreme centralization and fragmentation within the EOP developed.

President Gerald R. Ford moved promptly to restore cabinet and agency involvement in policy processes, a move recommended by many, including congressional leaders and the National Academy of Public Administration (NAPA) in its 1974 Watergate report.[6] Ford's domestic policy staff was used in part to coordinate interagency task forces, but those groups were chaired by cabinet officials or other agency heads. One Ford administration EOP unit, the Economic Policy Board (EPB), became central to policy development.[7] The EPB met over five hundred times in little more than two years. It functioned through systematic and predictable processes, linking EOP and agency resources across a broad range of domestic affairs and international economic policy. The EPB executive director reported directly to President Ford, and sustained presidential and cabinet involvement was achieved.

Domestic policy under President Jimmy Carter was characterized by incoherence and even disorder. Yet, key EOP policy staffers Stuart Eisenstadt and Jack Watson were generally regarded outside the Carter White House as among the president's most capable assistants. Interagency task forces facilitated extensive EOP/agency interaction. Cabinet departments were endlessly involved in policy formulation—and in disputes. In part, the Carter problem was caused by some trivialization of the policy staff role. Carter pulled back at midterm from his initial heavy involvement of the cabinet, and his Domestic Policy Staff became increasingly used for casework and for short-term political and legislative activities at the expense of policy development and synthesis. By contrast, two Carter departmental aides, Ben W. Heineman, Jr., and Curtis

---

6. Frederick C. Mosher, *Watergate: Its Implications for Responsible Government* (Washington, D.C.: National Academy of Public Administration, March 1974).

7. Roger B. Porter, *Presidential Decision-Making: The Economic Policy Board* (Cambridge: Cambridge University Press, 1980).

Hessler, recommended an EOP restructuring around four activities: economic policy, domestic affairs, budget and management, and political affairs.[8]

A clear Carter difficulty was weak EOP leadership outside the Domestic Policy Staff. Eisenstadt and Watson stood out in part because of their Carter cohorts: Bert Lance and James McIntyre at OMB, Frank Moore in Legislative Affairs, Hamilton Jordan as assistant to the president and Jody Powell as press secretary. The agencies included some strong domestic policy figures, notably Joseph Califano, but generally the administration was a collection of disparate elements that never jelled.

As bequeathed to Reagan in 1981, the EOP policy apparatus contrasted with the orthodoxy of its Reform Era and New Deal origins on all three long-term issues noted earlier. First, the balance in policy leadership in the separation of powers system had tilted decisively from Congress to the executive branch and, within that, from the operating agencies to the EOP. A reversal of that trend following Watergate somewhat crippled Ford and Carter, but the 1980 election was a call to return to strong presidential leadership.[9] Second, deinstitutionalization of the BOB as a professionally expert policy staff organization, which started under Kennedy and Johnson, culminated under Nixon with creation of the Domestic Council and the partisan politicization of the council, OMB, and key administrative positions in agencies.[10] Under Carter, partisan staffing continued as the norm in the EOP and in administrative and program management positions at departmental and bureau levels. The Civil Service Reform Act of 1978 resulted in deinstitutionalization at the top of the career civil service, opening the way legally for further partisan politicization not only in the EOP but at key operating levels throughout government.[11] Third, the EOP policy apparatus became fragmented, a problem that started under Johnson as a result of his style. Creation of the Domestic Council under Nixon ratified policy separation from OMB, but it failed to work cohesively. Ford's successful reliance on the Economic Policy Board demonstrated the feasibility of a coordinated policy apparatus that did not need to usurp cabinet, agency, or congressional involvement. But under Carter the Domestic Policy staff withered in influence, and both EOP and

8. Ben W. Heineman, Jr., and Curtis Hessler, *Memorandum for the President: Managing the Domestic Agenda in the 1980s* (New York: Random House, 1980).

9. Gregory B. Markus, "Political Attitudes during an Election Year: A Report on the 1980 NES Panel Study," *American Political Science Review*, vol. 76, no. 3 (September 1982), pp. 538-560.

10. Richard P. Nathan, *The Plot that Failed: Nixon and the Administrative Presidency* (New York: John Wiley & Sons, 1975).

11. Chester A. Newland, "Crucial Issues for Public Personnel Professionals," *Public Personnel Management*, vol. 13, no. 1 (Spring 1984), pp. 15-46.

agency policy machinery became disconnected. For the new Reagan administration, the inherited EOP policy apparatus appeared to be of little use.

EOP Transition Planning

Four characteristics of the Reagan administration's effort to create a framework and a climate for domestic policy coordination emerged during the transition and have persisted. First, strategic implementation of Reagan's agenda has been the undeviating purpose, policy guideline, and evaluation standard. Second, a conception of a strong presidency has been adhered to with sustained, deliberate attention to congressional relations, including Reagan trips to Capitol Hill before and after the inauguration; personal presidential telephone calls somewhat in the fashion of President Johnson, but more limited and controlled; structuring and expert staffing of machinery for legislative liaison; strategic political actions, including targeting of elections; and dramatic presidential use of the media. Third, EOP/cabinet collegiality—teamwork—has been sought and, with conspicuous exceptions, significantly achieved. Fourth, in the design of the official policy management apparatus, efforts have been made to create coordinated but differentiated networking structures and processes, all oriented to agenda enforcement.

Extensive use of transition teams was the first generally visible agenda implementation action by the incoming Reagan administration, signifying clearly the purpose for which EOP and other executive branch policy machinery would be used. From before November 1980 through January 1981, however, the transition leadership extensively evaluated other alternatives to accomplish the purpose of governmentwide enforcement of Reagan's ideology.

Transition Leadership and the Search for Structure

Edwin Meese, III, headed the Reagan transition. A longtime associate and personal friend of Reagan, Meese was the most trusted guardian of the faith in limited government and self-governance and had worked throughout Reagan's campaign on plans for the transition and the initial period in office. Yet, some key decisions remained at the outset of the transition about how to organize the policy apparatus. Meese was initially a staunch proponent of a "Super Cabinet," hoping to adapt Reagan's California experience to Washington, D.C. However, the Super Cabinet idea was opposed by James Baker, III (later appointed as Reagan's chief of staff), among others. While the search remained open, at election time the National Academy of Public Administration sent Meese a new academy publication, *A Presidency for the 1980s*.[12] After seeing it, Meese met in early November 1980 in Washington with academy members to review recommendations for strengthening the institutional presidency. NAPA recommended creation of EOP policy councils, similar to those proposed in the Carter period by Heineman and by Hessler. At the meeting, Meese seemed concerned to avoid Nixon's error of neglecting cabinet officials as a result of White House centralization. At the same time, concern was evident about problems associated with the Carter presidency, which seemed to many to be plagued by contradictions and incoherence within and between agencies and the EOP.

Most crucial to the final decision to reorganize the EOP's Domestic Policy Staff into an Office of Policy Development with several Cabinet Councils was a memorandum prepared for Meese by Roger Porter of the transition staff. Porter, who had served as executive secretary to President Ford's highly successful Economic Policy Board, recommended organizing the EOP around four major functions: economic policy, domestic affairs, budget and management, and political affairs. That recommendation corresponded to suggestions to Meese by NAPA. More important, it had the support of the future secretary of the Treasury Department, Donald T. Regan, and of the Baker contingent.

Transition Teams

While the search for an EOP structure continued at the transition headquarters, another important dimension of agenda implementation was initiated immediately following the election. Nearly 100 citizen task forces of Reagan loyalists were dispatched to federal agencies throughout the government. Reagan's teams were composed less of substantive policy experts than of ideological campaign workers, many seeking jobs, and they were organized to link agencies governmentwide into one agenda implementation network.

Under the direction of William E. Timmons, Reagan's transition chief for executive branch and congressional relations, the teams were organized into five issue clusters: economic affairs, national security, human services, resources and development, and legal-administrative. The Carter administration gave the Reagan teams relatively full access to agency budget and operating files. They were not given access to individual personnel files, but in many cases, as in the Office of Personnel Management (OPM), they requested

---

12. National Academy of Public Administration (NAPA), *A Presidency for the 1980s* (Washington, D.C.: NAPA, November 1980).

them of most senior career people and interviewed key personnel prior to entering office. Agencies prepared detailed briefing books to acquaint the teams with policy and organizational issues and practices. The Reagan teams, in turn, submitted reports to the central transition office and later to the EOP. In most agencies, these reports concentrated on the perceived need for cutbacks or elimination of programs, budgets, and personnel and on private-sector deregulation. In three cases—the Community Services Administration (CSA), the Department of Education, and the Department of Energy—total agency abolition was proposed. Access to those reports was strictly limited. A set was available to the Office of Policy Development, and, along with notebook compilations of campaign promises on which Reagan's assistant for policy development, Martin Anderson, and others routinely relied, they provided important, often required, initial policy guidance.

Related to the transition teams was movement of a few "Kitchen Cabinet" figures into the Reagan EOP. Lyn Nofziger obtained use of an office in the Old Executive Office Building (OEOB) for William Wilson and others for liaison with Pendleton James's White House Personnel Office. Some, like Wilson and Charles Wick, were awaiting clearance of their own appointments; others, like Justin Dart and Earle Jorgensen, were simply providing transition support. But political fundraising and other volunteer activities soon created questions. On February 23, 1981, several of those senior volunteers were informed by White House Counsel Fred Fielding that if their activities in EOP were to continue they would be required to submit financial disclosure forms and undergo Federal Bureau of Investigation (FBI) clearances. They then disbanded as an OEOB/EOP group, but power of Reagan loyalists over personnel appointments was soon increased by other methods.

Reagan's use of partisan transition teams within agencies and his subsequent subcabinet appointments patterned politically after them brought a changed dimension to the basic issue of agency/EOP relationships in policy matters, the issue being creation of an ideological network for agenda enforcement. The partisan team framework later impacted upon the functioning of Cabinet Council secretariats and working groups and also focused partisan power in policy implementation deep within the bureaucracy. A new level of politicization and deinstitutionalization was achieved, reaching well beyond the OPD and OMB and into subbureau levels across the government.

Initial Policy Structure and Phase I Plan from the Transition

Strategic versus reactive behavior was a presidential policy management challenge raised in November 1980 with the Reagan transition leadership. Two crucial subordinate issues were discussed. First was the matter of whether long-term policy research and analysis were at all possible in the EOP. If the answer was yes, the next question was whether long-range efforts, near-term policy development and formulation, and day-to-day political/policy decision responsibilities were best divided or combined into one policy apparatus.

During the transition, these issues were presented by NAPA to Meese and other Reagan officials in a set of recommendations that favored a multiple EOP domestic policy structure. NAPA proposed creation of three units, not counting OMB and White House Office components: (1) a new policy research and analysis staff with long-term horizons of two to twenty-five years, (2) a new economic affairs staff (not displacing the Council of Economic Advisers), concerned with domestic and international matters, and (3) a domestic affairs staff, through reorganization and reduction of the existing Domestic Policy Staff, which in 1980 employed approximately sixty people.

The Reagan administration decided to perform some of these functions through differentiated but related policy structures. With respect to formal policy machinery, an Office of Planning and Evaluation (OPE) was created. Ostensibly, OPE was to engage in somewhat longer-term strategic policy planning, but in fact as an outgrowth of the election and transition organizations, it was involved mostly in political intelligence related to the president's agenda, schedules, and plans, with hardly anything like the long-term research responsibility as suggested by NAPA. The Domestic Policy Staff was reorganized into the Office of Policy Development (OPD) for near-term policy management, especially to facilitate a network of EOP/cabinet/agency interactions. Organization and staffing of the White House Office and formation of a Legislative Strategy Group provided the framework for day-to-day decision making.

During the election campaign, the first OPE director, Richard S. Beal, worked with Reagan's pollster, Richard Wirthlin. During the transition, those two, with David Gergen and others, set to work on what was to become a series of analyses supporting strategically oriented presidential actions. Beal, a political scientist and a former Brigham Young University professor and Fulbright scholar, was appointed January 20, 1981, as special assistant to the president and OPE director. Nine days later his office delivered to Meese and others the administration's Phase I plan. Largely written during the transition and titled *Phase I Plan: The Final Report of the Initial Actions Project*, the closely held, unpublished plan stressed the importance of strategic actions during Reagan's first few months as president. It began as follows:

The direction of the country remains unsatisfactory to a majority of Americans. Hoping for change, they elected Ronald Reagan to preside over a restructuring and redirection of public policy for the country. The public sense of urgency requires that the President immediately undertake to steer a new course.[13]

To show how all the preinaugural and subsequent transition planning that went into setting up the EOP translated into actual practice, this paper now turns to the patterns that emerged in four spheres of EOP policymaking activity: the top presidential advisers, the Office of Planning and Evaluation, the Office of Policy Development and its Cabinet Councils, and the Office of Management and Budget's nonbudgeting policy roles. Each of these arenas illustrates the character of the Reagan response to one or more of the ongoing issues that have arisen in EOP organization and management.

Presidential Advisers: Long- and Short-Term Policy Roles

A persistent policy problem of the presidency is how to reconcile long-term priorities with short-term realities; in other words, how to achieve a reasonable measure of consistency and continuity of direction in presidential policy leadership in an environment of political and other forces that favors situational and reactive behavior.

It is only a slight oversimplification of the Reagan White House to say that this dilemma is highlighted by the different roles performed by Edwin Meese on the policy side and by James Baker and Michael Deaver on the day-to-day operations side. Whereas journalists may cite personality conflicts in the White House, the real difficulties may reside in inherent role conflicts of the presidency that are accounted for by the Reagan presidential policy apparatus.

The most significant Reagan White House network consists of Meese, Baker, and Deaver—the Reagan troika. Meese is responsible for the long-term implementation of the Reagan agenda—overseeing the policy development and cabinet affairs operations. He has staffed those functions with people like Roger Porter, Ralph Bledsoe (special assistant to the president and executive secretary to the Cabinet Council), Wendell Gunn (special assistant to the president and executive secretary), and initially, Richard Beal, each disciplined to favor deliberate presidential behavior over knee-jerk reaction. As explained later with respect to OPE, "strategic and long term" in the Reagan EOP generally connotes adherence to the agenda and to political

---

13. Office of Planning and Evaluation, Executive Office of the President, *Phase I Plan: The Final Report of the Initial Actions Project*. (Unpublished internal White House document.)

actions to support it, not neutral analysis in futures projections. Holding the administration to the agenda has provided high consistency and continuity of direction, although at high policy and political costs. Because that consistency has resulted from ideological adherence to a fixed agenda, kept in focus principally by Meese's crucial role, if Meese should depart the White House, the policy apparatus would be greatly affected.

Baker and Deaver, as contrasted to Meese, fill roles that virtually compel reactive behavior. The Baker side of the Reagan White House has attracted political campaign-type expertise. While less helter-skelter than the frenzied Johnson White House, the Baker side clearly contrasts with the measured, agenda-oriented Meese side. It is decisive and more politically sensitive to the present.

The Baker side gets to the president more frequently than does the Meese policy operation, in part because Baker's staff deals with the here and now.[14] In most recent administrations, such urgent daily matters have nearly monopolized attention, and the Reagan structure favors that tendency. In a February 17, 1981, memorandum to the cabinet and senior White House staff, Meese and Baker defined a key part of the structure as follows:

> To coordinate the efforts of all departments, agencies, and offices involved, we need to pull together the various plans and activities related to the economic recovery program. . . . The contact person for all material from the White House staff will be Dick Darman. The contact for members of the Cabinet will be Craig Fuller.[15]

Dick Darman, on the Baker side, largely controls what reaches the president. Nevertheless Meese and the agenda make the difference with respect to policy in the Reagan presidency. By force of his long-term, trusting relationship with the president, Meese succeeds in getting the policy side on the president's schedule and in keeping the Reagan agenda as the focus of cabinet and policy affairs.

Michael Deaver, as deputy chief of staff in control of presidential appointments, scheduling, East Wing, and personal support functions, is also powerfully placed. His role likewise puts him within the Baker here-and-now side, but his responsibility for image also dictates some concern for the longer run.

Several linking mechanisms operate within the Reagan White House to diminish bifurcation. The president and his agenda are the principal glue. Reagan appears to define his own role as much as any recent president, and

---

14. Dick Kirschten, "Under Reagan, Power Resides with Those Who Station Themselves at His Door," *National Journal*, vol. 16, no. 8 (February 25, 1984), pp. 361-364.

15. Quoted in Lawrence I. Barrett, *Gambling with History: Reagan in the White House* (Garden City, N.J.: Doubleday Co., 1983), p. 89.

he seems largely to define and value the different Meese/Baker roles. Reagan is congenial and likes congeniality, but he insists on a responsible subordinate structure to get work done, both to open up and resolve differences—*collegially.*

The National Security Affairs (NSA) apparatus and foreign policy are beyond the scope of this assessment of domestic policy machinery, but those operations also illustrate the point that congeniality and collegiality are highly prized by Reagan. The replacement of Secretary of State Alexander Haig by George Schultz is one obvious indicator. The official and personal roles of William P. Clark also illustrate this. First at the State Department and then as National Security Affairs adviser from January 1982 when he replaced Richard Allen to November 1983 when he was replaced by Robert C. McFarlane, Clark had an impact that Reagan valued at the White House well beyond NSA. The troika of Meese, Baker, and Deaver became the Big Four with the addition of Clark. Nonetheless, McFarlane's appointment, like the earlier designation of Baker as chief of staff, indicated the importance of functional as well as personal role considerations in a collegially oriented Reagan White House. Both those role aspects—official and personal—while often ignored by journalistic assessments of the Reagan White House, which tend to focus instead on personalities and conflicts, are important to an understanding of Reagan policy operations.

Two White House/EOP groupings that function as collegial linking pins are the Legislative Strategy Group (LSG) and the Budget Review Group (BRG). The LSG grew in part from a February 21, 1981, paper written by Darman to Baker that stressed the need for a focused legislative strategy for a "planned string of successes."[16] The LSG was formed with Baker and Meese as cochairpersons. Darman became LSG secretary, sharing staff-support responsibility with Craig Fuller. The president's assistant for legislative affairs (first Max Friedersdorf, then Kenneth Duberstein, followed by M. B. Oglesby) is an LSG principal, along with Meese and Baker as cochairpersons, Darman as LSG secretary, Fuller (shares staff-support responsibility with Darman), Gergen, and, initially, Elizabeth Dole, former head of the White House Office of Public Liaison, later the secretary of Transportation. The Budget Review Group, a variation of the LSG at first, also functions with Richard Darman as secretary, with other members including Baker, Meese, Stockman, and Regan. Clearly, the Baker action side of Reagan's White House dominates the LSG, but not without major Meese/policy-side participation. Both the LSG and its variant, the BRG, are the key coordinators of

---

16. Barrett, *Gambling with History*, p. 89.

policy decisions. Differences in perceptions exist in the EOP about the president's relationship to the LSG, with some criticism that it reacts to legislative pressures without Reagan's involvement and other reports that that seldom occurs.

Assessment of actions of the Reagan troika may be strengthened by yet another, interpersonal (not personality) role dimension. By many accounts, Deaver has the most contact of the three top advisers, both officially and formally, with Reagan—but in an interpersonal relationship somewhat like a son. Baker functions with regular high access, officially and formally, but without long-term role linkages. Meese, like Deaver, interacts not only in a formal agenda/policy role but also in a personal relationship, but more like a younger brother. While those role differences are highly significant, Meese, Baker, and Deaver worked from the start at developing collegial White House interaction. Breakfasts in Baker's office at seven-thirty, for example, became routine in the first year. That regularity stopped later, but more formal linkages like the LSG and the proximity of Fuller's and Darman's operations have encouraged collaborative processes and behaviors in crucially interdependent but different White House roles—the long term and the here and now.

To reiterate, in the Reagan presidency, the long-term Reagan agenda persistently defines the policy. Meese, in his agenda/policy role, is frequently criticized for staying the Reagan course or losing the ball in the face of contrary political forces and other realities, as in the Social Security reform situation, noted earlier, or the 1983 Civil Rights Commission episode, in which Reagan's view ultimately prevailed.[17] Baker, in turn, is the target of agenda loyalists for his sensitivity to other perspectives. The resulting conflicts are less ones of personality or loyalty than of roles in an administration where, to an unprecedented extent, a fixed agenda—clearly that of the president—determines how the policy apparatus is used.

"Strategic Planning" Under the OPE

The long-term versus short-term issue is also illustrated in what happened to the Office of Planning and Evaluation once the Reagan administration took office. Although the OPE was not formed as the sort of institutionalized long-range research and analysis staff envisioned by NAPA, its functions became distinguishable from the OPD. Its initial charter was broadly stated as "as-

---

17. For an example of common journalistic criticism, see Juan Williams, "Aides Concede White House Fumbled Civil Rights Panel Episode," *Washington Post*, November 26, 1983, p. A-4.

sisting the counsellor in projecting strategic activities for the president, based on evaluations of significant national, international, and political phenomena and conditions'' and ''planning at the level of the president, which gives focus to presidential behavior that can be communicated publicly, and gives perspective to the domestic, foreign, budgetary, and political activities of the president.''[18] After the transition, the OPE prepared a series of follow-ups to the Phase I plan, commencing on an issue-oriented Phase II report on February 13, 1981, then an implementation Phase III report, and working through a Phase V plan for the period May 15 through September 30, 1982. The Phase I plan remained as a key administration guide in 1983. Besides the Strategic Planning Memoranda (SPMs) relating to current and future phases of the president's overall agenda, the OPE produced a number of planning and evaluation documents. Also, under Beal, it worked on EOP applications of advanced information and communications technology to enhance domestic, international, and security policy processes.

The OPE was established as a tiny staff agency with only six positions, five originally carved out of the OPD, and reduced to four in fiscal year (FY) 1982. In classic EOP fashion, Beal relied in part on detailees and interns for staff. But the OPE functioned actively on what the White House termed ''strategic planning'' during the first months of Reagan's term. With respect to domestic policy, strategic planning appeared to mean principally using polling data and other indicators to plan Reagan's schedule of political speeches, appearances, and other behaviors. It also meant evaluating OPD performance and policy actions related to the Reagan agenda.

In 1982 Beal left the OPE to become special assistant to the president working in crisis management support and planning in National Security Affairs, reflecting many of his interests while in the OPE. With his departure, the OPE's involvement in international and security affairs shrank, so that by late 1983 it was again significantly oriented to public, opinion-related political intelligence, looking toward the 1984 election. Under Beal's successor Bruce Chapman, former Washington State secretary of state, the OPE moved to a closer working relationship with the OPD.

Experience with the OPE supports two conclusions relevant to structuring long-term EOP policy research and analysis capacity. First, the White House need for future-oriented information and strategic planning is great, but the market is small. Second, the creation, functions, and survival of this sort of presidential staff unit may be very much a function of political circumstance and personality.

---

18. Memorandum from Richard S. Beal to Jim Jenkins, ''Information on OPE,'' June 15, 1982.

Although the Reagan administration, particularly through Meese, is more inclined to an interest in some longer-term policy/agenda considerations than its recent predecessors, immediate needs still tend to drive out long-range issues. Strategic planning is virtually a code term for agenda tracking or polling analysis. To outside observers, relatively modest value appears to have been placed on OPE products, with the exception of the Phase I plan, Beal's development of strategic technical support and planning capacity in international and security affairs, and analysis of support of presidential speaking schedules and political activities. The OPE was near extinction in 1982 when it was perceived to be too distant from the "here and now." It survived as a unit only because it became reoriented to public opinion analysis, re-election issues, and EOP political sensitivities.

Office of Policy Development and Cabinet Councils

As noted earlier, the OPD and the Cabinet Councils, along with OMB, are ostensibly the *principal* policy organizations in the Reagan EOP, and experience of previous administrations was considered in their design. The councils are the vehicles designed to deal with the problem of involving agency, cabinet, and EOP resources in presidential policy activities oriented to agenda implementation, and, as such, they are the chief topic in this section. First, however, the two EOP levels above the councils are discussed: the assistant to the president for policy development, and the OPD and its director.

The Assistant for Policy Development and the OPD

Edwin Meese has brought continuity and presidential authority and access to the policy side of the Reagan White House. Subordinate to Meese, however, some significant discontinuity has occurred. The three appointees who served as Reagan's assistant for policy development in his first three years as president have differed considerably in background and style.

Martin Anderson, the Reagan campaign economic adviser who had previously been with the Hoover Institution and on the faculty of Stanford University, served the first year. He demonstrated little interest in managing the forty-person OPD staff, which was formally directed by Edwin Gray and in fact informally coordinated initially by the OPD's deputy director, Ronald Frankum, a close associate of Meese. Anderson was more interested in vigorously advancing the libertarian opposition to governmental interference in individual liberties and economic affairs. He provided general policy leadership through involvement in the Cabinet Councils, participating in meetings more than anyone else. But, save for a couple of the Cabinet Councils, the OPD often floundered during that first year. Except for loose coordination, the OPD was managed primarily within separate Cabinet Councils if such capacity were present, as in the Cabinet Council on Economic Affairs (CCEA). Anderson was out of place, if one considers that a manager of OPD was what was needed in part. He left in frustration soon after his close associate, Richard Allen, departed.

Edwin Harper, Reagan's deputy director of OMB, succeeded Anderson in February 1982. Unlike Anderson, Harper had a reputation as a manager, although OMB and the Reagan administration almost wholly neglected governmentwide management matters when Harper was at OMB, and internal management of that office languished. Harper was less ideological and more pragmatic as a free-market Republican conservative than Anderson. Like Anderson, Harper was soon discounted and disparaged in the press by the Baker side of the White House,[19] and he left in spring 1983 to reenter private business. Harper's principal impact may have been a consistent effort to develop ways for the president to appear engaged in Cabinet Council activities, including visible policy leadership scenarios. For example, he encouraged the CCEA to structure opportunities for Reagan's involvement.

After Harper left, the policy position remained vacant until the end of September, 1983 when John A. (Jack) Svahn was appointed. Svahn had been part of Governor Reagan's circle in California and had been named Reagan's Social Security Administration (SSA) commissioner in 1981. He later moved to the Department of Health and Human Services (HHS) as deputy secretary under Margaret M. Heckler, but he was unwanted and relatively unused there. At the White House, Svahn compared philosophically to Anderson as a Reagan domestic agenda loyalist, but he had a reputation as a more active and knowledgeable manager with a capacity for the anonymity that has characterized that Reagan White House position.[20]

Below the level of the policy assistant to the president, the OPD was created as the successor to Carter's Domestic Policy Staff. From its origin in 1970 as Nixon's Domestic Council, that staff has been ''Hatched'' by statute, but in fact all of Reagan's appointees except for a few agency detailees are loyal Reagan partisans, including only one senior person from career service. A complete turnover of OPD staff occurred in the 1981 change of administrations, with the abrupt dismissal even of most nonpartisan Schedule-A secretarial and support personnel, many with extensive civil service experience.

---

19. Dick Kirschten, ''Don't Look for Sparks to Fly from White House Domestic Policy Office,'' *National Journal*, vol. 15, no. 50 (December 10, 1983), pp. 2566-2567.
20. Ibid.

The OPD started out with dysfunctional layering: an initial OPD director Ed Gray, with vague performance, an energetic deputy Ronald Frankum who was close to Meese and who initially provided principal leadership, and below those two levels, five Cabinet Councils, each headed by an executive secretary. By 1983 the OPD structure shook down to half a layer. Roger Porter continued as CCEA executive secretary but also became OPD director. That office became largely administrative for all the Cabinet Councils whose executive secretaries dealt directly with Svahn on various substantive matters.

All Cabinet Council executive secretaries and other OPD officials under Reagan have appointments as special assistants to the president, in addition to their organizational positions. In short, the OPD is not institutional; it is personal and partisanly political, as the policy office has been since creation of the Domestic Council, despite Title III Code provisions and some talk in 1970 of creating continuity of career expertise and professionalism in the presidential policy apparatus.

The Cabinet Councils

President Reagan, like many newly elected forerunners in the presidency, stressed cabinet government during the transition as his chosen vehicle to achieve coordinated unity of direction in his administration. To that end, Cabinet Councils became a chosen mechanism to balance EOP and agencies' involvement in policy processes.[21] In fact, as they developed, the councils did become important to facilitate coordination of secondary-level domestic policy development, interpretation, and implementation. But neither the councils nor the OPD, which they constitute as a whole, became the principal center of highest policy processes. The councils and the OPD never achieved the capacity to provide general policy direction; they became principally preoccupied with details required to carry out Reagan's agenda. More than other forces, the budget initially drove other policy, not the reverse.

After an initial summary of Cabinet Council structure, two aspects of the councils' activities that show these qualities are noted here. First, subjects considered and actions taken by the councils are reviewed. These activities illustrate the secondary-level character of the councils' work and their roles as coordinators of these nonetheless crucially significant policy activities,

---

21. President Reagan described the councils as a "means for deliberate consideration of major policy issues that affect the interests of more than one department or agency." Office of Planning and Evaluation, Executive Office of the President, *Strategic Evaluation Memorandum #18, Cabinet Councils and Domestic Affairs Management: An Evaluation*, June 8, 1982, p. 9. (Unpublished internal White House document.)

heretofore often neglected. Second, participation of officials in the councils' activities is summarized, showing further their importance in coordinating Reagan agenda implementation.

The Seven Councils and Their Diversity.   In February 1981, the new administration announced creation of five Cabinet Councils: Economic Affairs (CCEA), Commerce and Trade (CCCT), Human Resources (CCHR), Natural Resources and Environment (CCNRE), and Food and Agriculture (CCFA). A sixth Cabinet Council on Legal Policy (CCLP) was established in January 1982, and a seventh on Management and Administration (CCMA) was announced in September 1982. By fall 1983, two of those Cabinet Councils were dormant—CCNRE and CCFA; two were only marginally active—CCHR and CCLP; one was moderately and consistently active—CCCT; one was strongly active—CCMA; and one—CCEA—was extremely busy, with a record of activity for the three years matching all the others combined.

Some structural dimensions are common to all of the councils, even though they operate very differently. Most significantly, as subgroups of the cabinet, the president chairs all the councils. Each has a designated cabinet-level chairperson pro tempore who directs the council and chairs sessions when the president is not in attendance. OPD staff members serve as executive secretaries to the councils and provide limited staff support and coordination.

Differences between the councils are most evident in the functioning of their executive secretariats and working groups. Secretariats are typically composed of assistant secretaries and comparable-level officials drawn from departments and agencies of the council principals. Working groups function to provide the councils with interdepartmental expertise. Characteristic differences in how these support structures work are these: In 1983, the CCMA executive secretariat was regularly meeting bimonthly; by contrast, the CCEA seldom relied on that structure and used twenty working groups instead in 1983, compared to CCMA's use of three. More importantly, as noted, some councils have never been very active and others have virtually vanished, while CCEA, CCMA, and CCCT have remained active.

Cabinet Council Subjects and Actions.   Subjects and actions taken by the Cabinet Councils show that while many are of great importance, they are typically of a secondary order of policy.

Subjects of Cabinet Council actions during the first fifteen months of operations may be described under the following eleven categories of "governmental activity," as defined generally in an OPE evaluation.[22] It is clear from this list that the Cabinet Councils deal with a host of matters that scarcely

---

22. Ibid., pp. 33-34.

fit the term *policy development*; they are more concerned with facilitating implementation of agendas.

1. *Preparing or approving legislative proposals or positions*
   Examples: Thrift industry, on the CCEA's agenda twenty-two times, leading to the Restructuring Act of 1981; tax policy and the Economic Recovery Tax Act of 1981, on the CCEA's agenda seven times; the Clean Air Act, on the CCNRE's agenda seven times

2. *Acting on budget cost items and issues (but not the annual budget)*
   Examples: Dairy price supports (CCFA); federal credit policy (on the CCEA's agenda ten times in 1981); minority business (CCCT); procompetition health care proposals (CCHR); strategic petroleum reserve financing (CCNRE)

3. *Approving regulatory policies and issues*
   Examples: Child nutrition meal patterns (CCHR); Davis-Bacon Act changes (CCEA); family planning (CCHR)

4. *Taking administrative actions*
   Examples: Surplus cheese disposal (CCFA); outer continental shelf leases (CCNRE); national urban policy (CCHR)

5. *Preparing for international meetings*
   Examples: Ottawa summit (CCEA, CCCT), Cancun summit (CCEA, CCFA), and Versailles summit (CCEA); Lopez-Portillo meeting (CCCT)

6. *Developing international economic positions*
   Examples: International investment policy (CCEA); Polish debt (on the CCEA's agenda seven times in 1981)

7. *Initiating or reviewing issues studies*
   Examples: Coal exports (CCCT); the Gold Commission (CCEA); and LANDSAT/METSAT transfer to the private sector (CCCT)

8. *Reviewing and clearing reports to Congress*
   Examples: National energy policy (CCNRE); national urban policy (CCHR); and small business and competition (CCCT)

9. *Deciding governmental management issues*
   Examples: PATCO strike (CCEA); Federal Employee Health Benefits Program (CCHR); and reorganizations of departments of Energy (CCNRE) and Education (CCHR)

10. *Reviewing status reports*
    Examples: Review of economic indicators such as unemployment, wages, savings, inflation, and specific industry trends (automobiles, airlines, and so forth) (CCEA and CCCT)

11. *Determining broad presidential agenda positions*
    Examples: Balanced Budget Amendment (CCEA); monetary policy (CCEA)

Cabinet Council actions on agenda items in the first fifteen months of operations were grouped by the OPE in the following seven categories, with percentages of their occurrence: presidential policy decisions, 4.4 percent; recommendations resulting in a later presidential policy decision, 10.8 percent; strategy, 9 percent; council decision, 17.7 percent; review/discuss, 30 percent; further study, 25.1 percent; and postpone, 3.1 percent.[23] According to that analysis, a total of 15 percent of items resulted in presidential decisions during that time period. Presidential decisions on Cabinet Council items increased slightly after the first fifteen months, owing to changes in CCEA processes and the creation of the CCMA. Of thirty issues dealt with by the CCMA during its first year, fifteen went to the president, and he made decisions on twelve. Activities of the councils with respect to frequency of meetings and participation are discussed in the subsection following. Statistical summaries of those matters and of the substance of Cabinet Council meetings, like the statistic on presidential decisions, have little comparative merit because of the complexity of the apparatus.

Subjects given little consideration by the Cabinet Councils are also revealing. Most crucially, annual budgets have received little general attention by them, except for last-minute information sessions. The FY 1983 budget, for example, was not reviewed by the CCEA until three days before its formal submission to Congress. In that respect, OMB has exercised greater policy influence in the Reagan administration than has the OPD and the Cabinet Councils, although that power balance appears to have shifted from extreme OMB domination the first year to more broadly shared power in the third and fourth years. OMB Director Stockman participated in many Cabinet Council sessions during the councils' first fifteen months of operation (31 percent of the total), but the budgetary process functioned outside of that apparatus to control policy in line with Reagan's agenda.

Other subjects of minimal Cabinet Council concern in the initial months were internal governmental management and intergovernmental relations. Ne-

---

23. Ibid., p. 22.

glect of governmental management ended in September 1982 when the CCMA was created and changes of direction were made at OMB. Reagan federalism issues were considered in the OPD with respect to specific important policies—namely, block grants and urban policy (in the CCHR). A separate EOP Intergovernmental Relations Office was supposed to handle general aspects of the field, but it had little positive impact on Reagan's policy. Apparently owing to ideological antipathy to "Washington insiders" and governmental professionals, the Reagan intergovernmental relations staff had limited contacts with the Big Seven state and local government interest groups. Robert Carleson in the OPD was closer to policy processes with respect to Reagan federalism, functioning as a principal architect of the policy. But external liaison on the policy was ineffective. Reagan's first pronouncement of urban policy was prepared in HUD and in the EOP with virtually no external consultation, and it proved to be an ideologically based political disaster from which the president was forced to disassociate himself.

Cabinet Council Meetings and Participation. Frequency of council meetings and participation in them indicates the importance of some as coordinating mechanisms for implementing the Reagan agenda. The infrequency of meetings and minimal accomplishments of others indicate their low value as parts of the EOP policy apparatus and suggest the need to revise the OPD structure.

By November 1983, as noted, three Cabinet Councils were meeting most actively: the CCEA, which has accounted for 49 percent of meetings of all councils, convening on an average of twice weekly except during holiday and vacation periods; the CCMA, which met twenty-one times in 1982–1983; and the CCCT, which has met from one to four times per month. The CCHR met only three times after its creation, from March to June 1981. It then skipped meeting for five months but held twelve meetings from December 1981 to May 1982. It met infrequently after Secretary Richard S. Schweiker left HHS in 1982. The CCNRE and the CCFA, both dormant in mid-1983, met a few times in 1981–1982. CCLP, created in January 1982, has held few meetings, but it continued to function in 1984.

Numbers of meetings must be considered along with other indicators of the councils' activities in order to evaluate them. Personalities, subject matter, and chances of presidential attendance are crucial variables. For example, the CCHR has met infrequently compared to the CCEA. Secretary Margaret Heckler, CCHR chairperson pro tem since January 1983, appears to prefer to handle matters within HHS; on the other hand, she participates actively in CCMA meetings (perhaps because those always involve Meese and often the president). Participation of principals in the CCHR, as in the CCFA, has been lower from the start than in other councils. Also, Carleson, CCHR executive secretary until fall 1983, preferred to complete staff work at lower levels, using the council infrequently for decisions and the secretariat for control. CCHR topics have generally appeared as one-time agenda items, not as longer-term matters as in the CCEA. The percentage of presidential actions on CCHR items during the first fifteen months of its existence is high (9 percent) compared to the CCEA (1 percent); but as noted earlier, such comparative statistics are nearly meaningless (2 of 22 items for CCHR and 3 of 224 for CCEA).

Other differences among councils are important to note. The few meetings of the CCLP after the first three have generally involved the president because of the close relationship between Reagan and Attorney General William French Smith. Former Secretary James Watt's erratic style and tendency to exclude people from the CCNRE was in contrast to Secretary Regan's systematic, deliberate, and participative CCEA leadership. As noted earlier, the CCEA does not rely heavily on the secretariat, but it makes extensive use of its twenty working groups, under Roger Porter's systematic management. The CCMA, by contrast, relies heavily on its secretariat, which met forty times in its first year, twice as often as the council. Also, the CCMA executive secretary, Ralph Bledsoe, meets individually with the OPM director and the GSA administrator or their deputies, as well as with the OMB deputy director, and regular reports are reviewed from those agencies on agenda priorities.

Participation by high-ranking officials in Cabinet Council meetings varies significantly. A summary of attendance in the first fifteen months of meetings is provided by table 1. Those statistics show that the initial chairpersons pro tem took seriously their responsibilities for managing the councils. Top individual attendance at all Cabinet Council sessions during those initial months ranked as follows: (1) Martin Anderson, 65 percent; (2) Murray Weidenbaum (chairman, Council of Economic Advisers), 60 percent; (3) Donald Regan, 59 percent; (4) Malcolm Baldridge (secretary of Commerce), 52 percent; (5) Drew Lewis (secretary of Transportation), 49 percent; (6) Vice-President George Bush, 43 percent; (7) William Brock (U.S. trade representative), 42 percent; (8) John Block (secretary of Agriculture), 42 percent; (9) Raymond Donovan (secretary of Agriculture), 38 percent; (10) David Stockman, 31 percent. Meese attended 18 percent of the sessions and Baker 7 percent. As noted earlier, the president attended 14 percent of council meetings in that period.

An OPE evaluation of the operation of the Cabinet Councils during their first fifteen months resulted in a recommendation to develop "systematic means for the President to give earlier, more direct and pro-active direction to Cabinet Council activities, and identify ways to communicate the Presi-

TABLE 1

ATTENDANCE AT CABINET COUNCIL MEETINGS
(First fifteen months, by member category)

Cabinet Council	Total Meetings	President Reagan (%)	Chairperson Pro Tem (%)	Principal Member (%)	Other Member (%)	Ex Officio (%)
CCEA	100	7	95	53	14	33
CCCT	31	26	97	43	13	41
CCHR	15	27	100	32	7	32
CCNR	31	16	100	40	9	29
CCFA	10	20	100	20	13	22
CCLP	3	0	0	1	0	0

SOURCE: Office of Planning and Evaluation, Executive Office of the President, *Strategic Evaluation Memorandum #18, Cabinet Councils and Domestic Affairs Management: An Evaluation*, June 8, 1982, p. 17. (Not a public document. No revisions made here of OPE data.)

NOTE: The CCLP data here are too limited to be of value, since that Cabinet Council had just begun operation when these statistics were collected.

dent's role to the press and to the public.''[24] The evaluation concluded that the councils had taken the initiative on most policies and issues, with little evidence of direct response to presidential direction or guidance. Edwin Harper urged such efforts by the CCEA as the most active council, and agendas were structured during subsequent months to enhance the image of presidential participation. A second OPE recommendation, creation of the CCMA, also resulted in increased Reagan involvement, as noted earlier. As chairperson pro tem of that council, Edwin Meese has facilitated presidential involvement, with regular quarterly reviews.

The OPE's 1982 assessment suggested including important noncabinet agencies like the Veterans Administration and the Environmental Protection Agency in the councils. Working groups have regularly included participation from various subcabinet agencies. Creation of the CCMA brought the OPM and GSA in as principals of that council. The OPE also urged reexamination of the councils to determine whether workload and attendance imbalances might require restructuring some of them.

OPD and Cabinet Council Evaluation

From the outside, Reagan's Cabinet Councils appear to facilitate heretofore neglected secondary-level domestic affairs coordination. The Reagan

---

24. Ibid., p. 41.

agenda and budgeting drive policy, and the OPD and Cabinet Councils function within that framework to coordinate and structure subordinate policies and related activities. The CCEA, CCCT, and CCMA, particularly, and others to some extent, have succeeded in bridging the EOP and government agencies, with high cabinet-officer involvement. But the bridging serves not to voice original or challenging inputs from subordinate experts in agencies or elsewhere in the EOP so much as to keep agencies exposed to the EOP's agenda orientation and to provide for agency actions to reconcile policies to it. A highly visible example in 1983–1984 of a hostile posture toward alien viewpoints was the sharp White House rebuke of CEA Chairperson Martin Feldstein for questioning the wisdom of Reagan's persistent rejection of tax increases to diminish deficits. Nevertheless, within the bounds of the Reagan agenda, considerable debate over alternatives is encouraged in the Cabinet Councils.

The policy network, in short, does not set the general direction; it follows it, working out policy details strictly secondary to the president's fixed views of government.

Even within that context, a changed configuration of councils may be in order. Pre-Reagan assessments noted earlier, by NAPA, Porter, Heineman, Jr., and Hessler, recommended fewer councils. The first three and one-half years of Reagan's term indicate that consideration could be given to limiting the number of councils to three: economic affairs, other domestic policy, and governmental administration. A fourth function, long-term policy research, may be needed, but the OPE experience and the practices of past administrations demonstrate that short-term priorities preclude that sort of activity, probably making it impossible as an aspect of the presidential domestic policy apparatus.

Reagan's Office of Policy Development and related policy machinery, like OPD's forerunners since the creation of the Domestic Council in 1970, have been staffed on the bases of personal and partisanly political considerations. All of the key OPD personnel serve not simply in organizational offices but as personal assistants or special assistants to the president—after passing strict political litmus tests. Virtually all would be removed by a change of administration. Thus, institutionalized continuity of the EOP policy apparatus appears improbable at the end of the Reagan administration. By defining policy development in ideological terms and structuring and staffing EOP and agency operations accordingly, the Reagan administration has virtually assured that its imprint will endure only so long as it remains in office.

Of more immediate concern is that by orienting the policy apparatus to ideological staffing and agenda activities, the Reagan administration has also limited its effectiveness while in office. Many key policies have failed; others have survived only because Reagan's ideology has been compelled by Congress to yield reluctantly to other forces. For example, Reagan's 1980 campaign promised both elimination of deficits and reduced unemployment as key elements of his agenda, and the Economic Recovery Act of 1981 and its accompanying provisions were adopted on the bases of supply-side economics and government cutback ideology, in disregard of extensive contrary expertise in the private sector and in government. But the policy resulted in deficits over three times greater than any previous record, and those are projected to continue for years. Also, unemployment rose to sustained levels exceeded only in the Great Depression. Only congressionally initiated modifications of the 1981 tax cuts the next year kept deficits from soaring another $90 billion annually.

The administration's handling of Social Security in its first two years hurt Republican congressional candidates in 1982 and brought few improvements in the system. Robert J. Samuelson, economist and columnist, characterized the failure as follows in 1983: "No issue better highlights the President's reluctance to grapple with contemporary realities than social security. . . . The President operates from deeply held principles and prejudices, but these mainly reflect old ideological combats and economic realities."[25] The EOP/OPD policy apparatus contributed little on its own initiative to a solution of this enormous domestic policy concern. Only after being forced into a loser's corner did the administration join bipartisan forces with Congress to turn the issue over to a National Commission on Social Security Reform to formulate acceptable, necessary changes.

Adherence to ideology and reliance on narrow partisanship in EOP staffing has also crippled other policies that are crucial to the Reagan agenda. Among the most notable of these is regulatory reform, discussed in the following review of OMB policy roles.

OMB: Nonbudgeting Policy Roles

Three of Reagan's policy priorities—deregulation, changed procurement practices, and internal governmental management—are responsibilities largely assigned to OMB. Management of these polices reveals much about continuing struggles within the EOP for leadership in presidential policy activities. The old BOB "had it all" with respect to budget, central policy staffing, and administrative management leadership. Fragmentation of the EOP policy apparatus since the 1960s has continued as a problem, and some would favor

---

25. Robert J. Samuelson, "Old Realities," *National Journal*, vol. 15, no. 4, p. 175.

reintegration of functions in OMB or in some new governmental body. To a large extent, the real policy power shifted to OMB in Reagan's first year because of use of the budget as the principal vehicle to implement the agenda. As noted early in this paper, that OMB budgeting role is not discussed here, but is assessed in Schick's paper in this book. Regulatory reform—deregulation to free up private enterprise and state and local governments—was secondary in Reagan's agenda only to his 1981 Economic Recovery Act package, and it too became the responsibility of OMB. That is discussed briefly here, along with two other Reagan policy concerns assigned to OMB.

Regulatory Policy Management

In his first White House press briefing, Reagan announced creation of a task force on regulatory reform chaired by Vice-President George Bush. Regulatory reform has remained one of the president's highest policy priorities, based on four principles: (1) harnessing of market incentives; (2) reduction of burdens on state and local governments; (3) modification of regulations where social costs exceed benefits; and (4) streamlining of regulatory procedures.

A major staff was created for this purpose by drastically reducing OMB's "management side" and expanding the small activity created by the 1980 Paperwork Reduction Act into a vigorous Office of Information and Regulatory Affairs. Under the direction of a political appointee, Christopher DeMuth (a former Nixon Domestic Council staffer and director of the Harvard Faculty Project on Regulation), the OMB Office staffed the Bush task force. It also greatly expanded OMB regulatory review under Reagan's February 1981 Executive Order 12291, which elevated some political pressures and regulatory decisions from regulatory agencies to OMB, greatly increasing politicization there.

From the outset through 1983, two categories of OMB regulatory review have received the greatest publicity and are typical of OMB's expanded policy role: first, the Occupational Safety and Health Administration's (OSHA's) cotton and grain elevator dust regulation and, second, intervention in the EPA. In June 1981, OSHA cotton-dust standards were upheld by the Supreme Court, and a Congressional Research Service study challenged the legality of OMB's regulatory review. But DeMuth successfully persisted through 1983 in obstructing issuance of OSHA grain-dust regulations, with documented reports by the *Washington Post* of direct industry lobbying in OMB.[26] The

---

26. Felicity Barringer and Howard Kurtz, "OMB Delay of Grain Elevator Standard Hit," *Washington Post*, November 11, 1983, p. A-15.

propriety of such OMB regulatory policymaking was questioned by Senator Robert T. Stafford (R-Vt.), chairperson of the Senate Environment Committee, with respect to intervention in November 1983 in the EPA: "Recent history suggests that it is both inappropriate and counterproductive for OMB to seek to pressure EPA in matters regarding public health and the environment. It is not OMB's role to determine Congressional intent in this matter."[27]

Despite such objections to OMB policymaking at the expense of statutorily mandated agency authority, regulatory reform has been claimed as one of Reagan's most successful efforts by OMB's own assessment. In April 1982, DeMuth's office reported a one-year reduction of federal rulemaking by one-half and of the size of the *Federal Register* by one-third. In August 1982, OMB claimed savings of $9 billion to $11 billion in one-time costs and $6 billion in annual recurring costs, all due to deregulation. Claimed as most successful among those efforts were $1.1 billion in regulatory relief of the automobile industry by changing or revoking thirty-two regulations and proposed rules of the National Highway Traffic Safety Administration (NHTSA) and of EPA.[28] However, by Reagan's third year, deficiencies on two grounds were criticized by industry advocates of deregulation: failures to push regulatory reform legislation and inadequacies of legal casework handled by political amateurs lacking the regulatory expertise required to win in the courts. For example, in June 1983 the Supreme Court unanimously overturned administration actions that had eliminated the NHTSA air-bag rule. At that same time, a challenge to revocation of the five mile-per-hour bumper standard was also before the U.S. Court of Appeals for the District of Columbia.

The issues here with respect to presidential policy apparatus are the three classic ones: EOP/agency policy roles and interrelationships; personal and political versus institutional staffing of OMB and EOP offices and regulatory agencies; and centralization of policy machinery versus the alternatives. Reagan administration practice demonstrates the extent of change from Reform Era orthodoxy. In regulatory reform, Reagan's OMB has functioned not simply as a staff arm of the president but has usurped statutorily assigned policy functions of agencies to enforce the Reagan agenda centrally. Also, its staffing is partisan and the organization is transitory, not institutional, in contrast to the former BOB model. It lacks technical expertise in areas for which such agencies as the NHTSA, EPA, and OSHA are responsible, but it is expert in terms of political dimensions of regulatory reform and the Reagan agenda.

---

27. Quoted in Cass Peterson, "OMB Letter Calls EPA Too Cautious," *Washington Post*, November 19, 1983, pp. A-1, A-12.

28. Michael Wines, "Reagan Plan to Relieve Auto Industry of Regulatory Burden Gets Mixed Grades," *National Journal*, vol. 15, no. 30 (July 23, 1983), pp. 1532-1537.

Procurement Policy Machinery

President Reagan issued Executive Order 12352 on procurement reform on March 17, 1982, and procurement management is a policy priority of OMB's Reform '88. That priority stems in part from the reality that much governmental activity that is financed by federal funds is performed by private contractors, universities, and state and local governments. In December 1980, Frederick C. Mosher estimated that "less than one-tenth of the federal budget is allotted to domestic activities that the federal government performs itself."[29] Mosher's article was distributed to Meese and to OPD staffers in January 1981. Procurement reform had long been a priority of Congress, but prior to Reagan the executive branch had been slow to act on it.

In 1969 Congress had created the Commission on Government Procurement out of exasperation with executive branch inactivity in that area. For another dozen years OMB and advocates of the presidential loyalty model resisted congressional involvement, while OMB provided only sporadic and limited leadership. Again in 1979, Congress acted to withdraw regulatory authority from OMB's Office of Federal Procurement Policy (OFPP), because it saw the OFPP as acting as a centralizing agency instead of facilitating reform for improved, decentralized, agency procurement. Only then did OMB take action. The Carter administration nearly completed new legislative proposals; Reagan's OMB rejected those and came up with the 1982 executive order.

The General Accounting Office (GAO) continued in 1983 to favor restoration of OFPP regulatory authority.[30] Agencies typically favored decentralization. NAPA in late 1983 favored the agency viewpoint but supported continued OFPP leadership.[31]

Agency actions under Reagan's 1982 executive order were scheduled as part of the FY 1985 budget/management review, a major development, since past efforts to combine specific policy implementation and budgetary review have been relatively unsuccessful. For the first time, OMB's budget and management review staffs combined comprehensive efforts on behalf of systematic enforcement of a governmentwide presidential policy priority. This

---

29. Frederick C. Mosher, "The Changing Responsibilities and Tactics of the Federal Government," *Public Administration Review*, vol. 40, no. 6 (November/December 1980), pp. 541-548.

30. General Accounting Office (GAO), *Selected Government-Wide Management Improvement Efforts—1970 to 1980* (Washington, D.C.: GAO/GGD-83-69, August 8, 1983), p. 17.

31. National Academy of Public Administration (NAPA), *Revitalizing Federal Management: Managers and Their Overburdened Systems* (Washington, D.C.: NAPA, 1983).

action broadened OMB's and, in turn, the EOP's capacity to control policy implementation.

Federal Government Management Policy

Federal government management policy was generally neglected by Reagan during his first eighteen months in office, except for a narrow control approach by OMB and presidential appointments to place administrative management under Reagan's personal/partisan control both centrally and at operating levels within agencies. In September 1982, steps were taken to end the neglect, by creation of the Cabinet Council on Management and Administration and announcement of a new OMB initiative, Reform '88. The substance of those related management developments is beyond the scope of this paper.[32] But two issues related to the presidential policy apparatus are highlighted here: (1) actions to deinstitutionalize the inspectors general (IGs) and (2) OMB's loss of leadership to the Cabinet Council on Management and Administration (CCMA). Two relevant proposals for reorganization of OMB are also noted.

First, attacks on fraud, waste, and abuse nearly defined the emphasis of Reagan's initial federal management concern, continuing a major Carter administration policy priority. The Reagan policy was launched with the precipitate firing of all of the IGs appointed under the new Inspectors General Act of 1978. That act sought to make the IGs independent, with requirements to report to both Congress and their departmental secretaries. Reagan nonetheless fired them, asserting that "it is vital that I have the full confidence in the ability, integrity and commitment of each appointee."[33] The House of Representatives Government Operations Committee charged that the firings violated the 1978 Act. Criticisms became rife about politicization of the IGs to avoid having "watchdogs." Reagan then reappointed six IGs along with ten new ones, all with governmental experience. A twenty-three-member President's Council on Integrity and Efficiency (PCIE), coordinated by OMB's deputy director, was also created on March 23, 1981, with all the appearance of an attempt to stem a reaction to adverse publicity.

That IG episode and the developments subsequent to it came down on one side of the presidential apparatus issue of institutionalization versus politicization: Reagan successfully made the IGs personal, presidential appoin-

---

32. For a discussion of the substantive issues, see Chester A. Newland, "Federal Government Management Trends," *Bureaucrat*, vol. 12, no. 4 (Winter 1983-1984), pp. 3-13.
33. Quoted in Pete Early, "Inspectors General: Effective Watchdogs," *Washington Post*, July 13, 1982, p. A-17.

tees, undermining the intended institutional character of the IG function in the first transition after the 1978 act.

The second issue related to presidential policy apparatus to be discussed here is that OMB has lost much of its management policy leadership to the CCMA. OMB's "management side" withered during Reagan's initial months in office, through heavy loss of resources to regulatory review and other functions and through a deliberate narrowing of concerns. OMB did reestablish meetings with the assistant secretaries for management and administration, a practice of the Johnson, Nixon, and Ford years, but these were mostly concerned with a limited range of waste, fraud, and abuse activities, including important new accountability provisions. During Reagan's first eighteen months, the OPE persistently urged increased attention to federal administrative and program management for implementation of Reagan's agenda, and the CCMA was finally created under Meese's leadership. Only with this development did OMB demonstrate renewed interest in management leadership. Reform '88 was announced the same day as the formation of the CCMA. However, it was a hurried initiative lacking in definition and substance and comprised an incoherent collection of nine existing activities and vague hopes. Working conferences with agency IGs, assistant secretaries, the CCMA, and others later brought substance to the OMB program, but considerable leadership in management policy nonetheless shifted from OMB to the CCMA, where it remained early in 1984.

Two 1983 recommendations for OMB reorganization focus on perceived deficiencies in its management role and are based on a generally rejected concept from before the New Deal that policy and implementation may be separated. One proposal, by the President's Private Sector Survey on Cost Control (PPSSCC—the Grace Commission), recommended creating an Office of Federal Management (OFM) to replace OMB.[34] The Grace proposal called for a budgeting office to be placed under OFM, along with attenuated GSA and OPM units (with most staff-operating functions decentralized to agencies). A second proposal, by NAPA, suggested an opposite approach from that highly centralized administrative staff model. NAPA also called for creation of an OFM, but one formed by taking the neglected management activity out of OMB.[35] The result would be recreation within the EOP of a budget office and the addition of a separate management office. NAPA would have policy functions as it had recommended in 1980, separate from both the budget and management office.

---

34. President's Private Sector Survey on Cost Control (PPSSCC), *Task Force Report on Federal Management Systems* (Washington, D.C.: PPSSCC, June 13, 1983).
35. National Academy of Public Administration, *Revitalizing Federal Management*.

Besides the classic issues about EOP apparatus, these two proposals for restructuring OMB point up two crucial subissues: (1) Is the central budgeting process—which is largely a negative control process as practiced—consistent with positive policy development and management functions, or are those activities best separated? and (2) How are budgeting and policy development interrelated? Which drives what? and How may those functions best be structured in the EOP apparatus?

It is clear from the FY 1985 combined budget and procurement policy review that OMB's budgeting process can be used at the micro level to enforce the Reagan agenda, although that is a pale reflection of its more sweeping use for earlier cutbacks. Whether used surgically, as in the FY 1985 example, or as a meat ax, as in 1981, the budget remains the key instrument to enforce policy. Therefore, where and how that function is structured is crucial to the policy process. President Reagan's Grace Commission demonstrated little understanding of the complexities of that process in the EOP or elsewhere in government.

Presidential Policy Apparatus Issues

With Reagan's agenda as the policy, the Reagan policy apparatus is strictly secondary to that. Within that context, however, the policy apparatus has the important function of coordinating the administration's actions from the president through subcabinet operating levels. With respect to the three classic issues of EOP policy machinery noted throughout this discussion, three conclusions stand out from the Reagan experience.

First, the Reagan policy apparatus is structured and staffed around strictly partisan and personal presidential loyalty, largely excluding professional expertise. The gradual politicization and deinstitutionalization of the EOP since the late 1960s has culminated under Reagan in an unprecedented partisan presidential system that reaches from the White House deeply into agency-operating levels. Institutionalized expertise and professionalism are rarely present at high levels within the EOP or elsewhere, making virtually certain a complete turnover in the policy and implementation apparatus with a change of administration. The Reagan administration has demonstrated almost no appreciation of institutionalization as a means to achieve lasting force or continuity beyond its time in office.

Second, dispersion of policy responsibilities characterizes the formal policy structure under Meese, where much of the power is located. Principal power also resides in OMB, which exercised greatest clout during Reagan's first year. The fragmentation in the EOP appears to be overcome only owing to the compelling control of the Reagan agenda. If that focused policy direction were absent, restructuring of the complex and loosely organized EOP policy apparatus would be essential. Even the Reagan experience suggests consideration of three basic EOP domestic policy development units: domestic and international economic affairs; other domestic policy; and governmental administration. Budgeting as policy would and will persist as an issue, but a return to EOP unity in BOB/OMB seems highly unlikely. Also, although needed, long-term EOP policy research and analysis seem impossible, since short-term political considerations are increasingly hostile to the institutionalized expertise, professionalism, and reflection required for long-range approaches.

Third, despite persistent conflicts, a high measure of collegial interaction has been achieved between the EOP, cabinet officers, and top policy levels within agencies. Cabinet Councils for the most part have helped to facilitate that. EOP/agency conflict has been common in OMB policy control activities, however, resulting in persistent criticisms of inappropriate EOP/agency/congressional imbalance in policy processes.

In sum, the Reagan presidency has achieved an exceptional measure of sustained policy direction, accounted for by the president's fixed agenda. The policy apparatus implements the agenda, which in large measure has taken the form of an ideology. Only after damaging policy failures has the administration acceded reluctantly to broader political considerations to modify its fixed positions. Thus, as an ideology the Reagan agenda has proved to be a major obstacle to its own implementation. Whether more limited government and self-governance might be more nearly achieved if pursued in the American political system as a flexible philosophy rather than as an unyielding ideology remains untested.

COMMENTS   *Ben W. Heineman, Jr.*

Marrying Politics And Policy

Leo Tolstoy's *Anna Karenina* begins: "Happy families are all alike: every unhappy family is unhappy in its own way." A paraphrase of that famous sentence states the bedrock principle on which any discussion of policy management in the Executive Office of the President must begin: The successes of policy management are alike because they are built on a happy marriage between policy and politics; failures of policy management are failures in their own ways because marriages between policy and politics are not consummated for many reasons.

Reconciling the tensions, even antagonisms, between the world of policy (what is desirable) and the world of politics (what is feasible) is, in my judgment, the supreme act of political leadership. EOP policy management is a crucial process for trying to make that marriage work. In starkest terms, a successful policy process must provide a coherent view of the striking complexities and contradictions of national policy; it must relate that policy perspective to the many levels and facets of present politics; and it must seek to move present politics toward a desired policy, while finding a balance between high-risk and lower-risk initiatives for the president.

The need to marry policy and politics is at the core of the four issues of governmental structure and process raised by Chester A. Newland. Yet he does not give that crucial connection its due. To be sure, a political leader's fusion of policy and politics is much like Louis Armstrong's retort when asked to define jazz: "If you got to ask, you can't know." Clearly, the happy marriage of policy and politics is determined by key factors that all of us can recognize but none of us can prescribe, such as the president's personality, the chemistry between his key appointees, the tides of history, and good luck. Yet certain core prescriptions have emerged from the post–New Deal presidencies. These prescriptions have been underscored and made concrete by lessons from the Carter administration's difficulties—difficulties that the Reagan administration has tried to avoid.

169

I will summarize some of the more salient prescriptions according to the four issues raised by Newland, but I will take those issues two at a time.

The EOP and the Cabinet

Newland asks how to achieve a reasonable balance in policy development between the agencies and the EOP, a question closely tied to the issue of how to organize and run the EOP. In briefest terms, I believe that the following principles provide a framework for solving the puzzle of cabinet-EOP relations and EOP structure over which so much ink has been spilt (at least with respect to policy development as opposed to policy implementation). The principles are based on differentiating four roles in the policy development process: process-management, advice giving, decision making on discrete issues, and strategic thinking/decision making.

- The administration should have an overall strategy of governing that, among other things, divides the major issues it will face into first-, second-, and third-order initiatives and establishes a time sequence for dealing with them.

- On first-order issues, which should be limited to five or so in domestic affairs, the president makes virtually all significant decisions. The decision process is managed within the EOP, and advice is given by both relevant agencies and relevant EOP units.

- On second-order issues, which should number about twenty-five, the president makes the basic decision on the shape of the policy, but subsequent decisions on details are made at a subpresidential level, probably within the EOP. (For these purposes, I consider the Treasury Department secretary—as head of the troika—to be, in effect, part of the EOP.) Again, the agencies have full access to provide advice. Unless the issue is dominated by a single department or agency, the decision-making process is managed within the EOP.

- On third-order issues, the president, in essence, merely identifies the issues as important to the record of his administration but leaves virtually all decision making to others—because his ideology or campaign promises have already given shape to those issues or because the issues are controlled by decisions made on first- and second-order issues. On issues cutting across departments, decision making takes place in the EOP. On department or agency-specific issues, decision making is primarily the task of the secretary or agency head.

- These first-, second-, and third-order issues are handled in one of three policy channels: first, economic affairs headed by the Treasury secretary as chair of the troika; second, budget and program coordination under the aegis of the OMB director; and third, domestic affairs headed by a top presidential assistant. The "domestic affairs" channel should be limited to the ten to twenty first- and second-order domestic issues that do not go through the economic or budget channels. Within these channels, subgroupings of affected departments and EOP units will deal with specific issues.

- The political threads of the administration are joined in the hands of an assistant for political affairs who oversees relations with Congress, state and local governments, the interest groups, party officials, and the media. This office must participate extensively in policy formulation in the three substantive channels.

- Crucial to the operation of this system of policy development is the president's chief of staff, who is responsible primarily for developing the strategy of governing; for ensuring that policy is consistent with that strategy; and for making the (often arbitrary) decisions about which issues should be handled in which channels and at which levels. The chief of staff must also mediate or arbitrate second- or third-order issues short of the president when advice givers strongly dissent from the initial, subpresidential decision maker. The crucial system of delegating second- and third-order decisions away from the president, and of making the delicate system of centralization and decentralization work, depends on the chief of staff's functioning, in effect, as deputy president.

On this set of issues—EOP/cabinet relations and EOP structure—the Carter administration was, in many respects, not a success. There was no sustained strategy of governing; little appreciation of priorities; significant squandering of the president's time on second- and third-order issues; no clear system of subpresidential decision making; uncertainty about which channel would handle which issue; fragmented political advice; an inability to join policy and politics, in part because the political advisers were untutored in policy (and often did not seem to care); and the absence of a chief of staff who could function as a de facto deputy president.

In its first twelve to eighteen months, the Reagan administration, on the other hand, tried to act in a manner somewhat consistent with the principles just suggested, according to the accounts of Newland and others. The president, whether for biological or managerial reasons, concentrated his energies on first- and second-order issues (although it appears that he is often out of touch, even on these crucial issues, and functions only as an effective spokesman for staff decisions). Much of the subpresidential decision making seemed to occur in relatively well-defined channels of activity—in other words, in the Cabinet Council on Economic Affairs for economic policy and OMB for a range of budget and other policy issues. The political strands were tightly interwoven in the hands of James Baker, III. And the Baker-Meese-Deaver triumvirate functioned loosely as a collective deputy president, trying to coordinate policy and politics, making final decisions short of the president, and overseeing the strategy of governing.

But problems also surfaced or increased in severity over time. As noted, the president's penchant for delegation was viewed by many as a gloss for his lack of involvement in, even lack of knowledge about, decisions on first-order issues, let alone secondary ones. Significant strains developed within the triumvirate, tensions that were due, in part, to Meese's unsteady handling of the "domestic affairs" channel and uncertain supervision of the OPD. That channel has been less coherent and less well-defined than the economic and budget channels, and, in fact, has been the source of some major gaffes (as in the administration's initial Social Security proposals).

I do not read Newland as disagreeing with any of the principles summarized here. But with respect to the prescriptive part of Newland's paper, he has not paid enough attention to some key issues: the president's different levels of involvement in policy development depending on the relative importance of various issues; the differing EOP and agency functions of advice giving, process managing, decision making, and strategic thinking; the complexities of the system of subpresidential decision making, which I have only hinted at; and the crucial role of the chief of staff as a referee and arbiter in that subpresidential system.

Prospects for a Strategic Presidency

Newland's paper poses two other questions about policy development that must be answered together: how to manage a strategic presidency when the political environment often requires quick, reactive behavior, and what are the respective roles of the president's personal staff and the EOP's institutional staff.

On the issue of how to manage a strategic presidency, a few core principles on which there appears to be general agreement may be briefly stated.

- Initially, presidential strategy needs to be defined. It is, in my view, an attempt to join the four basic dimensions of executive government—policy, politics, process (how things get done), and structure (who does them)—in a four- or eight-year time frame.

- Politics is not just short-term reaction but, seen properly, also involves understanding the political map of America and trying to build strategic coalitions and shape a new consensus to support innovative policy. Thus, politics has a crucial strategic element just as policy does.

- Policy management within the EOP is only part of the broader processes of policy innovation and implementation. As to policy innovation, which is largely the subject of Newland's paper, securing external support for White House policy or adapting policy proposals to congressional or other political pressures is just as important as is the process of developing policy within the executive branch—a process to which the Reagan administration, via the Legislative Strategy Group, has given greater weight than did the Carter administration. Thus, policy management as part of policy innovation cannot be separated from strategic political thinking, and policy "types" must work constantly with political "types" in shaping issues both before and after the president announces his policy—points that, I feel, deserved greater emphasis by Newland.

- An administration needs to articulate a strategy for itself in order to provide the necessary framework for deciding future issues arising in all four dimensions of executive government—and for reducing the inevitable intra-administration conflict over what is in the president's interest. For maximum effect, this strategy must be communicated to high-level appointees in the early days of an administration, which, in turn, means that the most important task of the transition is to develop the strategy of governing. Major personnel decisions should be made as quickly as possible after the election (which assumes much preelection planning), leaving two full months for strategic thinking. Moreover, the strategy, although organic in detail, should be reformulated in its essential terms only once—presumably at midterm if at all—unless there is a major crisis.

- The chief of staff/deputy president must, short of the president, reconcile the inevitable conflicts between short-term political and policy needs and longer-term political and policy aspirations as reflected in the strategy of governing. The deputy president—and the president— are where the policy and political tensions merge and where they must be resolved in a broader strategic framework.

Given the fundamental need for a presidential strategy, there can be only one answer to the related question posed by Newland about the type of individuals who should manage the EOP/administration policy machinery: they must be loyal to the president and attuned to his politics. This is so because, as I have emphasized, the core of a strategic presidency is the joining of policy *and* politics. In addition, the fundamental task of the EOP must be to act as the strategic center for the presidency. The EOP must be capable at its highest levels of surveying the entire terrain of the domestic presidency (and of the "international" presidency, too) and of plotting a four-year path across that terrain. The concept of a strategic presidency is built, in part, on the need to integrate operationally in the EOP that which in the past has often been distinguished conceptually: "personal" and "institutional" staffs, politics and policy, "budget" and "policy" considerations, and economic and social issues (not to mention foreign and domestic concerns).

Loyalty to the president need not mean lack of professional, policy competence, nor need it mean excessive preoccupation with transient politics. Presidential appointments to both the personal staff and to the "institutional" elite—for example, to the highest levels of economic, OMB, and domestic affairs staffs—must have a high degree of professional competence. The political people must have a well-grounded knowledge of and aptitude for policy, just as the policy people, in addition to requisite technical skills in leading the institutional staff, must have a firm knowledge of and aptitude for politics. And both political and policy personnel must have a strong sense of longer-term issues as a filter for the political and policy pressures of the moment. That, at least, is the ideal that each administration must try to realize.

The Carter administration had obvious difficulties in following the principles of a strategic presidency. Lacking strategic coherence and often even the means for trying to formulate a strategy of governing, Carter's presidency was heavily criticized for its fragmentation, its zigzags, and its confusing signals—to such an extent that Carter's basic competence was a major issue in the 1980 presidential campaign. The Reagan administration, possessing at least a degree of strategic coherence, will present to the country in the 1984 campaign the basic question of whether its policies and politics are appropriate to this moment in our nation's history. Nonetheless, it should be remembered that the administration lost the initiative on basic taxing and spending issues to the Congress after its first year. President Reagan's lack of involvement in his own government could also become an important issue for the electorate.

I do not believe that Newland would disagree with the core principles of a strategic presidency as stated here, except that he would perhaps wish for a greater "institutional" presence at the top of the policy management machinery. But a strategic presidency requires personnel in key policy positions who, while professionally competent, are nonetheless fundamentally attuned to the politics of the president's policies. "Institutional" continuity will not necessarily suffer, because there are numerous policy professionals outside government waiting for a new tour of duty. Especially in an era where there are sharp differences between administrations on the role of government, turnover in key policy personnel is almost inevitable.

Finally, it must be stressed that the principles of governmental structure and process that are the focus of Newland's paper must be understood against the backdrop of the policy and political conflicts of particular historical moments. It is a testament to the Reagan administration's technique of governing—as opposed to its substance—that, despite major divisions within the Republican party (and despite not a few blunders and squabbles), this administration generally has managed to give the impression of a united, coherent front.

But, if one believes, as I do, that the Reagan administration has so far avoided some of the most profound policy conflicts—such as the deficit—that inevitably lie ahead, then no amount of skill may prevent the administration from being rent by conflict between opposing camps. Indeed, in late 1983 and early 1984, an unusual amount of public bickering among high-level economic officials in the administration over budget and taxes was an indication of the growing internal discomfiture with what the administration had previously wrought. Technique may ameliorate, but it cannot smooth away, the profound conflicts in policy and politics that exist in our political system today. Those conflicts may, in the end, disrupt technical skills used in manipulating the structures and processes of executive government. That could be the story during Reagan's second term.

Yet such a story would hardly be surprising. As suggested at the outset, issues of governmental process and structure are shaped by policy and politics at least as much as process and structure shape policy and politics.

COMMENTS   *Stephen J. Wayne*

Politics Instead Of Policy

Chester A. Newland has written an excellent paper detailing President Reagan's policy management apparatus. He describes a labyrinth of offices, councils, and groups, a veritable arrangement and disarrangement of processes and committees—formal and ad hoc, hierarchical and multilayered—designed to facilitate the policy process with as little interference as possible from outside the administration.

The purpose of this organization has not been to develop policy in the manner of contemporary presidents (Johnson through Carter), who used the process to help enumerate their objectives, establish their priorities, and construct and reconstruct their policy agendas. The Reagan administration had already declared its objectives, set its priorities, and articulated much of its agenda before taking office. What remained to be done was to implement and sell that policy.

One objective of the mechanism has been to help the president implement his decisions by providing him an assessment of viable options. Another goal has been to mobilize support for these decisions within the administration. A third objective, to build external coalitions, has been the principal task of the operational White House staffs, such as congressional liaison and public liaison, although the policy units have input here as well.

To develop workable options, the administration turned to experts within the executive branch. To keep these options within Reagan's prescriptive framework, the White House required these experts to pass a litmus test of loyalty. To minimize the impact of traditional forces that affect and afflict presidential policymaking, the administration rewarded teamwork, penalized noncollegial behavior, and coopted or ignored departmental interests. Newland's paper explains how this has been accomplished, how the mechanism has worked to discourage new domestic programs, to promote internal harmony and cooperation, and to contain and mute pressures that deviate from the administration's basic course.

176

OPD: Breaking With Tradition

If the past were indicative, one could have expected the Office of Policy Development (OPD), the successor to Nixon and Ford's Domestic Council and Carter's Domestic Policy Staff, to develop programs as its primary responsibility. It has done little of this on its own. Instead, this office has been concerned mainly with managing the president's domestic casework and providing institutional support for the Cabinet Councils.

The break with tradition can be explained by the domestic goals of consolidation and retrenchment and by the instruments used to accomplish them: budget cuts, personnel reductions, and regulation oversight. It would be hard to imagine a highly visible policy shop churning out scores of legislative proposals in an administration that wanted to shrink the federal government's role in the domestic area.

The anomaly and frustration of working on such a staff has already taken its toll. Reagan has had three assistants for policy development in three years. There has also been considerable turnover among middle-level aides. These personnel shifts have further impeded the visible output of the OPD and the less-visible influence it has been able to exert within the administration.

The operation of the OPD raises some interesting questions: Is a separate presidential office necessary and/or desirable to perform these coordinating, liaison, and staffing functions? Could the job be adequately or even more effectively handled by career professionals (such as those from OMB)? More important, what is the effect of not having a separate domestic policy adviser (sometimes critic, sometimes advocate) in the high echelons of the White House? (I am assuming that White House Counselor Edwin Meese, III, the chief policy adviser to the president, was more of a broker, coordinator, and overseer and that his duties were so broad as to preclude his in-depth involvement on a wide range of policy matters.) What does this suggest about the kind of issues that will or will not get the president's attention and the kinds of treatment that policy matters will receive in this White House?

Role of the Cabinet Councils

To address the latter question one must turn to the Cabinet Councils, a unique variation on the familiar theme of cabinet government. The councils bring relevant department heads and their principal assistants together on different levels to develop and integrate interagency policy—an important function, to be sure, but as Newland tells us, one that has worked unevenly in this administration. He suggests that differing personalities and functions explain the varying levels of activity in the council—to which I would add a third explanatory variable, that of proximity to presidential priorities. In areas of high priority, economic affairs, and governmental management, Cabinet Councils have met regularly, have dealt with key issues, and have made recommendations to the president. In areas of lower priority, they have not.

The principal incentive for activity in the councils appears to be presidential interest and the need for a policy forum, a coordinating mechanism, and the dual objectives mentioned earlier: the presentation of a range of options and the promotion of internal harmony. That two students of organization and management, Roger Porter and Ralph Bledsoe, have assumed administrative responsibility for the economic and management councils has undoubtedly contributed to their functional success.

Whether the Cabinet Councils actually expand presidential discretion or limit it is a question that needs to be explored. A related issue is the extent to which President Reagan is dependent on his councils' and counselors' judgments in making his own decisions. A third potential problem and an old one is the "group-think" aspect of a discussion among loyalists in which department interests are downplayed, an administrative perspective is promoted, and certain goals and assumptions are not debated or even debatable, certainly not within the president's presence. The fear is the danger that George Reedy wrote about more than thirteen years ago.[1] I have no doubt that the Cabinet Councils are helping to fortify the president's objectives and to implement them, but I question their sensitivity to a range of public interests and needs while doing so.

OMB and OPE

Two other policy units need to be mentioned: the Office of Management and Budget and the Office of Planning and Evaluation. The former has had a major impact on the policy apparatus in the Reagan administration; the latter has not.

The use of the budget as a packaging mechanism and as the vehicle for imposing the cuts in domestic programs has effectively reduced the roles and influence of other units within the EOP at the same time that it has increased

---

1. George Reedy, *The Twilight of the Presidency* (New York: New American Library, 1970).

the role of OMB. Moreover, the Reagan administration's imposition of a more centralized executive budgetary process, controlled by David Stockman and influenced by key presidential aides, has extended further OMB's clout, to the detriment of departments and agencies within the executive branch. OMB has operated as independently as any presidential agency ever has, with the result (as Newland correctly points out) that OMB's budgetary decisions drive the domestic policy process rather than vice versa.[2]

In contrast to OMB, the OPE has had a limited impact beyond its initial scenario for the rapid deployment and implementation of Reagan's new agenda. Newland suggests the traditional reason for the lack of influence: Short-term considerations tend to force out long-term planning. However, in this administration quite the opposite has occurred. Long-range goals have managed to structure and contain short-range considerations. This would suggest that this administration needs a long-range perspective for strategic, not substantive, policy concerns. Hence, the problem for the OPE is that it may be located on the wrong side of the White House hierarchy, with Meese rather than with Baker.

In sum, from a short-term political perspective and on the basis of the administration's goals, the domestic policy apparatus seems to be working well. It has enabled Reagan to stay his course and his administration to appear to speak with a single voice. Internal dissent has been muted (albeit with the threat of polygraphs), and the "going-native" syndrome, whereby secretaries advocate their department's interests, has been contained (although not eliminated). The public understands the direction of the administration and the presidential force behind it. Reagan is seen as a strong leader despite his penchant to delegate and his tendency to wait for decisions to "perk up" to him. The contrasts with Ford and Carter are striking.

From the perspective of effective administration and responsive governance, the verdict is less clear. A system in which most policymaking units do not generate new programs or do so marginally and reactively does not impress me as fulfilling the needs of the institution that has become the principal policymaker of our national government. Nor has the responsiveness of the system been demonstrated. Can and will it adjust to changing public pressures and environmental impacts? Can and will it admit to the adverse effects its policies have had on certain groups within the society? Is pragmatism in the pursuit of ideology possible?

Within the legislative arena, pragmatism certainly has played a role; the president has been forced to make numerous compromises. Within the ex-

---

2. See paper by Schick in this volume.

ecutive arena, however, ideological purity has more often prevailed, with policy remaining closely tied to the president's beliefs about the role of government within the domestic sphere. Of course, there has been some backing off, but there has been no reversal of Reagan's basic philosophical thrust. Even the 1984 election has not altered the administration's basic goals, although these goals have affected its salesmanship. Thus, staying the course may be both the short-term strength and potentially the long-term weakness of domestic policy development in the Reagan presidency.

PRIVATE-SECTOR INITIATIVES IN THE REAGAN ERA: NEW ACTORS REWORK AN OLD THEME

Renée A. Berger

On October 5, 1981, President Ronald Reagan announced his private-sector initiatives strategy. In a speech before the National Alliance of Business (NAB)—a group that had been created during the administration of Lyndon Baines Johnson to increase private-sector involvement in government efforts to reduce unemployment—Reagan outlined a two-part program to establish a special presidential task force and to initiate a comprehensive effort to be undertaken by the cabinet.[1] The President's Task Force on Private Sector Initiatives (herein referred to as the Task Force) was to be a blue-ribbon panel composed of thirty-five civic leaders (later increased to forty-four). Its purpose, the president explained, would be "to promote private sector leadership and responsibility for solving public needs, and to recommend ways of fostering greater public-private partnerships."[2] The directive for the cabinet stipulated that it was to "review agency procedures and regulations and identify barriers to private sector involvement . . . (and) develop pump-priming and seed money programs that offer incentives for private sector investment." Furthermore, the cabinet was to "provide technical knowledge to develop private initiatives" and was to examine "existing programs . . . to determine which could be more productively carried out by the private sector."[3]

So began an effort that proved to be not only highly visible and controversial but extremely difficult to define. To sort out the president's and his

---

1. *Public Papers of the Presidents of the United States: Ronald Reagan*, Remarks at the Annual Meeting of the National Alliance of Business, 5 October 1981, (Washington, D.C.: Government Printing Office, 1981).
2. *Public Papers of the Presidents*, National Alliance of Business, p. 885.
3. *Public Papers of the Presidents*, National Alliance of Business, p. 885–886.

aides' intentions and describe the results of those intentions, one must examine the history predating the NAB speech, as well as the administration's subsequent actions.

The private-sector initiatives strategy has evolved over three phases. Phase one, the planning stage, began during the presidential transition period with a paper written by John McLaughry (who eventually was appointed to a White House policy position). The paper advised the creation of a private initiatives program.[4] In January 1981, the idea of the private-sector initiative was further advanced in a memorandum to White House Chief of Staff James A. Baker, III, from Robert Mosbacher, Jr., who had been an aide to Senator Howard Baker. In the memorandum Mosbacher expressed concern over the impact of the budget cuts and the need for business to take on new responsibilities for solving community problems.[5] Phase two began in October 1981 with the creation of the Task Force. Phase three, which is still evolving, began in January 1983 after the Task Force's termination.

Owing to the fact that the history of these initiatives has never been fully documented (no magazine articles have been published describing the first phase and only two articles have focused on the second phase),[6] the account here has been reconstructed from interviews with senior White House aides affiliated with the private-sector initiative effort, and from comments provided by Task Force members on early drafts of this paper, and from interviews with executives of key nonprofit organizations and research institutions affected by the private-sector initiative program, staff of the Task Force, and federal-agency personnel responsible for implementing the private-sector initiative program. This paper also draws on my personal experience coauthoring several studies on public-private partnerships and serving as a division director for the Task Force.

Past Presidential Interest in Private-Sector Initiatives

Before analyzing the Reagan private-sector initiatives strategy, it is useful to examine the context in which it evolved. Ronald Reagan's political platform promised to rejuvenate the economy and improve the morale of a citizenry that had been told by President Jimmy Carter that it was suffering from

---

4. Jay Moorhead, interview with author, October 1984.

5. Robert Mosbacher, Jr., telephone interview with author, November 1983.

6. Marvin N. Olansky, "Reagan's Second Thoughts on Corporate Giving," *Fortune* (20 September 1982), pp. 130–136; and Richard J. Margolis, "Great Expectations, Questionable Results," *Foundation News*, (March/April 1983).

malaise. Reagan's proposed program had several components: tax cuts, expenditure reductions in nondefense areas, deregulation, and a philosophy of promoting individual initiative. In general, the president proposed that there be a massive shift to market-oriented policies, that government be brought closer to the people, and that self-reliance be encouraged. Fundamentally, the administration's entire program was rooted in private-sector initiative.

With the creation of a presidential task force, the private-sector initiative effort was boosted to public prominence. Presidential task forces and advisory commissions have often been formed to defuse a politically sensitive issue (e.g., Lyndon Baines Johnson's Kerner Commission on the urban riots) or to promote a president's favorite subject (e.g., John F. Kennedy's mental health commission). In establishing his private sector initiatives Task Force, Reagan combined the promotion of one of his favorite subjects—private-sector initiative—and the defusing of a rising public storm over the budget cuts.

Other presidential initiatives taken in the past have promoted philanthropy and the related subject of volunteering. In particular, during both World Wars I and II, the federal government was directly involved in organizing volunteers to assist in activities ranging from health care for soldiers to entertaining them. The concept of federal involvement in organizing volunteers for non-wartime programs emerged in the Kennedy administration with the creation of the Peace Corps in 1961.

In November 1962 President Kennedy announced the formation of a President's Study Group for National Service, a group that nurtured the idea of a domestic peace corps. A bill to establish such a corps was drafted but was eventually killed in Congress, after which the study group reconvened and searched for new models to present to Congress. Kennedy's death temporarily stemmed the initiative, but it regained a foothold under President Johnson as the VISTA program within the Office of Economic Opportunity.

Notably, this emergent government role in volunteering offered a framework for Johnson to expand his agenda by asking the business community to assist in tackling unemployment. This request led to the creation of NAB, an organization that both then and now relies on business executives volunteering time to make its efforts operational. In addition, during this period the U.S. life insurance industry undertook a unique initiative to organize a massive program to inject $2 billion into urban areas. This was not a government-organized initiative but did receive the encouragement of the president and cabinet. Today, like the NAB, the insurance industry's Center for Corporate Public Involvement carries out private sector initiatives to mitigate unemployment and urban decline.

In 1971 the Nixon administration formed ACTION—an umbrella organization including the Peace Corps, VISTA, and several other volunteer programs utilizing senior citizens (Foster Grandparents Program) and business executives (Service Corps of Retired Executives). By late 1971, most federal departments had begun volunteer programs. At the same time, Congress mandated the creation of a private-sector agency—the National Center for Voluntary Action—to assist and educate the public about volunteering.[7]

Under President Carter the emphasis shifted beyond volunteering to voluntary organizations (nonprofit, particularly community-based organizations) and to the new concept of a "partnership" between government and the private sector. The Carter administration's centerpiece for action in this area was its national urban policy, bearing the title "A New Partnership to Conserve America's Communities." This partnership proposed encompassing the public sector as well as business, nonprofit organizations, and neighborhoods, for the purpose of stabilizing the economies of cities in decline, as well as encouraging opportunities for growth. A central aspect of this new partnership was to leverage public funds by requiring private-sector financial participation, particularly for urban economic development in distressed cities. In 1978 private-sector involvement in solving public employment needs was added to the Comprehensive Employment and Training Act (CETA). Title VII authorized the creation of local private industry councils that invited local business executives to participate in solving unemployment.

The concept of private-sector initiatives thus has a long history predating the Reagan program. Over time, the concept has grown more expansive—both in terms of the groups participating (initiatives now encompass youth, senior citizens, and business executives) and the constituencies affected (these now include the poor, the elderly, children, the unemployed, cities in distress, and even new businesses in need of technical assistance). All of Reagan's recent predecessors used conventional policy tools—budget, legislation, organizational structure, and leadership— to assert their priorities in this area.

The Reagan Approach

Reagan's private-sector initiative is not only more expansive but includes innovative dimensions not present in earlier efforts. For one thing, Reagan has maximized the symbolism of presidential leadership, using the presidency

---

7. Susan J. Ellis and Katherine H. Noyes, *By the People: A History of Americans as Volunteers* (Philadelphia: Michael D. Prestegord and Co., 1978), pp. 177–226.

to highlight leaders as role models and to persuade them to encourage their constituencies to engage in private-sector initiative. In a sense, President Johnson's appeal to create the NAB had the same basis. However, with Reagan the scale is broader—calling on business, labor, religious groups, and so forth. In addition, an organizational structure has been created to give the concept White House status as well as to blend the initiative with other administration actions.

The Reagan private-sector initiative program could logically have been a part of the administration's "new federalism" proposal. In fact, Mosbacher's appeal to James Baker initially was referred to Richard Williamson, the White House official in charge of the new federalism effort. New federalism suggested a realignment in the delivery of services, and private-sector initiative implies that there is a role for the private sector—specifically, the for-profit firm—in service delivery. Beyond an initial meeting of Mosbacher with Williamson, however, the administration did not capitalize on this logical link.

The motivation for private-sector initiative was to soften the impact of the budget cuts by demonstrating that the private sector—the business community—could help solve community needs. The initiative can be viewed as a cousin both of Reagan's economic policy as well as of new federalism, although the program's administrative handling never clearly placed it within a policy context. As is discussed later in this paper, the administration may well have lost a major opportunity by failing to give the program full policy credence.

Policy commitment is traditionally measured by evidence of legislative activity as well as budgetary assistance. Other measures include organizational structure (scale and status) and leadership activities. It is problematic to determine whether the Reagan private-sector effort should be regarded as a policy. On the one hand, the program was not placed in a policymaking office, its staff did not have policy backgrounds, opportunities for utilizing legislative clout were steadfastly avoided, and a proscription was placed on accessing public funding. On the other hand, a special White House office was established, a presidential task force was created, an advisory council is now in place, the president routinely speaks on private-sector initiative, and a private-sector initiatives structure has been established across agencies. Since 1983 strictures on using public funds have been relaxed, but the legislative docket is still largely moribund. Over time the private-sector effort has taken on features associated with policy, but it has never been comprehensively organized as such.

Overall, it can be said that the private-sector initiatives effort has suffered from a lack of clarity as to what it was expected to accomplish and how it was to proceed. Furthermore, the range of policy tools at the White House's disposal was applied slowly and unevenly. On matters of budget and legislation, in particular, the private-sector initiatives effort has fallen silent in the face of philosophical restraints and political sensitivities.

The section following describes more fully how the White House Office of Private Sector Initiatives and the President's Task Force on Private Sector Initiatives developed, how they operated, and what consequences they had. This is followed by a discussion of other Reagan programs that have emerged within the federal agencies under the rubric of private-sector initiatives. A final section assesses the significance of the private-sector initiatives of the Reagan era.

The White House and Task Force Efforts

Phase One: Planning

One concept shared by the original architects of Reagan's private-sector initiatives strategy was that the budget cuts were facing a hostile public and that there would be a need to mitigate the impact of these cuts. Given Reagan's private-sector orientation, it is logical that the administration would look to the private sector for assistance in "selling" the budget. As noted earlier, a key element in the planning stage began with Robert Mosbacher, Jr.'s, memorandum in January 1981 to James Baker, suggesting that the expertise of the business community be tapped in solving community problems. In March Mosbacher stated his case in a *New York Times* editorial:

> We can no longer afford to view the Government as the first, last, and only resort for the treatment of myriad social and economic problems. Rather, amid the hand-wringing over how and where to cut the Federal budget, it behooves us to find new and innovative ways to deal with old problems. . . . The most efficient and practical alternative is the American business community.[8]

After the initial meeting with Richard Williamson, Mosbacher's proposal was referred to Elizabeth Dole, then director of the White House Office of Public Liaison, who was in charge of a "business coalition" strategy designed to recruit the business community's support of the president's economic package. This was the first of several critical junctures that shaped the private-sector initiative. Why the proposal was referred to Dole rather than staying

---

8. Robert Mosbacher, Jr., "How Business Can Help," *The New York Times*, (6 March 1981).

with Williamson or being referred to the White House policy office is a matter of conjecture, and is one indicator suggesting that this was intended to be a public relations strategy more than a policy-oriented effort.

Many business executives were wary of Reagan and of the untested theory of "supply-side" economics. To calm their anxieties Dole had orchestrated gatherings comprised of corporate and trade association executives in order to develop a network and to facilitiate lobbying on behalf of the administration. The respective responsibilities for organizing a private-sector program effort and a business-coalition strategy were given to two aides in Dole's office.

The idea of a private-sector initiative program was then presented to the president at a private dinner with senior White House staff and Senator Howard Baker. Reagan, it was reported, welcomed the concept and expressed his willingness to make public statements supporting the effort.

Given the green light, Dole's aide assigned to the private sector initiative and Mosbacher met with members of the business community and with executives from business associations such as the Business Roundtable, the National Federation of Independent Businesses, and the National Association of Manufacturers. These meetings were designed both to obtain input from the business community and to stem a growing concern that the corporate sector would be caught in an untenable position of high expectations that they could not meet.

In another memorandum to James Baker dated May 28, 1981, Mosbacher offered a proposal for "a modest, realistic private sector program in the area of employment, which we believe has a high probability of success and a relatively low risk of exposure or embarrassment to the Administration." Mosbacher outlined an organizational strategy of forming a "steering committee of approximately 15 to 25 top representatives of small, medium, and large businesses" who would implement a specific goal "to employ as many of the 325,000 displaced CETA workers as possible."[9]

James Baker, however, was occupied full-time with the legislative demands of the economic package. Mosbacher therefore asked Senator Howard Baker to urge the White House to move ahead with planning a program. Mosbacher reported that the senator sent a letter to Michael Deaver, deputy chief of staff, emphasizing the "priority" of a private-sector program.[10] The senator was successful in reactivating the effort, with Michael Deaver put in charge.

---

9. Robert Mosbacher, Jr., memorandum to James Baker, 28 May 1981.
10. Robert Mosbacher, Jr., telephone interview with author, January 1983.

This was the second critical juncture. The shift from James Baker to Deaver suggests again that public relations was a key impetus. Under Reagan, policy responsibilities fell largely to Presidential Counselor Edwin Meese, III, and also to Baker, whereas Deaver has dealt principally with the president's image. White House aides have characterized Deaver's designation in this role as "natural," stating that "he has been with the president for twenty-seven years. The topic had personal meaning for the president and through Deaver, its priority could be ensured." These aides contend that had the proposal been placed in the policy area, it would have risked becoming a peripheral aspect of the economic program. Deaver, they note, guaranteed proximity to the president and ensured that the initiative would be on Reagan's calendar.[11]

Deaver has in fact proven successful in keeping private-sector initiatives high on Reagan's agenda. Deaver's interpretation of the effort was revealed in the subsequent negotiations with the American Enterprise Institute (AEI), which had been studying grass-roots private-sector initiative for over five years and had gained a reputation early in the Reagan administration as the president's think tank. The AEI was asked to take a lead role in a private-sector initiative program, and Reagan sent a letter to William Baroody, Jr., the president of the AEI, making this request official.[12] The AEI then rapidly organized internally to create a Center for the Study of Private Initiative.

However, in mid-summer 1981 James Rosebush, the director of business liaison at the Department of Commerce and former manager of contributions at Standard Oil of Ohio, was loaned to the White House to work under Deaver on the private-sector initiative. Deaver, Rosebush, and Mosbacher agreed that business should take the lead and that action should take precedence over conducting a study. When I questioned a senior staff member at the AEI about the administration's actions, he explained that at that time, the administration didn't fully "appreciate [the AEI's] nonpartisanship and the role of research."[13] The AEI had received "encouragement"[14] for its effort, and Baroody would eventually be appointed to the Task Force. But the effort soon shifted dramatically to the business-led, action-oriented program that Rose-

---

11. White House staff aides (anonymity requested), interview with author, November 1983. On the roles of Deaver, Baker, and Meese, see also paper by Newland in this volume.

12. Ronald Reagan, letter to William Baroody, Jr., 19 June 1981.

13. Staff member of the AEI (anonymity requested), telephone interview with author, November 1983.

14. Staff member of the AEI, telephone interview with author, November 1983 describing meetings held between senior White House aides and AEI senior researchers during May–June 1981.

bush was to organize under Deaver's direction. This is one of two manifestations of senior aides' misinterpreting the role of think tanks.

Meanwhile, in summer 1981 the Committee for Economic Development (CED)—a nonpartisan research organization comprised of chief executives from business and of university presidents—was finishing drafts of two publications on public-private partnerships that were the products of two and a half years of field work in eight cities.[15] This in-depth study was motivated by findings from a 1977 CED study of urban policy that concluded: "The federal government should encourage—at the very least it should not frustrate—both active efforts and developing potential of local leadership to bring together public and private resources for the productive resolution of the problems of the cities."[16] Also in 1978 the CED published a seminal review of public-private partnerships and their role in relieving unemployment.[17]

The president of the CED met with senior aides at the White House to learn about the White House strategy and to inform them of the impending publications. At this meeting, aides asked the CED if it would lend staff to assist the White House effort. It appears, then, that the White House regarded both the AEI and the CED as potential staff resources.

The growing distance between the White House effort and outside think tanks was enlarged, however, by two Urban Institute studies. In summer 1981 the Institute released an analysis of the impact of the federal budget cuts on nonprofit organizations, in which it was estimated that nonprofit groups would lose $27 billion over the 1981–1984 period. A second study on charitable giving analyzed the projected impact of tax changes resulting from the 1981 Economic Recovery and Tax Reform Act and concluded that charitable giving, particularly of wealthy individuals, would decline.[18]

For an administration about to launch a major initiative to promote private-sector involvement, the Urban Institute conclusions were ominous. In simple terms, the nonprofits are widely regarded as the "third leg" of the

---

15. These manuscripts were eventually published as: R. Scott Fosler and Renée A. Berger, *Public-Private Partnership: An Opportunity for Urban Communities* (New York: Committee for Economic Development, 1982); and R. Scott Fosler and Renée A. Berger, eds., *Public-Private Partnership in American Cities, Seven Case Studies* (Lexington, Mass.: D.C. Heath and Company, 1982).

16. *An Approach to Federal Urban Policy*, (New York: Committee for Economic Development, December 1977), p. 30.

17. *Jobs for the Hard-to-Employ: New Directions for Public-Private Partnerships* (New York: Committee for Economic Development, 1978).

18. Lester M. Salamon and Alan J. Abramson, "The Federal Government and the Nonprofit Sector: Implications of the Reagan Budget Proposals" (Washington, D.C.: The Urban Institute, 1981), and Lester M. Salamon and Charles T. Clotfelter, "The Federal Government and the Nonprofit Sector: The Impact of the 1981 Tax Act on Individual Charitable Giving" (Washington, D.C.: The Urban Institute, 1981).

public-private partnership, yet the Institute cautioned that administration policies were weakening that leg. The administration's counterpoint was that the Office of Management and Budget (OMB) made these cuts as part of the overall economic program. To justify these actions the administration claimed that many of the programs were ineffective and that an improved economy would strengthen the nonprofits. However, there had been no consultation between OMB and the aides planning the private-sector initiative strategy—thus suggesting that the policy implications were never considered.

The administration's generally unproductive interactions with the AEI and the CED, and the discomfort resulting from the press attention given to the Urban Institute studies, appear to have magnified White House aides' suspicion that social scientists created more problems than solutions. Charles Wick, head of the International Communications Agency and one of Reagan's first appointees, characterized the feeling prevalent among senior advisers when he stated, "social scientists have never had to meet a payroll. That's what brought us to this calamitous point in our history. . . ." Wick believed that more social scientists were not the solution, that what was needed was the "innate common sense" of a Ronald Reagan.[19] So single-minded was the opinion among top White House aides (many of whom had business backgrounds) that social scientists "think" but do not "do," that the Task Force was asked to be action oriented and not to produce a report. The problem, however, was that there was no clarity regarding what *action* was supposed to mean. (This is discussed in the next section of this paper.)

By late August 1981 Rosebush had completed an "action plan" for the president and his senior staff, outlining the organizational arrangements and proposed schedule for implementing a private-sector initiatives program. The approach was approved, and Rosebush officially became the president's assistant for private-sector initiatives. Although the appointment demonstrated the president's high regard for the effort, Rosebush was given no staff or budget, under the rationale that federal funds should not be used to support the initiative. Philosophy and politics thus may well have initially undermined the development of a viable program.

A two-stage strategy emphasizing constituency building was planned to launch the program: a breakfast meeting with the president and his senior

19. Charles Wick is quoted in Sidney Blumenthal, "Whose Side is Business on Anyway?" *The New York Times Magazine* (25 October 1981), p. 93. A similar argument had been advanced, though not so stridently, about the problems of the Great Society programs. For example, Daniel Patrick Moynihan argued in *Maximum Feasible Misunderstanding* (New York, N.Y.: Free Press, 1970) that social scientists had been responsible in part for the confusion over the meaning of citizen participation, and he advised that social scientists are most effective performing policy evaluation, not policy design.

aides, attended by chief executives of major nonprofits as well as business executives and foundation executives, at which the idea of the Task Force would be discussed; and a showcase speech at the National Alliance of Business. The breakfast meeting was brief and allowed no opportunity for dialogue about the expectations that business would confront or about the concerns of nonprofits. And although some might have perceived that there was initial unanimity, whatever unity may have existed did not survive once the program began to develop.

In summary, this first phase of action planning reflected the business backgrounds and promotional orientation of its primary architects. There was unanimity that the effort would be action oriented and that it would be promotional. One year later Deaver explained, "We originally thought the private-sector initiatives campaign should go through AEI." In the tumultuous environment of summer 1981, however, public relations needs escalated. Deaver explained this shift by saying, "We needed a showcase."[20]

It would be ingenuous to believe that the administration was solely interested in public relations. Mosbacher's May memorandum described a specific program to alleviate unemployment. The issue the Task Force would confront was: If the effort was to be more than public relations, what else should it be? Further, although action was to be the modus operandi, what did action dictate? The Task Force was to find itself explaining what it was not—that is, it was not to be a way of "filling the budget gap"—rather than what it was. Action became defined as not producing a report with policy recommendations.

Phase Two: Operations

The centerpiece of the second phase of the administration's private-sector initiative strategy was the President's Task Force on Private Sector Initiatives. Four dimensions of the Task Force are reviewed here: the mandate, management culture, organizational structure, and products.

Mandate. In his October 1981 announcement of the creation of a Task Force on Private Sector Initiatives, President Reagan stated that he was instructing his cabinet to review impediments and to develop seed programs and incentives for private-sector investment. C. William Verity, Jr., chairman of the executive committee of Armco Steel, was named to the post of Task Force chairperson.

Although the common thread in voluntarism is benevolence, the dilemma for the Task Force was deciding what role government could play in en-

---

20. *Fortune*, p. 132.

couraging individual and institutional benevolence. The White House was strategically positioned to focus attention and provide recognition for benevolent acts. This, however, could be accomplished without a task force. Furthermore, although the government ofered legislative and budgetary mechanisms to implement its initiatives, the administration resisted utilizing these mechanisms.

The executive order creating the Task Force was signed October 14 and stated that the Task Force was to provide advice on "methods of developing, supporting and promoting private-sector leadership and responsibility for meeting public needs." Further, the Task Force was to provide "recommendations for appropriate action by the President to foster public-private partnerships and to decrease dependence on government." The order stated, "The Task Force shall serve as a focal point for private sector action addressing public problems."[21]

The process of organizing the membership of the Task Force was marked by uncertainty. Originally, the White House selected thirty-five members. Task Force Chairperson Verity did not have a hand in the original selections, but he was given the opportunity to expand the membership to forty-four. Owing to the fact that Verity was not consulted in the selection process, his authority over the group could not be guaranteed, and his capacity to lead would suffer.

Strategically, the composition of the Task Force was bipartisan; a number of constituencies were represented including nonprofit organizations, religious leaders, blacks, hispanics, corporations, government officials, and so forth. Many of the Task Force members were prominent leaders in their respective fields, such as John Gardner and Richard Lyman from the nonprofit sector, businessmen William Norris and James Rouse, and the Archbishop of New York, Terence Cardinal Cooke. Thus, the Task Force makeup helped to ensure political credibility, public support, and media coverage. Nevertheless, the diverse and powerful membership could not compensate for ambiguity both in the mandate and in the Task Force management process and organizational structure.

In addition to enlarging the membership, the chairperson set about planning the overall agenda. Two prominent Task Force members provided consultants to assist in drafting the agenda. John Filer, chairman of Aetna Life and Casualty and former head of the 1970s' Filer Commission on philanthropy, provided a political consultant who had been a chief lobbyist for

---

21. *Public Papers of the Presidents of the United States: Ronald Reagan*, Executive Order 12329—President's Task Force on Private Sector Initiatives, 14 October 1981 (Washington, D.C.: Government Printing Office, 1981), p. 929.

Jimmy Carter. And Arthur Levitt, Jr., the head of the American Stock Exchange, offered the help of the director of the American Business Conference—a group devoted to assisting entrepreneuers. The December 2 inaugural meeting of the Task Force was essentially a showcase event, with little opportunity for dialogue. Members were presented with a mission statement and an organizational structure, both of which they summarily approved. But Task Force members commented later that they felt that few of the members realized the implications of what they were supporting.

The Task Force's key missions were stated as follows:

1. To identify existing examples of successful or promising private initiatives and public/private partnerships and to give these models national recognition in order to promote their broader use.

2. To encourage increased and more effective use of the human and financial contribution resources of religious groups, businesses, unions, foundations, and philanthropic organizations, including more creative use of leadership, management expertise, training and volunteer work.

3. To encourage the formation and continuation of community partnerships—private sector organizations working with local government—to identify and prioritize community needs and then marshal the appropriate human and financial resources.

4. To identify government obstacles to private initiatives and make recommendations for their removal, and to formulate new incentives to inspire and incite the private sector to undertake new initiatives.

5. To contribute to the development of public policy in areas of concern to the Task Force. [22]

On December 3, the *New York Times* reported, "President Reagan established a Task Force on Private Sector Initiatives today to seek ways to help take up the slack left by the deep cuts he has made in Federal spending." [23] This perception is exactly what the president, his advisers, and Verity were laboring to prevent. The White House had been particularly concerned not to raise expectations that business—financially or otherwise—would be expected to fill the gap from the budget cuts. In addition to such a perception being a political liability, it was philosophically and pragmatically unacceptable.

---

22. Documents from the President's Task Force, collected by the author.
23. *The New York Times*, 3 December 1981.

Philosophically, the president and his aides had argued that the cuts in nondefense areas were both to be a part of the economic recovery package and to eliminate programs they regarded as wasteful. Pragmatically, the aides were aware (from their early meetings with the business community) that corporate giving averaged $3 billion annually and that with profits declining, growth in this area could not be expected. Furthermore, even if the administration had sought a dollar-for-dollar replacement—and it would be naive to believe this were the case—contributions would have had to increase tenfold. Nevertheless, Verity and the Task Force were confronted from the outset by a press corps demanding to know specific goals. The sweeping mission statement, the president's smorgasbord of case examples cast within the rubric of voluntarism/private-sector initiative/public-private partnership, and the timing of the Task Force's creation unfortunately fed this perception.

An article in the *National Journal* typifies the reporting about the Task Force. In describing the December 3 press conference officially announcing the Task Force membership, the *Journal* stated:

> Verity wasted little time in stressing that it was not the Task Force's purpose to fill some budget gap created by the cuts in federal funds. . . . However, the press kit contained a speech Verity delivered to the Midwest Governors' Conference . . . [where he] suggested a spotlight be placed on corporate philanthropy by establishing an honor roll of businesses that have 2, 3, 4, and 5 percent pre-tax giving policies.[24]

There was not a linear relationship between the cutbacks and the call for increased corporate community involvement, yet the press drew this connection repeatedly.

Somewhat later Jack Meyer, director of the AEI study on private-sector initiatives, tried to clarify the issue:

> To begin with, we should address the misleading, but prevailing notion that each dollar cut from federal government spending "disappears" and must be "replaced." Neither the American business community nor the non-profit portion of the private sector can or should try to compensate for the slowdown in the growth of federal social spending on a "dollar-for-dollar" basis.[25]

The Task Force, however, continually found itself diverted by having to defend and explain its mandate.

In its attempt to be broad and to encompass the full range of potential activity and constituencies affected, the mission statement avoided delineating

---

24. Dick Kirschten, "Reaganomics Puts Business on the Spot: Now It Must Either Put Up or Shut Up," *National Journal* (19 December 1981), pp. 2229–2232.

25. Jack A. Meyer, "Private Sector Initiatives and Public Policy: A New Agenda," in Jack A. Meyer, ed., *Meeting Human Needs: Toward a New Public Philosophy* (Washington, D.C.: American Enterprise Institute, 1982), p. 4.

particular problems—for example, unemployment, child care, illiteracy, hunger, and so forth. The only specific project proposed was to create a data bank of examples of private-sector initiatives. The mission statement, it should be underscored, was developed with bipartisan input and may well have been a reflection of a mutual desire to find common ground while leaving the specifics to the Task Force members.

Task Force committees, too, were not project specific but were broader in orientation. For example, committees were created on the topics of community partnerships, contributions, liaison with government and national organizations, the marshaling of human resources, communications, impediments, incentives, and governors. Only the models committee had a project—the data bank. Although several Task Force members argued for a focused and project-specific approach, they were unable to get such a proposal on the agenda for discussion by the entire Task Force. This was owing to an early decision by Verity to let the Task Force committees operate independently of the whole, thereby granting them freedom to act but preventing group consensus.

The following example illustrates the problems that arose from this lack of specificity in operating procedures. In February 1982 the contributions committee passed a recommendation urging businesses, within four years, to double the level of cash contributions for public service programs. A goal of tax-deductible contributions totaling at least two percent of pre-tax net income was established. (The law provided for special tax considerations up to 5 percent of pre-tax profits, but 1981 legislation increased the ceiling to 10 percent.) The Task Force also asked corporations to double their involvement in community service activities through employee volunteer programs.[26] Given that there were no clearly specified rules, the committee faced a dilemma of how this recommendation could be a policy statement of the Task Force. This dilemma shed light on two other problems:

1. There was no decision-making process to make a Task-Force–wide policy statement—a fact that angered those who substantively disagreed with the statement as well as those who agreed with it but sought a fair decision-making process.

2. Members' roles and responsibilities had not been defined, resulting in an opportunity for some to define their own. Although in theory all members were equal, this ambiguity left the door open for more assertive members.

26. *Response* (Washington, D.C.: Center for Corporate Public Involvement, January 1983).

Moreover, the subject of the recommendation—corporate philanthropy—reopened the debate over whether or not the Task Force mandate was to "fill the budget gap" with private-sector dollars. It is ironic that in what appears to be an attempt to keep everyone happy and to avoid controversy by not picking a specific project, Verity found himself confronting conflict. Externally, the statement magnified the administration's political sensitivities. Internally, it highlighted the indistinctness of the mandate and the chairperson's reluctance to establish a clear decision-making process for policy statements.

Five months had passed since the NAB speech, but a clear mandate and a decision-making process to achieve full consensus had yet to be outlined. As the clock ticked away, the ambiguity would heighten, ultimately affecting the products of the Task Force.

Management Culture.   As the ethos of the Task Force took shape, two sources of confusion perpetuated the original ambiguity concerning what the Task Force was expected to accomplish. The first source of confusion had to do with whether this president-appointed body was supposed to produce a report. The Task Force members got mixed signals. In January 1982, President Reagan stated: "I told Bill Verity 6 weeks ago, I don't want a committee report. Give me action and results. Get the private sector in the driver's seat so we can start using market incentives and philanthropy to find lasting solutions to community problems."[27] But presidential commissions are typically designed to produce a report based on considerable study and hearings, which offers a legislative package to affect public policy. Numerous members of the Task Force had formerly served on commissions, and several were simultaneously serving on other commissions; indeed, Task Force member John Filer had headed a private commission to study voluntary giving. Thus, it can be assumed that Task Force members who had served on presidential commissions would expect to focus their attention on producing a report, and that precedence might have led other members to such an assumption. Both the executive order and the mission statement, moreover, had expressly asked for "recommendations," which, it would seem, required study and a report. Thus, when the chairperson explained that the Task Force was to be action oriented and that the president did not want a report, his appeal was not understood by the members.

The second source of confusion arose out of the differing backgrounds and organizational experiences of the Task Force members. The Task Force

27. *Public Papers of the Presidents of the United States: Ronald Reagan*, Remarks at the New York City Partnership Luncheon in New York, 14 January 1982 (Washington, D.C.: Government Printing Office, 1982), p. 29.

was composed of representatives of three types of institutions: for-profit, nonprofit, and public sector. Apparently the Task Force never fully understood or addressed the different values that underlie these three spheres. Although it is not the purpose of this paper to expound on management culture, a brief comparison of public-sector and corporate styles is pertinent to an understanding of the group dynamics of the Task Force and to its influence on the final products. Whereas public-sector style emphasizes dialogue and allows for open challenges to leadership, corporate style avoids conflict in the boardroom, and the leadership of the corporate chief executive is rarely openly called into question. In the public sector, the leader seeks to appeal to multiple constituencies; in corporations the leader is primarily concerned about the bottom-line interests of the investors. The corporate sector is risk rewarding, while the public sector is risk averse.

Meetings of the Task Force on Private Sector Initiatives utilized a corporate style of management. The chairperson's authority was not publicly questioned; meeting time was consumed with committee reports, leaving minimal time for dialogue; and decisions were made by the chairperson (as would be his prerogative in the corporate setting, even when consultation had been sought), without appealing for clear consensus. The most dramatic evidence of the exclusivity of authority was demonstrated by Verity's decision that consensus would not be sought for the final document to be submitted to the president. This was a logical extension of corporate decision making, where authority is clear and the operating rule is optimize, not compromise.

The stylistic differences were also manifested in another Task Force product: the data bank of case examples of private-sector initiatives. The data bank, initially designed by the head of a national nonprofit organization, was established at the beginning of the Task Force. But it was managed by corporate executives, with college interns feeding information into the system. The decision at the outset was to keep the information brief and simple. This was another reflection of a style difference: corporate executives prefer their information in a terse format and rely on simple, straightforward case examples to highlight a point; public-sector style, on the other hand, often prefers lengthy justification and backup information. Moreover, there was no systematic process for validating the data. For public-sector people, valid information is essential; for the private sector, validation was assumed to be the user's responsibility—that is, the market would determine whether or not the information was satisfying consumers. These managerial conflicts were never resolved.

Organizational Structure. Organizationally, the Task Force administration, personnel, and budget suffered from a lack of clear definition of roles, lines of authority, total budget, and spending priorities. On the one hand, the internal administrative structure for the Task Force members was established early and appeared tidy despite the vagueness both of the mandate and of members' roles. On the other hand, creating the structure for the external relationship to the White House consumed the entire first quarter of Task Force operations. Although the White House sought the benefits of its association with the Task Force, it also labored to establish a structure independent in financing and administration in order to permit the Task Force to receive private funds. Instead of creating a new nonprofit organization to achieve legal and financial separation, the Task Force made arrangements to utilize an existing organization—VOLUNTEER: The National Center for Citizen Involvement. (George Romney, a Task Force member, was also the chairperson of the board of VOLUNTEER.) Essentially this was a bookkeeping arrangement. It was an innovative approach; but the first three months of operating time had already been lost.

Strategically, the White House Office of Private Sector Initiatives thus positioned itself as structurally independent from the Task Force, but this was more illusion than reality. The White House and Task Force were in fact interdependent, requiring each other's resources to achieve their goals. For instance, the White House Office of Private Sector Initiatives staff worked with the Task Force staff in organizing White House meetings with leaders from national associations, such as religious groups and trade associations. These meetings were conceived by Task Force members and held at the White House. They were typically attended by approximately 150 people and showcased private-sector projects. In addition, the White House used the data bank to identify possible sites for presidential visits to highlight private-sector initiatives. For the Task Force, the White House affiliation helped to open doors, though at times the assumed political affiliation sparked resistance.

Although the Task Force office was located across the street from the Office of Private Sector Initiatives, and staff in the two offices routinely worked together, in actuality, the White House senior aides for private-sector initiatives generally did not attempt to influence daily operations of the Task Force. Indeed, none of the Task Force staff were political appointees.

On matters of personnel, both the White House Office of Private Sector Initiatives and the Task Force were undergoing change. In February 1982, James Rosebush became First Lady Nancy Reagan's chief of staff, a job transfer that critics cite as further evidence of the public relations origins of the private-sector initiatives. The appointment of Jay Moorhead as Rosebush's successor (Moorhead, a thirty-year-old political appointee had formerly worked in the White House personnel office and as an organizer for the Republican party) raised further questions among critics as to the administration's understanding of the effort and of its commitment to it. Neither Deaver nor Moorhead was policy oriented. Moorhead had other sizable barriers to overcome: an office without a budget, only one other professional staff member, a task force of illustrious American leaders with an unclear mandate, and an increasingly impatient and suspicious public.

The personnel arrangements for the Task Force initially proceeded on the premise that loaned executives would be available—in microcosm, a practical test of the Task Force philosophy. In February the chairperson loaned a trusted assistant and marketing specialist to become the permanent executive director, replacing an interim director earlier loaned by one of the Task Force members. Given the new director's close relationship with Verity, he could not only be expected to work well with the chairperson, but his marketing skills would be beneficial in the area of promotion. However, the new director had no substantive background in private-sector initiatives and no experience in management. In terms of other staff, John Filer made available an expert in corporate philanthropy; another staff member was the director of a national volunteer organization; two staff members were loaned from government; and corporate staff were loaned to set up and maintain the data bank. Other staff joined the Task Force when private-sector funds were raised; they were paid as consultants. There were never more than eight senior staff. The remaining staff were largely volunteer interns. The functional areas of work were liaison, corporate philanthropy, volunteers, community partnerships, and public relations. Public relations and the data bank were the two most heavily staffed components, with as many as six people each; other program areas had only one or two full-time staff. Overall, the number of staff was inadequate to the Task Force mandate.

Beyond staff being assigned to assist Task Force committees, no functions or organizational chart were specified. Like the chairperson, the executive director resisted establishing either clear lines of communication or opportunities for staff to have dialogue. Staff meetings were not regularly scheduled, and less than fifteen were held.

The ability of the staff to carry out their responsibilities was severely hampered by the ambiguity of what they were to accomplish, the lack of staff assistance, and the lack of funds. Eventually, staff did define their functions and attempted to raise funds to implement programs, but the designated termination date of early December 1982 restricted the ability to accomplish proposed activities.

Thus, the personnel situation was riddled with uncertainty and obstacles. Critics argue that philosophical biases and political sensitivities could have been overcome, that other presidential commissions have been given an adequate complement of staff and funds.[28] Furthermore, had the planners thought more about how "action" could be carried out, the loss of the first quarter of the year's time might not have occurred.

Finally, the budget presented problems. Public funds had been set aside to support basic office needs such as space, postage, and copying. No public money, however, was available for staffing needs or for programs, and funds had to be raised for these purposes from the private sector. Total contributions were $506,000. Despite the prevailing belief that all staff were loaned, $355,000 was expended for consultants and payroll. Therefore, the Task Force tacitly recognized that expertise needed to be purchased, despite its operating thesis that volunteers and loaned executives would be both available and capable of efficiently performing tasks otherwise done by hired experts. The remaining expenditures were for travel, printing, and meetings.

Although the idea of a private-sector-funded effort was politically and philosophically attractive, it ultimately created a range of practical problems. For example, if a conference, publication, or other project was to be more than just an idea, funds needed to be raised and adequate time had to be allotted to do this.

In addition, corporations as well as foundations were inundated with requests for funding, which they claimed were coming both from organizations that had lost their federal funds, and from other groups that were trying to avoid government dependence. The strategy of using private-sector funds for the Task Force may have sounded safe, but it pitted the Task Force against groups that in theory it was supposed to be assisting. In sum, the issue arises of why there was a lack of sound financial planning in a task force that was purported to be a presidential commitment of the highest priority.

Products.   There were, to be sure, innovative dimensions to the Task Force. Philosophically it was to be a model of its mission: there were loaned personnel from corporations and government, funds were raised from the private sector to support its operations, and equipment was loaned by corporations and government. Strategically the action orientation proved to generate considerable activity—though it is difficult to directly correlate these efforts with Task Force impacts. The action focused on process. Had a thesis of change been articulated—and one was not—it appears that the White House and Task Force leadership would have contended that change could result from exhibiting leaders as role models, and that persuasion was preferable to getting bogged down in traditional approaches to bringing about change through regular policy channels.

---

28. Several Task Force members made these observations to me privately during the Task Force and in interviews in November 1983–February 1984.

By summer 1981, subsequent to the interactions with AEI, it was clear that the Task Force would be action oriented. But the specifics had not been detailed. It was a major disappointment to some Task Force members that they were to produce neither policy initiatives nor a legislative package. Action, they felt, did not have to be at the exclusion of policy. Had the White House and the Task Force decided to move on both fronts—action and policy—the Task Force might well have been a decisive force for change. Over time, it became clear that the overarching mission given to Moorhead was action, and that policy was subordinate to this agenda.

Action in the case of the Task Force translated into serving as an information broker, engendering networks, and promoting new approaches particularly at the state and local levels of government for solving community problems. The emphasis throughout was on using leaders to exhort other leaders, providing recognition and endorsing efforts, and promoting self-reliance—especially at the state and local levels. This was a new model of operations for a presidential task force.

The Task Force coordinated meetings of leaders of religious organizations, trade associations, community-based organizations, and community colleges, as well as meetings of governors' aides, corporate chief executives, congressional aides, and numerous other groups. In addition, the press was aggressively cultivated, resulting in a flood of articles and television spots. A monthly newsletter was produced, as well as three other publications: a brochure on volunteering, a booklet on corporate community involvement, and a book on alternative investing in community and economic development entitled *Investing in America*.[29]

As an information broker, the Task Force operated a data bank. Despite the data bank's technical weaknesses (depth of information, accessibility, and questions of validity), the concept remains useful. Unfortunately, records providing an accounting of the bank's use were not maintained. It is important to note, too, that the information brokering placed the responsibility for action back in the hands of the users; this was not a mechanism to provide technical assistance.

The Task Force was in a unique position to utilize the White House as well as the high profiles of its members as a magnet for events. Thus, the network effort focused on hosting meetings of institutional groups, of youth volunteers, and of corporate chief executives together with community-based

---

29. Renée Berger et al., eds. *Investing in America: Initiatives for Community and Economic Development* (Washington, D.C.: President's Task Force on Private Sector Initiatives, 1982); "Volunteers: A Valuable Resource" (a brochure on volunteering); and "Corporate Community Involvement" (a booklet on reviewing corporate strategies for giving programs).

organization leaders. The meetings ranged from the traditional White House one-hour "walk-through," where the president would make a brief appearance and several Task Force members would make speeches, to a one-day-and-a-half conference on corporate social investing. In each case the thrust was that it takes leaders to make a difference—and that those assembled were the leaders. This was the role-modeling and persuasion approach. Again, no technical assistance was offered attendees; follow-up was to be their own responsibility.

Also, states and localities were encouraged to start their own task forces and private-sector initiatives groups. To prompt action at the state level, Reagan sent a letter to all governors asking them to establish the state equivalent of the presidental Task Force, with membership to come from both the public and private sectors. Follow-up on this suggestion from the presidential Task Force was limited to one meeting of governors' aides and to information brokering. At the termination of the Task Force, over forty states had committed themselves to establishing task forces.

These state task forces ranged from large-scale efforts to dubbing a staff member with an additional title. As of August 1983 White House records showed that less than half of these task forces survive; however, the scope of their activities has never been catalogued. Massachusetts, for example, launched a major task force that produced a report and a set of legislative recommendations; the task force also proposed a center for training and technical assistance in "partnerships." The Massachusetts effort survived a political change in its governorship, demonstrating both that the concept could be nonpartisan and that a state-led initiative could sustain itself. Pennsylvania's Governor Thornburgh created a 50 member task force, whose extensive activities incorporated some of the best features of the original White House Task Force. Why these two states pursued such efforts successfully while others did so only lukewarmly or not at all is a matter of speculation, however.

Finally, Task Force members were urged to speak out in favor of private-sector initiatives and, where feasible, to promote the formation of task forces locally. This strategy resulted in the creation of a few local task forces (San Francisco's and Houston's are notable examples that were started by Task Force members and are still flourishing), as well as of corporate executive partnerships devoted to civic problems.

Unfortunately, no systematic effort has been made to monitor initiatives that have emerged throughout the nation. Some groups evaporated as quickly as they were formed; others still survive. The president's Task Force provided a context of legitimacy for these groups and an opportunity for presidential endorsement. Beyond such encouragement, however, the attitude was that local groups are best at solving their own problems. The opportunity still remains to identify those efforts that took root and to determine what made them successful.

How "action" displaced policy is also seen in the preparation of the Task Force's final report. Despite the president's call for action instead of a report, the idea of producing a report surfaced repeatedly. Reasons for this include White House ambiguity about how the Task Force should proceed; the fact that "recommendations" had been requested in the executive order and the mission statement; the subculture of commission expectations for a report; and the influence of Task Force members who saw an opportunity to affect policy. However, aides in the Office of Private Sector Initiatives did not perceive themselves as policy initiators. Rather, policy-related issues were routinely referred to the Office of Management and Budget for analysis. At the Task Force, the senior staff who were experienced in policy had their time diverted to "action" projects.

Nevertheless, a policy development expert was hired. This was a non-political appointment that was approved by the chairperson and a bipartisan group of Task Force members. The White House could not technically prevent the appointment, but if it so desired it could have pressured the chairperson not to allow it. Jay Moorhead, however, chose not to interfere. During the summer of 1982 the Task Force policy expert conducted meetings on an individual basis with Task Force members. A draft of a conceptual policy framework was submitted to Task Force committee chairpersons in early September, their approval being critical for the Task Force meeting later that month (the last formal meeting before the closing ceremonial session in December). The framework was approved by the chairpersons.

At the September meeting, however, Task Force members John Gardner and Richard Lyman queried why a report was being written when the chairperson had repeatedly asserted that the president did not want one. These members were expressing the feelings of others that the time remaining between September to December was inadequate for dialogue and for meaningful consensus on a policy framework. Conceivably, the confusion over a policy report might have been avoided had Verity better communicated the role of the policy development expert to the Task Force members. Also, evidently the members had not been notified that the chairpersons had approved the conceptual framework. Thus, an opportunity for consensus over a policy structure evolved but quickly dissipated because it was not seen as an opportunity.

It was subsequently decided that a summary of the Task Force's activities would be written and presented to the president, but that there would be no policy statement. It was decided, furthermore, that if committees chose to make recommendations, they could include them in the committee summaries;

however, they would not be Task-Force-approved recommendations. For instance, a report on legislative impediments and incentives was written by a law student in concert with two aides of Task Force members Senator David Durenberger and Representative Barber Conable. The report was approved by the appropriate Task Force committee but was designated as an appendix—available separately from the White House. In a sense, once the decision was made that there would be no policy statement (which would have included the legislative document), an attempt was made to bury policy-oriented statements.

It was furthermore agreed that Verity would write a letter to the president about the Task Force's efforts. This letter and the report would be reviewed by the communications committee in the name of the entire membership.

The policy development expert soon found himself in a job without a task. The assignment to write a summary of activities fell to the public relations staff, with input from senior staff. Ambiguity therefore ultimately undermined the opportunity for the Task Force to be more than an information broker, a networker, and a promoter of local initiative. Furthermore, the chairperson would assert his corporate prerogative of making his own decisions regarding the letter and its contents. As such, the chairperson recommended that the data bank be continued; that the president continue to articulate the need for private-sector initiative; that an interagency committee chaired by a cabinet officer be established to "encourage increased sensitivity in policy making to impact on initiative, voluntarism, and private sector involvement" and to "encourage cabinet initiatives which increase agency reliance on the private sector and public/private partnerships, in program development and implementation"; that the Office of Private Sector Initiatives be strengthened and become a "focal point for federal government initiatives"; and that a new bipartisan advisory council be established.[30]

The Task Force terminated in December 1982. Two weeks after the termination of the Task Force, *Newsweek*'s year-end feature was titled, "The Hard-Luck Christmas of '82: With 12 million unemployed and 2 million homeless, private charity cannot make up for federal cutbacks." The article described the activities of the Task Force, quoting Verity as saying "the last thing in the world we could try and do was fill the gap. The gap remains. We're up against the wall."[31] Thus, despite the Task Force's attempt to

---

30. C. William Verity, Jr., made these recommendations in the final summary of the Task Force, "Building Partnerships: The President's Task Force on Private Sector Initiatives," December 1981–December 1982, p. 5.

31. "The Hard-Luck Christmas of '82," *Newsweek* (27 December 1982), p. 15.

overcome the shadow of the budget cuts, the public's image of the Task Force and expectations for it appear to have remained the same.

One month later, Reagan lauded the Task Force's activities in his State of the Union address. He stated that the Task Force had "successfully forged a working partnership involving leaders of business, labor, education, and government to address the training needs of American workers," and he credited the Task Force with helping "thousands of working people . . . [make] the shift from dead-end jobs and low-demand skills to the growth areas of high technology and the service economy."[32] The Task Force had certainly tried to accomplish the former, though it did not focus on training. However, the latter goal had been pushed off the agenda from the start.

Senior aides in the Office of Private Sector Initiatives were pleased that the president had chosen to praise the program, viewing this as a writ of importance within the White House. As for the inaccuracies, these were excused as an error of "tense." With numerous White House offices vying for the president's attention, it was perceived as more important that the program received air time than that the coverage was exaggerated.[33]

Phase Three: Implementation

In January 1983 the Office of Private Sector Initiatives underwent another personnel change when Jay Moorhead left government and was succeeded by James Coyne, a former congressman. The third phase of the private-sector initiatives strategy, which began after the Task Force ended and is still evolving, is marked by some organizational and programmatic activity.

Over time, the private-sector initiative strategy appears to have spread throughout the administration. Whereas the Office of Private Sector Initiatives had been the focal point especially during the time of the Task Force, several agencies have now developed their own interpretations of private-sector initiatives. In some cases these initiatives are loosely associated with the White House through routine, required reports that are submitted to the Office of Private Sector Initiatives. However, contact with the White House is minimal and infrequent, and the agencies generally function with relative freedom. Office of Private Sector Initiatives' priorities have been asserted in the agencies' organizational structure and programmatically. The organizational structure operates through cabinet secretaries, who are given the authority to delegate staff and who typically set their own priorities. The following pro-

---

32. U.S. Congress, House. *The President's Address on the State of the Union before the Joint Session of Congress*, 97th Cong., 2nd sess., 26 January 1983.

33. White House aides (anonymity requested), interview with author, January 1983.

vides a sample of the efforts of the Office of Private Sector Initiatives during this evolving third phase of the private sector initiative program.

Office of Private Sector Initiatives.   The White House wasted no time in January 1983 in establishing an internal working group under Michael Deaver. However, as of December 1983 this group had met only once—the result, it is speculated, of other priorities being perceived as more urgent by Deaver.[34] After the Task Force was dissolved, the White House did not announce the creation of the new Advisory Council on Private Sector Initiatives until June 28, 1983. Explanations for this lack of haste included James Coyne's newness in the position of presidential assistant, as well as the desire to exert more caution as a result of the lessons from the Task Force difficulties.

The Advisory Council's makeup differs from that of the Task Force. Of the council's thirty-nine members, nine are from the public sector—including seven cabinet secretaries, the director of ACTION, and Deaver. The remaining members are from the private sector, but they are not the Fortune-500 names that were a big part of the Task Force's identity. As of October 1984, the Advisory Council had met four times. Seven committees have been established: communications/marketing, education, family/community, impediments/incentives, international, networking, and work place. Committee assignments were not formalized until October 1983, but during the following year, the committee met an average of five times each. They appear, moreover, to be operating in an environment that is more permissive—as manifested by the willingness to employ government funds to leverage some of their programs, and the willingness to initiate new projects.

A key change is that the White House has overcome its philosophical rigidity and political sensitivity regarding utilizing federal funds to encourage private-sector initiatives. The administration appears to have recognized that to realistically initiate efforts, federal funds have to be accessed. Although the White House Office of Private Sector Initiatives has no funds for grants, they can—and have—sought to influence federal departments. Thus some grants awarded by the Department of Health and Human Services as well as other departments may be traced back to White House influence. But it is important to understand that this clout does not guarantee releasing department funds nor ensure White House control over recipients. Two examples, a data bank and a job-search program, are instructive.

The data bank, as mentioned earlier, was the only explicit project of the Task Force that had been specified at the outset. Data collection also was regarded as an appropriate role—the government traditionally has been a

---

34. White House aides (anonymity requested), interview with author, January 1983.

repository of data bases. Moreover, the data bank was essential to fulfilling the Task Force's information-brokering role and was a manifestation of the administration's approach to private-sector initiative: present a leader who provides the role model, use persuasion and peer pressure, and provide case examples to sketch the concept.

Although the quality of the data was a source of conflict, the White House agreed to provide federal funding to be leveraged with private-sector monies so that the data base could be maintained. This marked a major departure for the Office of Private Sector Initiatives: public funds would be used to support private-sector initiatives. In 1983, though one organization had already been officially authorized (and promised $300,000 in federal funds) to operate the data bank, another emerged and was given $150,000 in federal funds, on the premise that private-sector funds would eventually be raised. In March 1984 the two organizations merged to form an independent organization, Partnerships Data Net, combining a joint public- and private-sector funding base.

Regarding the job-search program, the Office of Private Sector Initiatives played an instrumental role in gaining cooperation from the Department of Labor to authorize $1.5 million to help displaced workers find jobs. This was to be supplemented by $260,000 from the Department of Commerce for technical assistance. The Labor Department contracts were designed to flow through the National Alliance of Business and the Human Resource Development Institute of the AFL-CIO. A nonprofit research institute that had done an evaluation of a job-search club was to operate as the technical assistance provider. In a nutshell, the program used the thesis that jobs are available but that workers do not know how to market themselves.

As of early 1984, fifteen "demonstration" job-search clubs were anticipated and three were already operational. By late spring, however, the technical assistance provider, NAB, and the White House were unable to get the Labor Department to release the funds for the project. It has since been terminated.

These two cases, the data bank and job-search program, and the fact that the White House could not control the bureaucracy, nor grantees, are in part a result of the pluralism of our system of governance. Important too, is that the White House had overcome its rigidity toward using federal resources to help meet its priorities, just as Carter and preceding presidents had done. There is a curious logic, however, to the Reagan administration, caught in a philosophical contradiction of using federal funds to promote private-sector initiative. To some degree, Carter neutralized this problem by calling the concept a "partnership." In reality, Reagan programs have become partnerships, but this fact is clouded by the anti-government tone of the administration and the connotation of "private-sector initiative," that is, without a public-sector role.

The Office of Private Sector Initiatives has utilized its access to the president principally for recognition and promotional endeavors. Most notably, an awards program for recognizing outstanding volunteer service was launched early in Reagan's first term with the assistance of VOLUNTEER: The National Center for Citizen Involvement and has continued. The role modeling approach was followed again in 1984 in the creation by the Advisory Council of a "Presidential Citation for Private Sector Initiatives." The president also proclaimed 1984 as the Year of Adopt-a-School and advocated an adult literacy campaign. A challenge program convening forums through local Chambers of Commerce to develop business education programs has been conducted in three cities. The role of the Office of Private Sector Initiatives in promoting partnerships in education is thus largely confined to informal networking and holding meetings and conferences. In addition, forums informing employers of day-care options have been held in over 20 cities. International initiatives include efforts to promote economic development in Grenada and a fellowship exchange program with Japan. While all these efforts have been effective in stimulating significant press and television attention, it is difficult to ascertain their precise impact on the development of local programs.

In summary, during phase three the role of the Office of Private Sector Initiatives has been to put into place an organizational structure within the federal bureaucracy, to undertake selected program initiatives, and to continue promotional efforts. The office has not sought to influence budget priorities within OMB, nor has it offered legislation that might affect private-sector initiative. Its strategy appears to go further than did the Task Force, but it has yet to tackle its mission by utilizing the full array of tools available to policymakers.

Private-Sector Initiatives in the Agencies.   Some private-sector initiatives by the Reagan administration were given inspiration by the efforts of the Task Force and White House Office of Private Sector Initiatives, but did not operate under their guidance. Over the past two years several agencies have established private-sector initiative liaisons or have created a separate office for such activities. The liaison idea was originally a Task Force strategy. Many of these liaisons are principally political appointees with minimal knowledge of the private-sector initiatives concept, but the agencies nonetheless have endeavored to develop programs. Many of these programs are in the early stages; it is difficult to determine patterns, therefore, and premature to discuss their impacts.

Some of these agency efforts predate the Reagan administration. The Department of Housing and Urban Development had established an office for public-private partnerships during the Carter administration. Although this office focused on neighborhood issues, another division was implementing the Urban Development Action Grant (UDAG)—a program that the Reagan administration has continued. Described simply, the UDAG combines public- and private-sector funds for urban economic development. HUD also serves as the lead agency for an interagency agreement with Partnerships Data Net to develop and provide for public and private groups case examples of a wide range of partnership initiatives.

Both the Economic Development Administration (EDA) and the Small Business Administration (SBA) have a history similar to HUD in the private-sector initiatives area. During the Carter administration these agencies played a key role in funding a range of development efforts. Their interest in promoting public-sector–private-sector collaborative activities has continued during the Reagan administration. The EDA has funded projects to help network public- and private-sector leaders in midsize cities. The SBA established a separate office for private-sector initiatives and staffed the effort with professionals. Its projects include working with county supervisors in California to create small-business incubators in cooperation with Chevron Oil, Crown Zellerbach, and the San Francisco Chamber of Commerce; helping the state of Ohio develop a new pool of equity capital for the state's small companies; and, with HUD, finding ways to better utilize community block-grant funds for small business. In 1984 this SBA office launched a program to encourage the development of small business incubators. Conferences, a newsletter, and booklets on incubators have been produced.

Thus, although the record is uneven, it appears that several departments have encouraged their staffs to establish programs. Unlike the first two phases of Reagan's private-sector initiative strategy, this implementation period allows for "pump priming" with federal funds. Indeed, the period of rhetoric and promotion that dominated the initial phases of private-sector initiatives shows signs of evolving into an organizational structure with programmatic content.

Conclusion

As noted earlier, it is naive to believe that the Reagan administration created the private-sector initiatives effort as a dollar-for-dollar replacement of the budget cuts. On the other hand, the strategy explicitly sought both to soften the blow of the cuts as well as to capitalize on an attitude that was central to the administration's ideology about the private sector—namely, that local business and individual initiative could be channelled to meet community needs. The history of the private-sector initiative efforts suggests the following conclusions:

1. The effort was not initially conceived as a policy. It was not assigned to a policy office and was not under the command of individuals with policy capability. In 1983, however, it appears that the ground work laid over the prior two years set the stage for initiatives that have now assumed the shape of policy.

2. The administration succeeded in expanding upon a concept that had its roots in President Kennedy's volunteer programs and that had grown into Carter's public-private partnerships. Reagan's program added corporate philanthropy—monetary and noncash giving of time and equipment, as well as corporate leadership—under an umbrella called private-sector initiatives (whose roots appear to start with Johnson's NAB initiative). This important conceptual advance, however, was undermined by the Reagan administration's ambiguity and apparent unfamiliarity with the subject, as well as by the poor timing of the creation of the Task Force.

3. In addition to an awareness that the administration was not attempting to fill the gap outright, it is important to recognize that despite the Task Force's "policy statement" recommending that corporate giving be doubled, it is doubtful that this ambitious goal could have been achieved. The Filer Commission had made this "2 percent" recommendation in the 1970s,[35] and change did not result then. Corporate giving, regardless of these mandates and pressures, has stayed at 1 percent of pretax profits for well over a decade. Furthermore, corporate monetary giving has appeared not to change significantly even with modifications in the tax code. A Council on Foundations study of chief executives and corporate giving concluded that tax breaks played a relatively unimportant role in corporate decisions about philanthropy.[36] Also, given the consistency of the 1 percent figure, changes in the overall economic climate do not

---

35. *Giving in America: Toward a Stronger Voluntary Sector: Report of the Commission on Private Philanthropy and Public Needs* (Published by the Commission, 1975).

36. Arthur H. White and John S. Barthlomeo of Yankelovich, Skelly, & White, Inc. for the Council of Foundations, *Corporate Giving: The Views of Chief Executive Officers of Major American Corporations* (Washington, D.C.: Council on Foundations, 1982).

seem to influence monetary giving. However, it appears that changes in the tax code regarding equipment donations have succeeded in increasing this type of giving. Data, however, suffer from collection and from methodological problems.

4. The administration's highlighting of private-sector initiative has received significant press attention. While impossible to quantify or correlate, the resultant leadership pressures and networking have created opportunities for information exchange where few had existed before.

5. The private-sector initiative effort thus far has been an assortment of pluses and minuses. It has succeeded in encouraging public discussion on the subject, but it has taken only limited advantage of exploiting opportunities for legislative or budgetary changes. Although organizational structure and leadership have been effectively utilized, their full potential in this area have yet to be realized.

6. Presidential task forces and commissions tend to fade quickly from memory. The innovation of this Task Force (in addition to broadening the concept of private-sector initiative) was its novel structure—a quasi-nonprofit status—and its action approach, which has continued in other administration efforts. These innovations were undermined by lack of clarity, but they deserve recognition and study.

COMMENTS   *Denis P. Doyle*

A Missed Opportunity

Although I agree in large part with Renée Berger's comprehensive account of the development of the Reagan private-sector initiatives, I would emphasize more than she does three factors that shaped the process and outcomes of the Task Force on Private Sector Initiatives.

A Diverse Membership

First, the diverse, unpredictable membership of the Task Force. In addition to C. William Verity as chairperson, the Task Force's forty-four members were selected to be bipartisan—after heated debate in the White House inner circle about the relative assets and liabilities of bipartisanship in this delicate area. The membership included people with diverse political views, and was not limited to individuals sympathetic to the Reagan administration. John Gardner, Leon Sullivan, Dick Lyman, Ellen Strauss, and James Rouse are hardly Reagan supporters. Indeed, their reaction to the Reagan budget cuts ran from skepticism to outright opposition.

Once the bipartisanship decision was made, the president could not expect to be able to control the Task Force. It is not surprising, therefore, that certain members of the president's inner circle viewed the entire enterprise as highly sensitive—it was clear that the potential for political harm—if not for disaster—was as realistic as was the prospect of political gain. Given the public visibility and access to the media of many of the Task Force's more prominent members, there was continuing concern in the White House that the whole process might backfire, that a strong-willed and articulate Task Force member, for example, might seize the opportunity to make political hay at the president's expense. This concern about political fallout was what reinforced the administration's conviction that the Task Force should be action oriented and should not concern itself with "writing reports that will only gather dust," as Chairperson Verity was fond of saying. In all likelihood the administration

212

was more concerned about reports that did not gather dust, that would turn up in the evening news broadcast and morning newspapers. The Reagan administration definitely did not want a group of social scientists making waves.

Reaction of Business Community

As Berger points out, the *New York Times* responded to the Task Force's first meeting by describing it as seeking ways "to help take up the slack left by the deep cuts [the President] has made in Federal spending." This characterization made both the White House and the business community nervous, and with good reason. The scale and scope of the proposed Reagan cuts were so enormous that there was simply no way the private sector could fill the gap, even if the economy had been robust. In the best of times, corporate contributions to charity and philanthropy have hovered around $3 billion per year. As a supplement to government social programs, $3 billion is a great deal of money: As replacement funding it is a pittance. Just as the Reagan administration was concerned about adverse political reaction if the Task Force were viewed as a return to nineteenth-century private charity, the business community was concerned that it would be expected to pick up the tab for government cuts. As Berger points out, the Reagan administration was attempting to marshal arguments about the essential fairness and appropriateness of its cuts, but it never escaped the temptation of using the rhetoric of "filling the gap." As Berger notes, Verity was proposing a corporate "honor roll" for big donors at the same time that he was suggesting that the gap could not be filled.[1]

Role of Moderate Members

The third factor affecting the Task Force was the role of its moderate members. As Berger points out, the most dramatic example of Verity's skill

---

1. This controversy over whether the private sector could fully compensate for government cuts might have been avoided if the Task Force had been more receptive to existing analysis of private-sector capabilities. While the president's Task Force was moving forward, the American Enterprise Institute was preparing a comprehensive book on the subject, *Meeting Human Needs*, edited by Jack Meyer (Washington, D.C.: 1982). In the book, Meyer observed that "we should address the misleading, but prevailing notion that each dollar cut from federal government spending 'disappears' and must be 'replaced.' Neither the American business community nor the nonprofit portion of the private sector can or should try to compensate for the slowdown in the growth of federal social spending on a 'dollar-for-dollar' replacement basis."

in maneuvering among the varying orientations represented by the Task Force was his unchallenged decision to submit a brief final report to the president, one that would not be reviewed and approved by the full Task Force. The reason that Verity was able to bring off so clever a move was the ambivalence of the more liberal members of the Task Force. It was, in fact, the work of a spontaneous liberal "caucus" that finally prevented the submission of a comprehensive Task Force report. Just as the Reagan White House was afraid that Task Force members might use the platform presented by the Task Force to rail against the Reagan budget and social programs, so too liberal Task Force members were afraid they would be co-opted by Reagan and find their names affixed to a report in which they had no confidence. A small number of moderate Task Force members pressed Verity for a comprehensive final report, a proposal he strongly resisted. But as the work of the Task Force neared its end, Verity began to lose ground and was clearly prepared to accede to the demand. As much to his surprise as anyone's, the liberal "caucus" killed the idea outright, losing whatever chance they might have had to go on record with their views on the Reagan budget and social programs.

A Case of Failed Potential

As Berger notes, the principal accomplishment of the Task Force was to stick to its commitment to action and escape the necessity of producing a policy document that might, for a variety of reasons, have embarrassed the administration. The Task Force's final report to the president was artfully crafted to say nothing of consequence, to offend no one (or everyone, as the case may be), and to slip out of the public consciousness as one of the least memorable of recent presidential commissions. The ceremony of the major public meetings organized by the Task Force, the illustrious nature of its membership, its access to the White House, and the personal interest of the president combined to make the Task Force a continuing media event; in the end the Task Force failed to attract serious journalistic attention. There was little careful reporting and no probing questioning of what the Task Force was about and of what its objectives were.

This outcome could have been different. A task force with a distinguished membership and one given adequate direction, proper staffing, and a coherent conceptual framework could have made a lasting contribution to national life. Scholars at the American Enterprise Institute (AEI), for example, have advanced a number of ideas over the past decade to strengthen the private sector by creative collaboration with the public sector. The institute has repeatedly put forward ideas for social programs that would utilize what AEI refers to as "mediating" structures, the intermediate social organizations—the family, local community, mutual associations, religious organizations, and so on— that stand between the individual and the megastructures of modern society, especially the corporation and the state.[2]

The real issue that should have been before the Task Force was that of identifying those government strategies that would strengthen rather than weaken the capacity of the private sector to respond to human needs. Both experience and research show that the provider of choice in times of need— whether in areas of health, nutrition, employment, moral support, or financial assistance—is the private sector. People in distress turn first to family, friends, churches and synagogues; fraternal and benevolent associations; and employers and former employers. Only as a last resort do they turn to government. Because the line of demarcation between government and the private sector has blurred so much in the past fifty years, a wide range of government policies is available to strengthen the private sector, the family, and the individual in meeting our larger social obligations. The President's Private Sector Initiatives Task Force had the opportunity to make a lasting contribution to national debate and to the formulation of public policy in this area; it will be remembered, if at all, for its failure to exploit the opportunity before it.

---

2. See *To Empower People*, by Peter L. Berger and Richard John Neuhaus (Washington, D.C.: 1977), the most well known of the AEI's publications in this area; and the more recent AEI book by Jack Meyer, *Meeting Human Needs* (Washington, D.C.: 1982), which raises many of the same issues in a more practical, less theoretical framework. In addition to the work of AEI scholars and Fellows in this important area, there is the outstanding book by the Brookings Institution economist Charles Schultze, *The Public Use of Private Interest* (Washington, D.C.: The Brookings Institution, 1977). In sum, there is no shortage of ideas on the subject.

COMMENTS *John B. Olsen*

Assessing An Unfinished But Promising Experiment

With the inauguration of the Reagan administration and in the face of a complex set of economic problems, new national policies were implemented, including moving from categorical programs to block grants, minimizing federal mandates, and withdrawing federal support from selected social programs. Simultaneously, much more attention was given to the role that the private sector may play. In this context, Renée Berger has contributed a valuable case study that, within its inherent constraints, provides an illuminating account of how the Reagan administration has influenced the management of the White House—and by inference that of other units of the executive branch—by emphasizing the private-sector initiatives. A timely analysis, Berger's paper deserves commendation as being both fact-based and eminently readable. It is especially thought-provoking in posing this question: Has the Reagan administration private-sector initiative been an extraordinarily promising opportunity that was missed, or is it yet another example of the remarkable self-discipline of an administration whose commitment to a limited agenda may be its most important first-term legacy?

Before discussing some fundamental issues raised by Berger's paper, I would like to note here several thoughts that occurred to me while reading it. While these points are not crucial to Berger's findings and conclusions, they perhaps deserve consideration by those pursuing the subject further.

- Does the "long history predating the Reagan program" of private-sector initiative during times of peace trace back only to the Kennedy administration, or should earlier antecedents receive more attention?

- Berger provides an important insight: Ambiguity in purpose begets ambiguity in results. However, is there evidence that other presidential commissions were conceived with more perfect mandates, management processes, and organizational structures?

216

- Berger offers a series of interesting contrasts about public-sector style versus corporate style. But although provocative, it would appear that these statements should be refined, or else they may detract from the analysis by summoning conclusions on the basis of evidence never presented. For example, how much dialogue takes place in cabinet meetings at both the state and federal levels of government? Is there any credible research to support the assertion that corporate chief executive officers are solely concerned with "the bottom-line interests of the investors?" If we accept the "risk-averse" nature of the public sector, how does one explain the Kennedy space program—does every bold national venture of this kind depend on the threat of a greater evil to claim resources in our democracy?

To return to some of the more basic issues of this paper, the reader is compelled to conclude that there is an apparent need for our academic institutions and think tanks to: (1) address some of the fundamental governance issues raised by this Reagan private-sector initiative case; (2) define what would be an appropriate standard for judging the success or measuring the progress of such initiatives; and (3) encourage the development of pertinent management tools and the application of extant knowledge.

Regarding the fundamental governance issues, what is the proper role of public, private, and quasi-public/private sectors in the decision making and implementation of governmental programs? Some contend that years of research and millions of dollars of expenditures have not convinced the majority of our citizens that the benefits of the myriad of federal programs justify the associated budget costs. Recent events suggest that many of the mandates and laws that generate federal programs derive from traditional congressional processes which fail to legitimate those enactments with broad-based public support. Thus, it is both timely and essential to explore the meaning of a limited national agenda. Of course, the formulation of such an agenda, and the goals and strategies that it implies, will cause us to reassess the capabilities both of the three branches of the federal government and of the other levels of government. For example: What priorities might better guide the legislative branch to overcome a disposition more to oversight than foresight? Is the need for a national agenda/goals/strategies more manifest as a consequence of the successful economic development policies advanced by the Japanese? The implications and ramifications of proposed policy options such as increasing taxes, especially on business, and encouraging corporations to increase their giving, require study. Since the electorate in some fashion bears the cost, the matters of equity and efficiency will have to be analyzed more forthrightly. Finally, how will this balance between public- and private-sector initiatives be reconciled with laws and practices such as the Freedom of Information Act and the use of the legislative subpoena?

Regarding the matter of an appropriate standard for judging the success or measuring the progress of private-sector initiatives, the fact remains that—except for winning an election—all other means for assessing governmental performance are tentative, inconclusive, or inadequate. Although the paper informs us that "few states are likely to emulate the scale of" the private-sector initiative effort in Massachusetts, how are we to determine what constitutes success in Massachusetts? Recognizing that all important public policy issues involve making value choices, and that such choices "are not receptive to empirical analysis," what is to be recommended?

Regarding the development of pertinent management tools and the application of extant knowledge, the need for a public policy research agenda is convincing. For instance, why did the White House have to initiate an effort, however inadequate, to collect relevant data on the experiences of private-sector initiatives when annually numerous theses and dissertations are produced at public and private institutions of higher education on less demonstrably useful topics?

The Berger paper brings into focus what may prove to be the most significant policy initiative of the Reagan administration. Perhaps the administration's current efforts and subsequent initiatives by others will benefit from this very worthwhile attempt to distill the lessons learned and place in perspective the larger issues involved.

PART THREE
POLITICAL SUPPORT

THE REAGAN PHENOMENON AND PUBLIC ATTITUDES TOWARD GOVERNMENT

Everett Carll Ladd

Pollsters are forever asking American citizens what they think about governmental policies, political events, leadership performance, the economy, and many other related topics. Cumulatively, the results of this massive national opinion research are illuminating. Sometimes, though, the sheer volume of data seems to overwhelm those who turn to the polls for guidance on "what Americans are really thinking." There are so many surveys done from so many analytical perspectives, with so many biases, conscious and unconscious; so many excellent questions and so many that are misleading—both to the original respondents and to those seeking to make sense of the answers and their apparent contradictions.

It is useful, therefore, to stand back a bit, review the diverse data on public attitudes and assessments, and look for the shape of the larger "forest." In the following pages, I address these topics:

1. Was the Reagan administration elected with a "mandate" to change the fundamental direction of American public policy? One version of this question, especially popular in 1980 and 1981, asks whether the United States has "swung to the right."

2. If Ronald Reagan was handed a mandate, how has it held up over three years of his policies and leadership? Are there signs that Americans' policy preferences have undergone any basic changes over those of three years ago?

3. Have public attitudes toward American government and social performance been shifted significantly by "the Reagan experiment?" Is the confidence gap getting wider, is it closing, or is it unaltered?

The Mandate of 1980

The 1980 presidential balloting—which Adam Clymer has called, correctly I think, "perhaps the most over-interpreted in American history"[1]— was widely seen to reflect a dramatic shift in the public's preferences for candidates and policies. The United States supposedly "swung to the right." It followed almost inevitably that the inauguration of Ronald Reagan as the country's fortieth president would be seen to initiate the "Reagan Revolution."

In fact, Reagan's election represented a strong call for moderate change. Far from signaling a sharp departure in voter preferences, it built upon two key developments of the preceding decade: (1) Electoral dealignment, the weakening of party loyalties, and the diminishment of public confidence in traditional partisan answers; and (2) growing public ambivalence on many major policy questions, especially on the role of government itself. While these developments did not augur a "new Republican majority," their extension and elaboration in the 1980 balloting further weakened the New Deal Democratic coalition and ended its status as a reliable national majority.

Dealignment

A number of related factors attest to the weakening of voter ties to political parties. For some time, there has been a pronounced growth in the number of Americans who think of themselves as independents, rather than as adherents of one of the political parties. Whereas surveys by the Gallup Organization in the early 1950s, for example, showed the proportion of self-described independents to be approximately 19 percent to 20 percent, by the 1970s this proportion had climbed to the 30 percent to 35 percent range.[2] The 1980 General Social Survey, conducted by the National Opinion Research Center (NORC) of the University of Chicago, found that 38 percent of the public identified themselves as independents, and a poll taken by Market Opinion Research for the Republican National Committee in September 1980 placed independents at 40 percent of Americans—compared with Democrats at 37 percent and Republicans at 24 percent. Among both younger Americans

---

1. Adam Clymer, "Contradictory Lessons of '82 Election," *New York Times*, November 4, 1982, p. 1.

2. The Gallup question is phrased, "In politics, as of today, do you consider yourself a Republican, a Democrat, or an Independent?" The entire collection of Gallup Polls, comprising more than 1,200 separate surveys reaching back to the 1930s, is contained in the archives of the Roper Center for Public Opinion Research, Storrs, Connecticut. The distributions cited in the text are derived from scores of individual surveys within this collection.

in professional jobs and those who have attended college, independents are now an absolute majority. According to Gallup polls in late 1980, for example, 50 percent of college graduates under thirty years of age are independents, as are 50 percent of men and 50 percent of women under thirty who hold professional occupations.[3] This substantial growth in the number of self-described independents has been paralleled by large increases in actions that indicate independent political behavior—that is, crossing of party lines and ticket splitting in election contests.

Even more revealing of the rapid progress of electoral dealignment are data showing that the majority of Americans, including those who continue to think of themselves as Democrats or Republicans, no longer either rank the parties highly or believe that it makes a substantial difference which party wins. For example, a CBS News/*New York Times* poll asked respondents in August 1980: "Do you think there are important differences in what the Democratic or Republican parties stand for?"[4] Only 40 percent replied in the affirmative; and the proportion was not much higher among Democratic and Republican identifiers—43 percent and 47 percent, respectively. Also, in July 1980, only 28 percent of the public gave the Democratic party a "highly favorable" rating in a Gallup survey, a score down from 35 percent in 1970 and 42 percent in 1967. The Republicans' support also fell comparably: just 17 percent gave the GOP a "highly favorable" rating in the summer of 1980, as compared with 25 percent in 1970 and 34 percent in 1967.[5]

One of the more dramatic illustrations of the weakening of citizen allegiance to the parties is found in a survey conducted by the University of Connecticut's Institute for Social Inquiry near the height of the presidential campaign, in September 1980. Respondents were asked, "Which party, the Republicans or the Democrats, does the better job [handling a specified set of problems] or don't you think there is much difference?" Depending on the problem area, between 52 percent and 70 percent indicated that they really did not see much of a difference. On some of the questions there was a pro-Democratic margin, on others a pro-Republican edge, but these differences were incidental to the main finding: large majorities simply did not think one party was better than the other. Only 29 percent perceived a partisan difference

---

3. The Gallup question is phrased, "In politics, as of today, do you consider yourself a Republican, a Democrat, or an Independent?" (see footnote 2).

4. In another survey conducted in 1980, this time by the Gallup Organization, the following question was asked: "For the various political offices, did you vote for all the candidates of one party, that is, a straight ticket, or did you vote for candidates of different parties?" Of the respondents, 62 percent were identified as ticket-splitters, compared with just 38 percent voting a straight ticket. This Gallup Poll was taken between November 7 and November 10, 1980.

5. These data are from a Gallup Poll release dated July 13, 1980.

of consequence on the matter of handling inflation, 33 percent on reducing unemployment, and a somewhat higher share but still a minority of 47 percent on the handling of foreign affairs. Connecticut Republicans were somewhat more inclined to see a party difference and to favor their own party than were Democrats, but even here what was most striking was the size of the proportion that did not believe there was much of a difference. At a time when the Democrats controlled the presidency and both houses of Congress, with the country in the midst of double-digit inflation, and the Republican presidential candidate stressing inflation as the top economic issue, 63 percent of Connecticut Republicans said they did not see much of a partisan difference on the matter of controlling inflation.[6]

A dealigned electorate is like an unanchored boat—it can be easily blown one way or another. In 1980 American voters were highly volatile, moving this way and that over the course of the campaign. Without the secure guidance of strong party ties, record numbers decided how to vote very late—37 percent during the last week of the campaign according to a Gallup post-election poll.[7]

In a realignment, some old divisions within the electorate weaken, but new ones appear in their place. In a dealignment, however, the old lines of cleavage erode without any new and enduring ones arising in their stead. For some time there has been an erosion of historic party attachments, but the 1980 presidential election extended this feature of dealignment. Many of the differences in the vote of various social groups that were so much a part of the New Deal configuration—including those defined by religion, ethnicity (except for blacks), and region—were scarcely evident in the 1980 voting.[8]

In every regard, the processes of dealignment were clearer in 1980 than in any preceding election.

Ambivalence

The pull of opposing values and perspectives is clearly evident on the basic question of the role of government and its appropriate interventions in American economic life. Survey findings demonstrate that by the early 1970s Americans of all classes and most social positions had come to accept two basic propositions: first, that there is no alternative to a major role by gov-

---

6. These data are taken from Connecticut Poll no. 9, conducted by the Institute for Social Inquiry, University of Connecticut, September 11–16, 1980.

7. Survey by the Gallup Organization, November 7–10, 1980.

8. Everett C. Ladd, "The Brittle Mandate: Electoral Dealignment and the 1980 Presidential Election," *Political Science Quarterly*, vol. 96, no. 1 (Spring 1981), pp. 1–25.

ernment in regulating the economy, providing social services, and assuring
economic progress; and second, that these generally desired interventions by
government frequently cause problems.

The broad support of Americans in all social strata in 1980 for the
"service state" is shown by data from the earlier-mentioned General Social
Surveys, conducted by NORC. NORC had asked respondents whether they
think government spending in various sectors is too high, too low, or about
right.[9] Responses showed that support for government service was at or near
record levels in 1980 in virtually all of the specified program areas (see
table 1). Large majorities of Americans believed that current spending was
either too low or about right on controlling crime; combatting drug addiction;
health; education; defense; environmental matters; the problems of big cities;
meeting the needs of blacks; and the space program. Only with foreign aid

TABLE 1

PUBLIC OPINION ON PUBLIC SPENDING, 1980

Percentage of Majorities Who Say We Are Spending

Too Little on:		Too Little or About the Right Amount on:		Too Much on:	
Halting crime	(72)	Halting crime	(94)	Foreign aid	(74)
Drug addiction	(65)	Drug addiction	(92)	Welfare	(59)
Defense	(60)	Health	(92)		
Health	(57)	Education	(89)		
Education	(55)	Defense	(88)		
The environment	(51)	The environment	(84)		
		Big cities	(76)		
		Blacks	(74)		
		Space exploration	(57)		

SOURCE: National Opinion Research Center, 1980 General Social Survey (Chicago: NORC, University of Chicago, 1980.) For text of the survey question, see footnote 9.

---

9. The text of the NORC question was as follows: "We are faced with many problems in this country, none of which can be solved easily or inexpensively. I'm going to name some of these problems, and for each one I'd like you to tell me whether you think we're spending too much money on it, too little money, or about the right amount. First (an item is read), are we spending too much, too little, or about the right amount on (the item)? (A) Space exploration program, (B) Improving and protecting the environment, (C) Improving and protecting the nation's health, (D) Solving the problems of the big cities, (E) Halting the rising crime rate, (F) Dealing with drug addiction, (G) Improving the nation's education system, (H) Improving the conditions of Blacks, (I) The military, armaments and defense, (J) Foreign aid, (K) Welfare" (National Opinion Research Center, *1980 General Social Survey*) Chicago: NORC, University of Chicago, 1980.

and welfare did majorities of the public maintain that current spending was too high.

Various other measures employed by other survey organizations verified that the NORC findings were a reliable rendering of public sentiment: Americans wanted government to do a great deal in many different areas. But at the same time, confidence in government performance and in political leaders had dropped sharply. Surveys showed that large majorities of the public blamed government for skyrocketing inflation. There was a widespread sense that the government was clumsy, inefficient, and wasteful.[10]

It was not at all clear, then, which of the two principal partisan approaches to government found greater favor with the American people. The conventional wisdom in 1980 held that Americans were notably disenchanted with government—and thus were much closer to the Republican position. In some areas that definitely was so. The popular sense of government as a "problem" squared clearly with established Republican doctrine and thus contributed positively to the fortunes of the GOP. But at the same time, people had not stopped looking to government for solutions and assistance. Americans of all classes expected high levels of service and performance by government. This commitment conformed with traditional Democratic doctrine and was of electoral benefit to the Democratic party, although the presidency was lost. Overall, the American people had become ambivalent with regard to the state.

Had Americans turned decisively against government and adopted a generally conservative response on matters involving public spending for social programs, the 1980 presidential election might well have evidenced a realignment ushering in long-term Republican ascendency. This did not occur because the public's antigovernment mood was balanced by its progovernment mood. Ambivalent about the contemporary state, Americans in 1980 were also of two minds about the contrasting philosophies of the two parties. Over the last half-century or so in this country, conservatism has been a political and philosophical stance critical of government, while liberalism has endorsed ever-expanding governmental responsibilities and roles. The American public in 1980 was not affirming a commitment to either of these perspectives. Rather, it was vigorously incorporating aspects of both. Although one could

---

10. For an extended analysis of popular ambivalence, see Everett Carll Ladd, *Where Have All the Voters Gone?* (New York: W.W. Norton & Co., 1982); idem, "The New Divisions in U.S. Politics," *Fortune*, vol. 99, March 26, 1979, pp. 88–96; idem, "What the Voters Really Want," *Fortune*, vol. 98, December 1978, pp. 40–48; Everett Carll Ladd and Seymour Martin Lipset, "Public Opinion and Public Policy: Trends and the Likely Climate for the 1980s," in Peter Duignan and Alvin Rabushka, eds., *The United States in the World of the 1980s*, (Stanford, Calif.: Hoover Institution Press, 1980); and Ladd and Lipset, "Anatomy of a Decade," *Public Opinion*, vol. 3, no. 1, December/January 1980, pp. 2–9.

selectively read aspects of either side and proclaim either a rightward swing or a victory for liberalism, there were no legitimate grounds for doing either. Americans who were comfortable with traditional liberal or conservative dicta were rare.

The full emergence of a basic tension or dualism in public attitudes toward government in the United States followed naturally from the linking of conflicting ideological legacies with recent powerful experiences. One of the great political misperceptions is that the American tradition is antistate. The founders of our republic were an unusual breed philosophically. They were passionately committed to the state—as the architects of an effective new national union under the Constitution—but they were also certain that a government unchecked would usurp and tyrannize. This mix of pro- and antigovernment perspectives taught the public to revere coherent and active national government—and to be vigilant against governmental abuse. Americans may be the only people who began their modern political experience without strong ideological traditions either uniformly for or against the state.

Recent experience has greatly enlarged the scope and meaning of this unique legacy. During the New Deal, the national government assumed a variety of new responsibilities and won general approbation for its performance in meeting them. With society's increasing affluence in the post-World War II years, popular expectations of what should be achieved in both the private and the governmental sectors naturally rose. Americans came to expect more leisure time, more consumer goods, higher standards of living—and, in addition, more governmental service in protecting the environment, in extending educational opportunities, in helping those in need, in assuring adequate incomes in old age and retirement, and the like. Without any profound bias either for or against the state, large majorities of the public saw the government's role in achieving a fuller life inextricably mixed with the various private roles. For them, the proper questions were "Is it practicable?" and "Does it work?"

The other side of this nonideological posture toward the state has involved a readiness to criticize government whenever its actions seemed not to work or not to advance a better life. Over the course of the 1960s and 1970s, as American government greatly expanded, it presented a much bigger target for criticism.

Groping Toward a New Political Economy

As the preceding discussion has demonstrated, the American public did not "swing to the right" in 1980, and the Reagan administration did not receive a mandate from the electorate to implement what for the last half-century or so have been called conservative policies. In no sense did the public want to return to a past policy approach. This is not surprising, of course. Not since the Populists in the 1890s has the United States experienced a *reactionary* movement able to compete for control of the government. Our national outlook and values have usually been—and are still too forward-looking and optimistic for any genuinely reactionary impulse to prosper.

But by 1980 Americans had come to conclude that "something new" was needed in the country's public policies. Citizens were clearly dissatisfied with the pattern of governance of the preceding decade or so, a dissatisfaction that in no sense was merely a response to the shortcomings of one or more political figures (it was not, for example, just an anti-Jimmy Carter reaction). "Something new" meant something different from the approach to political economy that the Democratic party had pioneered in the 1930s and that had evolved in the ensuing decades. Without expressing much confidence in the Republicans' capacity to define a successful new approach, the public showed its substantial displeasure with the Democrats' "old time religion."

Many Democratic leaders understood this. What gave them such concern was their sense that their party was floundering intellectually and that the country had turned decisively against their approach to governing. In July 1980, New York Democratic Senator Daniel Patrick Moynihan argued that his party had become a stale force stubbornly defending the big establishment of modern government: ". . . there is a movement to turn Republicans into Populists, a party of the People arrayed against a Democratic Party of the State." Moynihan went on to call this role reversal "terrifying" for the Democrats and one that might signal "the onset of the transformation of American politics." He conceded, further, that "all of a sudden, the GOP has become a party of ideas."[11]

For some time, of course, intellectuals like Moynihan had been highly critical of aspects of the performance of the modern state and of the Democrats' response to these perceived inadequacies. But during the 1980 election concern with deficiencies in Democratic "ideas" became widespread across the party. Senator Gary Hart, who managed George McGovern's presidential campaign in 1972 (and who in 1983 had tried to channel the newer currents of Democratic liberalism in his presidential bid), agreed with Moynihan that "the liberal wing of the Democratic party has run out of ideas." "It has been operating," he said, "on the Roosevelt momentum of programmatic, bureaucratic solutions to the domestic agenda," even though such currents as "increased taxpayer resistance to the growth of the costs of governmental

---

11. Daniel Patrick Moynihan, "Of 'Sons' and Their 'Grandsons,' " *New York Times,* July 7, 1980, p. 15.

programs, inflation, the realities of international economics, and a lot of other factors . . . have been catching up with that momentum.''[12]

Some Democratic leaders, it should be noted, did not like the claim that their party was lacking in ideas. As former Democratic National Chairman John White put it, ''The trouble is we are a party of too many ideas.''[13] But behind such semantic differences, there was general agreement that the 1980 results reflected not just upon Jimmy Carter but also upon Democratic ''ideas''— the way the party approached the task of governing the country.

Above all, many Democrats agreed, the party's economic ideas or economic approach was its greatest failing. Persistent high inflation and diminished economic growth called into question the Democratic claim to being the party of prosperity. The high inflation of the 1970s was deeply resented in the United States, a country that had no experience with it historically outside of war. Frustration with inflation could be seen across the social spectrum, but it was especially acute among the Democrats' traditional constituents—the less affluent. Working-class Americans, fully as much as those in the upper-middle class, had come to believe by 1980 that the very workings of contemporary government, more than actions of business and labor, had caused the inflationary surge. The electoral impact of the extraordinary shift in class perceptions of government and of the Democrats' handling of government was felt in 1980 as the party suffered its greatest losses among Americans who thought they were in trouble economically.

''Compared to a year ago,'' a CBS election-day poll asked respondents, ''Is your family's financial situation better today, worse today, or about the same?''[14] Among those who thought they were better off, Jimmy Carter was preferred to Reagan by 53 percent to 37 percent, while among that third of the electorate who believed their economic position had declined, Reagan led the president by a massive 64 percent to 25 percent (see table 2). The Republican nominee made significant inroads in 1980 into the traditionally Democratic working class, splitting the blue-collar vote evenly with Carter, but most strikingly he did best among blue-collar workers who thought their economic position was deteriorating. When a Republican who had long been the leader of his party's conservative wing and who ran an avowedly conservative campaign drew his greatest support from Americans—including blue-collar workers—who felt they were in trouble economically, rather than from those satisfied with their success, one sees how far the erosion of confidence in the Democrats and their economic answers had progressed.

---

12. Senator Gary Hart, interview with author, December 2, 1980.
13. John White, interview with author, December 3, 1980.
14. CBS News, election-day poll, November 4, 1980.

TABLE 2

AMERICANS' PREFERENCE FOR 1980 PRESIDENTIAL
CANDIDATES, BY PERCEPTION OF FINANCIAL SITUATION

"Compared to a year ago, is your family's financial situation better today, worse today, or about the same?"

	Percentage of Respondents Who Preferred:		
	Jimmy Carter	*Ronald Reagan*	*John Anderson*
Among all voters			
Those who thought they were better off financially than a year ago	53	37	8
Those who thought their financial position was unchanged	46	46	7
Those who thought they were worse off financially than a year ago	25	64	8
Among blue-collar workers only			
Better off	73	22	2
Unchanged	55	39	6
Worse off	30	62	5

SOURCE: CBS News election-day poll, November 4, 1980.

The Democrats' problem in 1980 was part of a much larger one in the area of political economy. Simply put, the Democrats were the party of Keynesian economics. So long as Keynesianism seemed to work, it was hard to challenge the Democrats' contention that they were the party of prosperity. But when Keynesianism ran afoul intellectually, the Democrats got into trouble politically.

David Vogel argues that a resolute pragmatism has distinguished the American approach to questions of political economy: "The American public has supported whichever 'side' has offered the most effective program for promoting real economic growth." From the 1870s through the 1920s, Vogel maintains, the ascendency of private business and its success in limiting governmental intervention ultimately rested on business's capacity "to manage successfully the transformation of America from an agrarian to a modern industrial society." The Great Depression changed all this, however. In Vogel's words:

> Americans supported the reforms of the New Deal because they represented an effective alternative for restoring the viability of the American private sector. . . . What gave political credibility to liberal forces in America during the quarter-century following the second world

war was their ability to argue effectively that the expansion of the welfare state and the adoption
of the principles of Keynesian economics were not only compatible with economic prosperity,
but essential to it.[15]

Rather than encouraging individual thrift, John Maynard Keynes had
argued in 1936 in his celebrated *General Theory of Employment, Interest,
and Money*,[16] that government should help generate consumption through
means such as public works programs, which put money into the hands of
poorer citizens. Furthermore, Keynes contended, government spending should
not be paid for by economizing in other areas. When demand is lagging
because large numbers of people lack money to buy the things they need,
government should run a deficit—that is, spend more than it takes in from
taxes—to provide economic stimulus. It is not even necessary, said Keynes,
for the increased expenditures to be productive in the usual sense. According
to Keynes, high unemployment and lowered production occur when many
people are without the money to purchase what they need. By deficit-spending
and thus pumping money to those who need it, the government would stimulate
increased consumption, more jobs would be created to produce goods to meet
this demand, and investment in new plant facilities would become attractive
again.

Keynesianism sounded almost too good to be true: Politicians who created
new social programs, especially to help those in need, and who spent for
such programs more than they asked people to pay in taxes, were not being
profligate or crassly buying votes; they were stimulating the economy, increasing productivity, lowering unemployment, and generally making everyone more prosperous. Understandably, many politicians were not reluctant
to receive this advice. And what made Keynesianism so unassailably alluring
was the fact that, *in the economic context in which Keynes wrote, it was right.*

The General Theory was not "general" at all, but, rather, a highly
specific response to the needs of one period. Most economists recognize that
that period is now past. The American political economy of the 1980s differs
drastically from that of the New Deal era, and the search is on for another
"new economics" to replace Keynes's.

What major changes have challenged the Keynesian approach? For one
thing, it is now much harder to defend the proposition that increased
governmental intervention in the economy, including social welfare spending
and business regulation, is mostly salutary. Whether or not the United States

---

15. David Vogel, "The Inadequacy of Contemporary Opposition to Business," *Daedalus*,
vol. 109, no. 3 (Summer 1980), pp. 47–57.
16. John Maynard Keynes, *The General Theory of Employment, Interest and Money*, New
York: Harcourt, Brace & World, 1965), (first published in 1936), p. 383.

has reached the optimal level of governmental activity, from most perspectives the country is much closer to it now than it was a half-century ago.

Unemployment was an overwhelming problem in the 1930s—standing at 20 percent in 1935 and nearly 15 percent at the end of the decade. Since World War II, the task of creating jobs rapidly enough to meet the huge growth in the labor force—resulting from both a general rise in the working-age population and a major jump in the proportion of women working outside the home—has continued to be formidable. During the 1982–1983 recession, unemployment climbed into the double-digit range for the first time since the outbreak of World War II; and even with economic recovery in late 1983, the unemployment rate was over 8 percent. Still, at no time since World War II has unemployment been out of control as it was in the Depression years; and various governmental programs, notably unemployment compensation, have at least somewhat cushioned the impact of being out of work. At the same time, however, inflation rose in the 1970s to record levels and at times has appeared, to the public and many economists alike, to be on the brink of surging out of control. *Deflation* had been more common than *inflation* through much of U.S. history. Even in the 1950s and early 1960s price increases were moderate. From the late 1960s through 1980, however, inflation was devastating. In 1981 the dollar would purchase little more than one-third as much as it had just sixteen years earlier. These economic experiences left Americans in a mood for change, although uncertain just what approach was needed.

The 1982 Elections: The Brittle Mandate is Extended

In the 1982 congressional elections, the public had its first formal opportunity to reaffirm or recast the tentative, somewhat ambiguous mandate it had extended two years earlier. The electoral result was generally viewed as indecisive. The Democratic Party made gains in governorships and in the House of Representatives but it did not gain massively. The Reagan administration was told to "change course," but it was not repudiated. "The Center, Rediscovered," was the way the *New York Times* put it.[17] James Nuechterlein argued in *Commentary* that "the message of the election was an ambiguous one," and that "the results of the election point to no clear policy

---

17. "The Center, Rediscovered," *New York Times*, editorial, November 7, 1982.

mandate. . . ."[18] Many other analysts saw a rebirth of prudent moderation, a return to balance after the lurch to the right in November 1980.

In fact, the 1982 vote was a remarkable reaffirmation of the message the electorate conveyed in 1980. Moreover, it furthered the electoral developments—including overall policy ambivalence, insistence on a new approach to political economy, and partisan dealignment—that had shaped the vote two years earlier. The reaffirming character of the 1982 elections is even more impressive because it occurred "against the grain" of a foundering economy. In a sense, then, just as the 1980 results were overstated and oversold, those of 1982 have been made to appear more ambiguous than they were.

It was almost a foregone conclusion that the 1982 election would be a referendum on national policy and direction. Too much had been made of the great departures of the preceding two years for it to be otherwise. The Democrats, smarting from their electoral defeat of 1980 and their program setbacks of 1981 and 1982, and sensing a singular opportunity given the country's economic woes, wanted a referendum on "Reaganomics," a theme thoroughly exploited in the media. Although the Reagan administration was uncomfortable about interpreting the vote as a referendum, it recognized correctly that the election would be given such a cast regardless. The administration thus chose to make a virtue of necessity: "Stay the course" became Reagan's theme.

In the 1980 election, voters had expressed the view that the Democrats' approach to political economy was flawed, and that a new Republican departure should be endorsed, even though that party's capacity to govern successfully was viewed skeptically. Did the public reaffirm or repudiate those judgments in 1982? An especially striking indicator that voter dissatisfaction with the Democrats' approach had persisted is found in answers to the question, "Which of the two political parties do you think is better able to handle the nation's economic problems?" (see table 3). This question was asked nationally in the NBC News election-day poll and of samples of voters in thirteen states as well. Historically, the Democrats' margin over the Republicans has been large and persistent on this type of question. Add to that the troubled state of the economy in 1982, with the GOP in power, and one might have expected a substantial majority to say the Democrats were to be preferred economically. Not so. Only 36 percent nationally said the Democrats were best equipped, compared to 35 percent who picked the Republicans, 18 percent who did not see any difference, and 11 percent who were not sure

---

18. James Nuechterlein, "The Republican Future," *Commentary*, vol. 75, no. 1 (January 1983), p. 1.

TABLE 3

PUBLIC OPINION—WHICH PARTY CAN BETTER HANDLE ECONOMIC PROBLEMS

"Which of the two political parties do you think is better able to handle the nation's economic problems?"

Responses of:	Democrats Best (Percentage)	Republicans Best (Percentage)	No Difference (Percentage)
All voters nationally	36	35	18
California	35	36	19
Connecticut	35	36	18
Florida	35	39	17
Illinois	35	34	19
Maryland	42	29	21
Massachusetts	46	22	22
Michigan	38	33	20
Minnesota	34	35	19
New Jersey	35	32	22
New York	35	29	22
Ohio	38	28	22
Texas	36	41	13
Virginia	35	37	16

SOURCE: NBC News election-day poll, November 2, 1982.
NOTE: Percentages do not total 100 percent because "no answer" and "not sure" responses have not been displayed.

or were not answering (latter percentage not shown in the table). Even in a Democratic state like Michigan, which was especially hard hit by the recession, only 38 percent said the Democrats' approach to economic problems was better—just 5 percent more than preferred the GOP's approach (see table 3.)

Was the Democrats' glass half full, or the Republicans' half empty? If only a little more than a third of respondents endorsed the Democrats as the party better able to handle economic problems, the proportion picking the GOP was no higher. Still, it seems fair to reemphasize that meeting economic needs has been the Democrats' strong suit ever since Franklin Delano Roosevelt, and that the 1982 conditions were tailor-made to elicit a perception of them as the party of prosperity—since the economy was not doing well under the Republicans.

The other part of the 1982 referendum was its broad-brush assessment of the Reagan administration's approach. Throughout the 1982 campaign, Americans were unhappy about the state of the economy and were critical of many Reagan administration policies. On the question of whether the administration's general approach deserved endorsement or rejection, however, the 1982 verdict was to continue the experiment begun two years earlier. Table 4 shows responses to a CBS News/*New York Times* national sampling in late October 1982 comprising a series of three questions on the impact of Reagan economic programs. In answer to the first two questions in this poll—"Have you personally been helped or hurt by Ronald Reagan's economic program?" and ". . . do you think the economic program has helped or hurt the country's economy so far?"—those saying "hurt" outnumbered "helped" by approximately two to one. On the third question, however—"Do you think the economic program eventually will help or hurt the country's economy?"—the answers revealed the intent to continue. Sixty percent said the economy would be helped, compared to just 27 percent who thought it would be hurt in the long run. Although the proportions varied from one survey to another over the course of the 1982 campaign, in every instance in which this or a comparable question was asked, at least a plurality of respondents said they thought the long-term impact would be salutary (see tables 4 and 5).

CBS News and the *New York Times* conducted election-day polls in twenty-seven states (table 5). With the exception of Utah, a plurality of voters in every instance maintained that thus far the Reagan program had hurt their state's economy. However, in twenty-three of the twenty-seven states surveyed—Massachusetts, Rhode Island, Tennessee, and West Virginia were the four exceptions—a majority held that Reagan's program would eventually help. When an ABC News election-day poll asked, "Do you think Reagan's program of cuts in federal spending and cuts in income taxes will help or hurt the economy?" 55 percent said it would help, as against 45 percent who said it would hurt.[19] Again, it bears reemphasizing that these assessments were made against an immediate backdrop of economic news that could hardly be deemed encouraging.

Voters in every state where NBC News polled on election day maintained that "Reaganomics" should be given more time or, in the opinion of a small minority, that it had already succeeded (see table 6). As indicated in the table, the proportion thinking more time should be given, rather than a verdict of "failure" rendered, was 52 percent to 35 percent in California, 57 percent to 31 percent in Texas, and 55 percent to 33 percent in Connecticut. Even in Michigan and Ohio, states reeling from the recession, clear pluralities of voters thought more time should be given—by 51 percent to 38 percent in Michigan and 49 percent to 37 percent in Ohio. Nationally, the split was 53 percent to 35 percent.

19. ABC News, election-day poll, November 2, 1982.

TABLE 4

PERCEIVED EFFECTS OF THE REAGAN PROGRAM

"Ronald Reagan's economic program includes both budget cuts and a cut in taxes. Have you personally been helped or hurt by Ronald Reagan's economic program?"

Reagan Economic Program Has:	Response (Percentage)
Helped	17
Hurt	38
No effect (volunteered view)	39
No opinion	6

"Whatever its effect on you, do you think the economic program has helped or hurt the country's economy *so far*?"

Reagan Economic Program Has:	Response (Percentage)
Helped	30
Hurt	55
Too early to tell (volunteered view)	6
No opinion	9

"Do you think the economic program eventually will help or hurt the country's economy?"

Reagan Economic Program Will:	Response (Percentage)
Help	60
Hurt	27
No opinion	13

SOURCE: CBS News/*New York Times* poll, October 23–28, 1982, of a national sample of 1,437 registered voters.

Views such as those just cited reflect in part the continuing high salience of inflation in the minds of many Americans. Republicans have generally got their best economic marks as inflation tamers, and the one economic boast that the Reagan administration could make persuasively in the 1982 campaign was that it had brought inflation down. With the rate of unemployment climbing to over 10 percent, and this rise dominating economic news during the campaign, the inflation issue might well have been temporarily eclipsed. But when on election day, NBC News asked whether it was more important for the federal government to control inflation or to control unemployment, the electorate split down the middle. And, in the same poll, when voters were asked a companion question on their own economic interests—". . . in terms of your own personal finances, would you rather see the federal government

TABLE 5

PERCEPTIONS OF THE REAGAN PROGRAM BY STATE

"Has the Reagan economic program helped . . . hurt . . . or had no effect?"
"Will Reagan's economic program eventually: Help the economy? Hurt the economy?"

State	*Percentage of Voters Who Believe Reagan Economic Program Has:*			*Percentage of Voters Who Believe Reagan Economic Program Will Eventually:*	
	Helped	*Hurt*	*Had No Effect*	*Help*	*Hurt*
Alabama	24	56	19	55	45
Arkansas	25	52	24	53	47
California	41	46	13	60	40
Connecticut	32	51	18	55	45
Illinois	18	64	18	54	46
Iowa	21	62	17	58	42
Maine	30	53	17	55	45
Massachusetts	NA	NA	NA	50	50
Michigan	19	63	18	53	47
Minnesota	30	55	15	57	43
Mississippi	38	48	13	59	41
Missouri	32	54	14	55	45
Montana	32	55	13	59	41
Nebraska	39	45	16	66	34
Nevada	35	48	17	65	35
New Jersey	27	57	16	52	48
New Mexico	33	51	16	57	43
New York	25	58	17	51	49
Ohio	27	59	14	55	45
Rhode Island	18	69	13	47	53
Tennessee	26	59	14	47	53
Texas	NA	NA	NA	59	41
Utah	48	39	13	72	28
Virginia	40	49	11	57	43
Vermont	NA	NA	NA	58	42
West Virginia	20	65	15	47	53
Wyoming	40	44	16	71	29

SOURCE: CBS News/*New York Times* election-day poll, November 2, 1982.

help control inflation or unemployment?"—the results dramatically confirmed inflation's continuing centrality (see table 7). By 59 percent to 33 percent nationally, and by solid majorities in every state surveyed, voters said that government's success in licking inflation was of greater importance

TABLE 6

PUBLIC OPINION ON REAGANOMICS: SUCCESS OR FAILURE?

"Which statement is closest to your opinion? Reaganomics is a success;
Reaganomics is a failure; Reaganomics needs more time."

Responses of:	Give Reaganomics More Time (or Already a Success) (Percentage)	Reaganomics a Failure (Percentage)
All voters nationally	53	35
California	52	35
Connecticut	55	33
Florida	55	33
Illinois	52	36
Maryland	50	39
Massachusetts	42	42
Michigan	51	38
Minnesota	56	31
New Jersey	52	35
New York	47	39
Ohio	49	37
Texas	57	31
Virginia	52	34

SOURCE: NBC News election-day polls, November 2, 1982.
NOTE: Percentages do not total 100 percent because "no answer" and "not sure" responses have not been displayed.

to them personally than controlling unemployment. Moreover, clear majorities of every occupational group (outside of those unemployed), of union members as well as of those not belonging to unions, and of every income group except the poor, stressed the preeminence of inflation as a problem over unemployment (see table 8). High inflation had markedly changed public perceptions of the political economy.

At the time of the 1982 elections, Americans were fairly optimistic about national leadership and direction, even with the economy in a serious recession. Numerous diverse measures attest to this. For example, the election-day polling of CBS News/New York Times and ABC News showed majorities of voters—albeit small ones—favoring Reagan over either of the two most prominent Democrats, Edward Kennedy or Walter Mondale. "If the 1984 presidential election were held today, would you vote for Ronald Reagan or Ted Kennedy?," the CBS News/New York Times poll asked voters; by 53 percent to 47 percent they picked Reagan. The trial heat came out exactly the same when Reagan was pitted against Mondale. (In December 1982, a Gallup Poll produced a discrepant finding, with Mondale and John Glenn

TABLE 7

PUBLIC OPINION ON CONTROLLING INFLATION VERSUS CONTROLLING
UNEMPLOYMENT: BY VOTERS NATIONALLY AND BY STATE SAMPLES

"In thinking about the national economy, is it more important for the federal
government to help control inflation or unemployment?"

"And in terms of your own personal finances, would you rather see the federal
government help control inflation or unemployment?"

	For Nation		For Self	
Responses of:	Control Inflation (Percentage)	Control Unemployment (Percentage)	Control Inflation (Percentage)	Control Unemployment (Percentage)
All voters nationally	44	46	59	33
California	46	45	59	33
Connecticut	47	43	64	29
Florida	50	44	65	28
Illinois	43	46	57	34
Maryland	43	49	62	32
Massachusetts	38	53	60	33
Michigan	40	52	55	40
Minnesota	46	45	61	31
New Jersey	47	46	62	30
New York	41	48	62	30
Ohio	41	49	55	37
Texas	53	36	65	26
Virginia	44	44	61	30

SOURCE: NBC News election-day polls, November 2, 1982.
NOTE: Percentages do not total 100 percent because "no answer" and "not sure" responses
have not been displayed.

leading Reagan.) When a *Los Angeles Times* poll asked, in a survey conducted
just after the election, "do you think President Reagan is going in the right
direction today . . . or do you think he has gotten off on the wrong track
. . . or do you think he's somewhere in-between?," only 21 percent said,
"he's on the wrong track."[20]

The electorate's positive assessment of political leadership in late 1982
apparently contributed to its overall optimism. The degree of optimism/

20. The *Los Angeles Times* survey was conducted from November 14–18, 1982. A total
of 1,475 adults were interviewed by telephone. The question referred to in the text read in its
entirety: "Considering the nation's economy taken as a whole, do you think President Reagan
is going in the right direction today . . . or do you think he has gotten off on the wrong
track . . . or do you think he's somewhere in-between?" Forty-five percent of all respondents
said "in-between"; 32 percent answered "right direction"; 21 percent said "wrong track"; and
2 percent stated that they were not sure.

TABLE 8

PUBLIC OPINION ON CONTROLLING INFLATION VERSUS CONTROLLING
UNEMPLOYMENT: BY OCCUPATION, UNION MEMBERSHIP, AND FAMILY INCOME

"And in terms of your own personal finances, would you rather see the federal
government help control inflation or unemployment?"

	Inflation (Percentage)	Unemployment (Percentage)
By occupation		
Professional/man	72	28
White collar	66	34
Blue collar	58	42
Farmer	66	34
Student	54	46
Housewife	66	34
Retired	64	36
Unemployed	30	70
By union membership		
Union member	55	45
Not union member	69	31
By family income		
Less than $8,000	48	52
$8,000–$14,999	54	46
$15,000–$24,999	63	37
$25,000–$34,999	67	37
More than $35,000	75	25

SOURCE: NBC News election-day poll, November 2, 1982, of 11,618 voters.

pessimism—whether in regard to one's personal situation or that of the nation—seems to be shaped significantly and independently by two different variables: first, people's sense of their country's political health and direction and, second, their sense of how the economy is doing. Both factors are pervasive. When both assessments are down, as they were in 1974—with the economy buried in recession and the polity in Watergate—the public is necessarily pessimistic. Conversely, when both assessments are up, optimism rises. Frequently, of course, one gets differing mixes of these two variables—as in 1982—when the economy clearly was not doing well but the public's sense of political direction was far from negative.

Polls conducted by the Roper Organization over the past decade give an interesting indication of the interaction of these two defining components of optimism/pessimism. Each December, Roper has asked these two questions of national samples: "Do you expect [next year] to be a better year for you than [the last year], about the same, or not as good as [the last year]?"; and

"Thinking about the country as a whole, what kind of year do you think [next year] will be for the nation—better than [the last year], about the same, or not as good as [the last year]?"

In December 1974 in response to the Roper questions, Americans were highly pessimistic in both personal and national terms. For example, 51 percent said that the next year would not be as good for the nation, while only 16 percent thought it would be better. This pessimism would contrast with the mood in December 1976, when, with the country out of recession and a new president just elected, personal and national optimism soared. In December 1978 pessimism had again risen, while in December 1980 the public was once again more optimistic (see table 9). During this time a striking set of two-year alternations, then, was tied to the fluctuations of economic performance and to the degree of satisfaction with national political leadership. The latter was understandably higher as new presidents took office following the elections of 1976 and 1980. In 1982, however, the pattern of two-year

TABLE 9

OPTIMISM/PESSIMISM OF AMERICANS, 1974–1983

"Do you expect [next year] to be a better year for you than [the last year], about the same, or not as good as [the last year]?"

	Percentage of Responses by Year					
	1983 December	1982 December	1980 December	1978 December	1976 December	1974 December
Better	56	46	46	46	52	36
About the same	37	42	37	39	37	39
Not as good	4	8	10	12	6	23
Don't know	3	4	6	3	5	5

"Now, at the start of this interview I asked you what [next year] looks like to you in personal terms. Thinking about the country as a whole, what kind of year do you think [next year] will be for the nation—better than [the last year], about the same, or not as good as [the last year]?"

	Percentage of Responses by Year					
	1983 December	1982 December	1980 December	1978 December	1976 December	1974 December
Better	47	37	38	23	47	16
About the same	39	42	40	42	40	27
Not as good	10	17	16	31	10	51
Don't know	3	4	6	4	4	5

SOURCE: Polls conducted by the Roper Organization (*Roper Report 84–1*), latest that of December 3–10, 1983.

alternations finally broke. In both personal assessment and expectations for the country, Americans showed the optimism they had exhibited in 1980 and 1976. Burns Roper called attention to this in releasing his data. Personal expectations, he wrote, are "a good deal closer to the level of ebullience that existed as President Carter was about to take office than they are to the gloomy levels that existed at the time of the last big recession in 1974." Similarly, Roper noted, expectations for the nation "come much closer to expressing . . . optimism than to expressing the kind of pessimism that existed at the time of the last recession."[21] Of course, what made December 1974 such a gloomy time for Americans was not simply the recession but the shock of Watergate, with a sense of the polity reeling out of control. In December 1982 the economy was arguably worse off than it had been eight years earlier, but the public's relative confidence in national leadership and direction produced a more upbeat mood.

In 1982 the public believed that its mandate for moderate change aimed at reining in government was being responded to, although imperfectly. The inflation rate, which has become in Western democracies a kind of litmus test for whether the political economy is under control, had dropped significantly. Given these positive inputs, the public's composite sense of self and nation was fairly optimistic, even in the face of real economic dissatisfactions.

Public Attitudes and Assessments in Spring 1984

In the year and a half that has elapsed since the 1982 elections, American political attitudes have changed little. Of course, the Reagan administration appears to be in a stronger electoral position now than in November 1982— but this is simply a short-term response to immediate events, such as the improving economy. To be sure, elections are won and lost on just such short-term moves in voter sentiment, and I do not mean to downplay their importance. In this paper, however, I have attempted to look at more deep-seated attitudes on government and governing—and here not much is occurring. The ambivalence in American attitudes toward government has not been reduced at all, and given the sources of these conflicting views, it is hard to know what future developments might diminish the tensions. The public moved in the 1970s toward the position that some changes were needed in the political economy—directed at lowering inflation and stimulating economic

---

21. Roper Organization, *Roper Report 83–1*, December 1982. The surveys reported on comprise in-person interviews conducted in December of each year, of national samples of 2,000 adults. Quotation is from the Roper Organization release dated January 1983.

growth. Its views here remain unaltered. The Reagan administration has benefited politically, not from the view that it has found the right formula, but from a general receptivity to the "experiment" in which it is participating.

One sees the strength of this inclination to try "something new" in the public's responses to a question posed by Mark Penn and David Schoen, interviewers for *The Garth Analysis*: "Thinking about the next few years, do you think that the administration's economic program will eventually improve the economy, will eventually worsen the economy, or will eventually not have much effect?"[22] When Penn and Schoen first posed this question, in August 1982, 54 percent of respondents said "improve," 21 percent "worsen," and the rest "not much effect" or "don't know" (see table 10). In December 1982, with the recession at its worst and the administration buffeted by criticism, 48 percent said the program would eventually improve the economy, while just 26 percent said it would hurt it. It is hard to find more compelling proof of the public's yearning for a new approach and its "patience" in seeing it through. The fact that in their latest survey (October 29–November 4, 1983) Penn and Schoen found the improve/worsen ratio to be 55 percent to 14 percent—the best ever from the administration's standpoint—is hardly noteworthy: if the public was willing to bear with the Reagan program in December 1982, of course it would be willing a year later when the economy had strengthened.

The public still has economic complaints, of course. Polls show that the huge federal deficits are a source of particular unease. But the deficit problem is not significantly affecting the Reagan administration's standing—because the public does not apportion partisan blame. When Penn and Schoen (for *The Garth Analysis*, asked a national sample in February 1984 who they thought was to blame "for the current budget deficits—President Reagan, previous presidents, Congress, or general economic conditions," only 12 percent said "Reagan."[23] In fact, only 16 percent of Democrats said they blame the president. The issue just does not have a partisan cut at present.

Levels of Public Optimism/Pessimism Toward Government

After three-plus years of Ronald Reagan's leadership and policies, have Americans become more or less confident about the prospects for sound and

---

22. Penn and Schoen Associates, *The Garth Analysis*, August 1982.
23. Penn and Schoen Associates, *The Garth Analysis*, February 1984.

TABLE 10

PERCEIVED FUTURE EFFECTS OF THE REAGAN PROGRAM

"Thinking about the next few years, do you think that the administration's economic program will eventually improve the economy, will eventually worsen the economy, or will eventually not have much effect?"

	Percentage of Responses			
	Improve	Worsen	Not Much Effect	Don't Know
All respondents				
August 1982	54	21	17	8
October 1982	54	23	17	6
December 1982	48	26	20	7
February 1983	55	18	20	7
June 1983	55	16	21	7
August 1983	49	15	28	7
October/November 1983	55	14	23	9
Respondents by selected groups				
(October/November 1983)				
Party				
Democrat	45	17	26	12
Republican	75	6	14	4
Independent	54	14	25	7
Income				
Less than $7,000	42	19	26	13
$7,000–$14,999	51	14	24	11
$15,000–$24,999	49	15	29	7
$25,000 and above	63	11	19	7
Education				
Less than high school	40	18	26	16
High school	54	11	25	10
College	59	14	20	7
Race				
White	58	12	21	8
Black	34	25	33	9
Sex				
Male	62	12	21	6
Female	49	15	25	11
Region				
Northeast	53	13	27	8
South	57	13	22	9
Midwest	55	13	22	9
West	57	16	19	8

SOURCE: Penn and Schoen Associates, *The Garth Analysis* (November 1983). Survey work done by Penn and Schoen; date of field work of the latest survey was October 29–November 4, 1983.

successful governance? This question has the appearance of being important—and it would be if it had not previously been answered so convincingly. The public's responses during the dozen or so years before Reagan took office gave us a firm reading. What were those responses? First, on a great variety of questions specifically designed to measure "confidence," optimism/pessimism, "political alienation," distrust, and the like—Americans showed themselves critical and complaining. Seymour Martin Lipset and William Schneider have reviewed these data.[24] Second, Americans showed that their basic, underlying confidence in and commitment to their social, economic, and political system was undiminished. Through the Vietnam War and Watergate, through energy shocks and double-digit inflation, the public did not waver in its fundamental assessments. It fumed a great deal; it clearly did not believe that those in command were doing as well as they might (but who could have believed that?). Seemingly, the public had become more cynical about the powers that be—perhaps because of the problems of performance already referred to and perhaps in part because the message of the mass news media encourages political cynicism.[25] But if dissatisfied with current performance and somewhat distrustful, the public had not withdrawn its strong historic commitment to the ideas, values, and institutions on which the society was built.[26]

Nothing has happened in the three years the Reagan administration has been in office to change at all this general structure of public response. It would have been startling indeed if anything had—since the structure had been so securely established.

What has happened, of course, is that the "political marks" given the administration—how well the public thinks Reagan and his associates are conducting the affairs of state—have gone down and up in response to various actions and events. This pattern happens in every administration; it is an

24. Seymour Martin Lipset and William Schneider, *The Confidence Gap* (New York: Free Press, 1983).

25. Everett Carll Ladd, "The Polls: The Question of Confidence," *Public Opinion Quarterly*, vol. 40, no. 4 (Winter 1976–1977), pp. 544–552; Ladd, "The Matter of Public Confidence: Inadequate Data and Untested Theories" (Paper prepared for the annual meeting of the American Association for Public Opinion Research, Buck Hill Falls, PA, May 19–22, 1977; Ladd, "The American 'Sense of Nation' " in *Political Culture in the United States in the Seventies: Continuity and Change* (Frankfurt/Main: Center for the Study of North America, 1981).

26. I have reviewed the complex assortment of survey data that support these conclusions in other publications, including *Public Opinion* magazine. For reports of studies that suggest the contemporary mass news media have contributed to the growth of a kind of political cynicism, see Michael Robinson, "Public Affairs Television and the Growth of Political Malaise," *American Political Science Review*, vol. LXX, no. 2, (June 1976), pp. 409–432; and Arthur Miller (et al.), "Type-set Policies: Impact of Newspapers on Public Confidence," *American Political Science Review*, vol. 73, no. 1 (March 1979), pp. 67–84.

assessment of immediate governing and economic performance—not a reflection of deeper attitudes toward governance. We know that, especially in response to an improving economy, the administration is now getting better leadership grades than it did in late 1982 and early 1983. In general, presidential approval scores taken in the polls show Reagan at about the approval level he enjoyed in the fall of 1983, scores that are quite high and that reflect a recovery in popularity that many did not expect. According to Gallup data, Reagan's approval rating—the percentage of the adult populace approving his handling of the presidency—was higher in his thirty-eighth month in office (March 1984) than that of any other post-World War II president except Dwight D. Eisenhower at comparable times in their presidencies.[27]

Before leaving the broad question of public confidence, a note of caution is in order. One should always assume that respondents intend by their answers to various questions on social optimism and political confidence to convey only the moods. These moods are often filled with contradictions—for example, satisfaction and dissatisfaction existing side by side—and are inchoate. When one adds to this the fact that the questions themselves frequently are remarkably vague, one can see why one gets such a smorgasbord of answers.

Consider, for example, the public's responses to the widely used "right track/wrong track" question: "In general, do you think that things in the U.S. are going in the right direction, or are they off on the wrong track?" (see table 11). What does the response "wrong track" mean? A stinging indictment? A minor rebuke? It almost certainly encompasses both. The only thing one can be certain of is that the mood being reflected shows at least some dissatisfaction.

Polling on this question has generally shown ups and downs in some reasonably predictable response to national experience, economic and political. Thus "right track" answers were proportionally very low in 1973 and 1974, for example, at the time of Watergate, inflation, and the recession; and low again in early 1980, reflecting in part unease with Carter's leadership and the Iranian hostage situation. But while the *direction* of change in responses to this question is fairly consistent and predictable from one survey to another in the work of any given survey organization, the absolute *proportions* differ widely from one survey organization to another.[28] Any

---

27. Gallup Organization, "Opinion Roundup: Reagan and His Predecessors," *Public Opinion*, vol. 7, no. 1 (February/March 1984), pp. 32–34.

28. Compare, for example, the findings from recent askings of the "right track/wrong track" question by ABC News/*Washington Post*, the Roper Organization, CBS News/*New York Times*, and Penn and Schoen Associates in "Opinion Roundup. Pollsters: Right Track, Wrong Track, or Off the Track," *Public Opinion* (February/March 1984), p. 30.

TABLE 11

PUBLIC'S RESPONSES TO "RIGHT TRACK/WRONG TRACK" QUESTION

"In general, do you think that things in the U.S. are going in the right direction, or are they off on the wrong track?"

	Percentage of Responses		
	Right Direction	*Wrong Direction*	*Don't Know*
Party			
Democrat	40	39	20
Republican	73	15	12
Independent	55	31	14
Income			
Less than $7,000	29	43	28
$7,000–$14,999	41	36	23
$15,000–$24,999	46	39	14
$25,000 and above	65	23	12
Education			
Less than high school	36	36	28
High school	47	32	21
College	60	29	12
Race			
White	57	27	17
Black	23	62	16
Sex			
Male	61	24	15
Female	45	37	18
Region			
Northeast	54	32	15
South	54	29	17
Midwest	50	31	19
West	54	31	15

SOURCE: Penn and Schoen Associates, *The Garth Analysis* (November 1983). Survey work done by Penn and Schoen; date of field work of the latest survey was October 29– November 4, 1983.

satisfactory explanation of such differences must take into account that the question is reflective of superficial swings or articulations of public mood. Seemingly small differences relating to question wording and question placement yield major response differences. However, the "internal" relationship of group responses to the right track/wrong track question are what one would expect. Thus both the poor and blacks are much more likely to say "wrong track" than are both the more prosperous and whites (see table 11).

Conclusion

There is a stable, predictable structure to public attitudes relating to governance. The basic elements of this structure may be described as the following:

1. Americans are confident about their central political values and institutions and have remained so through the often troubling experiences of the past fifteen years. They do complain, of course—less often when things are going well for the nation and more often when things are not going well.

2. Americans are not at all inclined to embrace either New Deal-style liberalism or conservatism. Reagan was elected in the midst of a national policy mood that was distinguished by ambivalence and searching. The 1980 Reagan electoral mandate did not represent a "swing to the right"; rather, it was a reflection of the fact that the public *has* lost confidence in the answers and performance of the Democratic/Keynesian approach to the political economy. The impulse to "try something different" in order to control inflation and promote growth is far from casual.

The political results are also far from casual. The Democrats have been having special problems with the presidency: they have won it in only three of the last eight elections (spanning 1952–1980). Moreover, they have won it decisively only once in this period—in 1964 when the GOP nominated a man (Barry Goldwater) who was not the choice even of a majority of Republicans. Every publicly available national poll as of this writing (May 1984) showed Reagan ahead of both Walter Mondale and Gary Hart. While two of the Republican presidents of the last thirty years—Eisenhower and Reagan—have enjoyed great personal popularity, the Democrats' problem with the presidency goes deeper than this.

3. Still, there has been no realignment of the "classic" sort, such as occurred in 1928–1935, when the Democrats moved from minority status to majority status in all offices from the state houses to the presidency. The New Deal realignment was sui generis—nothing like it had ever occurred before, and nothing like it can be expected again. The dealignment discussed at the beginning of this paper is a prime reason why the Democrats' ongoing problem with the presidency is unlikely to extend to a full realignment, with the Republicans the majority at every level. It is always exceedingly difficult to assemble a stable new partisan majority; it is virtually impossible to do so when citizen ties to parties generally are eroding, as they have over the last two decades.

The model for the years ahead is not that of 1928-1935. Rather, it is an electoral variant of the economist's classical free market. Consumers (voters) pick and choose among products (candidates) without restriction or constraint (from strong party ties). This is not to suggest that it is impossible for one party consistently to win out in the electoral free market—the market is free, not random. To win continually though, a party must continually convince a majority of voters that it is better than its rival.

Daniel Yankelovich

When Reaganomics Fails, Then What?

Everett Carll Ladd's lucid paper on the meaning of the "Reagan Revolution" prompts at least two questions on the part of a commentator.

First, "Has Ladd got it right?" Ladd has had to plough through masses of survey data and partisan commentary. That he has sifted the pieces and fit them together coherently is no small accomplishment. My own assessment, based both on the data in Ladd's paper and on other findings, is that Ladd has solved a confusing puzzle in a masterful fashion. All of the data I have analyzed support four conclusions, as outlined in Ladd's review. These are as follows:

1. The 1980 election should not be interpreted as a swing to the right, which would imply that the American electorate had changed its political hue from moderate-liberal to conservative and that Ronald Reagan was elected because voters had come to share his ideological outlook. Ladd correctly emphasizes that this did not happen.

2. Ladd also correctly and conclusively rejects the explanation of the Reagan victory offered by partisans from the other end of the political spectrum, namely, that the Reagan victory was due primarily to the voters' repudiation of Jimmy Carter.

3. Ladd also accurately identifies the source of the Reagan victory. Reagan's ascendancy capped a long process of growing voter disaffection with the liberal Democratic strategy, a strategy that links a "welfare state" role for the federal government with Keynesian economic policies for managing the economy. A Keynesian premise provides the link—the assumption that deficit spending for social purposes will stimulate consumer demand and hence economic growth.

   So long as the Keynesian approach worked, the moderate center—which was nonideological and pragmatic—supported an essentially liberal doctrine even though it was not itself particularly liberal in outlook. As that strategy showed increasing signs of wear and tear, the electorate began to consider alternative choices. In 1980, with the liberal strategy in disarray, the moderate center decided it was best to abandon an approach that was no longer working and to give the competition a try. The center has now thrown its provisional support to a conservative doctrine—so long as it is seen to work.

4. Ladd documents his contention that the moderate center is ambivalent about the role of government in carrying out either a liberal or a conservative agenda. This ambivalence reflects the experience of the past two decades, an experience that has led the public to reaffirm liberal goals but at the same time to become deeply skeptical about liberal methods. Thus, the electorate supports a positive role for government in meeting a wide variety of social and economic needs yet is critical of government's performance in carrying out this role. This makes for a complex situation but not a confusing or contradictory one. It is the partisan tendency to superimpose an ideological interpretation on the public's straightforward practical stance that makes the stance appear confusing.

Although Ladd makes a number of other points as well, the four points summarized here are the important ones to get right—and Ladd does this with impressive skill.

The Reagan Alternative and Our Future Governance

The second question that may be raised in connection with Ladd's paper is, "What does Reagan's program portend for our future governance?" Following are several thoughts that occurred to me on reading Ladd's analysis.

The liberal approach that Ladd associates with Keynes held sway for almost a half century. It enabled liberal Democrats—about one out of five voters—to win the support of the moderate majority, thereby locating the center of gravity of American politics slightly to the left of center. The Keynesian strategy was a stroke of political genius: it arranged things so that what was good for the welfare state was also good for the economy, and vice versa. And it did so in a manner that precisely conformed to the needs and circumstances of the times.

That harmony of purpose no longer exists. The growth of the welfare state imposes heavy constraints on the economy, while the slow growth of the economy chokes off the support the welfare state needs if it is to thrive. This mutual antagonism can be seen even more clearly in Western Europe than in the United States. In countries like Sweden and Britain, what was once synergism has grown into cannibalism. The demands of the welfare state constrain the economy, and the slow tempo of economic growth starves the welfare state of nourishment. European social democrats are bereaved: Few had realized how utterly dependent the welfare state was on an affluent and vital economic base.

In considering our country's own future, we must ask whether the Reagan alternative to the Keynesian strategy will prove viable. Can it do what needs to be done through conservative strategies? Can it reconcile the economic imperatives of growth, competitiveness, and vitality with the social imperatives of equal opportunity, fairness of burden sharing, and a helping hand to those who need it? Will it be, in its own fashion, the functional equivalent of the Keynesian strategy? And if not, what will be the consequences?

It should be remembered that voters did not support the Reagan strategy on its merits. Reaganomics has yet to prove itself to voters, and Reagan social policy is largely negative—a matter of dismantling other peoples' solutions to problems rather than addressing the problems themselves. Indeed, far from reconciling social and economic imperatives, Reagan has obliged the electorate to swallow a bitter remedy—to sacrifice social welfare to improve our economic health. A majority of voters support Reagan's economic approaches even though they are seen as unfair, on the grounds that they are supposed to be good for the economy. But suppose they prove not to be good for the economy? Suppose that economic and societal needs are driven even farther apart? Suppose the results are ambiguous and inconclusive?

In my judgment, one or several of these "supposes" will turn out to be true. Reaganomics combined with Reagan's social policy will not provide a successful replacement for Keynesian strategy. For lasting electoral appeal, the country needs an approach that will do for the 1990s what the Keynesian strategy did in its own time—revitalize the economy while simultaneously addressing our growing social needs. Evaluated in this light, the Reagan approach is unlikely to meet the test. When it fails, the electorate will abandon it abruptly and without sentiment. Voters like Ronald Reagan and his leadership style, but on matters of economic policy, the test is exclusively pragmatic. As Ladd has shown, the electorate is not a body of ideological conservatives who will stay with an approach simply because it is congenial to their economic faith.

When the Reagan strategy does falter, in order for the country to avoid a long period of churning and near-chaos, it will be necessary to have a ready substitute for Reaganomics. The country cannot return to the Keynesian strategy of the past. I believe that one or several other strategies can be evolved, but this will not happen unless it is recognized that the need is urgent.

COMMENTS   *David E. Price*

Parties In The Reagan Years

This commentary provides a brief assessment of how the parties have fared during the Reagan administration, using Everett Carll Ladd's paper on public attitudes toward government as a point of departure. While Ladd's findings apply mainly to the parties in the electorate, I will examine also the developments within the parties in government and party organizations, primarily at the national level.

Parties in the Electorate

Regarding the parties in the electorate, the principal news is what has *not* happened. Polls in 1981 that showed sizable gains in Republican identification—a one-year increase of four percentage points in the share of the electorate professing Republican loyalties and a drop of eight percentage points in the share of Democratic identifiers—led some to anticipate "the most important political development in half a century: the Republican realignment."[1] But by the time of the 1982 midterm elections, leading national polls showed (and the election results reflected) a return to the partisan balance recorded in mid-1980.[2] As Ladd suggests, public attitudes about the role of the state have been too ambivalent and inconsistent to support decisive shifts in either partisan direction. Nor have the Reagan administration's economic policies been efficacious or attractive enough to give partisanship a new policy basis the way New Deal Keynesianism once did.

The Reagan years may nonetheless have contributed to the shifting and settling of partisan allegiances. This may be more a matter of *reinforcing*

---

1. Adam Clymer and Kathleen Frankovic, "The Realities of Realignment," *Public Opinion*, vol. 4, no. 3 (June–July 1981), p. 42.
2. Gallup Organization, *Gallup Poll* release dated March 10, 1983.

basic New Deal patterns, however, than of bringing new issues to the fore.[3] We do not yet have sufficient evidence on this point. Studies of the increasing coherence and consistency of voters' policy views after the 1950s—and of the greater congruence between voters' policy and party preferences since that time—stress the stimulative and educative impact of the ideologically polarized 1964 election.[4] Might the Reagan years have a comparable impact? Both the 1980 campaign and the administration's conduct have sought to graft onto traditional Republican economic conservativism the social conservatism of the New Right on issues such as abortion, busing, and school prayer, and a hard line in international affairs. But the main policy focus has been economic. Democratic politicians and publicists have long assumed that to focus attention on "bread and butter" issues would automatically work in their favor—and indeed most Americans do remain "operational liberals," favoring a variety of governmental programs and services even when they call themselves conservatives. But Reagan has demonstrated that economic issues can be given mass appeal from the conservative side, with a focus on inflation and taxes displacing the traditional Democratic emphasis on economic and personal security. Thus Republican gains may come more through shifts in voters' perceived economic and class interests than through any displacement of the New Deal agenda with noneconomic issues. The polls suggest that such shifts have not greatly altered the balance of party strength, at least in terms of individuals' identifications. But the polls also show that significant differences have developed between the two parties' identifiers in their views on a wide range of issues, particularly those involving the role of government.[5]

Ladd emphasizes the steady march of electoral *dealignment*. As Walter Dean Burnham and others have stressed, the weakening of voter attachments to the parties may have made "realignment" in the classic sense highly unlikely. Electoral enthusiasms and disaffections have increasingly focused on specific issues and candidates rather than on enduring party ties. Many of the indicators of detachment from party—split-ticket voting, for example, and reliance on personality or issues rather than on the party label in voting—continue to move in the direction of disaggregation, although other indicators, such as the numbers of "independent" identifiers and of those expressing

3. See James Sundquist, *Dynamics of the Party System*, rev. ed. (Washington, D.C.: The Brookings Institution, 1983), 444–449.

4. Gerald Pomper, *Voters' Choice* (New York: Dodd, Mead & Co., 1975), p. 178.

5. Everett Carll Ladd, "A Party Primer," *Public Opinion*, vol. 6, no. 5 (October–November 1983), p. 58; see also "Opinion Roundup," *Public Opinion*, vol. 6 (October–November 1983), pp. 27, 34–37.

unfavorable attitudes toward the parties, show some signs of leveling off.[6]
Some have suggested that if the parties make increasingly distinctive and
coherent electoral appeals, their bases of mass support and their electoral role
might be revitalized. But it is unclear how far this trend toward distinctive
partisan images and appeals might go. Nor is it clear that voter perceptions
of clearer party stands or increases in the congruence of voters' policy and
party preferences necessarily lead to increased voter *reliance* on party cues.[7]
At best, then, the Reagan years may have seen some deceleration of the
dealignment process, but at a level that leaves the parties in the electorate in
a seriously weakened state.

Party Organizations

The signs of renewal in party organization are more hopeful than in the
parties in the electorate, although the strength of a party at one level is
ultimately related to its health at the other. The institutional development of
national party organizations, as well as comparable developments in many
states, have continued during the Reagan years. Tables 1 and 2 give an
indication of the levels of campaign funding the national party committees
have undertaken in recent years and of the scale of their staff operations.
Extreme disparities between Republican and Democratic operations are still
apparent. But both the Democratic National Committee (DNC) and the Democratic congressional campaign committees have begun to emulate the Republicans' successes in expanding their financial base and increasing the
support and services that they can offer candidates.[8] While this is not a flawless
model of organizational renewal—for example, it ignores the vitality of parties
as local associations—it nonetheless represents a successful adaptation to the
modern campaign environment.

The national party organizations have generally enjoyed more growth
and prominence when they were *not* in possession of the White House. As
DNC Chairman Robert Strauss once put it, "If you're a Democratic party

---

6. See the discussion in David E. Price, *Bringing Back the Parties* (Washington, D.C.:
Congressional Quarterly Press, 1984), pp. 10–18.

7. See Pomper, *Voters' Choice*, p. 183.

8. See Price, *Bringing Back the Parties*, pp. 38–46, 246–249; Larry Sabato, "Parties,
PACs, and Independent Groups," in Thomas Mann and Norman Ornstein, eds., *The American
Elections of 1982* (Washington, D.C.: American Enterprise Institute, 1983), pp. 82–86; and
Dom Bonafede, "Democratic Party Takes Some Strides Down the Long Comeback Trail,"
National Journal, October 8, 1983, pp. 2053–2055.

TABLE 1

RECEIPTS AND CONTRIBUTIONS BY NATIONAL PARTY COMMITTEES (FEDERAL ACCOUNTS ONLY), 1979–1982

	1979–1980			1981–1982		
	Net Receipts[a] ($ millions)	Number of Contributors	Contributed to (or Spent for) Candidates ($ millions)	Net Receipts[a] ($ millions)	Number of Contributors	Contributed to (or Spent for) Candidates ($ millions)
Democratic National Committee	15.1	60,000	4.0	16.2	220,000	0.2
Democratic Congressional Campaign Committee	2.1	15,000	0.6	6.5	72,000	0.8
Democratic Senatorial Campaign Committee	1.7	3,000	1.1	5.6	39,000	2.4
Total Democratic Committees	18.8		5.7	28.4		3.4
Republican National Committee	76.2	870,000	6.2	83.5	1,600,000	1.9
National Republican Congressional Committee	28.6	700,000	3.2	58.0	1,200,000	7.5
National Republican Senatorial Committee	23.3	175,000	5.4	48.9	270,000	9.3
Total Republican Committees	128.1		14.9	190.5		18.6

SOURCE: For committee receipts and contributions, Federal Election Commission reports. For donor base, estimates by committee staff and by *National Journal*, May 23, 1981, p. 923.

a.   Figures are for receipts minus transfers. Refunds, however, are included in Federal Election Commission receipt totals. Republican National Committee data suggest this may result in an overstatement of Republican committee receipts by as much as 2 percent.

TABLE 2

PRECAMPAIGN STAFFING LEVELS, NATIONAL PARTY COMMITTEES

	Republican	*Democratic*
National committees		
Administrative	99	37
Finance	105	23
Political	100	39
Communications and research	57	7
Total	361	106
House campaign committee	95	31
Senate campaign committee	85	21

NOTE: Data, furnished by committee sources, represent staffing levels as of September 1983.

chairman when a Democrat is president, you're a Goddamn clerk.''[9] But there are strong indications that the Reagan presidency has not been nearly as damaging to the Republican National Committee (RNC) as was, say, Nixon's, or as were Johnson's and Carter's for the Democrats. Reagan's first national chairman, Richard Richards, had a rather insecure tenure and his words upon leaving office in 1982 had a familiar ring: "Every clerk at the White House thinks he knows how to do my job."[10] But his successor, Frank Fahrenkopf, has enjoyed greater White House access and confidence, partly because of a new arrangement whereby Senator Paul Laxalt (R.-Nev.), a presidential intimate, serves as "general chairman," coordinating the work of the RNC and the Republican congressional campaign committees.[11]

The RNC's role, of course, displays less independence and different emphases than it did when the Democrats were in power. Policy and research operations, for example, have shifted from the touting of Republican alternatives and critiques of the Carter record to "good news" reports designed to shore up the troops and opposition research on prospective Democratic candidates. But the RNC has had sufficient resources, and has enjoyed enough support across the party by virtue of the services it has provided, to allow it to avoid the kind of eclipse that the national committee of the in-party has all too often suffered. And the role of the GOP's congressional campaign committees has, if anything, become even more important. Without the

---

9. Quoted in Joseph Califano, Jr., *A Presidential Nation* (New York: W.W. Norton & Co., 1975), p. 153.

10. *Congressional Quarterly Weekly Report*, October 9, 1982, p. 2657.

11. Dom Bonafede, "Laxalt's RNC Follows a Simple Rule: A Minority Must be Better Organized," *National Journal*, June 18, 1983, pp. 1270–1273.

activities of these committees, encouraging attractive contenders to run and providing generous support and essential services once they were in the race, the party's midterm losses almost certainly would have been substantially greater than they were.[12]

The Parties in Government

The role of Republican party committees in recruiting and financing candidates has probably encouraged party regularity in Congress. But such aid has had few strings attached, and the party has supported a number of mavericks who nonetheless were critical to the balance of party control. The party loyalty and presidential support scores of Senate Republicans reached modern highs in Reagan's first year. Party unity has since lessened in both chambers, but the slight upward trend visible over the past decade has continued. This no doubt reflects the polarizing effects of Reagan's proposals, but it is also indicative of the strengthening of party institutions and the more assertive leadership styles that have been evident in both houses since the mid-1970s.[13]

One of the least successful DNC operations has been the National Strategy Council, a body formed in 1981 that some hoped would provide a forum for policy debate and development. But this gap has to some extent been filled by congressional Democrats, who have developed the party's policy machinery to an unprecedented (though still modest) degree. The most conspicuous initiatives have come from the Committee on Party Effectiveness of the House Democratic Caucus and a task force on long-term economic policy formed by the Senate Democratic Policy Committee. The reports of these groups broke some new ground in the area of industrial policy but achieved less in other areas. The House Caucus enjoyed only limited success in its efforts to influence the agendas of the standing committees, but its work enabled the party to put forward a far more substantive and unified appeal— in forums ranging from the 1982 midterm conference to State of the Union responses to the 1984 platform deliberations—than it could have otherwise.[14]

---

12. See Gary C. Jacobson, "Reagan, Reaganomics, and Strategic Politics in 1982: A Test of Alternative Theories of Midterm Congressional Elections" (Paper delivered at the annual meeting of the American Political Science Association, Chicago, September 1983).

13. See Price, *Bringing Back the Parties*, pp. 51–57, 64–69, 72–75.

14. *Ibid.*, pp. 279–284. See also the two major reports of the House Democratic Caucus: "Rebuilding the Road to Opportunity: A Democratic Direction for the 1980s" (September 1982), and "Renewing America's Promise: A Democratic Blueprint for Our Nation's Future" (January 1984); and the report of the Senate Democratic Caucus, "Jobs for the Future: A Democratic Agenda" (November 1983).

In sum, while one can identify little that the Reagan administration has done directly to enhance the parties' prospects, it has shown more respect for party roles and institutions than did several of its predecessors. And in the meantime, the curious pattern of contradictory trends has continued: party "decline" on many fronts but new signs of organizational resilience and successful adaptation.

A NEW PRESIDENT, A DIFFERENT CONGRESS, A MATURING AGENDA

Charles O. Jones

Ronald Reagan's victory over Jimmy Carter in 1980 was viewed by most observers as stunning. Not since Grover Cleveland's loss to Benjamin Harrison in 1888 had a Democratic incumbent lost to a Republican challenger. In his critical examination of the media coverage of the 1980 presidential race, Jeff Greenfield reports:

> Even on the last days of the campaign, after the debate, and after the false hopes raised by the possible release of the hostages, the polls showed a very close race, although movement to Reagan was detected by NBC and ABC. . . . No network, no news organization, came close to predicting anything like the ten-point, eight million vote spread for Reagan, much less the electoral landslide of the sweeping Republican gains in the Senate and the House.[1]

States that had been breathtakingly close the week before were won handily by Reagan (e.g., Illinois, Michigan, Ohio). Other major states like New York were not even considered as potentially going for Reagan—yet the new president won there by 51.4 percent of the two-party vote. As election analyst William Schneider put it: "The surprise of the November 4, 1980, presidential vote was that it was so decisive."[2]

Decisive Republican presidential victories are not uncommon, however. Despite a commanding Democratic advantage in party identification of voters,

I wish to acknowledge the support of the White Burkett Miller Center of Public Affairs, University of Virginia, in preparing this paper. I am also grateful to Roger H. Davidson, Norman J. Ornstein, Lester M. Salamon, James L. Sundquist, and Stephen J. Wayne for their helpful comments.

1. Jeff Greenfield, *The Real Campaign: How the Media Missed the Story of the 1980 Campaign* (New York: Summit Books, 1982), p. 294.

2. William Schneider, "The November 4 Vote for President: What Did It Mean?" in Austin Ranney, ed., *The American Elections of 1980* (Washington, D.C.: American Enterprise Institute, 1981), p. 212.

Republican presidential candidates have fared well in the last eight elections: four overwhelming wins (1952, 1956, 1972, 1980), one narrow victory (1968), two narrow losses (1960, 1976), and one debacle (1964). The 1976 election should have been more instructive than it was for understanding 1980. In the first post-Watergate presidential election, Gerald R. Ford, a genial compromise vice-presidential appointee who pardoned Richard M. Nixon almost won! A shift of 5,560 votes in Ohio and 3,690 votes in Hawaii would have elected him president. Though replaying history as quasi-experiments is as dangerous as it is intriguing, one cannot help speculating that, without Watergate, we would have had uninterrupted Republican presidencies from 1968 to the present.

A more engaging task, however, is to examine the underlying conditions that have led to Republican success in presidential elections. Politics in America have changed. That is the broader development focused on in this paper. A more specific purpose is to explore the context within which the Reagan administration has communicated its agenda to and exerted its influence with Congress. A central theme is that a new domestic policy agenda had been emerging since the late 1960s, but had been resisted by recent Democratic Congresses. The new issues were in reaction to the domestic breakthroughs of the Great Society and thus were more consolidative in nature—making government work better, seeking to control a budget that had come to have a life of its own, and evaluating the efforts of regulatory interventions into the marketplace. The Nixon-Ford and Carter administrations comprehended the change but each had difficulties on Capitol Hill—the Republicans for obvious partisan reasons, the Democrat for special reasons associated with his personal political background and style. In terms of the policy agenda, the 1980 election was bound to be interpreted as having a significant effect, given the clarity of the issue stands taken by Ronald Reagan. And the incremental shift that was already occurring in the direction of the consolidative issues just cited was made dramatic by the surprising returns.

This paper examines the current status of presidential-congressional relations in domestic policy by discussing the following topics:

1. How Reagan came to Congress (stressing the implications of the 1980 election for the policy agenda and the organization of the White House).

2. How Congress came to Reagan (stressing the organizational and personnel changes of the previous decade and the impact on Capitol Hill of Reagan's election).

3. How each institution dealt with the other (stressing the strategic situation for presidential control of congressional choice, the problems associated with response in Congress, and various measures of presidential-congressional interaction and support).

How Ronald Reagan Came to Congress

In his essay on the 1980 election, Wilson Carey McWilliams observed, "It didn't mean much." For him "Carter was a humorless bungler and Reagan was an amiable simpleton, 'the Ted Baxter of American politics.'" He concluded:

> The election may, of course, prove to have far more profound and far-reaching consequences for American politics, but no such portents are visible. We will have to wait and see.[3]

As events have shown, McWilliams missed the signs of change. For some decades, Ronald Reagan had been making his case—"Government is not the solution to our problem. Government is the problem."[4] While this was not exactly a new theory, still a great deal of policymaking between 1933 and 1981 had been predicated on the opposite premise. Thus it was Reagan's plan essentially to reverse the trends of past decades. A Brookings Institution analyst, A. James Reichley, concluded, "Ronald Reagan has brought to the presidency an unusually coherent social philosophy,"[5] and he identified four major tenets of the Reagan philosophy: supply-side economics (with budget cuts), decentralization of domestic programs, a strengthened defense, and a return to traditional morality. Here was a prescription for change—and for high conflict.

Despite alternative interpretations of the meaning of Reagan's victory— some analysts claiming that it was a vote more against Jimmy Carter than for Reagan[6] and others asserting that "the underlying structure of conservative preferences" explained the outcome[7]—Reagan clearly chose to proceed on the latter view and to act early to implement his campaign promises. In fact,

3. Wilson Carey McWilliams, "The Meaning of the Election," in Gerald Pomper, ed., *The Election of 1980* (Chatham, N.J.: Chatham House Publishers, 1981), p. 170.

4. Ronald Reagan, "Inaugural Address," January 20, 1981.

5. A. James Reichley, "A Change in Direction," in Joseph A. Pechman, ed., *Setting National Priorities: The 1982 Budget* (Washington, D.C.: The Brookings Institution, 1981), p. 229.

6. Gregory B. Markus, "Political Attitudes During an Election Year: A Report on the 1980 NES Panel Study," *American Political Science Review*, vol. 76, no. 3 (September 1982), p. 560.

7. Warren E. Miller and J. Merrill Shanks, "Policy Directions and Presidential Leadership: Alternative Interpretations of the 1980 Presidential Election," *British Journal of Political Science*, vol. 12, part 3 (July 1982), p. 352.

he had no other choice. Reagan had, after all, achieved a decisive triumph in the Electoral College (90.9 percent of the vote). There is a self-enforcing quality to presidential elections that is amplified by decisive wins in the Electoral College, a factor that has been too frequently overlooked in analyses of various administrations' policy performances. In Reagan's case, the clarity of his image and message also contributed to expectations that he would make bold policy moves. Princeton political scientist Fred I. Greenstein correctly concludes that:

> A Reagan victory that encompassed more than 90 percent of the electoral vote and carried with it the first Republican control of the Senate since 1954 and a thirty-three-seat Republican surge in the House *looked* like a landslide. Reagan's aides inevitably treated the outcome as a mandate for his specific policy proposals, and, with far less justification, *much of the press and many members of Congress accepted this reading of the election results.*[8]

Reagan's challenge during his first year in office was to enact his program without creating unachievable expectations for subsequent years. All presidents face a variation of this squeeze, which presidential scholar Paul C. Light describes as the "cycle of decreasing influence" and the "cycle of increasing effectiveness."[9] Presidents enter office with as much support as they are ever likely to have. But as Lyndon B. Johnson observed: "A President must always reckon that his mandate will prove shortlived."[10] So he must act fast. Early success can be his undoing, however, if president watchers decide to judge him thereafter according to standards set when he is at the peak of his influence with Congress. This is a major dilemma for a four-year president (even more so for an eight-year president). But defeats are as relative as victories and, as we shall see, *congressional restructuring during the 1970s made it difficult to judge who won when the president lost.*

Just as generals seek to avoid the mistakes of the last battle, so, too, do presidents organize to avoid the criticisms of their predecessor. Jimmy Carter had large Democratic majorities in both the House of Representatives and the Senate, yet he did not work comfortably with these majorities and was severely criticized for his congressional relations. The Reagan administration was determined not to make the same mistakes. As a consequence of Reagan's more political style, it was not long before a president with the most radical program since Franklin Delano Roosevelt's in the 1930s was actually being

---

8. Fred I. Greenstein, "The Need for an Early Appraisal," in Fred I. Greenstein, ed., *The Reagan Presidency: An Early Assessment* (Baltimore: Johns Hopkins University Press, 1983), p. 15. (First emphasis is Greenstein's; second is mine.)

9. Paul C. Light, *The President's Agenda: Domestic Policy Choice from Kennedy to Carter* (Baltimore: Johns Hopkins University Press), 1982, pp. 36–37.

10. Lyndon B. Johnson, *The Vantage Point: Perspectives on the Presidency* (New York: Holt, Rinehart & Winston, 1971), p. 443.

praised on Capitol Hill for his approach. Max Friedersdorf, Reagan's assistant for congressional relations, assembled a team that had wide experience on Capitol Hill, including several people like himself, who had previously served in congressional liaison posts in the executive (see subsection later in this paper on "Reagan's Liaison with Congress"). Thus, former President Carter made yet one more contribution to the ascendancy of his successor. Carter's distant relationship with Congress encouraged members to view Reagan's approach with favor, thus giving the new president an advantage not normally available to a Republican.

Reagan's electoral margin, the sizable gains made by Republicans in Congress, the Republican takeover of the Senate, and the negative image of Carter's relations with Congress all contributed to a political and policy atmosphere supportive of change. Reagan's strategic problem was to manage these advantages so as to secure the changes he had proposed without losing control of the agenda in subsequent years.

How Congress Came to Ronald Reagan

Beyond the question of how Reagan came to Congress is the separate question of how Congress came to Reagan. In particular, the Congress that Reagan confronted was significantly different from Congresses of the past. As is argued in this section, congressional change itself, in terms both of party representation and of institutional reforms, facilitated pursuit of the Reagan agenda and made it difficult for opposing viewpoints to prevail. Thus whereas Reagan was unable to maintain the momentum of his first year, it was even more difficult for congressional Democrats to take initiatives thereafter. They had to work with the Reagan agenda and in that context the debate itself represented a victory for change. Among other effects, it resulted in Democratic presidential aspirants having to worry about budget deficits, governmental effectiveness, tax increases, and program cuts (including defense). By the end of the first session of the 97th Congress, the agenda shift was complete.

It is important to emphasize that Reagan ran *with* his party in the 1980 election. Gerald R. Ford had run with his party in 1976, but he did not win. The two most recently elected presidents before 1980—Richard M. Nixon and Jimmy Carter—ran alongside their respective parties but not really with them. The Reagan organization resolved not to make this error. Were Reagan to win, therefore, he could expect, at a minimum, a willingness on the part of congressional Republicans to give his program a chance. As it happened, of course, the election results provided much more than that.

It is generally conceded that presidential coattails no longer have the influence they once had. Still, interrelated developments coincided in the 1980 election, making inevitable the conclusion that the tide had shifted—an avowed conservative had won the presidency and many stalwart liberal senators had lost to their more conservative opponents. Defeated incumbent Senator Frank Church (D-Idaho) spoke for many when he observed, "The conservatives are in charge now. This is what they wanted and the people have given it to them."[11] And congressional scholars Thomas E. Mann and Norman J. Ornstein concluded, "There can be no question that the electorate in 1980 opted for a much more conservative Senate."[12]

There are really two levels of postelection interpretation for members of Congress: that of the more general mood of the electorate—what it all meant; and that of the specific returns for individual members. Senator Church spoke to the former. A plausible contrary interpretation would have been hard to find. Not even the retrospective theory of voting could be used to suggest that somehow the American voter was expressing a convoluted liberal message in 1980.[13]

Senate Results and Reagan

The Senate results were as stunning as those for the presidential contest. Combined they produced an irresistible force to let the president have his way in 1981.[14] Here are some of the results:

---

11. Quoted in *New York Times*, November 6, 1980, p. A-29.

12. Thomas E. Mann and Norman J. Ornstein, "The Republican Surge in Congress," in Austin Ranney, ed., *The American Elections of 1980* (Washington, D.C.: American Enterprise Institute, 1981), p. 294.

13. The notion that the election reflected a conservative shift may actually be consistent with the seemingly contrary interpretation that the electorate was expressing dissatisfaction with President Carter. In his report on the 1980 national election study, Gregory Markus concludes that the voters were not supporting a conservative program—at least not Reagan's. He believes that "Carter's loss can be attributed to pervasive dissatisfaction with his first-term performance and doubt about his personal competence as a political leader." But performance and competence are not issue-less activities. Given the agenda shift discussed earlier, they may well relate to capacities to cope with the consolidative issues of the time. If so, Markus may be both right and wrong: right in failing to spot "a mandate for the conservative ideology in general and Reagan's positions on the issues in particular," wrong in failing to acknowledge that voters wanted more competence in managing an oversize government (a consolidative message, if not strictly conservative). See Markus, "Political Attitudes During an Election Year," p. 560.

14. The point has been made that Democratic senatorial candidates as a whole outpolled their Republican rivals and that "many individual races were extremely close" (see Mann and Ornstein, "The Republican Surge," p. 293). While unquestionably true, the results were nonetheless interpreted at the time as representing a shift to the right.

1. Reagan ran ahead of Republican candidates in twenty-two of thirty-four states, even with John Anderson's vote included.

2. Reagan ran ahead of eight of the remaining twelve Republican candidates when the two-party vote only is counted.

3. Of the remaining four Republican candidates, Reagan ran only slightly behind two candidates (Robert Dole and Jeremiah Denton) when counting the two-party vote.

That leaves only Charles McC. Mathias, Jr. (Maryland) and Mack Mattingly (Georgia). The former ran well ahead of Reagan (twenty-two percentage points ahead of his three-way vote; eighteen points ahead of his two-way vote). The latter defeated the embattled Herman Talmadge in Carter's home state (where Reagan reduced the incumbent president's percentage by over ten points). On the Democratic side, four returning incumbents had their margins reduced over 1974. Another four actually increased their margins over 1974.

House Results and Reagan

In the House of Representatives, the Democrats retained their majority, but there were important changes in a more conservative direction. For example, many of the Democrats who were not reelected had relatively low conservative coalition scores.[15] Some of these Democrats were important House leaders (John Brademas, James C. Corman, Al Ullman, Thomas L. Ashley, Frank Thompson, Jr., Harold T. Johnson). There was ample evidence in House returns to contribute to the interpretation of a conservative trend in national mood.

But, as was the case with their Senate counterparts, did individual House members view Reagan as an important factor in their election or reelection? Here the evidence is less conclusive for the House than for the Senate. Reagan ran ahead of successful House Republican candidates in just 38 congressional districts, behind in 150, presumably even in the other 4. When the two-party vote was computed, Reagan ran ahead in 59 districts of the 192 where Republicans were successful.[16]

Other relevant data would include how well Reagan ran in relationship to all Republican candidates, how well he ran relative to Ford in 1976, and

15. Charles O. Jones, ''The New, New Senate,'' in Ellis Sandoz and Cecil V. Crabb, Jr., eds., *A Tide of Discontent: The 1980 Elections and Their Meaning* (Washington, D.C.: Congressional Quarterly Press, 1981), p. 108.

16. Norman J. Ornstein, Thomas E. Mann, Michael J. Malbin, and John F. Bibby, *Vital Statistics on Congress, 1982* (Washington, D.C.: American Enterprise Institute, 1982), p. 54.

how well returning Democratic candidates did as compared to 1978.[17] A review, for example, of the results for one state in each of the five major regions of the country—Florida in the South, New Jersey in the East, Wisconsin in the Midwest, Texas in the Southwest, and Washington in the West—shows that Reagan ran well. In the seventy congressional districts in these states:

1. Reagan ran ahead of forty-four of the Republican candidates in the sixty-three congressional districts where there was two-party competition.

2. Reagan ran ahead of Ford in fifty-four of the seventy districts counting his three-way percentage and ahead of Ford in sixty-seven of the seventy districts counting his two-way percentage. Only the New Jersey Tenth, the Wisconsin Fifth, and the Texas Twentieth districts showed a lower two-party percentage for Reagan compared to Ford.

3. There were thirty-three returning Democrats who had Republican opposition in both 1978 and 1980. Of these, seventeen experienced a percentage loss in their margins in 1980.

In no case would we expect that a member would automatically fall in line in support of the president owing to election returns. That is not the way our system works. Rather, the election returns within the district could be expected to encourage members to be more or less receptive to presidential wishes. House members are obviously the most attentive observers of developments in their respective districts. At the very least, the results from the sample districts just examined encouraged members to pay heed to the Reagan phenomenon. And in two of these states—Florida and Texas—members could be anticipated to do even more. In Florida, Reagan ran ahead of Ford in all fifteen districts by an average of 8.3 percent—counting only his three-way percentage. And in Texas, Reagan ran ahead of Ford in twenty-three of twenty-

---

17. Additional relevant data would be what the voters themselves were doing. Congressional elections specialist Gary Jacobson reports that "people who voted for the other party's presidential candidate were a good deal more likely to vote for its House or Senate candidate as well; about half of the presidential defectors also defected in congressional elections. . . . About 80 percent of the defectors were Democrats voting for Reagan, so this pattern must have helped Republican congressional candidates. . . . The results of the 1980 survey indicate that nontrivial coattail effects were present." [*The Politics of Congressional Elections* (Boston: Little, Brown & Co., 1983), pp. 135–136.]

four districts by an average of 7.1 percent—again relying on his three-way percentage.[18]

In evaluating the electoral prisms through which members of Congress viewed President Reagan, it is important to stress their receptivity to his ideas and their willingness "to give the president a chance." The reasonableness of this position tends to mask how far-reaching were its implications. For giving Ronald Reagan's program a chance was to accept (in the president's words) "dramatic change." Though there was ample Democratic criticism following the submission of the FY 1982 Reagan budget, House Speaker Thomas P. O'Neill, Jr., predicted that "we will ultimately send a bill to the president that he will be satisfied with."[19] What eventually was sent more than satisfied the president. It also locked in place a new agenda that would dominate debate for the succeeding years of the Reagan administration.

The New Congress and Reagan

Congress is, above all, an institution of representation whose natural inclination is to perfect that capability. Yet during the 1970s, circumstances forced this bulky institution to assume a more active role in governing the nation.

In his perceptive treatment of "the decline and resurgence of Congress," Brookings scholar James L. Sundquist observed:

The constitutional crisis of the Nixon period wrenched the legislators out of their complacency and thrust responsibility on them. . . . The conflict also generated new attitudes in Congress—the new assertiveness. But it did nothing to change the structure of incentives that control and motivate congressmen, for it did not alter in any way their relations with their constituencies, did not lessen their representational responsibilities. As time passes and the memory of Nixon and his "usurpations" fades, and congressmen live with presidents they respect and trust, the links in the old causal chain are likely to reappear. The will to govern will again wane. The

---

18. It is interesting to note that the Democratic delegations from these two states had much higher presidential support scores in 1981 on the average than did Democrats overall: 55 for Texas Democrats and 58 for Florida Democrats, compared to 42 for all Democrats. In 1973, following the Nixon landslide, the comparable scores were: 42 for Texas Democrats, 43 for Florida Democrats, and 35 for all Democrats. Calculated from data in *Congressional Quarterly Weekly Report*, January 2, 1982, pp. 22–23; *Congressional Quarterly Weekly Report*, January 19, 1974, pp. 104–105.

19. Quoted in Gail Gregg, "Reagan Proposes Dramatic Reduction in Federal Role," *Congressional Quarterly Weekly Report*, March 14, 1981, p. 445. In comments on this chapter, congressional scholar Roger H. Davidson makes the point that "Reagan's strong showing in congressional districts was less important than the tons of mail that appeared on the Hill demanding simply that legislators support the Reagan budget and tax packages." I judge these developments to be complementary in encouraging congressional support at a crucial time.

capabilities that are missing will not be acquired, because the members will not be willing to sacrifice their individual freedom and, in the literal sense, their irresponsibility.[20]

As a result of Nixon's attempts to create whole government within the White House, followed by the near collapse of the presidency as a consequence of Watergate and the growing frustration among members of Congress that their institution was poorly equipped to manage its own business, a series of reforms was inaugurated—some of which were incompatible. The House increased the authority of Democratic party leaders while further decentralizing the committee structure and joining the national mood for increased direct public and group participation in its decision making. The Senate sought to streamline its committee structure but also submitted to pressures to provide more opportunities for participation by junior senators and to "let the sunshine in." Congressional ambivalence on its role in the political system was apparent in every change made.

The effect of these reforms has been analyzed by many scholars, and most conclude, with Norman J. Ornstein, that "Congress has become an *open system*."[21] My own analysis classified House reforms as contributing further to expressiveness (the representational function) and to organizational or policy integration. My conclusions were:

(1) the overwhelming majority of these reforms were intended to provide more opportunities for more members to express themselves in the legislative process; (2) many reforms had the effect of increasing the potential for integration but they were designed primarily for expressive purposes; (3) the Budget and Impoundment Control Act of 1974 was the only reform for which the primary intention was organizational and policy integration; and (4) policy integration typically was not an intended consequence of reforms, further evidence in support of the view that the principal aim of the 1970s reforms was to promote expression, not integration.[22]

Here was a Congress undergoing considerable change. The manifold motivations for reform ensured ambiguous institutional purposes. Was Congress to create its own budget? If so, then the "missing capabilities" Sundquist speaks of would have to be supplied. Was a political party to direct policy development in the House? If so, then newly crowned subcommittee chairmen would have to, as Sundquist notes, "sacrifice their individual freedom." Or were we to have a kind of superpluralism in which the sanctity of

20. James L. Sundquist, *The Decline and Resurgence of Congress* (Washington, D.C.: The Brookings Institution, 1981), pp. 457–458.

21. Norman J. Ornstein, "The Open Congress Meets the President," in Anthony King, ed., *Both Ends of the Avenue* (Washington, D.C.: American Enterprise Institute, 1983), p. 203. (Emphasis Ornstein's.)

22. Charles O. Jones, "House Leadership in an Age of Reform," in Frank Mackaman, ed., *Understanding Congressional Leadership* (Washington, D.C.: Congressional Quarterly Press, 1981), p. 131.

subcommittees would replace that of committees in an earlier age? If so, then the norms of specialization and reciprocity would have to be reapplied. As it happened, we were to have none of these exactly, yet Reagan initially confronted a Congress that was trying for them all.

In conclusion, the two most important factors affecting how Congress would react to the Reagan presidency were their interpretations of his victory and Congress's institutional capacity as a result of the earlier reforms. Most members of Congress came to Reagan impressed by his personal showing nationally and in their states and districts. That case is strong for the Senate, which went Republican for the first time in twenty-eight years, but it can be made for the House, too, where southern Democrats in particular were encouraged to acknowledge the president's popularity. The institutional Congress came to Reagan nearly exhausted from reform and from efforts to consolidate structural, procedural, and personnel changes. With ambitions running high and purposes more ambiguous than usual, Congress was prepared to entertain strong and purposeful leadership from the White House. Working this open and incoherent system would not be easy, but the advantage initially was clearly with the president.

Working Together

The strategic conditions for presidents working with Congress vary greatly from one administration to the next. What does not vary is the critical need for the president to control the expectations of his performance. In particular, as touched upon earlier, the chief executive needs to prevent expectations from overshooting his capacity to meet them. On the other hand, the president must also take advantage of favorable circumstances to enact his program. The ideal approach, of course, is to enact a program that will influence future expectations by establishing the subsequent agenda. A successful first year in office is essential to accomplish this goal. President Reagan had to move swiftly to take advantage both of his own electoral success and of the willingness of Congress in those early days to act on his program. Richard P. Nathan describes the results, and their impact, as follows:

> The Reagan administration seized the moment in 1981. Under the impetus of budget revisions, the administration achieved a major change of direction in national policy for domestic, and particularly social, programs. The decay rate of the administration's legislative success in this area has been commented upon. . . . However, in my view, these setbacks do not have as much importance as do the fundamentally changed tone and approach to domestic

policy-making and its execution that were brought about under Reagan. Reagan's conservative movement, I would argue, has had its greatest success in the field of domestic policy.[23]

I agree with Nathan's perspective. Despite both victories and defeats, Reagan's control of the congressional agenda insured his leadership throughout. He won over others but lost to no one in particular. Nathan identified split-party control between the House and Senate, deft White House management, the agenda shift, and pressure for spending cuts created by tax reductions as crucial explanations for presidential control.[24] Again, I agree.

To explore this topic further, it is useful to review Reagan's initial approach to Congress and then to examine briefly the years 1981–1983 in terms of the framework suggested here (that of controlling expectations and managing congressional choice).

Reagan's Liaison with Congress

In studying four other recent presidents, I became convinced that

political and personal conditions help to explain presidential *styles* of relating to Congress, and these styles, in turn, contribute to determining which *techniques* are used to get the legislative program enacted.[25]

For convenience I identified four styles of presidential dealings with Congress:

Lyndon B. Johnson: majority leader as president
Richard M. Nixon: foreign minister as president
Gerald Ford: minority leader as president
Jimmy Carter: political layman (or possibly missionary) as president.[26]

These styles suggested a further useful classification between a partnership model of congressional contact and a more independent model.

Presidents Johnson and Ford understood and attempted classic bargaining . . . but differed markedly in their political resources. Presidents Nixon and Carter were uncomfortable with the politics of exchange, depending instead on a form of persuasion that preserved distance between them and the members of Congress. Despite individual differences within this set of four presidents, [there are] similarities among two pairs—Johnson and Ford accepting a

---

23. Richard P. Nathan, "The Reagan Presidency in Domestic Affairs," in Fred I. Greenstein, ed., *The Reagan Presidency: An Early Assessment* (Baltimore: Johns Hopkins University Press, 1983), p. 78.
    24. Ibid., pp. 77–78.
    25. Charles O. Jones, "Presidential Negotiation with Congress," in Anthony King, ed., *Both Ends of the Avenue* (Washington, D.C.: American Enterprise Institute, 1983), pp. 104–106.
    26. Ibid.

partnership or inside model of congressional contact, Nixon and Carter preferring an independent or outside model.[27]

Note that these models are not coincident with political party; nor are they ideologically or programmatically based. In addition, it bears emphasizing that both partnership presidents were in the White House by accident— Johnson in the more familiar position of taking over as an elected vice president, Ford in the extraordinary position of having been "elected" to the vice presidency by Congress. Finally, note that the independent style is bound to cause problems for a president. Nixon and Carter—despite their different parties and different programs—were plainly not liked on Capitol Hill. If they were uncomfortable in the company of members of Congress, it is equally true that the members were uncomfortable with them.

Clearly these two models do not exhaust the possible styles of presidential contact with Congress. In fact, the preceding comments suggest these models may be uncommon and associated with the extraordinary political conditions of the era. The Reagan style may fit within a more common model—that of *classic separation*. Presidents relying on this third model (for which there may be many individual styles) are unlikely to get as close to Congress as in the partnership model, nor are they likely to be so distant as in the independent model. Further, they are inclined to depend on experienced professionals as political translators and negotiators.

What, then, is the Reagan style? I judge it to be that of *communicator as president*.[28] Communication is an article of faith with the actor. It is a highly political style that is dependent on the two-way flow of information, intention, and understanding. It requires involvement by the president not only in direct contacts with Congress but in managing other sources of their information (e.g., from the public, interest groups, and the media). It demands sensitivity to what messages may represent in regard to political and policy developments. Above all, this style depends on maintaining open channels, even with one's adversaries. True presidential-congressional conversation must continue. The communicator as president cannot be too thin-skinned. Thus, for example, if the speaker of the House publicly criticizes the president, means must be found to prevent this incident from interfering with direct communication. The play's the thing for the communicator as president. You cannot even open if the actors do not show up.

---

27. Ibid, p. 124.

28. In my aforementioned essay (Jones, "Presidential Negotiation"), I used the label "actor as president." That is appropriate, too, but I think communicator is more apt, and it avoids the confusion over the president's previous career. Lou Cannon refers to Reagan as the "Great Communicator" [*Reagan* (New York: G.P. Putnam's Sons, 1982), chapter 20].

The president did not wait to be inaugurated to establish communications with Capitol Hill. First, as noted earlier, he actively ran with congressional Republicans. Soon after his election he sought the services of Tom Korologos —a Hill veteran—to assist in liaison during the transition. Korologos, in turn, chose a highly professional team to begin making the rounds and to schedule presidential contacts—all in the pre-inaugural period. Stephen J. Wayne, in his review of congressional relations during the first year of the Reagan administration, quotes Korologos as saying: "We had to lasso him [Reagan] to keep him off the Hill."[29] Clearly the president himself was the single greatest asset in establishing good relations right from the start.

By definition, congressional liaison is crucial for the communicator as president. This suggests that Reagan would have created a professional liaison office whomever he succeeded; following Carter simply meant that his liaison staff had an easier job. Once in office, Reagan chose Max Friedersdorf to head the White House liaison office. Friedersdorf suited the president's style perfectly. Not only could he carry the message to the Hill and expect an audience, but he could educate the president about all aspects of Congress and advise him about when and how to be involved. But Friedersdorf's first task was to create a team of Hill-wise personnel. The results impressed everyone. For example:

Powell Moore: Chief Senate lobbyist; worked for Senator Richard Russell (D-Ga.), Department of Justice, and White House congressional liaison in Nixon and Ford administrations.

Kenneth Duberstein: Chief House Lobbyist; worked for Senator Jacob Javits (R-N.Y.) and as director of congressional relations for the Department of Labor and the General Services Administration.

William Gribbin: Deputy to Friedersdorf; worked for Senator James L. Buckley (Cons.-R-N.Y.) and the Senate Republican Policy Committee.[30]

---

29. Quoted in Stephen J. Wayne, "Congressional Liaison in the Reagan White House: A Preliminary Assessment of the First Year," in Norman J. Ornstein, ed., *President and Congress: Assessing Reagan's First Year* (Washington, D.C.: American Enterprise Institute, 1982), p. 50.

30. Others on the initial liaison team included David Swanson, Senate lobbyist; Pamela Turner, Senate lobbyist; John Dressendorfer, House lobbyist; M.B. Oglesby, House lobbyist; Nancy Risque, House lobbyist; David Wright, House lobbyist; Sherrie Cooksey, legislative counsel; and Nancy Kennedy, administrative assistant. Information taken from Dick Kirschten, "The Pennsylvania Avenue Connection—Making Peace on Capitol Hill," *National Journal*, vol. 14, no. 10 (March 7, 1981), p. 385. See also Wayne, "Congressional Liaison in the Reagan White House," pp. 52–56.

There have been staff changes since the initial organization, the most notable being two changes at the top.[31] Subsequent appointments were also made on the basis of Hill experience, however.[32]

The success of this team is a story oft-told. In one of the most detailed accounts, Wayne describes an efficient and savvy operation that played to rave reviews.[33] The work of the liaison team on the Hill is only part of the story, however. A great deal of effort went into guaranteeing that the federal departments and agencies did not go off on their own. Thus, all liaison appointments had to be cleared in the White House. This was a presidency determined to coordinate its own messages—another vital element for the communicator president. As one former Republican liaison official observed in a conversation with me on this topic: "The Reagan Administration didn't make Carter's mistake. All of the top people were appointed through the White House and that is the way you have to do it."

This determination to ensure a liaison team staffed with Reagan loyalists suggests another point about the Reagan approach. Lou Cannon speaks of "the delegated presidency":

> He [Reagan] had a secure and uncluttered concept of the presidency, inspired by his mythic remembrance of Franklin Roosevelt and molded by his practical experience as public speaker and governor of California. Out of the governorship came a delegative style of decision-making which reflected both impressive strengths and formidable limitations.[34]

One must connect two actions, however, to understand the "delegated presidency." *Delegation follows careful appointment.* As one Department of Labor bureaucrat explained to me: "Delegation for Reagan doesn't mean that we do what we want. It means that his appointees do what he wants."

As with any congressional liaison personnel, the president can make them look good or bad. Ronald Reagan has made them look good. He has been a willing partner in lobbying for his program. Ornstein points out that "the open system [in] Congress requires much more frequent use of the most precious presidential resource—the president himself."[35] While these efforts may be burdensome for the president in dealing with Congress, they can have a real positive effect. Ornstein again comments:

---

31. Duberstein succeeded Friedersdorf, then Oglesby succeeded Duberstein and currently heads the liaison team.

32. See Bill Keller, "Duberstein Starts at Fast Pace as Top White House Lobbyist," *Congressional Quarterly Weekly Report*, May 1, 1982, p. 972.

33. Wayne, "Congressional Liaison in the Reagan White House," pp. 44–65.

34. Cannon, *Reagan*, p. 371.

35. Ornstein, "The Open Congress," p. 205.

> While members of Congress have changed, they are still human beings who respond to attention and favors, who understand political give and take, and who remain respectful and a bit awed by the presidency.[36]

Decentralization thus creates more work, but the effort can pay off. Committee chairmen may no longer be in a position to deliver for the president, but neither are they in a good position to deliver against him. Constructing majorities one vote at a time is tedious but it can be done. The former Republican congressional liaison person quoted earlier commented, "Now they have more people and they get less done." But the changes in Congress require more staff effort in order to form cross-party and cross-issue coalitions, and coalitions do not necessarily last. They must be constructed for each issue.

In sum, the first impressions, both on and off Capitol Hill, of Reagan's work with Congress were uniformly favorable. Above all, the president was at ease with members of Congress—at least he projected that image. His demeanor was one of cordiality and respect, and he chose wisely in his director of congressional liaison—one who commanded respect on the Hill and who was bound to create a professional team in the service of the presidential program.

The First Three Years

As a nondetail president, Reagan has been successful in being associated with big, chunky issues—the budget writ large, tax cuts, Social Security, defense buildup. In so doing, he has been able to focus congressional and media attention as few presidents before him. The 1981 budget reconciliation and tax-cut stories—crucial issues of Reagan's first year—have been well told by others, most notably budget specialist Allen Schick. What interests us here is that by stressing the budget early in his term, the president was able to dominate the legislative process in Congress thereafter. As Schick observed:

> Congress responded by behaving more as a budget office than as the legislative branch. The Senate took almost 200 votes on budget issues in 1981, not including the roll calls on regular appropriations bills and the budget battles fought over authorizing legislation. . . . More than two-thirds of the recorded votes in the Senate were on budget-related matters.[37]

Republican unity in both houses was extraordinary—an average of nearly 98 percent support in the House on seven key votes and 97 percent support

---

36. Ibid.
37. Allen Schick, "How the Budget Was Won and Lost," in Norman J. Ornstein, ed., *President and Congress: Assessing Reagan's First Year* (Washington, D.C.: American Enterprise Institute, 1982), p. 15. See also chapter by Schick in this volume.

in the Senate on nine key votes. This unity resulted in outright victories in the Senate and made House wins possible when combined with conservative Democratic support. The White House relied on the new congressional budget process to maintain its priorities and its momentum. The budget resolution, reconciliation, and the new budget timetable all worked to favor the president's program. One need only imagine what might have happened to the president's budget under the old congressional system; it would have been distributed among the authorizing and taxing committees, and the appropriations sub-committees, never to have been seen whole again.

So the president was able to use congressional procedures to his advantage. As Schick points out, however, Reagan "won the battles but lost the budget."[38] The president who made big government his principal issue pre-pared a taxing and spending formula that created mind-boggling deficits. Therefore, the budget battles had only just begun. Like it or not, and most did not, members of Congress would have to cope with issues at the macro level, where they are the most uncomfortable and the least well structured (see discussion later in this chapter).

Thus, in this first crucial year President Reagan created the issues that dominated executive-legislative conversation for the rest of his term. On the other hand, he committed himself to a solution that was unlikely to (and did not) show positive results in the short run and that reduced his options. Setting a course based on a hunch about the market and its relationship to the tax structure, he had to wait to see whether he was right or not, meanwhile protecting the conditions set in 1981 that were presumably essential for the theory to work. The effect for the president was to establish a predictable pattern—pressure for additional budget cuts on domestic programs, support for defense increases, resistance to any tax increases.

This relatively passive role in subsequent years served as an encourage-ment for congressional initiative. House Democrats were unlikely to grasp the opportunity, however. Even if the House leadership had been able to overcome significant internal divisions on policy issues, they were checked politically by the Republican Senate and the White House. Senate Republi-cans, on the other hand, were actively filling the gap. In fact, as the president waited for his program to work, leadership in deficit reduction was assumed by Senators Robert Dole, chairman of the Finance Committee, and Pete Domenici, chairman of the Budget Committee. Dole steered a "revenue enhancement" bill through the Senate in 1982, an election year. President Reagan eventually supported the bill and worked with House Speaker O'Neill

---

38. Schick, "How the Budget Was Won and Lost," p. 14.

to ensure sufficient bipartisan support to pass the bill in the House. In so doing, Reagan was credited once again with an almost magical touch in congressional relations. Insiders knew of Dole's genius in getting the tax package passed; the general public was told of Reagan's "victory" in working with Speaker O'Neill to fashion a majority.[39]

One should not get the impression that the president could do anything he wanted with the 97th Congress. What I have emphasized is that Reagan was supremely successful in completing the agenda shift, to such an extent that high-level budget politics dominated his relations with Congress. But he was notably unsuccessful in tackling other cumbersome issues. Social Security was certainly a big part of the budget scene in 1981. Reagan's proposals for financing the system in the future were soundly defeated that year, with the Democrats carrying the issue into the 1982 congressional elections. It became clear that neither the White House nor Congress could manage the politics of this issue, and a special commission was appointed. Reagan and O'Neill monitored the commission's work and, in the end, this extrainstitutional device was able to circumvent the political stalemate.

Another initiative, Reagan's "new federalism" plan was, if anything, even more complex than his Social Security proposal. While it engaged the states and Congress in a debate on the manifold issues associated with the development and administration of domestic programs, it did not, as a plan, make any progress on Capitol Hill. It did provide a slightly different cut at the budget issues, however, and may have had secondary effects that were beneficial to the president's overall program.

Congressional response to presidential initiatives reveals that the Reagan agenda of consolidative and contractive issues displayed Congress at its worst. Despite its reforms, Congress is not well structured for doing comprehensive, comparative program analysis of the type required by the new agenda. Rather, it is designed to represent and ventilate issues, with each chamber contributing a different mix of functions. Agreements and disagreements develop as proposals are tested for their effects by those with parochial or specialized interests. The new budgetary process was designed to overcome the limitations of this system and was used by Reagan in 1981 to achieve his goals. But the resistance by the traditional committee structure to decision making at this level is very great. Rather than building agreements over time, the budgetary process sought to force agreements very early in the session. Congress was thus asked to do its work in reverse: to agree first, then represent and ventilate.

---

39. A second effort by Senator Dole in 1983 was unsuccessful. As deficits increased, the president resisted all invitations by Senate Republicans to support a deficit reduction program. The momentum was never sufficient to encourage presidential involvement.

It probably was entirely predictable that Congress just would not want to do it that way. If forced to do so, the natural tendency, then, is for the members merely to go through the motions.

As emphasized earlier, most reforms in the 1970s were not integrative at all but more expressive or representative in nature. This greater fragmentation and participation can result in diverse policy innovation but very limited *institutional* response to presidential initiative. The subcommittee bill of rights, turnover of chairmen, sunshine procedures, and addition of staff are changes that permit Congress to identify alternatives and test ideas with greater sophistication than ever before. Therefore one may expect thorough, even technical, review of presidential proposals. But Congress is not prepared to develop and support specific alternatives. Its disaggregative capacities were fine-tuned just as the agenda became highly aggregated in the budget. The consequences, as witnessed over the first three years of Reagan's term, have been the gradual disintegration of the budgetary process and the emergence of scores of members in business for themselves. Where the political situation has called for congressional responses to presidential passivity, Congress itself has often been immobilized by partisan and individual entrepreneurship.[40]

By January 1983, Reagan's presidency was at a low ebb. The Democrats had increased their numbers in the House, making Republican-southern Democratic majorities much more difficult to fashion. The president's popularity had dropped to its lowest point—with just 35 percent of the Gallup Poll respondents approving of his handling of the job.[41] Commentators wrote uniformly bleak assessments of Reagan's political and policy future. *National Journal* columnist Dick Kirschten spoke for most when he wrote that:

> Heading into the second half of his term, Reagan is beset by charges of unfairness and insensitivity. His standing in the public opinion polls is sagging, and legislators on Capitol Hill are distancing themselves from the White House. Even before the new and clearly more independent 98th Congress is sworn in, the President's legislative mastery has begun to ebb. . . . The mood in Washington has changed vastly since the heady first months of the Reagan Administration, when the President adroitly pulled off a series of startling legislative coups. . . .[42]

Kirschten then acknowledged that "after two years of Reaganaut rule, the government . . . unmistakably bears the stamp of this unabashedly ideological President. . . ."[43] No one doubted that the 1982 election results and the

40. Interestingly, Congress received high marks for its action on budget issues during the first six months of 1984. A tax package was even passed.
41. Reported in *Public Opinion*, vol. 6, no. 2 (April/May 1983), p. 40.
42. Dick Kirschten, "President Reagan After Two Years: Bold Actions but Uncertain Results," *National Journal*, vol. 16, no. 1 (January 1, 1983), p. 4.
43. Ibid.

persistence of a stubborn recession would make the 98th Congress very different from the 97th. As Kirschten indicates, however, the new Congress would still be reacting to the Reagan agenda—an agenda made even more urgent by the slow recovery of the economy. And the president began his third year in office with low public expectations for success. Yet somehow—perhaps circumstantially—President Reagan managed to have his low point just where it would do him the most good—that is, as a base from which to improve for the 1984 campaign.

Presidential Support and Party Unity

Ronald Reagan achieved a policy breakthrough in his first year and then engaged in a holding action. Having firmly established a new agenda, he was in a position to permit others to experiment with solutions. The changes in presidential-congressional relations during Reagan's first three years are illustrated by the budget politics for each year. In 1982 the Republicans in each house formulated compromise substitutes to Reagan's proposed budget that eventually passed. In 1983 the initiative shifted to the House Democrats, who enacted a budget resolution more generous to domestic programs, less generous to defense, and including new taxes. President Reagan proved unyielding, however, in support of his formula. Senate Republicans were therefore put in a difficult position, and the budget process in that chamber nearly collapsed. The final budget resolution passed 50-49, with the support of 38 percent of the Republicans (a marked change from the near-unanimous support in 1981) and 63 percent of the Democrats. *Congressional Quarterly* reporter Diane Granat describes presidential-congressional relations in 1983 as follows:

> Congress and President Reagan generally kept to their own turf in 1983—each branch going about its business with little involvement from the other side.
>
> Unlike the first two years of the Reagan administration, when the president essentially wrote the economic script, Congress conducted its 1983 debate on deficits without Reagan's overt participation.[44]

No presidential year is exactly like another in working with Congress. For Reagan, however, the first three years differed more dramatically than most—again as a consequence of the remarkable first year. Analyses of presidential support and party unity scores from 1981 to 1983 provide an

---

44. Diane Granat, "Partisanship Dominated Congressional Year," *Congressional Quarterly Weekly Report*, November 26, 1983, p. 2467.

aggregated review of these years.[45] Tables 1 and 2 document the shifts that occurred. Presidential support in the House fell significantly in 1982 and again in 1983 (table 1). In 1982 there was a consistent decline in support among both Democrats and Republicans. After the 1982 elections, however, the shifts were very different (see 1983 in table 1). The Democrats, whose numbers were greater, had a significantly lower support score, while the Republicans provided a higher support score than in 1981. The increase in House

TABLE 1

PRESIDENT REAGAN AND CONGRESS—SUPPORT SCORES, 1981–1983

| | Year | | | |
	1981	*1982*	*1983*	*Average*
House				
Democrats	42	39	28	36
Republicans	68	64	70	67
Senate				
Democrats	49	43	42	45
Republicans	80	74	73	76
Overall	82	72	67	74
House	72	56	48	59
Senate	88	82	86	85

SOURCE: Various issues of *Congressional Quarterly Weekly Report.*

TABLE 2

PARTY UNITY IN THE REAGAN YEARS, 1981–1983

| | Year | | | |
	1981	*1982*	*1983*	*Average*
House				
Democrats	69	72	76	72
Republicans	74	69	74	72
Senate				
Democrats	71	72	71	71
Republicans	81	76	74	77

SOURCE: Various issues of *Congressional Quarterly Weekly Report.*

45. The limitations of these scores are widely understood. For details on how the scores are developed and their limitations see any issue of the *Congressional Quarterly Weekly Report* that presents the scores and George C. Edwards, III, *Presidential Influence in Congress* (San Francisco: W.H. Freeman and Company, 1980), pp. 50–53.

Republican support, however, was not sufficient to offset the sizable drop in Democratic support.

The party unity scores provide a different measure of the declining support for the president (see table 2). House Democrats showed steady increases in party unity from 1981 to 1983. Further, there was a sharp increase in the number of votes on which party majorities differed—the highest percentage increase in such votes since 1975 (no doubt then associated with the large increase in the number of House Democrats in the 1974 election).

On the Senate side, presidential support (table 1) dropped off among both Democrats and Republicans in 1982 but the composite (overall) score in the Senate remained high—at 82. In 1983 the partisan scores showed little change, but the president actually won a higher percentage of roll calls than in 1982. One might have expected that the decline between 1981 and 1982 would have been among moderate Republican senators. While it is true that those moderates with the lowest support scores in 1981 had even lower scores in 1982, still the principal explanation for the reduced support among Senate Republicans was that conservatives had lower scores. In 1981, ten senators who voted on at least 85 percent of the presidential support roll calls had scores of 75 percent or below, and all but one of these were bona fide moderates. In 1982, twenty-three senators met these conditions, twelve of whom were bona fide conservatives (including even Jesse Helms). As *Congressional Quarterly* reporter Nadine Cohodas explained: "Some of Reagan's most conservative GOP colleagues wavered in the ranks, particularly over his last initiative of the year, a highway bill that included a gasoline tax hike."[46]

It is instructive also to review the presidential support scores of the four post-World War II Republican presidents during their first three years in office. Table 3 shows the importance of Republican support for President Reagan as compared with his recent Republican predecessors. The Senate Republican scores for Reagan are very close to those during the Eisenhower administration (the Republicans had a narrow majority in both houses in 1953–1954). House Republican support for Reagan was less than that for Dwight D. Eisenhower during his first two years. Reagan's support increased impressively in 1983, however, whereas House support dropped significantly for Eisenhower in his third year.

---

46. Nadine Cohodas, "Presidential Support Study Shows Reagan Rating Fell 10 Percentage Points in 1982," *Congressional Quarterly Weekly Report*, January 15, 1983, p. 95.

TABLE 3

PRESIDENTIAL SUPPORT SCORES, POST-WORLD WAR II REPUBLICAN PRESIDENTS IN
THEIR FIRST THREE YEARS

President	House		Senate		Composite	Average
	D^a	R^b	D	R		
Eisenhower						
1st year	55	80	55	78	89	
2d year	44	71	38	73	83	82
3d year	53	60	56	72	75	
Nixon						
1st year	48	57	47	66	74	
2d year	53	66	45	60	77	75
3d year	47	72	40	64	75	
Ford						
1st year	41	51	39	55	58	
2d year	38	63	47	68	61	58
3d year	32	63	39	62	54	
Reagan						
1st year	42	68	49	80	82	
2d year	39	64	43	74	72	74
3d year	28	70	42	73	67	

SOURCE: Various issues of *Congressional Quarterly Weekly Report* and volumes of *Congressional Quarterly Almanac*.

a. *D*, Democrats.
b. *R*, Republicans.

On the other hand, none of the other three Republican post-war presidents experienced as large a falloff in House Democratic support as did Reagan. President Reagan began with a relatively low support percentage, just 1 percent above that for Ford in the nearly five months he served in 1974. By contrast both Nixon and Eisenhower did quite well, though the latter suffered a sharp decline in his second year.

Table 4 confirms the increase in party unity for both sides of the aisle. Again the similarity between Reagan's and Eisenhower's first three years is striking. The average unity score for each party in each house was over 70 (with nine of twelve scores above 70 for Eisenhower; ten of twelve above 70 for Reagan—see those boxed in table 4). During the Nixon and Ford years, 70 was broken only once (the second year of the Ford administration, by House Republicans). Indeed, only six scores were above 65 during those years. It should also be pointed out that the percentage of party-unity roll

TABLE 4

PARTY UNITY SCORES, POST-WORLD WAR II REPUBLICAN PRESIDENTS IN THEIR
FIRST THREE YEARS

President	House		Senate	
	D^a	R^b	D	R
Eisenhower				
1st year	74	84	74	82
2d year	66	74	64	80
3d year	72	69	72	75
Nixon				
1st year	61	62	63	63
2d year	58	60	55	56
3d year	61	67	64	63
Ford				
1st year	62	63	63	59
2d year	69	72	68	64
3d year	66	67	62	61
Reagan				
1st year	69	74	71	81
2d year	72	69	72	76
3d year	76	74	71	74

SOURCES: Various issues of *Congressional Quarterly Weekly Report* and volumes of *Congressional Quarterly Almanac*.

NOTE: Boxed scores indicate scores over 70.

a. *D*, Democrats.

b. *R*, Republicans.

calls was also higher during the Eisenhower and Reagan years than during the Nixon and Ford years (though the percentage of such votes decreased each year for Eisenhower, decreased slightly the second year for Reagan, and then increased dramatically in 1983).

Composite scores of this type must be used cautiously, however. They are useful primarily to confirm other evidence or to suggest additional areas for exploration. These scores confirm the changes that occurred following the

1982 elections and suggest some of the interesting differences between the
Reagan presidency and those other Republican presidencies in the post-World
War II period. Among other things, Ronald Reagan was successful in getting
the support of his party in Congress (by the scores presented in tables 1–4).
His overall record is more like that of Eisenhower than of the other two
Republican presidents of the period.

Conclusion

Ronald Reagan came to the White House with a clear vision of what he
wanted to accomplish. He had sufficient electoral support and communication
skills to establish his agenda and to maintain it throughout the first three years
of his term. Congress came to Ronald Reagan impressed with his electoral
showing, prepared to support his formula for economic recovery, and ill-
equipped as an institution to provide alternatives at the level of the full
budget.[47] Support of the Reagan approach during the first year locked Congress into the consolidative agenda, and new social programs were no longer
entertained or even proposed.

Reagan's style of dealing with Congress is identified here as that of the
communicator as president—a style consistent with the classic separation
model of presidential-congressional relations. According to this model, the
president views his role as separate from that of Congress but by no means
as fully independent. He is likely "to rely on the full range of negotiating
strategies—from classic bargaining to precise and resolute translations of the
national interest."[48] He is more likely than those employing the partnership
model to use outside strategies, yet he is not at all uncomfortable engaging
in direct negotiations with congressional leaders. Open channels are essential
for the communicator president as the means for the conversation that is
essential to political understanding. Yet such a president expects to gain an
advantage through a politics of communication (and Reagan has typically
enjoyed that advantage).

Upon reflection, it seems apparent that this communicator president has
succeeded in establishing a new context for congressional choice—that of
macro budget and economic policy. But agenda setting is not the whole of
governance. Proposals are needed to deal with the problems that have been

---

47. Individual efforts, such as those by Senators Domenici and Dole, are nevertheless
possible. Indeed, it appears that the budgetary process may have provided an additional training
exercise for prospective presidential candidates in the Senate.

48. Jones, in King, ed., *Both Ends of the Avenue*, p. 126.

identified, and these proposals must then command sufficient support to be enacted. It is easier for the president and members of Congress to produce proposals than it is to generate the support needed to enact them. Partisan splits and structural contraints, as discussed earlier, interfere with majority building. It may well be that the Social Security commission format is the only way out for major issues—that is, a format permitting political leaders to overcome the limitations sustaining what is generally acknowledged to be an unacceptable status quo.

What can be said, in conclusion, about the Reagan contribution to governance in regard to presidential-congressional relations? First and foremost Reagan has been successful in managing the context for congressional choice. He has not always been successful in building support for his true policy preferences—particularly not after 1981—but he surely got congressional attention. Policy talk on Capitol Hill was different after 1981. President Reagan was responsible for completing the shift to the consolidative agenda.

Second, one detects in the Reagan performance a willingness to work within the party structure. One expects conflict between a president and his own party's congressional leaders. Such conflict is hardly even news—and it existed for Reagan, notably in 1983. But the presidential support and party-unity scores provide evidence to confirm a basically sound working relationship between the president and his congressional party. That would appear to be good news for those preferring a stronger role for political parties.

Third, in accepting that problems are different and that the government's role in meeting the needs of its citizens has changed, both Congress and the presidency appear now to be searching for new methods of decision making. The National Commission on Social Security Reform is the most obvious example of such a new format, but the procedures for passing the 1982 tax reform bill and other unusual budgetary interactions are also cases in point. It must be acknowledged that redirecting a government is not easy. The new consolidative/contractive issues inevitably create conflicts within a system designed to expand. So a period of adjustment is to be expected.

Finally, President Reagan has reintroduced classic separation-of-power politics into presidential-congressional relations. His particular version stresses a communicator's style that is reminiscent of Franklin Delano Roosevelt's. In fact, there is nothing particularly innovative about this approach.[49] It has been tried successfully many times in the past. Yet in the last twenty years, the partnership and independent models of presidential-congressional relations

---

49. President Reagan has demonstrated an unusual, though not surprising, capacity for using the media to his advantage. This advantage has undoubtedly contributed to his success in classic separation politics.

have predominated. It seems apparent, however, that classic-separation politics is more suited to the American system (among other features it encourages greater responsibility). President Reagan deserves credit for promoting it at a critical juncture in the life of both the executive and legislative branches.

COMMENTS *Norman J. Ornstein*

The Impact Of A More Republican Congress

Charles O. Jones's paper examines the current status of presidential-congressional relations in domestic policy by discussing how Ronald Reagan came to Congress; how Congress came to Ronald Reagan; and how each institution dealt with the other. This is a sensible form of organization, and, as usual, Jones has it basically right. In commenting, I will take each of these three areas and elaborate on some themes that I think deserve more attention.

How Reagan Came to Congress

First, on how Ronald Reagan came to Congress, Jones stresses that Reagan began his term with a number of important advantages, particularly as a minority party president, including his electoral margin, the sizable increases in congressional Republicans, the Republican takeover of the Senate, and the negative image of Carter's relations with Congress. I would put considerably more stress than does Jones on the Republican gains in Congress and particularly on the *perception that stemmed from those Republican gains*, especially because of the unexpected nature of the results.

Republican congressional gains were a key to Reagan that overshadowed his own election landslide. We have only to look back to 1972 to see a presidential landslide that did not work to the advantage of a minority president, precisely because it carried with it no significant congressional gains. Richard Nixon in 1972 outdistanced Ronald Reagan in 1980 by every conceivable measure—ten percentage points in the popular vote and a bigger advantage in electoral votes over his opponent. But because Nixon's landslide was not a *Republican* landslide, it was interpreted in the narrowest terms.

The 1972 election was a defeat for George McGovern first, a Nixon victory second, and a Republican party victory not at all. Ronald Reagan, on the other hand, brought with him thirty-three new Republicans to the House and a dozen new Republicans to the Senate—and, of course, the first

288

Republican Senate in more than a quarter of a century. Thus, Ronald Reagan's victory was first a Democratic defeat and a Republican victory—meaning, to most observers, the rejection of the Democratic Party (including the New Deal, the Fair Deal, the Great Society, and so forth), then a Jimmy Carter defeat and a Ronald Reagan victory.

The notion of 1980 as a Democratic party defeat was underscored by the surprise of the Senate election. By election eve, most political experts had seen the trend shifting in the final week of the campaign and believed that Ronald Reagan would win the presidential contest. Most experts also saw a substantial Republican gain in the Senate, but the overwhelming consensus was a Republican Senate gain of no more than five or six seats. Virtually no one believed that Republicans had a significant chance of gaining the nine or ten seats required to take a majority. When they gained twelve seats, exceeding the wildest dreams of Republican strategists, the impact was multiplied.

The Republican victory in the Senate occurred because Republicans won the overwhelming share of "toss-up elections." It could easily have gone the other way. A shift of less than fifty thousand votes in seven states would have swung Senate seats back to the Democratic column, leaving the Republicans with a net gain of five and the Democrats with a fifty-four to forty-six majority in the Senate. The 1980 election would then have been interpreted much more as a Jimmy Carter defeat than a Democratic party defeat, and the attitudes of both Democrats and Republicans in Congress, as well as the attitudes of press, pundits, and the president, would have been much different. No doubt, the whole nature of the policy process in 1981 would also have been affected.

How Congress Came to Reagan

Regarding how Congress came to Reagan, Jones rightly stresses the House and Senate election results and their impact on the Congress that Reagan faced in 1981. It is important as well to emphasize the tremendous impact that a Republican Senate—and especially a *new* Republican Senate—had on the policy agenda in 1981. Congress controls the domestic policy agenda, at least in terms of timing and content. A president may be able to use his command of national attention and of the air waves to put a new issue on the national agenda (as Nixon did, for example, with family assistance and federalism). But Congress decides when such issues get debated and when they receive votes, as well as the substance of the bills that will be voted on. Under most recent presidents, of course, Democratic Congresses have controlled this agenda—Congresses with members and leaders who were veterans to majority rule and who had a history of independent action and of pursuing their own agendas through several presidents. For Republican presidents like Nixon and Ford, this was particularly frustrating, but it was upsetting as well for a president like Jimmy Carter who found independent majority Democrats in Congress unwilling in many instances to pursue his agenda in the form or with the timing that he preferred.

Ronald Reagan had an enormous advantage over other recent presidents. Fifty-one of the fifty-three Republican senators in 1981 had never been in the majority in the Senate. Most had expected to remain in the minority for the duration of their Senate careers. Most were therefore grateful to Ronald Reagan for helping them move into an unanticipated majority status, and most saw Ronald Reagan's policy success in the White House as essential to their ability to hold their Senate majority. On the other hand, no Democratic Senate in recent memory saw *its* political future as dependent on the policy success of a president.

Unlike other recent Republican presidents, Ronald Reagan had a piece of the congressional agenda and was able to use it. Republicans in the Senate, acting as loyal soldiers, used their offices and resources to the president's best advantage. They devised the strategy of using reconciliation to get a single, encompassing, and binding vote on budget cuts. They were willing to overturn 100 years of political tradition and have the Senate act first on budget matters, thus forcing the House to act on an agenda and with a timing that was to its great disadvantage. It is unlikely that any of those great early policy successes—the first budget resolution, the reconciliation package, the tax bill—would have been achieved in anything like the form proposed by Reagan without that control of the agenda used to the president's advantage by his enthusiastically loyal Republican majority senators.

By 1982, however, Republican senators were beginning to see that their futures might not be inextricably linked with that of Ronald Reagan, and many were trying to distance themselves from his policies. Others, like Robert Dole and Pete Domenici, defied Reagan, proposing and implementing a budget and a tax increase that were not designed by the White House and that went against the tide set one year earlier. But at least for that one crucial year, Reagan had an advantage denied most modern presidents.

An Advantage is Not Enough

However, as Jones persuasively notes in examining how Reagan and Congress worked together, having an advantage alone is not enough with the new, open Congress. With power and initiative decentralized and democratized, Congress is more complex, more unpredictable, and more diffused than ever before. A president must have the skill, sensitivity, and character to understand and exploit this Congress if he is to gain policy and political success. Ronald Reagan had personal qualities that enabled him to succeed in 1981—and to make failure in 1982 look like success. (Jimmy Carter, on the other hand, was capable of making his policy successes look like failures.) Reagan developed a congressional liaison team that was experienced and sensitive to the changing nature of Congress. Reagan—in Jones's words the communicator as president—had the personal qualities to work with Congress and to establish solid communications with Capitol Hill. All of these elements have worked to Reagan's advantage.

Nevertheless, these assets could not help Reagan achieve sweeping policy changes after August 1981. Partly, it is the way our political system operates. Partly, it is the nature of the open Congress. Partly, it is the limits on policy change imposed by public opinion. And, partly, it is Ronald Reagan. After his first initiatives, Reagan has not returned with additional, sweeping changes but appears content to consolidate and make permanent what he has achieved, using his 1981 achievements as a base.

Reagan has been fortunate in that he has a Congress willing to move into a policy vacuum when one exists. This, too, is an offshoot of the split-party Congress. Senate Republicans since 1982 have felt the weight of majority responsibility heavily on their shoulders—and have responded responsibly. When President Reagan for all practical purposes dropped out of the budget process in 1982, Senate Republicans—in the closest version since 1910 of congressional government—wrote their own budget and their own tax bill, thus saving themselves and Reagan from economic and political deadlock and/or chaos. Congress's disposition to act in this fashion fits Reagan's style—that curious blend of political pragmatism and ideological rigidity, of passionate aggressiveness and studied passivity.

This style defines the Reagan presidency. In my view, Ronald Reagan was a John F. Kennedy and a Lyndon Baines Johnson in 1981; since then, his style has befit Dwight D. Eisenhower. The 1984 campaign was run in a manner comparable to the 1956 Eisenhower campaign. The accomplishments of 1981 was underscored and emphasized, to be sure, but a major theme was that Ronald Reagan will maintain prosperity and peace and will not rock the boat. We no longer have Reagan the revolutionary. That may fit the pragmatic side of Reagan's personality, but it also fits the realities of American politics today and tomorrow.

But The System Still Won

Charles O. Jones's paper reminds us emphatically of something that perhaps all of us recognized at the time but have not had much occasion to reflect on since: The Reagan years began with one of the most auspicious outlooks for presidential-congressional relations in recent history. In early 1981, American citizens had every reason to believe that the U.S. government, which requires a high degree of harmony between the executive and legislative branches for decisive action on domestic matters, would be able to cope effectively with the problems that beset the country.

Consider the things Jones identifies that the American governmental system had going for it in 1981:

- A clear, unambiguous Republican party program enunciated by the party's newly elected president.

- A landslide electoral victory, which had converted that program into a mandate.

- The biggest Republican presidential-year gain in the House since 1920 and in the Senate since 1868,with a GOP takeover of the Senate.

- A Congress (including the Democratic majority in the House) that was disposed to accept the election mandate and to let the president have his way.

- A president who exhibited great skill in dealing with Congress and who was willing to work hard at cultivating and influencing its members.

- A superbly staffed and effective congressional liaison office.

In the opening three-quarters of his paper, Jones draws a picture of a governmental system in which nearly everything that could go right was going right—in contrast to the preceding Carter years, when almost everything that could go wrong did so. The circumstances of 1981 were more like those of Franklin Delano Roosevelt's Hundred Days or the heyday of Lyndon Baines Johnson's Great Society than those of Jimmy Carter's wasted term or the conflict-ridden years of Richard M. Nixon and Gerald R. Ford.

One might have assumed, then, that in the rest of his paper Jones would describe how the government, under President Reagan's leadership, proceeded smoothly to carry out the mandate of the 1980 election and to do what had to be done to meet the needs of the new decade. Right? No, wrong. In his concluding pages, Jones draws quite another picture, one of a governmental system that even in those favorable circumstances did not work well.

True, President Reagan got the main outlines of his budget through Congress—a major achievement by any standard, even though many of his specific recommendations were defeated. But that was 1981, and the budget victory represents about the sum of his achievements since. On Social Security, Jones reminds us, the president was defeated. In addition, his new federalism plan got virtually nowhere. In 1982 he was forced to revise his fiscal policy and to accept a tax increase. And by 1983 Jones describes Congress as "immobilized by partisan and individual entrepreneurship," and the president as a leader who has found it easier "to produce proposals than it is to generate the support needed to enact them," resulting in a sort of policy drift in a sea of uncontrolled deficit spending.

Policy Drift and the Deficit

Jones could have expanded on the last of these points, which is the truest measure of systemic failure during Ronald Reagan's first three years. Enactment of a radically new budget policy was, as already stated, the proudest achievement of the Reagan administration. Yet, two years later, almost nobody in public life would defend the outcome of that policy, and the government appeared powerless to alter it. The president denounced the deficit as too high for either the short-range or long-range good of the country, and demanded that it be reduced. So did the secretary of the Treasury. So did the chairperson of the Council of Economic Advisers. So did every responsible leader of Congress, of both parties, in both houses. So, for that matter, did numerous expert observers outside of government. And many more citizens can be expected to voice their opposition, as the full effects of an increase of $50 billion to $100 billion in annual interest payments begin to be comprehended.

The president made clear that he wanted to bring down the deficit through more cuts in domestic spending—but the Congress rejected that course.

Various congressional leaders had proposals for lowering the deficit, some of which were quite specific. But, as Jones aptly points out, Congress put forward no *one* proposal, and it was not about to, for the president had announced in advance that he would veto any measure that either increased the projected revenues or reduced the intended military buildup—and any bill emerging from Congress was sure to do both of those.

So the policy drift continues into 1985. Meanwhile, in the 1984 election, the electorate was not able to hold anyone responsible. The president blamed the Democrats in Congress, and the Democrats blamed the president. The Republican orators lambasted House Speaker Thomas P. O'Neill, Jr., making him the villain who gave the country these horrendous deficits, while Walter Mondale and his fellow Democrats pinned the fault on Reagan. And both sides were largely right in denying responsibility, because in truth nobody was responsible.

Postelection Prospects

Now that election is over, the prospect is not necessarily better. Reagan still confronts a Democratic House, one that will be less docile than was the House of 1981. This time, it will be determined from the outset to resist and discredit the lame-duck president. The Senate, with a two-seat gain by Democrats, will be less reliable as a bulwark of presidential support. Thus, the outlook is for four more years of policy confusion and irresponsibility in the literal sense, during which time the deficits have the potential to choke off recovery, not just in this country but worldwide, bringing on the grievous political consequences that always attend economic reverse.

One must ask: if the "Great Communicator," after two landslide victories, with a clear mandate, and all the necessary skills in dealing with Congress, cannot make the American system work, who can? The answer from modern American history is that no leader, or set of leaders, can make it work for long.

In Reagan's case, the system permitted the people not only to give the president a mandate but at the same time to elect a House of Representatives controlled by the opposing party, whose mission was, naturally, to discredit and defeat the president. A government divided between the parties is ordained to stalemate and deadlock, yet divided government has come to be the rule rather than the exception—having prevailed in twenty of the thirty-two years from 1954 through 1986. Put another way, five times since 1954 have the people chosen a Republican candidate for president, but each time they have denied the victorious GOP either the opportunity to govern or the responsibility and accountability for governing—by placing one or both houses of Congress (usually both) under control of the Democrats.

It was the system that allowed the people in 1982 to reinforce the partisan deadlock after only two years by strengthening the opposition party in Congress in the mid-term election. That, too, has become the normal state of affairs. Only once in this century has the midterm election reaffirmed the mandate that had been given to either party in a landslide election two years earlier; that was the Democratic victory in 1934 that strengthened Franklin Roosevelt's hold on Congress and made possible the completion of the New Deal. Every other midterm election has led to deadlocked government (if one disregards the exceptional circumstances that followed President John F. Kennedy's assassination in 1963). This is now a commonplace, accepted fact of political life; every administration knows that anything significant it hopes to accomplish must be achieved in its first two years, and probably in its first year, before the inevitable stalemate overtakes it. If an administration spends any time trying to make up its collective mind as to what it wants to do, as in the case of the Carter administration in 1977, it is destined to be lost for the whole four years.

These two systemic difficulties that have so obviously thwarted President Reagan and the Republican party during his term are rooted in the Constitution. They are compounded, also, by extra-Constitutional features of the American governmental system, arising from political culture and traditions, that serve to reduce the cohesion, effectiveness, and accountability of government. These include the weakening of political parties as the mechanism that binds the executive and legislative branches; the rampant individualism and institutional fragmentation of Congress; the deterioration of the civil service, particularly at the top levels; and, one may add, the independence of the Federal Reserve System.

Those who blame Ronald Reagan or anyone else for a failure of leadership if the government displays an incapacity to cope with great problems—such as today's uncontrolled deficit—should look to the institutional structure in which a president finds himself embedded. There may not be much that even a superman could do.

INTEREST GROUPS AND THE REAGAN PRESIDENCY

Harold Wolman and Fred Teitelbaum

Introduction

Studies of comparative politics frequently emphasize the importance of interest groups in American political life relative to that of other Western democracies. Group theory—a dominant paradigm in American political science—argues that interest groups play a critical role in the political process in determining public policy outcomes.[1] Changes in the comparative influence of interest groups or in the level of government at which decisions are made—since the relative influence of various groups is not the same at every level of government—could alter public policy outcomes and create new winners and losers.

It is alleged also that interest groups affect important macro-policy outcomes such as the size of government, the level of government spending, and the growth rate of the gross national product (GNP). Some critics, for example, contend that high levels of government spending result from the activities of special-interest groups and that spending can be brought under control only when the influence of these groups is curbed. Finally, the proliferation of interest groups—and particularly of single-issue interest groups—is said to have raised the level of political conflict and dramatically increased the difficulties of governing.

Ronald Reagan's administration came to office determined to reduce interest-group influence on American political life, at least insofar as this influence was felt to contribute to the growth of government spending, to political overload, and to the disproportionate advancement of "liberal" causes.

---

1. David Truman, *The Governmental Process* (New York: Alfred A. Knopf, 1951), p. 502.

This paper reviews the actions of the Reagan administration with respect to interest groups and the consequences of these actions on interest-group policy objectives, resources, and lobbying strategies at the federal and state levels. It then discusses the implications of these actions for the governability of American society, for government spending, and for the distribution of winners and losers emerging from the policy process.

We conclude that the role of interest groups—at least in the human services area, which is the focus of this study—has indeed been altered, at least in the short run. During the first three years of President Reagan's term, interest groups exerted a reduced influence on government spending and struggled to readjust their strategies. However, we are skeptical that a fundamental change has occurred in the overall role and importance of interest groups in the American polity. What many have perceived as a decrease in the significance of interest groups is more likely a shift in the relative influence of various groups, with previously dominant liberal groups losing and more conservative groups winning, as would be expected in a conservative administration. In addition, we question whether the short-term effects—particularly the reduced impact on spending decisions—will be lasting. Paradoxically, we project that over the long run, the result of these readjustments by interest groups—especially in terms of greater grass-roots mobilization and an expanded presence at the state level—may strengthen interest groups' impact on public policy and may increase the level of conflict in the political system.

We predict, furthermore, that a decentralization of policy such as that advocated and partly put in place by the Reagan administration will result in a different set of winning and losing interests than would result from the present relatively centralized system. At least in the short run, many groups that were previously effective at the federal level—particularly in the human resources area—have been at a disadvantage at the state level because they are not properly organized there. In the longer run, in the absence of major changes in the comparative influence of various interests, a widespread decentralization would imply that the interests of the poor, above all, would be diminished in relation to other interests in low-income states and states with high minority and poverty populations.

The Significance of Interest Groups in Contemporary American Politics

Why should we be concerned about what has happened to interest groups during the Reagan era? What do interest groups do? What impacts do they have, and what functions do they serve to justify focussing attention on them?

Interest Groups and Political Overload

American politics, more than those of most democracies, have long been characterized as interest-group politics, in which organized groups are thought to play a key role in determining the outcome and distribution of public policy issues. The "group theory" of politics was one of the earliest and most widely recognized models in political science. Expressed in its most pristine and simplistic form, group theory argues that:

> what may be called public policy is actually the equilibrium reached in the group struggle at any given moment, and it represents a balance which the contending factions or groups constantly strive to tip in their favor . . . the legislature referees the group struggle, ratifies the victories of the successful coalition, and records the terms of the surrenders, compromises, and conquests in terms of statutes.[2]

While few today would agree that interest groups hold such sway over the political process, few would deny their importance.[3] The last two decades have seen an expansion of the interest-group system to include a variety of previously unorganized or weakly organized groups, such as consumer groups, public interest groups, socially and economically disadvantaged groups, and various ethnic minorities. Daniel Bell and other neoconservative scholars have contended that the growth in this type of group representation has resulted in an increasing set of demands on public officials, leading to further political conflict and a near paralysis of government. Bell asserted that:

> the major conflicts, increasingly, are not between management and labor within the framework of the economic enterprise but between organized interest groups claiming their share of government largesse. The political cockpit in which these battles are fought is the government budget. . . . One large question that the American system now confronts is whether it can

---

2. Earl Latham, "The Group Basis of Politics: Notes for a Theory," in H. R. Mahood, ed., *Pressure Groups in American Politics* (New York: Charles Scribner's Sons, 1967), p. 41.

3. Some recent political science literature has tended to minimize the influence of organized groups on the policy process, at least so far as direct lobbying is concerned. On the basis of a detailed case study of foreign trade legislation, one work has expressed "reservations about the extent of influence that has characteristically been attributed to pressure groups" (Raymond A. Bauer, Ithiel de Sola Pool, and Lewis Anthony Dexter, *American Business and Public Policy* [New York: Atherton Press, 1963], p. 396). In his study of lobbyists and lobbying, Milbrath is less equivocal in his conclusions: "The weight of the evidence . . . suggests that there is relatively little influence or power in lobbying per se. There are many forces in addition to lobbying which influence public policy; in most cases these other forces clearly outweigh the impact of lobbying." (Lester Milbrath, *The Washington Lobbyists* [Chicago: Rand McNally, 1962], p. 354).

find a way to resolve these conflicts. Lacking rules to mediate rival claims, the system will be under severe strains.[4]

Robert Lubar pits the argument more dramatically. Discussing Bell's "revolution of rising entitlements," he observes:

> Those who sought redress from government insisted that they were entitled to it as a matter of right. In an age that encouraged self-assertiveness, no right seemed too farfetched to assert . . . the deluge of demands put an intolerable strain on governments at all levels. Since one group's rights can be another group's infringements, conflicts were inevitable.[5]

Sociologist Amitai Etzioni and others have argued, however, that an increase in demands on the political system is an inevitable and not necessarily undesirable price paid for the extension of political participation to a greater variety of groups.[6]

Interest Groups and Government Spending

The growth of interest-group activity is frequently pointed to as an important cause of the rise in government spending. Interest-group activity and the organization of semiautonomous "iron triangles," or "subgovernments," linking interest-group concerns with those of congressional committees and executive agencies, have been cited by political scientists as encouraging logrolling and excess spending.[7]

Economists with a public-choice orientation have also argued that the interaction of special interests with a majority-rule decision system leads to logrolling and to governmental spending that oversteps public preference.[8] A synthesis of various strands of the public-choice argument is as follows: To gain support (campaign contributions, campaign endorsements, or votes) from

4. Daniel Bell, "The Revolution of Rising Entitlements," *Fortune*, April 1975, p. 99.

5. Robert Lubar, "Making Democracy Less Inflationary," *Fortune*, September 22, 1980, p. 82.

6. Amitai Etzioni, "Societal Overload: Sources, Components, and Connections," *Political Science Quarterly*, Winter 1977–1978, p. 619.

7. Robert Hawkins, President Reagan's appointed chairperson of the Advisory Commission on Intergovernmental Relations, expresses this view in "American Federalism: Again at the Crossroads," in Robert Hawkins, ed., *American Federalism: A New Partnership for the Republic* (San Francisco: Institute for Contemporary Studies, 1982), pp. 9–10. Although the actual origin of the term *iron triangle* is uncertain, the term has become part of the conventional wisdom about the way the nation's capital operates.

8. For a review of this literature, see Dennis Mueller, *Public Choice* (Cambridge: Cambridge University Press, 1979), chapter 8; see also James Q. Wilson, *Political Organizations* (New York: Basic Books, 1973), chapter 16. Economist Mancur Olson has carried the argument about the impact of interest groups a step further. He argues that the incentives facing organized groups strongly suggest that societies with large numbers of special-interest groups will experience not only excessive government spending but also a low rate of economic growth.

various interest groups, legislators attempt to enact legislation furthering the interests of groups whose favor they seek. The conjunction of many different groups with access to legislators and a majority-rule decision-making structure permitting logrolling inevitably leads to passage of a variety of special-interest legislation and government spending that exceeds public preference. This occurs because although the benefits of the legislation accrue to a particular interest, the costs are borne by the general public and are thus largely invisible.[9]

Interest Groups and Policy Outcomes

The interplay of interest groups with government institutions throughout the federal structure has long been assumed to be an important factor in determining public policy outcomes. The question inevitably arises: Which groups are the most influential and which the least in the political struggle— in other words, who are the winners and who are the losers? To what extent has President Reagan, particularly through his decentralization initiative, changed the environment in which the group struggle occurs and thus permanently altered the identity of the winners and losers in American politics?

Identifying the winners and losers is complicated by the nature of the federal system. Influence depends on effective access to the decision-making process, and federalism has helped to create multiple points of access. As political scientist Robert Dahl observes, those who lose at one level of government frequently seek to recoup their losses at other levels:

> Organizations may succeed in achieving at the lower levels what they could not gain at the national level. . . . Within the state itself the same process goes on. Groups who lack influence with city governments may turn to the state legislature; urban groups unable to gain what they want at the state level may concentrate on the city administration.[10]

Olson argues that members of groups have an incentive to seek public benefits (through additional public spending or other public action), even if the result is a lower level of welfare for society as a whole. Groups will seek additional benefits to the point that their members' share of the marginal cost of providing additional benefits equals their members' marginal benefits. Except where a group is "encompassing"—that is, where it comprises a substantial portion of the population—"there is for practical purposes no constraint on the social cost such an organization will find it expedient to impose on the society in the cause of obtaining a larger share of the social output for itself" (Mancur Olson, *The Rise and Decline of Nations* [New Haven: Yale University Press, 1982], p. 44).

9. Others argue, however, that any overspending resulting from passage of special interest legislation is more than offset by underspending on programs for which benefits are general rather than concentrated.

10. Robert Dahl, *Pluralist Democracy in America* (Chicago: Rand McNally, 1967), p. 385.

As this comment suggests, some groups are likely to be systematically more influential at one level of government than at others.[11]

The Setting: The Reagan Administration and Interest Groups

It is reasonably clear that the number of interest groups increased rapidly during the 1960s and 1970s.[12] More importantly, the political presence of these groups in the nation's capital increased. Kay Lehman Schlozman and John T. Tierney, using a sample of 200 organizations listed in cumulative indexes of the *National Journal*, found that while only one-fifth of the organizations had been formed after 1960, three-fifths had opened a Washington, D.C., office since then and two-fifths had done so since 1970.[13] Many of these groups were small and single-interest-oriented, and, to some extent, they represented a partial enfranchisement of some of the interests previously left out of the interest-group system.

The increased presence of interest groups gave rise to concern over their impact in American politics. In his farewell address, President Jimmy Carter observed:

> We are increasingly drawn to single-issue groups and special interest organizations to ensure that whatever else happens our own personal views and our private interests are protected. This is a disturbing factor in American political life. It tends to distort our purposes. . . . Because of the fragmented pressures of these special interests, it's very important that the office of the president be a strong one.[14]

---

11. David Truman observes that "In consequence of the structural peculiarities of our government some groups have better and more varied opportunities to influence key points of decision than do others. . . . The existence of a federal system itself is a source of unequal advantage in access. Groups that would be rather obscure or weak under a unitary arrangement may hold advantageous positions in the state government." (*The Governmental Process*, pp. 323–323.) Harmon Ziegler and Wayne Peak make the same point by arguing that "federalism does not involve a struggle between the nation and the states, but rather a struggle among interests which have favorable access to one of the two levels of government." (*Interest Groups in American Society* [Englewood Cliffs, N.J.: Prentice-Hall, 1972], p. 48.)

12. See the discussion presented in Jack Walker, "The Origins and Maintenance of Interest Groups in America," *American Political Science Review* LXXVII (June 1983), pp. 394–395.

13. Kay Lehman Schlozman and John T. Tierney, "More of the Same: Washington Pressure Group Activity in a Decade of Change." Paper delivered at American Political Science Association Convention, Denver, September 2–5, 1982, pp. 12–13. See also Walker, "Interest Groups in America," pp. 394–395.

14. "President Carter's Farewell Address," reprinted in *Congressional Quarterly Weekly Reports*, January 17, 1981, p. 156.

President Reagan and his appointees shared these concerns and came to office dedicated to changing what they considered to be the perverse impact of interest groups.[15] This impact, as the Reaganites saw it, included not only political overload and government paralysis, but also the tendency of interest groups to generate growth in government programs and spending, all to the benefit of liberal forces in society.

Thus David Stockman, director of the Office of Management and Budget (OMB), saw the reduction of the political congestion caused by the concentration of issues and interest groups at the national level as an important priority:

> We are overloaded at the national level. We simply can't make wise decisions on the thousands of issues that come before us. There has to be a better division of labor and a redelegation of decision-making to lower levels of government.[16]

Robert Carleson, a White House official in the Reagan administration, saw a need to reduce federal outlays by attacking the iron triangles that, he felt, sustained this excessive spending:

> We have consciously set out to force political decisions and the struggles that accompany them down to the state and local level. The so-called iron triangles in Washington for too long have had a virtual monopoly on political influence in Congress and the agencies.[17]

In addition, the Reagan administration felt that the Washington, D.C., interest-group system was biased toward liberal groups advocating social programs. As the president himself remarked:

> It's far easier for people to come to Washington to get their social programs. It would be a hell of a lot tougher if we diffuse them and send them out to the states. All their friends and connections are in Washington.[18]

Finally, some of the Reaganites believed that many of the social-advocacy groups had been sustained through federal grants and contracts and that the federal government was, in effect, paying groups to lobby it. Howard Phillips, executive director of the Conservative Caucus, urged "eliminating the power of the federal bureaucracy . . . to subsidize activist organizations which are working . . . to render irrelevant the election results."[19]

---

15. *Congressional Quarterly Weekly Report*, June 5, 1982, pp. 1, 328.

16. Quoted in Claude E. Barfield, *Rethinking Federalism* (Washington D.C.: American Enterprise Institute, 1981), p. 24.

17. Barfield, *Rethinking Federalism*, p. 24.

18. Quoted in Stephen V. Roberts, "Budget Axe Becomes a Tool of Social Change," *New York Times*, June 21, 1981, p. 2.

19. Quoted in Rochelle F. Stanfield, "Defunding the Left May Remain Just Another Dream of Conservatives," *National Journal*, August 1, 1981, pp. 1, 374.

The Changing Environment for Interest Groups

The Reagan administration undertook specific actions to eliminate the supposed adverse impacts of interest groups. In addition, trends predating Reagan's term also affected interest groups, bringing about important changes not only in the environment these groups faced, but also in the way they behaved and, ultimately, in their impact. These actions and trends are examined in the remainder of this section.

Decentralization.   Upon taking office, President Reagan began an explicit effort to decentralize responsibility and decision-making authority from the federal to the state levels. The president's block-grant proposals were the primary vehicle to this end, although federal funding reductions and deregulation reforms also reinforced the decentralization objective. As the remark just quoted from the president makes clear, Reagan desired and foresaw both lower public spending and, in particular, less spending on social welfare programs favored by "liberal"-oriented groups as a result of decentralization to the states.[20]

Early in his term, President Reagan unveiled a first step to accomplish these goals by proposing that almost ninety categorical programs totaling $15 billion be combined into three block grants to the states, with substantial reductions in funding. Interest groups with a stake in the categorical programs that were proposed for block granting—primarily, those in the health, social services, and education areas—initially fought hard for exclusion from the blocks, for once in the block, funding for their unique programs would no longer be guaranteed (serving the president's objective of reducing the pressure for increased federal expenditures). Some groups were successful in avoiding being blocked, thus protecting their interests. Congress increased the number of block grants to nine, reduced the number of categoricals included in the block grants to fifty-seven, eliminated large programs from the blocks, and reinstituted some strings.[21] The net result was a $1.4 billion, or a 12.6 percent, reduction in budget authority for the blocked programs relative to their fiscal year (FY) 1981 levels.

Defunding the Left.   In addition to the decentralization efforts, the administration also launched a variety of strategies intended to reduce federal support for "liberal" advocacy groups. These included the proposal to eliminate the legal services program, a Great Society initiative that had served

20. Roberts, "Budget Axe," p. 2.
21. For a description of the new block grants and the categorical programs consolidated into them, see John L. Palmer and Isabel Sawhill, eds., *The Reagan Experiment* (Washington, D.C.: The Urban Institute, 1982), chapter 6.

as an important means, through the vehicle of the class action suit, for conveying the interests of the poor to the political system; the reduction in federal grants and contracts to professional associations, public interest groups, and nonprofit service-provider groups for research, technical assistance, and even program operation purposes; and the effort to curtail the lobbying of groups receiving federal funds.

This last initiative, which was a proposed OMB regulation, created considerable controversy. It would have prohibited organizations receiving federal grants from using those funds for a variety of overhead purposes that are currently routine. For example, it would no longer have been permissible to use federal aid to pay for the rental of any office in which 5 percent or more of the space were used for political-advocacy purposes. (Political advocacy was defined not simply as lobbying and campaign activities, but also as efforts to "influence governmental decisions through an attempt to affect the opinions of the general public" and "communication with any member or employee of a legislative body.")[22] The proposed regulation was opposed by business-oriented and professional groups as well as social-advocacy ones. It was thus withdrawn, and a defanged, less controversial substitute proposed in its place.

Fiscal Discipline. Although the two decades leading up to the late 1970s had seen relatively rapid economic growth and corresponding increases in federal revenues, President Reagan faced an economy experiencing slow economic growth and modest revenue increases. He responded by immediately proposing massive tax reductions and substantial increases for defense spending. These proposals, as eventually adopted, cause the federal resources available for domestic spending to shrink rather than to grow. Thus, the president originally proposed $40 billion in domestic spending reductions from the Congressional Budget Office's (CBO's) FY 1982 current policy baseline budget; as finally enacted, the FY 1982 budget incorporated $31.6 billion in domestic program reductions from the CBO baseline.[23]

Shrinking resources provide a much different environment for interest-group activity than do growing resources. In this connection, Theodore Lowi has distinguished between distributive and redistributive "arenas of power."[24]

---

22. *Federal Register*, vol. 48, no. 16, January 24, 1983, p. 3349.

23. John L. Palmer and Gregory Mills, "Budget Policy," in John L. Palmer and Isabel V. Sawhill, eds., *The Reagan Experiment* (Washington, D.C.: The Urban Institute, 1982), pp. 77–78.

24. Theodore Lowi, "American Business, Public Policy Case Studies, and Political Theory," *World Politics*, vol. 16 (1964), pp. 667–715. The terms *distributive* and *redistributive* refer not to the actual ultimate impact of the policies but to the way the policy impact is perceived by actors while they are involved in decision making. Lowi's original article has generated a body of work modifying his typology. While many of these modifications represent improvements, they are essentially refinements of Lowi's initial insight and, accordingly, we confine our discussion to Lowi's work.

Distributive politics consist of a disaggregation of benefits, such that losers cannot easily be identified; logrolling is the characteristic decision process and the results are perceived as non-zero-sum. Conversely, in the redistributive arena, winners and losers are clearly perceived, and the battles fought involve the clash of important social interests, such as business versus labor and the rich versus the poor, rather than large numbers of small interest groups and associations.

Distributive politics are interest-group politics: they flourish when the economy is growing and the budget is not highly constrained. Redistributive politics are much more likely to occur under conditions of budget constraint. The supposed upward impetus that interest groups impart to federal spending is much less likely to occur when the major issues of the day are redistributive in nature.

Changes in the Structure of Fiscal Decision Making. President Reagan was not the first president to come to the White House dedicated to reducing federal expenditures. However, previously the mechanics of the congressional budget process had frustrated such efforts. In particular, the divorce of spending decisions from revenue-raising decisions imposed little constraint and contributed to the essential feature of distributive decision making—in the sense that the game was non-zero-sum and no visible losers needed exist.

By enacting the 1974 Congressional Budget Act,[25] Congress attempted to replace this ineffective budget control procedure with a new, more coordinated process that related spending to revenues so as to provide a total picture of the federal budget. In a nutshell, the act stipulated that in the course of a specified time period before September 15, the House of Representatives and the Senate were to pass first a concurrent resolution setting total spending and revenue levels and providing nonbinding spending targets for each function, followed by various appropriations bills, and then a second concurrent resolution specifying final spending and revenue levels. If necessary, a reconciliation bill was to be passed by October 1 to adjust the spending in the appropriations bills to the budget targets.

By 1980, however, the limitations of the new process were obvious— the target spending figures set for each function in the first resolution were being largely ignored, and the reconciliation process was taking place too late and in too short a period to allow for sufficient adjustment. The major change made, which was introduced during the Carter administration and expanded

---

25. For an extensive discussion of the Congressional Budget Act and Reagan's use of it, see Allan Schick, *Reconciliation and the Congressional Budget Process* (Washington, D.C.: American Enterprise Institute, 1981); see also the paper by Schick in this volume.

upon enthusiastically by the Reagan administration, was to have the reconciliation bill follow the *first* budget resolution, thus locking in the spending and revenue levels of the first resolution. In the reconciliation process committees were required to report out any substantive legislative changes necessary to meet spending targets. Reconciliation thus was extended to apply to authorizing legislation, including entitlement programs, rather than solely to appropriations. All the proposed changes from the various committees were then packaged into a single reconciliation bill whose totals were to conform to those of the budget resolution.

These alterations in the budget process, and Reagan's successful and rapid use of the process in 1981, had two significant effects. First, by moving the decision on binding spending and revenue levels to the beginning of the budget process, Congress was forced to alter its spending orientation from one that was distributive to one that was redistributive. Before 1981, Congress was able to avoid head-on clashes among competing interests by enacting a series of appropriations bills and multiple-authorizing legislation and by separating spending from revenue-raising measures. Reagan effectively used the modified process to combine all decisions into one package, thereby compelling Congress to make decisions about budget priorities early in the process. What had previously been determined through a multiplicity of disaggregated decisions was now decided in a single vote and, for the first time, under a strict budget constraint. Expenditure reductions in the reconciliation bill had to total the targets in the first budget resolution. Second, by extending the focus of the congressional budget process to authorizing legislation as well as appropriations, Congress was forced to deal with entitlement programs, outlays for which constitute over half of federal spending.

Other recent changes in congressional structure have also had a marked effect on interest groups. Briefly, the important points of access that interest groups must pursue to influence congressional action have proliferated dramatically. By the late 1970s, pressures for reform had resulted in the demise of the rigid seniority system, the proliferation and increased autonomy of subcommittees, the opening up of committee and conference sessions, the referral of bills to multiple committees, and the general weakening of party leadership. These changes meant that interest groups could no longer concentrate on only a small number of committee chairpersons or party leaders to do their bidding. They also had to deal with the subcommittee chairpersons and, when multiple referral of bills occurred, with several committees and subcommittees.

In addition, the enhanced powers of the new House and Senate Budget Committees meant that it was no longer sufficient for interest groups solely to lobby key authorizing and appropriations committee and subcommittee members and staffs to protect their interests; much more emphasis had to be placed on the Budget Committees. Even successful courting of all of these committee members, however, does not ensure favorable action, as the reconciliation act encompassing virtually the entire federal budget, is frequently closely contested on the floor, making the votes of individual members critically important.

Changes in Interest Group Behavior and Impacts

How did the changes discussed in the previous section affect interest-group behavior?

Interest groups lobbying for additional federal spending for their programs were clearly placed on the defensive, particularly by the president's artful use of the reconciliation process. As mentioned, the "front-ending" of the reconciliation process forced Congress to examine the budget as a whole and prevented the disaggregation of spending into specific programs into which distributive politics could intervene. As one observer noted:

> The steamroller has leveled a wide path. This year, many hundreds of lobbying groups that had built strong relationships over the years with authorizing and appropriations committee members and aides have found themselves not so much without a sympathetic ear as without a way to leverage that sympathy to get more money.[26]

Congressional Quarterly described the results:

> The engine of Reagan's budget cutting victory last year was the so-called Gramm-Latta reconciliation measure which packaged savings in a single test of budgetary solidarity . . . without it, interest groups would have isolated votes on their programs on which they focus their lobbying and measure lawmakers' friendship. "Last year, whenever members were forced to look at the specific programs, we could win," said a House aide supportive of social programs.[27]

On the other hand, interest groups opposed to federal spending increases were given a great boost. Many business-oriented groups that oppose high government spending in general but do not focus on individual programs found that the new congressional budget decision-making structure had become much more amenable to their views. In fact, business organizations were able to maintain a remarkably high consensus in favor of the spending cuts contained in the reconciliation bill.

---

26. Linda E. Demkovich, "It's a Whole New Budget Ball Game, But Lobbyists are Playing by Old Rules," *National Journal*, October 10, 1981, pp. 1, 806.

27. *Congressional Quarterly*, February 20, 1982, p. 305.

On the revenue side, the 1981 tax cut provided a forum for traditional interest-group behavior, with various groups attempting to add provisions favorable to them. The experience in 1982 was different, however. Faced with the necessity for a tax increase but unwilling to impose general increases on individuals or business, Congress searched for "revenue enhancements" in the form of a series of increases affecting specific interests. Thus, groups with tax-reduction interests were placed somewhat in the same situation as the "spending" interest groups had been the previous year. They could not play the distributive tax game, which is playable when tax cuts are possible; instead they were forced to compete against each other to avoid tax increases. As one business lobbyist noted, "Various organizations that were formerly opposed to any tax increase are getting into the mode of 'Don't tax me, tax thee.' "[28]

Faced with this new set of circumstances, interest groups modified their behavior in a variety of ways. To obtain information on these changes, we interviewed twenty-five Washington, D.C.–based interest groups that are primarily spending groups rather than tax reduction or process-oriented groups. These groups are involved in health and social services/income support, education, and the human services field in general, and their memberships are composed of clients as well as private providers, relevant professionals, and state and local government.[29] We focused on human-services-oriented groups precisely because these organizations appear—from their own testimony and from articles in the press—to have been most affected by the changes detailed in the previous section. There is no presumption that findings for these groups necessarily hold for groups in other areas. It must be emphasized, too, that the groups interviewed in no way constitute a representative sample of all human services interest groups. Resource and time constraints precluded any attempt to interview interest groups in sufficient numbers for a reasonable sampling error. Neither was this sample drawn in a "scientifically systematic" fashion. However, we hope that the answers to our open-ended questions,

28. *Congressional Quarterly Weekly Report*, June 5, 1982, pp. 1, 328.

29. Interest groups interviewed include: AFL-CIO; American Association of Retired Persons; American Association of School Administrators; American Federation of Teachers; American Health Care Association; American Library Association; American Personnel and Guidance Association; American Psychiatric Association; American Public Health Association; American Public Welfare Association; Children's Defense Fund; Children's Welfare League; Coalition for Health Funding; Council for Exceptional Children; Day Care Council of America; League of Women Voters; National Association of Private Psychiatric Hospitals; National Association of Social Workers; National Conference of State Legislators; National Education Association; National Mental Health Association; National PTA; U.S. Conference of Mayors; U.S. National League of Cities.

which are detailed over the next several pages, will provide insights into how such advocacy groups have responded to their changing environment.

Policy Objectives

From the mid-1960s until the beginning of the Reagan administration, interest groups advocating a greater federal program and/or fiscal presence in the social services/income support, health, and education areas frequently were successful in promoting their policy objectives. However, the speed of the Reagan push to cut domestic spending, enhanced by a perceived voter mandate to do so, put these interest groups on the defensive. Instead of budget debates that centered on which programs would be slated for how much growth, Reagan's budget shifted the discussions to which programs would be cut more. This recasting of the budget debate forced affected interest groups to transfer their emphasis from arguing for more money to lobbying to prevent their programs from falling under the budget ax. Nearly all the groups interviewed asserted that their policy goals had been altered this way, whether they were client-, professional-, or provider-oriented. Typical comments included:

> Our policy objectives have moved from initiatives such as Title XX and Welfare Reform more to preventing cuts. Our objectives reflect political reality—growth in domestic [welfare] spending no longer will occur. Now our focus is on simplifying programs in a positive sense and preventing further cuts in a negative sense. (American Public Welfare Association)
>
> Under Carter we hoped to pay more attention to the quality aspect of education of the handicapped and to expand gifted and talented programs. Under Reagan, we are just trying to maintain programs at current levels of funding as opposed to trying to improve quality. (Council For Exceptional Children)
>
> Essentially prior to the Reagan Administration, we were attempting to improve a variety of areas. . . . Now we are trying to hold on to what we have. (AFL-CIO)

Lobbying Strategies: Federal Level

Just as changing public sentiment toward a growing public sector and huge deficits caused interest groups to alter their policy objectives, recent changes in congressional procedures and power relationships have compelled these groups to modify their lobbying tactics in several ways. First, the Congressional Budget Act process as refined in 1980 and again in 1981 diluted the power of authorizing and appropriation committees and subcommittees— the traditional points of access for interest groups. The greatly expanded power of the Budget Committees resulting from these changes meant that interest groups had to deal with yet another series of actors to protect and further their objectives. Most of the respondents noted that they had to spend significantly more time with the Budget Committees.

> The ability to submit one budget and make reconciliation took a lot of power from the authorizing committees. . . . Now I have to go to all the people on the Budget Committees. (National PTA)
>
> We are putting much more emphasis on both the Budget and the Appropriations Committees than we did before. That is because dollars are the game now; new ideas aren't. (American Personnel and Guidance Association)
>
> The job is much more difficult because of decentralization. . . . For us now, it is a constant process that takes in every member of Congress. (National Education Association)

Promoting positive sentiment within Congress toward specific programs is a much more difficult chore for interest groups than it was several years ago. Whereas previously an interest group could promote or defend its programs by arguing its merits, the new budget structure has transformed consideration of programs into much more of a fiscal context, a process Allan Schick has termed "the fiscalization of legislative debate."[30] One of our respondents observed that

> the whole concept of what authorizations are has changed a lot. Authorizations now are keyed to what can get through the budget process rather than what needs are. (American Federation of Teachers)

In addition, because reconciliation instructions specify spending targets in terms of functional categories, it is difficult for interest groups to get relevant committees to focus on individual programs to the extent they did only a few years ago. As a consequence, iron-triangle relations around a specific program have become much less relevant and lobbying on that program's behalf more problematic.

> You are now an insignificant piece in the totality when they go the reconciliation route through the budget process. It is hard to get them to focus on you. (American Psychiatric Association)
>
> The Omnibus Budget Reconciliation Act made lobbying for any individual program very difficult. (American Public Welfare Association)

The difficulty in focusing attention on individual programs in the course of the congressional budget process has resulted in changes in lobbying strategies: The congressional budget process is concerned with entire functional areas rather than individual programs; interest groups wishing to protect their programs must attempt to increase resources for the entire function. Clearly this is the case with programs that have been block-granted as well, since these programs no longer exist as separate entities. As a consequence,

---

30. Schick, *Reconciliation and the Congressional Budget Process*, p. 34.

nearly two-thirds of the groups we interviewed indicated that their organizations are much more likely to participate in coalitions with other groups than in the past. This tendency appears to have also resulted in part from the magnitude and scope of the cuts proposed. Defensive coalitions may be a natural response to threats.

> Twelve years ago there were lots of ad hoc coalitions and then the number receded. Reagan mobilized them. . . . What binds these groups together are Reagan's cuts and block grants. (National Association of Social Workers)
> There are more and broader coalitions driven together by the common bond of the need to fight cuts and block cuts. (Children's Defense Fund)
> The block grant has changed the way we lobby to some extent. It has made working with other education associations and groups more important because we all share a stake. (American Library Association)

It is notable also that the push for coalition building cuts across provider, client, and professional groups, prompting alliances among them.

Finally, many of the interest groups in our sample have become more reliant on mobilizing grass-roots support to fend off proposed budget cuts and block grants. This phenomenon appears to have two causes. First, to overcome the magnitude of the proposed cuts, groups have responded by increasing efforts to educate their own memberships and to mobilize public support against these proposals. Thus many interest groups have attempted to engage their memberships in letter-writing campaigns aimed at specific members of Congress. The hope was that as legislators have become more independent politicians and, consequently, more sensitive to constituent interests, this tactic might generate support in opposition to the cuts. Second, the budget process now results in a single floor vote on the reconciliation bill that contains almost the entire budget in one document. Consequently, to influence the decision on the budget, votes not just from key committee chairpersons but from all members of Congress have to be sought. This requires a grassroots campaign.

> We have tried to educate and activate our own grass roots membership. . . . through accelerating the development of the congressional contact team operation. We have three contact people in each congressional district. (National Education Association)
> Prior to 1980, the national office didn't spend much time with grass root activity. Now, there's not much the national office could do without the grass roots. We spend a lot of time now trying to educate and involve grass roots to bring pressure on Congress. (National PTA)
> We are attempting to sensitize our people to become better fighters. We have initiated a political education and training program. (American Personnel and Guidance Association)

Lobbying Strategies: State Level

Some of the interest groups we interviewed indicated that federal budget cuts and the implementation of the block grants have meant that, compared with the past, more of the important decisions about their programs are being made at the state than at the federal level. Other groups, however, still see the federal government as the level whose decisions most affect their interests. Among these latter are some groups in the social welfare area who feel that the block grants have dealt mostly with minor programs and the amount of actual decentralization has been minuscule. Thus, the American Association of School Administrators responded:

> We originally expected more of the important decisions to be moved to the state level. But we honestly haven't noticed it. Our organization hasn't focused more on the state level. Most of our objectives are still national: retain the Department of Education, oppose the school prayer amendment, oppose the tuition tax credit, provide adequate funding for a broad range of education programs.

The National Education Association representative also observed that "The education block grant hasn't devolved decisions to the states as much as the administration says."

Nonetheless, several groups noted that more of the action is now at the state level. In a few cases, groups have simply changed their objectives, acknowledging that they cannot affect a decentralized process from Washington, D.C. One lobbyist observed:

> We have shifted away from an interest in service delivery. We used to be interested, but the block grant killed that. There is no way you can track that from the federal level. (American Psychiatric Association)

The education block grant, in particular, has caused problems for some organizations because the critical allocation decisions are decentralized to the *local* rather than the state level. Thus the American Federation of Teachers observed:

> Teacher organizations have always concentrated on the state level and we are used to working there. But the education block grants are hard to affect at the state level. Decisions are made at the local level, but the amounts are so small that lobbying is not useful there.

Despite these problems, several groups stated that they were making efforts to build up their state lobbying capacity. The National Mental Health Association, for example, created a new position with the responsibility of working with the state divisions on public policy issues, including preparing issue newsletters, and technical assistance reports and providing assistance on how to lobby. Other groups also indicated that they had increased their mobilization efforts at the state level:

> We are much more active on the state level. During the fall of 1981 and spring of 1982, we worked hard with our local chapters to form Human Services Coalitions. (National Association of Social Workers)

The state chapters have become more active. There has been a tendency in the last several years for state associations to hire the partial services of a lobbyist; recent developments have accelerated this trend. (American Library Association)

We have tried to get our state federations more involved—trying to educate them more on block grants. (AFL-CIO)

To be effective at the state level, interest groups located in Washington, D.C., must have a physical presence in the state capitals. The critical questions, therefore, are whether these advocacy groups have state and/or local affiliates and whether such affiliates are professionally staffed. Nearly all the groups we interviewed had state chapters and, in some cases, local affiliates or chapters in most or all of the states. Exceptions were the Children's Defense Fund, which has only two state counterparts, and the Children's Welfare League, which has affiliates in twenty-five states.

The groups vary widely, however, in their staff capacity to lobby at the state level. Many have paid staff in only a few states and most do not have full-time lobbyists. At one extreme are groups like the National Education Association and the AFL-CIO, which are essentially organized in all states. Somewhat more common are groups like the League of Women Voters, which has paid staff in twenty-five states but very few paid lobbyists, and more typical still are organizations like the Council for Exceptional Children, which, although it has chapters in all fifty states, has paid staff in only ten and a paid lobbyist only in California.

Interview data from the national and state levels do in fact suggest that advocacy groups generally have become more active in state capitals than they once were, and that this increased activity was initially a result of federal budget cuts and the new block grants. With affected interest groups being forced to deal more with state officials in block-grant areas, many groups in the states developed formal or informal coalitions to handle procedural matters dealing with block-grant implementation. Human service coalitions composed of a wide variety of groups have sprung up in more than half the states. In most cases the first activity of these coalitions was directed toward guaranteeing that publicized public hearings would take place, that civil rights requirements would be followed, and that coalition membership would be represented in state advisory committees.

In large part to ensure that the coalitions would be maintained, the meting out of funding reductions was approached in a pro rata fashion. This strategy was largely successful, in part because state officials initially were reluctant to set service priorities, which would have created the impression among recipients that the state was responsible for their funding cuts. Rather, pro rata cuts were adopted so that it was clear that the initial dollar decreases were solely due to federal actions. As the states begin setting priorities among the blocked programs, it is likely that interest-group coalitions will experience dissension among their members, possibly causing the coalitions to dissolve. Thus the American Personnel and Guidance Association observed:

> At the national level, coalitions are fine: the goal is simply more money for the block grant. At the state and local levels where the block grant funds are handed out, there is lots of competition. At the local level, we will be competing against well-entrenched education groups such as vocational education, the handicapped, Title I.

Interest-Group Resources

This section has so far discussed the response of interest groups to changes in their environment. We now turn to the impact these changes have had on the viability of interest groups.

The earlier-mentioned reduction in federal funds for research, training, and technical assistance obviously caused problems for some groups, with severe repercussions for others. In the latter category, for example, was the National League of Cities, which received $3.6 million in federal funds out of a total 1981 budget of $7.2 million. By 1983 a spokesman reported that the League was receiving almost no federal funds and that the number of people on staff had dropped from 120 to approximately 50. Other major state and local government groups had essentially the same experience. For example, the U.S. Conference of Mayors spent $2.6 million from federal grants and contracts in 1981 and only $915,000 in 1983, reflecting a dramatic decline in federal funding. The conference's staff fell from 110 to 42 during that same period. In addition, the National Conference of State Legislators suffered a 33.8 percent drop in federal grants and contracts and a staff reduction from 140 to 100 between FY 1981 and FY 1983.

However, many of the human resource groups we interviewed were not directly affected by cutbacks in federal funds. Only three organizations in our sample other than state and local public interest groups reported any significant reduction in federal support, primarily because federal funds were never a significant proportion of their total budgets. The most striking case was that of the Day Care Council of America, which, according to its spokesperson, had received 70 to 80 percent of its revenues from federal funds. These funds declined rapidly during the Reagan administration and the organization collapsed, voting to go out of business. The Children's Welfare League, half of whose budget consisted of federal funds, received no federal funds in 1983, and despite raising its dues, cut the size of its Washington, D.C., staff in half. The American Public Health Association also was forced to reduce its staff, owing to lost federal contracts, but the association actually increased its government relations personnel from one to three people and indicated that it had become much more active politically.

Our general finding, that most human resource groups are not dependent to any great degree on federal funds, is consistent with the conclusion reached in a 1981 *National Journal* survey, which found that

> the groups that rely the most on federal funds—to operate programs, collect and evaluate data and help their constituents comply with federal laws—are not social action organizations but ones that represent the 50 states and the local governments. Half or more of their budgets, they say, come from federal grants and contracts. . . . Many social action groups, by contrast, get little or no federal money; few get as much as half of their income from Washington.[31]

Interest-group resources, particularly for professional associations, might also be affected by reductions in federal support for programs that the group members administer. Layoffs and attrition resulting from these program cuts might in turn affect the membership of or dues paid to these groups. However, while a few of the groups we interviewed reported membership declines, only in one case was this attributed directly to federal cuts; in most cases the recession or idiosyncratic reasons were cited. In a few cases membership *increases* were reported as a result of growing opposition to the president's programs.

Discussion and Analysis

In the beginning of this chapter we discussed the importance of interest groups in terms of their effect on public outcomes and distribution, the level of government spending, and the amount of political conflict. This section examines the implications of changes in interest-group behavior during the Reagan administration in each of these areas.

Interest-Group Politics: Is America More Governable?

Do the events of the Reagan era suggest that an important and permanent change has occurred in the role that interest groups play in American politics—in other words, do such groups now play a diminished part in determining political outcomes? Has there been a reduction in the demands that interest

---

31. *National Journal*, August 1, 1981, p. 1374. However, a more recent study by the *National Journal* suggests that those client advocacy groups that relied heavily on federal grants and contracts may have suffered disproportionate losses in federal funds. *National Journal*, August 6, 1983, p. 1632.

groups can effectively place on political decision makers and a consequent increase in the governability of the American political system?

The question is complex, for interest groups interact with the political system through a specific set of structures that affect their behavior and influence. Clearly, the changes in the framework of congressional decision making with respect to spending decreased the ability of interest groups to affect spending outcomes. Distributive politics, the natural arena for group politics, became redistributive politics. However, this hardly suggests an across-the-board demise of interest-group politics; interest groups continued to play their traditional roles in other policy arenas, such as in the 1981 tax act that accompanied the major spending reductions.

More important is how long one can expect redistributive politics to prevail. The political environment that sustained redistributive politics required more than simply a change in the structure of congressional budgetary decision making. Such changes, after all, do not occur in a political vacuum. While the process is clearly advantageous to conservative interests and disadvantageous to liberal spending interests, it is also likely that the process succeeded primarily because President Reagan was able to call on an effective majority in Congress in favor of reducing spending at the expense of domestic programs. This does not mean that the structural changes were irrelevant or unimportant in bringing about the reductions; indeed, they provided the means for the president to transform his political support in Congress into effective public policy. Had Reagan been forced to rely instead on the more traditional, disaggregated budget process, it is probable that his success would have been much less impressive.

Nevertheless, experience since 1981 supports the contention that the viability of the front-ended reconciliation process is tied strongly to policy preferences. With the decline in the president's public support and the change in the House as a result of the 1982 midterm elections, congressional support for this self-imposed discipline has flagged. In addition, there are strong reasons for believing that the structural changes will be weakened as a result of internal congressional dynamics. The front-ended reconciliation process lodges enormous decision-making power in the hands of the two Budget Committees at the expense of the authorizing, appropriating, and revenue-raising committees. It is unlikely that such a disproportionate internal sharing of legislative opportunities can sustain itself.

Finally, as noted early in this paper, the apparent reduction in the importance of interest groups during the Reagan years is more likely a shift in the relative influence of various groups: Activist spending-oriented groups are losing; more conservative groups, frequently opposed to more government activity, are winning. It is not surprising that in the Reagan administration, conservative and business groups have more effective access to decision makers than they did in the Carter administration and that liberal and labor groups have relatively less. However, there is no reason to believe that this represents any fundamental change in the structure of influence within the American political system. Moreover, events during the Reagan era may actually be increasing the importance of group activity: many groups are enlarging their government relations and lobbying staffs, as well as their grassroots activity. Our evidence also suggests that for state government the level of politicization and political conflict is increasing and may rise dramatically as interest groups establish a more organized and professionally staffed presence at the state level. Thus, there appears scant evidence for the supposition that interest groups are being tamed and that America is becoming more governable.

Do Interest Groups Mean More Government Spending?

The extent to which interest groups have contributed to escalating government spending is hotly debated. A variety of explanations have been proposed for the growth of public spending, including changing public opinion (the public may prefer higher spending levels), the dynamics of economic development (Wagner's Law), the ratchet effect of crisis-induced tax increases (the Peacock-Wiseman hypothesis), and the growth-oriented objectives of bureaucratic behavior.[32]

Furthermore, on its own merits, the theory that interest-group activity causes growth in public expenditures is less than convincing. Jack Walker examined the origins of more than 550 Washington, D.C.-based interest groups, using data from questionnaires he had sent them. He found that

> more than half of the 46 groups representing the elderly in my study were formed after 1965, the year of the great legislation breakthroughs of Medicare and the Older Americans Act. Many other groups in fields like education, mass transportation, and environmental protection also sprang up *after* the passage of dramatic new legislation that established the major outlines of public policy in their areas. In all of these cases, the formation of new groups was one of the *consequences* of major new legislation, not one of the *causes* of its passage.[33] [Emphasis added.]

As Cynthia Cotes Colella and David R. Beam observe:

---

32. For a discussion of the various theories, see U.S. Advisory Commission on Intergovernmental Relations, *The Federal Role in the Federal System: The Dynamics of Growth*, Report A-78 (Washington, D.C.: Advisory Commission on Intergovernmental Relations, August 1981), chapter 5.

33. Walker, "Interest Groups in America," p. 403.

> The importance of such [interest] groups very often lies not in their greatly exaggerated abilities to create and successfully advocate new policies but rather in the ability of policies to sustain new interest groups. Once established, a group will inevitably work to sustain the policy that gave it life.[34]

If Walker and Colella and Beam are correct, then the theory relating interest groups to public spending must be revised: Interest group activity does not cause high levels of public spending; rather, it serves to sustain existing levels, perhaps leading to increases at the margins and certainly impeding efforts to reduce spending.

It is widely thought that interest groups achieve these objectives through operation of the earlier-mentioned informal subgovernment or iron triangles, consisting of interest groups, administrative agencies, and congressional sub-committees.[35] Timothy Clark, writing in the *National Journal*, observes:

> It has become a truism in the past decade that any change in government programs is hard to achieve because of the combined opposition of middle level bureaucrats, members of highly specialized congressional panels and lobbyists for the beneficiaries of government programs. The triangles also have been called subgovernments, a word suggesting the autonomy they often attain over programs they consider their own. There are hundreds of them in Washington, often invisible to the general public but acting quietly and constantly to preserve their interests.[36]

How have these so-called iron triangles been affected by events during the Reagan administration, and is the effect likely to be permanent and to lead to lowered government spending in the long term?

---

34. Cynthia Cates Colella and David R. Beam, "The Political Dynamics of Intergovernmental Policymaking," in Jerome J. Hanus, ed., *The Nationalization of State Government* (Lexington, Mass.: D. C. Heath, 1981), p. 139.

35. The iron triangle concept has been criticized as both simplistic and outmoded. Hugh Heclo argues that Washington, D.C., politics is characterized not by iron triangles, but by "issue networks," consisting of individuals who interact intermittently with each other around a specific issue. It is these individuals' interest in and commitment to the issue rather than their institutional position that determines their participation. "Iron triangles and subgovernments suggest a stable set of participants coalesced to control fairly narrow public programs that are in the direct economic interest of each party to the alliance. Issue networks are almost the reverse image in each respect. Participants move in and out of the networks constantly. Rather than groups united in dominance over a program, no one, so far as one can tell, is in control of the policies and issues. Any direct material interest is often secondary to intellectual or emotional commitment . . . the true experts in the network are those who are issue skilled (that is, well-informed about the ins and outs of a particular policy debate) regardless of formal professional training. More than mere technical experts, network people are policy activists who know each other through the issues." Hugh Heclo, "Issue Networks and the Executive Establishment," in Anthony King, ed., *The New American Political System* (Washington, D.C.: American Enterprise Institute, 1978), pp. 102–103.

36. Timothy B. Clark, "The President Takes on the 'Iron Triangles,'" *National Journal*, March 28, 1981, p. 516.

Our review of recent developments suggests that the role of interest groups in affecting budgetary outcomes *has* diminished during the Reagan administration. The evidence we have presented suggests that interest groups were put on the defensive and in a situation where their traditional resort to iron-triangle protective devices was unavailable. The front-ending of the reconciliation process effectively bypassed the normal forms for iron-triangle activity—the authorization and appropriations subcommittees—thus largely preventing traditional distributive budgeting, with its emphasis on logrolling. Indeed, individual groups were forced to enter into broad coalitions of interests, with the coalitions contending against one another—a characteristic of redistributive politics.[37]

The critical question is whether the front-ending of the reconciliation process will remain the structure under which resources are effectively allocated among the various governmental functions—which brings us back to the previous discussion in this paper. Again, the answer must be that the structure has been far less effective since the 1982 midterm elections, which dissolved a sustainable majority, and that it is unlikely to work at all with a majority in favor of expanded spending.

The creation of block grants may have had a more permanent structural impact on federal budgetary expansion. The history of block grants suggests that they make distributive politics more difficult and result in lower funding levels than would have been the case in the aggregate for the prior unblocked programs. However, experience also suggests that block grants are subject to recategorization at the federal level as individual groups reassert their claims for special set-asides. It is too early to determine whether the Reagan block grants will follow this pattern.

The difficulties encountered by human-resource interest groups at the federal level during the Reagan era have, as we have seen, caused many of them to intensify their efforts at the state level. This suggests that, after an initial period of organization, the hypothesized impact of interest groups on spending levels and governance should begin to be felt at state levels—if, indeed, the original hypotheses are true.

---

37. Redistributive politics does not, of course, *necessarily* imply budget constraint; if the main issue is the total size of the budget and is, in effect, a clash between low tax interests and spending interests, it is not inevitable that the former will emerge triumphant. However, once a budget constraint is agreed on, the allocation among budget priorities within that constraint is a zero-sum game, provided the structure does not permit relaxation of the constraint.

Policy Outcomes: Who Wins and Who Loses?

There has been almost no systematic research into the question of which groups are more influential at the state level and which at the federal level. However, there is a prevailing scholarly opinion on this topic, derived primarily from the logic of American electoral politics. It is that urban interests, low-income groups, blacks, ethnic groups, and labor unions, which are centered in the large, urban, industrialized states and whose support is crucial in presidential elections, have been cited as frequently concentrating their lobbying efforts at the national level.[38] Many business-interest groups, on the other hand, are more likely to turn to the state capitals to press their concerns.[39]

E.E. Schattschneider carries the argument a step further by contending that the *scope* of conflict—the number and kind of groups involved in any given conflict—varies among the local, state, and federal levels of the political system, therefore affecting their respective policy output:

> One way to restrict the scope of conflict is to *localize* it, while one way to expand it is to nationalize it. . . . It follows that debates about federalism, local self-government, centralization, and decentralization are actually controversies about the scale of conflict. . . . The nationalization of politics inevitably breaks up old local power monopolies and old sectional power complexes.[40]

Grant McConnell elaborates on this thesis by arguing that the lower the level of political system, the more closed it is likely to be to participation by nonprivileged groups:

> In legislatures, for example, logrolling is the product of the great complexities of established and anticipated personal obligations. The resulting web is woven from admirable human traits— friendship and gratitude—but rationality and concern for those not immediately involved are rare and slender threads in it.[41]

In McConnell's view, the closed nature of state and local political systems accounts for why some groups are more active and influential at the federal level.

> One of the most serious problems of a system of decentralized political units in a liberal society is the consequent uneven sharing in power. Some segments of the population are excluded from effective participation in the benefits of the political process because, as Madison

---

38. Thomas Dye, *Politics in States and Communities* (Englewood Cliffs, N.J.: Prentice-Hall, 1969), pp. 62–63.
39. Michael D. Reagan, *The New Federalism* (New York: Oxford University Press, 1972), p. 74.
40. E.E. Schattschneider, *The Semi-Sovereign People* (New York: Holt, Rinehart & Winston, 1960), pp. 10–11.
41. Grant McConnell, *Private Power and American Democracy* (New York: Alfred A. Knopf, 1967), p. 194.

observed, small units have less diversity than large units; they thus allow greater opportunities for the oppression of those who are already weak. This is not merely a matter of extreme action by small majorities, as Madison seemed to suggest, for power often derives from factors other than sheer numbers. The force of whatever element in the unit is powerful is accentuated to the degree that the unit is small and homogeneous, whether its power is founded on numbers, wealth, or even violence. . . . Thus farm migrant workers, Negroes, and the urban poor have not been included in the system of "pluralist" representation so celebrated in recent years. . . . Such protection as they have had has come from the centralized features of the political order—parties, the national government, and the Presidency.[42]

Winners and losers thus are likely to differ—and, according to Schattschneider and McConnell, differ in systematic ways—at the federal, state, and local levels.

Political science analysis therefore suggests that a decentralization of decision-making authority to the states such as President Reagan has advocated and attempted to pursue will result in a change in winners and losers, even without changes in available funding. The assumption generally held is that overall the losers will be groups such as minorities, the poor, urban interests, and labor organizations. Studies of the consolidation of federal categorical programs into block grants indicate that state politics impose a "spreading effect" on the intrastate distribution of funds, which works to the disadvantage of groups that have been the focus of federal categorical programs. In a review of the literature on the effect of block grants, Harold Wolman concluded:

Block grants result in a spreading of resources both geographically and with respect to recipient groups. They thus tend to move resources from . . . central cities . . . to suburban and small town areas. They also tend to diminish the focusing of categorical programs on low-income and minority groups by distributing benefits more widely.[43]

Decentralization of decision-making authority to the states through block grants and other devices may thus bring about an important change in the relative ability of groups to affect public policy. Although most groups in our survey indicated that the actual amount of decentralization has so far been small, some in the human resource area viewed the trend with some trepidation.

We are probably much better off when issues are decided at the national level rather than at the state level. (American Psychiatric Association)

The AFL-CIO is likely to be more effective at the federal level than at the state level. This is partly because state legislatures aren't very sophisticated, but it's partly a political problem as well. We just aren't as politically strong in a lot of states. (AFL-CIO)

---

42. Ibid., pp. 348–349.
43. Harold Wolman, "The Effect of Block Grants," Working Paper 3083–1 (Washington, D.C.: The Urban Institute, September 1981), p. 45.

On the other hand, groups whose primary focus has always been at the state and local levels view decentralization with greater equanimity. The National Education Association, for example, observed:

> It's hard to say whether we fare better at the federal level or the state level. Because of our structure, we're not disadvantaged by going to the state level. We know we have to play a role in each.

One way to assess the probable impact of decentralization on winners and losers is to attempt to examine the relative strength of interest groups in the various states. Unfortunately, there are virtually no systematic studies of how interest-group influence varies by state.[44] John C. Wahlke, Heinz Eulau, William Buchanan, and LeRoy Ferguson sent questionnaires to state legislators in four states asking them to name the most powerful groups in state politics. They found that business interests were mentioned most, followed by education, then labor.[45] Wayne Francis later repeated the procedure for all fifty states and found that the most frequently mentioned groups were the AFL-CIO, state teachers' associations, manufacturing associations, state farm bureaus, truckers, and utilities, but that responses varied substantially from state to state.[46] Sarah Morehouse reviewed the literature on the politics of individual states and found that business was overwhelmingly considered the dominant group in state politics, followed by labor, farm, and education groups.[47]

The Wahlke et al. and Francis studies suffer from obvious difficulties, since they represent only *perceptions*, rather than direct measures, of political influence. Moreover, the studies are faulty even as rankings of *perceived* influence, because the survey instruments used did not specify scope of influence, that is, the policy area to which influence is directed. (Influence is likely to differ among interest groups from one policy area to another; the most influential group in state tax policy will most likely not be the most influential in highway or education policy.) Such drawbacks are not unexpected, given the difficulty of developing valid and reliable operational measures for a concept that is in itself less than clear.

---

44. The only systematic effort to address this question, albeit only with respect to business interests, is made by Lester M. Salamon and John J. Siegfried, "Economic Power and Political Influence: The Impact of Industry Structure on Public Power," *American Political Science Review*, vol. 71 (1977), pp. 1026–1043.

45. John C. Wahlke, Heinz Eulau, William Buchanan, and LeRoy Ferguson, *The Legislative System* (New York: John Wiley & Sons, 1962), pp. 313–315.

46. Wayne L. Francis, *Legislative Issues in the Fifty States: A Comparative Analysis* (Chicago: Rand McNally, 1967), pp. 41–42.

47. Sarah Morehouse, *State Politics, Parties, and Policies* (New York: Holt, Rinehart & Winston, 1981), pp. 107–113.

An alternative approach to assessing decentralization's impact is to drop any pretext of measuring the relative strength of interest groups and to focus directly on how well specific interests are served by public policy. (It is likely that interest-group activity is related to how well interests fare in a state, but many other factors probably operate as well.) Such an effort might provide an indication of which interests would likely dominate (or be dominated) in different states if policy decisions now made at the federal level were decentralized to the states, a situation implying a much more extensive decentralization than has, in fact, occurred to date. However, such a decentralization clearly is a major long-range objective of President Reagan, who has been quoted as saying:

> I have a dream of my own. I think block grants are only the intermediate step. I dream of the day when the federal government can substitute for [block grants] the turning back to local and state governments of the tax sources we ourselves have preempted at the federal level so that you would have those tax sources.[48]

In fact, accurate predictions of winners and losers under a thoroughgoing decentralization would occur only if such a decentralization were not also to result in an altered structure of decision making. If, for example, the decentralization were to call forth much greater participation in state politics by some interests than by others, the existing set of winners and losers in a state might be substantially changed. Some modification in the structure of state decision making would indeed be likely. However, the exact nature of such changes cannot be predicted; analysis of the existing structure of influence in the states is the best starting point for any analysis of the distributive impacts of decentralization.

Existing research on this subject can take us part of the way. The primary object of this research, conducted during the late 1960s and early 1970s, was to examine the extent to which "political" variables as opposed to "socioeconomic" variables affect state policy outcomes. During the course of this research, work by Dawson and Robinson, Dye, Sharkansky, Hofferbert, and others established a strong link between per capita income and social-welfare policy outputs.[49] Dye, for example, found simple correlation co-efficients of .74 between state per capita income and average monthly state Aid to Families

---

48. Quoted in Barfield, *Rethinking Federalism*, p. 62.

49. See, for example, Richard E. Dawson and James A. Robinson, "Inter-party Competition, Economic Variables, and Welfare Policies in the American States," in *Journal of Politics*, XXIII (1967); Thomas R. Dye, *Politics, Economics and Public Policy: Policy Outcomes in the American States* (Chicago: Rand McNally, 1966); and Ira Sharkansky and Richard Hofferbert, "Dimensions of State Politics, Economics and Public Policy," American Political Science Review LXIII (1969). For a review of this literature, see Thomas R. Dye, *Understanding Public Policy* (Englewood Cliffs, N.J.: 1975), chapter 12.

of Dependent Children (AFDC) payments and .80 between income and average weekly unemployment payments.[50] Sharkansky and Hofferbert found a simple correlation of .69 and a partial correlation of .43 between state affluence and state welfare-education policy (both variables derived from factor analysis of a wide range of variables).[51] This work suggests that the interests of the poor are likely to be better served in states with high per capita income and less well served in states with low per capita income.

This work provides an excellent starting point. However, we wished to expand this type of analysis to identify a fuller range of interests and to examine how well these interests are served across states that differ in terms of percent minority population and percent poverty population, as well as in terms of per capita income. (Existing research focuses primarily on income, industrialization, and urbanization as state socioeconomic variables.) In addition, we wished to examine the strength of interests *within* states as well as how well interests are served by certain types of states relative to other states.

We undertook a preliminary exercise to examine the structure of influence by identifying various interests and evaluating them in terms of the extent to which the interests were served by favorable public policy.[52] The result is, in fact, an output measure of interest success rather than an input measure of interest-group influence. As an example, the interests of the poor were measured, at least partially, by AFDC benefit levels and by recent rates of change in these levels.

The interests with which we were concerned included the poor, the wealthy, business, labor, teachers, students, and large cities. *Interests*, as the term is used here, refer to the shared concerns of people or places rather than to policy sectors such as education, health, or social services.

We compiled two categories of interest-group influence in our analysis of the various states. The first category included *those states in which a particular interest is best served by public policy*. Thus, if our concern was the interest of poor people, we identified those states with the highest AFDC benefit levels (adjusted for cost-of-living differences) and examined recent rates of change in these levels.

The second category included *those states in which the interest was strongest relative to other interests in the state*. In general, this was done by

50. Dye, *Politics, Economics and Public Policy*, p. 125.
51. Sharkansky and Hofferbert, "Dimensions of State Politics," p. 875.
52. For the report of this preliminary research, see Harold Wolman and Fred Teitelbaum, "Interest Groups and Interests in the Reagan Era," CDP Discussion Paper (Washington, D.C.: The Urban Institute, November 1983).

comparing the policy output to state per capita income (or, as appropriate, average weekly earnings), using the latter figure as a proxy for all other interests in the state. Thus, an interest was deemed to be stronger (relative to other interests in the state) in state A as compared to state B, if the ratio of the policy output (e.g., AFDC benefit level) to per capita income were greater in state A than in state B. Another way of looking at this ratio is as an "effort score" measuring the extent to which a state provides a policy output relative to its capacity to do so. The policy output measures we used for the various interests are included in table 1.

Our findings, summarized in table 2, leave little doubt that it is better to be a poor person in a wealthy state that has relatively few poor people than in a poor state with many poor people. Indeed, the data broadly suggest that the interests of the poor, labor, pupils, and teachers are inadequately served in states with low per capita income and in states with a high percentage of poor people or minorities.[53]

TABLE 1

POLICY OUTPUT MEASURES USED FOR VARIOUS INTERESTS

Interest	Policy Output Measure
The Poor	1. Maximum AFDC benefits for family of four (adjusted for regional cost-of-living differences) 2. Percentage of poverty population receiving AFDC 3. Medicaid expenditure per recipient (adjusted for state-by-state cost-of-health-care differences) 4. Medicaid recipients as a percentage of poverty population 5. A "generosity index," consisting of an average rank-order score on measures 1–4 for each state
Labor	Maximum disability payments for total disability
Business	Business taxes as a percentage of business income
Teachers	Average teacher's salary, adjusted for regional cost-of-living differences
Pupils	State-local per-pupil revenue
Large Cities	State per capita general support to large cities as a percentage of state per capita general support to all municipalities

53. These characteristics tend to reinforce one another and to be concentrated in the southern United States. The correlation between 1980 state per capita income level and the percentage of a state's population in poverty in 1980 is $r = -.58$; the correlation between 1980 state per capita income and the percentage of a state's 1980 population that is minority is $r = .06$; the correlation between poverty population in 1980 and minority population in 1980 is $r = .58$.

This in itself is, of course, hardly unanticipated, since wealthier states have more resources with which to provide benefits. What is unexpected, however, is that, with the exception of teachers, the interests of these groups also are weak *relative to other groups within these states*—that is, states with low per capita income, high poverty, and high minority populations provide lower benefits *relative to their income* to the poor, labor, and students than other states do. By contrast, the interests of business are *best* served (and stronger relative to other groups) in these same states.

Given the above findings, it is no surprise that, in regional terms, the South was an unfavorable location for the interests of the poor, labor, and students, but that business there fared well. In the Northeast the interests of the poor, students, and large cities fared particularly well relative to other interests, while the interests of business (in terms of tax burden) were particularly poorly served. Labor's interests relative to business were strongest in the West.

It is possible that the pattern of how well interests are served and how strong they are relative to other interests might best be captured by grouping the states by ideology or political culture. Although we have no variable permitting us to test this hypothesis, it is likely that a grouping of the states by region is, in effect, a grouping by political culture. Indeed, simple inspection of the data suggests that, for example, if Maryland and Delaware are removed from the grouping of southern states and if Indiana, Missouri, Arizona, and Nevada—four states with conservative traditions—are added to the remaining southern states, a strong pattern emerges. For example, seventeen of these eighteen states (all but Oklahoma) ranked below the median for AFDC payments adjusted for cost-of-living differences; eleven of the eighteen ranked below the median for adjusted Medicaid payments; eleven of the eighteen for adjusted teacher salary (fourteen of the eighteen if unadjusted for cost-of-living differences); seventeen of the eighteen for state-local per pupil revenues; and fifteen of the eighteen for maximum disability payments.

It bears reemphasizing that it is uncertain that the patterns described in this study would persist under the radical decentralization of decision-making authority envisioned by President Reagan. Certainly the various interests would try to increase their influence through organizational efforts, campaign contributions, and other means, and some interests would be more successful than others. Nonetheless, the conclusions reached provide a suggestive starting point for analyzing the distributional impact across and within states of such a decentralization.

TABLE 2

CORRELATION (r) BETWEEN MEASURES OF INTERESTS AND STATE CHARACTERISTICS

Interest	State Per Capita Income, 1983	Percentage of State Population in Poverty, 1980[a]	Percentage Minority Population, 1980
Poor			
Adjusted AFDC payment, 1983	.58	− .68 (− .67)	− .44
Percentage of poverty population receiving AFDC, 1983	.48	− .39 (− .35)	.14
Adjusted Medicaid payments per recipient, 1982	− .04	− .21 (− .24)	− .34
Percentage of poverty population receiving Medicaid, 1982	.41	− .34 (− .29)	.01
AFDC effort score, 1983[b]	.22	− .55 (− .56)	− .52
Medicaid effort score, 1982[b]	− .15	− .14 (− .13)	− .30
Difference between tax rates for middle-income people and the poor, 1980	.22	− .20	− .09
Labor (business)[c]			
Maximum disability payment, 1983	.53	− .30 (− .25)	− .12
Disability effort score, 1983[d]	.44	− .25 (− .17)	− .09
Business			
Business taxes as a percentage of business income, 1979	.37	− .33	− .13
Teachers			
Adjusted average teacher's salary, 1983	.70	− .19 (.16)	.25
Teacher salary effort[e]	− .12	.11 (.23)	− .01
Pupils			
State-local per-pupil revenue, 1983	.76	− .50 (− .56)	− .23
Pupil effort score, 1983[f]	.35	− .39 (− .40)	− .40
Big Cities			
State general support to big cities: state general support to all municipalities, 1981	− .01 (1980)	.24	.64

NOTES: See next page.

Conclusion

Any effort to assess the impact on interest groups of events during the Reagan era must distinguish between immediate and longer-range effects. In the short run, the influence of spending-oriented special-interest groups has indeed been diminished, primarily as a result of political support for overall budget constraint and use of the revised congressional budget process to translate that support into budget reductions.

However, the decline in the influence of these groups is unlikely to herald a permanent diminution of their role in the political process. The decline is substantially the product of both a conservative administration and a Congress to which liberal human-resources-oriented groups have little access and influence. This situation is not surprising; nor is it likely to endure.

Indeed, the overall legacy of the Reagan administration may be an increase in interest-group activity. In response to changes in their established means of influencing policy, human-resources interest groups have done more coalition building, have attempted to mobilize their memberships through more grass-roots activity, and have expanded their presence at the state level. These responses point to a strengthening of interest groups over the long term, and possibly to increased political conflict at the state level.

While the overall role of interest groups is unlikely to be weakened, a continued decentralization of policymaking to the states does imply a different set of winners and losers. At least in the short run, many groups that are influential and effective at the federal level—particularly in the human resources area—would be at a disadvantage at the state level because they are not at present effectively organized there. Overall, a widespread decentralization would imply that certain interests—the poor and labor, especially— would be disadvantaged relative to other interests in low-income states and in states with a high percentage of poor people or minorities.

NOTES TO TABLE 2:

a. Figures in parentheses in this column represent the correlation between *1980* values of the row variables and the column variable.

b. AFDC and Medicaid effort scores are calculated by dividing state AFDC benefit levels and state Medicaid expenditures per recipient respectively by state per capita income.

c. Business interests can be interpreted as the inverse of labor interests on this measure.

d. Disability effort score is the state maximum disability payment divided by state average weekly earnings.

e. Teacher salary effort score is the state average teacher salary divided by state per capita income.

f. Pupil effort score is state-local revenue per pupil for each state divided by the state's per capita income.

COMMENTS   *Michael J. Malbin*

Governability, Iron Triangles, And Scarcity

The major conclusion I draw from Harold Wolman and Fred Teitelbaum's paper is one the authors chose not to stress, although they may well agree with it. It is that interest groups, far from being independent actors in the national policymaking process, change their objectives, shift their institutional focus, and modify their lobbying strategies in response to forces beyond their control. Some of these forces were produced by the state of the economy, some by a skillful president's ability to control the policy agenda, and some through self-consciously adopted changes in Congress and in other governmental institutions.

This observation affects my reaction to three other general points: governability, iron triangles, and the future.

On Governability

Wolman and Teitelbaum come to the carefully qualified conclusion that the Reagan administration's policy changes will not have much of an impact over the longer term in making the United States a more governable country. I agree: The United States is not *more* governable because of the Reagan administration's policies. But that begs a more basic question. Is the nation governable or not? I believe the United States has been governable under President Reagan, was governable under President Carter, and will remain governable under future presidents unless something radical happens to change the situation fundamentally. President Carter's complaints about stalemate do not make his claims about ungovernability accurate; they only serve to highlight his own problems of leadership.

The U.S. government has always made it easier to preserve the status quo than to bring about basic change. That this is so was the result of a deliberate decision by the framers of our Constitution about the form and ends of government, not an accidental blundering into ungovernability.[1]

President Reagan has shown that basic change remains possible under the present system. What this change demands, to offer an oversimplification, is determined presidential leadership that produces strong popular support. When President Reagan's popularity was high, he was able to shift the course of defense spending markedly, he cut taxes, and he reduced the growth rate for discretionary domestic spending. When his popular support became more equivocal, he had to compromise some of his original objectives, but even then, he preserved the basic thrust of his tax and defense policies. Interest groups have been forced to operate within the basic framework set by Ronald Reagan's ability to control the terms of political debate. The groups may be as active as ever but, as Wolman and Teitelbaum indicate, their activity must now be conducted in the name of less ambitious objectives than in the past.

On Iron Triangles

An important basis for the charge of ungovernability has been the so-called iron triangle thesis. Wolman and Teitelbaum maintain that the role of iron triangles is no different on distributive questions than it was before the Reagan administration. Perhaps not. But as with governability, I am not satisfied with so comparative a conclusion. The reason, as before, is that I question the utility of the iron triangle metaphor for the years before Reagan. Iron is an impermeable metal and triangles are closed figures. During the Carter administration Hugh Heclo wrote, accurately I believe, that the system was far too open and permeable to permit such a metaphor.[2]

The iron triangle thesis assumes a consistent, supportive relationship among interest groups, executive branch bureaus, and congressional subcommittees. There is no question that such relationships sometimes exist. But the relationship depends decisively on the political perceptions and interests of the chairpersons and members of the relevant subcommittees. These interests and perceptions, in turn, depend both on the members' opinions and on the political climate of the day in their districts.

1. See Alexander Hamilton, James Madison, and John Jay, *The Federalist*, Nos. 10 and 51, *passim*, any edition.

2. Hugh Heclo, "Issue Networks and the Executive Establishment," in Anthony King, ed., *The New American Political System* (Washington, D.C.: American Enterprise Institute, 1978), p. 102.

The triangle notion cannot begin to explain why automobile manufacturers lost to Ralph Nader when he was a lone wolf before Senator Warren Magnuson's Commerce Committee in the 1960s or why the industry continues to lose before Representative Henry A. Waxman's House Commerce Subcommittee on Health and the Environment today. How can a metaphoric triangle explain the different reception that large natural gas producers receive before Senator James A. McClure's Senate Committee on Energy and Natural Resources and Representative John D. Dingell's House Committee on Energy and Commerce?

What is more, the triangle thesis fails utterly to take account of the permeability of Congress. Perhaps the thesis once had some validity when some chairpersons controlled their committees and committees won without challenge on the floor. But neither of these conditions holds today. The sloppiness of congressional committee jurisdiction almost assures that contrary views on major issues will be aired somewhere and then brought to the floor. Interest groups are, to be sure, important, but the metaphor, I am afraid, obscures more than it reveals in explaining just how or why. Moreover, the main point it ignores—the independent role both of public opinion and of the opinions of political leaders—is precisely the one that is open to change through a president's power of persuasion.

On the Future

Finally, Wolman and Teitelbaum suggest that relations between the federal government and interest groups will return to their old ways once President Reagan leaves office. I am not so sure. The paper noted a number of changes in group behavior since January 1981. Almost all of the important ones have stemmed from the difference between operating in conditions of budget scarcity and operating in conditions of plenty. Scarcity plus congressional budget reform plus presidential leadership force groups to focus on budget totals by function. Scarcity also means intergroup conflict once the totals are set. And scarcity, to paraphrase Wolman and Teitelbaum's quotations from the AFL-CIO, means a shift away from promoting new ideas to defending old ones. Or, more accurately, it means a shift away from promoting new ideas whose implementation costs money.

Whether this situation will change after Reagan will depend on whether a new administration—even one that wants to spend more on domestic programs—will operate under conditions of scarcity. That in turn will depend substantially on whether the indexing of personal income tax rates ever goes into effect. Stuart Eizenstat, President Carter's chief White House staff advisor for domestic policy, has called tax indexing the most important of all of Reagan's 1981 policy changes.[3] I believe he was right. Before indexing, the phenomenon known as bracket creep meant that federal revenues grew faster than the rate of inflation. This invisible tax increase produced enough new revenues each year to pay for entitlement cost-of-living adjustments (COLAs) with something left over. But indexing tax rates means, depending on the real rate of economic growth, that visible tax increases may have to be passed just to finance COLAs. If indexing is repealed before the public feels its benefit, then the structural situation may return to the status quo that existed before Reagan. But once indexing is in effect, the change will not be easy to reverse. The effects, I expect, will be felt in tax bills as well as spending bills, with future tax politics resembling more the redistributive politics of 1982 than the distributive politics of 1981. All groups—whether businesses looking for tax breaks or human services groups that want to spend more money—will be forced to compete with each other. Taxes may increase in such an environment to support governmental growth. But they will not be increased silently so long as indexing remains on the books. Indexing may not prevent distributive logrolling, but it will change logrolling's political costs for each member of Congress.

---

3. Remarks before a January 7, 1982 American Enterprise Institute conference, "President and Congress: Assessing Reagan's First Year."

Assessing The Strength Of Interest Groups

The primary objective of Harold Wolman and Fred Teitelbaum's study was to determine how policies and actions of the Reagan administration affected interest groups in the human resources area, but it also provides a valuable window on the character and depth of what has been called the "Reagan Revolution."

The number of interest groups has grown rapidly over the past two decades, with many of these groups concentrating on one issue or a set of issues. Well before President Reagan took office, a number of analysts and policymakers complained that these developments were making policymaking much more difficult. The Reagan administration not only shared this concern, it exhibited considerable eagerness to do something about it. The administration seemed especially determined to restrain the number and influence of liberal, human-resources-oriented groups who were believed partly responsible for the rapid growth in the federal government's social program expenditures.

Four types of administration actions were either aimed directly at reducing the influence of these groups or achieved this effect secondarily. They were (1) advocacy of greater decentralization, mainly through increased use of block grants, (2) reduced federal grants and contracts that helped support human-resources-oriented interest groups, (3) reduced funding for many human resource programs, and (4) drastic changes in the budget decision-making process in Congress. Wolman and Teitelbaum report that although some of these groups were adversely affected by the administration's actions, and a few of these folded with the elimination or reduction of federal grants and contracts, most were not measurably hurt and some were even strengthened by these actions.

These valuable, if undramatic, findings confirm a widely held belief that interest groups are flexible and can adapt quickly to changes in the political arena. According to Wolman and Teitelbaum, at least four major changes occurred as a result of the administration's actions that appear likely to strengthen the human-resources-oriented interest groups. The changes are the following:

- The groups reduced somewhat their reliance on federal money to support their activities.

- They increased their efforts to mobilize their clients or constituencies to participate in influencing policymaking.

- They increased their emphasis on coalition building among groups with common interests.

- They substantially increased their attention to state and local political arenas where a growing share of public policy decisions are being made.

Drawbacks of the Study

In spite of the study's many strengths and the light it sheds on interest groups' behavior, one might reasonably question the significance of some of its findings on at least two counts. One is the study's apparent assumption that the first year of the Reagan administration, and especially the unusual circumstances surrounding the initial budget reconciliation resolution (Gramm-Latta), provide adequate evidence that major changes occurred in the interest groups studied. I would challenge this view. The first year of the administration was jolting and disorienting for virtually all actors in the policymaking process, a development not entirely new to the political arena. The authors note that hundreds of traditionally powerful interest groups were unable to benefit from their influence because of the administration's virtual stampede of the budget-making process. However, by the administration's second year the budget process had begun to return to normal with most interest groups resuming their routine involvement. Therefore, the changes in that process, and even the defunding activities of the administration, may reasonably be seen as prompting a brief departure from routine, with relatively short-lived effects on the interest groups studied.

Another count is that the paper tends to overstate the impact of the Reagan administration's actions on the groups studied. Granted, a number of those actions have underscored the vulnerability of many human-resources-oriented groups, thereby inducing some of the changes reported in the study. But even in these cases, it is not clear to what extent the changes are entirely products of administration actions. For example, the emphasis of decentralization of authority through block grants had been around for about a decade before the Reagan administration, and with it a gradual broadening of interest-group foci. The administration's vigorous advocacy of this approach and its modest success in creating new block grant programs merely gave a fresh boost to an ongoing process. The study might have been more cautious, therefore, both in its portrayal of how much change has occurred and in attributing these changes to the Reagan administration. By placing their observations in a historical context, the authors might have better clarified the character and extent of administration-induced change.

One of the most interesting features of the study is its bold and creative attempt to measure the relative influence of various interests at the state level. The authors appropriately characterized the undertaking as a "preliminary first-cut exercise." Although helpful in many respects, however, the effort clearly has major problems. To measure the strength of major interests like the poor, the wealthy, labor, and teachers, the authors used output measures (policy outcomes) rather than input measures (group influence). Although the difficulties with the latter emphasis are clear—especially given the constraints of this study—it is not evident that the output measures reveal much about the relative influence of the groups and the organizations that represent them. Thus, the finding that the interests of the poor, labor, and students are poorly served in states with low per capita income and a high percentage of poor and minority individuals is neither surprising nor revealing. Moreover, many of the output measures carry strong ideological and historical overtones that make their unqualified use as measures of group influence highly suspect. Other measures, such as spending for education and welfare, reflect differences among states in financial resources, at least as much as they reflect differing levels of group influence.

All things considered, the study's flaws are understandable consequences of the effort to analyze events as they happen and to break new ground in the process. They are far outweighed by the worthwhile insights the study provides into how changes in policies and policymaking affect interest-group behavior. Equally important, the study suggests that at least with respect to the human resources area, the Reagan Revolution has not profoundly altered the character of interest-group politics.

PART FOUR

POLICY IMPLEMENTATION

THE REAGAN ADMINISTRATION AND THE RENITENT BUREAUCRACY

Laurence E. Lynn, Jr.

Although every president wishes to gain the upper hand over the federal bureaucracy, Ronald Reagan has made perhaps the most determined effort of any recent president to bend the permanent government to his will. His methods have included mobilizing broad public support for his policies, making aggressive use of the budget to reshape policy priorities, and imposing hiring freezes and reductions in force to shrink the size of government. His most notable departure from the leadership methods of his predecessors, however, has been in the deliberate way he has used his power of appointment to fill senior executive positions in federal departments and agencies with loyal advocates of his policies.

Typically, incoming administrations have professed to seek strong, well-qualified people for top executive positions. Actual appointments, however, depart from a strict criterion of merit to allow for the variety of political pressures affecting the appointment process: the need to reward specific constituencies and contributors, the success of some cabinet appointees in negotiating the right to control the appointment of subordinates, and the wish to have appointees who will be dedicated to the president and to his political philosophy. The usual result is cadres of appointees who exhibit divided loyalties and uncertain reliability. Anticipating this result, presidents are reluctant to delegate or decentralize control over policy to political appointees or even to view the use of their appointment power as more than peripheral to the achievement of their policy goals.

All field interviews were conducted by Paul Starobin of Harvard University's John F. Kennedy School of Government. Starobin's skills in eliciting useful information and producing summaries of what he learned were indispensable to completion of this study.

Departing from this view, the Reagan administration appeared from the outset to embrace the notion that faithful supporters in key executive positions could be a potent tool of administrative leadership. The primary qualification for appointment—overshadowing managerial competence and experience or familiarity with issues—appeared to be the extent to which an appointee shared the president's values and would be reliable and persistent both in transfusing these values into agency practices and in executing central directives bound to be unpopular in his or her agency. The right appointees could, it was believed, significantly advance the president's cause in the face of opposition expected from a government long in moderate or liberal hands.

Reagan's emphasis on the role of his appointees in the administrative management of the federal bureaucracy raises several interesting questions. Has Reagan effectively used the power of appointment to advance his cause? How have the efforts of his appointees affected the activities of their departments or agencies? Have the changes brought about by these appointees been consistent with Reagan's goals? Consistency aside, how have these changes influenced the effectiveness, efficiency, and overall capabilities of these agencies? What factors explain differences in the performance of Reagan appointees? What are the lessons of the Reagan experience for future administrations?

These questions are addressed in this paper by analyzing the accomplishments of five Reagan appointees to subcabinet positions. The emphasis here is on identifying (1) the changes in the activities of each agency that appear to be associated with the management actions of the appointees, (2) the factors that appear to account for each appointee's performance, and (3) the consequences for agency performance of the changes brought about by each appointee. Evidence from these five cases is used to draw conclusions about Reagan's success in using his appointment authority and about the implications of the Reagan experience for future administrations. First, however, it is important to discuss the concept of core activities and the factors contributing to executive performance.

Political Executives and Organizational Change

Government organizations are created to carry out specific public purposes, which are spelled out with varying specificity both in the organization's authorizing statutes and in appropriations acts and are further amplified or delimited in executive orders, in regulations, and in the internal routines and practices of the agency. To make these purposes a reality, bureaucratic structures and routines are established to allocate authority and responsibility within the agency and to set the standards for specific tasks that are to be performed.

Those activities relating directly to fulfilling the organization's purposes may be termed the organization's *core activities*, consisting of actions or practices such as promulgating standards, conducting inspections, awarding grants and contracts, making benefit payments, and administering or protecting a natural resource or geographical area such as a park or military base. Organizational interests and the organization's "culture" gradually materialize around these core activities. Operational routines and standards are created to support them. The way core activity is carried out defines the purposes or mission of the organization as its employees see it.

The concept of core activity provides a useful basis for measuring the performance of Reagan appointees in altering the behavior of their agencies. The nature of appointees' influence may be defined in terms of their success in making lasting changes in the character of core activity that are consistent with Reagan's policy preferences. Evaluating executive performance in terms of core activity permits a comparison of the executives' conceptions of their goals and of their approaches to achieving them. It becomes possible to ask: How well have these executives identified the main business of their agencies, and how well are their ideas formulated to bring about change in their agencies' basic operations? Among those executives who focus on core activities—many may focus on peripheral issues—it may be further asked: What factors seem to account for a pattern of success and failure? If the executives had fundamental change in core activity in mind, for example, did they also have the skills and resources to carry it out?

Questions such as these can be framed in terms of a model that links change in governmental behavior to the political appointee's role in bringing it about. The effectiveness of a political appointee in changing the behavior of his or her agency (behavior is defined here as core activity), can be postulated as depending on four distinct factors. First is the appointed executive's *managerial skills and experience*. A public executive's performance might be expected to depend in part on his or her facility in carrying out the ordinary tasks of public management. Potentially valuable skills include the traditional managerial tasks—planning, organizing, communicating, motivating subordinates, and the like; skill in relating to the agency's political environment—such as building legislative support, negotiating, and sensitivity to varied and changing interests; and, finally, technical competence with respect to the problems and issues facing the agency—that is, the extent to which the executive understands and can intelligently intervene in the substance of the agency's activities. Experience in government, moreover, especially in positions of executive responsibility at the federal or state level, might be expected to be an asset to an appointee confronting the ambiguities, pressures, and uncertainties of a federal executive post. Knowing what to anticipate and how to act can greatly shorten the time needed to master the specific demands of the job.

The second factor affecting the appointee's effectiveness in carrying out core activity is the executive's *personality*. As used here, personality encompasses the appointee's habitual responses to the job situation, including his or her styles of thinking, of identifying and solving problems, and of relating to people and to tasks. The underlying proposition here is that, all other things being equal, appointees with a high level of cognitive and emotional development—in other words, with high tolerance for and an ability to be creative in the face of ambiguity and uncertainty, with sensitivity to the needs and motivations of subordinates and employees, and with a liking for open and candid relationships—will be more effective than those who lack these characteristics and who alienate subordinates, disrupt agency routines, and misconstrue issues.

High levels of managerial skill and desirable personality traits may substitute for one another. An inexperienced and unskilled manager may nonetheless succeed if he or she has a personality that stimulates trust and cooperation or a charismatic personality that inspires effort. Similarly, less adaptable, more aloof individuals may still succeed if they are skilled administrators able to earn respect for their expertise and technical skill.

The third factor is the nature of the *opportunity to accomplish change* that is inherent in the situation. Circumstances internal or external to the agency may favor or oppose changes in core activity. Cataloguing the possibilities is difficult because an agency's readiness and ability to incorporate changes in its basic operations is likely to depend on numerous variables: Employee attitudes and values may be more or less accommodating to new ideas; organizational structures and processes may be more or less malleable, as may the issue networks that support or monitor agency activity; and authorizing statutes may be difficult or impossible to amend, or they may permit little discretion in interpretation. Thus, depending on the setting and the problems to be confronted, accomplishing change may be harder in some agencies than in others.

Fourth is the appointee's *design*, in other words, his or her expressed goals or intentions with respect to the behavior or performance of the agency, together with the specific means chosen to implement them. Some executives will quickly identify core activities and the organizational structures and processes that support them and design a strategy for change aimed directly at these activities. Other executives, however, may measure their influence in terms of specific decisions rather than in terms of agency routines or practices. The objective of the head of the National Highway Traffic and Safety Administration, for example, might be the rescission of the regulations prescribing air bags in automobiles rather than changing the philosophy and process of setting vehicle safety standards. Or a political executive might have as an objective the installation of zero-base budgeting or some other management reform rather than changes in core activity, under the theory that management is properly process- rather than task-oriented.

Conventional management theory might suggest that design is a joint product of several facets: personality, primarily determining which phenomena in the agency setting are classified as "problems" or are otherwise selected for managerial attention; opportunity, primarily determining the general approach to problems; and skills, determining the precise tactics to implement the approach. But there are other possibilities. Of special interest to this study, for instance, is the possibility that appointees' designs are products of a general ideological orientation—either that of the appointee, of the president, or of both. That is, no matter what the particular circumstances, an appointee's design may feature, for example, less regulation, more reliance on market mechanisms, stricter eligibility requirements, or less bureaucratic discretion.

One might expect some correlation—or a minimum of variation—among these factors for a given group of appointees, provided that the appointments reflected a careful matching of personalities, skills, and opportunities and that appointees were given latitude to choose their own designs. The appointments process seldom approaches this degree of rationality, however, and certainly has not appeared to do so in the Reagan administration. Thus among Reagan appointees we expect considerable independent variation among these four contributors to executive performance.

Design of the Study

The data for this study consist primarily of information obtained from interviews with five executives appointed to their positions in 1981 and other individuals associated with five federal agencies: the Employment and Training Administration (ETA) of the Department of Labor; the Forest Service in the Department of Agriculture (FSDA); the Mine Health and Safety Administration (MHSA) of the Department of Labor; the Federal Communications Commission (FCC); and the National Highway Traffic and Safety Administration (NHTSA) of the Department of Transportation. Five agencies constituted the maximum number of which sufficiently detailed information could be obtained within available time and resources.

These agencies and their selected appointees were chosen to be interviewed for four reasons: (1) Each appointee has appeared to reflect Reagan's philosophy and intentions in making appointments to subcabinet positions. Moreover, in matters of program, each generally reflects Reagan's conservative ideology, has dutifully executed administration policies concerning budget and staff reductions, and has formulated specific goals consistent with Reagan's general policies; (2) Each agency is headed by or is within the administrative jurisdiction of a Reagan appointee who, once in office, has expressed definite ideas about changing the agency beyond merely carrying out Office of Management and Budget (OMB) and White House directives; (3) The appointee and a representative group of other appointed and career officials within the agency agreed to be interviewed; (4) Preliminary investigation suggested significant variation among the five appointees in the four factors discussed here as influencing their performances as well as their success. Thus, these five agencies and the appointed executives can be said to be representative of Reagan's apparent beliefs about the potential contributions of his appointees to the furtherance of his policies.

For each agency, interviews were conducted with the selected executive and with other appointed officials, career employees, former political appointees, members of legislative staffs, interest-group representatives, and other individuals—General Accounting Office (GAO) officials and agency consultants, for example—who are knowledgeable about the agency's activities.[1]

The interviewer sought the following types of information from each interviewee: (1) the appointee's goals and objectives; (2) the methods chosen by the appointee to carry out his purposes; (3) opinions concerning the apparent effect of the appointee's managerial actions; (4) opinions concerning the consequences of changes in agency activity on agency performance; (5) any other information bearing on the appointee's style of leadership and management. Apart from this outline, the interviews were open ended.[2]

The resulting data were then searched for information concerning each appointee's managerial skills and experience, personality, opportunity, de-

---

1. The appointees agreed to be interviewed on the record; many others agreed only on the condition that their names not be revealed. Inevitably, interviewees betrayed biases; many of their assertions could not be adequately corroborated. Every effort was made, however, to check the veracity of sources and to verify appointees' views.

2. In most instances permission was received to record the interviews on tape, even when the interviewee requested anonymity. Where appropriate, the interviewer supplemented his information with documentary evidence, such as speeches, testimony, and other interview transcripts. Comprehensive assessment of all activities in every agency proved impossible. Emphasis was placed on activities in which appointees expressed considerable personal interest and initiative.

sign, and accomplishments that seemed to directly relate to the appointee's managerial efforts. The resulting assessments were necessarily doubly subjective. They reflect, first, the opinions of observers rather than objectively drawn indicators or measures. Second, they reflect the author's judgments concerning the proper interpretation and value of these opinions. The pictures of these appointees and agencies that emerged from the interviews were quite robust, however. While other interpreters of the data would doubtless differ concerning nuances, it is unlikely that they would arrive at altogether different views.

Five Executives and Their Stories

As background for the analysis to follow, this section summarizes the stories of the five executives included in the study.[3]

Albert Angrisani and the Employment and Training Administration

Thirty-five-year-old Albert Angrisani was appointed to the position of assistant secretary of labor for employment and training. A vice-president of Chase Manhattan Bank, he had a bachelor's degree in political science, a master of arts degree in finance, and a certificate in accounting. He would be responsible for managing the department's Employment and Training Administration. By all accounts, his political contacts, not his business acumen or his experience with staffing programs (he had none of the latter), led to his appointment. He had helped Secretary of Labor Raymond Donovan manage Ronald Reagan's presidential campaign in New Jersey, and he was to become Donovan's chief assistant at the Department of Labor.

ETA awards some $30 billion annually in grants and contracts to private firms, nonprofit groups, and state and local governments for operating employment and training programs. It is a highly politicized agency, "corrupt" and "wasteful" in the view of many agency observers. Over the years, control over contracting had shifted both between Washington, D.C., and the field and between program officers and financial officers. The agency had been the subject of numerous GAO audits, reorganizations, and management evaluations, and there had been little stability and a minimal sense of professionalism except in the Job Corps, which had a strong mission orientation.

---

3. Unless otherwise cited, quotations in this section of the paper may be assumed to be from interviews with the author. Officials not identified in the text requested anonymity.

Angrisani would be under continuing pressure from the White House and from OMB to end the fraud and waste that were frequently cited in the media.

Short, heavy-set, and youthful, Angrisani projected self-confidence, ambition, and a distrust of bureaucrats. This distrust was reflected in his comment, "We have people who have tenure in their jobs. They're totally inefficient." He viewed himself as a tough-minded businessperson. "The difference between me and my predecessors is, I'm a manager, not a manpower specialist," he said. He saw ETA's Comprehensive Employment and Training Program as "just another big welfare program,"[4] and conservatives expected him to clean up the mess. He expressed great faith in business management systems: "You can have the best person in the world in charge of a system, and if that system is incapable of functioning right, that person's going to fail." Critics described him as a "bully" who was terrible at relating to people.

Of necessity, one of Angrisani's primary goals was to phase out or redesign programs that were not in accord with the president's philosophy. For example, he carried out Reagan's decision to terminate the Public Service Employment Program, and he assisted the White House and Senate Republicans in replacing the Comprehensive Employment and Training Act (CETA) with legislation providing for block grants for job training dispensed through private industry councils. He also directed an OMB-dictated 20 percent reduction in force, and he was prepared to cut the staff even further.

In addition, Angrisani set about making the procurement process more "efficient" and less susceptible to corruption. "The first thing a manager has to have is control," he said. He thus required that all contracts, including those modifying existing contracts, be approved by a staff created in his office. (A computer in his office gave him access to the status of each of the thousands of ETA contracts, and for a while he looked at everything himself.) He created a special task force to reduce the backlog of audits, and he shifted responsibility for contract administration from program officials to financial officials. (He commented that "financial people are basically the same everywhere; there is something in their nature . . . that you can count on.") Furthermore, he established a model procurement process that encouraged competition and limited the discretionary judgments of contracting officials. Contracting officers in ETA program offices in headquarters ("political hacks," Angrisani called them) were stripped of their authority, and contracting authority was shifted to the Financial Control and Systems Management Division. Contracting officers in the regional offices were placed under the surveillance of headquarters.

---

4. Quoted by Mark Huber, "Angry AC," *Conservative Digest*, November 1982, p. 42.

Reactions to these moves were predictably mixed. ETA veterans referred to Angrisani's hand-picked staff as "Snow White and the Seven Dwarfs." Some seasoned procurement officials expressed outrage at what they saw as Angrisani's ham-handed approach, even suspecting him of deliberately sabotaging the agency's procurement activities—"strangling them," said one, "then letting them breathe a little." In the field offices there was considerable confusion, fear, and resentment; in one regional office, the Job Corps director had to answer his own phone, and his staff, depleted to 12 persons, worked in one large room with torn-up carpets and empty desks scattered about. Yet even critics conceded that Angrisani deserved credit for eliminating the audit backlog. A GAO official called him "one of the good guys" for "tightening things up" and making the agency more management conscious. In 1983, Angrisani resigned his ETA post and left government service.

John Crowell and the Forest Service

A lawyer and an outdoors enthusiast, John Crowell was appointed assistant secretary for natural resources and the environment at the Department of Agriculture—the official responsible for overseeing the Forest Service. Crowell, who at this writing still remains at the Forest Service, has been one of the most controversial of Reagan's appointees. In his previous career with the timber products industry, he had been charged with shady dealings in an antitrust case involving timber companies. His Forest Service confirmation was opposed by twenty-five senators. He bristled at the opposition: "I am not a lawyer who was just plucked out of some law firm because I had worked on a Reagan campaign. And I'm not an ideologue. . . ." Yet his conservative philosophy of deemphasizing the concept of wilderness in favor of economic values was clearly in line with Reagan's own philosophy.

Headed by a nonpolitical chief forester, the Forest Service is a highly decentralized, quasi-military organization dedicated to administering the national forests. Foresters comprise most of the agency's 28,000 employees, they typically have a college degree in forestry, and the agency espouses the dictum that "the (person) on the ground knows best what to do." Said one forester, "We're close to the ground. We can feel things. We have a certain amount of righteousness about us, too. The cost shouldn't dictate how you treat the land. You take care of the land, in a physical sense, a practical sense."

Although an exploiter of resources and active in the National Forest Products Association, Crowell quickly earned the respect of the Forest Service. Observers of the agency saw him as a leader by example, a straight arrow, not cocky, and a good listener. Unlike Angrisani, he had no wish to shake up his agency. "I'm not going to be a dictator," he said. Crowell thought it important to give managers "clear ideas about his philosophy" and to "develop credibility and respect" among people in the agency. During the period under study he exhibited a lawyerly, case-by-case, detail-by-detail way of thinking, based on the attitude that persuasion is a matter of marshaling facts. He was not known as a conceptualizer, a strategic thinker, or a poker player. And he appeared to look at politics as a necessary but burdensome chore.

Crowell had two primary and related goals: to increase the timber harvest from national forest lands and to incorporate "economics" into the national forest planning process and into other agency activities. "It is inevitable," he said, "that we have to get more of our wood from the national forests. It's just bad management for us to get into a situation where we've got a housing boom coming along and don't have enough wood coming out of the forest to supply it."

He saw no need to amend the National Forest Management Act, believing that the act's legislative history made it clear that departures from the act's timber harvest policy should be undertaken wherever necessary in the interest of good management. His strategy was to increase the budget for timber sales at the expense of both the research and the state and private forestry budget. Yet, although supported in his views by the secretary and undersecretary of agriculture, he was unable to offer a convincing rationale to OMB for seeking increased timber sales during a severe construction recession (all he could come up with was that old growth forests needed to be cut), and Congress was unresponsive to a budgetary tradeoff that appeared to favor the Northwest at the expense of the Southeast (which benefited from the state and private forestry account). Crowell obviously failed in this initiative, a failure that he readily concedes.

Crowell was somewhat more successful in promoting economic values in the planning process. He promoted this objective not by creating a team of economists, planners, and policy analysts in his office or by dictating that people with these qualifications be hired in the Forest Service. Crowell and his aides were reluctant to interfere with the Forest Service's personnel system in such a way as to risk charges of politicization. Rather they moved the service in this direction indirectly by requiring the service to perform more economic analysis.

Vice-President George Bush's Task Force on Regulatory Relief, created in 1981, had identified as a "high priority for review" the Carter administration's rule guiding the planning process (the Reagan White House viewed the rule as too broad and vague and as affording wilderness advocates too much scope for influencing the process). With White House support (and its acquiescence to Crowell's compromises with environmental groups) the Department of Agriculture revised the guidelines for the national forest planning process to increase emphasis on economic analysis. Crowell also issued specific guidance to the Forest Service as to what he expected. "He meant business," said an observer. "There are a lot of memos that go out to the Forest Service that get lost. This one did not get lost."

One career official in the field observed,

> We find him a very fine and capable leader. But I would not say the Forest Service has fundamentally changed as an institution as a result of John Crowell. Our duties have not changed. I think that the forest supervisor is very conscious of Crowell—the supervisor is in the meetings a lot, travels to Washington, and reads a lot of paper. And yes, the supervisor does direct the ranger. But the ranger lives in the forest . . . is a relatively independent person and is a doer, and his allegiance is to the natural resources, not to some political philosophy.

Ford B. Ford and the Mine Health and Safety Administration

Ford B. Ford, who was appointed assistant secretary of labor responsible for the Mine Health and Safety Administration, came to the job with a reputation as having "White House connections." With a degree in production management and control from the University of California, he spent over twenty years in California state government. Five of those years were spent as Governor Reagan's chairperson of the Occupational Safety and Health Appeals Board and as the employer advocate on the board. When he was not reappointed by Reagan's successor, Ford lobbied the board on behalf of businesses as vice-president of the California Institute of Industrial and Government Relations. He was a believer in Reagan's mission.

The Mine Health and Safety Administration is responsible for enforcing the Federal Mine Safety and Health Act of 1977, as amended, a classic piece of command and control legislation. The agency was built around coal and metal/nonmetal mine inspection and the detection, correction, and punishment of violations. Its corps of inspectors consists primarily of former miners, organized into sixteen relatively autonomous districts, who have been described as "physical people" who "know how to mine coal and inspect mines." The inspectorate is clearly the power center of the agency. Although heterogeneous in their loyalties to labor or management, inspectors and their supervisors form a relatively close-knit culture, loyal to each other and to the agency's mission.

Variously termed "a nice guy," "inoffensive," "low key," "unaggressive," and "bland," Ford was viewed by critics as a "yes man" to Reagan and to Vice-President Bush's Task Force on Regulatory Relief. Nonpartisan observers of the agency, however, saw in him a great determination and a healthy instinct for doing the intelligent thing, and called him a "driven" man who knows where he wants to go. He was given high marks for respecting and listening to the career staff and for relying on them, rather than bringing in outsiders (for instance, he chose his deputy from the career ranks).

Before taking the federal position, Ford studied the agency closely and carefully formulated a strategy. "Clearly," he said,

> MHSA's effectiveness should not be measured in the number of inspections conducted, citations issued, or penalties collected, but in the reduction of injuries and illnesses. And a broadly focused, coordinated approach that encourages an active partnership between managers, workers, and the government is the best way of achieving those reductions.

The existing statute seemed to require the confrontational approach Ford abhorred. The American Mining Congress was urging the vice-president's Task Force on Regulatory Relief to seek changes in the 1977 Federal Mine Safety and Health act to foster cooperation among industry, labor, and government to improve workplace safety. Ford detected no consensus to change the act, however, and he decided to interpret it as broadly as possible.

Ford thus decided to consolidate inspections, civil penalty assessments, and education and training under the district managers, thereby increasing their authority and, incidentally, creating a potential base of support for the reorganization. This reorganization stimulated some temporary internal conflict. The administrator for the coal area, for example, liked the idea of having education and training under his wing, whereas Ford's deputy feared that the education and training function might be decimated in the process. Reorganization also coincided with a number of other actions, including administration-imposed budget cuts that were perceived as adverse by the inspectors, who accused the administration of "going soft" on safety. Then came a series of mine disasters, which galvanized the agency's critics, who charged that Ford's reorganization "results in less inspections, more responsibility, less violations written, lower assessments, and a more relaxed attitude toward mine health and safety." Though slowed down somewhat, the reorganization generally was put into effect with the overall support of the mining industry.

Ford encountered fewer difficulties with another internal change, that of requiring a conference between mine and MHSA officials before citations were issued. His move, however, to change the system of appraising inspectors' performances by, among other things, replacing reports on the number of inspections with reports of accident and injury reductions as a performance criterion stimulated the greatest opposition. Some administrators worried that inspectors would bribe operators not to report accidents. Inspectors also were uneasy about the new and less precise role they were being asked to play, and opposition to reductions in the staffing of the inspectorate intensified. Said one expert:

> The inspectors don't like the new system one bit. They've got to do all kinds of new things that they're not trained to do (such as holding conferences with mine operators). In particular, they are not interpersonal types, they are not managerial types, they are not trained to sit nose to nose with the operator and talk with him.

A different view, however, came from a district manager, who thought inspectors should learn to act like "gentlemen" and behave themselves at the mine site. Ford, he believed, is not going to let the inspectors get away with pushing the operator around; inspectors, he said, will have to learn how to "handle authority."

Ford's actions therefore sparked controversy and discontent. Inspectors appeared to be unhappy and angry. A nonpartisan agency observer commented, however, that Ford "turned that agency around without any major disturbance." Ford himself believes that "we've gone just about as far as we can [with] policy without infringing on the law." In the summer of 1983, Ford was promoted to the position of under secretary of labor.

Mark Fowler and the Federal Communications Commission

Mark Fowler came to the post of chairperson of the Federal Communications Commission from a career in the broadcasting industry. A former lawyer for a Washington, D.C., firm representing mostly small-size radio stations, he adopted the outlook of a small businessperson. He was also communications counsel for the Reagan presidential campaigns of 1976 and 1980 and was sponsored for a federal appointment by Reagan intimate Charles Z. Wick. His belief in the virtues of the marketplace as a protector of freedom of the press was qualification enough for the FCC appointment.

The FCC has become one of the most visible agencies of government. Organized into four largely autonomous operating bureaus—for broadcasting, cable television, common carrier, and private radio—the agency is formally independent of the executive branch and is headed by a five-person commission. Rapid advances in telecommunications technology transformed the agency from a preoccupation with awarding licenses to very high frequency (VHF) television and to amplitude modulation (AM) and frequency modulation (FM) radio applicants to a concern with access to the entire spectrum of new services. Fast change made the agency staff apprehensive, all the more so as it became obvious that the proliferation of new services made the rationale for restrictive regulation of the old services much less persuasive. In addition, the fact that every major or controversial FCC action is publicized in some part of the communications field, if not in other fields, makes lawsuits likely.

As a fervent believer in the free market and an ideologue, Fowler views the FCC as Big Brother and a dinosaur, an inefficient, lackadaisical agency. His inflexible commitment to principle becomes palatable to friend and foe alike, however, because of his folksy, outgoing, and buoyant personality. He is a preacher but is not pontifical, and he is good natured and willing to hear criticism. Rather than confronting the bureaucracy, he believed in establishing clear expectations, in rewarding people for fine performance and in providing constructive criticism when warranted. However, even his defenders see him as a babe in the woods.

Fowler had several specific goals. First, to make the FCC more responsive, he wanted to articulate its mission so clearly that even the smallest division could see where its activities fit into the big picture. He approached this task by creating a management-by-objective (MBO) system. Second, he wanted to extend "freedom of the press" to the electronic media by securing repeal of Section 315 of the Communications Act of 1934, as amended, which required the commission to enforce the "fairness doctrine" and the "equal time" clause. Third, he wanted to streamline licensing procedures so as to increase access to the communications media. Each of these goals was related to Fowler's larger purpose: reducing FCC interference in the free-market process.

Fowler moved swiftly to install his MBO system in 1981, successfully establishing in the minds of FCC watchers that the agency was now management conscious. A lengthy GAO report issued the year before had condemned FCC management and lent impetus to this initiative. FCC bureaus were required to produce action plans and were expected to adhere to them. The aide who was responsible for holding bureaus to their action plans was installed in an office next to Fowler's and had virtually unlimited access to him.

Unlike Ford, Fowler acted quickly to name loyal Reaganites to key FCC jobs; ten to thirteen offices and bureaus received new chiefs who were "free-market advocates actively working toward unregulation." At the same time Fowler took steps to "reach out to the employees" of FCC through incentive awards, pay increases, and other recognitions. According to one observer "even if people disagree with him, they like him," although his perceived opposition to affirmative action has antagonized some women and minorities.

Fowler's proposal to repeal Section 315 encountered a brick wall in Congress. Although the broadcasting content rules had respectable critics, the move was portrayed by opponents as a great boon to the three networks. Fowler's insistence on the amendment was irritating to many in Congress, and his handling of this and other issues earned him a reputation as being politically naive. "Some people just know how this town works," a Senate aide said. "Mark wasn't one of them." As a result, administration critics were made more suspicious of the FCC's enforcement of the Communications Act, despite the fact that operating results do not reveal any differences between complaint rulings under Fowler and rulings under previous commissioners.

In a continuation of practices begun under his predecessor and facilitated by congressional amendments to the Communications Act, Fowler placed great emphasis on simplifying applications procedures. Extensive review by lawyers, engineers, and other specialists was replaced by "machinelike" processing by paraprofessional broadcast analysts. Morale among agency professionals suffered because of this deregulation emphasis. Said one: "We feel it. We see it. We hear it. Lawyers are doing very routine work. . . . if you're going to be a grade-13 attorney, then you need to be doing certain kinds of complex work." Yet there is a greater volume of work to be done— for example, in AM and FM licenses—because the number of applicants had increased markedly.

Under Fowler, who as of this writing still remains at the FCC, the commission's basic functions have not changed; the agency's resources continue to be devoted chiefly to processing applications and responding to complaints. Many FCC watchers are convinced, however, that the agency is "more responsive" under Fowler. Many of the changes are subtle. Said one agency veteran:

> You can't put out of your mind that they want to abolish the content rules. We all know it. We're cognizant of the commissioner's desires. We will try to do that within the limit of the law. How? I don't know. Our procedures are based on precedent.

Raymond Peck and the National Highway Traffic and Safety Administration

Raymond Peck was appointed director of the National Highway Traffic and Safety Administration from the position of director of regulatory affairs for the National Coal Association. A lawyer who had practiced for several years in New York, he came to Washington, D.C., in 1971 and served successively as environmental counsel at the Department of Commerce, director of the Office of Energy Regulation and Legislative Policy in the Treasury Department, and deputy assistant secretary for energy and minerals in the Department of Interior. He was an unknown in the automobile safety community. However, his reputation for fearlessly confronting environmentalists in opposing strip-mining regulations appealed to Reagan, who placed his high priority on the NHTSA's providing regulatory relief for the automobile industry in the face of opposition from Ralph Nader and his staff of zealous watchdogs of the agency.

Though the agency is divided into components emphasizing vehicle safety and driver safety, the Ralph Nader-slated orientation of NHTSA is toward regulating motor vehicle design, not promoting safe behavior by drivers. Ninety percent of the agency's employees, a diverse group of engineers, scientists, and lawyers, work in Washington, D.C. Many are bright, independent, and outspoken, much quicker to challenge political leadership than the top staff of other agencies. Said one, "we are the agency with the highest ideological content . . . within DOT [Department of Transportation]. The rest of the department builds stuff."

The first thing Peck told his staff, said this employee, was that he was "very bright" and a "very quick study." To most observers Peck appeared combative, self-assured, suspicious, and hard to pin down. He saw no need for a personnel shakeup at NHTSA, but he claimed not to be "blindfolded as to the possibility of duplicity on the part of the staff." "He is an extremely bright guy," said one, "but he is his own worst enemy." By instinct neither an ideologue nor a manager, Peck thought he possessed the qualities the White House wanted—a "litigator," not "gun shy," and someone who could see the job as challenging, tough, fun.

Peck's primary goal was to shift emphasis away from standards, such as that requiring the installation of airbags by car manufacturers, and toward promoting safety awareness, such as the voluntary wearing of seat belts; in other words, "to restore balance to the agency" by creating a proper mix of technical safety standards and behavior modification. Neither Peck nor the White House viewed NHTSA's statutory mandate to establish vehicle safety standards that are reasonable, practical, and appropriate as an obstacle, as it appeared to allow wide latitude in designing regulations. Another of Peck's goals was to achieve better cooperation between the agency and industry. By all appearances, however, he had no specific plan to achieve these goals. When he became interested in an activity, he tended to become personally involved regardless of agency routines, and he exhibited a lawyerly, argumentative, wits-matching style. When uninterested, he remained uninvolved. Thus his personal style, rather than his ideas, his strategy, or his accomplishments, became the basis for his reputation.

Among Peck's personal interests was promoting the use of seat belts, in part, associates believe, to challenge the preeminence of Joan Claybrook, Peck's highly visible predecessor. When NHTSA staff expressed skepticism, he planned his own seat belt campaign. Ignoring traditional traffic safety advocates and other potential allies, he hired a private consultant to create a Traffic Safety Foundation to raise funds for safety awareness programs. However, the vehicle safety community and its congressional allies pounced on Peck in hearings to investigate the foundation, and the enterprise was abandoned. Even Republicans were dismayed by Peck's "filibustering" and irritating personality. Peck was able to gain President Reagan's participation in his campaign to encourage seat belt use and to discourage drunk driving, and seat belt advocates in NHTSA cooperated, but Peck never gave the campaign either a goal or a solid political base.

To promote changes in agency priorities, Peck convened a weekend conference to discuss the possibilities. A memorandum recording decisions reached at the conference was not published until he was leaving office in May of 1983, and Peck never showed serious interest in it. A similar fate was met by a proposal for joint industry-agency research on side-impact protection and steering column design; following a law suit brought by Joan Claybrook, the project was canceled.

Said an automobile industry spokesperson,

> The only difference between the Claybrook era and the Ray Peck era is that under Peck we got a fair hearing. . . . but I don't think the changes were fundamental. The changes were all reversible. If Joan Claybrook and the Democrats came in in 1984, I think we would go right back to the adversary position we were in before.

The industry did not have to wait that long. Following Peck's resignation in the summer of 1983, and the promotion of his deputy to replace him, NHTSA watchers immediately detected a revival of enthusiasm for safety regulations (as well as a decline of enthusiasm for deregulation in the White House). Peck and his goals were gone and forgotten.

Reagan's Managers as Change Agents

The extent and character of change promulgated by these five officials varied widely from agency to agency, as table 1 makes clear. Some change attributable to these appointees occurred in each of the five agencies, however. Each appointee made a deliberate, sustained effort to bring about change, and each found some kind of leverage over agency activity through which his personal influence could be and ultimately was felt.

However, the particular reinforcements employed by the Executive Office of the President (EOP) had significant consequences for these managers' influences on their agencies and on their agencies' constituencies. President Reagan, by creating ties that bound his appointees to his philosophy of gov-

TABLE 1

FIVE FEDERAL MANAGERS AND THE RESULTS THEY ACHIEVED

Agency Official/ Core Activity	Skills/ Experience	Personality	Opportunity
Employment and Training Administration			
Albert Angrisani			
(awarding grants and contracts)	Inexperience in congressional poli- tics; good bureau- cratic instincts; few managerial skills; good grasp of grant and contract administration	Strongly adversar- ial; action-oriented, impulsive; oriented toward progress rather than people	Authority central- ized; weak sense of mission; little professionalism (except for job corps); history of flux in character of agency opera- tions—thus little cohesion or cul- tural identity
Forest Service			
John Crowell (administering national for- ests)	Politically naive; highly competent manager; no gov- ernment experi- ence; highly competent in re- source administra- tion; long associated with timber industry	Organization- builder; product- oriented; a "tradi- tionalist" in attitude toward manager's respon- sibilities; deter- mined, decisive, yet flexible; re- spectful of staff	Authority decen- tralized to field or- ganization; strong sense of mission; professionalism; distinctive organi- zational cultures; well-organized constituencies; considerable stability

TABLE 1 (continued)

Design	Results
Increase control over procurement by centralizing approval of requests for proposals (RFPs), sole-source justifications, contract awards, contracting modifications; shift control over contracting from program officials to financial managers; promulgate standard procurement model to reduce scope of contract officer discretion; expedite audit resolution	Shift of control over procurement to central office and from program to financial officials Evidence of lengthening of procurement cycle; increase in paperwork Significant disruption of agency routines and sharp decline in career staff morale; apparent increase in staff workloads and reduction of contract monitoring because of personnel cutbacks
Seek immediate increase in timber harvest by increasing timber sales budget, reducing state and private forestry and research budgets; change of policy of multiple-use, even-flow management; increase emphasis on economic values in planning forest uses by revising the planning process, insisting on economic analysis from field staff	No increase in planned timber sales or change in forest management policy Increased emphasis on economic analysis in planning; increased appreciation of economic issues by career foresters

TABLE 1 (continued)

FIVE FEDERAL MANAGERS AND THE RESULTS THEY ACHIEVED

Agency Official/ Core Activity	Skills/ Experience	Personality	Opportunity
Mine Health and Safety Administration			
Ford B. Ford *(inspecting mines)*	Good political instincts; capable manager; state government, but no federal government experience; little knowledge of mining industry	Organization-builder; a "traditionalist" in attitude toward manager's responsibilities; open, a listener, low key	Authority decentralized to field organization; close-knit protective organizational culture: low level of professionalism
Federal Communications Commission			
Mark Fowler *(awarding spectrum)*	Poor political instincts; adequate management skills; Washington, D.C., lawyer: well-developed appreciation of communications issues	True believer; outgoing and good natured; process-oriented	Authority decentralized to four functional bureaus; conservative, parochial agency culture; plural executive-rule by majority
National Highway Traffic and Safety Administration			
Raymond Peck *(establishing vehicle safety standards)*	Politically maladroit; ineffective as a manager; several years of federal government experience; no particular technical competence	Egoistic, wary; lawyerly rather than conceptual or ideological	Authority highly centralized; organizational culture infused with ideology, high sense of professionalism; strong sense of mission

TABLE 1 (continued)

Design	Results
Reduce command and control emphasis in enforcement by enhancing authority, discretion of district manager to issue citations; take steps to increase health and safety by changing role of inspector through performance appraisal, institution of conferences with company officials	Significant change in inspection/enforcement process; shift of bureaucratic power toward district supervisors; some attitudinal change in field: many no longer see themselves as "just cops"
Seek statutory repeal of "fairness" and "equal time" doctrines; install and use management by objectives to establish direction and accountability; require bureaus to prepare action plans; increase access to communications media by making licensing process less judgmental and by reducing discretion of bureaucrats; appoint Reagan loyalists to key posts	Bureau autonomy somewhat reduced: increased sense of accountability and of awareness of performance and responsiveness to outside inquiries; morale of career staff improved; continued trend toward streamlined procedures; less reliance on lawyers: increased applications—thus some increases in backlogs No repeal of section 315, though some congressional moves toward deregulation: deemphasis on "fairness doctrine"; heightened suspicion of administration in Congress and among consumer groups
Reduce emphasis on vehicle safety standards by suspending, moderating, or delaying vehicle standards; institute cooperative research to increase cooperation between government and industry; use motivational research, safety-awareness research to achieve behavior modification—for example, seat-belt use; reallocate priorities between vehicle standards and highway safety by planning "retreats"; broaden quarterly agenda of meetings between industry representatives and agency to include policy issues	Some standards modified; passive-restraint decision overruled Little change in agency emphasis on safety standards, though slightly increased appreciation of behavioral modifications among career staff; some new thinking Planned increases in cooperative research canceled

ernment—for example, enlisting them in budget and staff reduction and deregulation—appeared to attenuate the influence on agency performance of each appointee's skills, ambition, and personality. Each appointee was acting as an agent for the president's policy preferences, and none showed much inclination to go into business for himself.

Thus the president and his EOP advisers were able to project their influence deeply into the bureaucracy, thereby occupying a substantial amount of executive "space" and leaving much less to chance or to the whims of appointees. In analyzing the interview data, one senses that Reagan's practices of appointing like-minded subordinates and reinforcing their belief that, although assigned to remote provinces, they are united in a common cause have helped to further his policies. Far from limiting his appointees' persuasion to bringing the bureaucracy into line with his policies, the president used them as agents provocateurs, enforcers, and proconsuls in the agencies. Intimidation and the threat of reductions in force (RIFs) and budget cuts undeniably caught the attention of career bureaucrats.

For example, with the exception of Mark Fowler, whose agency's budget was beyond the purview of OMB, each appointee became an agent of an effort led by OMB Director David Stockman to force retrenchment on the federal bureaucracy, and all but Angrisani were associated with implementing deregulation in line with guidance from Bush's Task Force on Regulatory Relief. Managerial moves associated with implementation of Reagan budgetary or regulatory policies thus generated more controversy and opposition than might otherwise have been the case. Ford B. Ford's patient efforts to alter the character of mine inspections, for instance, which could be justified on their own merits, were criticized all the more severely because they were viewed as part of the president's crusade to disembowel enforcement of health and safety statutes. By the same token, many of these managers' moves were taken seriously and supported, both inside their agencies and in Congress, because they were seen as associated with a popular and determined president's policies.

Loyalty to the president's goals, however, was not inconsistent with open, trusting, and participative approaches to agency management by those presidential appointees. Only Angrisani confronted his agency's employees, openly distrusted them, and kept his distance from them. By contrast, Ford, Fowler, Crowell, and, to a lesser extent, Peck, sought to make full use of the human resources in their agencies, and they went out of their way to motivate subordinates to be cooperative. Promoting change in government, far from requiring confrontation and conflict, is doubtless inhibited by adoption of a "we-they" attitude.

Although some kind of externally provoked change was the rule rather than the exception in these agencies, their experiences also demonstrate convincingly that change is a slow, costly process attended by controversy and exceedingly demanding of executive effort. Though one can imagine a group of public executives who might exhibit greater economy, facility, and acumen in approaching their tasks than these five, it is hard to imagine any public executive succeeding by moving more boldly, ambitiously, or dramatically against the resistances he or she faced. That policy change under most circumstances comes about through incremental change is nowhere better illustrated than in these five agencies.

These generalizations notwithstanding, there was still considerable room for individual influence. The executives in this study differed in skills and personality, in the kinds of opportunities they faced, and in the quality of the designs they chose to exploit these opportunities. These differences, summarized in table 1, help explain the pattern of changes occurring in these agencies, although the interactions among the changes are complex.

Factors in Managerial Success

The most extensive changes in core activity appear to have occurred in the Mine Health and Safety Administration. By shifting power from mine inspectors to district supervisors through reorganization, and by redefining the role of the mine inspector, Ford succeeded in fundamentally altering his agency's approach to and attitudes toward its primary mission, that of inspecting mines. At the opposite extreme, Raymond Peck appears to have had relatively little effect on his agency's emphasis on and approach to establishing motor vehicle safety standards. Accomplishments of the other three executives appear to lie somewhere in between those of Ford and Peck. Significant, though not necessarily far-reaching, changes occurred both in the core activity of the Employment and Training Administration, where Angrisani succeeded, through a design similar to Ford's, in modifying the agency's approach to contracting, as well as in the core activity of the FCC, where Fowler has apparently increased his agency's sense of accountability, has changed its licensing process, and has reduced its emphasis on command and control regulation. Crowell, at the Forest Service, has reinforced already growing awareness among foresters of economic values in planning, although as yet without tangible results. However, during the period covered by this study, Crowell failed to achieve his primary objective, that of increasing timber sales (an objective, incidentally, not directly related to the agency's primary mission).

How to account for this pattern of success and failure? At first glance, managerial skills, including political sophistication and an open and respectful attitude toward one's organization, seem to be decisive. Ford had many of the skills and the personality of one who would be commonly called a "good manager." Though low key, he appreciated and used his organization to good effect. Among the five appointees, moreover, he was the only one with exceptionally good political instincts. Peck, in sharp contrast, would not be widely regarded as a "good manager" because he lacked skill both in the tasks of management and in political maneuvering. Moreover, his personality made him unpopular with many persons inside and outside the agency. His success was limited to actions—such as refusing to sign regulations—in which he could directly exercise his authority. Ford and Peck, one could argue, earned their just desserts: a good manager got good results, a poor one failed.

In terms of the other three appointees, although neither Angrisani nor Fowler could be fairly labeled as altogether lacking in managerial qualifications, neither their skills nor their personality notably qualified them for managerial roles in the public sector. Angrisani accumulated a substantial roster of critics outside of his inner circle, and Fowler, although well liked, was not viewed as a strong or authoritative figure. Yet each achieved notable results. As compared to Fowler and Angrisani, Crowell seemed to have the potential to be an effective manager, despite his lack of political acumen. Among the five, for example, Crowell earned the highest regard among his career subordinates. Despite his potential, however, Crowell's achievements were clearly inferior to all except Peck. If these results are any indication, possession of managerial skills and a good managerial personality may not be powerful predictors of success in public management.

The picture of factors in success or failure becomes somewhat clearer when comparing the opportunities these appointees faced, in other words, the relative ease or difficulty of accomplishing change in core activity in these five agencies. Agencies in which authority over core activity is decentralized to dispersed sites in the field, in which career personnel have strong professional identities, and in which career personnel participate in tightly woven issue networks of well-organized constituencies probably constitute the most difficult challenges to a political appointee. On the other hand, an agency executive who has significant authority over core activity and confronts relatively weak organizational cultures and disorganized, powerless constituencies has a greater opportunity to bring about change.

If opportunity is so conceived, Crowell probably had the least promising opportunity. Core activity was highly decentralized, and the status quo was reinforced by a strong organizational culture. Crowell's relatively homogeneous group of college-educated foresters could be expected to offer considerable resistance to externally imposed changes that threatened their sense of how their jobs ought to be done and their control over field activities. Crowell also had to contend with well-organized interest groups—environmental groups and the wood products industry—who had substantial economic and ideological stakes in agency activity. The dispersal of agency activity meant substantial congressional interest in agency affairs.

The Mine Health and Safety Administration also had highly decentralized core activity and a strong, though more heterogeneous, agency culture. The principal difference between the Forest Service and the MHSA was the latter agency's obscurity. Unlike the Forest Service, MHSA activities were centered in relatively few congressional districts, and the economic interests were less powerful. Barring a mine disaster, Ford labored on a bureaucratic back street, and for that reason faced a less confining situation than Crowell.

In the other three agencies, authority over activity was centered for the most part in Washington, D.C., physically and bureaucratically closer to the offices of the political appointees. Fowler nonetheless faced problems. He was only one of five commissioners, though supported by a Republican majority, and his four bureaus possessed considerable autonomy. Rapid technological and economic changes in the communications industry, and their attendant uncertainties, increased the problem of pursuing a proactive policy. Change at the FCC was far from certain.

Angrisani and Peck both had more favorable situations. Angrisani had considerable leverage over his agency's core activity. Though numerous procurement decisions were made in the Labor Department's regional offices, he captured control over his agency's procurement process relatively easily. As mentioned earlier, the ETA was widely regarded as a problem agency ripe for leadership, reform, and good management. The National Highway Traffic and Safety Administration was a somewhat tougher nut. Zealously guarded by Ralph Nader-inspired advocates of strong federal regulation of car and highway safety, the agency was staffed with a disparate group of well-educated professionals who identified strongly with the agency's objectives and established means for achieving them. Nonetheless the agency's core activity, that of setting standards, was relatively accessible to an appointed executive; standards could not be issued without Peck's approval. Thus Peck had the necessary authority over the issuance of standards to exert substantial influence on how and why and, to a lesser extent, when they were prepared.

Taking opportunity into account brings a little more coherence to the search for explanations for managerial success and failure, and, in particular, to the importance of the appointee's personal strengths and weaknesses. Ford's skills and political acumen seem well suited to his moderately difficult assignment. In the same vein, Angrisani faced a significantly more promising situation, and his modest managerial endowment, especially his financial management orientation, was sufficient to enable him to make headway in restructuring the procurement process. He confronted something of a power vacuum, and his authoritarian, process-oriented personality led him to coerce his relatively helpless subordinates into submission. Fowler, too, was equal to the challenge posed by his situation. He was liked better than his predecessor, and his persistence, consistency and facility with bureaucratic routines were successful in deflecting the FCC toward different policy orientations. In contrast, Crowell's managerial capacity was insufficient for a challenge of much greater magnitude than any of the others faced. His efforts earned him respect but not results. It is not far fetched to imagine that a manager with Crowell's endowments might have done well in Peck's agency. Angrisani, on the other hand, might have been sunk by the turbulence he would have generated in more renitent agencies such as those of Ford or Crowell.

A comparison of these executives' designs—that is, the particular goals they chose to pursue and the means by which they pursued them—sheds more definitive light on their achievements. Considering these managers' varying accomplishments, it is not surprising that their designs also differed substantially in quality. Ford and Angrisani quickly achieved a pronounced effect on their agencies' core activities—mine inspections and procurement, respectively. Ford adopted a creative, complex strategy for changing his agency. By increasing the authority and the discretion of district supervisors in overseeing the inspection process, he sought to reduce the command and control emphasis in enforcement of the laws governing mine safety and health. At the same time, he redefined the role of the mine inspector—making him an agent for safety rather than an enforcer of rules—and reinforced this role by focusing heavily on the process of appraising the inspector's performance. Although capitalizing on pressures already present to deregulate mine safety enforcement, Ford was skilled in translating these pressures into a program for change.

Angrisani's goal was to make contracting more "efficient" and less subject to favoritism and other abuses by imposing more stringent criteria over contract awards and by standardizing the procurement process. He pursued these objectives by increasing the role of his office in approving procurement actions, by shifting authority over contracting from program officers to financial officers, and by promulgating a standard procurement model to reduce contract officer discretion in making awards. The flaw in this design is that it is internally inconsistent; procedural changes aimed at reducing fraud, waste, and abuse conflict with the objective of streamlining the process and of making it less arbitrary and uncertain. His failure to notice this inconsistency was responsible for considerable confusion and resentment in his agency.

Crowell and Fowler both had clear goals; Crowell's was to increase timber sales from the national forests and Fowler's was to reduce the federal role in regulating broadcast content and to increase access to communications media. Both appointees, however, chose ill-advised strategies to achieve these goals. Crowell attempted to increase budgetary allocations for timber sales at a time when there was little apparent rationale for such a policy. And Fowler sought congressional repeal of the "fairness" and "equal time" doctrines despite advice that pursuit of this goal, for which there were better strategies, would be jeopardized by the ensuing controversies. Crowell's design included little else than the attempt to increase timber sales and when it collapsed he had nothing of real consequence left to emphasize. He failed to recognize that to achieve his goals, he would have to change the duties of the forest ranger. Fowler's strategy, which included internal changes, was more diverse, and he was less vulnerable to the failure of any particular aspect of it. For example, he sought to increase the sense of direction and accountability within the FCC by relying on a management-by-objectives process and by requiring each bureau to prepare action plans. He endeavored also to increase access to the communications media by making the licensing process less judgmental. In these pursuits, which were concerned with the core activity of licensing, he was much more successful.

Peck had a reasonable goal: shifting the emphasis of his agency away from issuance of stringent vehicle safety standards toward stimulating increased public awareness of safety through behavior modification. His plan for achieving this goal was vague and diffuse, however, and he did not appear to devote sustained attention to it. Some vehicle standards are different than they would otherwise have been because of his interventions, but his efforts to increase cooperative research between government and industry and to reeducate his career subordinates through a planning process came to nothing. Of the five designs, Peck's was the least precise and coherent.

Design, or, to use a more familiar term, strategy, thus emerges as an important factor in managerial success. Of the three most successful managers, Ford alone had a relatively well-conceived design, and the designs of Fowler and Angrisani had strengths sufficient to counterbalance their weaknesses. The two least effective managers, Crowell and Peck, had relatively poor designs. Indeed, an inadequate managerial strategy led to failure for a relatively good manager, Crowell, facing a difficult situation.

What conclusions can be drawn about determinants of managerial success or failure? Table 2 summarizes the foregoing discussion by rating each appointee as excellent, good, fair, or poor for each variable considered important

TABLE 2

FIVE FEDERAL MANAGERS AND THE RESULTS THEY ACHIEVED: A SUMMARY
ASSESSMENT

Agency Official	Skill	Personality	Opportunity	Design	Accomplishments
Albert Angrisani	Fair	Poor	Good	Good	Fair
John Crowell	Good	Excellent	Poor	Poor	Poor
Ford B. Ford	Good	Good	Fair	Excellent	Excellent
Mark Fowler	Fair	Fair	Good	Good	Good
Raymond Peck	Poor	Poor	Excellent	Fair	Poor

in an appointee's success. The information in the table suggests the following conjectures: good to excellent accomplishments are associated primarily with good to excellent designs and not directly with good to excellent skills or personality. Creating good designs may be difficult, however, and the degree of difficulty may be associated, in turn, with the difficulty of the opportunity. Both Ford and Crowell needed a sophisticated design to accomplish their goals in a decentralized agency. The problem of design for Angrisani and Fowler was less difficult. The experiences of these four suggest the importance of skills and personality—perhaps especially political skills and qualities of imagination and flexibility. *The greater the challenge—that is, the more difficult the opportunity and thus the more sophisticated the design needed to exploit it—the greater the premium on managerial skills and personality.* Although he had much going for him in terms of outside support, Ford's success can nonetheless be attributed to his personality and skills as a manager. Neither Angrisani nor Fowler needed managerial qualities equal to Ford's in order to succeed in relatively less challenging circumstances. Inspired and supported by a strong, ideologically consistent administration, these appointees were sufficient to their tasks. By contrast, Crowell, as capable as he was, lacked the political skill and the flexibility to give him a real chance to alter the practices of his venerable agency.

Policy Change and Agency Performance

The suggestion that an executive has been successful in changing his agency's core activity should not be taken to imply that the overall performance of the agency has therefore improved. Ford B. Ford's administration of the Mine Health and Safety Administration drew sustained criticism from organized labor and from some internal critics who suggested that safety has been jeopardized by Reagan's and Ford's policies.[5] All five Reagan appointees have been criticized for failures to enforce existing statutes and for sacrificing the public interest in favor of more parochial, selfish, or ideological interests. Fundamental change is bound to be controversial, especially when there is a polarization in relations between political parties or between the president and Congress, and change agents are almost certain to be surrounded by conflict. The question is whether there are any objective, or less relative, criteria by which to appraise the changes brought about by the appointees. What has been their impact on the quality of governance?

Available information is unfortunately insufficient to permit any comprehensive judgments, or even very good guesses, as to how these five appointees have affected the quantity, quality, or unit cost of their agencies, services, apart from the effects on these variables brought about by centrally imposed budget and staff reductions. It is not possible, for example, to determine whether Angrisani's policies affected the number of trainees, job placements, or trainee earnings or whether Ford has affected the safety of mines. And judgments as to whether Fowler's success in dampening his agency's enthusiasm for the "fairness" and "equal time" doctrines or on whether Crowell's success in increasing his agency's sensitivity to economic values has enhanced or retarded his agency's performance depend on one's views as to the wisdom of the policies being changed.

Nevertheless, the study interviews provide scattered information, largely of an impressionistic nature, bearing indirectly on changes in agency performance. The morale of career employees, and by implication their productivity, declined sharply in the ETA, the MHSA, and the NHTSA. Ford appeared to be building a base of support for his policies at the MHSA, however, and Peck was viewed more in sorrow than in anger and appeared to do no lasting harm at the NHTSA. Angrisani's rough treatment of the ETA seemed to have some damaging effects on performance. By centralizing and constricting the procurement process, Angrisani appeared to create a number of perverse effects, including heightened delays, increased resort to sole source awards and contract extensions, and meaningless paperwork. Impartial observers believed, however, that these disruptions were a small price to pay for what they saw as greatly heightened agency concern for management. In contrast, Fowler's actions at the FCC appeared to be working. Though processing delays increased, the cause appeared to be the greatly increased volume of applications for licenses. FCC watchers reported an improved agency re-

---

5. Ford B. Ford, "An Update on MSHA: Reorganization and Regulatory Perform," *American Mining Congress Journal*, April 1982, p. 24.

sponsiveness to various inquiries, and employee morale, which had been low under Fowler's predecessor, rose under Fowler.

Of interest, however, is that each appointee had to confront the issue of whether or not his agency's authorizing statute would constrain his freedom to act. Angrisani and Fowler both sought changes in authorizing legislation, though Fowler was unsuccessful. The other three appointees (Fowler, too, after he saw the futility of obtaining legislative changes, made conscious decisions to stretch interpretations of authorizing language as far as necessary to accommodate their policy views, even if commonly accepted interpretations of intent were breached in the process. And all were at least partially successful in this regard.

Did Reagan's electoral mandate justify a sustained assault on previously accepted versions of legislative intent? Should a presidential appointee ask, "What does the law, as interpreted by a clever general counsel, permit?" rather than "What did the legislature intend?"—making due allowance for the vague and inconsistent nature of most statutes? Reagan's is not the only administration, of course, to seek relief from the chafing of legislative intent— nor should our Constitution and system of laws be regarded as narrowly binding—but the extent of the Reagan administration's efforts to evade the law instead of confronting the legislature makes it doubtful that its approach to administrative management can be unequivocally branded "good governance."

The evidence, then, does not support claims either that Reagan's appointees, as opposed to Reagan's budgetary or personnel policies, have caused widespread deterioration in agency performance or that they have made federal management generally more efficient and more businesslike. If anything, they have demonstrated the extent to which federal statutes can be reinterpreted to permit significant organizational change.

Improving Managerial Performance: The President's Role

These five appointees do not, of course, an administration make. A significant number of Reagan appointees have made spectacular exits from public service or have fallen from grace for real or perceived transgressions. While most Reagan appointees were part of the effort to cut back and deregulate, some, especially in the area of defense, were engaged in expanding governmental activity. Expansion makes different demands on executives than does contraction, and an appraisal of the success of such executives engaged in expansionist change might identify different variables. The five appointees in this study may be taken to broadly represent Reagan's domestic appointees, however, and lessons derived from their performance can be instructive for future administrations.

Reagan's practice of appointing like-minded subordinates and of expecting loyal service from them has served him reasonably well. Although his appointees' performances were uneven, on balance all moved the government in directions consistent with his policies. How their particular contributions rank in terms of changes attributable to RIFs and budget cuts depends on the administration's overall purposes, but a good case can be made that an administration committed to reshaping governmental roles and performance will place substantial emphasis on its cabinet and subcabinet appointees and their potential roles in bringing about fundamental change.

The record of Reagan's five appointees, however, supports the impression that the power of appointment is an uncertain instrument of presidential influence. Presidential advisers might well have hoped for greater achievements from this group of officials. The Reagan administration is changing the government, but not nearly to the extent that it might have if these officials as a group had been more capable. Opportunities were missed in at least four of the five agencies.

It is likely, moreover, that actual performances departed from expectations in unpredictable ways, given the administration's insufficient prior knowledge of these appointees. Presidential recruiters seldom assess skills, personality, and opportunity in the depth that this study suggests is relevant. Nor is a candidate's likely design ordinarily ascertained. The cost of undertaking such assessments would be significant. The question is whether the benefits in terms of appointee contributions to presidential goals would be worth it.

The results of this study can only suggest the answer to this question. The attributes of these appointees are sufficiently pronounced so that careful investigation of references would probably have revealed most of them. Assessing the precise nature of the opportunities for which appointees are to be sought might be more difficult and costly, but the insights gained thereby could be valuable; skilled and patient managers could be placed where these qualities are particularly necessary in accomplishing presidential purposes. Advance insight into a candidate's competence at designing a strategy may be the most difficult capability of all to obtain. Evidence that a candidate has created good designs in other responsible positions is an imperfect but useful indicator of how he or she will perform in government. Unlike skills and personality, however, appointees' strategies are not altogether beyond presidential control once they are in office, and continuing oversight by OMB and the president's policy staffs can aid appointees' performances.

President Reagan helped his cause by choosing appointees who shared his vision and by communicating and implicitly enforcing his sense of purpose among subordinate political executives. If Reagan and his recruiters had had a more explicit understanding of how lasting change in governmental activity is achieved, they might have used the power of appointment to even greater effect. Investing in an effort to match skills, personality, and opportunity, and assisting appointees in designing managerial strategies, could yield significant benefits to the president's program.

An Executive's Success Can Have Costs

Laurence E. Lynn, Jr., has made my task easy by producing a very direct, no-nonsense paper. The questions are succinctly posed, the definitions are clear, the methodology is well executed, and the conclusions are reasonable. In an area of study noted for fluffy homilies, Lynn comes close to offering hard evidence on political management in the executive branch. One might wish that he had taken more direct account of the currently fashionable literature on "decremental management" (i.e., the idea that management strategies and styles differ systematically during periods of government cutbacks versus periods of growth). But that is only a quibble with what is otherwise a solid piece of work.

Need for Peripheral Vision

At the same time, larger issues regarding the effects of Reaganism on the federal bureaucracy were not dealt with appreciably in the paper, an omission that is understandable in light of Lynn's research design. Basically the paper tries nobly to do two somewhat different things. One purpose is to report on Reagan's efforts to use presidential appointees to change bureaucratic behavior. The second aim is to test a theory of executive effectiveness in five federal agencies. As the paper acknowledges, the evidence yielded in pursuing the second purpose is not sufficient to produce significant conclusions addressing the first purpose. We learn that appointees' strategies (as these strategies match up with opportunities that make greater or lesser demands on skill) are the key to explaining effectiveness. We learn that in one agency—and to a lesser extent in two others—appointees have succeeded in producing changes roughly in line with presidential thinking. To arrive at a more general conclusion about Reagan's effects in the bureaucracy would require not simply more cases but a longer time span and a fuller picture of bureaucratic behavior. Lynn's attempt to test a theory of management thus does not permit peripheral

371

vision; it dictates that we study the problem in a monofocal or linear way, looking at specific appointees' goals, at appointees' personal strengths and weaknesses, at specific agency contexts and opportunities, and at the designs chosen by these appointees and the resultant outcomes. This is fine so far as it goes, but it is only one perspective and a fairly narrow one at that. What we do not see are the same events in the context of the larger organizational life of government.

I exaggerate slightly. Occasionally, the paper does suggest some unintended side effects. For example it is noted that one of Reagan's "good" performers (Albert Angrisani at the Employment and Training Administration) succeeded in his goal of imposing more centralized financial management, but that he did so at the price of increasing the amount of paperwork and producing time-consuming bottlenecks in administration. But given the paper's emphasis on the effectiveness of individual appointees, these other results are not developed extensively. What this study cannot provide is a well-rounded appreciation of the the effects of Reaganism in the bureaucracy. Let me give some purely hypothetical examples to illustrate what I mean by peripheral vision on the organizational life of government.

View from Within

First, within an organization, an appointee may be highly "effective" in achieving his or her and the president's agenda, with little regard to ensuring longer-term organizational health. A suggestive list of these costs is not difficult to imagine:

—The appointee's agenda may have displaced organizational attention and resources from a preexisting and more promising agenda of change. It is in the nature of things that each new appointee heavily discounts his or her predecessor's bright ideas.

—The appointee's success in creating change in one part of the organization may have imposed strains and produced reactions in other parts, with a lowering of organizational performance as a whole. Almost by definition, a successful appointee must be preoccupied with only those features of the organization that are directly relevant to his or her desired change.

—A successful appointee may have created divisions among permanent staff that reduce the capacities for effective cooperation and advice when the next appointee comes along with a different agenda. This is not an implausible result, since strategic-minded appointees are likely to exploit favorable segments of opinion in the organization and to profit from sidetracking or ending the careers of bureaucratic opponents with different opinions. Yet it may be precisely the demoralized segments that the next appointee needs most to draw upon. The result is an imbalanced organization that can walk with only its right or left feet.

I do not think these examples are farfetched. Given appointees' short tenure in office; given that appointees who are high achievers for their presidents are likely to be fairly single-minded in their devotion to the agenda at hand; given that most appointees will have no enduring personal stakes in the longer-term well-being of the agencies they head—given all these things, I think we should want to know much more about the organizational costs of political executives' success. We should be especially sensitive to this issue in an administration that (rhetorically at least) denigrates the idea of a positive, vigorous civilian government.

View from Without

A second area in which peripheral vision would be useful is outside the appointee's own organization. Again it is easy to imagine a list of liabilities that can be produced by appointees who are "successes" in translating their agenda into bureaucratic behavior:

—The greater an appointee's bureaucratic effectiveness, the more this success may have the effect of mobilizing outside political opponents. The appointee becomes an inadvertant fundraiser for interest groups, a point of integration and focus for otherwise fragmented congressional critics, a supplier of case material for litigious opponents, and so on.

—Few political appointees succeed in carrying out their designs without making compromises along the way. Whether the constraints imposed by such side payments, commitments, and other deals are worth the success achieved is of course an open question. It is an especially problematic one from a White House perspective. Even if the "success" is what the president would have wanted had he known all the details himself (a dubious assumption), the inevitable result is to tie the president to a set of understandings that reduce his future room for political and bureaucratic maneuver.

—Successes achieved by appointees occur within a particular bureaucratic setting (one appointee tightens up central financial management; another one increases discretion in the field inspectorate). Our governmental system is especially weak in ensuring that initiatives by the various segments of the bureaucracy bear reasonable relationship with one another. The result is that a large number of uncoordinated successes may serve to increase the muddle of the whole.

This matter of holistic effects is perhaps the most appropriate point on which to conclude, for it is the same question of governance that is addressed by this volume as a whole. If governance results from the joint interaction of many different parts, it follows that the appropriate unit of analysis is not appointees in bureaus, or interest groups, or the presidency, or the administration's program in Congress, or the actions of the courts. The appropriate unit of analysis is the cluster of interrelated parts that produces the results by which we are governed. Reaganism affects governance by deploying ideologically committed appointees who not only pursue agendas but also affect organizational capacities; which helps mobilize outside groups and alliances; who then defend themselves through the courts and promote judicial activism; which then encourages members of Congress and their staffs to write legislation specifying legislative intent (or to duck the issue at hand); which then affects White House calculations as to legislative strategy—and so on and so on. Governance is a web of actions, reactions, and anticipations spread across the political landscape. Evaluations of management "success" need to take account of this larger view.

Political Administration Is Legitimate

Should politicians control the bureaucracy? This is one of the least studied, yet most critical, questions of American governance. Laurence E. Lynn, Jr., has applied an imaginative framework to his study of the Reagan administration's efforts to penetrate and control federal agency operations. In what is to my mind one of the most original papers in this book, Lynn focuses on five Reagan appointees, telling us in each case what they did and whether, according to his definitions, they succeeded in changing what he refers to as the "core activities" of their agency. He attempts both to use and to make theory. He judges Reagan's results as mixed, and he presents a conceptual apparatus for understanding and assessing the relationship between executive branch politicians (in this case, Reagan's subcabinet appointees) and career civil servants.

Reagan's Administrative Strategy

Of the two major questions that the papers in this volume attempt to answer—what has Ronald Reagan achieved, and how has he achieved what many consider to be his chief accomplishments—it is to the second of these that Lynn's study is directed. How did Reagan do it? What institutional levers and political strategies were used? How well were they used? One of the main institutional strategies that Reagan has employed is an administrative strategy. More than any president since World War II, Reagan has attempted to push his ideas into agency operations—to achieve some or some part of his objectives by administrative action. Lynn describes how the Reagan administration has endeavored to do this by appointing like-minded, energetic subcabinet officials who are committed to the administration's objectives and who are willing to challenge career officials in order to incorporate these ideas into the administrative processes.

To appreciate Reagan's success in these terms, a well-known point bears emphasizing, which is that it is extremely difficult to make changes in our American, Madisonian governmental system with its multiple checks and balances. Ours is a highly competitive political system in which many actors from many vantage points can and do resist change. Taking this point into account, I give Reagan higher marks than does Lynn for the success of his administrative strategy. Lynn, for example, grades Assistant Secretary of Labor Albert Angrisani with qualifications. While I have personal reservations about some of the things Angrisani achieved, I am more impressed than Lynn by the way he took on the entrenched bureaucracy of the Employment and Training Administration. Angrisani was actively involved in, and strongly supported, the Reagan–David Stockman efforts to reduce the size and cost of ETA programs, to change their ideological orientation, and to "defund the left" in the agency's contracting operations.

After Angrisani's appointment but before he took charge, senior officials at the ETA told me that he would be like all the others: He would sputter and grope to change things for six months, and then everything would settle down and be just as it was before with the same people in charge. However, Albert Angrisani was not like the others, and the same people are not in charge today; some of them are no longer with the agency. I know of other examples involving social programs in grant-making agencies where Reaganites have applied similar strategies with similar successes. ETA career officials did not like Angrisani; the process was not a smooth and happy one, but change did occur. Reagan's policies penetrated this bureaucracy.

Lynn deals primarily with the operational aspects of Reagan's administrative strategy among the five appointees. The remainder of my comments will focus on the theoretical lessons of Reagan's approach. To begin with, is it right for President Reagan to use political appointees in the administrative arena?

On this question I am no shy flower, nor am I in my usual role as dispassionate analyst. I think it is appropriate and, in fact, desirable in our governmental system for political appointees to be involved in administrative processes. I believe, furthermore, that when the wheel of government rotates again to the liberal side on domestic issues, this is precisely what social policy liberals must do in their turn.[1]

---

1. For an excellent discussion of shifting public policy moods and approaches, see Albert O. Hirschman, *Shifting Involvements: Private Interest and Public Action* (Princeton, N.J.: Princeton University Press, 1982).

Max Weber said bureaucracy is "government by experts."[2] Certainly there is no getting around the need for expertise in the modern state. Today, technocratic power centers are found both in and outside of government. Yet when the political going gets toughest, the issues that become politicized almost always are *value* issues, not technical questions that can be answered definitively. Often knowledgeable experts argue both sides of issues. In such cases, in which intensely controversial matters frequently arise involving agency operations, the concept of an administrative strategy comes into play. I argue that it is appropriate under these conditions for political officials to *attempt* to influence these decisions. They do not always win. There are other players, too, but political appointees have every right to participate in the decision-making process on administrative issues that involve the goals and values of the government they serve.

Why the Strategy is Legitimate

The Reagan administrative strategy, carefully planned in advance by E. Pendleton James and Counselor to the President Edwin Meese III, is an expression of what the electorate frequently says it wants—leadership and change. Whether or not the public agrees with the leadership and change that resulted, the Reagan administration used effective, legitimate strategies to further its ideas. Now, the burden is on me to say why I think an administrative strategy is legitimate.

Several ideas connect here. My essential thesis is that in a highly change-resistant political system with a technologically advanced economy, in which many complex social value issues interact, and where many policy decisions are made in administrative processes, executive branch politicians (and this applies also to governors, mayors, and county executives) should give *greater attention* to administrative processes. Our laws often permit agency heads wide latitude in defining policy by enabling them to write and implement regulations and by a myriad of other ways in which appointees influence the rules, procedures, and the strategy and tone of agency action. Moreover, the dangers of such an administrative strategy tend to be overstated. The U.S. political system, as has been emphasized here, is open, accessible, and highly competitive, and there are many ways in which excesses in pursuing an

---

2. Max Weber, *The Theory of Social and Economic Organization*, ed. Talcott Parsons and trans. A. M. Henderson and Talcott Parsons, paperback ed. (Glencoe, Ill.: The Free Press, 1964).

administrative presidency (or a gubernatorial or a mayoral) strategy can be identified and rooted out. In fact, the most conspicuous excesses of the Reagan administration's administrative presidency strategy support my point. James Watt, former secretary of the Department of the Interior, and Anne Gorsuch Burford, former head of the Environmental Protection Agency, were so heavy-handed in their agencies that the activities of opposition groups and the popular outcry they engendered led the Reagan administration to remove these officials and to retreat in substantive terms from its own policy goals in these areas.

The other side of the coin of an administrative strategy is the contention that such activities are an intrusion on the proper role of career officials. This issue, discussed in Edie N. Goldenberg's paper in this volume, raises again the perennial question in political science of whether, as Woodrow Wilson argued, a distinction should be made between policy and administration: Are politicians supposed to work on policy issues but stay out of administration?

In my view, Paul H. Appleby was right when he said we cannot separate policy and administrative issues and that whether a given issue is a policy issue is basically a function of how controversial it is.[3] For example, the decision to locate a police substation in my urban neighborhood may sound like a technical issue to some people, but it is one on which mayors, council members, and many urban political groups are likely to have strong and differing views. They make it a policy issue.

It is in these terms that many of the tasks that government agencies perform that involve the work of career officials become policy issues—that is, the tasks become policy matters because they are regarded as critical and controversial. For instance, the types of jobs that welfare recipients should be required to accept are not chiseled in stone. This question is value-laden and therefore has become a policy issue now being played out in the administrative process. Numerous actors in the policy process seek to have a voice in this decision. Given the Reagan administration's specific viewpoint on welfare, it is appropriate for presidential appointees in the responsible agencies to attempt to influence these agencies to act in a way that reflects the Reagan stance. Their role, I repeat, is to attempt to influence governmental operations and procedures. They do not operate by fiat. Such a role for political officials is neither dangerous nor inappropriate. As Wallace Sayre, Paul Appleby, Pendleton Herring, Herbert Kaufman, Hugh Heclo, and others have taught us, governmental agencies do not exist in a political vacuum. They are in-

---

3. Paul H. Appleby, *Policy and Administration* (University, Ala.: University of Alabama Press, 1949), p. 13.

fluenced by many actors—Congress, the courts, interest groups, the bureaucracy itself, the press. There are many ways in which important players in these issue networks can counter administrative strategies pursued by people like Albert Angrisani, John Crowell, Ford B. Ford, Mark Fowler, and Raymond Peck, as Lynn's paper so ably demonstrates.

THE PERMANENT GOVERNMENT IN AN ERA OF RETRENCHMENT AND REDIRECTION

Edie N. Goldenberg

One of President Ronald Reagan's oft-expressed priorities is to cut the size, cost, and scope of the permanent government in the area of domestic policy. A second goal is to encourage those career employees who remain to respond enthusiastically to presidential leadership. President Reagan and his political appointees cast the civil servant in the role of an administrator. In so doing, they embrace the idea of a policy-administration dichotomy. They do not want permanent employees to act as policy entrepreneurs or to exercise discretion. Rather, President Reagan wants, to limit their activity to that of responding to the policy initiatives that emerge from political appointees.

In order to pursue these goals, President Reagan imposed a hiring freeze immediately upon taking office, and a number of his appointees ran reductions in force (RIFs) in their agencies. Reagan not only made political loyalty a necessary condition for appointment to cabinet and subcabinet positions, but he also increased the number of political appointments at lower levels. He supported proposals that would reduce federal employee benefits, that would correct for overgrading (and therefore overpaying) of employees, and that would contract out to the private sector a wide range of activities currently provided in-house. These were among the most dramatic initiatives undertaken by the Reagan administration for the explicit purposes of reduction and control.

Of course, the actual consequences of these initiatives may be quite different from what was intended. For example, reductions in force may actually increase cost in the short term, since those who are fired receive severance pay and other benefits, while those who remain sometimes receive high levels of pay in low-level jobs. Moreover, less dramatic actions may be more consequential for the future of the permanent government in the long run. For instance, raising executive salaries and hiring new recruits noncompetitively may be more significant in the long term for the quality of the public service. In addition, criticizing government employees and the public service in general may further erode public confidence in government, may demoralize government workers, and may discourage potential future recruits.

It is still too soon to assess definitively the impact of Reagan initiatives on the career service. The task is complicated further by the fact that some actions were set in motion before President Reagan assumed office. Nevertheless, this paper provides a preliminary assessment of the actual and likely effects of the Reagan administration on the career service. The assessment, in three parts, identifies lost opportunities for improvement in this administration as well as the results of new programmatic directions. Any judgment of the administration's efforts in this area requires a vision of what the career service ought to be and an evaluation of whether particular presidential actions contribute to or hinder the realization of that vision. The first section of this paper, therefore, discusses various perspectives on what the career service in our system can and should be. The second section examines the actual and likely effects of various changes stimulated by the Reagan administration. The final section considers the overall probable impact of these changes on the permanent government.

Role of the Career Service

The variety of federal jobs is astounding. In addition to the thousands of white-collar employees—secretaries, clerks, accountants, claims examiners, attorneys, internal revenue agents—an amazing number of forgotten specialties exist that are not usually associated with career service. Federal employees work, for instance, as physicians, funeral directors, bakers, microbiologists, museum curators, groundskeepers, horse wranglers, and glassblowers. In the face of such occupational diversity, meaningful statements about the average federal employee are difficult to make.

Most of the heated debate over the role of civil servants is directed at a relatively small subset of employees, the roughly one hundred thousand personnel who are responsible for managing the bureaus, regional offices, and other installations where much of the government's public business is conducted. There is little argument over how a letter should be typed or filed, but important disagreements emerge over whether the letter should be written in the first place and what it should say. These are the decisions of supervisors and their managers who set policy either explicitly or implicitly as their daily actions accumulate into patterns of behavior.

In spite of the obvious importance of the actions of these one hundred thousand managers, there is no widely accepted view of what their role should be. It is commonplace to note that the framers of our Constitution never anticipated such a large and diverse civil service as exists today. Neither the Constitution itself nor other documents of the period provide a cogent description of the place of the bureaucracy in our system; instead, the role of the civil servant was left to evolve without explicit guidance.

Most democratic theorists see some form of political control over the bureaucracy as essential, but such control does not have to be exerted solely by the president. One of the many questions left unanswered in the Constitution is how much control over the civil service should be exerted by whom. The Constitution specifies that executive departments will be headed by officials appointed by the president, with the advice and consent of the Senate. As political scientist James Q. Wilson reminds us, however, Congress was left to decide how these officials can be removed, and the decision was controversial.[1] Vice-President John Adams had to cast a tie-breaking vote in the Senate to give the president sole right of removal. Since the early days of the Republic, opinions have diverged on whether or not the executive departments should be wholly subordinate to the president. Our system's structural design makes complete subordination virtually impossible.

Among the differing views on the essential role of the civil service, four broad perspectives have been discussed and debated in normative and empirical terms: civil servants as passive extensions of the presidency, civil servants as active supporters of the presidency, civil servants as brokers of conflicting interests, and civil servants as protectors of the public interest. Each of these roles warrants elaboration here, particularly in terms of the impact of administration actions on the ability of permanent employees to perform them.

Extension of the Presidency

Whoever inhabits the White House tends to believe that civil servants should be hierarchically subordinate to the president. This view is especially appealing to those who cling to the idea of a policy-administration dichotomy, with the politicians (meaning the president and his appointees) making decisions and civil servants merely executing them through administrative action.

---

1. James Q. Wilson, "The Rise of the Bureaucratic State," *The Public Interest*, no. 41 (Fall 1975), pp. 77–103.

The vision of civil servants as subordinates of the president dates back to the constitutional period, but it gained renewed momentum in response to the fragmentation that resulted from the good-government reforms of the late-nineteenth and early-twentieth centuries. Independent boards and commissions and merit-system protections for employees insulated the career service from the influence of executive leadership. As social scientist Herbert Kaufman has pointed out, there were many criticisms of this fragmentation, including that it "bred chaos," "fomented conflict," "opened gaps in the provision of service," "was costly," and "led to irresponsibility."[2] A solution that appealed to some reformers was to strengthen the executive by pulling administrative functions, including personnel management, back under the president.

Establishing effective presidential control over the executive branch is one of the greatest challenges a president faces. The provisions of the Civil Service Reform Act of 1978[3] were designed in large part to provide additional tools to presidents and their appointees to control top-level civil servants in the bureaucracy. These reforms made it easier not only for political appointees to move career executives around within their own agencies but to hire career and noncareer executives of their choice and to shift executive-level positions into areas of high priority. Appointees now also have more flexibility in establishing pay rates for executives and managers. The Reagan administration was the first to have these provisions available from the outset, and, as is discussed later in this paper, they have been applied vigorously.

As tidy and compelling as is the idea that the civil service can or should be merely a passive extension of the presidency, not everyone agrees with it. A sharp distinction between policy and administration is more myth than reality. Career civil servants set policy every day in the course of exercising necessary discretion on the job. Since these civil servants are trained as professionals and develop expertise over years of experience, they are often better equipped than political appointees to identify promising policy directions. In certain circumstances, civil servants are expected to resist the directions of their political appointees. When laws are broken or agencies are grossly mismanaged, civil servants are supposed to "blow the whistle" and make the problem public. Legitimate whisteblowing is recognized in presidential policy statements and is protected by law. Many believe that for government to operate effectively, civil servants must be active rather than passive, and that their activity will inevitably involve them in policymaking.

---

2. Herbert Kaufman, "Emerging Conflicts in the Doctrine of Public Administration," *American Political Science Review* (December 1956), pp. 1057–1073.
    3. Public Law 95-454, October 13, 1978.

Active Supporters of the Presidency

Politicians assuming federal posts in Washington, D.C., immediately face three separate budgets—the current one, the one before Congress, and the one in preparation by the Office of Management and Budget (OMB)—in addition to a host of other complexities related to running the programs under their jurisdiction. If these politicians bark orders without seeking advice from their career subordinates, their successes will be few and their failures may be embarrassing. Even under normal circumstances, passive support by civil servants rarely is enough to allow presidential appointees to accomplish their objectives. This is because civil servants understand the technical details of getting things done in government. After all, they designed the complex personnel, budget, information, and contracting systems, and they have had years of experience operating under them. Civil servants also are expert at responding to the growing number of legislative requirements: they know what is required when and by whom. Their positive support and guidance is thus crucial, especially for the numerous political appointees with little previous government experience.

Because of the fragmentation of authority that is built into our political system, cooperation within and across agencies is also essential to accomplish most important tasks. Such cooperation depends upon trust that is established over time in relatively stable working relationships. Most civil servants, especially those in older agencies, follow career paths that start at the bottom and move up an agency's bureaucratic ladder. Over the years, these employees develop effective networks and credits based on helping others along the way. Through the people they know in other agencies, they can learn about developments before they happen and can strike agreements about divisions of responsibility and action. Based upon their knowledge of past experience, civil servants can often predict which interest groups will become active and which members of Congress will become exercised over particular issues. The civil servant, if anyone, provides organizational memory.

In contrast, political appointees rarely arrive with an effective network in place. They have to build one. If they stay only two or three years, they may just have time to develop the relationships they need in order to accomplish something before they leave.[4] Meanwhile, their career subordinates can help get things done sooner.

What may be less obvious about the importance of civil servants is the influential role they can play in setting sensible policy directions in the first

---

4. Hugh Heclo, *A Government of Strangers* (Washington, D.C.: The Brookings Institution, 1977), p. 104.

place. Given their professional training and technical and organizational savvy, civil servants are uniquely able to identify problems and fashion programs that can work, anticipating difficulties that may cause other approaches to fail. They can serve their political appointees by providing policy ideas, some of which are already well-formulated and waiting to be plucked from file drawers at the first sign of interest from above. (Of course, these signals sometimes come from outside the agency, from Congress, from the courts, or from interest groups.)

Brokers of Conflicting Interests

With the separation of powers, especially between the executive and legislative branches, civil servants receive orders from multiple masters. Federal agencies owe their existence and budgets to Congress as well as to the president. Each agency has its own separate statutory base and laws to administer. Each deals with a different set of subcommittees in Congress, and each has its own set of clients, supporters, and detractors outside the government.

Given the often conflicting policy preferences of the president and Congress, and the frequently vague guidance in the law, the civil servant's task in responding to political priorities has never been straightforward. Unable to reach consensus on highly charged issues, Congress intentionally passes some difficult decisions to departments and agencies by omitting critical but controversial details from legislation. Because decisions have to be made before programs can begin, political appointees and their career subordinates make them, shifting the focus of political debate and controversy away from Congress and to their executive agency. In the process, bureaucrats sometimes find themselves directly involved in highly political situations.

Hugh Heclo describes the usual bureaucratic response as one of "gradualism."[5] Left to establish a course of action, civil servants try to accommodate all strenuous objections in order to protect their programs. This tends to produce incremental policy adjustments that temper (and sometimes frustrate) the sharper alterations that some political leaders would prefer. On the other hand, civil servants strike a compromise among various legitimate political actors. It is in this sense that they become brokers of clashing interests in political conflicts.

Of course, the nature of the compromise they reach may serve their own interests. Elected leaders come and go, but civil servants remain. They know they will be called upon to explain and defend their programs to Congress

---

5. Ibid, pp. 143–144.

and to political appointees in the future. They also know that their own livelihood and the livelihood of the people who work for them depend on how effective a defense they can muster. They have to motivate subordinates to take programmatic action, and motivation becomes difficult if orders shift dramatically every two or four years. Therefore, they resist embarking in directions they believe are indefensible, especially if they see those directions as radical departures attractive to only one of the two parties.

Contradictory and vague instructions create both problems and opportunities for civil servants. Trying to please multiple bosses is rarely easy, but, within certain boundaries, bureaucrats can refer to whatever guidance they wish in order to support the directions they believe are best. They can and do exercise discretion that sometimes departs from presidential and congressional guidance, and when they do, they inevitably justify this departure in terms of the "public interest."

Protectors of the Public Interest

In reaction to the incompetent and unethical behavior of political bosses and their patronage appointees, the idea of insulating the bureaucracy from political control gained acceptance in the late-nineteenth century. Merit provisions were adopted to hire the most talented people available and to protect them from political abuse and control. The neutral competence of a professionalized bureaucracy was expected to solve problems efficiently. According to this view, civil servants could provide the long-term planning and sustained action that was absent in a system dominated by politicians with short-term horizons.

The need for a professionalized civil service only increased as the problems of the twentieth century became more complex and the government required more and more specialists and technocrats. Today, most career executives in the United States hold advanced degrees.[6] Scientists and engineers, doctors and lawyers practice their professions in the public sector. Their training instills in them certain values, standards, and models about how the world works that guide their actions on the job and that evolve further into notions about what serves the public interest. Unless political appointees are credible as experts themselves, they can find that leading their highly trained career employees in new directions is not easy.

---

6. *Federal Employee Attitudes—Phase 2: Follow-up Survey, 1980* (Washington, D.C.: Government Printing Office, 1983), p. 42. Demographic data from the U.S. Office of Personnel Management's (OPM's) Federal Employee Attitude Survey revealed that 69 percent of the executive respondents held graduate degrees. Twenty percent were trained in law, 18 percent in engineering, and 15 percent in business.

Such tensions did not seem to bother early reformers, who saw political leaders—because of their frequent need to be reelected—as too susceptible to pressure from special interests. With tenure, civil servants were expected to be more independent of special interests and therefore freer to run public programs in the broader public interest. As Kaufman points out, one goal of reformers was to reduce the vulnerability of agencies to political leaders and to demands for special favors by constituents whom appointees hesitate to offend.[7]

On the other hand, people differ in their views of what constitutes the public interest, and there is no guarantee that the views held by career professionals are more accurate or more desirable than those held by elected officials. At least officials can be thrown out of office for unpopular views. Indeed, civil servants who are completely insulated from the electoral process create problems of democratic accountability.

Making civil servants more responsive to the public is one concern underlying work on representative bureaucracy. For example, demographic representativeness rather than professional training is considered by some to be the key to protecting the public's interests. However, no scholarly work has yet demonstrated that citizens are better served by bureaucrats who share their demographic characteristics than by those with different backgrounds.[8] Nevertheless, much of the work describing the demographic makeup of the bureaucracy assumes such a connection.

These four alternative views of the role of high-level civil servants in our political system are neither mutually exclusive nor completely compatible with each other. Each contains insights into the important functions that civil servants do and should perform if the system is to function effectively. And each may be used as a broad benchmark against which President Reagan's initiatives can be assessed.

Reagan Initiatives

President Reagan and his appointees have proposed and implemented initiatives with significant implications for the permanent government. The

---

7. Herbert Kaufman, "Reflections on Administrative Reorganization," in Frederick S. Lane, ed., *Current Issues in Public Administration* (New York: St. Martin's Press, 1978), pp. 68–77.

8. In fact, data have been presented suggesting that civil servants hold views at variance with their socioeconomic counterparts outside of the government. See Joel D. Aberbach, Robert D. Putnam, and Bert A Rockman, *Bureaucrats and Politicians in Western Democracies* (Cambridge, Mass.: Harvard University Press, 1981), chapter 3.

most dramatic of these have been directed at civilian personnel—especially those in nonpostal domestic agencies—who make up less than half of the total federal work force. Many of these initiatives are complex and serve multiple purposes. For ease of discussion each is presented here under one of three general headings: reducing the size and scope of government; increasing presidential control over civil servants; and recruiting and retaining desirable employees.

Reducing the Size and Scope of Government

As mentioned earlier, immediately upon taking office, President Reagan imposed a retroactive hiring freeze on federal agencies and announced that he would reduce federal civilian employment in nondefense agencies by nearly one hundred thousand people. President Jimmy Carter had already scheduled personnel reductions in his 1981 and 1982 projections, but Reagan promised to slash even deeper and to concentrate his cuts on domestic agencies. Meanwhile, the Department of Defense (DoD), which had fallen from 56 percent of total civilian employment in 1960 and 1970 to 41 percent by 1980, was slated for an unspecified personnel increase. Between 1980 and 1986, President Reagan proposed increasing the national defense share of federal spending from 23 percent to 38 percent. If past practice holds true, such a boost will produce a significant increase in the size of the civilian work force in the DoD.[9]

The reorganizations, RIFs, and shifts in budget and policy priorities that resulted from Reagan's actions forced or encouraged many employees in targeted agencies to leave government service. For example, the Community Services Administration (CSA) was abolished as of October 1981. Although the Department of Health and Human Services (HHS) assumed some of the CSA's functions, the successor office in HHS employed only about one-third as many people as had the CSA at the time it was disbanded.

Pronounced changes in budget priorities forced transfers of personnel. Between 1980 and 1983, real government spending shifted from domestic programs (other than Social Security and Medicare) to defense.[10] Because some programs are more labor-intensive than others, budget modifications do not always translate directly into personnel. However, changes of such magnitude usually do, and these were no exception.

---

9. Robert W. Hartman, *Pay and Pensions for Federal Workers* (Washington, D.C.: The Brookings Institution, 1983), p. 4.

10. See Council of Economic Advisers data cited in John M. Berry, "Politics, Ideology Underlie Deficit Dispute," *Washington Post*, December 1, 1983, p. A-7.

Large-scale reductions in the size of the federal work force have occurred previously when the Department of Defense has had to be scaled back at the end of a war. Reagan's reduction program was different, however, in that it focused on domestic agencies. Regular monitoring by the Office of Personnel Management (OPM) shows that more than twelve thousand employees lost their jobs as a result of RIFs conducted during fiscal years 1981 and 1982. Additional layoffs occurred in 1983, with more planned for 1984. Thousands of people were bumped from one job to another after the formal RIF rules were imposed, and thousands of others left the government voluntarily. Many of the forced separations were in the Departments of the Interior, Health and Human Services, Commerce, and Agriculture, as well as in the General Services Administration (GSA), but smaller agencies such as the OPM also ran RIFs. And in 1981 the Department of Transportation (DoT) fired thousands of air traffic controllers following their strike.

Budget cuts, RIFs, and the hiring freeze reduced the size of the federal work force in domestic agencies. By September 1983 there were approximately ninety-two thousand fewer people (seventy-one thousand full-time equivalents [FTEs]) in nonpostal domestic agencies than there had been in January 1981.[11] Also by September 1983 the Tennessee Valley Authority, the Departments of Commerce and Education, the Interstate Commerce Commission, the Consumer Product Safety Commission, and the Federal Trade Commission were each more than 25 percent smaller in terms of employees than they had been two years earlier. The OPM and GSA were not far behind. DoD was the big winner, increasing in size during that period by over fifty-five thousand employees (about 7 percent). The size of DoD's civilian work force has also continued to grow during fiscal year (FY) 1984. DoD's growth has offset much of the domestic decline in terms of employment. As a result, the civilian work force overall is only about 1 percent smaller in 1984 than when President Reagan took office.

Reductions in force have disproportionately affected women and minorities working for the federal government, and dollar savings from RIFs are yet to be realized. Women were more likely than men, and minorities more likely than nonminorities, to be fired in the 1981 and 1982 RIFs.[12] The costs of administering RIFS, of continuing to pay higher salaries even after people were reassigned to lower-level jobs, and of paying severance and other

---

11. "Reagan Administration Very Close to Achieving Employment Reduction Goal a Year before Target Date," U.S. Office of Personnel Management *News*, January 10, 1984.

12. U.S. Merit Systems Protection Board, Office of Merit Systems Review and Studies, *Reduction-in-Force in the Federal Government, 1981* (Washington, D.C.: Government Printing Office, June 1983), pp. 27–28.

benefits have been so substantial that RIFs have not saved money in the near term.

Three other types of initiatives related to controlling the size and scope of the federal govenment are under way, but it is still too early to assess their effects. First, OMB revised its circular A-76 to encourage contracting with the private sector in cases where services can be provided at lower cost than by in-house federal workers. By easing the rules on required comparisons of federal costs and private-sector bids, and by requiring agencies to conduct reviews in an effort to identify those jobs that might be contracted, OMB's instructions should encourage more contracting in the future.

Most contractable jobs appear to be in the defense area. Contracting out work activity offers the potential both for increasing DoD's effective work force without adding more civil servants and for spending more money without increasing personnel. Since 1950, the size of the federal civilian work force has remained relatively stable, while total federal outlays have grown markedly. The federal government expanded its scope of activities but relied on other parties to carry them out. For example, state and local government employment over this period has grown rapidly, along with federal grants-in-aid to state and local governments.[13] The size of the work force in the private sector that is dependent on federal contracts has remained more elusive. It is large and will grow larger as a result of the combination of vigorous contracting and sizable defense budget increases.

Moreover, because contracted jobs will tend to cluster in certain occupations, extensive contracting may also change the occupational mix in the federal sector. Early signals suggest that contracting may occur in white-collar areas such as library management and computer programming, which would constitute a significant shift in contracting practice. Meanwhile, the federal government will need more people such as contract officers and auditors in monitoring jobs in order to ensure that contract work is of high quality and low cost.

The second initiative related to controlling the size and scope of government was the President's Private Sector Survey on Cost Control—also known as the Grace Commission—which has produced more than forty reports with thousands of cost-cutting recommendations for different aspects of federal operations. For example, the commission suggests closing inefficient

---

13. Lester A. Salamon, "Rethinking Public Management: Third-Party Government and the Changing Forms of Government Action," *Public Policy*, vol. 29, no. 3 (Summer 1981), pp. 255–275; Frederick C. Mosher, "The Changing Responsibilities and Tactics of the Federal Government," *Public Administration Review*, vol. 40, no. 6 (November/December 1980), pp. 541–547.

federal installations, consolidating OMB with the OPM and GSA into a new management office, and cutting more than one thousand employees from the Office of the Secretary of HHS. Not surprisingly, the commission's recommendations have generated considerable controversy. The comptroller general and the director of the Congressional Budget Office have questioned the accuracy of the commission's estimates of expected savings, while others have disputed the wisdom of various recommendations. Depending on which of the suggestions are adopted, the consequences for the size and scope of the career service could be substantial.

The Grace Commission is only the latest in a long series of studies arguing that there is substantial overgrading in the work force, especially at the middle management levels of GS-11 through GS-15.[14] The Reagan administration plans to cut the number of workers in those grades by approximately 8 percent by downgrading approximately forty thousand positions governmentwide over the four years beginning with FY 1985.[15] The OPM led the way by announcing that its own claims-examiner positions will be downgraded. Because downgraded employees can retain their grade and pay levels for two years, downgrading jobs with people in them will not yield immediate dollar savings. However, when jobs become vacant, they will be refilled at a lower grade level, thus saving money with attrition. The details of how grade changes will be made are still unclear, but the potential exists for blocking the career advancement of talented employees, including presidential management interns and other new recruits with graduate training.

The third initiative involves a series of far-reaching proposals for personnel reforms in the areas of pay, retirement, and other benefits, which, if enacted, could greatly lessen government costs. For example, one OPM proposal recommends raising the retirement age and calculating retirement annuities based upon the highest five years of pay rather than the highest three years.[16] Another recommends that the total compensation of federal workers—fringe benefits plus wages—be linked to the compensation of comparable workers in the private sector. Such changes would reduce costs for the government and would lower compensation for workers.

President Reagan recommended a 3.5 percent pay increase in FY 1984 for white-collar employees, which became effective January 1984 rather than

---

14. U.S. Civil Service Commission, Bureau of Personnel Management Evaluation, *A Report on Study of Position Classification Accuracy in Executive Branch Occupations under the General Schedule* (Washington, D.C.: Government Printing Office, July 1978).

15. David Hoffman, "Downgrading 40,000 Federal Jobs," *Washington Post Weekly Edition*, November 28, 1983, p. 37.

16. The size of an employee's retirement benefit is based upon the highest average salary earned during any three consecutive years of employment.

October 1983. This is considerably below the 21 percent increase estimated to be required on average in order to keep federal pay rates comparable to those in the private sector.[17] However, the Carter administration also refused to propose pay increases at the comparability level, and there has been bipartisan criticism of the way comparability is calculated. The year 1976 was the last year that federal pay was adjusted in terms of the comparability calculation. Since then, the gap between federal and private-sector pay for similar jobs has been growing, especially at the upper levels.

Previous presidents also proposed—unsuccessfully—many of the salary and benefits reforms now touted by the Reagan administration. President Carter recommended adopting the total compensation approach, adding state and local employees to the set of private-sector workers used to determine comparability, and adjusting some federal salaries according to local wage rates. He drew his proposals from recommendations to President Gerald R. Ford by the Rockefeller Panel, which had relied upon a 1975 study by the Civil Service Commission.[18]

To those earlier suggestions, President Reagan has added the idea that federal compensation should be set only at 94 percent rather than 100 percent of nonfederal compensation, in recognition of the greater attractiveness of federal jobs. Establishing this "6 percent advantage" would require legislation. The Reagan administration has already had a substantial impact on the size and scope of many domestic agencies, as well as on the growth of DoD. Additional proposals, if enacted, could bring about even broader changes than have been realized to date.

Cost-cutting initiatives have implications for the ability of civil servants to function effectively in three of the four roles earlier discussed. First, a large increase in contracting should be accompanied by increases in the number of government workers with contracting, monitoring, and auditing skills. Yet, there is little evidence of planning for additional hiring or training in these areas. Without it, the quality of the contracts and the accountability of contractors will suffer. The ability of civil servants to protect the public interest will therefore be impaired if so much of the government's money is spent by third parties who are left to operate largely free of government oversight. Second, active support of the president by career personnel is made more difficult during RIFs when employees are bumped out of the jobs they know well. Perhaps this explains why so many of those bumped to new jobs were

---

17. *Federal Pay Comparability Act of 1970, 5 U.S.C. 5301.* Under this act, federal pay rates are supposed to be comparable to rates in the private sector for the same levels of work.

18. Robert W. Hartman, *Pay and Pensions for Federal Workers* (Washington, D.C.: The Brookings Institution, 1983), p. 79.

quickly returned to their old jobs. Third, the brokering role of civil servants is under vigorous attack by this administration, which is striving to make government workers responsive only to executive direction. Budget and personnel cuts were targeted for organizations seen to be pursuing congressional rather than presidential priorities.

Increasing Presidential Control over the Bureaucracy

A second major objective of the Reagan administration has been to guarantee that career civil servants are responsive to executive direction. Richard P. Nathan demonstrates how effective this administration has been in placing loyalists in cabinet and subcabinet positions.[19] The data in figure 1 show that this administration has filled a higher proportion of allowable noncareer Senior Executive Service (SES) appointments than did the last administration. There was an expected sharp decline in the total number of noncareer appointees when President Reagan first took office, and it took a few months to make the first several hundred hires. By December 1981 the number of noncareer appointees was over five hundred and thirty, approaching the highest levels achieved during the Carter administration.[20] Since then, the numbers have continued to increase, exceeding seven hundred by December 1983.

As of September 1983 noncareer appointees for the first time constituted over 10 percent of the executive population.[21] Although there is a 10 percent limit written into law, under both Presidents Carter and Reagan the OPM has interpreted the limit as based upon allocated rather than established or filled positions. Since there are generally more than one thousand unfilled but allocated positions at any time, they yield an additional one hundred noncareer possibilities over what would be permitted if the 10 percent were applied to the total number of executives actually in jobs.

Moreover, by September 1983 the number of "limited-term" executive appointments, which are also exempt from usual career controls, was up to seventy governmentwide, a substantial increase over the previous year. In

---

19. Richard P. Nathan, *The Administrative Presidency* (New York: John Wiley & Sons, 1983), pp. 74–76.

20. A number of noncareer executives were permitted to convert to career status at the time that the Senior Executive Service was established. That may have depressed the "real" number of noncareer executives serving the Carter administration. However, most of the people who converted were career civil servants in every sense of the word. The numbers of partisan, noncareer executives have clearly increased under President Reagan.

21. In January 1984 the OPM revoked the power of agencies to appoint noncareer executives, so that the number of executives could be controlled centrally.

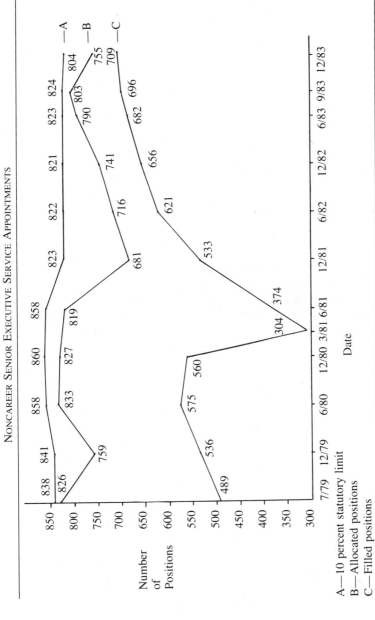

Edie N. Goldenberg

395

FIGURE 1

NONCAREER SENIOR EXECUTIVE SERVICE APPOINTMENTS

A—10 percent statutory limit
B—Allocated positions
C—Filled positions

SOURCE: Executive Personnel and Management Development Group Management Information System (EPMDMIS), U.S. Office of Personnel Management.

addition, by August 1983 the number of Schedule-C political appointees to lower-level positions was 14 percent higher than the number under President Carter at a similar point in his administration, and was greater than the total number employed under Carter at any time during his four-year term. In some agencies the increases in the numbers of Schedule-C appointees were much greater: at the U.S. Information Agency, by April 29, 1983, there were forty-three Schedule-C appointees, as compared with eleven during the Carter administration; at the Department of State, the number had increased from fifty-four to seventy-nine, and at the OPM from eight to nineteen.[22]

What is especially striking about these figures is that the increases in the number of political appointees under President Reagan have occurred primarily in the very domestic agencies where the total number of career employees has declined. That is, in those agencies targeted for major shifts in program priorities, the ratio of political to career employees appears to be significantly higher than before. A look at executive figures alone, for example, reveals that between September 1980 and September 1982, the percentage of executive appointees who were noncareer or limited grew from 7 percent to 18 percent in the Consumer Product Safety Commission, from 35 percent to 40 percent in the Department of Education, from 33 percent to 50 percent in the Federal Home Loan Bank Board, from 5 percent to 19 percent in the General Services Administration, and from 5 percent to 23 percent in the Federal Trade Commission. Occasionally a small percentage increase is important from the perspective of political control, such as occurred within the National Aeronautics and Space Administration (NASA), which changed from having no noncareer senior executive appointees in 1980 to having eight such appointees two years later.[23]

Moreover, political appointees have greater leverage over their career subordinates than ever before, and the OPM is actively trying to increase this leverage. Under the Civil Service Reform Act of 1978, the OPM no longer has to certify that a job merits executive designation or that an individual is technically qualified to do the job. Those responsibilities now reside with the agencies themselves. The abolishment of ranks for executive positions means that executives can now be assigned to a wide variety of positions, including jobs in different geographic locations. Refusing to move is grounds for removal or early retirement. Yet geographic reassignments are often seen as

---

22. Bernard Rosen, "Effective Continuity of U.S. Government Operations in Jeopardy," *Public Administration Review*, vol. 43, no. 5 (September/ October 1983), pp. 383–391.

23. U.S. Office of Personnel Management, *Biennial Report to the Congress on the Senior Executive Service* (Washington, D.C.: Government Printing Office, 1980 and 1982).

punitive not only because they are so costly for the executive but because the executive is sometimes given less responsibility and the reassignments can be required on extremely short notice.[24]

In FY 1980 the first full year under the Senior Executive Service provisions, there were approximately 1,000 executive reassignments. The number was lower during Reagan's first year, in large part because new political appointees are legally prohibited from forcing the reassignments of career executives within 120 days of assuming office. During FY 1982 the number of reassignments jumped to 1,226, and in 1983 the number was about 1,100.[25]

Although relatively few reassignments have required geographic moves (about 15 percent), some that did were highly publicized. These "horror" stories may have created the incorrect impression that forced geographic moves were widespread. Career executives realized quickly that forced moves are possible, legal, and largely unpreventable if the agency heads want to use them. In those agencies where geographic reassignments have been prevalent, such as the Department of the Interior, executives became concerned because they had little say in the reassignment process. For example, GAO found that eight of the twenty-two executives in the Department of the Interior who had been reassigned said that they had no say in their relocations.[26] In some agencies, executives left public service to avoid moving. Others assumed less visible postures to protect themselves against reassignment.

In sum, the Reagan administration has already achieved an impressive degree of political presence and control over the career service, although obviously this control varies from agency to agency. The use of noncompetitive authority rather than competitive examinations to hire recent college graduates has opened up the possibility of political influence over thousands of new employees too. Political control supports the view of the civil servant as a passive extension of the president; it increases the risks for careerists who criticize administration plans or who try to accommodate views other than those of their political appointees; and it threatens civil servants who pursue their own visions of the public interest or who try to carry out the intent of the law as they understand it.

---

24. Toni Marzotto, Carolyn Ban, and Edie N. Goldenberg, "The Senior Executive Service and Political Control of the Bureaucracy," in David H. Rosenbloom, ed., *Public Personnel Policy* (Port Washington, N.Y.: Associated Faculty Press, 1984), pp. 15, 16.

25. U.S. General Accounting Office, *Detailed Statement for the Record by Charles A. Bowsher, Comptroller General of the United States, before the Subcommittee on Civil Service of the House Post Office and Civil Service Committee*, November 7, 1983.

26. Ibid.

Recruiting and Retaining Desirable Employees

When President Reagan assumed office, he was faced with two difficult recruitment and retention problems. First, at the upper end of the salary scale, executive salaries were capped at a level that made attracting outsiders difficult, and there were strong financial incentives for the most mobile federal executives to retire early. They could qualify for retirement benefits, which, unlike capped salaries, are adjusted regularly in response to the cost of living. And, at the same time, they could earn additional salary at another job. Second, at the lower end of the pay scale, President Carter's administration had agreed to a consent decree that resulted in a phaseout of the Professional and Administrative Career Examination (PACE), a carefully validated occupational test used to hire at the entry level for over one hundred separate occupations. The decree left the Reagan administration with a problem—to devise some method of hiring that did not result in the underrepresentation of minority groups. The administration's response in each case has important implications for the quality of the career work force in the future.

The Reagan administration's attention has been fixed primarily on the first of these problems. By the end of March 1983, more than 40 percent of the career executives who had converted to the Senior Executive Service in July 1979 had left the service, roughly twenty-five hundred of them.[27] As the data in table 1 show, nearly half of these executives left before President Reagan took office. Studies of exiting executives in FY 1979 and FY 1980 showed clearly that salary restrictions were the most widely cited reason for leaving federal service.[28] The largest bulge in voluntary retirements occurred in February 1980, which was a "high-3" year for those who had received pay raises in February 1977. But the total number of departures remained high during the transition period as well. Until late 1982 the number of resignations was sufficiently high to keep total departures near 300 executives per year, even with retirements falling substantially.

By 1976 nearly half of all male retirements from the federal service were occurring before age sixty, as compared with less than 10 percent in the private sector. By 1980 federal retirees were even younger.[29] In September 1981 OPM Director Donald Devine, testifying before Congress about executive pay, argued that the average age and length of service of senior exec-

---

27. Ibid.
28. U.S. Office of Personnel Management, *Federal Employee Attitudes—Phase 2: Follow-up Survey, 1980* (Washington, D.C.: Government Printing Office, 1983), pp. 1, 9–10.; U.S. Office of Personnel Management, *Statement of Dr. Donald J. Devine, Director, before the Committee on Governmental Affairs of the U.S. Senate*, September 14, 1981.
29. Hartman, *Pay and Pensions*, pp. 73–74.

TABLE 1

CAREER EXECUTIVES IN SENIOR EXECUTIVE SERVICE LEAVING FEDERAL GOVERNMENT

	Resigned[a]	Discontinued Service Retirement	Optional Retirement	Disability Retirement	Reduction in Force[c]	Death	Other[a]	Total
7/13/79–12/31/79	70	28	165	2	—	6	3	274
1/01/80–6/30/80	69	9	407[b]	8	—	6	6	505
7/01/80–12/31/80	93	18	284	12	—	9	5	421
1/01/81–6/30/81	158	20	146	2	—	12	13	351
7/01/81–12/31/81	162	33	69	3	1	7	7	282
1/01/82–6/30/82	122	47	94	9	6	4	16	298
7/01/82–12/31/82	99	18	52	3	1	9	4	186
1/01/83–6/30/83	78	15	102	3	1	10	5	214
7/01/83–12/31/83	73	18	56	2	1	4	14	168
7/13/79–12/31/83	Total 924	206	1,375	44	10	67	73	2,699

SOURCE: Executive Personnel and Management Development Group Management Information System (EPMDMIS), U.S. Office of Personnel Management.

a. Not including reemployed annuitants who resigned or left for other reasons. Annuitants are counted once only at time of retirement.
b. February 1980 was end of retirement "high 3" for those whose pay was adjusted in February 1977 from $39,600 to $47,500.
c. Individuals separated in a RIF and eligible for discontinued service or optional retirement are reported in those categories.

utives was falling because they were retiring as soon as they became eligible. He saw this as a threat to the quality of the career service.[30]

One of the most underreported initiatives of the Reagan administration has been its successful effort to raise executive salaries. In December 1981 the pay cap was lifted from $50,112 to $58,500, an increase of 17 percent. In December 1982 the cap was raised again, this time to $67,200. Some federal executives are making one-third more today than they were when President Reagan took office. More than any other single act, this has slowed the retirement exodus from the executive ranks. So long as further pay increases are forthcoming, retirement rates should remain at a lower level in the future.

Moreover, the Reagan administration also relaxed rules on executive bonuses. Under the 1978 law, career senior executives can receive lump-sum performance bonuses of amounts up to 20 percent of their basic salary. Until recently the number of bonuses is limited by law to 50 percent of the total executive slots allocated to an agency. Beginning in 1980 Congress and the OPM further limited the number of allowable bonuses to 20 percent of eligible executives. This lower limit was extremely unpopular among senior executives, many of whom felt that they had been betrayed. They had joined the Senior Executive Service and had given up a certain amount of job security on the promise of bonuses that Congress quickly withdrew. The lower limit was not renewed in FY 1984, and the OPM has issued guidelines suggesting that the number of awards could approach 30 percent to 35 percent of an agency's eligible executives. In late 1984, the limit was removed altogether, leaving the decision about distributing a bonus pool of money with political appointees in the departments and agencies.

Improving executive compensation is consistent with all four of the views of appropriate career roles. Whether executives are passive extensions of the president, active supporters, brokers, or protectors of the public interest, they need knowledge, skills, and abilities to perform well. The most experienced executives were leaving government service at an alarming rate prior to these increases. Under the current retirement rules, regular salary increases will be needed to keep the rate of voluntary departures under control.

At the other end of the pay scale, prospects are less encouraging. The PACE problem was not immediate, owing to the hiring freeze. Once the freeze was lifted in March 1981, the government began hiring again. In place of PACE, the Reagan administration is allowing noncompetitive hiring that does not carry career security. Since the OPM has given agencies the authority

---

30. U.S. Office of Personnel Management, *Statement of Dr. Donald J. Devine, Director, before the Committee on Governmental Affairs of the U.S. Senate*, September 14, 1981.

to hire and at the same time has closed a number of job information centers to save money, applicants now have to look agency-by-agency and even installation-by-installation to learn which jobs are available. The jobs they find pay considerably less than comparable jobs in the private sector. Entry-level employees in professional, administrative, and technical occupations were already receiving 20 percent less in 1980 than their private-sector counterparts.[31] Since then, the gap has widened. With the prospects of no job security, of blocked promotion potential as a consequence of job down-grading over the next four years, and of reduced health and retirement benefits at higher cost, the attractiveness of federal jobs must surely be fading.[32]

Although salary increases for executives help maintain a quality work force, the actions that have been taken in entry-level hiring do not. As the federal government becomes less attractive as an employer, the most talented new recruits go elsewhere. Yet the demands on career civil servants are heavy. The problems left to the public sector are the most difficult to solve, and the political environment of public activity makes solutions even harder to effect. The potential to discourage talent is certainly among the most serious long-term threats of the administration's personnel initiatives.

Other threats include a neglect of training and development needs in the current work force and a failure to mount an effective research program in public management. The emphasis by central management agencies under President Carter on executive and managerial training and on research has largely withered under President Reagan. Defense agencies, traditionally strong in these areas, will probably remain so, but most domestic agencies are not strong in this respect and will not improve much without encouragement. Thus an important opportunity is being lost to improve the quality of the public service of the future.

Finally, public opinion of government workers remains negative. Study after study demonstrates that the morale of the federal work force is low, and even newly retired, long-time civil servants are cautioning today's college graduates about careers in the public service.[33] Of course, negative appraisals of government service did not begin with this administration, but little creative

---

31. Hartman, *Pay and Pensions*, p. 22.

32. For an examination of many of these problems, see National Academy of Public Administration, *The Selection of College Graduates for the Federal Civil Service: The Problem of the Pace Examination and the Consent Decree* (Washington, D.C.: National Academy of Public Administration, March 1984).

33. For a review of some of these studies, see Bernard Rosen, "Effective Continuity of U.S. Government Operations in Jeopardy," *Public Administration Review*, vol. 43, no. 5 (September/October 1983), pp. 383–391.

effort has been forthcoming to reverse the trend. If anything, the problem has been made more severe.

Impact on the Permanent Government

The Reagan initiatives can be considered first in terms of the objectives the administration set for itself and second in terms of their implications for the functioning of the career service. The administration appears to be accomplishing most of its major objectives. It has not reduced the size of government overall, but it has shifted budget and personnel from the domestic to the defense agencies. The initiatives with the greatest potential for reducing personnel costs are still in the proposal stage. Political presence, and presumably control, is greater now than before, especially in certain targeted domestic agencies. The exodus of top talent has slowed, and current pay rates make recruiting new executive talent easier than it might have been otherwise.

In terms of the four visions of the role that civil servants should play, the picture is mixed. On balance, the Reagan administration has succeeded in enhancing the role of the careerist as a passive extension of the presidency. In some agencies, even the most senior civil servants are excluded from policy discussions; they await their orders from political appointees. Because civil servants prefer to be trusted and involved, and because they do not want to be forced out or given nothing to do, most are anxious to comply once they determine what is expected of them. Those who are not anxious to comply have close political supervision.

The Reagan administration has been less successful in winning the active support of the civil service. The analysis that careerists can offer of political realities both in Congress and in the agency's traditional constituencies is less relevant to political appointees who are convinced that the traditional relationships among Congress, bureaucrats, and interest groups need to be altered. The independent, professional judgments that civil servants can make of policy directions are not particularly welcome unless these judgments support the ideological preferences of the agency's leadership.

Given that many of the goals of this administration are threatening to civil servants—to their jobs, their benefits, and the programs that they believe in—widespread active support would be surprising. Its absence was hardly noticed during 1981 when administration attention was focused on cutting budgets. Positive support has become more valued since the administration has turned to initiate programs of its own. The large number of reassignments, resignations, and retirements of senior civil servants, and the bumping from job to job of other employees during the RIFs, inevitably disrupted well-established networks and forfeited some organizational memory and technical competence.

Civil servants' roles in taking independent action and in brokering various political interests are probably more difficult under the Reagan administration than before. It is clearly risky for civil servants to buck presidential direction in order to support congressional or other perspectives. Several whistleblowers did emerge at the Environmental Protection Agency and the Department of the Interior, but despite the protections in the 1978 Reform Act, whistle-blowers continue to face grave job risks. It has never been easy for civil servants to oppose administration policy. Today, it is probably even harder because there is closer political supervision than before and there are many more legitimate ways for political appointees to retaliate if they are displeased with their subordinates.

From a representative-bureaucracy perspective, the OPM statistics show a modest gain for women and minorities in the civilian work force, in spite of losses during the RIFs. In the executive ranks, women are nearly as well represented as they were under the previous administration, but minorities have lost some ground since the end of President Carter's term. With little knowledge of the policy positions of these minorities, it is foolhardy to speculate about whether they are more responsive to the interests of minorities in the public.

Effective functioning by civil servants in several of their roles is made more difficult because of the formation, growth, and activities of their political action committees (PACs). In 1982 twelve federal employee PACs set new records for campaign contributions. Two of them, the National Association of Retired Federal Employees (NARFE) and the National Association of Letter Carriers (NALC), each contributed more than one-half million dollars toward electoral campaigns, which was the total amount distributed by all federal employee PACs in the 1978 elections. Democrats received most of this money.[34] Although the overwhelming majority of civil servants do not belong to any union and do not contribute to PACs, the partisan activity of the few may strengthen the view held by some conservatives that government employees resist their leadership. This could complicate future relationships between civil servants and Republican officeholders, making active support and dis-interested brokering more suspect. Partisan inclinations could also subject to legitimate criticism claims by civil servants that they are acting as specialists in support of the public interest.

Finally, the future ability of the career service to perform effectively in any of its four roles is threatened. The public service today is less appealing

---

34. See *Federal Times* (1983) and the Federal Election Commission data cited therein.

as a place to start a career than in the past, and the Reagan administration's initiatives, in sum, only compound that unattractiveness. At the same time, a larger and larger portion of the federal budget is being funneled to third parties who spend it relatively free of public scrutiny. The civil service lacks the capacity to provide effective oversight. If this capacity is not improved, the permanent government may become largely irrelevant to much of the federal government's business in the future.

Denigration Of The Public Servant

"The government of the United States is run not by career ministers but by amateurs." So begins the preface to the recent book of the National Academy of Public Administration on presidential appointments.[1] The statement is somewhat exaggerated. A substantial part of the government is in fact run by career officials and under laws that permit little discretion; and a good many noncareer officials are in fact professionals, not amateurs. Yet the central fact remains: a relatively small number of political appointees, whose tenure is typically temporary, are presumed to govern the activities of between 4 million and 5 million mostly permanent federal employees in the civil service, the military services, and other career systems.[2] The politically appointed and presumably responsive executives amount to less than one-tenth of 1 percent of total direct federal employment.[3] This discussion addresses the roles and problems of those in the regular (classified) civil service who comprise a little under one-half of all direct federal employees.

How can or should so few direct so many? To what extent should the many be permitted to direct each other? How can or should their goals and behaviors be changed in response to the desires and commitments of the elected president and his political appointees? And what is or should be the role of the civil service in our system?

Edie N. Goldenberg suggests four possible roles of the civil service against which to evaluate the Reagan administration. I will comment on the following three: the civil service as a passive extension of the president; as

---

1. Jackson Walter, "Preface," in National Academy of Public Administration, *America's Unelected Government: Appointing the President's Team* (Cambridge, Mass.: Ballinger Publishing Co., 1983), p. xi.
2. If the 600,000 employees of the U.S. Postal Service are included, the total is near 5 million; if not, it is around 4.25 million.
3. This does not include those employees of state and local governments and of the private sector who are indirectly paid by the federal government. These employees would probably more than triple the total.

an active supporter of the president; and as a protector of the public interest. These are useful conceptual tools, but they seem to me rather vague and to a considerable extent antagonistic to each other, oversimplified, and incomplete. All are a matter of degree and direction and are not absolutes.

The first role—passive support of the president—is roughly what political scientist Emmette Redford described as overhead democracy: the following of directions as they filter down through hierarchical channels.[4] In its most literal definition, passive support assumes little thought on the part of the recipients and executors of these directions and no intellectual or affective concern about their nature and consequences. The acceptance of this doctrine has been declining ever since Andrew Jackson indirectly propounded it a century and a half ago. An increasing proportion of the leaders and practitioners in the permanent government are highly educated professionals who have been taught to think for themselves according to the rational precepts of their profession. Yet, as Goldenberg suggests, there is little doubt that numerous Reagan administration appointees have been vigorously acting on this concept of the role of the permanent civil service in a number of the most contentious fields of federal activity.

In Goldenberg's discussion of the role for the civil service as an active supporter of the president's objectives, insufficient evidence is given to the part played by federal employees in the development and analysis of policies or of their role in helping to solve problems, although Goldenberg later refers to the Reagan administration's discouragement of policy inputs on the part of civil servants. My own limited observations and contacts suggest that the administration's failure to seek and consider or even listen to experienced and knowledgeable civil servants has been a principal source of malaise and disaffection in and of separation from public service in recent years.

Another of Goldenberg's proposed roles of the civil service is as a protector of the public interest—presumably vis à vis whatever group is in power. Her concern about the public interest seems to take a mainly negative view of political influence: the legal insulation of civil service personnel from politics, protections from whistle-blowing penalties, and helping to avoid embarrassing situations between administrations and members of Congress who disagree. Aside from acknowledging, as Goldenberg does, that there are different perceptions of what constitutes the public interest, a more positive view would acknowledge that the perceptions of a public servant with long experience in his or her field have some validity and importance and that the civil servant's ideas should be heard and considered whether or not they are

4. Emmette S. Redford, *Democracy in the Administrative State* (New York: Oxford University Press, 1969), pp. 70–71.

in full accord with the policy objectives of the current political leadership. If the civil servant's views are overruled, many purists would say he or she should either accept and pursue the political judgment of his or her superiors or get out. (Other less severe puritans might urge staying on and fighting from within.) But the idea that the opinions of those who have been on the job, who have confronted the problems before, and who have differing views on how these problems should be handled should therefore be disregarded seems to be both arrogant and self-defeating, since it deprives the current political officeholder of informed opinion and advice. It is also demeaning to the career public servant. My impression is that the current discontent among upper-level bureaucrats today often stems from the fact that they are not advised that a changed or new policy is being considered, they are not consulted on its wisdom, and they do not enter the decision-making process. However, after the decision is made they are called upon to develop the argument and the data to justify it, and then to carry it out.

Goldenberg concludes that the Reagan administration has been reasonably successful in respect to the first role of the civil service: generating passive support of the president. But she avers that it has been much less so in engendering active support for administration goals or in protecting the public interest. It should be reemphasized that the Reagan administration has not paid much attention to what I see as the positive aspect of the public interest role: contributions by permanent public servants of their knowledge, opinions, and wisdom in deciding and developing public policy. Civil servants are specially qualified to make such contributions because of their education, training, and experience. If we do not oblige those in the higher civil service to play such a significant role, we have wasted a great deal of effort and money over the past half-century in educating and professionalizing our permanent public employees.

This issue is delineated clearly when one contemplates the competing definitions of a professional civil servant. Recently, an alumnus of the Office of Management and Budget described to me a current career official of that organization as a "real pro." When I asked what he meant, he said that the official supported the administration's proposals with skill and enthusiasm even though he did not believe in them. In other words, the official—as well as my friend who was speaking of him—viewed his professional mission as that of an advocate: approximately the same as an attorney and equivalent to Goldenberg's concept of "active supporter of the president." The question raised for career public servants is profound: Is their appropriate posture that of an advocate of positions taken by their superiors on which they may or may not agree? Or does it encompass searching for and supporting the best policies and practices in the public interest as perceived by the civil servants themselves and not necessarily by their superiors?

There is nothing new about these questions or about the skepticism and distrust held by the Reagan political leaders toward the career service. Every new administration has similar tendencies, particularly in its early months and years. However, the lack of confidence displayed in career public servants is particularly acute today because the causes espoused by the present administration are such a break from the past and are so threatening to current programs, organizations, and personnel. Can or should a high-level career official give his or her maximum support to measures that would damage or destroy programs in which he or she has deep intellectual, political, or ideological stakes? In the longer term will a career official who is working enthusiastically for elements of the Reagan program be able to apply equivalent energies to essentially opposite objectives in 1989 if a Democrat is elected president?

The reduction of influence and discretion of civil servants on matters of policy and program is another way of expressing one of the three principal goals of the Reagan administration as set forth by Goldenberg, that of increasing executive (or political) control over the civil service. In this aim, the administration has apparently been successful, although it is questionable how permanent is the change. Another goal, according to Goldenberg, was to reduce the size and scope of government, with an incident reduction in the number and costs of civil servants. The reductions in employment in the domestic service and particularly in certain targeted agencies have been substantial and painful, but they have been partially and perhaps totally offset by increases of both civilian and military personnel in the defense agencies. The third objective identified by Goldenberg is recruiting and retaining "desirable" people. If by desirable people Goldenberg means those in sympathy with the president's philosophy of government or those more willing to follow instructions without question, she is probably right about the president's aims. But if she means people more qualified for their jobs in the traditional sense of individuals with creativity and initiative, little or nothing in the record— with the exception only of raising the cap on federal pay for executives— indicates that the administration sought to hire or retain such individuals. Moreover, the administration has done a great deal to discourage them: criticizing and ridiculing them in public, holding down their pay, seeking reductions in their fringe benefits, eliminating competition for many entering jobs, and generally denigrating the public service as a challenging career opportunity for the young.

It is not surprising that Goldenberg did not include among the aims of the Reagan administration the strengthening of the merit system. Some of the behavior of the current administration in fact suggests goals opposite to the aspirations of civil service reformers. There are now many more political appointees in the Senior Executive Service than ever before. In the OPM, the central agency that oversees the administration of the civil service, there are more than forty political appointees. Indeed, the principal qualification of many of these senior-level OPM appointees appears to be their experience in partisan political campaigns. One executive resigned his post in order to run a Republican senatorial campaign, then returned to it in open defiance of the spirit of the Hatch Act. The OPM has done little or nothing to improve development and training programs, to improve labor-management relations, to improve employee morale—now probably at its lowest point since the era of Joseph McCarthy in the early 1950s—or to encourage personnel research.

It is a bitter irony that the centennial anniversary of the first civil service reform act of 1883 should have been celebrated at the midpoint of a presidency that has done so little to further the act's aims.

Alan K. Campbell

No Permanent Damage

Using the evidence presented in the paper by Edie N. Goldenberg and the comments by Frederick C. Mosher, I will examine current attitudes of federal career civil servants from a somewhat different perspective. Too frequently, in my view, changes made or advocated for the civil service system are assumed to have equal impact on the attitudes of all federal public servants. It is important, too, to ask whether the reality of what the Reagan administration has done or advocated justifies the kinds and intensity of concern by civil servants that Goldenberg and Mosher have described.

These comments review, first, Reagan proposals and policies that affect the conditions of federal employment. Second, the role of the high-level career civil servant in management decisions and in policymaking at the highest levels is discussed. Third, Reagan initiatives to reform management practices are described.

The Reagan Proposals and Policies

The most important determinant of the general morale and attitudes of the bureaucracy is conditions of employment. Federal employees—and all other public and private-sector employees, for that matter—have in common a primary concern about the conditions affecting their day-to-day work, job security, pay, and benefits. Studies of public management tend to ignore this basic fact and emphasize issues like the supposed policy-administration dichotomy or the appropriate policy role of the higher civil servant, protections for whistleblowers, and believed abuses in transfers, hiring, and promotions.

I had assumed, for example, before becoming chairman of the Civil Service Commission, that the overwhelming majority of career civil servants would prefer to have as their superiors other careerists. That is not necessarily the case. Political appointees are often more responsive to their employees' concerns than are their career managers. The reason is that short-term political

410

appointees seldom have any interest in the development and maintenance of professional management practices. In fact, they seldom possess much management experience. In other words, we often assume a commonality of interest among the different management levels in the system that simply does not exist.

On conditions of employment the Reagan administration has advocated a set of changes, perhaps the most frightening to civil servants being the attack on their job security brought about by the Reagan efforts to reduce the size of government through formal reductions in force and through informal pressures on people to leave. Another threat is seen in the proposed method of setting federal pay, which entails a shift to total compensation comparability with the private sector rather than just pay comparability. Some of the proposed changes in retirement and health benefits are also relevant here, as in the reduction in the opportunities for promotion.

Practically all of President Reagan's recommendations in these areas have roots in previous administrations. For example, total compensation comparability had been advocated by the Nixon, Ford, and Carter administrations and was first recommended by the 1972 Presidential Pay Commission when it suggested adding benefits to the compensation package that would be measured against private-sector compensation. The only feature added by the Reagan administration was to recommend reducing the figures resulting from the comparability analysis by about 6 percent, on the grounds that government employment provides greater job security. Even this proposal to provide a pay offset has long been advocated by OMB, with strong support from the career employees in that agency. The proposal was presented to the Reagan people when they arrived, just as it was offered to me when I became head of the Civil Service Commission in 1977, and it had been sitting on the shelves at OMB for some years before that.

In the benefits area the need to do something about the federal retirement system has been recognized for years. The option of early retirement, the level of benefits, and their indexing have made the federal system one of the most generous retirement systems in the American economy.

It was inevitable that the Reagan proposal to place federal employees in Social Security would be unpopular. The failure, however, to develop a supplemental retirement program was not only unfortunate, it was grossly unfair. In the case of RIFs, the administration has recommended in determining retention rights that not only tenure and veteran status should be taken into account, as is now the case, but, in addition, performance on the job— a position that most students of personnel management would heartily endorse.

The Reagan administration has failed, by and large, to get its proposals adopted. The most remarkable thing about these proposals is not their content but the political incompetence of the administration in pushing them. The lack of movement is due largely to the confrontational environment created by the administration with the federal work force. If there is any area in which the Reagan administration has been politically inept, it is in the personnel area. In my judgment, one of the primary reasons for this failure was the rejection by the leadership of the OPM and OMB, as well as by the White House staff, of the benefits to be gained by using the knowledge of their career staffs. When I was at the Civil Service Commission, I used that knowledge continuously and found it helpful and effective. Many in the current administration refuse on ideological grounds to seek it.

Policy-Administration Dichotomy

This leads to my second point, which is the policy-administration dichotomy and the rhetorical adoption by this administration of the belief that a wall must exist between policymakers and administrators. It was a puzzle to me that the current head of the OPM, who holds a doctorate from Syracuse University's Maxwell School, could argue in one of his first speeches after taking office for a firm demarcation separating policy and administration. This position became partially comprehensible when I learned that he did his doctoral work in political behavior and parties, not public management.

Public servants usually assume policymaking begins at the level of their position and moves upward from there. Be that as it may, no student of public administration would argue that a sharp line can be drawn between policymaking and management. The administration's statements supporting a policy-administration dichotomy have tremendously hurt the morale of the top people in the career civil service and have undermined these individuals' ability to help the administration.

Such a line does not and cannot exist. In agencies—such as EPA and OPM—where enforcing such a separation has been tried, the agencies experienced much more trouble in performing their responsibilities than in agencies where there has been a willingness to use the expertise of senior career people.

Reform of Federal Management Practices

My third topic is the reform of management practices. It is odd that an administration that sees itself as representative of the business community has been so ineffective in bringing improved management practices to the public service, practices that, incidentally, were made much easier to accomplish by the Civil Service Reform Act of 1978. For instance, the administration has advocated moving performance appraisal further down into the system, but there has been no effective implementation of performance appraisal where it is now required. The use of bonuses has, moreover, been ineffectual. And the administration abolished the productivity improvement program that was just getting off the ground when Reagan took office.

Looking, then, at all three of the issues, a major question arises: Why this overall picture of failure? Why the inability to get appropriate improvements adopted in the area of employment conditions, such as those that would bring about some progress toward total compensation comparability? Why so little action on the retirement system? Why the lack of understanding of the interaction between politics and professional management people? Why the lack of any movement in the area of management improvement? The only answer I can suggest is the employment of ideology where it is not relevant and political ineptness.

In conclusion, I think it fair to argue that a new consciousness on the part of top-level civil servants has emerged during the past three years, consciousness that has enhanced their sense of ownership of the system and of the responsibilities entailed. A case in point is the creation of the Senior Executive Association. As Goldenberg points out, in regard to pay levels, the Senior Executive Service has done very well under the current administration. In 1980 the top pay for the senior executives was about $52,000–$53,000; it is now about $69,000. This is a well-kept secret, perhaps intentionally because of the fear of what the public response might be. The Senior Executive Association gets much of the credit for that increase. The Public Employee Roundtable is also beginning to play a useful role. Their concerns go beyond just conditions of employment to broader issues of effectiveness.

In my judgment the permanent government has not been permanently damaged. Its resiliency will quickly show itself again, at such time as appropriate changes are made in either the leadership of agencies or at higher levels.

NEW FEDERALISM, OLD REALITIES: THE REAGAN ADMINISTRATION AND INTERGOVERNMENTAL REFORM

David R. Beam

American politics is hard on the purveyors of "grand designs." The history of the past decade, in particular, abounds with ambitious governmental reforms that never matured or were stillborn. Among these can be counted major departmental reorganization initiatives, energy independence plans, welfare reform schemes, and coordinated urban policies.

It is still too early to offer a final judgment on the Reagan administration's vaunted "new federalism" plan, aimed at reversing the historical trend of national governmental expansion and restoring greater authority to the states. But, considering actions to date, it is clear that official intentions once again far out-stripped actual achievements. The Reagan administration has left a strong mark on federal-state-local relationships, but no dramatic reversal of past policies has been accomplished or seems likely. Indeed, the president's most drastic proposals for federalism reform have now been set aside.

If a less demanding standard is applied, neither can it be said that the administration's policies have reduced the tensions and frictions that have marked intergovernmental relations. Although many state and local officials shared the president's desire to readjust the balance of responsibility within the federal system, the specific actions and proposals advanced under the banner of new federalism sparked much opposition and controversy among their intended beneficiaries. Despite political hyperbole, the problems of government that the new federalism addressed were real. Palatable and effective remedies, however, have yet to be found.

Governance Issues in an Intergovernmental Perspective

The 1960s and 1970s saw a dramatic expansion in the national government's domestic activities and an especially striking growth in the number and financial magnitude of intergovernmental programs funded by the federal government but administered by states, local governments, and community organizations. During the Great Society era, landmark statutes were adopted in fields such as education, health care, community development, and employment training, along with a host of lesser, but interrelated, programs in the same fields. Over 200 grant programs were enacted during President Lyndon Baines Johnson's five years in office alone. Grant outlays began to mount rapidly, from $7 billion in 1960, to $24 billion in 1970, to $91.5 billion in 1980. The period from the mid-1960s onward also was marked by numerous regulatory initiatives, especially in health and safety, environmental protection, and nondiscrimination.[1] Some 53 major regulatory laws were adopted in the 1960s and 130 more in the 1970s.[2]

Although intergovernmental relations had been a continuing concern of policymakers since the mid-1950s, the number and character of these concerns expanded sharply with the rapid growth of new federal programs. The drive to eradicate poverty, to improve education and health care, and to banish discrimination quickly became entangled in administrative difficulties. Mayors and governors protested the duplication, complexity, and intrusiveness of proliferating categorical grants,[3] while policy analysts stressed the complexities of "implementation" and questioned the effectiveness of many social interventions.[4]

Managerial and intergovernmental reforms thus moved to the center of the political agenda in the 1970s. The period stressed "rationalizing" policies, aimed at correcting past errors and inefficiencies, rather than the pursuit of new objectives.[5] Although the federal government grew steadily—indeed, by

---

1. William Lilley, III, and James C. Miller, III, "The New 'Social Regulation,'" *The Public Interest*, no. 47 (Spring 1977), pp. 49–61.

2. Ronald J. Penoyer, *Directory of Federal Regulatory Agencies*, 3d. ed. (St. Louis: Center for the Study of American Business, Washington University, 1981), p. 12.

3. For a thorough discussion see Donald H. Haider, *When Governments Come to Washington* (New York: Free Press, 1974), pp. 52–62.

4. Jeffrey L. Pressman and Aaron B. Wildavsky, *Implementation* (Berkeley, Calif.: University of California Press, 1973); Alice M. Rivlin, *Systematic Thinking for Social Action* (Washington, D.C.: The Brookings Institution, 1971); William Gorham and Nathan Glazer, eds., *The Urban Predicament* (Washington, D.C.: The Urban Institute, 1976).

5. This concept is presented more fully in Lawrence D. Brown, *New Policies, New Politics: Government's Response to Government's Growth* (Washington, D.C.: The Brookings Institution, 1983). See p. 7.

some measures, more rapidly than in the 1960s—Presidents Nixon, Ford, and Carter all attempted to control and streamline the federal apparatus. Richard M. Nixon's administration advanced the first new federalism program, which was intended to decentralize a significant measure of program responsibility, and proposed a comprehensive consolidation of seven federal departments into four new "superagencies." President Jimmy Carter, who ran for office as an outsider who would clean up the "horrible" federal bureaucracy, made administrative improvements—including zero-base budgeting, civil service reform, and (once again) departmental reorganization plans—the hallmark of his administration.[6]

This managerial focus reflected a need to come to terms with the new pattern of service delivery. The federal government had come to rely heavily on "third parties"—including state and local governments as well as private, nonprofit organizations—to administer "its" domestic programs.[7] The latter, in turn, had grown increasingly dependent upon federal resources and increasingly constrained by federal requirements. Such extreme interdependence posed problems. Although intergovernmental partnerships had been a feature of American government since its founding, past initiatives had been limited in number and narrower in functional scope. What emerged in the late 1960s and 1970s was a peculiar and most "uneasy kind of partnership . . . in which the negative power of each partner to block or harass was much stronger than the positive power to move in desired directions."[8] To some observers, the changing style of government operations suggested a need to rethink the precepts of public management, even to formulate an entirely new body of administrative thought and practice.[9]

This concern about administrative performance was mirrored in the political arena. As the demands on government grew, the capacity of government appeared to be stagnating.[10] The term *atomization* was used to describe the splintering of political power among diverse interests and *overload* to char-

---

6. See David R. Beam, "Public Administration is Alive and Well—and Living in the White House," *Public Administration Review*, vol. 38, no. 1 (January/February 1978), pp. 72–73.

7. Lester M. Salamon, "Rethinking Public Management: Third-Party Government and the Changing Forms of Government Action," *Public Policy*, vol. 29, no. 3 (Summer 1981), pp. 255–275.

8. Walter Williams, *The Implementation Perspective* (Berkeley, Calif.: University of California Press, 1980), p. 44.

9. Frederick C. Mosher, "The Changing Responsibilities and Tactics of the Federal Government," *Public Administration Review*, vol. 40, no. 6 (November/December 1980), pp. 541–548.

10. James L. Sundquist, "The Crisis of Competence in Government," in Joseph A. Pechman, ed., *Setting National Priorities: Agenda for the 1980's* (Washington, D.C.: The Brookings Institution, 1980), pp. 531-563.

acterize the effect of too much pressure and too many decisions on the policymakers themselves.[11]

At the close of the 1970s, disenchantment with government was deep and widespread. To Theodore White, who has chronicled each presidential campaign since 1960, the election of 1980 "marked the end of an era." "What had come to issue," he wrote, "was the nature of the federal government's power."[12] Still, if the New Deal, conceived as a coherent philosophy of government, had died, no alternative public philosophy was on hand to replace it.[13] Rather, the nation was "between idea systems."[14]

The Reagan Approach to the Intergovernmental Agenda

Ronald Reagan, perhaps the most ideologically committed of any recent president, stepped into this ideological void determined to set new directions. Changes in federal and state responsibilities were a cornerstone of his plan. In formulating the new federalism, President Reagan borrowed some concepts from the initiatives of others, but in most respects his approach differed radically from those of the past. Stated succinctly, most past reform proposals have sought to simplify the management of intergovernmental programs while retaining the commitment to national aid for a broad range of state and local services. The Reagan administration departed from this pattern by aiming instead for what federalism theorists term a "devolution" of responsibility. National financial support, as well as national rules and standards, were to be reduced or eliminated wherever possible. In a sense, the president's ambitions were more in line with the tradition of separated federal and state functions under "dual federalism," which reigned as constitutional doctrine until the 1930s, than with the more recent ideal of joint federal-state action under "cooperative federalism." As Reagan declared in his inaugural address: "It is my intention to curb the size and influence of the federal establishment and to demand recognition of the distinction between the powers granted to

11. Anthony King, "The American Polity in the Late 1970s: Building Coalitions in the Sand," in Anthony King, ed., *The New American Political System* (Washington, D.C.: American Enterprise Institute, 1978), p. 391; Advisory Commission on Intergovernmental Relations, *A Crisis of Confidence and Competence* (Washington, D.C.: Government Printing Office, 1980), pp. 21–25.

12. Theodore H. White, *America in Search of Itself: The Making of the President, 1956–1980* (New York: Harper & Row, Publishers, 1982), p. 7.

13. Samuel H. Beer, "In Search of a New Public Philosophy," in Anthony King, ed., *The New American Political System*, (Washington, D.C.: American Enterprise Institute), pp. 5–44.

14. John Herbers, "Americans Seem to Be 'Between Idea Systems,' " *New York Times*, December 30, 1979, p. 12.

the federal government, those reserved to the states or to the people."[15] In his view, a better national government would be a much smaller national government.

At the same time, it cannot be said—as various opponents charged— that Reagan desired to "repeal the New Deal" or to reinstate the Articles of Confederation. Rather, his harshest criticism was directed at more recent social programs. One close inspection of his budget proposals suggested that Reagan might be most comfortable with the status quo ante of the Eisenhower years.[16]

The scope of this paper does not allow a full description of the new federalism in either ideological or historical terms. The discussion following therefore examines the administration's proposals and actions in six major areas of continuing intergovernmental concern, offering comparisons with the efforts of other reformers.

Expenditure and Tax Restraints

If any single goal can be said to dominate Ronald Reagan's approach to intergovernmental issues, it is that of a desire to reduce federal domestic expenditures and taxes. Certainly this has been his most long-standing commitment. During an earlier bid for the Republican nomination, candidate Reagan proposed in 1975 a $90-billion-dollar plan to turn back a host of federal programs to state and local governments, along with the resources to pay for them.[17] He made a similar pledge upon receiving the Republican nomination in 1980.[18]

Expenditure and tax restraints also were the focal points of the administration's proposals during the crucial honeymoon year of 1981. The economic recovery plan proposed in February embellished long-lasting commitments to fiscal conservatism with newer ideas borrowed from supply-side economics. Expenditure and tax cuts were presented as the key to eliminating unemployment and controlling inflation—necessary steps for attacking what the

15. Ronald Reagan, "Inaugural Address," Washington, D.C., January 20, 1981.

16. Samuel H. Beer, "Foreword," in John William Ellwood, ed., *Reductions in U.S. Domestic Spending: How They Affect State and Local Governments* (New Brunswick, N.J.: Transaction Books, 1982), pp. xiii–xxii.

17. Ronald Reagan, "Let The People Rule," Remarks to the Executive Club of Chicago, McCormick Place, Chicago, Ill., September 26, 1975.

18. First ballot nomination, July 16, 1980, Republican National Convention, Detroit, quoted in Richard S. Williamson, *Federalism in Perspective: A Republican Monograph* (June 1982), p. 10.

president termed the "worst economic mess since the Great Depression."[19] Even before the administration took office, David Stockman, director of the Office of Management and Budget (OMB), started working on a plan to reduce federal spending by $40 billion. Since the defense budget and "social safety net"[20] programs were exempt, this meant that most of the cuts had to come from grants-in-aid and general government operations.

No previous administration has made a large-scale reduction in federal assistance the major goal of its intergovernmental policy, although most recent presidents have attempted to control burgeoning outlays for public assistance or have attacked "excessive" expenditures in other specific fields. With the adoption of the landmark Omnibus Budget Reconciliation Act (hereafter, Reconciliation Act) during the summer of 1981, the Reagan administration extended a trend to reduce the growth of federal aid that had been initiated in the Carter administration, achieving the first absolute reduction in federal aid outlays recorded in decades. Federal aid spending fell from $94.8 billion in fiscal year (FY) 1981 to $88.2 billion in FY 1982. Major components of the $6 billion decrease included a $2.6 billion decline for employment and training assistance and a more than $1 billion dip in highway grants.[21]

Federal tax revenues, too, were greatly reduced with the adoption of the Economic Recovery Tax Act, signed into law on August 13, 1981. Prospective revenue losses from this act, which provided for the largest tax cut in history, were then estimated at over $1 trillion through 1987. Because many state and local income taxes are tied to federal tax schedules and rules, this measure also reduced their revenues.[22]

Despite the historic reversal of aid growth trends, available evidence indicates that the cuts have had less of an effect on states and localities than political rhetoric might suggest. For example, in Stamford, Connecticut, where a detailed survey was conducted, researchers found that "there was only the most modest evidence of real impact on city agencies, the community's

---

19. Ronald Reagan, "Address on the State of the Nation's Economy," Washington, D.C., February 5, 1981.

20. The "social safety net" was never clearly delineated, however. For a discussion, see James R. Storey, "Income Security," in John L. Palmer and Isabel V. Sawhill, eds., *The Reagan Experiment* (Washington, D.C.: The Urban Institute, 1982), pp. 383–384.

21. Advisory Commission on Intergovernmental Relations, "Federal Aid to States Registers First Decline," news release, April 28, 1983. A detailed analysis of the major cuts affecting state and local governments is presented in John William Ellwood, ed., *Reductions in U.S. Domestic Spending: How They Affect State and Local Governments* (New Brunswick, N.J.: Transaction Books, 1982), pp. 131–311.

22. See Robert F. Cook, "The Economic Recovery Tax Act and Its Effects on State and Local Revenues," in John William Ellwood, ed., *Reductions in U.S. Domestic Spending*, pp. 71–86.

nonprofit organizations, and the public. In each case the effects of federal policy changes were incremental—certainly not the stuff of 'revolution.' "[23] A similar conclusion was reached in the most comprehensive study to date on the effects of the cuts, based upon observations of some fifty-four states, cities, and counties. According to this report, "the cuts were not as large as was expected when the 1981 budget reconciliation act was being debated. . . . State and local governments were more concerned with the deep recession and resulting fiscal problems than with federal aid cuts in federal fiscal year 1982."[24]

Still, opposition to domestic spending cuts stiffened in the wake of the 1981 Reconciliation Act. State and local officials protested the administration's "meat-ax" approach to aid reductions and asked to be spared from more.[25] They were shocked when a Treasury Department aide suggested that no specific tax turnbacks, beyond the reductions already enacted, would be forthcoming.[26] State governors made it clear that they wanted to be consulted before other actions were taken and called upon the president to identify the functions he considered to be primarily federal, to be balanced against the list of responsibilities he wanted to shift to the states.[27]

Congressional resistance to further aid cuts also rose in late 1981. The FY 1983 budget was pronounced dead shortly after it was announced,[28] and Congress went on to write its own. Although the president proposed new reductions, aid outlays (at $93.5 billion) in the adopted 1983 budget were $12 billion higher than requested and more than $5 billion greater than in the preceding year. The FY 1984 budget projects modest dollar increases through FY 1986 (see table 1). Much of this increase may be attributed to the continuing growth in Medicaid spending, as well as a significant rise in transportation expenditures stemming from the adoption of the Surface Transportation Act in 1982. Regarding the latter act, President Reagan departed from his new federalism principles to give grudging support to a traditional congres-

---

23. G. Donald Ferree, Jr., W. Wayne Shannon, and Everett Carll Ladd, "Stamford, Connecticut Weathers Reaganomics," *Public Opinion*, February/March 1983, p. 17.

24. Richard P. Nathan, Fred C. Doolittle, and Associates, eds., *The Consequences of Cuts: The Effects of the Reagan Domestic Program on State and Local Governments* (Princeton, N.J.: Princeton Urban and Regional Research Center, 1983), p. 6.

25. B. Drummond Ayres, Jr., "Key Supporters of Reagan Assail His Concept of 'New Federalism,' " *New York Times*, December 2, 1981, p. B8.

26. David S. Broder, "Tax Turnbacks to States Is Done, Aide Says," *Washington Post*, October 23, 1981, p. A14

27. Governor George Busbee, "Where is That Federal 'Partnership?' " *Washington Post*, September 24, 1981, p. A19.

28. Helen Dewar, "Baker Suggests Income Surtax As Reagan Budget Called Dead," *Washington Post*, February 23, 1982, p. A4.

TABLE 1

FEDERAL GRANT-IN-AID OUTLAYS,
1950–1986

Fiscal Year	Amount (In $ billions)	As Percentage of GNP[a]
1950	2.3	0.9
1955	3.2	0.8
1960	7.0	1.4
1965	10.9	1.7
1970	24.0	2.3
1975	49.8	3.3
1980	91.5	3.6
1981	94.8	3.1
1982	88.2	2.9
1983 estimate	93.5	2.9
1984 estimate	95.9	2.7
1985 estimate	99.2	2.6
1986 estimate	102.5	2.5

SOURCE: Executive Office of the President, Office of Management and Budget, *Special Analyses, Budget of the United States Government, Fiscal Year 1984* (Washington, D.C.: Government Printing Office, 1983), p. H-16.
  a.   GNP, gross national product.

sional-style response to the problem of decaying transportation infrastructure. Financed by a five-cents-a-gallon increase in the federal motor fuels tax, the act offers a major expansion of federal support for the construction and repair of highways, bridges, and mass transit systems. Some state officials condemned the action for preempting a badly needed source of state revenues.[29]

As the 1985 budget season approaches, the war on domestic spending seems to be abating—at least until the election has passed. Budget Director David Stockman indicates that, overall, the president has won about half of the cuts he sought, but at the same time is unlikely to obtain congressional support for the other 50 percent.[30] Like any other half-full, half-empty glass, this one is subject to mixed appraisals. The Reagan administration has succeeded in dramatically slowing the growth of federal aid. Federal taxes were reduced sharply, while many states moved to increase their revenues in 1983—

---

29. See Governor Richard A. Snelling, "Stop the 'Quick Nickel' Gas Tax," *Washington Post*, December 12, 1982, p. C7; also Governor-Elect Anthony S. Earl, "Why the Gas Tax Hike is a Bad Idea," *Washington Post*, December 2, 1982, p. A27.
30. Quoted in David Hoffman, "Reagan Won Half of Cuts Sought, Stockman Reports," *Washington Post*, October 22, 1983, p. A3; also Steven R. Weisman, "Big Domestic Cuts Seen As Unlikely In Reagan Budget," *New York Times*, October 23, 1983, pp. 1, 48.

a shift in the desired direction. But this achievement is less impressive when measured against the president's own announced intentions. As he completes his first term, federal grant outlays will still be slightly higher than when he took office—though representing a smaller proportion of domestic expenditures and of the gross national product (GNP). Many of the president's most drastic proposals—including termination of aid for legal services and for mass transit operating subsidies, the replacement of urban grants with "urban enterprise zones," and abolition of the Economic Development Administration and the Departments of Education and Energy—remain unachieved.

Grant Consolidation

As an accompaniment to the drive to reduce federal domestic expenditures and taxes, every Reagan administration budget to date has also proposed the consolidation of categorical aid programs into new, broader, and more flexible block grants. Such a strategy has been supported by intergovernmental reformers since the days of the Commission on the Organization of the Executive Branch—the first Hoover Commission, in 1949—and was advanced with special ardor by President Nixon. Prior to 1980, three block-grant programs were created by grant consolidation (for public health in 1966, employment training in 1973, and community development in 1974), and others were established for law enforcement (1968) and social services (1975). However, the number of specific-purpose categorical programs continued to rise steadily, totaling some 534 in early 1981, up from 379 in 1967. Most of these grants were small: as of 1981, 80 percent of the funds flowed through just 25 programs.

Grant consolidation has long been advocated as a good technique for streamlining both federal and recipient management. According to this strategy, red tape can be reduced by merging closely related programs in a single functional field; at the same time, state and local governments are provided the flexibility they need to attack priority problems. When Ronald Reagan took office there were some 113 separate federal education aid programs, in addition to 63 programs offering health-care services and 52 programs in economic development. Many observers regarded some consolidation as desirable.

The Reagan block-grant proposals differed from past patterns in two key respects.[31] First, many of Reagan's proposals were linked to substantial fund-

---

31. For a discussion of these and other points, see Timothy J. Conlan, "Back in Vogue: The Politics of Block Grant Legislation," *Intergovernmental Perspective*, vol. 7, no. 2 (Spring 1981), pp. 8–15.

ing reductions, whereas earlier consolidations were supported in part because they included financial "sweeteners." As a consequence, much of the debate on the Reagan proposals focused upon their fiscal stringency, not their programmatic merit. Indeed, the president said repeatedly that he viewed consolidation not as an administrative improvement but as the first step toward a total phaseout of federal involvement in the fields designated.

Second, nearly all of the new Reagan programs emphasized the role of the states, and some relied on states to administer federal funds that had previously been directed to cities or counties. In contrast, grant consolidation proposals advanced successfully in the past have not greatly altered existing programmatic linkages between Washington, D.C., and recipient jurisdictions (for example, local governments were the primary beneficiaries of the community development and manpower block grants adopted during the Nixon years). The shift proposed by Reagan generated opposition from local officials, who frequently view their respective states with as much or more suspicion as they view the federal government. In prior years many city officials had in fact urged an expanded federal role because states had failed to take sufficient interest in urban problems. On the other hand, the primacy of the states under the new federalism is in accord with traditional American practice, as well as with that of most other federal nations, which typically bar national grants to local governments.

Despite the negative rumblings resulting from Reagan's proposals, it was in the area of grant consolidation that the administration won its most prominent successes. The 1981 Reconciliation Act bypassed congressional skeptics and established, in one fell swoop, more block grants than all past efforts combined. Nine new block grants were formed by merging seventy-seven categorical programs (see table 2). Another sixty programs were simply eliminated.

Still, the block grants that emerged from the reconciliation process were more restrained than those first proposed. Some of the larger categorical grants, most notably Title I education assistance for disadvantaged persons and educational aid for handicapped individuals, were deliberately excluded. In the health field, the president had proposed merging twenty-five programs into two; Congress created, instead, four different block grants out of twenty-one earlier programs.[32] Some block grants retained so many requirements as to be essentially categorical. Furthermore, most of the consolidations were comparatively small: Only five of the block grants embraced as many as a

---

32. Judith Feder, John Holahan, Randall R. Bovbjerg, and Jack Hadley, "Health," in John L. Palmer and Isabel V. Sawhill, eds., *The Reagan Experiment* (Washington, D.C.: The Urban Institute, 1982, pp. 291–293.

TABLE 2

BLOCK GRANTS CREATED BY THE
OMNIBUS RECONCILIATION ACT OF 1981

Block Grant	Programs Superseded	FY 1982 Appropriations (In $ millions)
Community development— small cities	4	952
Elementary and secondary education	37	519
Preventive health and health services	6	84
Alcohol, drug abuse, and mental health	10	432
Maternal and child health services	9	291
Primary care	2	215[a]
Social services	1	1,974
Community services	7	225
Low-income home-energy assistance	1	1,400

SOURCE: David B. Walker, Albert J. Richter, and Cynthia Cates Colella, "The First Ten Months: Grant-in-Aid, Regulatory, and Other Changes," *Intergovernmental Perspective*, vol. 8, no. 1 (Winter 1982), pp. 8–11.
  a. FY 1983.

half-dozen categoricals and two involved administrative changes in a single program; just two involved outlays of over $1 billion annually.

It is too soon to tell much about the impact of this large-scale policy experiment. However, despite concerns that the states would be unable to handle their responsibilities, a General Accounting Office (GAO) field study found that most were "making reasonable progress" during the transition stage, relying on past experience and making few changes in administrative procedures.[33] Reduced grant funds made some cuts necessary, but states seem to have avoided arbitrary actions that would have disproportionately hurt persons with very low incomes.[34] Views on administrative improvements

33. U.S. General Accounting Office, *Early Observations on Block Grant Administration* (Washington, D.C.: Government Printing Office, 1982), p. i.
34. "Block Grants in the First Year," *The Urban Institute Policy and Research Report*, vol. 13, no. 2 (Summer 1983), p. 15.

differ. OMB has claimed an 83 percent drop in the paperwork burden imposed on state and local governments,[35] and some state officials agree. On the other hand, the National Governors' Association has protested that "the most vexing problem being experienced in block grant administration is the shortfall between federal promises and results. The President's original concept of much greater state control has not materialized."[36]

By all accounts, local governments have thus far received few benefits from consolidation. Although federal requirements have been lifted, most states have not reduced—and some have augmented—their own rules and procedures, which are often perceived as being at least as restrictive as federal regulations.[37] Some large urban jurisdictions have experienced substantial drops in aid receipts as a result of new state allocation formulas in combination with federal funding cuts.

These early findings are consistent with experiences under previous block grants, which suggest that consolidation may be a weak reed on which to hang hopes for federalism reform. On the whole, state and local governments have been less innovative than might be hoped in the use of their new-found flexibility; furthermore, Congress and the bureaucracy have, over time, tended to reinstate national controls through a gradual process of "recategorization."[38] (Some signs of the latter tendency have already appeared.)[39] Although the new block grants were enacted with comparatively few national strings and controls, Congress may demand additional information so that it can assess program performance, and it is likely to respond to any perceived abuses by increasing national supervision. Then, too, perhaps because past block grants fragmented the political coalitions supporting federal funding, the grants did not expand in size or scope over time.

Block grants also are difficult to enact, notwithstanding the president's successes in 1981. Under usual circumstances, consolidation proposals need to be carefully crafted to withstand the skepticism of Congress and opposition from interest groups. Such resistance has surfaced in the treatment of the

---

35. Richard S. Williamson, "Block Grants: One Year Later," *Journal of Legislation*, vol. 10, no. 2 (Summer 1983), p. 289.

36. National Governors' Association, *1982 Governors' Guide to Block Grant Implementation* (Washington, D.C.: National Governors' Association Center for Policy Research, 1982), p. 47.

37. Catherine Lovell, "Effects of Regulatory Changes on States and Localities," in Nathan, Doolittle, and Associates, eds., *The Consequences of Cuts*, pp. 176–178.

38. See Advisory Commission on Intergovernmental Relations, *Block Grants: A Comparative Analysis* (Washington, D.C.: Government Printing Office, 1977.

39. "Feeling Categorical, Congress Moves to Trim Ch. 2 Block Grant," *Education Times*, October 31, 1983, p. 4.

administration's more recent initiatives. In 1982 the president proposed expanding three existing social service block grants and establishing seven new or substantially modified programs in fields such as education for handicapped persons and child welfare. Only one new block-grant program, a replacement for the controversial Comprehensive Employment Training Act (CETA) program, was adopted. Congress showed no interest in any of four "megablock" grants proposed in 1983, which were intended to consolidate thirty-four programs—among them nine earlier block grants and revenue sharing—or in several smaller consolidation proposals.

Reagan's recent record on consolidation, then, is no better than that of his predecessors. Nor does it appear that future block grants will be easily adopted. What once was regarded by many as a politically neutral technique for simplifying aid management is now likely to be viewed as an instrument of conservative ideology. Because of their narrower political base, further consolidations may prove even more difficult to establish.[40]

Welfare Reform

Welfare programs have been a persistent intergovernmental concern ever since the national government first entered the field during the depths of the Great Depression. Under provisions of the landmark Social Security Act of 1935, matching grants were offered to states to support their programs of aid to several categories of the "deserving poor." Franklin Roosevelt was no fan of welfare, however, and hoped that it would wither away with economic recovery and the expansion of contributory social insurance programs. Instead, policymakers of the 1960s and 1970s were haunted by rising welfare outlays and, more troubling still, an increasingly large number of poor women and children dependent upon government for financial support.

Criticism and concern rose, too. Former Health, Education and Welfare Secretary Joseph A. Califano described welfare administration as a "nightmare," noting that in Atlanta 229 forms are used in the application process for Aid to Families with Dependent Children (AFDC).[41] He and many others have condemned as inequitable a system that results in diverse benefits, which

---

40. For a thorough analysis, see Timothy J. Conlan, "The Politics of Federal Block Grants: From Nixon to Reagan," *Political Science Quarterly*, forthcoming 1984.

41. Quoted in Advisory Commission on Intergovernmental Relations, *Public Assistance: The Growth of a Federal Function* (Washington, D.C.: Government Printing Office, 1980), p. 92.

ranged in 1976 from $370 in Wyoming to $3,033 in Hawaii per poor resident annually.[42]

Proposals for welfare reform have had ideologically mixed sponsorship but a remarkably consistent orientation. As early as 1962 conservative economist Milton Friedman suggested replacing categorical welfare grants with a much simpler "negative income tax" system providing uniform benefits nationwide.[43] Sargent Shriver, the head of Lyndon Johnson's Office of Economic Opportunity, showed interest and launched a series of income-maintenance experiments. Later, the drive for reform was championed by President Nixon, who made a guaranteed minimum income, termed the Family Assistance Plan, a centerpiece of his domestic policy. Most recently, President Carter advanced a Better Jobs and Income Act that would have consolidated AFDC, Food Stamps, and Supplemental Security Income into a single cash system with a basic federal benefit floor.

Welfare, however, has proven difficult to restructure; all of the efforts just mentioned resulted in comparatively limited changes. Food Stamp amendments in 1971 and 1973 extended coverage across the nation and standardized benefits. A guaranteed minimum income for aged, blind, and disabled persons was enacted in 1972, fulfilling a limited portion of the Nixon plan. But the Carter initiative ran aground as estimates of the additional cost of a federal takeover rose to as much as $20 billion. Thus, comprehensive welfare reform still seemed a distant goal as the 1970s ended.

Searching for a way around the deadlock, several organizations—including the Advisory Commission on Intergovernmental Relations, the National Governors' Association, and the National Conference of State Legislatures—devised a new approach. In 1980 they proposed a trade-off of federal financial support and functions, whereby the federal government was to assume responsibility for the full cost of all public assistance programs (long regarded by the states as a national concern) and the states and localities would relinquish grants in other fields, including perhaps education, law enforcement, and transportation. Such a move, these groups argued, would both strengthen the welfare system and clarify the allocation of functions between governmental levels, improving policymaking and administration by reducing the tangle of small categorical grants.

---

42. Joel Havemann and Linda E. Demkovich, "Making Some Sense Out of the Welfare 'Mess,' " *National Journal*, January 8, 1977, pp. 46–47. See also Helen F. Ladd and Fred C. Doolittle, "Which Level of Government Should Assist the Poor?" *National Tax Journal*, vol. 35, no. 3 (September 1982), pp. 323–336.

43. Milton Friedman, *Capitalism and Freedom* (Chicago: University of Chicago Press, 1962), chapter 12.

This approach ran afoul of the incoming president's own predilections, however. Welfare, in Ronald Reagan's view, is a state and local function, not a national one. Indeed, in 1975 he said: "If there is one area of social policy that should be at the most local level of government possible, it is welfare. It should not be nationalized—it should be localized."[44] Although most welfare reformers emphasize the inequities resulting from the present system of federal-state matching grants, the Reagan administration has been more concerned with holding down welfare expenditures, eliminating fraud, and reducing welfare dependency. These objectives, it believes, would be better advanced by state-run instead of national programs—and the president points to his own experience in California as evidence. In taking this position, however, the Reagan administration stood essentially alone. In the face of state and local pressure, the president advanced a possible compromise. In his 1982 State of the Union message, he proposed a narrower functional swap, including federal assumption of all costs for the $30 billion Medicaid program but a turnback of responsibility for AFDC and Food Stamps.

Congress reacted to this second round of new federalism initiatives with disinterest and hostility. Many members, including some Republicans, regarded the proposal as a diversionary tactic for avoiding action on continuing unemployment and on the exploding deficits that had resulted from the previous year's tax cuts.[45] Social program advocates were aghast: "The worst thing you can do," said the Coalition on Block Grants and Human Needs, "is to decentralize responsibilities you know will be neglected because of lack of political will."[46] In contrast, many governors regarded the administration's initiative as a good first step and praised the president for putting the question of federalism reform "on the table." At the same time, they were disappointed with the specifics. Arizona Governor Bruce Babbitt hailed the proposal as "an excellent start" and the beginning of a great national debate, but he also accused the administration of "a lack of guiding principles" about which programs ought to be run at the national level and which by state and local governments.[47]

Throughout the spring and summer of 1982, top administration officials met with a group of state and local spokesmen to devise the specifics of a

---

44. Ronald Reagan, "Conservative Blueprint for the 1970's," reprinted in *Congressional Record*, vol. 121, 94th Cong., 1st sess., 1975, p. 31186.

45. See Helen Dewar, "Hill Republicans Say New Reagan Direction Leaves Them Adrift," *Washington Post*, February 1, 1982, p. A3; and David S. Broder, "Federalism Plan Fails to Shift Focus Away From Economy," *Washington Post*, January 28, 1982, p. A1.

46. Quoted in Neal Peirce, "The States Can Do It, but Is There the Will?" *National Journal*, February 27, 1982, p. 377.

47. Bruce Babbitt, interview on *Meet the Press*, National Broadcasting Company, January 31, 1982.

legislative package. After repeated delays and alternative proposals from both camps, the negotiations broke down.[48] The governors were unwilling to accept a programmatic turnback that included AFDC or, especially, Food Stamps, and challenged the administration's estimates of projected cost savings. Given fiscal pressures produced by the continuing recession, they were concerned about any proposal that might exacerbate their budgetary problems; their interest in federalism reform waned as economic worries rose. The administration itself was divided on the Medicaid takeover; some feared that its costs could be hard to control, and technical questions about the operation of a nationalized program could not be resolved. No legislation was ever forwarded to Congress. By the end of the year, after periodic obituaries, the trade-off proposal was dead.[49]

Some far-more-limited changes in AFDC, Food Stamps, and Medicaid were made by the 1981 Reconciliation Act. Most of the changes were intended to reduce welfare costs by restricting eligibility and were directed specifically at the "working poor," who have some outside income, not the neediest recipients. As a consequence, the number of households receiving aid has held steady, or has been reduced, despite rising poverty and unemployment levels. The Medicaid amendments reduced the federal contribution and at the same time granted states long-sought flexibility to contract with specific health-care providers; the authority to impose nominal charges upon the recipients of services; and the option of supporting patients in their own homes or foster homes, rather than institutions.[50] States seem to be restraining Medicaid outlays by making advance agreements with hospitals on the cost of services or enrolling beneficiaries in prepaid health maintenance organization plans. It is generally accepted that some action was needed—Medicaid's costs had risen about 15 percent annually through most of the 1970s. At the same time, some critics fear that the quality of health care for the poor may suffer as a result of the new measures.

Overall, welfare remains an intricately shared function, neither state nor national. The changes made thus far fall short of the objectives set by either

---

48. For summaries of the negotiations see National Governors' Association, *Governors' Priorities: 1983* (Washington, D.C.: National Governors' Association, 1983), pp. 37–44; and Richard S. Williamson, "The 1982 New Federalism Negotiations," *Publius*, vol. 13, no. 2 (Spring 1983), pp. 11–32.

49. "Reagan's Idea of Federalism Called 'Dead,' " *New York Times*, December 13, 1982, p. B17.

50. Linda E. Demkovich, "States May Be Gaining in the Battle To Curb Medicaid Spending Growth," *National Journal*, September 18, 1982, pp. 1584–1588; Randall R. Bovbjerg and John Holahan, *Medicaid in the Reagan Era: Federal Policy and State Choices* (Washington, D.C.: The Urban Institute, 1982).

President Reagan or other welfare and intergovernmental reformers. The continuing division of opinion makes any sort of comprehensive reform unlikely.

Revenue Sharing

Revenue sharing—a broad, general-purpose support grant with limited strings and controls—was the cornerstone of the original new federalism, that of the Nixon administration, although the concept had originated in earlier years. Congressman Melvin Laird, a Wisconsin Republican, introduced the first modern revenue-sharing bill in 1958, and the idea was later endorsed by a task force led by Walter Heller, Lyndon Johnson's chief economic adviser. Johnson never embraced the proposal, but it found advocates in Congress and was adopted in 1972 with President Nixon's strong backing.

The concept of general-purpose aid has won support from many public-finance experts as a way to reduce "vertical" and "horizontal" fiscal imbalances. In principle, it recognizes that the national government possesses the strongest, most elastic, and most equitable tax base, while state and local governments face the heaviest demands for services. "Prosperity," Walter Heller once wrote, "gives the national government the affluence and local governments the effluents."[51] At the same time, a properly constructed formula could guarantee that federal funds are offered to the jurisdictions least able to provide adequate public services from their own resources. The American program has never been large enough, nor sufficiently well targeted, to fully meet these objectives, but such equalizing general-support grants are central to the intergovernmental fiscal systems of other federal nations such as Canada, Australia, and West Germany.

Revenue sharing also appeals to many political conservatives, as well as to state and local officials, as a strategy for reducing federal strings and controls. This accounted for Richard Nixon's fervent advocacy. Ronald Reagan has never shared this view, however, and he targeted the program for termination in his 1975 turnback package. He rejects the notion that the national government should redistribute resources between states that are relatively well off and those that are not. Rather, he argues that citizens in a federal system have a right to "vote with their feet": "If a state is badly managed, the people will either do one of two things: they will either use their power at the polls to redress that, or they'll go somewhere else."[52]

---

51. Walter W. Heller, *New Dimensions of Political Economy* (New York: W. W. Norton & Co., 1967), p. 129.

52. Quoted in "Reagan to the Nation's Governors: The Federal Aid Cupboard is Bare," *National Journal*, November 28, 1981, p. 2111.

Under the original general revenue-sharing (GRS) program, a total of $6 billion in essentially string-free grants were given to each of the fifty states as well as some 39,000 general purpose units of local government: cities, counties, and townships. But in 1980, state governments—then enjoying what turned out to be temporary revenue surpluses—were dropped from the program and funding was reduced to $4.6 billion.

When President Reagan took office, local officials early on sought assurances that revenue sharing would enjoy a special, protected status—one they believed it merited in an administration dedicated to reducing national control. Reagan assented, but his commitment has always seemed lukewarm. In late 1981 he proposed that GRS funding be reduced $550 million as part of a 12 percent across-the-board domestic cutback. The proposal brought an immediate objection from state and local officials, who termed it a "breach of faith."[53] Although supporting reauthorization of the program in 1983, the administration warned that it would veto a House of Representatives-passed bill that included funding increases. And, despite its general commitment to a strengthening of the states, the administration has not sought to bring them back into the program. Local governments, as well as the states themselves, favor reinstatement.

What has been termed a kind of "super" revenue sharing was a major component of the administration's 1982 new federalism initiative. Along with the welfare trade-off or swap, the president proposed that proceeds from the federal windfall profits tax on oil, as well as various excise taxes, be placed into a $28 billion trust fund, and then allocated among the states on a "hold harmless" basis, which would avoid sharp changes in receipts. At the same time, some forty to sixty grant programs were to be terminated. Unlike general revenue sharing, however, the trust fund was to be temporary. After four years, both it and the federal taxes supporting it would begin to phase out, leaving it to the states to determine whether or not to replace lost revenues and services. GRS, along with nearly all other federal-local programs, was designated part of the turnback package.

Proposed at a time of worsening budget and economic conditions, the revenue turnback idea became snarled in a debate over "winners" and "losers." Some state officials believed that the funds offered would prove insufficient to maintain existing services in the long run. Those without oil resources, in particular, were unable to see how they could benefit from a "turnback" of the windfall profits tax. Local officials feared that their own receipts would fall under the state-administered program. Both argued that

---

53. B. Drummond Ayres, Jr., "Reagan and Cuts in Revenue Sharing," *New York Times*, October 2, 1981, p. A29.

the turnback would leave hundreds of small categorical grants untouched, doing little to rationalize the overall grant system.[54]

These objections, and others, were reflected in reactions on Capitol Hill. Senator David Durenberger, the Republican chairperson of the Senate Intergovernmental Relations Subcommittee, was openly critical. In his view, the national government has a responsibility to ease fiscal disparities among the states. The freedom to "vote with your feet," he said, "is an important freedom, but not a sound foundation for a functioning federal system," adding that low-capacity states may not be able to boost their tax rates without reducing their attractiveness to potential investors and employers.[55] As an alternative to the president's plan, he proposed setting aside a share of federal income tax revenues in a permanent trust fund, to be allocated among the states in a manner that would help equalize their fiscal capacities. State and local officials generally favored this approach.

Like its bedfellow, the welfare trade-off, the President's tax turnback proposal was never forwarded to Congress. GRS was reauthorized for three years, with few changes, at the end of 1983. But the underlying issue of interstate differences in tax resources may be a continuing source of intergovernmental tension throughout the 1980s. Disparities are large and growing, chiefly as a consequence of the new affluence of the energy-rich states: for example, Alaska now enjoys a per capita tax base more than seven times higher than the poorest state, Mississippi. Moreover, the current grant system, as a whole, tends to distribute funds to states that are best able to help themselves.[56] Despite the Reagan administration's disinterest, these differences are perceived by many as serious inequities and are likely to lead to new proposals for national remedies.

Administrative Standardization and Simplification

Along with grant consolidation and revenue sharing, most past intergovernmental reformers have advocated managerial procedures to simplify and coordinate the administration of aid programs. These procedures typically were instituted through OMB management circulars setting standards to be followed by every department and agency. For example, circular A-85, pro-

54. See Rochelle L. Stanfield, " 'Turning Back' 61 Programs: A Radical Shift of Power," *National Journal*, February 27, 1982, pp. 369–374.

55. Senator David Durenberger, "New Federalism: Back to Basics," *American Education*, March 1983, p. 11.

56. A thorough analysis of these issues is presented in Albert Davis and Robert Lucke, "The Rich-State-Poor-State Problem in a Federal System," *National Tax Journal*, vol. 35, no. 3 (September 1982), pp. 337–363.

mulgated in 1967 after a much publicized "governors' revolt," guaranteed state and local officials an opportunity to be consulted during the design and implementation of intergovernmental programs. Another circular, A-95, was intended to ensure that different federal agencies did not fund duplicative or conflicting development projects. It created a system allowing state and local governments and planning agencies to comment on grant applications from their region. Circular A-102, along with its multitudinous attachments, standardized every step of the grant process from application to audit. The joint funding procedure (circular A-111) established a procedure for "packaging" aid resources from several federal sources into a single grant, overseen by just one federal manager.

New organizational structures were created to implement these (and other similar) management processes during the 1960s and early 1970s. Local areawide planning commissions were offered extensive financial aid; Federal Regional Councils, composed of each department's senior regional officials, were established in ten newly standardized federal administrative regions; and the old Bureau of the Budget was converted into a new Office of Management and Budget.

These procedures and mechanisms exemplify a consistent thrust of federal policy that originated during the Johnson years, was given special emphasis by the Nixon administration,[57] and renewed by President Carter.[58] Consistency notwithstanding, most evaluations have found that the processes thus established never were fully effective. For instance, despite the name change, OMB continued to be dominated by its budget side, and federal agencies did not always adhere to its directives. Still, these management measures were generally considered useful, if in need of bolstering. In 1980, for example, a distinguished group of administrative experts recommended that a new and stronger federal assistance administration staff be created within OMB.[59]

President Reagan, on the other hand, seems to be of a different mind. Under his new federalism, many grants management questions have been left to state discretion. Nearly all of the earlier procedures cited here have been

---

57. See Advisory Commission on Intergovernmental Relations, *Improving Federal Grants Management* (Washington, D.C.: U.S. Government Printing Office, 1977), pp. 161–166 and 181–185.

58. The major study undertaken during the Carter years appears in Office of Management and Budget, *Managing Federal Assistance in the 1980s* (Washington, D.C.: Government Printing Office, 1980).

59. National Academy of Public Administration, *A Presidency for the 1980s*, reprinted in Hugh Heclo and Lester M. Salamon, eds., *The Illusion of Presidential Government* (Boulder, Colo.: Westview Press, 1981), p. 328.

replaced, weakened, or eliminated, along with the institutions that managed them.

The 1981 block grants were exempted from most of the management circulars. Federal agencies have offered little guidance on the interpretation of statutory requirements, leaving it to the individual states to devise their own applications, processes, and reporting systems. The A-95 process has been discarded, and federal agencies have been instructed to utilize whatever consultation process each state may establish. Although many state and local governments welcomed the promised relief from paperwork burdens, they have also expressed skepticism about the workability of systems instituted independently by some twenty-nine different federal agencies and the fifty states, without any central enforcement mechanism. Local governments have voiced concern that their views may not be reflected in the new state-initiated procedures. Some participants fear that the new strategy will be more complex and less effective than the one it was intended to simplify.

Before President Reagan took office, Circular A-85 had been replaced with a less formal consultation process under Executive Order 12044. This executive order was rescinded in early 1981; as a consequence, state and local governments no longer enjoy any special status in federal rule making. The joint funding circular (A-111) was revoked in early 1983. Circular A-102 is currently being reviewed, apparently with an eye to eliminating requirements. The Federal Regional Councils were first reduced in size and later abolished. OMB's intergovernmental staff unit was disbanded after a reorganization of the office's managerial side and, while its former functions have been entrusted to the management improvement staff, there is little ongoing monitoring of agency implementation.

The same treatment was accorded some newly proposed procedures. The Reagan administration discontinued work on a draft circular intended to standardize and coordinate federal administration of "crosscutting" requirements—such as nondiscrimination guarantees—that apply to many or all grant programs.[60] Improvements in this area had been a priority concern of many state and local government officials. Instead of strengthening OMB oversight of agency policies, the administration published a directory of crosscutting requirements.[61] The implication, one observer commented, is that the states

---

60. Office of Management and Budget, "Proposed Circular on Managing Generally Applicable Requirements for Assistance Programs: Request for Comment," *Federal Register*, November 7, 1980, Part VIII.

61. Office of Management and Budget, Intergovernmental Affairs Division, *Directory of Generally Applicable Requirements and Administrative Management Standards* (Washington, D.C.: Government Printing Office, 1982).

themselves must decide how seriously to take each of these fifty regulations and must guess whether and how federal agencies will assess compliance.[62]

The administration's deemphasis on grants management processes has been the least noted component of its intergovernmental strategy. Yet it, too, represents a significant departure from past practice. If the number of aid programs had in fact been reduced as severely as proposed, better grants management procedures might well be superfluous. As matters stand, however, it may be expected that state and local governments will continue to press for clear, simple, and uniform federal procedures and guidelines.

Regulatory Reform

With the growth of federal regulation during the late 1960s and 1970s came repeated calls for regulatory reform. Regulation, it appeared, was too often overbearing, too rigid, too expensive. For this reason, every president since Nixon has instituted some process for reviewing the costs and benefits of rules proposed by the agencies.

By and large, these regulatory reform efforts were concerned with the seeming economic inefficiency of federal requirements affecting business firms. However, unlike the "old" economic regulation that typified the Progressive era and New Deal, much of the new social regulation is aimed at or implemented by state and local governments. By the time Reagan took office, state and local officials were voicing concern about the cost and intrusiveness of national requirements. Federal "mandate mandarins," protested New York's mayor Edward I. Koch, had hung a "mandate millstone" around the necks of the nation's cities.[63]

The incoming administration was the first to accord much attention to this aspect of the regulatory problem. Two days after taking office, the president announced the creation of a Task Force on Regulatory Relief, chaired by Vice President George Bush and charged with reviewing pending and past regulations. Like business and consumer groups, state and local governments were invited to suggest particular rules for possible modification. A week later, President Reagan put a temporary freeze on nearly 200 regulations promulgated toward the end of the Carter administration. A February 1981 executive order required agencies to carefully assess the costs and benefits

---

62. Catherine Lovell, "Effects of Regulatory Changes on States and Localities," in Nathan, Doolittle, and Associates, eds., *The Consequences of Cuts*, p. 185.

63. Edward I. Koch, "The Mandate Millstone," *The Public Interest*, no. 61 (Fall 1980), p. 6.

of new rules, including those affecting state and local governments, and charged OMB with policing compliance.[64]

Despite the fast start, however, achievements were modest. A first-year review concluded that when "judged against the results expected by the public because of campaign rhetoric . . . the Administration's regulatory reform program to date appears shallow, weak and poorly focused."[65] Other commentaries noted that the administration had slowed the rate of issuance of rules but achieved few major alterations.[66] The campaign, furthermore, seemed to be losing momentum, and some critics thought that the prospects for substantial reform looked dimmer than when Reagan had taken offce.[67] Recently, Murray L. Weidenbaum, a regulatory policy expert who served as President Reagan's first chairperson of the Council of Economic Advisers, concluded that "the similarities between the regulatory system of mid-1983 and that of January 1981 are far greater than the differences. . . . Only a fraction of the regulatory reforms envisioned at the beginning of 1981 have been accomplished."[68]

Still, the regulatory relief campaign has realized some successes. An official progress report in August 1982 identified twenty-four completed actions in programs affecting state and local governments, including the greatly streamlined regulations developed for the new block grants and changes in the method for calculating wages to be paid workers on federally assisted construction. Total savings were estimated at $4 billion to $6 billion in investment costs and $2 billion in annually recurring costs.[69] No major new regulatory statutes have been enacted since the administration took office, and it is enforcing environmental, civil rights, and occupational health and safety rules less vigorously than its predecessors. Indeed, changes in the way agencies enforce rules may be the administration's chief victory.[70]

On the other hand, long-lasting statutory changes have been few. Most regulatory reformers stress the need for a careful review and modification of

64. Executive Order 12291, February 17, 1981.

65. "The Reagan Administration's First Year," *Regulatory Eye*, vol. 3, no. 1–2, p. 3.

66. Michael Wines, "Reagan's Reforms Are Full of Sound and Fury, but What Do They Signify?" *National Journal*, January 16, 1982, pp. 92–98.

67. Robert W. Crandall, "Has Reagan Dropped the Ball?" *Regulation*, September/October 1981, p. 15.

68. Murray L. Weidenbaum, *Confessions of a One-Armed Economist* (St. Louis: Washington University Center for the Study of American Business, 1983), pp. 43–44.

69. Presidential Task Force on Regulatory Relief, *Reagan Administration Achievements in Regulatory Relief for State and Local Government* (Washington, D.C.: Presidential Task Force on Regulatory Relief, August 1982), p. i.

70. Lovell, "Effects of Regulatory Changes on States and Localities," in Nathan, Doolittle, and Associates, eds., *The Consequences of Cuts*, p. 187.

existing laws. The administration has attempted little in this area, opting instead for revisions in agency rules that could be accomplished without congressional approval. The administration's major legislative goal—a revision of the Clean Air Act—has so far not been achieved.

Obstacles to the regulatory relief drive have arisen from interest groups, Congress, and the courts, as well as from the administration's own apparent missteps and inconsistencies. A good case study of these difficulties is offered by modifications in the Department of Transportation's (DoT's) rules implementing Section 504 of the Rehabilitation Act, which bars discrimination against handicapped persons in any federally assisted service. These rules, originally issued in 1979, required local transit systems to provide full access to existing facilities for patrons in wheelchairs and for other disabled riders—at a cost estimated at as much as $38 per trip.[71] State and local officials cited these provisions as a principal example of federal heavy-handedness and inefficiency. Aided by the decision of a federal appeals court, which found that DoT's rules lacked a clear statutory foundation, the administration, in 1981, issued new and much looser requirements. Cost savings were estimated at about $2.2 billion—more than that of any other single rule revision.

However, the Section 504 experience shows the limits of the regulatory relief campaign. Heated opposition from groups representing handicapped persons forced the Department of Justice to abandon its effort to rewrite governmentwide 504 standards in early 1983. Later that year, DoT and Justice proposed new transportation rules that were more prescriptive than those it had issued in 1981. These would require adequate service for all handicapped persons—those with mental and emotional as well as physical disabilities—at considerably higher costs.[72] The administration also has sought to extend 504 rules into a new and sensitive area—the treatment to be given infants born with serious disabilities—despite opposition from the medical community.

Pressures from the lobby for handicapped persons, coupled with congressional criticism, also forced the administration to drop its attempt to modify rules prescribing educational services to be offered to handicapped children. Local governments and school districts have long chaffed at the costs imposed by the 1975 Education for All Handicapped Children Act and the lack of adequate federal funding, although the rule changes proposed by the De-

---

71. Congressional Budget Office, *Urban Transportation for Handicapped Persons: Alternative Federal Approaches* (Washington, D.C.: Government Printing Office, 1979), p. xi.

72. See Michael Fix, "The Prospects for Regulatory Federalism," (Paper prepared for the 89th National Conference on Government, Baltimore, Md., November 12–15, 1983), p. 10. Milwaukee County, which has a model "paratransit" system for elderly and handicapped persons, would be forced to triple its current outlays to sustain existing service levels.

partment of Education in August 1982 exceeded what local governments and schools had requested. After heated protests by parent groups, and declarations of opposition from both the Senate and House, the new rules were withdrawn in what was described as "a rout for a major Reagan administration effort to reduce federal involvement in schools."[73]

Although much of the opposition to the regulatory relief drive has come from social and environmental groups, business interests also have been re- luctant to transfer additional regulatory authority to the states. Many prefer uniform national standards over varying state requirements. Indeed, one busi- ness critic has said that the new federalism has resulted in a "state regulatory nightmare," a "50-headed hydra."[74] To provide an illustration of these con- cerns, in November 1983 the Occupational Safety and Health Administration (OSHA) announced new rules requiring companies to inform their workers of potential dangers from the chemicals they handle. But whereas industry supports the new requirements, organized labor opposes them because they supersede the "right to know" laws of seventeen states, some of which are tougher than OSHA's standard.[75]

The courts, like interest groups, have also been a countervailing force. The administration has sought to lighten the burden on grantees, but the judiciary, with few exceptions, has interpreted laws in a manner that extends and intensifies grantees' obligations.[76] Recent decisions also have upheld laws regarding federal age discrimination, surface mining control, and public utility regulation in the face of Tenth Amendment challenges by the states. Overall, the executive and judicial branches appear to be marching to different drum- mers.

In August 1983 the Bush task force issued its final report and the drive for regulatory relief now seems to have been largely abandoned. Despite changes in block-grant rules, the modification of some specific requirements, and reduced levels of enforcement, the basic structure of intergovernmental regulation remains intact. Indeed, in the regulatory field, as in grant consol- idation, the administration's early frontal assault tactics may have polarized opinion and thus backfired. "Now signs abound," reported *Business Week*

73. Joanne Omang, "Bell Withdraws 6 Proposals for Educating Handicapped," *Washington Post*, September 30, 1982, p. A1.

74. "State Regulators Rush In Where Washington No Longer Treads," *Business Week*, September 19, 1983, p. 124.

75. "OSHA Rules Workers Must Be Told of Hazardous Chemicals," *New York Times*, November 11, 1983, p. A18.

76. For a review, see Thomas J. Madden and David H. Remes, "The Courts and the Administration: Marching to Different Drummers," *Intergovernmental Perspective*, vol. 9, no. 2 (Spring 1983), pp. 23–29.

in May 1983, "that these sweeping moves have created a bi-partisan backlash in Congress. The regulatory pendulum is swinging the other way."[77]

Retrospect and Prospect

Richard P. Nathan, whose monitoring studies have produced much useful information about the operational effects of many intergovernmental programs, has noted a widespread tendency to exaggerate the impact on states and localities of the Reagan administration's budget cuts. Liberals overstate the magnitude of these effects to help rally opponents; conservative supporters, in contrast, claim credit for changes they did not achieve.[78] This same description applies to many other aspects of new federalism. Despite some popular misperceptions, no large-scale devolution of federal fiscal or regulatory functions has been accomplished. Indeed, once the heat of battle dissipates, it is possible that the changes that have actually emerged from Congress since 1981 will be regarded as relatively moderate, incremental adjustments to the intergovernmental system.[79]

If the new federalism is examined in three rounds, the first, advanced in 1981, saw some remarkable legislative successes in grant consolidation and domestic expenditure reductions, as well as a large tax cut and a series of regulatory relief initiatives. These were carried along by the tide favoring dramatic action to stimulate the economy, as well as adroit political maneuvering by a president still enjoying a congressional honeymoon. But the usual rules of politics had been suspended, not revoked; resistance to the administration's initiatives rose by the end of the first year. The second and most important round of new federalism proposals, including the welfare trade-off and revenue turnback combination, in the end generated nothing but talk. Similarly, the extensive grant consolidations proposed as the third round in early 1983 made no headway. The administration now appears to have abandoned its efforts at comprehensive intergovernmental reform, at least until the election is over.

Many reasons for these difficulties may be identified. Participants in and close observers of the process are apt to blame their own tactical errors or

---

77. "A Bipartisan Swing to More Regulation," *Business Week*, May 30, 1983, p. 74.

78. Richard P. Nathan, Philip M. Dearborn, Clifford A. Goldman, and Associates, "Initial Effects of the Fiscal Year 1982 Reductions in Federal Domestic Spending," in John William Ellwood, ed., *Reductions in U.S. Domestic Spending*, p. 320.

79. This view is expressed by David B. Walker, "Incrementalism is Back!" *SIAM Intergovernmental News*, vol. 7, no. 2 (Summer 1983), p. 1.

the intransigence of others. The rush of action in 1981 produced early victories but generated resistance to further grant cuts, consolidations, or regulatory changes later on. Timing was surely faulty: The trade-off and turnback initiatives aroused hostility, in part, because they were advanced along with proposals to reduce aid outlays in a period of economic distress. The impression was created that *federalism* was nothing more than a code word for stringent expenditure cuts.

Other obstructions were created by the character of the proposals themselves. As the foregoing account indicates, President Reagan's initiatives, in essentially every area, differed from those advanced by other reformers, past and present. As a consequence, even potential allies were more often critical than supportive. Only in the area of grants management, where decisive action was possible by the executive branch alone, was the president able to accomplish most of his agenda.

If these tactical problems were the only roadblocks to reform, there might conceivably be strong prospects for the adoption of comparable initiatives by this administration, or a successor, later in the 1980s. However, there are other, more fundamental, constraints imposed by the character of public opinion. Attitudes toward the federal government and the role it has assumed in contemporary society are marked by a deep ambivalence. In 1967 a survey study found that 65 percent of respondents could be termed liberals on an "operational" scale involving specific policy questions, although 50 percent could be called conservatives on a scale of ideology.[80] That is, majorities valued small government but also wanted services that a large government can provide. This schizoid tendency has persisted ever since, finding partial resolution in the expedient of electing presidents who are more conservative than Congress—the members of which are expected to "bring home the bacon" for local constituents—as well as in the proliferation of interest groups whose attention is intrinsically focused on specific benefit programs.

The 1980 election reflected an altered balance between these inconsistent desires. Along with a Republican Senate majority, it produced a president who took conservative ideology more seriously than most of his electoral supporters and strove to put its dictates into practice. The effort to do so, however, collided with the practical consideration that large majorities continued to support high or rising levels of expenditure for many domestic services—though they wanted to squeeze out the "waste" and reduce taxes—and overwhelmingly favored maintaining many key environmental and social regulations. As a preelection survey report commented:

---

80. Lloyd A. Free and Hadley Cantril, *The Political Beliefs of Americans: A Study of Public Opinion* (New York: Simon & Schuster, 1968), p. 32.

Most Americans remain strongly committed to a large, even growing role for government. They still endorse new governmental initiatives—like a bigger federal role in health care. When people are asked about governmental expenditures . . . the proportion saying spending is excessive is very small, often as low as 10 percent, for virtually all programs.[81]

On the other hand, the same study showed that the public was dissatisfied with governmental performance, regarding it as intrusive and inefficient.[82]

The president's mandate for intergovernmental change thus was far thinner than he and many of his advisers supposed. It might well have been impossible to build an effective coalition for federalism reform under any circumstances, as history suggests; but it was certainly impossible to do so with measures and rhetoric that seemed to threaten the foundations of popular benefit and protective programs.

Tarnished by failure, the cause of federalism reform no longer finds many ardent supporters among officials at any level of government. The combination of rising defense outlays, financial pressure on the Medicare and Social Security systems, and projected record budget deficits is likely to restrain the growth of federal financial assistance to the states and localities. However, the odds remain strongly against any major devolution of federal revenue and programs of the kind Ronald Reagan has long desired.

---

81. Everett Carll Ladd, Jr., and Seymour Martin Lipset, "Anatomy of a Decade," *Public Opinion*, December/January 1980, p. 3.

82. Seymour Martin Lipset and William Schneider, "The Public View of Regulation," *Public Opinion*, January/February 1979, p. 6.

Hale Champion

The Big Impacts Were Indirect

David R. Beam's paper is an admirably comprehensive canvass of what has and has not happened in the Sargasso Sea of intergovernmental relations since Ronald Reagan came back down from the Santa Monica mountains in 1980. Beam's analysis underscores once again how invaluable is the role of both the Advisory Commission on Intergovernmental Relations (ACIR) and its expert observers. Students of government and governance spend proportionately too much time on the horizontal aspects of governance at the federal level and far too little on the vertical aspects, which, at least with respect to domestic programs of every kind, are of equal and often central significance. Beam's paper thus helps to redress the balance.

The paper's overall assessment of the effect of *direct* Reagan efforts at institutional reform in the intergovernmental arena seems cautiously negative. I see no reason for caution, especially if the key word is reform. Ronald Reagan's well-publicized "new federalism" initiatives never offered any prospect either for reform of the intergovernmental nonsystem or for residual change of any real consequence. But the *indirect* impact of the administration's fiscal and tax policies on state and local government fiscal capacity is major, of course, at least for the near future.

Rhetoric versus Actual Agenda

With respect to intergovernmental policies, Reagan confronts us with a classic problem. One must always distinguish carefully between what his rhetoric implies and what his basic agenda and actions really portend. There is almost always a difference, but it is extremely difficult to differentiate between the two because he does not seem either to perceive or to care about the distinction. Intergovernmental policy is an area in which the president himself has stated clear intentions but has offered proposals that often conflict with his intentions. He is, however, such a master at walking over wet paint that one has to use a magnifying lens to see the tracks.

The *new* "new federalism," for example, is really only a "grand design" in the president's rhetoric, which declares that authority, money, and flexibility should be turned back to state and local governments—close to the people. With minor exceptions, however, neither President Reagan's proposals nor his administration's actions have consistently matched his rhetoric. What we have is not devolution of authority, of flexibility, and of money in the intergovernmental system, but minimum authority, minimum flexibility, and especially, minimum money at *all* levels of government. Further, the president's actions indicate that the preferred level of government is simply the level perceived as most able and amenable to bring about a specific result or to further some social value of the president's choosing. Interestingly, this level is most often the state level, rather than the federal or local levels, no matter the fact that local government is closest to the people. This is not because Reagan loves state government more; he simply loves both the federal government and giving authority to the teeming masses of the cities less. More critical, however, is that Reagan basically is not seeking to shift governmental responsibilities anywhere as much as he is seeking to abolish or reduce interventions he does not like—and these are legion. As for reformist arrangements to bring needed harmony and efficiency into the realization of national purposes through subnational instruments, Beam is right in recognizing the administration's near-total failure in the further development of "cooperative federalism."

Impact of the New, New Federalism

The new, new federalism therefore was not a grand design, as a hasty reading of Beam's paper might suggest. I use the past tense advisedly: The president's initiative was not stillborn, but it never left the incubator. In the end, it was not even a developed scheme, much less "grand." The cities rejected any parental responsibility on sight, and the states followed suit after the blood tests. The proffered package or deal—which was all it ever was—had no consistent principles, nor even a persuasive rationale. It did have a purpose, however. (This administration is very strong on purpose, even when it is not being up-front about it.) The key purpose of the new, new federalism proposal was found not in its lip-service dedication to state and local wisdom and capacity but in its effort to cut further or at least to hold down domestic spending on programs the president did not like; and, in addition, to help justify and sustain reduced federal taxes, both now and for the indefinite future. The package's brief existence probably helped to serve those real purposes, but it did nothing to bring about any proclaimed, if confused, new, new federalism.

One could be more charitable, but not much. At best, one could describe the entire initiative as an attempt to proceed in stages through underfunded devolution in the present to unfunded laissez-faire in the future for the bulk of human service programs. Even this kinder view, however, still would not explain some of the administration's simultaneous executive actions that were taken without need of congressional approval. These actions were designed to impose the administration's values or to serve its desires, not to establish any well-conceived set of principles or even guidelines for intergovernmental management. The president was perfectly content to have the federal government decide on, even add to, the details of welfare program performance and to pay for enforcement (not services) when that would suit his preferences. When his administration felt that state and local government would not use discretion as he would, discretion was often denied. Remember, for instance, the federal edict that parents be informed of their children's birth control activities as a condition of federal funding assistance. There is no small-minded consistency there, or indeed, in a number of other comparable actions.

From Beam's evidence and my perspective, whatever legacy is to come from the administration's actions in intergovernmental relations and management—and a significant effect seems certain, at least in the short term—will relate to the effects of the tax and domestic spending cuts achieved in the summer of 1981. Most of those effects are indirect, but they are already evident, having not only diminished the size and character of the federal role but altered the balance between state and local governments in favor of the states, largely by changing the distribution of fiscal capacity. They have made it harder for both federal and local governments to get money, and have given the state governments less money but more tax leeway, setting up a kind of de facto halfway devolution. The impact on the federal role in domestic intergovernmental programs needs no further explication. If money makes the mare go, then lack of it leaves the mare in the stable. The new situation between state and local governments is only a little more complicated. Although the fiscal capacity disparities between local jurisdictions within states were already greater in many cases than those between the states, and are getting worse because of Proposition #13 and its imitations, the Omnibus Budget Reconciliation Act of 1981 gave the states the central discretionary role in distributing federal funds among localities and purposes. The room left in the income tax base by the tax cuts is much more accessible to the states than to cities, school districts, or other local jurisidictions than when it was used by the federal government. The federal income tax cuts also made it more difficult and costly for both states and cities to borrow for capital purposes—notably for much-needed infrastructure improvements—because the resulting deficits seemed to assure long-term interest levels above historic norms for tax-exempt municipal bonds.

Those are my major conclusions then—no impact from the new, new federalism initiative, but a major immediate, if indirect, effect from the Reconcilation Act and the tax cuts. I would take these also to be Beam's basic findings.

Unfortunately, none of the Reagan efforts showed any interest in the newer and, to me, potentially more interesting and rewarding reform possibilities raised by Frederick C. Mosher and Lester M. Salamon at about the time Reagan took office.[1] As Beam notes, these two scholars found that the enormous growth of grants-in-aid and other subsidy devices, especially in the Great Society and the Nixon years, made these the dominant domestic program mode. Mosher suggested that this development required a fundamental rethinking and reshaping of both federal management strategies and accountability systems. Salamon further suggested that policy analysts should look at the fifty-seven varieties of federal incentive, delivery, and enforcement devices invented during that time to see which were the most workable and why. Both recommendations were aimed at improving and simplifying the system for those who had to work in it, and both offered some promise of facilitating more "cooperative" behavior among levels of government rather than giving each level exclusive responsibility for domestic programs in a specific given area—for example, giving education to the states. Although neither Mosher nor Salamon offered much prescription, pending the outcome of the studies they advocated, Mosher's observations did point in at least one significant direction. Given that the present workings of intergovernmental programs require conflict resolution in political back channels, could we not get more of that work done correctly in the management channels by providing more discretion for interaction by the professionals involved at all levels of the system?

The legislative failure of the Reagan administration's new federalism centerpiece proposal, and Reagan's diminishing ability after 1981 to reduce the federal role even through the budget, probably mean there will be no breaking up of the federal-state-local delivery system into separate respon-

1. See Frederick C. Mosher, "The Changing Responsibilities and Tactics of the Federal Government," *Public Administration Review*, vol. 40, no. 6 (November/December 1980), pp. 541–548; Lester M. Salamon, "Rethinking Public Management: Third-Party Government and the Changing Forms of Government Action," *Public Policy*, vol. 29, no. 3 (Summer 1981), pp. 255–275.

sibilities for different programs. The implication, then, is that since almost everyone agrees that the present system is inadequate, we ought to concentrate on ways to improve it. Indeed, as Beam points out, the Reagan administration did try to do some tinkering of that kind, not in the Mosher-Salamon mode, but along the lines of the block-grant proposals in the Nixon administration.

Even in the advocacy of block grants, however, there was a hook in the flies that the administration was casting. Previous block-grant advocates usually came up with more money to ease the transition from categorical grants to block grants. However, Reagan's agent David Stockman, director of OMB, proposed 25 percent decreases, partly to save money but also to force the states to reduce or get rid of some of the categorical activities. The states were to carry the political burden of choosing the victims. Once again the administration's purpose seems at odds with its rhetoric. The administration was giving the states more authority but less money, and therefore less flexibility to exercise that authority. Congress went along, although only in part and very reluctantly, in the Reconcilation Act of 1981, but the movement has now all but stopped.

With respect to reducing federal regulatory requirements, the ACIR has already documented the failure to make major progress, and I think the commission's overall judgment is right. There even has been some retrogression, especially in health and welfare, but there also has been one action which, as opposed to the view of the ACIR, I think merits special applause. For a mix of reasons, the administration has reduced or ignored most of the comprehensive planning requirements of the A-95 variety. While the intent of these requirements was laudable, they have served more to complicate process than to avoid duplication or conflict, and they will not often be missed.

COMMENTS   *Marian Lief Palley*

Shifts In The Distribution Of Aid

The expansion of the fiscal and administrative scope of the national government in relationship to state and local governments has placed the intergovernmental grants system at the center of national domestic policy. Nearly
every domestic service is now "intergovernmentalized." In some policy areas
the federal government finances operations that are administered by state and
local agencies. In others, such as the environment or public health, the delivery
of basic public services requires administrative coordination, intergovernmental bargaining, and interdependent financing. The roles of the federal and
state governments are characterized increasingly by overlap and duplication.
State and local elected officials and program specialists actively try to shape
national policy, while federal officials monitor routine decisions at the state,
county, and local levels, or even make those decisions. "The functions of
the three levels of government are no longer distinguishable. Their revenue
sources are both interdependent and overlapping, and there often is a wide
gulf between the point of decision and the visibility of governmental action."[1]
Consequently, there is "a vast muddling of the appropriate fiscal, administrative, and servicing roles of governments in the system."[2] Now, more than
at any other time in our history, significant changes in policy require extensive
intergovernmental bargaining and joint financing.

   In a very perceptive paper, David R. Beam has looked at the state of
intergovernmental relations (IGR) during the Reagan administration and has
concluded that although the Reagan administration has left a strong mark on
local-state-federal relationships, no dramatic reversal of past policies has been
accomplished and no changes seem likely. To provide a framework for dis-

---

   1. George E. Hale and Marian Lief Palley, *The Politics of Federal Grants* (Washington,
D.C.: Congressional Quarterly Press, 1981), pp. 1–2. The introduction to this commentary relies
heavily upon Hale and Palley, chapters 1 and 2.
   2. David B. Walker, "A New Intergovernmental System in 1977," *Publius*, vol. 8 (Winter
1978), p. 133.

cussing Beam's argument, I wish to make some brief observations about the
contemporary operations of the intergovernmental system.

Workings of the Intergovernmental System

In *The Politics of Federal Grants*, George E. Hale and I suggested that
the best way to describe the intergovernmental grants process is to compare
it to the regulatory politics that operate in relation to the private sector. By
using this analogy one is able to stress fundamental political relationships.[3]
The central features of government regulation of business include (1) the
making of demands by private interest groups; (2) the indirect as well as direct
nature of government controls; and (3) the interdependence of the regulating
agency with the regulated industry. Similar dynamics seem to prevail in the
area of contemporary intergovernmental relations.

In regulatory politics, nongovernmental groups—including specialist and
constituency-based groups—often make demands on the government for certain activities. State and local governments and their agencies also act as
interest groups that seek support and regulatory concessions from the federal
government. As the scope of federal activity expanded during the 1960s and
1970s, more and more subnational governments and subnational agencies
were drawn to Washington, D.C., to seek assistance, while others accelerated
already-existing lobbying activities in the nation's capital. They learned many
lessons from the private sector, including the role of "iron triangles" in the
politics of business regulatory agencies. Intergovernmental policymaking now
operates similarly, with administrative agencies, congressional subcommittees, and a plethora of subnational officials, public interest groups (PIGs),
and other special-interest groups dominating the multiple spheres of decision
making. In some ways the subnational actors have improved on the techniques
of the private sector: multiple subnational groups as well as individuals provide
inputs into the system; and members of Congress often are not disposed to
ignore locally elected officials, who frequently have access to the media in
the representatives' home states.

This discussion leads one to draw several observations about intergovernmental relations during the Reagan administration. First "interest-group
liberalism"[4] is a vibrant force in intergovernmental politics and policy. Often
subnational actors are perceived to be very influential and are thus not easy

---

3. Hale and Palley, *The Politics of Federal Grants*, pp. 26–27.
4. See paper by Lowi in this volume.

to disregard. The interests they represent are varied and the potential for coalition building is great. The best-organized and "hooked-up" group interests are also those most likely to maintain or expand their publicly funded programs.

Second, intergovernmental programs develop in response to changing political relationships. Attacks on these programs are also rooted in shifting political sands. Put somewhat differently: Varying conditions and interest-group coalitions can successfully pressure for the development of programs; the breakdown of these programs is similarly dependent on multiple interactive behaviors. Once a program is in place, however, it is difficult to bring about its demise, although it may be eroded significantly. A corollary is that once an intergovernmental relationship is established it is very hard, though not impossible, to change it.

Finally, much of what has occurred in the area of IGR is not as significant as it might seem at first blush. Subnational governments do not want to end federal involvement, since this involvement brings federal money. Thus even though there has been a conservative counterattack on our liberal system by the Reagan administration, it has not been as effective in intergovernmental politics as its perpetrators had envisioned. Perhaps the subnational interest groups are too powerful to be put down; perhaps, too, the liberal tradition is too entrenched. Some programs have had their federal funding levels reduced; the programs that have received the sharpest financial blows have been those that assist the poor and the near poor. These programs are also the ones that have limited popular support and relatively weak constituency support.

Beam's paper begins by noting that most of the drastic proposals that the Reagan administration has put forward to alter the extensive federal involvement in IGR have been set aside, owing to a lack of external support and a minimal commitment from the administration itself. However, the tensions and frictions that have marked the political arena surrounding intergovernmental interactions continue unabated. Beam notes that although many state and local officials have been in favor of readjusting the balance between the federal government and the subnational governments, the "new federalism sparked much opposition and controversy among [its] intended beneficiaries. . . . the problems of government that the new federalism addressed were real. Palatable and effective remedies, however, have yet to be found."

Intergovernmental Relations in the Reagan Era

Beam discusses the new federalism in the Reagan administration from the vantage point of six major areas of continuing intergovernmental concern:

expenditures and tax restraints, grant consolidation, social welfare reform, revenue sharing, administrative standardization and simplification, and regulatory reform.

On the issues of expenditures and tax restraints, Beam suggests that the effects on state and local governments of the revenue cutbacks as a result of the Economic Recovery Tax Act of 1981 were less than expected—which is not to say that there were no effects. What Beam does not explore is how subnational governments have compensated for declining federal aid. Some state and local governments have had to raise their own taxes—which are often regressive—to maintain pre-1981 service delivery levels; in some states some programs have been permitted to languish. Beam notes that the major cuts are in employment and training programs and in the highway program. However, cuts have also been made in smaller programs that have had devastating effects on the provision of the affected services, specifically those for child care centers and community health and mental health programs. Although the revenue reductions are relatively small, these services have always been funded at much lower levels than the large programs, such as highways and employment—and because the smaller programs were funded primarily by federal aid, they had more to lose. Another fact not noted by Beam is that by virtue of not increasing funding for many state and local services, especially in health and welfare, the net effect has been a decline in available money for some programs—often those that provide services to the needy—due to the impact of inflation.

The second area Beam addresses is that of grant consolidation. Apparently state and local governments have not been terribly innovative with their new-found block-grant flexibility under the Reagan administration. However, it is important to note that available money for the programs included in the block grants has not increased. In fact, some of the block grants in the health and welfare areas have been funded at levels lower than the 1981 budget levels for the categoricals they replaced. Moreover, some programs cannot be eliminated because they are necessary; other programs may have substantial interest-group support in the state and local jurisdictions. These conditions do not leave much room for new and innovative subnational programming.

Beam next discusses welfare reform. The changes effected in the AFDC, Food Stamps, and Medicaid programs as a result of the 1981 Budget Reconciliation Act were intended to reduce welfare costs by restricting eligibility for public health-related and public welfare benefits and were directed primarily at the "working poor." Beam suggests that mixed opinion regarding the area of welfare policy makes comprehensive reform unlikely—despite the fact that most citizens disagree with the way the system now operates.

Beam fails to examine, however, the impact of the eligibility redefinitions on target populations. Thus he does not note that the cutbacks disproportionately affect both single women with young children—who have a greater risk of being in poverty than any other population subclass and who are the primary beneficiaries of AFDC—and older women, who are also at a disproportionately greater risk of being poor than other groups in the population. These are people who are traditional political nonparticipants and are thus minimally represented in the political system.

The fourth area Beam looks at is the revenue-sharing program. President Reagan is not very supportive of revenue sharing, and in fact targeted the program for termination. Beam states that Reagan's unease with revenue sharing stems from his rejection of the idea that fiscal imbalances between the states should be redressed by the federal government. In 1982, after acquiescing to the program's continuation, the administration proposed a "super" revenue sharing scheme based on a federal windfall profits tax on oil as well as other excise taxes. However, the idea did not gain sufficient support for it to float. It thus appears that the interest-group liberal model supporting the concerns of states and localities is operating despite Ronald Reagan's conservative counterattack on the system.

A fifth area Beam investigates is administrative standardization and simplification. He notes that under the new federalism it seems that it is the states themselves that must decide how to comply with federal regulations. However it is significant that to some extent uneven state and local compliance is not a new feature of our federal system. Given the tendency of federal agencies to form constituency relationships with grant recipients—in addition to the presence of ambiguous goals and staff constraints—federal regulation enforcement is not always vigilant. Federal agencies usually turn to informal bargaining as a way to resolve disputes, with the ultimate sanction being the withholding of funds. In practice, however, funds are rarely withheld because to do so would stop public services and further harm intended beneficiaries.[5]

Regulatory reform is the final area discussed. In Beam's words, "despite a fast start" at attempted deregulation, "achievements have been slim." In the three years since Reagan took office, no new major regulatory statutes have been enacted. This is not to say that programmatic regulations have not been implemented. In fact, many program-specific rules and regulations have been put into place by this administration. Certainly enforcement is less vigorous than it has been in previous administrations. Beam suggests that

---

5. Hale and Palley, *The Politics of Federal Grants*, p. 91.

changes in the way agencies enforce rules may be the administration's chief victory, since long-term structural changes have been few. Furthermore, interest groups have been able to block regulatory relief and the judicial system has also thwarted administration attempts in this area.

Reinforcing Liberal Verities

Beam's critique of intergovernmental relations under Reagan sheds light on some liberal verities. Professor Theodore Lowi of Cornell University has suggested that Reagan's conservatism manifests itself by attacks on both the welfare state and regulation and by tax cuts and rearmament.[6] Beam notes that the administration's uneven record in trying to cut programs, consolidate grants, and dismantle the welfare system may be attributed to the weight of pressures opposing these moves by interest groups and Congress. To take Beam's argument a step further, it becomes clear that when the budget ax is wielded successfully, it is aimed at those groups least able to "fight back"— nonorganized interests, the poor (especially poor women with children and poor blacks), American Indians, and other minorities. If one can see a direction that the Reagan administration is taking regarding issues of governance, one might suggest, as economist Robert Lekachman has, in *Greed is Not Enough: Reaganomics* that "the President and his co-conspirators have been conducting an undeclared war against Blacks, Hispanics, welfare clients, women, children, and blue collar workers. Under way is still another episode of class conflict between rich and poor."[7]

Do the efforts to bring about changes in intergovernmental relations signal permanent changes in governance, or is the Reagan administration's onslaught on the intergovernmental system simply a series of pragmatic efforts to use the liberal interest-group process on behalf of a socially and politically conservative presidency? The deepest domestic program cuts have been those targeted at the poor and the near poor. A conservative does not identify most of the poor as "worthy," deeming benefit reductions or eligibility redefinitions legitimate. Thus the successful cost reductions are consistent with the administration's ideological biases and are politically practical, since this

---

6. See paper by Lowi in this volume.
7. Robert Lekachman, *Greed is Not Enough: Reaganomics* (New York: Pantheon Books, 1983), p. 9

targeted population does not play an active role in our liberal political system. The actions of this administration do not imply a permanent restructuring or alteration in our system of governance. They do suggest a very successful manipulation of the political process, at least in the early months of Reagan's presidency.

PRIVATE-SECTOR INITIATIVES OR PUBLIC-PRIVATE PARTNERSHIPS?

Marc Bendick, Jr., and Phyllis M. Levinson

The push for private sector initiatives is as central to the Administration as cutting spending and taxes.

—Ronald Reagan, September 14, 1982

One of the abiding issues of governance in a pluralistic society is the relative degree of responsibility and appropriate roles to be given to the public and private sectors in fulfilling the community's needs for goods and services. The material welfare of modern industrial society is attended to by a mixture of public-sector and private-sector institutions: national and local governments; households; employers; profit-seeking firms; and nonprofit and voluntary organizations. During the 1980s the roles of the sectors have become subject to more explicit debate than was previously the case, partially reflecting such diverse societal developments as slower economic growth throughout the past decade; budgetary constraints and taxpayer revolts in the public sector (such as Proposition 13 in California); demographic changes (such as an aging population) that place increased pressure on public entitlements; and the rise of a neoconservative critique of the effectiveness of such ambitious governmental initiatives as Lyndon Baines Johnson's "Great Society."[1] When President Reagan assumed office in 1981, previous presidents had already sought to control the growth of government; state and local

---

1. For critiques of ambitious public programs even by persons who generally favor public action, see Henry J. Aaron, *Politics and the Professors* (Washington, D.C.: The Brookings Institution, 1978); William Gorham and Nathan Glazer, eds., *The Urban Predicament* (Washington, D.C.: The Urban Institute Press, 1976); and Robert H. Haveman, ed., *A Decade of Federal Antipoverty Programs* (New York: Academic Press, 1977).

governments were experimenting with various forms of reprivatization; and the European democracies were debating their own versions of a "revolt against the welfare state."[2]

Reflecting and accelerating these trends, one of the central themes of the Reagan administration has been to reduce the role of the federal government in social problem solving and community affairs and to increase the role of a variety of alternative institutions, including not only state and local government but also philanthropic and voluntary organizations, the business sector, and the charitable activities of individual citizens. As discussed earlier in this volume, President Reagan commissioned a President's Task Force on Private-Sector Initiatives and has emphasized this theme in numerous speeches and public appearances.[3]

It is important to examine the impact that these initiatives are likely to have on the roles and relationships of the public and private sectors in carrying out community functions. This paper looks at the Reagan approach to private-sector involvement in public problem solving from the perspective of the private-sector institutions upon whom Reagan has urged an enhanced role—corporations, foundations, religious institutions, nonprofit organizations, community groups, and individuals. It briefly describes the nature and magnitude of the public-oriented services they currently provide and the ways these activities are coordinated with those of the public sector. It then examines the prospects for increased activity by these institutions and the programmatic and institutional implications of such expansion.

The primary conclusion from this discussion is that the enhanced utilization of private-sector institutions may well increase the efficiency and effectiveness with which some public needs are met. However, this increased utilization is likely to occur and likely to contribute effectively to social problem solving only if the private sector is tapped primarily for its *unique capabilities in the delivery of some types of services* rather than for its *potential as a funding source*. Complementary relationships in which public resources are teamed with private skills are more promising than those in which either sector is viewed as a substitute for the other.

This conclusion, in turn, provides a basis for judging whether improved governance through better utilization of private institutions will be a permanent legacy of the Reagan era. In general, we conclude that the prospects are

---

2. See Organization for Economic Cooperation and Development, *The Welfare State in Crisis* (Paris: Organization for Economic Cooperation and Development, 1981) and George G. Wynne, *Learning from Abroad: Cutback Management* (New Brunswick, N.J.: Transition Books, 1983).

3. See paper by Berger in this volume.

disappointing, primarily because administration rhetoric and actions have not conformed to the principle just described. Attention to *private-sector initiatives* cast as alternatives to governmental action has distracted efforts from the development of various forms of *public-private partnership* wherein the longer-run promise for public use of the private sector is to be found.

The Controversy About Intersectoral Substitution

The Reagan administration itself would readily agree with at least the first part of this characterization, namely, that one of its central goals has been to shift the balance in the national life between governmental activities—especially federal ones—and those of nongovernmental institutions. As has been discussed extensively by other observers, one component of the administration's program for achieving this shift has been to reduce the federal role, both in terms of laws and regulations seen as intruding into the lives of citizens and/or the functioning of free markets, and in terms of budgets for federal programs.[4] The other component, which has received less analytical examination, involves a variety of efforts to encourage, expand, and reinvigorate the activities of nongovernmental alternatives.

President Reagan himself, both personally and through a Task Force on Private-Sector Initiatives that has been closely associated with him, has been the primary focus of this latter effort. During his first thirty-two months in office, Mr. Reagan featured the subject of private-sector initiatives in more than eighty-four separate speeches, public appearances, proclamations, or similar events, an average rate of nearly one per week. Table 1 lists seventeen examples of private-sector activities that enjoyed the spotlight of presidential attention as models to be emulated. The diversity of subjects involved—including employment, education, aid to the poor, community development, health care, support for the arts, and even international development assistance—suggests that private initiatives are being advocated as a general strategy for governance applicable to virtually any public problem. This conclusion has been confirmed on many occasions by the president himself, as typified by his statement on October 5, 1981:

> Isn't it time to take a fresh look at the way we provide [public] services? Not just because they cost so much and waste so much, but because too many of them just don't work? . . . In all my years as Governor, and now as President, I never found an agency, a program, a

4. See *America's New Beginning: A Program for Economic Recovery* (Washington, D.C.: Executive Office of the President, February 1981); and John L. Palmer and Isabel V. Sawhill, eds., *The Reagan Record* (Washington, D.C.: The Urban Institute Press, 1984).

piece of legislation, or a budget that was adequate to meet the total needs of human beings. Something is missing from the equation. I believe that something is private initiative and community involvement.[5]

For each of the exemplary projects included in table 1, a corresponding federal program is also listed, as well as the change in federal budgetary support for that program during the four years that Reagan has controlled the budget. In fifteen of seventeen cases, budgetary support has been reduced, for an overall average reduction of 38.9 percent.[6]

Much of the controversy surrounding private-sector initiatives in the Reagan program has centered on such pairing of cuts in public programs with administration praise for private efforts. Critics of the administration have suggested that the president has cited examples of private charity misleadingly, to imply that persons adversely affected by budget cuts have alternative private assistance available to them—thereby seeking to make reduced federal expenditures more acceptable to the voting public. The examples are misleading, the critics charge, because private efforts are far too small to "fill the gap" left by federal budgetary reductions on a multibillion-dollar scale.[7]

President Reagan has been quick to deny that he ever intended that the private sector should take up the slack for all of these budgetary cuts. According to the president on October 5, 1981:

> We're not advocating private initiative and voluntary activities as a half-hearted replacement for budget cuts. We advocate them because they're right in their own regard. They're a part of what we can proudly call "the American personality."

Or, equally, on January 14, 1982:

> I don't want to leave the impression that our administration is asking the private sector to fill the gap, dollar for dollar, for every reduction in the federal budget. We don't want you to duplicate wasteful or unnecessary programs. We want community models that have worked, models we can emulate and build on.

This line of reasoning is consistent with the fact that the president and members of his administration have attacked many federal domestic programs as

---

5. All quotations from President Reagan in this section of the paper are drawn from the *Weekly Compilation of Presidential Documents* (Washington, D.C.: Executive Office of the President, January 20, 1981 through November 30, 1983, various issues).

6. Budgetary figures refer to proposed budget obligations for fiscal year (FY) 1985 and actual budget obligations for FY 1981. They are drawn from Office of Management and Budget, *The Federal Budget of the United States, Fiscal Year 1982, Appendix* (Washington, D.C.: Government Printing Office, 1981); and *The Federal Budget of the United States, Fiscal Year 1985, Appendix* (Washington, D.C.: Government Printing Office, 1984).

7. See, for example, William A. Schamba, "From Self-Interest to Social Obligation," in Jack A. Meyer, ed., *Meeting Human Needs, Towards a New Public Philosophy* (Washington, D.C.: American Enterprise Institute, 1982), pp. 33-52.

TABLE 1

EXAMPLES OF PRIVATE-SECTOR INITIATIVES CITED BY PRESIDENT REAGAN DURING 1981–1983 AND THEIR CORRESPONDING FEDERAL PROGRAMS

Type of Program	Private-Sector Initiative[a]	Corresponding Federal Program	Change in Inflation-Adjusted Federal Budgetary Support for that Program 1980–1985[b] (Percentage)
Employment			
Job placement for the unemployed	Job-a-thons on local radio stations	U.S. Employment Service	−18.1
Summer jobs for youth	New York City Partnership Summer Jobs Drive 1983	Summer Youth Employment Program and Related Youth Programs	−85.7
Jobs for physically handicapped persons	American Express program to provide work equipment for homebound employees	Federal support of vocational rehabilitation programs	−71.0
Education			
Improvements in elementary and secondary schools	Corporate adopt-a-school programs	Chapter I federal aid to schools serving the disadvantaged	−31.7
Improvement in higher education institutions serving blacks	Corporate donations to traditionally black colleges	Institutional development programs for postsecondary institutions serving disadvantaged students	−30.7
Adult illiteracy	Operation Lift	Adult education grants to states	−51.0

TABLE 1—continued

EXAMPLES OF PRIVATE-SECTOR INITIATIVES CITED BY PRESIDENT REAGAN DURING 1981–1983 AND THEIR
CORRESPONDING FEDERAL PROGRAMS

Type of Program	Private-Sector Initiative[a]	Corresponding Federal Program	Change in Inflation-Adjusted Federal Budgetary Support for that Program 1980–1985[b] (Percentage)
Aid to the Poor			
Food for the hungry	Local food banks	Food Stamps	−9.8
Income for low-income families	Mormon church welfare program	Aid to Families with Dependent Children	−17.6
Medical services for those unable to pay	Medical services donated by individual physicians	Medicaid	+15.6
Community Development			
Housing rehabilitation	Jubilee Housing Corporation	Assistance contracts for low-income housing	−61.0
Disaster relief	Volunteer sandbagging during floods	Flood prevention loans, Agricultural Credit Insurance Fund	−100.0
Crime prevention	Neighborhood Crime Watches	Federal Law Enforcement Training Center	−6.6
Community recreation and sports facilities	Local fundraising drives	Recreation programs under the Department of the Interior	−94.8

TABLE 1—continued

Type of Program	Private-Sector Initiative[a]	Corresponding Federal Program	Change in Inflation-Adjusted Federal Budgetary Support for that Program 1980–1985[b] (Percentage)
Health Problems			
Medical research	Voluntary donations to the National Multiple Sclerosis Society	National Institute of Neurological and Communicative Disorders and Strokes	+21.0
Drug abuse	Keebler Baking Company and Warner Communications sponsorship of antidrug comic books	Federal drug abuse research, training, and services	−77.8
Miscellaneous			
Foreign aid to developing nations	Actions of voluntary agencies to rebuild Lebanon	Agency for International Development	−8.6
Cultural programming on radio and television	Texaco Corporation sponsorship of opera broadcasts	Federal support for the Corporation for Public Broadcasting	−35.0

a. Cited by President Reagan in a speech, public appearance, or proclamation between January 20, 1981 and November 30, 1983, as reported in the *Weekly Compilation of Presidential Documents* (Washington, D.C.: Executive Office of the President, various dates).

b. Percentage change in budget obligations between fiscal year (FY) 1980 (actual) and FY 1985 (proposed) as reported in Office of Management and Budget, *The Federal Budget of the United States, Fiscal Year 1982, Appendix* (Washington, D.C.: Government Printing Office, 1981); and Office of Management and Budget, *The Federal Budget of the United States, Fiscal Year 1985, Appendix* (Washington, D.C.: Government Printing Office, 1984); adjusted for changes in the Consumer Price Index between 1980 (actual) and 1985 (forecast).

unnecessary, overexpanded, or even counterproductive. If the president believes these activities are not worth doing in the first place, then he would hardly suggest that private funding should sustain them when federal funds are cut.

Despite these denials, however, it is difficult to discount the notion of implied sectoral substitution. At times, Mr. Reagan's own statements have been more specific. For example, he has frequently stated his belief that a negative consequence of growth of the government sector has been a displacement of preexisting private activities:

> We've let government *take away* many things we once considered were really ours to do voluntarily, out of the goodness of our hearts and a sense of community pride and neighborliness. I believe many of you *want to do these things again* (September 24, 1981, emphasis supplied).

When he then speaks of reversing this trend, he clearly implies that he expects a reduced government presence to be associated with an increased private one:

> With all the hard things that we have had to do to restore this economy, the cuts of many things that we wish didn't have to be cut, we at the same time are just embarking on a program where, from the White House, we are going to take action and form a task force throughout the country to mobilize volunteers and the force of the . . . private sector . . . to contribute, to take up the slack in many of the things that government perhaps shouldn't have been doing in the first place . . . (September 23, 1981).

Or, on February 18, 1981:

> Historically, the American people have supported by voluntary contributions more artistic and cultural activities than all the other countries of the world put together. I wholeheartedly support this approach and believe that Americans will continue their generosity. Therefore, I'm proposing a savings of $85 million in the Federal subsidies now going to the arts and humanities.

The theme of substituting the activities of one sector for the other is thus traceable in substantial part to the administration itself and is not merely an invention by opponents of federal budget cuts.[8]

The Revenue-Raising Capacity of
the Private Sector

Owing to the controversy that has centered on the theme of private-sector initiatives, it is worthwhile to try to answer empirically a question central to it: *Can* the private sector "fill the gap" left by federal budget cuts in domestic programs?

---

8. For more discussion on the ambiguous intent of the Reagan private-sector initiatives, see the Berger paper in this volume.

One study addressing this issue directly focused on the financial support given nonprofit organizations such as hospitals, universities, social service agencies, and neighborhood organizations.[9] It estimated that such organizations stood to lose approximately $33 billion in federal support over fiscal years 1982-1985 if President Reagan's then-current budget proposals were adopted. To maintain current service levels, private giving would have to grow over that period at the rate of 30 percent to 40 percent a year, three times faster than it has grown over the previous several decades. At the same time, if those organizations were to expand to fill gaps in services left by an additional $115 billion in cuts proposed for federal programs in the same fields in which nonprofits were active, then private giving would have to approximately double during each of those years, a rate eight times greater than the highest rate of growth ever previously experienced.

To understand the low probability of such growth rates, the three major private sources of revenues for public purposes—individuals, corporations, and foundations—are examined here in turn, as well as the factors governing their level of activity.

Individuals

Taken together, individuals account for the vast majority of voluntary donations for public-related purposes. Including both contributions by living individuals and bequests, individuals provide 90 percent of all charitable financial support, an amount that totaled more than $58 billion in 1983.[10] The giving of volunteer time is the other form in which individuals contribute substantially to public purposes. In a typical year, some 84 million Americans, or 37 percent of the total population, have provided at least some volunteer effort.

The psychological and social determinants of individual actions are, of course, complex, and it is not feasible to forecast whether their levels are increasing. However, several lines of reasoning suggest that philanthropic activity will have to experience a significant rekindling of the charitable spirit that President Reagan has exhorted Americans to exhibit simply to stay even. One such argument emphasizes the increasing impersonalization of modern life, in which the majority of the population lives in large urban areas with less face-to-face contact between community members; greater population

---

9. Lester M. Salamon and Alan Abramson, *The Federal Budget and the Nonprofit Sector* (Washington, D.C.: The Urban Institute Press, 1982).

10. Data on philanthropy in this section are from *Giving USA, 1984 Annual Report* (New York: American Association of Fundraising Counsel, 1984).

mobility; and greater diversity of characteristics between charitable donors and charitable recipients (along dimensions such as race). In such circumstances, charitable acts tend to become less self-motivating (that is, direct personal contact gives way to more impersonal actions such as writing a check to an institutional cause). The economists' "theory of public goods" suggests that such individual donors will be more inclined to let others do the giving and to be "free riders" on the charitable actions of others.[11] In the absence of arrangements to force everyone to participate in the provision of public goods—such as compulsory taxation—the amount of resources collected tends to diminish. In sum, to depend on individual altruism is difficult in an urban, diverse society because the personal linkages that provided reinforcement for charitable acts in a more rural, small-scale, stable society are fewer and weaker.

A second factor influencing the level of individual donations is the treatment of charitable gifts under the tax code. Although it is well-known that people do not give to charities just because the action is tax deductible, it is still the case that the amount they give is influenced by how much the gift costs them. As part of its economic package, the Reagan administration in 1981 obtained from Congress substantial cuts in personal income tax liabilities and related changes in tax laws. These changes, in turn, reduce the value of the tax deductibility of charitable gifts. It has been estimated that the total effect of these tax cuts will be some 9 billion dollars per year in reduced revenue for nonprofit organizations.[12]

A third factor is demographic changes in the American population. Future levels of volunteer time may be expected to be adversely affected by the shrinkage of the proportion of the population in categories traditionally contributing disproportionate amounts of volunteer effort. The youth population (aged 15 to 19) in the year 2000 will be only 7.1 percent of the national population, down from 9.3 percent in 1980; working-age females not employed outside the home will be 16.0 percent in the same year, down from 17.1 percent in 1980; and the younger retired population (age 65 to 74) will fall from 6.9 percent in 1980 to 6.6 percent in the year 2000.[13]

---

11. On the theory of public goods, see Mancur Olsen, *The Logic of Collective Action* (Cambridge, Mass.: Harvard University Press, 1965); and Burton A. Weisbrod, *The Voluntary Nonprofit Sector, An Economic Analysis* (Lexington, Mass.: Lexington Books, 1977).

12. Charles Clotfelder and Lester M. Salamon, *The Federal Government and the Nonprofit Sector: The Effect of Tax Cuts on Charitable Contributions* (Washington, D.C.: The Urban Institute, 1982).

13. *Provisional Projections of the Population of States by Age and Sex: 1980 to 2000* (Washington, D.C.: U.S. Bureau of the Census, 1983), p. 25, pub. no. 937.

These considerations taken together suggest that a scenario in which individual charitable donations—either of money or volunteer effort—escalate dramatically in the near future is not a likely one. Indeed, societal trends suggest a moderate downward trend in the level of giving. The same reasoning suggests that many factors other than displacement of private initiative by an expanding public sector figure into this result.

Corporations

Given the visibility of major corporations on the American scene, it is perhaps not surprising that much of the discussion of filling the gap left by federal budget reductions has focused on the business sector. Thirty-four percent of the seats on the President's Task Force on Private-Sector Initiatives, including that of the chairperson, were occupied by business executives. During 1981, 1982, and 1983, many large corporations reported experiencing a doubling or tripling of requests for support. However, since corporations provide only 5 percent of total charitable giving in the United States, the attention they received far outstrips their actual level of activity.

The origins of corporate giving date from railroad companies' support of Young Men's Christian Associations (YMCAs) to provide housing to railroad track layers in the latter part of the nineteenth century and diversion of corporate stockholder dividends to the Red Cross during World War I. Corporate charity was boosted by a ruling by the Internal Revenue Service in 1936 and a Supreme Court decision in 1953 allowing corporations to deduct charitable contributions from income subject to the federal corporate income tax. During the 1970s corporate giving achieved the status of conventional respectability, at least among major corporations, through policy statements by organizations such as the Conference Board, the Committee for Economic Development, and the National Association of Manufacturers. By the 1980s the majority of corporate chief executive officers, corporate stockholders, and the general public seem to accept the notion that corporations are institutions distinct from their stockholders and, to some limited extent, should play the role of a good citizen in their community.[14]

One major form of corporate charitable activity is cash contributions. In 1983 donations by American corporations totaled $3.1 billion. At the same

---

14. See Alice Muckler, ed., *Corporate Philanthropy: Philosophy, Management, Trends, Future, Background* (Washington, D.C.: Council on Foundations, 1982); Committee for Economic Development, *Social Responsibilities of Business Corporations* (New York: Committee for Economic Development, 1971); and Kenneth D. Walters, "Corporate Social Responsibility and Political Ideology," *California Management Review*, vol. 19, no.3 (Spring 1977), pp. 40–50.

time corporations provided assistance to public projects in many noncash forms, including loaning executives to provide management expertise to government agencies or community-based organizations; donating equipment, space, materials, or other surplus resources from the company's production activities; hiring and training hard-to-employ workers such as economically disadvantaged youth or physically handicapped persons; or providing financing at concessionary interest rates to minority businesses or community redevelopment enterprises.

A number of considerations suggest that the likelihood of rapid expansion of these activities is small. Despite the long history of the principle of corporate charity and widespread public advocacy by business leaders, at least two-thirds of all corporations in the United States (predominantly smaller ones) still make no charitable contributions. Among those that do contribute, the average level of cash giving is slightly more than 1 percent of pretax net income, a ratio that has not increased significantly in more than thirty years.[15] Most corporations operate their donations programs with small staffs and as a sideline activity. There are fewer than one thousand professionals in the entire United States engaged in corporate philanthropic activities. Even the most vocal corporate supporters of the concept have implemented their commitment on a scale generally designed to grow no faster than overall business revenues.

Were the corporate sector to decide to rapidly expand its charitable activities, it has the managerial resources to do so, of course. The constraint is not ability but motivation. The call to be more active because it is in the best interests of society as a whole—the theme President Reagan has struck—has failed in the past to provide that motivation. For example, in recommending that corporations double their level of cash donations from 1 percent of pretax revenues to 2 percent, the President's Task Force on Private-Sector Initiatives merely repeated an identical call issued, with little manifest effect, by the National Commission on Philanthropy (the Filer Commission) in 1975. Since the issuance of the Task Force's recommendations, a handful of major corporations have announced their intention to match the 2 percent goal, and several cities have developed new "Two Percent Clubs" of corporations achieving this standard. However, these are relatively isolated examples. A recent survey of chief executive offices of major American corporations elic-

---

15. An upsurge occurred in corporate giving expressed as a proportion of corporate profits, from 1.01 percent in 1981 to 1.51 percent in 1983. This sudden rise is attributable primarily to corporations maintaining their prior year's level of giving while experiencing reductions in profits due to a severe nationwide recession. It is unlikely that the higher ratio will be maintained as profits increase under an economic recovery.

ited the forecast that their companies' cash giving would grow at an average of about 6 percent per year (after adjusting for inflation)—but only if national recovery from the recession increased profits at the same time.[16]

The primary reason for this is that corporations justify their charitable activities less on the basis of the universal good of society than on the enlightened self-interest of their individual firms. At its most general level, this self-interest philosophy states that the business sector requires a stable, prosperous, just, and efficient society in which to operate, and therefore that all businesses should, through their contributions, help to create this desirable social and economic environment. More concretely, this philosophy is reflected in the fact that corporate contributions are typically targeted to uses promising at least some benefit to the donating firms. Newspapers, retailers, and local banks, for example, whose prosperity is tied to that of their local communities, tend to be the most prominent supporters of redevelopment programs in their cities' distressed areas. Petrochemical corporations provide financial support to higher education in the form of scholarships in chemical engineering. And financial support for public television comes disproportionately from corporations whose future depends on favorable public attitudes toward them; much less comes from corporations whose success is tied to public recognition of their commercial brands. This is not to say that corporate support never goes to causes with no potential payoff to the donor, but merely that as the public concern is further removed from a company's direct interests, a company's willingness to provide support diminishes. Even the 1 percent level of donations reflects, in many cases, at least some considerations of direct interest; and historically, that level seems to be as high as corporations are typically willing to go.[17]

Interacting with the tendency of corporations to be concerned about the payoffs of their charitable activities is the problem of public goods and the free rider, mentioned earlier in terms of individuals. From a self-interest point of view, the best outcome for a petrochemical company is to hire an engineer trained under a scholarship donated by its competitor. The tendency to avoid voluntary contributions to public causes tends to be counteracted by peer pressure—for example, within the personal circle of business leaders within a city. However, many of the trends affecting business in the 1980s tend to weaken such arrangements—for instance, the current restructuring of the

---

16. *Corporate Giving: The View of Chief Executive Offices of Major American Corporations* (New York: Yankelovich, Skelly, and White, 1982), pp. 85–88; see also Ralph L. Nelson, *Economic Factors in the Growth of Corporate Giving* (New York: National Bureau of Economic Research, 1970).

17. See *Corporate Giving*, pp. 62–65; and Muckler, *Corporate Philanthropy*.

banking and retailing industries away from locally oriented, locally owned enterprises toward impersonal national chains and the increasing pressure on profits and expenses experienced by firms facing international competitors.

The upshot of these considerations is that the most likely level of future commitment by the business sector to public problem solving is approximately that which has prevailed historically—a modest level of resources, treated as a sideline of mainstream business concerns, and directed in ways that are at least partially self-serving from the donor's perspective.

Foundations

The final 5 percent of giving in the United States—some $3.5 billion in 1983 is provided by private foundations. In contrast to both individuals and businesses, these institutions' central activity is philanthropy; and therefore, their motivation is less complex than in the case of other donors. The major issue then is simply one of resources. Annual foundation disbursements tend to remain at a relatively fixed ratio in relation to their total assets—currently at about 7 percent. These assets, in turn, tend to grow approximately as fast as the overall economy. Thus, this source of assistance may be expected to be a dependable source of private-sector initiatives but not one that grows much more rapidly than the total income of the nation.

The Revenue Outlook

Table 2 provides the "bottom line" for this brief review of private resources to meet public needs. It traces the past twenty-eight years in total charitable contributions per capita in the United States, after adjusting for inflation. The figures thus represent the level of resources, in terms of real purchasing power, available to meet the needs of each U.S. citizen. The table illustrates the cyclic problem of donations, with decreases in recessionary periods in the late 1950s, mid-1960s, and three times during the 1970s—at times when needs for assistance were rising. However, the long-run trend is one of substantial growth, with the level in 1983 standing 85.8 percent higher than it had been twenty-eight years before. This rate of increase outstripped that of total incomes per capita (measured by gross national product), which grew only 58.7 percent in the same period. Furthermore, increases in private giving coincided with growth in total federal expenditures per capita, which rose 125.0 percent over the same period.

Such data raise questions both about President Reagan's interpretation of history and his vision of the future. The growth of federal expenditures

TABLE 2

CHARITABLE CASH CONTRIBUTIONS IN THE UNITED STATES, 1955–1983, IN
INFLATION-ADJUSTED DOLLARS PER CAPITA

Year	Inflation-Adjusted Dollars per Capita	Percentage Change from Previous Year	Percentage Change from 1955
1955	50.05	—	—
1956	51.23	2.4	2.4
1957	54.42	6.2	8.7
1958	53.75	−2.2	7.4
1959	57.70	7.3	15.3
1960	58.63	1.6	17.1
1961	59.11	.8	18.1
1962	62.08	5.0	24.0
1963	65.73	5.9	31.3
1964	67.68	3.0	35.2
1965	65.78	−3.0	31.4
1966	77.22	17.4	54.3
1967	79.42	2.8	58.7
1968	83.99	5.8	67.8
1969	87.91	4.7	75.6
1970	90.15	2.5	80.0
1971	90.63	.5	81.1
1972	88.63	−2.2	77.1
1973	90.78	2.4	81.4
1974	87.71	−3.4	75.2
1975	84.21	−4.0	68.2
1976	86.94	3.2	73.7
1977	90.10	3.6	80.0
1978	91.14	1.2	82.1
1979	88.88	−2.5	77.7
1980	85.68	−3.6	71.2
1981	86.37	.8	72.6
1982	89.50	3.6	78.8
1983	93.00	3.9	85.8

SOURCE: Calculated from data in *Giving USA, 1984 Annual Report* (New York: American
Association of Fundraising Counsel, 1984). Adjusted for inflation using the Consumer
Price Index: 1967 = 100.

has been accompanied by an increase in voluntary contributions, rather than
the decline which the president's discussions of displacement imply. Apparently, Americans wish to increase their purchases of both "governmental
goods" and "charitable goods" as their incomes rise, just as they wish to
increase their purchases of personal goods and services. Presumably, such
growth will continue as incomes continue to rise—but probably at approxi-

mately the same incremental rate that has been experienced over past decades (or perhaps more slowly because of the various demographic, economic, and cultural changes referred to earlier in this paper).

The Efficiency and Effectiveness of Private-Sector Initiatives

The notion that some of the burden of resource generation can be shifted from the federal government represents only half of President Reagan's concept of the private sector's potential. He has also repeatedly asserted that programs operated outside of government are more efficient and more effective than federally based ones. An innovativeness in private efforts; the absence of expensive and unnecessary bureaucracy; the ability to identify accurately the "truly needy" through local or personal knowledge; the utilization of "costless" volunteers and surplus materials; the managerial expertise of private businesses—all these seem, in the president's mind, to contribute to efficiency and effectiveness.

To what extent are such assertions justified by experience? Following is an examination of the evidence for these assumptions with respect to each of the main categories of private actors involved—in this case, individuals, nonprofit organizations, and businesses.

Individuals

The most obvious advantage of individuals volunteering their time and energies to public-spirited endeavors is that of cost. The largest cost element in many cultural, educational, and social service programs is labor, and this is particularly true of "enrichment" activities where the effort can piggyback on physical plant and equipment already in place for an ongoing activity (for example, volunteer teachers' aides working in an ongoing classroom situation). In other types of community projects, such as large-scale redevelopment of a city's blighted downtown, public-agency labor costs are only a small proportion of total costs, but volunteer efforts by key individuals—such as prominent business executives, the publisher of the local newspaper, or an experienced developer—might provide expertise, momentum, clout, access, or other resources otherwise unobtainable at any price.

The variety of individual voluntary activities precludes generalizing about the degree of skills and dedication necessary for the job. In many cases— particularly those involving volunteers assisting members of their own families, neighbors, or others they know personally—there is reason to assume that personal interest could lead to a higher quality of service than, for example, that provided by a professional social service or health care agency; such personal interest would presumably be present to a weaker degree when the recipient of services is a stranger or is unknown to the volunteer. Counterbalancing these considerations is that volunteers may not possess technical knowledge or specialized equipment to perform tasks efficiently. Furthermore, they may use costly inputs, such as program materials or assistance from paid staff, and may be subject to problems of high turnover and lack of reliability.[18] Many human service needs, of course, are met without extensive specialized expertise, and public or professional agencies are often staffed largely by persons with little training. On balance, the delivery of many cultural, social, educational, and human service activities through donated effort, where available, probably compares favorably to more systematic governmental programs. This is probably true from the perspective both of the quality of service provided and the cost per unit of service.

The qualifying phrase "where available" in the previous sentence is important. One perennial problem with volunteer effort is that the greatest amount of resources typically are not available at the time and place of greatest need. For example, one locale of need for adult Boy Scout leaders is in distressed inner city neighborhoods where many boys will be growing up without adult male role models and where low incomes preclude family-supported camping trips and other culturally broadening experiences; on the other hand, volunteer leaders are typically more readily available in middle-class suburban areas. The geographical scale of modern urban areas, combined with the physical segregation of different racial, income, and cultural groups, means that reliance on volunteers tends to reinforce existing patterns of inequality.

A problem parallel to geographical mismatch is that of possible conflicts in values or cultural practices between potential volunteers and potential recipients of voluntary assistance. In many public programs, if a recipient can demonstrate eligibility for assistance, he or she has a legal right to benefits. Private programs, in contrast, may take the form of a charitable gift. If the recipient behaves in a manner in which the voluntary donor disapproves, then the volunteer can threaten withholding of assistance as a means to coerce the recipient.[19] Table 1 of this paper documented President Reagan's praise of a world where an indigent individual might depend on a volunteer doctor for

---

18. See Harry P. Hatry, *A Review of Private Approaches to the Delivery of Public Services* (Washington, D.C.: The Urban Institute Press, 1983), chapter 6.

19. For empirical evidence on value conflicts between donors and recipients, see Marc Bendick, Jr., "Vouchers Versus Income Versus Services: An American Experiment in Housing Policy," *Journal of Social Policy*, vol. 11, no. 3 (July 1982), pp. 365–377.

medical services, a local church for food assistance, and a corporation for a college scholarship. The loss of the potential for individual freedom of choice in such situations must be taken into account in the comparison of public and private alternatives.

The Business Sector

Many of the considerations discussed in relation to individual volunteers apply to businesses as well. A problem of mismatch in location arises because many corporations concentrate their contributions in their headquarter cities and major plant sites, leaving locations already in economic distress because of an absence of local employers at a further disadvantage. The problem of values mismatch also arises because corporate philanthropic donations tend to reflect both the personal preferences of corporate executives and a desire to avoid controversial causes that might embarrass the company. Thus, while a city's low-income residents might desire community-based advocacy groups in their neighborhoods, corporate donations tend instead to support "main-stream" groups such as the Boy Scouts or the local symphony orchestra.

Such distributional considerations aside, we can analyze the comparative efficiency of the business sector and the public sector by examining the experience with "contracting out" of public services to for-profit enterprises. Many public-sector activities in the United States, particularly at the local level, have been carried out by private contractors under bids won competitively from public agencies. Street paving, data processing services, refuse collection, legal services, hospital operations, and many other services have been provided this way. A number of these experiences have been subjected to careful analysis. Generally (although not universally) the results have been favorable; the service was typically provided at lower cost—and often at a higher level of quality or satisfaction as well—than was possible when the public agency itself fulfilled the role. However, this conclusion typically applied in cases where the service at issue was technical in nature, where it was produced with well-known processes, and where it was easily measured and monitored—such as street paving. When the same arrangements have been applied to complex human service needs—whether retraining the hard-to-employ, revitalizing ghetto communities, or transforming the life chances of the disadvantaged—then the record of private firms shows no consistently higher achievement than that of the public sector itself.[20]

---

20. Marc Bendick, Jr., "Privatization of Public Services: Recent Experience," in Harvey Brooks, Lance Liebman, and Corinne Schelling, eds., *Public-Private Partnership* (Cambridge, Mass.: Ballinger, 1984), pp. 153–174; and Hatry, *A Review of Private Approaches.*

A second arrangement under which business has undertaken a role in public problem solving is that of public-private partnerships for urban economic redevelopment. In these partnerships, profit-seeking real estate developers and other commercial interests join with governments to rebuild the physical structure and economic vitality of economically downtrodden areas of major cities—often the decayed downtowns. The private-sector participants bring to the venture some investment funds and a willingness to invest in the troubled area. The public sector typically contributes additional investment funds (often a combination of grants and interest-subsidized loans), as well as direct public investment (such as improvements in streets), improved public services, and the political and legal power to bring the project to fruition (through such means as the power of land condemnation). Notable examples of the success of such joint ventures can be observed in rejuvenated downtown areas of cities such as Baltimore, Boston, and Pittsburgh.[21]

In terms of what the experience of these partnerships implies for the role of the business community in solving public problems, it is important to understand that businesses enter into these joint ventures not primarily out of civic duty or public spirit but because of the profit opportunities available. Subsidies provided by the public sector, plus the ability of government to compel action, create attractive investment opportunities for private investors. Certainly the willingness of private firms to participate in these partnerships is crucial to the success of these ventures, as is the expertise in real estate development contributed by the private sector. But far from indicating a public-spirited willingness by private firms to sacrifice financial returns for the public good, this experience instead confirms the unwillingness of firms to venture far beyond normal business criteria of profitability. The majority of partnership projects financed by the federal Urban Development Action Grant (UDAG) program, for example, have been relatively safe forms of development, such as large downtown hotels, which are not located in the most distressed areas of cities and which are often nearly commercially viable even in the absence of subsidies.[22]

Even more striking examples of the limits of business charity are provided by the history of federal training schemes and federal tax subsidies to encourage private firms to hire disadvantaged youth, public assistance recipients, low-skill minorities, and other hard-to-employ workers. A small number of

---

21. See R. Scott Fosler and Renée A. Berger, *Public-Private Partnership in American Cities, Seven Case Studies*, (Lexington, Mass.: Lexington Books, 1982).

22. U.S. Department of Housing and Urban Development, *An Impact Evaluation of the Urban Development Action Grant Program* (Washington, D.C.: U.S. Department of Housing and Urban Development, 1980).

prominent corporations have engaged in a handful of highly visible "show-case" projects in which major manufacturing plants have been installed in ghetto neighborhoods or in which disadvantaged workers have been sought for special training opportunities.[23] However, the majority of firms have never participated in such activities, are not eager to undertake what they perceive as the risks or costs involved, and have remained resistant to participating even when government has provided extensive wage subsidies through tax credits or comprehensive screening and training to employment candidates prior to hiring. When firms have proven willing to hire workers assisted by government programs, this willingness has typically been greatest with workers who suffer relatively innocuous labor market handicaps—such as non-disadvantaged youth enrolled in cooperative education programs or persons with physical handicaps—rather than "hard-core" low-income, minority job-seekers.[24] Under the Reagan administration, the main body of federal employment and training programs was transferred from traditional public agencies (under the Comprehensive Employment and Training Act) to agencies directed by a board required to have a majority of business representatives (under the Job Training Partnership Act). Early indications are that this shift will have the effect of increasing the rate of successful jobs placements in the programs, in part due to greater accessibility to private-sector jobs that these privately directed programs will enjoy. However, it also appears that these business-directed programs are focusing their efforts on the least disadvantaged, most job-ready individuals who will have the greatest appeal for potential business employers.[25]

What do such experiences indicate about the role of business firms generally in solving public problems? In certain areas in which firms have direct experience—for example, urban revitalization in the case of real estate developers or employment generation for many types of firms—businesses often deserve high marks for the expertise and managerial competence that

23. See Marc Bendick, Jr., and Mary Lou Egan, "Providing Industrial Jobs in the Inner City," *Business*, vol. 32, no. 1 (January–March 1982), pp. 2–9.
24. For the experience of the Targeted Jobs Tax Credit program in this regard, see Randall Ripley et al., *The Implementation of the Targeted Jobs Tax Credit* (Columbus, Ohio: Ohio State University, 1982); and Marc Bendick, Jr. and David W. Rasmussen, "Enterprise Zones and Inner City Economic Revitalization," in George Peterson, ed., *Reagan and the Cities* (Washington, D.C.: The Urban Institute Press, forthcoming).
25. See Demetra Smith Nightingale, *State and Local Responses to Federal Employment and Training Policy Changes* (Washington, D.C.: The Urban Institute Press, forthcoming); Marc Bendick, Jr., "Employment, Training, and Economic Development," in John L. Palmer and Isabel V. Sawhill, eds., *The Reagan Experiment* (Washington, D.C.: The Urban Institute Press, 1982), pp. 258–262; and Phyllis M. Levinson and Marc Bendick, Jr., *How's Business in the Reagan Era?* (Washington, D.C.: The Urban Institute, 1983), chapter 6.

they bring to a public effort. But the extent to which they are willing to participate on a profit-sacrificing basis, while not nonexistent, is limited. Their willingness to participate on a larger scale is confined primarily to circumstances where public subsidies generate substantial profit incentives. Even then, the deeper the water of social trouble, the less likely they are to participate even when enticed by substantial subsidies.

Nonprofit Organizations

The idea that nonprofit organizations may deliver many types of services more efficiently and effectively than public agencies themselves has been popular for many years. Many existing governmental programs—particularly in the cultural, recreational, health, and social services fields—are in fact primarily arrangements for passing governmental resources to such organizations. Federal research contracts are awarded to nonprofit universities; church-based social welfare agencies place and supervise children in publicly financed foster care; local nonprofit arts organizations blossom under grants from the National Endowment for the Arts; disadvantaged workers are trained for employment opportunities under government contracts to community-based organizations such as the Urban League; patients are cared for in nonprofit hospitals with their bills paid by Medicare or Medicaid. In fiscal year (FY) 1980, federal support accounted for 35 percent of total revenues for the overall nonprofit sector and 58 percent of total revenues for nonprofit social service organizations.[26]

So common is this mode of service delivery that relatively few studies have compared the efficiency of such arrangements with that of direct governmental provision of services. In many cases, this comparison is difficult because of the qualitative nature of the products or services being produced. What is known from such studies, however, seems to suggest two major conclusions: First, an efficient public agency monitoring nonprofit operations, as well as clear contractual standards of performance are important in avoiding fraud and abuse and in preventing the use of resources to pursue objectives other than the intended ones. Second, as with individual volunteers, while standards of personal dedication may be high in such organizations, great variability is observable in the level of staff training, in the adequacy of equipment and services, and in other factors associated with professionalism and efficiency.[27]

---

26. Salamon and Abramson, *The Federal Budget.*
27. See Neil Gilbert, "Welfare for Profit: Moral, Empirical, and Theoretical Perspectives," *Journal of Social Policy*, vol. 13, no. 2 (April 1984), pp. 63–74.

In many cases, however, simple comparisons of efficiency are largely beside the point. The major objective in providing services through nonprofit channels is not to be more efficient in delivering a service that could be delivered in any case but rather to reach clients who would not deal with a public agency or to fulfill a role that a public agency could not fulfill. Indeed, the American Enterprise Institute (AEI) has built an entire philosophy of governance on this notion, under the rubric of "mediating structures." These structures are various community-based, grass-roots institutions that, by their small scale, unbureaucratic structure, and local knowledge can respond rapidly and accurately to local and individual needs in ways that large, formal institutions such as government agencies cannot.[28]

The Search for Public-Private Partnerships

The considerations and experience just reviewed do not support a claim that the private sector can universally outperform the public sector in efficiency and effectiveness. However, they do indicate many specific circumstances where the private sector can do equally well, and some where it can do substantially better. The major reasons for weakness in private-sector action, when examined carefully, are disguised forms of the problem of revenue generation, not the problem of efficiency and effectiveness *per se*. Thus, the second half of President Reagan's aspirations for private-sector action—that it could raise the level of program performance—seems fruitful to pursue, although the first half of his aspirations for it—that it can effectively generate resources to substitute for federal funding—is not. The challenge facing designers of institutions for meeting public needs then becomes one of how to combine the strength of the two sectors—revenue raising by the public sector and service delivery by the private-sector—in a complementary fashion. The concept of mediating structures offers one model for achieving this difficult synthesis.

Partisans of the mediating structures approach are not uncomfortable with the notion that these structures should be financed, subsidized, or encouraged by the public sector. Indeed, they generally advocate a range of reforms in public policies to increase the interdependence of the public and private sectors, rather than to reduce it. Their vision of the knowledge, skills, and efficiency that mediating structures can offer does not blind them to the

---

28. See Peter Berger and John Neuhaus, *To Empower People: The Role of Mediating Structures in Public Policy*, (Washington, D.C.: American Enterprise Institute, 1977); and Schamba, "From Self-Interest to Social Obligation," in Meyer, ed., *Meeting Human Needs*.

resource-generating problems of these structures. Thus, writings on this subject typically support increased governmental participation in public-private partnerships, more extensive tax incentives to foster public-related actions by businesses and individuals, and increased government contracting for private service delivery. The emphasis is less on "reprivatization" through disengagement of the public sector than on "pragmatic partnerships" in which complementary public and private capabilities are joined; the end result is empowerment of the private sector relative to the public sector as private actors exercise decision-making power over resources gathered (in part at least) through public means.[29]

President Reagan's own approach to these matters has focused more directly on reprivatization through explicit withdrawal of federal support. For example:

- ACTION is a federal agency that administers volunteer, service learning, and citizen participation programs (including Foster Grandparents, the Retired Senior Volunteer Programs, Young Volunteers in Action, Volunteers in Service to America, and the Vietnam Veterans Leadership Program). It provides technical assistance, training, demonstration funds, publicity and awards, and other activities to amplify the role of volunteers throughout American society. During 1980–1985, the years during which the Reagan administration has controlled ACTION's budget, that budget has declined 37.2 percent in terms of real purchasing power—about the same rate of decrease shown in table 1 to be typical for a range of federal domestic programs in the same years.

- The Urban Development Action Grant program is the main source of federal funds to match private investment in public-private partnerships for revitalizing distressed urban areas. The Reagan administration slated this program for extinction in its first round of budgetary cuts, and the program continues only because of congressional support.

- Many private charities rely extensively on mail solicitation for fundraising. In the Omnibus Reconciliation Act of 1981, the Reagan administration got Congress to agree to $158 million annually in reduced postal subsidies, thereby increasing signficantly the cost of such fundraising.

- The nation's primary welfare program for low-income families, Aid to Families with Dependent Children (AFDC), has been criticized for

---

29. See Berger and Neuhaus, and Ralph M. Kramer, *Voluntary Agencies in the Welfare State* (Berkeley, Calif.: University of California Press, 1981).

more than a decade for embodying too few incentives for welfare recipients to shift from public support to private efforts to earn their own living. As part of an initiative to reduce welfare expenditures by tightening eligibility rules for this program, the Reagan administration requested and obtained legislative changes that further reduced these work incentives.

- In the final year of the Carter administration, new federal child welfare legislation was passed to reduce the number of children held in short-term foster homes under the supervision of public social service agencies and to instead speed their placement into permanent private adoptive homes. The Reagan administration has refused to fund these activities at a level sufficient to achieve the shift in placements.

An equal number of examples can undoubtedly be identified in which the administration has supported initiatives that encompass an enhanced private-sector role. To cite just one example, in the field of housing assistance for the poor, the administration has urged cessation of federally financed construction of housing projects in favor of a system of vouchers under which low-income families rent housing from private landlords.[30] But their motivation in the case of housing vouchers is strikingly similar to their motivation in the case of the five other examples just cited: The administration supports the position that allows the greatest reduction in short-term federal budgetary support, regardless of whether or not the result is an increased role for the private sector in the long run. For reasons emphasized throughout this paper, the result of many of these cost-cutting measures is a weakening of private-sector initiatives, not the reverse.

The Legacy of the Reagan Era

In many pronouncements on public issues—not only on the subject of private-sector initiatives—President Reagan has referred to anecdotes from his youth in Dixon, Illinois. In that small-town world, personal charity and voluntary initiatives were central means of meeting public needs, both because they were all that was available and because they fit into a society where (among other things) the population was relatively homogeneous racially, face-to-face relationships kept the free-rider problem to a minimum, women typically were not employed outside the home, businesses were locally owned

---

30. See Bendick, "Voucher Versus Income Versus Services."

and locally oriented, and the difficulties that the community tried to meet were not complex (barn raisings, not large-scale urban revival; home visits to frail elderly relatives, not CAT scans for brain tumors). This paper suggests that the reason that government, rather than private initiatives, has grown to address more of society's problems over the course of the twentieth century is that many of these circumstances have changed, rendering many exclusively nongovernmental approaches both less feasible and less efficient, relative to governmental ones.

With the Great Society programs and other initiatives of the 1960s, the pendulum may have swung too far in the other direction, with too much faith placed in large-scale governmental initiatives and too little attention paid to the potential of private alternatives and the role of private institutions in mediating, delivering, or cosponsoring governmental efforts. During the 1970s, a search began for the middle ground with renewed interest in contracting out in social services, joint efforts in urban revitalization, tax incentives for private job development, locally based community development corporations, and other examples.

Such efforts have been by no means uniformly successful. But like any new approach, they improve with time and experience. And they represent versions of private-sector initiatives that are viable in the late-twentieth century in a way that replication of the arrangements from Dixon, Illinois, in the 1930s is not.

These public-private partnership approaches grew incrementally and experimentally throughout the Nixon, Ford, and Carter administrations, without undue fanfare or controversy. The Reagan years, in contrast, have been marked both by a confrontational atmosphere in which public and private efforts have become viewed as substitutes for rather than complements of each other and by very limited support by the administration for reforms in federal programs and policies to facilitate a sensible public-private division of labor. It is ironic that in an administration that has made private-sector initiatives central to its rhetoric, less progress has probably been made toward enhancement of the private role in public problem solving than would have occurred under the quiet, steady continuation of previous policies.

COMMENTS

Private Sector Initiatives: Straw Men Or Strong Men?

Unfortunately, the paper by Marc Bendick, Jr. and Phyllis M. Levinson does not rise above the rhetoric of the private-sector initiatives program it analyzes. The authors cannot resist the temptation to pick apart the administration's straw men. They conclude, not surprisingly, that the "private sector has unique capabilities in the delivery of some types of services," but that it has limited "potential as a funding source." The implication seems to be that the universe of private-sector initiatives would have been better served by benign neglect. While thorough, Bendick and Levinson's approach is plodding, and no analytic virtuosity is required to reach these conclusions. One wishes that the authors had turned their attention to weightier issues of philosophy, purposes, and alternative policies.

It is certainly true that the administration has done little to advance the philosophical or conceptual debate about the role and relationship of the two sectors. The administration's rhetorical and practical interests in the subject were restricted to the President's Task Force on Private Sector Initiatives. Made up of luminaries from across the political spectrum and directed by the politically adroit head of a midwestern steel company, the Task Force made avoiding research and analysis a virtue—it was to be "action oriented" and not produce documents that gather dust. This was a laudably practical ambition, but it became evasive at best, anti-intellectual at worst. It was never quite clear what the Task Force was to do. It had no clear set of guiding principles, no conceptual framework. The advantage of such an arrangement was that political travail was kept to a minimum; minority opinions do not appear in print any more than do majority opinions.

But the disadvantages are even more significant. Lacking either a guiding philosophy or a clear picture of what the private sector is, private-sector initiatives are too easily reduced to Babbittry, a list of corporate good works. Examples from the Task Force spring readily to mind. The most peculiar was its recommendation that corporate America increase its giving substantially. The fact that "compulsory giving" was oxymoronic—much the same as "wise president"—was never publicly voiced by any Task Force member. This lack of questioning persisted even though one Task Force member, the head of Control Data Corporation (CDC), strongly supported a wholly different and proven form of private-sector support for social programs. His corporation does not engage in charity; it locates plants in low-income areas to provide jobs for the hard-to-employ. Apparently, it has learned how to do good by doing well, to attend to both the "bottom line" and social responsibility. The CDC experience could provide a fruitful point of departure for analysis and debate about the appropriate roles of the different sectors, but it was not examined.[1]

The absence of this kind of debate and discussion revealed that the Reagan view of the private sector was seriously, even fatally, flawed, and represented merely a set of pietistic homilies that are inconsistent with the realities of modern life. Consider the implied expectation that there might be intersectoral substitution. No serious analyst would suppose that the "gap" created by federal cuts can or should be filled by the private sector, as long as the analysis is limited to programs specifically designed to help the poor. The reason is absurdly simple—the problem that the poor face is that they have no money. To cut their benefits on the theory that the private sector will step in requires the development of careful lines of reasoning that were not undertaken by the Task Force. One might have argued, for example, that the availability of welfare is a disincentive to work: make it tougher to qualify and people will be forced to overcome their inertia and get a job. Whatever its merit, the argument was not framed that way. Indeed, it was not framed at all.

In pointing out the weaknesses in the intersectoral substitution notion, Bendick and Levinson meet the Reagan administration on its own ground. But in so doing, the authors are reduced to a careful refutation of a proposition that is on its face unconvincing. The dissection of the private-sector initiative program proceeds very neatly. But that is no great achievement; one wishes the authors had turned their attention to more fundamental and constructive issues.

Examples exist in the administration's program as a whole of an implicit and productive strategy of intersectoral substitution, but these are not found in the programs for the poor. The quintessential case where it can be argued that the private sector should pick up the tab has to do with nonmeans-tested entitlements. The heart of the argument in favor of means testing such benefits is that the private sector can and should carry the freight. Thus, Medicare benefits should be means tested just as Guaranteed Student Loans (GSLs)

---

1. On the Reagan Task Force on Private Sector Initiatives, see also paper by Berger in this volume.

now are. At present, GSLs are a premier example of a de facto public-private partnership. Limited public funds are made available to low-and moderate-income students on very favorable terms, with the understanding that the publicly provided resources are only a portion of the total package that the student will be required to put together. The Reagan administration did not include such programs in its discussion of private-sector initiatives or of private-public partnerships, but Bendick and Levinson have nothing to say about them, either.

The last thing that private-sector initiatives need in the late 1980s is for them to get a permanent bad name simply because of one failure to develop a dynamic and convincing conception of what private-sector initiatives can mean. Private-sector initiatives are not just an expression of atavistic romanticism or an administrative instrument to accomplish public goals and objectives. If it is to mean anything, the private sector must be viewed as a fundamental alternative to government, a set of different, even competing institutions and associations that have a life of their own, independent of the state. We must assume President Reagan and his advisers have this in mind when they extol the private sector, even if the rhetoric of stump speeches is somewhat less sophisticated than one might like.

The example par excellence of private-sector initiative is the civil rights revolution, what might be best described as the last great moral victory of liberalism. Although given legal force and effect by the statutory changes begun by President Johnson and the judicial interpretations of Chief Justice Earl Warren and succeeding Supreme Courts, the real drama of the civil rights movement was its power to mobilize the forces of civic virtue and morality on its behalf, a development that was spearheaded by the most important of private institutions that escape the tender reach of the state, the church. By and large, the church in this case was black churches, a fragile collection of loosely organized institutions with little or no formal power. Their power was truly moral and spiritual, not temporal.

It was precisely at failures of the state—failures of omission and commission at several levels and in various manifestations—that the moral and political energy of the church-led civil rights movement was directed. The black churches remind us that the private-sector initiative idea has power because these institutions constitute a "mediating structure" standing between the harsh realities of the state and the individual, naked and alone.[2]

---

2. For a more complete description of the "mediating structures" notion see Peter L. Berger and Richard John Neuhaus, *To Empower People: The Role of Mediating Structures in Public Policy* (Washington, D.C.: American Enterprise Institute, 1977).

Private-sector initiatives may include a sense of "corporate responsibility," but in no sense is the corporation a substitute for state action; mediating structures do not exist to compensate for a feeble state. Central to the idea of mediating structures is the vision of human association that exists independent of the state. Its hallmark is self-help, self-reliance, and community building—charity is the least of it. But the idea of charity—one individual or group doing for those that cannot do for themselves—came to be seen as the centerpiece of the Reagan administration's private-sector initiatives program, and is therefore the focus of analysis for Bendick and Levinson. Of course the private sector cannot fill the gap. The authors' work demonstrates this effectively, but it is hardly a point that needs to be made, certainly not at length.

For most people—the man or woman in the street as well as the Washington, D.C., policymaker—the question is the appropriateness and effectiveness of government programs. The average citizen may ask: "Are recipients of public welfare deserving or undeserving?" or "Is workman's compensation an income insurance program or 'rocking chair'?" At a higher level of sophistication, the policy analyst asks, "Do government programs meet their objectives?" and "Are there more humane and effective ways to serve the social good?"

When the fundamental question is the appropriateness of government programs, it is clear that private-sector associations must be kept in mind. The black church, for example, is critical to the health of the black community, playing in an attenuated way the same function as the Catholic church in undergirding communities of central and southern European immigrants. Yet governmental policies are not designed to capitalize upon this extraordinary resource.

One way to consider the potential power of mediating structures is to turn conventional questions around. Take, for example, the Middle Income Student Assistance Act, which extended the Guaranteed Student Loan program to all families regardless of financial means. Fortunately, few excesses so wretched get enacted, and when a home magazine recommended borrowing GSL money for redecorating, it was clear even to Congress that the program could not survive. The issue became precisely the one that should be raised—which sector and which individuals should bear the burden, under what circumstances and to what effect?

But the question of private-sector initiatives must also be framed in a larger context than cost/benefit pragmatism alone, although that is surely a part of it. The bigger question is the role of the state in the late-twentieth century. That liberals should have come to support state preeminence is specially curious. Based on the conviction that he who governs least governs best, the American experience has been the very embodiment of mediating structures. Americans, a people with a passion for association, as Alexis de Tocqueville repeatedly observed, have been as committed to liberty as to equality. In the American context, liberty did not mean license. Liberty meant freely cooperating through patterns of voluntary association. The hereditary community and former association of the Old World was replaced in the New World by "natural" associations of individuals who were both free and equal.

When rightly understood, mediating structures, or private-sector initiatives, entail a dual commitment to personal liberty and joint action. They reflect the conviction that the state is not well suited to solve all problems, and indeed, often as not the state is the problem. The role of individuals and their mediating structures is to temper and ameliorate state power. This idea no longer enjoys much favor, except in "neoconservative" circles, but that in no way diminishes its intrinsic power or its historic legitimacy.

Even conservatives recognize that without bread, liberty is illusory, and if there is no other institution to protect the unfortunate and dispossessed, state action is warranted. But as Charles Schultze in *The Public Use of Private Interest* so eloquently demonstrates, there is no a priori reason to believe that the state must always rely exclusively or even largely upon state provision of goods and services to serve the public good.[3] The issue should not be cast as "private-sector initiatives *or* private-public partnerships," but as which policies can best strengthen the ability of the individual to function effectively in the modern world. The key to these policies is the mediating structure.

A gripping case in point is the disintegrating black family. Its precarious state is a profound issue for the black community and the nation as a whole. No modern, humane society can long tolerate the human suffering and waste associated with such pathology. Because we are all aware of the negative dimensions of weakened black family life, however, it is appropriate to remind ourselves of the power of the *healthy* family. In his most recent book, *Civil Rights: Rhetoric or Reality?*, Thomas Sowell reminds us that black family income hovers at about 65 percent of white family income, a disturbing statistic explained in large measure by age, family status, and education.[4] Intact black families in which both mother and father are present, however, enjoy income approximately 95 percent of that of comparable white families. Most startling—and most welcome—is that the income of intact black families

---

3. Charles Schultze, *The Public Use of Private Interest* (Washington, D.C.: The Brookings Institution, 1977).

4. Thomas Sowell, *Civil Rights: Rhetoric or Reality?* (New York: William and Mowon Co., Inc., 1984).

in which *both mother and father are college graduates* exceeds the income of comparable white families.

The importance of this finding is not its Horatio Alger dimension but its significance for public policy. Public programs are reasonably good at primitive forms of income redistribution, but they have been notoriously unsuccessful in dealing with social pathology. Indeed, certain contemporary social policies exacerbate rather than ameliorate the problems of the black family. The resources of choice that might strengthen the black family—the church, the fraternal and benevolent association, the neighborhood and community, the private school—are not institutions that public policy has been designed to strengthen. Indeed, existing social policies might be best characterized as ones that leave the limited Horatio Alger option as the only viable one; the successful black family is a triumph of personal integrity over hostile public policy.

The desire to shrink the size and reach of government is not necessarily motivated by a desire to escape social responsibility, nor need it be the result of a mean-spirited impulse to let the poor fend for themselves. In the twentieth century we have ample evidence that the all-powerful state too easily becomes the all-consuming state. Even in societies where the state has retained its humane impulses, state provision of services is by no means uniformly successful. But the more fundamental question that must be addressed has to do with independent forms of association and action, structures that command individual loyalty and provide support for the individual beyond the reach of the state.

One would think that the founding fathers' preoccupation with limited government and private association would be especially instructive in the late twentieth century, when excesses committed in the name of the state have never been so common or so terrible. Mediating structures and private-sector initiatives provide a conceptual framework within which the analyst may creatively examine social issues. Although such examination is not the same as identifying solutions, it is the first step toward finding them. Bendick and Levinson point out correctly that the Reagan administration failed to do so. The public policy debate is the weaker for the failure.

Edwin B. Knauft

The Gap Between Rhetoric And Substance

Marc Bendick and Phyllis Levinson have provided a scholarly, articulate analysis of the Reagan administration's attempts to invoke private-sector initiatives to address a number of current public needs. The authors also thoroughly examine the private sector's capacity for raising additional funds to carry out such initiatives, evaluate the operation of typical private initiatives, and, finally, discuss the respective roles of the public and private sectors in forming effective partnerships. The paper is noteworthy in that the informed critique of the administration's actions recognizes the limitations of translating isolated examples of successful partnerships into a successful national phenomenon.

The paper's first section focuses on the administration's efforts "to encourage, expand, and reinvigorate the activities of nongovernmental alternatives." An even stronger case might be made, however, to document the discrepancy between rhetoric and substance in stimulating meaningful private initiatives:

- There has not been systematic follow-up of the recommendations of the President's Task Force on Private Sector Initiatives. Particularly important opportunities to continue an effective liaison with governors' task forces in many of the states have been overlooked as have proposals to eliminate certain impediments to effective private initiatives. The President's Task Force was also discouraged from making policy recommendations that would serve to motivate and coordinate initiatives at the federal level.

- The Treasury Department has failed consistently to support income tax legislation that enables non-itemizers to deduct charitable contributions, even though conservative estimates indicate this device will produce an additional $2.5 billion for the voluntary sector.

- The Federal Office of Personnel Management has made every effort to exclude from the Combined Federal Campaign (annual charitable campaign for all federal employees) many nonprofits that serve some of the groups of citizens most affected by budget cuts.

- The Office of Management and Budget, while dealing with the valid issue of preventing federal grant dollars from being used by a nonprofit organization to lobby directly for additional grants, has extended this objective to impose broader constraints that might prevent such organizations from providing useful information to policymakers and legislators.

The second major section of the paper examines the revenue-raising capacity of the various segments of the private sector: individuals, corporations, and foundations. Through an extensive analysis, especially in the corporate area, the authors reaffirm the generally accepted conclusion that there is no reasonable potential for private-sector dollars to compensate for any significant portion of the budget cuts. Often such analyses concentrate only on the dollars, but Bendick and Levinson also treat the issue of the *character* of giving—will the designated dollars go to those organizations or groups in society that have been most affected by the withdrawal of federal funds? In individual giving, the point is made that people tend to give to organizations or causes for which they have the closest personal association, hence dollars are not necessarily directed to the areas where the cuts have had the greatest impact. For example, it is frequently overlooked that about 45 percent (or $24 billion) of all giving by individuals is for the support of religion.

Having clearly disposed of the notion that the private sector has the potential for increasing cash giving to an extent that would significantly offset the budget cuts, the discussion then moves to the more fruitful area of private initiatives carried out in partnership with the public sector. While recognizing the considerable potential for such partnerships, it would have been useful to identify factors that encourage their development:

1. There is a need for more model partnerships capable of local replication. The Local Initiatives Support Corporation (LISC), stemming from the experiences and leveraged funding of the Ford Foundation, is a prime example. Housing rehabilitation and commercial economic development projects underway in over a dozen cities are based on partnerships between neighborhood organizations, corporations, and local foundations. Another group is starting to explore the possibilities of a "human services LISC" that would apply some of the same concepts to the service-delivery field.

2. Insufficient attention has been given to the motivations for private-sector involvement. Some observers feel that corporate public in-

volvement, especially in the area of urban problems, is receiving less support from company executives than in the years immediately following the urban riots of the 1960s. Exhortations by national corporate membership organizations and at Task Force-sponsored presidential luncheons with executives are not sufficient incentives for action. The LISC model, however, enlists peer support in a community, builds on the "herd instinct" of companies to identify with a project that has good chances for success, matches local corporate grants with outside foundation and public money, offers the potential for recycling capital through revolving loan funds, and assures competent technical assistance in a field that falls outside of corporate expertise.

3. Successful public-private partnerships cannot in themselves solve the problems inherent in public service delivery systems. There is need for creative restructuring of how public services are organized and funded. The conventional public-sector response to the gap between needs and available resources is that there are only two possibilities: less service or more money. Ted Kolderie of the Hubert Humphrey Institute of the University of Minnesota proposes to address this dilemma through a traditional competitive-sector response: when revenues fall or costs rise, the challenge is to find a different approach that will do a better job at a lower cost. Kolderie points out the irony of a public sector not applying to itself the free market deregulation principle that it frequently mandates for the private sector—for example, the deregulation of the airline industry that consequently spurred competition and lowered prices.[1] Kolderie's concept is not "privatization" in the strictest sense of the term because the public still retains the responsibility both for deciding whether or not a particular service will be offered or a project carried out and for financing it. But in the implementation of the service or project, government needs to think of itself essentially as a buyer who is searching for the best contractor.

The final section of the paper by Bendick and Levinson neatly characterizes the President's view of private-sector initiatives as an attempt to apply to the whole nation those examples that apparently worked so well in a small midwestern town—Dixon, Illinois. By contrast, the authors have provided a

---

1. Ted Kolderie and Verne Johnson, "Public/Private Partnerships: Useful but Sterile," *Foundation News*, vol. 24, no. 2 (March–April 1984).

systematic analysis of the strengths and limitations of public-private partnerships as one response to social needs, with the constructive suggestion that
a key challenge is to develop a means of combining the revenue-raising
function of the public sector with the service-delivery ability of the private
sector.

ABOUT THE AUTHORS

David R. Beam is a senior associate of The Naisbitt Group. For more than ten years, he was a member of the staff of the Advisory Commission on Intergovernmental Relations, where he directed research for the Commission's studies of *The Federal Role in the Federal System: The Dynamics of Growth* and *Regulatory Federalism: Policy, Process, Impact and Reform.* He is coauthor of "Federalism: The Challenge of Conflicting Theories and Contemporary Practice" and *Unemployment: Intergovernmental Dimensions of a National Problem.*

Marc Bendick, Jr., is a senior research associate in the Human Resources Center of The Urban Institute. An economist, Dr. Bendick's writing and consulting have covered such topics as structural change in the American economy, low-income community revitalization, management reform in public assistance programs, enhanced job opportunities for the hard-to-employ, and public-private cooperation in public problem-solving.

Renée A. Berger is a consultant in international urban affairs, specializing in economic development and public-private sector relations. Her clients have included the American Enterprise Institute for Public Policy Research, Aspen Institute, Committee for Economic Development, Conference Board as well as the Organization for Economic Development and Cooperation (Paris, France) and the government of Australia. Ms. Berger is the author of numerous articles, and coauthored *Public-Private Partnership in American Cities: Seven Case Studies.*

492   THE REAGAN PRESIDENCY AND THE GOVERNING OF AMERICA

Alan K. Campbell is vice-chairman of the board and executive vice-president, Management and Public Affairs at ARA Services, Inc. He served as chairman of United States Civil Service Commission (1977–1978), and director of the United States Office of Personnel Management (1979–1980). Prior to government service, he was dean of the Maxwell School of Public Affairs at Syracuse University and of the Lyndon B. Johnson School of Public Affairs at University of Texas. He is author of several books and many articles in the fields of public administration and state and local fiscal behavior.

James W. Ceaser is associate professor in the Woodrow Wilson Department of Government and Foreign Affairs at the University of Virginia. He is the author of *Presidential Selection* and *Reforming the Reforms*.

Hale Champion is executive dean of the John F. Kennedy School of Government, Harvard University. He has been undersecretary of the U.S. Department of Health, Education and Welfare, director of finance of the state of California and director of the Boston Redevelopment Authority. He teaches public management with emphasis on managing domestic programs in the intergovernmental system.

Denis P. Doyle is a resident fellow at the American Enterprise Institute for Public Policy Research and director of AEI's Education Policy Studies program. He is a former assistant director of the National Institute of Education and served as the director of Planning and Program Coordination in the Office of Research and Improvement of the U.S. Department of Education. A senior consultant to the California legislature for eight years, he also served as a consultant to the Ford Foundation, the Institute for Educational Leadership, and the Academy for Educational Development. His publications include *Debating National Education Policy: The Question of Standards* and numerous articles on education.

Edie N. Goldenberg is an associate professor of political science and public policy at The University of Michigan. From 1978 through 1980, she was responsible for the U.S. Office of Personnel Management's evaluation of The Civil Service Reform Act of 1978. Dr. Goldenberg has written journal articles on a variety of topics in American politics and public policy. She is the author of *Making the Papers: The Access of Resource-Poor Groups to the Metropolitan Press* and coauthor of *Campaigning for Congress*.

Hugh Heclo is professor of government at Harvard University and former senior fellow at The Brookings Institution. He specializes in American public management and comparative social policy. Dr. Heclo is the author of *A Government of Strangers*.

Ben W. Heineman, Jr., a partner in the law firm of Sidley & Austin, is former assistant secretary for planning and evaluation at the Department of Health, Education and Welfare. He is coauthor of *Memorandum for the President: A Strategic Approach to Domestic Affairs in the 1980s*.

Charles O. Jones is Robert Kent Gooch Professor of Government and is associated with the White Burkett Miller Center of Public Affairs, University of Virginia. He is the author of books and articles on American politics and public policy and former managing editor of the *American Political Science Review*.

Edwin B. Knauft is executive vice-president of Independent Sector, a national forum to encourage giving, volunteering and not-for-profit initiative. Dr. Knauft was formerly vice-president, corporate social responsibility at Aetna Life and Casualty and has also been a visiting fellow at the Program on Non-Profit Organizations at Yale University and a senior consultant to the Council on Foundations. He has written and conducted research in the field of corporate grantmaking.

Everett Carll Ladd is executive director and president of the Roper Center for Public Opinion Research. He is also professor of political science and director of the Institute for Social Inquiry at the University of Connecticut, and senior editor of *Public Opinion* magazine. His latest book is *The American Polity*.

Phyllis M. Levinson is currently affiliated with the Potomac Development Corporation, real estate investors and developers. An urban planner, she was previously at The Urban Institute and the National Council for Urban Economic Development.

Theodore J. Lowi is John L. Senior professor of American Institutions at Cornell University. His research interests include political theory, public policy analysis, and American political behavior. Dr. Lowi is the coauthor of *The Pursuit of Justice* (with Robert F. Kennedy), *The Politics of Disorder*, and *The End of Liberalism*. His forthcoming book is entitled *The Personal Presidency*.

Michael S. Lund is a research associate at The Urban Institute in the Center for Governance and Management Research, where he is currently doing research on the alternative instruments of government action. Other research interests include the politics and organization of policy research, social welfare policy, and the public policies and politics of European democracies. Dr. Lund has taught at Cornell University, the University of California at Los Angeles, and the University of Maryland and has worked in various Washington agencies and Congress.

Laurence E. Lynn, Jr., is dean and professor at the University of Chicago's School of Social Service Administration and a member of the university's Committee on Public Policy Studies. He has served in policy and management positions in the U.S. Department of Defense, the National Security Council, the U.S. Department of Health, Education and Welfare, and the U.S. Department of the Interior. He has taught at the Graduate School of Business at Stanford University and the John F. Kennedy School of Government at Harvard University.

Michael J. Malbin is a resident fellow at the American Enterprise Institute for Public Policy Research. He is the author or editor of *Money and Politics in the United States: Financing Elections in the 1980s*; *Vital Statistics on Congress, 1982*; *Unelected Representatives: Congressional Staff and the Future of Representative Government*; *Parties, Interest Groups and Campaign Finance Laws*; and *Religion and Politics: The Intentions of the Authors of the First Amendment*.

Milton D. Morris is director of research and policy analysis at the Joint Center for Political Studies. A former senior fellow at The Brookings Institution, he has written extensively on comparative politics, government and politics of developing areas, and American politics. His books include *The Politics of Black America* and *Immigration: The Beleaguered Bureaucracy* (forthcoming).

Frederick C. Mosher is White Burkett Miller Professor Emeritus at the University of Virginia. Before his retirement in June 1984, he taught public affairs at the University of Virginia, the University of California at Berkeley, Syracuse University, and the University of Bologna (Italy). Dr. Mosher has held a variety of administrative positions in federal, state, local and international organizations. His main interest is public personnel administration, which is the subject of one of his books, *Democracy and the Public Service* and of a variety of reports and articles.

Richard P. Nathan is professor of public and international affairs at the Woodrow Wilson School, Princeton University, and director of the university's Urban and Regional Research Center. He currently heads a national field evaluation study of changes in federal aid under President Reagan and their effects on state and local governments and the people they serve. He is the author of *The Administrative Presidency.*

Chester A. Newland is professor of public administration at the University of Southern California's Sacramento and Washington Public Affairs Centers. He is a former president of the American Society for Public Administration and a member and former trustee of the National Academy of Public Administration. He was the initial director of the Lyndon B. Johnson Library, and served twice as director of the Federal Executive Institute.

John B. Olsen is senior vice-president of Mellon Bank and adjunct professor at the School of Urban and Public Affairs of Carnegie-Mellon University. He has had extensive career experience in both the public and private sectors, and was advisor to the Committee for Economic Development in the making of its major study: *Public-Private Partnership.* Mr. Olsen served as an elected member of the National Academy of Public Administration and is the coauthor of a book recently published by the Council of State Planning Agencies/ National Governors Association entitled: *The Game Plan: Governance With Foresight.*

Norman J. Ornstein is a resident scholar at the American Enterprise Institute for Public Policy Research. He is also professor of political science at The Catholic University of America, series editor of the television series, "Congress: We the People," (coproduced by WETA-TV and the American Political Science Association), and political consultant to CBS News. Ornstein's books include *The American Elections of 1982*; *The New Congress*; *Vital Statistics on Congress*; and *President and Congress: Assessing Reagan's First Year.*

Marian Lief Palley is professor of political science at the University of Delaware. She specializes in national urban policies, the intergovernmental grants process, and women's issues. Professor Palley is the author or coauthor of several books and articles. Her most recent books are *The Politics of Federal Grants*, *Urban America and Public Policies*, and *Women and Public Policies.*

David E. Price is professor of political science and policy sciences at Duke University. He is the author of *Who Makes the Laws?*, *Bringing Back the Parties*, and numerous articles on congressional policymaking, American political thought, and ethics and policymaking. He has served as a legislative aide in the U.S. Senate and as staff director of the Democratic National Committee's Commission on Presidential Nomination.

Robert D. Reischauer is senior vice-president of The Urban Institute. Before joining The Urban Institute in 1981 he served as the deputy director of the Congressional Budget Office. He left the Economic Studies Program of The Brookings Institution to help establish the CBO at its inception in 1975. Mr. Reischauer is the author of many publications dealing with the federal budget, social welfare policy, and intergovernmental fiscal relations.

Lester M. Salamon is director of the Center for Governance and Management Research at The Urban Institute. His current research interests are alternative instruments of government action, the processes of policy formulation and implementation, and the structure and role of private, nonprofit organizations. He has been deputy associate director of the Office of Management and Budget and associate professor of policy sciences at Duke University. Dr. Salamon's most recent publications are *The Illusion of Presidential Government, The Federal Budget and the Nonprofit Sector,* and "Voluntary Organizations and the Crisis of the Welfare State."

Allen Schick is professor of public policy in the School of Public Affairs at the University of Maryland. Mr. Schick specializes in studies on budget practices, American politics, and political institutions. He currently is directing a study of how industrialized democracies have adapted their budget practices to political and economic stress. His publications include *Congress and Money: Budgeting, Spending, and Taxing.*

James L. Sundquist is a senior fellow at the Brookings Institution. His views on the workability—or unworkability—of the American governmental system are expressed in several books, notably *Politics and Policy: The Eisenhower, Kennedy, and Johnson Years* and *The Decline and Resurgence of Congress,* as well as in journal articles and symposia.

Fred Teitelbaum is the chief planner for the Arizona Department of Health Services. He is a former senior research associate at The Urban Institute and director of research studies at the National Governors Association and has served in the Illinois and Pennsylvania state governments. His current research interests are in state health issues. Mr. Teitelbaum is the author of numerous articles on state policy and intergovernmental relations.

James M. Verdier is a lecturer in public policy at the John F. Kennedy School of Government, Harvard University. Prior to joining the Kennedy School faculty in 1983, he served for fifteen years in a variety of congressional staff positions, most recently as assistant director for tax analysis at the Congressional Budget Office.

Stephen J. Wayne is professor of political science and public affairs at George Washington University. A student of the contemporary presidency, he served as president of the Presidency Research Group and the National Capital Area Political Science Association. His books include *The Legislative Presidency*, *The Road To The White House*, *Studying the Presidency* (coeditor), and *Presidential Leadership: Politics and Policy Making* (forthcoming).

Harold Wolman is currently a visiting professor at the International Studies Unit of the University of Salford, Bedford College, London. A former senior research associate at The Urban Institute, a German Marshall Fund Fellowship recipient and director of policy and research for the White House Conference on Balanced National Growth and Economic Development, he is the author of several publications including *Learning from Abroad: Financing Urban Public Transportation: The U.S. and Europe* (with George Reigeluth) and *Housing and Housing Policy in the U.S. and U.K..* Dr. Wolman specializes in policy formulation and analysis, urban affairs, housing, community development, and fiscal policy and the budget.

Daniel Yankelovich is chairman and founder of Yankelovich, Skelly and White, Inc., a research and consulting firm specializing in monitoring social change. He is also president and cofounder of The Public Agenda Foundation. Mr. Yankelovich's current business board directorships include U.S. West (the Western offshoot of AT&T), the Meridith Corporation, Loral Corporation, and Reliance Group Holdings, Inc. He is the author of numerous books and articles on economic and social issues, including *Putting the Work Ethic To Work* (1983), *New Rules* (1981) and *Ego and Instinct* (1971).

PARTICIPANTS

Alan Abramson
The Urban Institute

David Beam
Advisory Commission on Intergovernmental Relations

Marc Bendick, Jr.
The Urban Institute

Renée Berger
Renée Berger and Associates

James Ceaser
University of Virginia

Alan Campbell
ARA Services, Inc.

Hale Champion
Harvard University

Roger Davidson
Congressional Research Service

Denis Doyle
American Enterprise Institute for Public Policy Research

Judith Feder
The Urban Institute

Edie Goldenberg
University of Michigan

Jack Goodman
The Urban Institute

William Gorham
The Urban Institute

Hugh Heclo
Harvard University

Ben Heineman, Jr.
Sidley & Austin

Charles Jones
University of Virginia

Bobbie Greene Kilberg
Washington Attorney

Everett Carll Ladd
University of Connecticut

Phyllis Levinson
The Urban Institute

Theodore Lowi
Cornell University

Michael Lund
The Urban Institute

Laurence Lynn, Jr.
University of Chicago

Michael Malbin
*American Enterprise Institute for
Public Policy Research*

Theodore Marmor
Yale University

Milton Morris
Joint Center for Political Studies

Frederick Mosher
University of Virginia

Andrew Mott
Center for Community Change

James Musselwhite
The Urban Institute

Richard Nathan
Princeton University

Chester Newland
University of Southern California

John Olsen
Mellon Bank

Norman Ornstein
*American Enterprise Institute for
Public Policy Research*

Marian Lief Palley
University of Delaware

John Palmer
The Urban Institute

George Peterson
The Urban Institute

Paul Peterson
The Brookings Institution

David Price
Duke University

James Reichley
The Brookings Institution

Robert Reischauer
The Urban Institute

Lester Salamon
The Urban Institute

Isabel Sawhill
The Urban Institute

Allen Schick
University of Maryland

James Sundquist
The Brookings Institution

Fred Teitelbaum
The Urban Institute

Susan Tolchin
George Washington University

James Verdier
Harvard University

Stephen Wayne
George Washington University

Laurence Weil
The Urban Institute

Harold Wolman
The Urban Institute

Daniel Yankelovich
Yankelovich, Skelly and White

HALF TITLE